Theravada Buddhism

Theravada Buddhism

Continuity, Diversity, and Identity

Kate Crosby

WILEY Blackwell

This edition first published 2014

Registered Office
John Wiley & Sons, Ltd, The Atrium, Southern Gate, Chichester, West Sussex, PO19 8SQ, UK

Editorial Offices
350 Main Street, Malden, MA 02148-5020, USA
9600 Garsington Road, Oxford, OX4 2DQ, UK
The Atrium, Southern Gate, Chichester, West Sussex, PO19 8SQ, UK

For details of our global editorial offices, for customer services, and for information about how to apply for permission to reuse the copyright material in this book please see our website at www.wiley.com/wiley-blackwell.

Library of Congress Cataloging-in-Publication Data

Crosby, Kate (Religion scholar)
Theravada Buddhism : continuity, diversity, and identity / Kate Crosby.
pages cm
Includes index.
ISBN 978-1-4051-8907-1 (cloth) – ISBN 978-1-4051-8906-4 (pbk.) 1. Theravada Buddhism.
2. Theravada Buddhism–Social aspects. I. Title.
BQ7185.C76 2014
294.3′91–dc23

2013021022

A catalogue record for this book is available from the British Library.

Cover image: A Tai Nuea monk in Wat Man Tao temple, Yunnan Province, China. He is reading a folding mulberry-paper manuscript in the Tham Lue script. Photo with the temple's permission and courtesy of David Wharton, Digital Library of Lao Manuscripts, Vientiane.
Cover design by www.cyandesign.co.uk

Set in 10/12.5pt Dante by SPi Publisher Services, Pondicherry, India

1 2014

MIX
Paper from responsible sources
FSC www.fsc.org FSC® C013604

For Claire

Contents

An extensive bibliography for this book is available at
www.wiley.com/go/theravadabuddhism

Acknowledgments

Much that I have learnt on the subject of this book comes from the preservers, practitioners, and observers of Theravada Buddhism, past and present. Over the past 25 years, I have received extraordinary hospitality and tireless explanations, both informally and in hundreds of interviews with many people from Bangladesh, Cambodia, India, Indonesia, Laos, Sri Lanka, Thailand, and within Diaspora groups who trace their origins to these countries as well as Burma, Malaysia, Nepal, and southern China. I cannot thank them enough. I am also grateful to the dedication of colleagues without whose writings and presentations this book could not have been written. It is a pleasure to conduct research in a field where so much painstaking and thoughtful work has been conducted and made public in such a relatively short amount of time. I know I have done justice to neither group in this contribution of mine.

Many audiences to whom I have spoken about aspects of the work contained in this book displayed patience, curiosity, and constructive frowns. In particular, I would like to thank my erstwhile students who have shaped this book over the years at the following places: the Buddhist Institute, Phnom Penh; Cambridge Muslim College; Cardiff University; Dongguk University, Seoul; University of Edinburgh; Lancaster University, England; McGill University, Montreal; the Oriental Institute, Theology Faculty and various year abroad programs, University of Oxford; the erstwhile Westminster College, now part of Oxford Brookes; the School of Oriental and African Studies (SOAS), University London; and, most recently, King's College, London – great teachers all.

For the research that has gone into this book, I owe thanks to several funders. The chapter on the Sangha, details about Bangladesh, and my ability to make some comparisons between Theravada countries owes much to a British Academy grant to compare disrobing practices across Theravada. Two grants from the British Academy Committee for Southeast Asian Studies several years apart allowed me to explore a wide range of Buddhist manuscripts and to look more closely at the literary traditions and practices of the Shan. My understanding of Shan Buddhism was also aided by a British Academy Key Speaker grant, a grant from the SOAS research committee and the SOAS Centre for Buddhist studies, as well as support from the Shan Cultural Association UK, to host an international conference on Shan Buddhism and Culture at SOAS in 2007. Chapter 11 is a substantially revised version of my article 'Gendered Symbols in Theravada Buddhism: Missed Positives in the Representation of the Female', which appeared in the *Hsuan Chuang Journal of Buddhist Studies*, No.9, March 2008c: 31–47. I am grateful to the

Hsuan Chuang Journal for permission to incorporate it here and Hsuan Chuang University for inviting me to consider the question it addresses in the first place. Some of the material on images came together thanks to the H.N. Ho Family Foundation's support of Buddhist Art Forum at the Courtauld. The chapters on meditation and *Abhidhamma* are in part the outcome of an Arts and Humanities Research Council Religion and Society grant. My longest stay in Sri Lanka was funded by the Commonwealth Scholarships program. My long stays in Cambodia were funded by the Arts and Humanities Research Board, as it was then, and the Heinrich Böll Foundation. The Seiyu Kiriyama post in Buddhist Studies that I held at SOAS during much of the writing of this book is funded by the Agonshu and was mediated by Tadeusz Skorupski.

In recent years, I have tagged along to participate in interesting activities and events and had the honour of meeting with intriguing places and people, in the company of – among others – Cheng Wei-yi, Phibul Choompolpaisal, Khammai Dhammasami, Nancy Eberhardt, Jotika Khur-Yearn, Long Sarou, Waskaḍuwē Mahindawamsa, Nagasena Bhikkhu, Nicola Tannenbaum, and David Wharton. This helped my thinking on some of the chapters that follow. I would also like to thank the following former colleagues at SOAS for their interesting work and conversations relevant to the subject of this book: Mike Charney, Amal Gunasena, Gustaaf Houtman, Andrew Huxley, and Atsuko Naono.

The following people read through individual chapters, made useful and supportive comments, and gave me further references: Erik Braun, Phibul Choompolpaisal, Angela "Hawk-Eye" Chiu, Alastair Gornall, Ian Harris, Kim Kyungrae, Kong Man Shik, and Graham Winyard.

Pyi Phyo Kyaw, Mike Charney, Phibul Choompolpaisal, Gustaaf Houtman, Kong Man Shik Kong, Jotika Khur-Yearn, and Andrew Skilton repeatedly provided me with access to electronic reading materials and vicarious access to the wonderful libraries at SOAS, the Bodleian, and the Oxford Buddha Vihara, which became particularly crucial while I was "between institutions." Several people provided me with access to their own writings at short notice during this time: Erik Braun, Wei-Yi Cheng, Steven Collins, Tilman Frasch, Jacques Leider, Justin McDaniel, Patrick Pranke, Martin Seeger, and Nicola Tannenbaum. Phibul Choompolpaisal helped me with Thai sources, Pyi Phyo Kyaw with Burmese sources, Jotika Khur-yearn with Shan sources, Long Sarou with Khmer sources, and Nagasena Bhikkhu with specifics about Bangladeshi Buddhism in multiple languages. Kong Man Shik collaborated with me in re-examining *Jātaka* as monastic documents. He was also highly informative about the fascinating differences between *vinaya* and meditation texts of different Buddhist canons and traditions. Wei-Yi "Polly" Cheng advised me on the latest developments among Sri Lankan *bhikkhunī* from the field in the summer of 2012. Patrick Pranke gave me details about Burmese intellectual history and literature. Justin McDaniel provided references on Thai Buddhism. Ian Harris pinned down further information about the history of *vipassanā* in Cambodia. David Wharton, always a mine of information and helpfulness, provided the cover photograph as well as details about the continuation of manuscript skills and meditation in Laos.

The steady completion of this book over the past year owes much to two people. I cannot overstate my gratitude to Pyi Phyo Kyaw for her assiduous help and unfailing enthusiasm. I owe much to her, especially on Burma and Abhidhamma – too much to acknowledge sufficiently through the in-text citation. Her contribution has come not only in the form of feedback, prompts, and corrections, but the provision of new information and discussions about parallels in Burma to practices and debates found elsewhere. She provided the charts in Chapter 7. We were also collaborating on a chapter on the adventures of Mahamuni images during the time this book was reaching its final stages, represented in Chapter 2 here also, although I failed to find a way of intertwining Queen Victoria's glorious blond locks, as depicted in a Burmese wall painting, into the narrative. She (Pyi, not Queen Victoria) read through the entire book, reading some chapters several times and was always willing to discuss not only detail but also theory and approaches to the study of Theravada. These included our growing shared interest in the mathematics of Theravada. Richard Arundel did sterling work in reading the manuscript of all chapters at the first draft and subsequently reviewed the structure of the whole book. He addressed both detail and the overall shape and balance. For rescuing the text from the tangled weeds of my habitual phrasing, monkey-mind repetitions, *anekagatacittatā*, and Buddhist hybrid English, I thank him on behalf on any non-Theravada specialists who can follow this book. He also showed extraordinary patience in adapting the revision process to my schedule and astute yet diplomatic goading when it faltered.

The final revisions were made possible by Andrew Skilton, who not only read several chapters in the early stages but checked the last changes in all chapters, as I implemented reader comments, standardized the format of the chapters to improve their accessibility for student readers, and succumbed to the temptation to add further details that intrigued me. Andrew also allowed me to reproduce and adapt the charts from his coursebook on Pali language and literature in Chapter 3 and provided me with the appropriately named product of my ancestral shores, 'Writers Tears.'

A final and extraordinarily fast read-through by Steven Collins caught a number of errors and highlighted a number of interesting references and points that I had missed.

I thank the staff at Wiley Blackwell for their patience and responsiveness. I am also grateful for their perspicacity in inviting Justin McDaniel and John Strong to be the no-longer anonymous readers. I could not have hoped for more encouraging, detailed, informative, and nuanced feedback, saving me also from several howlers. The further readings to which they drew my attention also shaped the final versions of several chapters.

I wish I were scholar enough to take fuller advantage of the efforts and kindness of these scholars, and of their own great writings in the field. I apologize for the howlers and omissions that remain.

The finishing of this book was made more prompt by the welcome and kindness of my new colleagues at King's, in particular Matt Ferguson, Paul Janz, Paul Joyce, and Xinzhong Yao. For assisting my journey southwards to the strand of the Thames, I would like to thank Brian Bocking, Steven Collins, Phyllis Granoff, Almut Hintze, Soonil Hwang, Gregory Schopen, and Nicola Tannenbaum.

For their wise counsel and support I would like to thank Anita, Brian, Claire, Dervilla, the other Henrietta, Lynn, Nikki, Sue, and Surana.

Finally, for having no interest in this work whatsoever and for their constant readiness for downtime, I thank Bella, Millie, Buzz, and "Puppy."

Kate Crosby, King's College, The Strand,
London, 10th April 2013

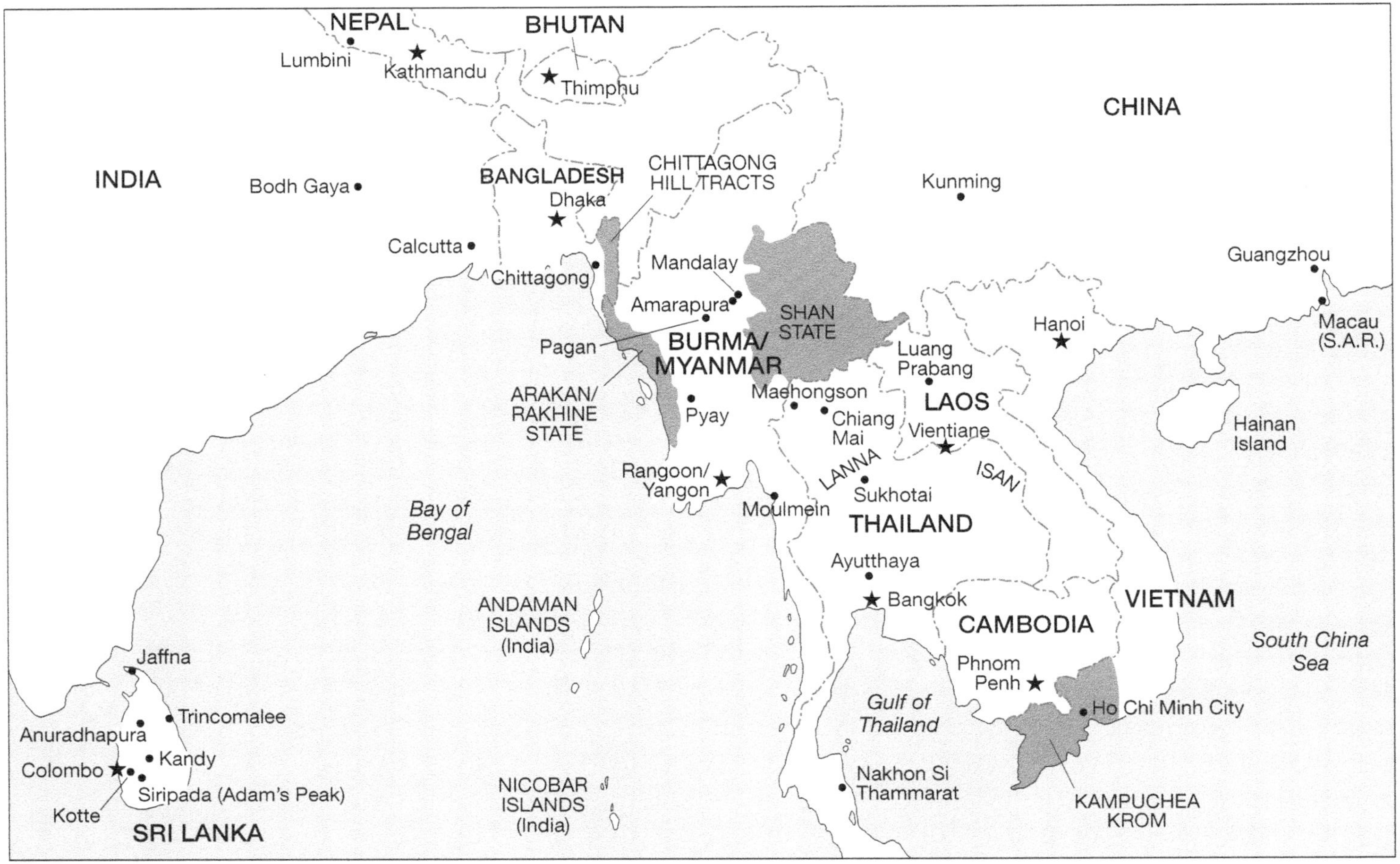

NEPAL
BHUTAN
Lumbini
Kathmandu
Thimphu
CHINA
INDIA
Bodh Gaya
BANGLADESH
CHITTAGONG
HILL TRACTS
Dhaka
Kunming
Calcutta
Chittagong
Mandalay
Amarapura
Guangzhou
SHAN
STATE
Hanoi
Macau
(S.A.R.)
Pagan
BURMA/
MYANMAR
Luang
Prabang
ARAKAN/
RAKHINE
STATE
Maehongson
LAOS
Pyay
Chiang
Mai
Vientiane
Hainan
Island
Rangoon/
Yangon
LANNA
ISAN
Sukhotai
Moulmein
Bay of
Bengal
THAILAND
Ayutthaya
Bangkok
VIETNAM
ANDAMAN
ISLANDS
(India)
CAMBODIA
South China
Sea
Jaffna
Phnom
Penh
Gulf of
Thailand
Ho Chi Minh City
Trincomalee
Anuradhapura
Kandy
Colombo
Siripada (Adam's Peak)
Kotte
SRI LANKA
NICOBAR
ISLANDS
(India)
Nakhon Si
Thammarat
KAMPUCHEA
KROM

Introduction

The simplest definition of a Buddhist is one who "takes refuge" in the "three refuges." The first refuge is the Buddha, who found the path to salvation in relation to which Buddhism as a religion developed. The second refuge is the Dhamma, the truth or teaching realized and promulgated by the Buddha. The third refuge is the Sangha, the communities of monks and nuns who have pursued and preserved the Dhamma, and provided religious and other support to the communities that materially supported them. Buddhism is the term now used for the religion of those individuals and communities that maintain and support the Buddha, Dhamma, and Sangha so that they continue to be available as refuges.

Theravada is the form of Buddhism that dominates the religious life of many communities in Cambodia, Laos, Sri Lanka, Thailand, the Union of Burma, and the Kampuchea Krom region of Vietnam. In Bangladesh, it is followed by the Barua, Chakma, Rakhine, and Marma ethnic groups, and in southern China by the Tais (Shan) of Yunnan. Historically it was also important in South India and the Maldives, and had a wider presence in South and Southeast Asia more generally. In the modern period, it has been adopted in Indonesia, adapted in India, and introduced into Nepal, traditionally a homeland of Vajrayana Buddhism, mostly among specific groups redefining their identity. At the end of the twentieth century and the beginning of the twenty-first century, increasing interest in Theravada led to its presence in the traditional homelands of Mahayana Buddhism in East Asia. It has also spread, through cultural influence, mission, and Diaspora, to other continents – to the Americas, Europe, Australasia, and, most recently, Africa.

Theravada is a community religion shaped by tradition, but the stereotype is that it is a religion of the book. The book in question is the "Pali Canon," a large collection of works regarded as the word of the Buddha who lived in north India in the sixth- to fifth-century BCE. For Theravada Buddhists, this is the highest authority on what constitutes the Dhamma (the truth or teaching of the Buddha) and the organization of the Sangha (the community of monks and nuns). Pali is a classical language formed in ancient India, and the Pali Canon is the only Buddhist Canon to survive in its entirety in an Indic language. This has given Theravada the reputation of being the earliest surviving form of Buddhism. Theravada identifies itself as the form of Buddhism that arrived in Sri Lanka and Southeast Asia in the middle of the third-century BCE after a rehearsal of the Pali Canon to ensure the purity and accuracy of the Dhamma it contained. This rehearsal is referred to as the "third council." At the same time the

Theravada Buddhism: Continuity, Diversity, and Identity, First Edition. Kate Crosby.

Sangha was also "purified" by the expulsion of wayward monks not able to profess this true Dhamma. This was done, Theravada sources tell us, with the help of the great Emperor Asoka. The missionaries that then arrived in Sri Lanka and Southeast Asia came under his auspices and included his own son, the monk Mahinda, and his daughter, the nun Saṅghamittā. It was they who established the Sangha of monks and nuns in Sri Lanka, fulfilling a prediction made by the Buddha on his mythical visits to the region. This origination myth provides the protocol for a relationship of mutual support between Sangha and state, as well as emphasizing Theravada's adherence to "original" Buddhism.

Three other features of Theravada inform its identity as "early." Firstly, while the Buddha is regarded as having been beyond human rather than an ordinary human being (contrary to some Western interpretations), the attitude toward him in Theravada is and remains realist (he really existed in the world) and relatively simple in comparison with understandings of Buddhahood and the greater proliferation of Buddhas that developed in other currently extant forms of Buddhism. Secondly, the Dhamma of Theravada, even in its most complex philosophical form (*Abhidhamma*), remains a type of realism: the external world that we experience is real. This contrasts with types of idealism that developed in other forms of Buddhism. Thirdly, the Sangha of Theravada retains visible forms of discipline associated with the Buddha's early disciples. These include a ceremony that marks the giving up of the trappings of lay life, cleanly shaven heads, relatively simple monastic "saffron" robes, not eating after noon, remaining celibate, relying to some extent on regular donations from laypeople, and, for the most part, abstaining from manual labor. Theravada's self-identification as early has been an important concept not only for personal belief and practice but also in the politics and economics of the religion and the region. It has allowed for a pattern of repeated reforms and it has informed the exporting of Theravada monks and teachings, especially meditation, to the wider world.

Problems with the Definition of "Theravada Buddhism"

Theravada Buddhism's reputation for being the earliest surviving form of Buddhism is developed in contrast to other forms of Buddhism, which are labeled "Mahayana" and "Vajrayana." These are the umbrella terms commonly used for the Buddhisms of East Asia and Central Asia/the Himalayas, respectively.

Those who become more familiar with any of these forms of Buddhism quickly realize that these categories are not fixed, exclusive, or comprehensive entities. In fact, there are deep problems with such categorization, which can make us blind to the fluidity, complexity, diversity, and richness of any actual manifestation of Buddhism in real people and communities. To label and define the living traditions that have emerged from two and a half millennia of history in this way is a form of essentialism. Essentialism, while often a useful tool of classification, can at its worst be a sinister tool of control.

In fact, it is only in the modern period that the term *thera-vāda*, literally "doctrine of the senior monks," came to be equated with the community religion of this region, becoming its official designation at the World Fellowship of Buddhists in 1950 (Perreira 2012: 561). The term *sthavira/thera* "senior monk" and its parallels in other languages were used by several branches of Buddhism, in their attempts to classify Buddhist divergence, to refer to an early division within the Buddhist fold between two groups: the *sthaviras*, and, usually, the Mahāsaṃghikas (Bareau 1955/2013: 23). The doctrinal positions preserved in the earliest layers of Theravada texts as well as Theravada's own historiography places it as a development within the *sthavira* side of that division. Within *one branch of sthavira/thera Buddhism*, the Mahāvihāra in Anuradhapura in Sri Lanka in the fifth-century CE, that is, 1000 years after the death of the historical Buddha, the term *thera-vāda* was used to refer to the teachings of senior monks, particularly those senior monks who gathered together immediately after the Buddha's death at a meeting called "the first council." The phrase was used in this way by the Mahāvihāra as it was codifying the preservation of its teachings (including the Pali Canon). The purpose of compiling these accounts of the first council at that point was to attribute to the Buddha's immediate disciples and their successors a process of rehearsing and recording the Buddha's teachings and rules in such detail that it could authorize the Pali Canon as it was rehearsed at the Mahāvihāra all those centuries later. The Mahāvihāra tradition also attributed to those early enlightened disciples the extensive commentaries that it had begun to systematize and "retranslate" into Pali at that time, the fifth-century CE. In the twelfth century, the Mahāvihāra monastic tradition came to dominate the Buddhism of Sri Lanka and would in turn strongly influence the textual and ordination lineages of Southeast Asia, across the forms of Buddhism that came at a later date still to be termed Theravada. Its claim to the authority of preserving the doctrine of the early senior monks was consolidated through a further period of reviewing this textual transmission and writing additional commentaries and handbooks.

The account of the first council, coupled with that of later councils, especially the third council connected with Asoka (mentioned earlier), validates the Pali Canon and commentaries, as the ultimate scriptural authority for Theravada Buddhism today. This in turn allows for the corresponding claim to earliness and authenticity on the part of Theravada. However, it is clear that the texts and the stories of their authenticity were the work of centuries. Moreover, there are also many other texts, written, visual, and aural, in many languages and media, that inform Theravada Buddhism as it is now practiced and as it was practiced over the centuries. Like other forms of Buddhism, what we now term Theravada is the process and product of two and a half millennia since the historical person referred to as the Buddha began preaching the teachings and institutions from which all forms of Buddhism developed. Within Theravada we frequently find doctrines, interpretations, and practices that have been more closely associated with Mahayana and Vajrayana. While these could be put down to the influence of Mahayana and Vajrayana on Theravada, the concept of Theravada as the religion of a community, ethnic group, and even nationality as a whole is a recent development. For most of the history of Buddhism, distinctions of doctrine and textual authority have been a matter of concern for a minority of scholars and practitioners, often coming to a head at points of crisis. The history of Buddhism in the region we now identify as Theravada shows different doctrinal and practice groups existing alongside and intertwined with one another. The current dominance of what is now defined as "Theravada" is the result of a number of factors, including which monasteries won in competitions to win royal sponsorship in the medieval period; and how Buddhist history came to be written at points of marked identity formation, that is, when big political changes led a group or community to redefine themselves. Key periods when this happened differ from region to region, but the eleventh to twelfth centuries marked one such watershed, as also did the nineteenth to twentieth centuries.

The definitions of Theravada that formed in the nineteenth to twentieth centuries owe much to changing conceptions of religion, rationality, science, and identity. Definitions of sameness and contrast became important in marking territory, ensuring allegiance and bolstering status at a marked period of shifting and contested power relations globally. This general picture has been complicated by and has interacted with Western Buddhist Studies scholarship that from the nineteenth through into the late twentieth centuries was also seeking to differentiate Buddhist traditions and schools and in the main did so on a purely doctrinal basis. The *locus classicus* that brought together the research that had been conducted in relation to the early schools of Buddhism by the time of its publication and went on to be the basis of further refinement in this area is the work of André Bareau (1955/2013). In it Theravada is identified as a later subgroup of the early schools emerging from the *sthavira* side of a conjectured early split between Sthavira and Mahāsaṃghika factions. Bareau then defines Theravada purely by the 222 doctrinal theses claimed as "orthodox" in the *Abhidhamma* book, the *Kathāvatthu*, compiled at the third council, even while observing how different the lived Theravada of different regions was on the ground (1955/2013: 275–326). East Asian and Western understandings of Theravada in this way, and the concomitant association of it with pre-Mahayana Buddhism, led to it being labeled as one of the *Hīnayāna* "inferior vehicle" schools, a pejorative term found in Mahayana *sūtras* to refer to the Buddhism of the opponents in those *sūtras*. It was in reaction to this identification that representatives from what was then termed the "Southern" branch of Buddhism began from the end of the nineteenth century to grapple with how to refer to the branch(es) of Buddhism represented in Sri Lanka and Southeast Asia (Perreira 2012: 510ff.), a process that led to the decision cited earlier to adopt Theravada as a collective label.

Rather than try to untangle the extent to which "Theravada" is *thera-vāda*, this book accepts the fluid definitions of Theravada to be found implicitly and explicitly among the people who identify themselves as Theravada Buddhists now and in recent history. It also accepts the fluid definitions of the Dhamma (truth), *sāsana* (transmitted teachings and associated institutions), and community (human and nonhuman) of those who contributed to the creation and continuity of the forms and manifestations of Buddhism on which "Theravada Buddhists" have been able to draw. What they believe(d), practice(d), and regard(ed) as authoritative is accepted here as Theravada belief, practice, and authority. This book therefore draws on a range of media and approaches, including fieldwork, for the evidence of what constitutes Theravada today. It draws on the evidence of texts and archeology for the views of those communities of the past that contributed to the current construction of Theravada.

Mostly the evidence we have for the past comes from textual collections preserved primarily by monks. While rich and diverse, such texts reflect the perspective of a minority, literate, usually monastic, usually male group, although shaped by the full range of humans and other beings and institutions with whom and which they interacted. This means that while the book aims to consider the views of animals and other beings as well as humans, children as well as adults, women as well as men, laypeople as well as monastics, and nuns as well as monks, the nature of the available evidence means that this quest is inherently doomed to failure. This particular challenge is greater for the past than for the present.

The fact that many Theravada Buddhists accept the idea that their form of Buddhism is earlier than other forms allows for debates over what is "true" or "orthodox" Theravada and what is "heterodox," in spite of the absence of a central authority for this issue either in the past or present since the Buddha himself "discarded his lifespan." Such debates are considered and questioned in this book in relation to the topics of the individual chapters. At the same time, there is no fixed distinction out there in the real world between Buddhist and non-Buddhist practices. For example, practices using protective string and recalling the spirits in Laos are found among those who identify themselves as Buddhists and those who do not. Feeding of ancestors is similarly found throughout Southeast Asia, among Buddhist and non-Buddhist families alike. Buddhists in Sri Lanka may find occasion to attend a Christian church whose patron saint has a reputation for assisting with matters of employment and Sri Lankan Catholic employees will allow their wrists to be bound with protective Buddhist string when prompted by an occasion at their workplace.

Distinctions between Buddhist and non-Buddhist practices can help us organize our knowledge and understand what we see. Yet what begins as a conceptual prop may then become a hindrance to a deeper understanding of the subject. In an inclusive study, which sees "what Buddhists do" as "Buddhist," such distinctions are difficult to address. On the one hand, we can analyze the history, political contexts, and rivalry that led scholars and reform Buddhists to emphasize some views and practices while rejecting others. We become wary of attempts to discard the constantly adapted practices and fluid pantheon of Theravada as we grow wise to agenda of exclusion and essentialism. In the case of the Buddhist pantheon, attempts – with varying degrees of success and failure – have been and continue to be made to exclude deities that can also be found in spirit religions, **animism**, and Hinduism. This is an agenda that relies on recent labels. The resulting categorization of these aspects of religious expression in the region is ahistorical. On the other hand, pragmatically we have to set ourselves some boundaries in order to limit even an inclusive study. One possible avenue is to define as Buddhist those practices that in some way make use of the Buddhist pantheon, Buddhist terminology, or the Buddhist Sangha (monastic community), but this immediately proves too narrow. Many rituals performed by Theravada Buddhists, such as those for fertility, childbirth, childhood, and female coming of age, make little reference to Buddhist doctrine, terms, or monks, but they shape the lives of Buddhists and may shape Buddhist ritual. Moreover, the rituals and practices of Buddhists are constantly reconfigured. This is very visibly true also of the pantheon. The Buddhist pantheon is a slow moving family of members, some similar, some disparate. While all nominally accept the Buddha as the head of the family, old members jostle with or welcome new arrivals, and it is not always the same who come and go, who form the heart of the action or stand at the sidelines. This book has not mastered these issues, but has tried to identify them where they impact each topic under consideration.

This book, then, explores the histories, texts, teachings, soteriological practices, social organizations, and rituals of Theravada, especially as found in Sri Lanka and mainland Southeast Asia. It touches on its aural and visual representations, and seeks to place what we see in its political context. In each chapter, a different aspect of Theravada is examined, with an eye to the continuities one may detect covered within the diversity that falls under the broad umbrella term of Theravada. Each chapter explores an aspect of how Theravada is defined by and is used to define the individuals and societies that accept it as an identifying label. The purpose of this book is to orient its readers such that they may contextualize any aspect of Theravada teaching, history, culture, or practice that they encounter. As such this book offers a broad overview. However, the book also aims to provide readers with sufficient detail that they are not taken unawares by the potentially bewildering array that makes up Theravada. This book therefore offers much detail to illustrate the great diversity of Theravada, historically and in the present, while suggesting how such details may relate to the overall picture. Of course, this book cannot cover every aspect or every angle, nor every historical turn taken, but it aims to map out sufficient highways and contours to make the reader's initial journey a smooth one. While seeking to err on the side of landmarks and highlights, the book also aims to draw the readers' attention to sufficient further guides for their own onward explorations.

The Structure of This Book and Its Use as a Coursebook

This book is structured to explore the historical and living expressions within Theravada following the tripartite framework of the three "refuges" that form the basic statement of a commitment to Buddhism. "I go to the Buddha for refuge" is explored in Chapters 1 and 2. The Dhamma (teaching) as a refuge forms the focus of Chapters 3–7. The Sangha (monastic community) as a refuge and the communities that create and support it are discussed in Chapters 8–12. While the book is neither a history nor an encyclopedic survey, it draws on diverse historical and geographical examples to explore these three refuges. This may lead to some odd juxtapositions as we move across centuries and between geographic regions at high speed. To make this less bewildering, most chapters are organized to some extent historically, looking at early and shared authorities on the topic in question first before looking at nuances and regional variations.

Within the section on the Sangha are three chapters dedicated to looking at women in Theravada (Chapters 9 and 10) and the potential of Theravada literature from a feminist perspective (Chapter 11). In reality, the topics included in these three chapters cut across the thematic divide even more than other chapters, but are included in the Sangha section because the possibilities of exploring them in any depth is thanks in large part to the heightened awareness of such matters generated by the debates concerning nuns and female power in recent decades. It is possible that dedicating three separate chapters to specifically female aspects of the religion is merely a continuation of the pattern of marginalization rather than inclusion: Why a dedicated section, why not complete integration? In reality, the overall bias of both primary and secondary sources, student interest in this topic, as well as the way certain types of marginalization have created separate patterns worthy of attention in their own right, mean that the topics warrant dedicated treatment in addition to the inclusion of a more balanced perspective in other chapters. The reverse bias, visibility neither through integration nor through focused attention, is so familiar in books on Theravada in general that it may strike only the sensitized reader as odd. The developments concerning nuns have come to a head since the publication of two earlier key textbooks that also combine textual, historical, and fieldwork material to give an account of Theravada Buddhism (Gombrich 1988 and Swearer 1995). While the developments are not so new – the successful reinstatement of the full nuns' lineage is fast approaching the adulthood of its twentieth anniversary – the antipathy of much of the male Sangha and, following their lead, lay society, particularly in mainland Southeast Asia, maintains public interest in this rebirth. I hope and anticipate that future books on the subject of Theravada will also pay greater attention to aspects of children and childhood. The section on the Sangha and the book as a whole closes with Chapter 12, which is on politics, for Theravada as we have it and see it has been shaped by, responded to, and taken an active role in the local, national, and international politics of the societies that it inhabits.

Twelve chapters correspond with the number of weeks in the semesters of some university systems. If a 10-week course is followed, then obvious candidates for merging are Chapter 4 with Chapter 3 and Chapter 11 with Chapter 10 (or to discard Chapter 11 as more theoretical than to do with historical or lived Theravada). Each chapter is also written to be accessible independently without the background provided in the preceding chapters and with cross-referencing throughout.

Other Studies of Theravada

Two previous overviews of Theravada have been important in the teaching of Buddhism in the English-speaking world. They are written with commendable clarity and complement each other in terms of coverage. They are Richard Gombrich's *Theravāda Buddhism: A Social History from Ancient Benares to Modern Colombo* (1988) and Donald Swearer's *The Buddhist World of Southeast Asia* (1995). A recent addition to the topic that appeared as I was putting the finish touches to this work is Asanga Tilakaratne's *Theravada Buddhism: The View of the Elders* (2012). It pays far more attention to early teachings than the current book, before turning to how this relates to practice, particularly from a Sri Lankan perspective, while its later chapters examine regional variations in the main Theravada countries. In the same year, Peter Skilling *et al.* published a collection of articles by different authors on different aspects of Theravada identity under the title *How Theravada Is Theravada?* Like this book, it seeks to look beyond monolithic representations and claims about Theravada and makes important contributions about the invention of Theravada as a tradition.

In addition to recommending these four books, I would like to highlight some absences or weak points in this book. Given that this book seeks to convey Theravada's rich diversity, there is relatively little here on the detail of Theravada's varied pantheons of the divine and divinized, the mythological, legendary, deceased and living sources of power, protection, and identity. Books such as Strong (1992), Holt (2004 and 2009), and McDaniel (2011) can supply this gap. Strong's book relates the specifics of Buddhist practice and narrative on the ground to a distinctive textual history that allows us to question in close detail the representation of Theravada as a single, monolithic culture. Holt's works reveal the diversity of Theravada pantheons across regions while also looking at the politics of definition and essentialization that continue to shape modern Theravada. McDaniel's work explores Buddhism from the ground up, rather than imposing top-down categories. Other areas of this book that I would like to have represented in more specific detail are the artistic, textual, and aural worlds of Theravada. A linear history for any given country or region is also missing, and comparison with other forms of Buddhism is confined to very specific points. I have tried to make good for these absences with a short list of films, books, articles, and web resources at the end of each chapter. There is no attempt to be exhaustive about websites and films, for the website of the Theravada Civilisations Project established by Steven Collins and Juliane Schober, which is among those listed, aims to add and update such information regularly.

While I have drawn on as much published scholarship as I was able to, a great deal of the material and discussion in this book is also based on my own experience and research in Theravada texts and communities, some of which is not published elsewhere. I have also drawn on the discussions with friends and colleagues about their experience and research. The reader's patience is requested for the lack of published, citable material for some statements.

Revisiting Conceptions of Theravada

This section identifies how the approach taken here may differ from that found in other writings on the subject. The subtitle *Continuity, Diversity, and Identity* indicates my agenda in writing this book. I aim to discard the static model that treats Theravada as a dinosaur. Each chapter, while addressing topics chosen to give an overview of key elements of Theravada, attempts to give some taste of that diversity and dynamism. Some pervasive stereotypes are challenged. The idea that Theravada Buddhists regard the Buddha as having been a mortal, human being and have eschewed the docetism and apotheosis of the founder found in other religions traditions, including other forms of Buddhism, is addressed in Chapter 1. The presence of the three paths of the *arhat, paccekabuddha*, and *bodhisatta/buddha* (in Sanskrit, the *śrāvakayāna, pratyekabuddhayāna*, and *(samyaksam)buddhayāna/bodhisattvayāna*) more commonly associated with the "Great Way," Mahayana (*mahā-yāna*), begins to draw our attention to the problematic nature of the equation of Theravada with *hīnayāna*. The idea that worship of the Buddha or of gods is not a core or orthodox component of Theravada is challenged in Chapter 2. The nature of the relationship between Pali and the Pali Canon and the Dhamma as actually accessed by Theravada Buddhists is explored in Chapters 3 and 4. The choices made by members of Theravada communities in their attempts to be good and dutiful Buddhists is explored in Chapter 5 in ways that question the use of the precepts as the primary guide to ethical or helpful conduct. The discussion takes into consideration ethnic, cultural, and religious diversity within the Theravada construction of appropriate and religious behavior. Chapter 6 looks at the dynamism of meditation, honed for centuries as humankind has developed its technologies of transformation, drawn on in the modern creation of Theravada identity and exported beyond the Buddhist framework. The historicity and changing dominance of practices is explored. Chapter 7 on *Abhidhamma*, Theravada philosophy and metaphysics, dismisses the notion that this is a minority, scholastic sideline, pointing rather to its widespread importance in defining beliefs and practice. The specifics of the *dhamma* theory, interdependent conditionality, and momentariness that characterize Theravada *Abhidhamma* again challenge the common equation of Theravada with *hīnayāna* and early Buddhism. Moreover, rather than remaining static, *Abhidhamma* continued to address philosophical, practical, and scientific developments. Chapter 8 provides an account of the place of Buddhist monasticism and monasteries within Theravada societies, which seeks to overturn stereotyping of Buddhist monks as "otherworldly" or "apolitical," yet acknowledges the Sangha's maintenance of ideals concerning *Nibbāna*, ethics and compassion. The common characterization of Theravada monks as focused on their personal path to liberation, in a theoretical contrast with the ideal of Mahayana monks and the role of the layperson, falls apart when one examines the extent to which monks and nuns' lives are shaped by their relationship to the communities in which they live and the services they provide for it. In spite of the rhetoric about continuity with the past and the purity of monastic lineage, it is observed that all of the current Theravada ordination lineages (*nikāya*) were established or defined relatively recently, since the mid-eighteenth century. In Chapter 9, the exploration of the history of and opportunities for nuns in Theravada pays attention to recent developments and how the deeply entrenched views on the subject in part arise because of Theravada's own, internal equation of its identity with that of early Buddhism. It begs questions of the identification of modern Theravada with historic sectarian difference in the pre-modern era and observes how patterns of centralized control and fear may be influencing decision-making in this area. Chapter 10 examines the theoretical and practical consequences arising from traditional notions of female versus male domains of power and the dominance of the male Sangha in Theravada institutional structures and religious expression. It draws attention to contrasting views concerning Theravada's role in providing a framework for egalitarianism or patriarchy. Chapter 11 is a theoretical chapter, which challenges a pervasive assumption that Theravada lacks the symbols and models of value to women that feminists have been able to find in Mahayana literature. At the same time, it questions the actual worth of such symbols in the light of their androcentric transmission. Chapter 12 addresses the interdependency between Theravada as lived religion and the small and large-scale politics of the societies that embody it. While the relationship between macro-politics and Theravada has been a theme much examined in sociological studies in the West, it may still come as a surprise to those whose previous study has focused on doctrine. The events of the post-world war era, particularly since the 1970s and 1980s, forced scholars within Theravada to consider the subject not only of Buddhist politics but of Buddhist violence (or violence perpetrated by Buddhists). The chapter also touches on a theme rarely explicit in either scholarship or insider rhetoric, namely, the micro-politics that shapes the daily lives of Buddhists, including monks and nuns. The stereotype of Theravada monks as divorced from such issues is hard to maintain.

This book, then, seeks nuance in the representation of Theravada. It aims to overturn a picture of it as static and monolithic to better describe the richness within Theravada and more closely represent the texture of the religion on the ground. While one might assume such attention to detail would be welcome to those thus represented, the opposite may in fact be the case. For, the stereotypes of Theravada as early and of monks as otherworldly serve a number of purposes within modern Theravada identities. The stereotype of Theravada as early, for example, authorizes claims to authenticity and superiority, claims which are tools in competition for power, control, or patronage at the local, national, and global level. This in turn generates an impressive living tradition of in-depth scholarship and hermeneutics concerning and building on canonical and commentarial literature in a classical language spanning over two millennia. The stereotype of monks as otherworldly keeps within reach and mind important ideals easily lost if one gauges all value in terms of GDP or personal advancement. On the other hand, the stereotype also serves those who would control and limit the effectiveness of the relatively large body of men that makes up the Sangha and the women who would add to their number in all those societies where Theravada is part of the national identity.

Geographical Terms

It is anachronistic to speak about historical Buddhism using modern geographical terms. In this book I nonetheless use modern state names even when talking about the past, unless I am writing about something that requires a differentiation between earlier centers of power. Thus, I refer to Mahinda arriving in Sri Lanka in the third century BCE, by which I mean the island that was only to acquire that name in 1972. Similarly, I refer to Thailand, rather than Siam or Ayutthaya, unless, for example, I am talking about the transition between Ayutthaya, Thonburi, and Bangkok as capitals. In the same vein, I follow the anachronistic practice of using "India," "Indian," and "Indic" to refer to the South Asian subcontinent and aspects of its history, religion, and culture, a practice common among classical Indologists who focus on the study of the culture of the subcontinent in the period most relevant to Buddhist history. As still widespread, I use the former name "Union of Burma," "Burma" in short, for the country officially renamed Myanmar.

There are ways in which Theravada practice relates to the broader approach to religion, healing, and social interaction of the different ethnic groups who define themselves as Theravada Buddhists. Some of the patterns also reflect historical dynamics and broader Indic or other cultural influences. We can see strong affinities, for example, between Arakanese and

Burmese Buddhism, and between Shan, Thai, and Lao Buddhism, and we can see other, less strong affinities, between Arakanese-Burmese Buddhism and Sri Lankan Buddhism, and between Shan, Thai, Lao, and Cambodian Buddhism. When writing about broad patterns I several times refer to "Tai-Lao" Buddhism. I use the term "Tai" to include the related groups of the Tai ethnic family, including the Shan of Burma and the various Tai groups of southern China, in contrast to the "Thais" of the modern nation-state of Thailand. (We can see this distinction elsewhere in scholarship, for example where the term "Thai-Lao" is used to refer to those of the Lao ethnic group resident in northern Thailand (Hayashi 2003: 1).) Another example of a regional pattern is the "calling of the spirits," a practice to recall the 32/19 spirits that belong to the human body, that is common to the various Tai–Lao–Khmer ethnic groups including the various branches of the Shan. I thus also occasionally refer to Tai–Lao–Khmer practices, to include the Khmer, who are mainly based in Cambodia and the Kampuchea Krom region of Vietnam. In modern Sri Lanka, Buddhist religion has become associated with the ethnic Sinhalese majority, even though historically Buddhism in the country was also practiced by Tamil-speakers. Even in the modern period non-Sinhalese may participate in Buddhist activities and events. I use the phrase "Sinhala Buddhism" to distinguish the Buddhism of the island from elsewhere without intending any historic prejudice in this regard. I make some broad distinctions between practice in mainland Southeast Asia and Sri Lanka, for example when discussing temporary versus lifelong ordination and attitudes to female power.

Non-English Terms, Text Titles, Transliteration, and Translation

The non-English technical terms given in this book for Buddhist concepts are in Pali, the sacred language of all current forms of Theravada, unless explicitly indicated otherwise or dictated by the specific context. On occasion this means that I use a Pali word, *kamma*, and the "Buddhist hybrid English" neologism *kammic*, where the Sanskrit-based terms *karma* and *karmic* have already entered the English language. I use the Pali Asoka, rather than the Sanskritic Aśoka or common transliteration Ashoka. A number of terms and phrases have become standard in the English used when referring to Buddhist practice but that may appear as incomprehensible jargon to the newcomer. The phrases "three refuges" and "taking the refuges" refer to a statement of faith or commitment to the three ideals/institutions that character Buddhism. These three refuges are the Buddha (spiritually enlightened religious founder of Buddhism), Dhamma (the teaching of the Buddha), and the Sangha (the Buddhist monastic community). The word precept refers to the various principles that Buddhists may choose to aspire to live to (rather than to rules prescribed from earlier). They are formulated as vows (in sets of 5, 8, or 10, see Chapter 5) and so the phrase "taking the precepts" means to make a statement of commitment to live by these principles. The phrase "merit-making" refers to the practice of consciously undertaking good deeds, and thus building up the benefits of good deeds (merit) that will have a beneficial effect on one's future. The phrases "transferring merit" and "merit-transference" refers to the act of sponsoring or performing good deeds on behalf of others, usually either the recently deceased or "all living beings," that is, the world as a whole. Part of the ritual that attends merit-transference is the naming of the beneficiary who may then benefit by becoming conscious of the good act being performed on their behalf, this positive consciousness itself then being considered a meritorious act (see Chapter 5). Buddhist monks are addressed and referred to with a number of honorifics. I confess I have been inconsistent in my use of these, often adopting the use of followers of specific individuals, for example, "Ledi *Sayadaw*" or "The Ledi *Sayadaw*," "*Phra* Payutto," "*Luang Pho* Sot," "Soma *Thera*," "*Ajan* Brahm," but elsewhere I use Pali ordinations names with or without the English "Venerable/Ven."

For Pali terms, the transliteration follows that of the Critical Pali Dictionary (Smith 1948). Other languages that appear in this book include Sanskrit and some of the regional languages of Theravada. The transliteration used often follows those in the sources referred to in the relevant section, although in some cases a standard system, such as the Royal Thai General System of Transcription for Thai, or, for Shan, a transliteration currently being trialed by the Bodleian Libraries, Oxford. Burmese words have been simplified and, where there is a standard English transliteration, it is used, as in the case of the names of many Sayadaws (not transcribed as *hsayadaw*) connected with meditation. Diacritics are used to represent the larger number of consonants and vowels in Pali and Sanskrit. There are exceptions for words that have become commonly used in English, such as Theravada, Mahayana, and Sangha. There are Pali terms that also occur in vernacular languages and it can be difficult to judge which transcription system to use. Sometimes the meaning is different in and even between vernaculars. One such term is ***ācariya*** (Pali), which means teacher and often occurs in the Pali Canon to refer to the teacher of, for example, meditation to a more junior monk in contrast to the ***upajjhāya***, who ordains the monk. In this book, we find it in Thai, where it is a term of address "teacher" more generally but also occurs associated with the names of monks, including those in the Ajan Chah Thai forest tradition. Because of the pronunciation in Thai of final –r as "n," it is sometimes transcribed as "*ajahn*" and in the Thai Royal transliteration system as *achan*. Here it is transliterated as Ajan, one of the two ways it is most commonly transliterated in association with the names of well-known teachers. In Khmer, the term as used here most commonly refers to the male lay specialists who help run temples and perform part of the services of a temple or of Buddhist rituals. So for Khmer the term is here transliterated as *achar*.

Names of texts tend to be divided up for ease of reading, for example, "the *Dhammacakkappavattana Sutta*," not "the *Dhammacakkappavattanasutta*," and I use the term *sutta* even where the term *suttanta* tends to be used for *suttas* from the *Dīgha Nikāya*, for example, "*Mahāparinibbāna Sutta*" not "*Mahāparinibbāna Suttanta*." Usually references to texts are to translations by named authors. Where only the initials of the texts are given without further explanation, this is to the Pali Text Society edition, for example, "*Dīgha Nikāya* (DN ii.123ff.)" refers to volume 2 of the Pali Text Society edition, page 123 following.

In this book, the terms "temple" and "monastery" are used interchangeably because most monasteries also house the building or buildings that function as the temple. Relatively few temples are not within monasteries. One example is the Temple of the Tooth, whose management alternates between two monasteries located on opposite sides of the lake in central Kandy. There are also "pagoda," temple buildings that developed out of the earlier *stūpa*, funerary mounds. The English word pagoda is used where these are buildings that may be entered, for example, "The Shwedagon Pagoda" in Burma, or where it is common to refer to them by the word pagoda, for example, "The Silver Pagoda" in Cambodia, in contrast to Sanskrit-English *stūpa* (Pāli *thūpa*) for the architectural monuments that are closed, even though both traditionally house relics. There are some monasteries and abodes for individual monks and nuns that do not function as temples because they are used only by forest monks who have undertaken to refrain from the usual social duties of monks and dedicate themselves to meditation. Even though they may admit the presence of laypeople to some degree, they do not have the facilities for laypeople to perform their religious practices. The word

"Wat" has become familiar in English to refer to monastic temple complexes in Tai–Lao–Khmer regions and is used in this way here. However, when the same word is used in a longer technical term, it is transliterated using the standard transliteration for that language, even though the pronunciation is the same. Thus "Wat Uṇṇalom" is the name of the temple in Cambodia that is the official residence of Supreme Patriarch Thep Vong, but a layman who provides astrological advice, teaches novices, or officiates at temple rituals is a "*vat achar*."

I use the term "spirituality" to mean the aspiration to engage in practices that support oneself and/or others toward the aims of the soteriological path as well as other altruistic aspirations and conduct. I am not cynical of this as an important motivation in human behavior and thinking. I do not use the term "religiosity" for this, since that has a far broader coverage, nor do I use the phrase "personal transformation" since this could obscure altruistic service of others. The term soteriology here is also used beyond its more familiar Abrahamic context, to refer to the path to liberation, even if there is no savior ("soter") to take one there.

References

Bareau, André. (2013 [1955]). *The Buddhist Schools of the Small Vehicle.* Translated from the French by Sara Boin-Webb, edited by Andrew Skilton. Honolulu: University of Hawai'i Press.

Gombrich, R.F. (1988). *Theravada Buddhism: A Social History from Ancient Benares to Modern Colombo.* London: Routledge & Kegan Paul.

Hayashi, Yukio. (2003). *Practical Buddhism Among the Thai-Lao. Religion in the Making of a Region.* Kyoto Area Studies on Asia. Kyoto: Kyoto University Press.

Holt, John Clifford. (2004). *The Buddhist Visnu. Religious Transformation, Politics and Culture.* New York: Columbia University Press.

Holt, John Clifford. (2009). *Spirits of the Place. Buddhism and Lao Religious Culture.* Honolulu: University of Hawai'i Press.

McDaniel, Justin. (2011). *The Lovelorn Ghost & The Magical Monk. Practicing Buddhism in Northern Thailand.* New York: Columbia University Press.

Perreira, Todd LeRoy. (2012). 'Whence Theravāda? The Modern Genealogy of an Ancient Term' in Peter Skilling, Jason A. Carbine, Claudio Cicuzza, Santi Pakdeekham (eds.), *How Theravāda is Theravāda?: Exploring Buddhist Identities.* Chiang Mai: Silkworm Books, 443–571.

Smith, Helmer. (1948). *Critical Pali Dictionary, Epilogomena to Vol. I.* Copenhagen: Royal Danish Acadmy of Letters and Sciences.

Strong, John S. (1992). *The Legend and Cult of Upagupta. Sanskrit Buddhism in North India and Southeast Asia.* Princeton: Princeton University Press.

Swearer, Donald K. (1995). *The Buddhist World of Southeast Asia.* Albany: State University of New York Press.

Tilakaratne, Asanga. (2012). *Theravada Buddhism: The View of the Elders.* Honolulu: University of Hawai'i Press.

Part One

Buddha

1

The Buddha and Buddhahood

Overview

The focus of this chapter is the enlightened being and teacher now generally known as "the Buddha." When distinguishing the Buddha of our era from other Buddhas of the past and future he is called **Gotama Buddha**. In exploring the life story and status of Gotama Buddha, we examine the religious and cultural background of early Buddhism and introduce some of the basic teachings and institutions of Theravada Buddhism. We shall examine the various ways in which the Buddha and Buddhahood was regarded and defined in Theravada Buddhism, how this developed, and how it contrasts with understandings of the Buddha in other branches of Buddhism and in the West. The chapter discusses how the Buddha is always seen as beyond human, the product of lifetimes of effort, and one example of those who realize the truth, rather than a unique, one-time occurrence. How his super-human status and character changes is examined in the light of the ways his portrayal accommodates the needs of different genres of canonical text. Such adaptation is also observed diachronically in later **Pali** and vernacular literature: notions of Buddhahood and omniscience developed and were more closely defined over time. Aspects of the biography and of biographical depictions of the Buddha are examined, including how these expand backward in time to include the earlier stages of the career of the Buddha-to-be (***bodhisatta***) in previous lifetimes and under former Buddhas, and extend forward, through his **relics** (***dhātu***) and images to inhabit the lands to which Theravada spread long after the Buddha's departure from life (his ***parinibbāna***).

Master of the Universe

A Buddha is the only type of being to have mastered the universe, the realm of rebirth, and is no longer subject to it. The living world in Buddhism is made up of humans, animals, and a whole host of nonhuman beings. There are multiple **hells** and heavens, a hierarchy of gods including the great, powerful gods of the Indian religious worldview, such as Brahmā, **Sakka** (Śakra / Indra in **Sanskrit**), the dominant gods of the **Vedic** period, and later Viṣṇu (in Sanskrit)

Theravada Buddhism: Continuity, Diversity, and Identity, First Edition. Kate Crosby.

and other gods of the Epic/purānic period. All these living beings, even the gods, are subject to the cycle of death and rebirth, ***saṃsāra***. When the merit acquired by those enjoying divine rebirths runs out, they will die, like other mortals. In the case of cosmologically significant gods, such as the king of the gods, Sakka, another being is reborn into the divine position as soon as it is vacated. Similarly, the demerit generated from the evil committed in former lifetimes by hell-beings will eventually run out, and they will be able to move on from hell. This view that good actions create a store of merit that leads to good experiences and rebirths (as fortunate humans and deities) and that bad actions create a store of demerit that leads to bad experiences and rebirths (as unfortunate humans, animals, and hell-beings) underlies much Buddhist religious behavior, which aims at "making merit," that is, performing good action. Such meritorious activity is also an important part of the path to becoming a Buddha. Since a Buddha has destroyed the unwholesome (***akusala***) mental states that underlie bad actions, a Buddha's conduct is inherently good. What is meant by good and bad action is looked at in more detail later and in Chapter 5.

Although in Buddhism, unlike in monotheistic religions, gods cannot offer salvation to humans, they are often portrayed as supportive of the Buddha and as helping to make his teaching, the **Dhamma**, which is salvific, available to others. But it is only a human being who experiences a sufficient balance of freedom and suffering to aspire to leave *saṃsāra* completely. It is only a Buddha who has found and put an end to this cycle. He (and it is always a he) has attained ***Nibbāna*** "Enlightenment," the literal connotations of which are both "bliss" and "extinction." Other terms for the Buddha's liberation include ***bodhi***/*sambodhi* "Awakening," *amata*, the deathless state – immortality in the sense of freedom from death, but not the retention of life – and *sabbaññutā* "Omniscience." Not only is the Buddha no longer subject to rebirth, he also has extraordinary powers, powers of cognition and of physical ability.

The power of the Buddha's mastery over *saṃsāra* can then be drawn on by his followers, not just for spiritual guidance but also for worldly matters. It is possible for other humans to gain individual Enlightenment, and freedom from *saṃsāra*, but only when a Buddha is accessible to make the Dhamma (teaching) available. This individual Enlightenment is called "arhatship" and an individual so enlightened an "*arhat*." There is another type of enlightened being according to Buddhism. The ***paccekabuddha*** "solitary Buddha," attains *Nibbāna* but, unlike the Buddha, does not make the Dhamma available for others. (For a discussion of *paccekabuddha* in the **canon**, see Anālayo 2010: 11ff.) The Dhamma, the "truth" or "teaching," is eternal, in that it expresses "the way things really are." It takes a Buddha to realize this truth. The further we are from the lifetime of the Buddha the harder it becomes to access the Dhamma, until eventually the world descends into an apocalypse. After this a new world order evolves and a new Buddha can arrive.

Each Buddha's quest had lasted many hundreds of lifetimes, his success predicted in the presence of previous Buddhas. The Buddha of our era is Siddhattha Gotama, who is described in Buddhist narratives as being born into a royal family in northern India in circa. sixth- to fourth-century BCE. For non-Buddhists, Gotama is spoken of as the "historical" Buddha, that is, founder of the religion that became Buddhism, whereas the preceding Buddhas are regarded as mythological. For Buddhists he is one in a line of Buddhas. Theravada Buddhism dates the death (*parinibbāna*) of Gotama Buddha to 218 years before the consecration of the **Emperor Asoka** of north India. Traditionally the *parinibbāna* has been dated to the year 544/543 BCE and that is the year that the "Buddhist Era" of Theravada dating begins. To convert "Buddhist Era" to Common Era (CE), in the dates of publications, for example, we subtract 544/543. However, by that calculation the Emperor Asoka lived in the fourth-century BCE. It has been possible to date Asoka quite accurately to the middle of the third-century BCE on the basis of the discovery and deciphering in the early nineteenth century of the inscriptions that he had engraved around his empire. His Rock Edict XIII mentions a list of kings to the northwest of his territory who are known to us from classical history: Antioch, Ptolemy, Antigonus Gonatus, Magas, and Alexander of Epirus (Pinsep in Thomas 1858: 16, Murti and Aiyangar 1951: 39–49). Scholars have therefore adjusted the Theravada chronology to date the *parinibbāna* of the Buddha to the early fifth-century BCE, that is, 478 BCE (e.g., Cunningham 1877: iii–iv) or 487/486 BCE. (Bechert 2004: 82. For a summary of the scholarship, see Hartmann 1991: especially 29–32). Texts belonging to a branch of Buddhism that prevailed in northern India calculate the Buddha's death as taking place far later, 100 years before Asoka. However, recent discoveries of archaeological remains from the mid-sixth-century beneath the **monastery** and the shrine commemorating the Buddha's mother **Māyā** at Lumbinī, identified in an **Asokan inscription** as the place of the Buddha's birth, may confirm the longer chronology (Coningham 2013).

In the final lifetime of Gotama Buddha, his quest for Enlightenment lasted six years, between the ages of 29 and 35. He had abandoned his life of luxury in response to four famous sights. The four sights were all the more shocking because of the sheltered life of luxury he had lived until that point on account of his father's desire to avoid his exposure to any of the harshness of life lest it inspire him to seek the spiritual life. The first three sights, a sick man, an old man, and a dead man, made Gotama realize the inevitability of suffering, aging, and death for all of us. The fourth sight, a serene mendicant who had "renounced" the world, inspired him to seek a way out of the cycle of rebirth, *saṃsāra*. These sights and his escape from the palace form the visual narrative of his life in Buddhist art. Such scenes depict the four sites, the harem and his wife **Yasodharā** with their new-born son, Gotama slipping away on his white horse Kanthaka the sound of whose hooves are muffled by the gods, Kanthaka dying from grief on being sent back with the groom, the god Sakka catching in a reliquary the lock of hair that the Buddha-to-be cuts off, and the god Brahmā, associated with **asceticism**, providing the eight "requisites" for a monk, which include the **robes** and bowl (Herbert 1993: 7, 28–31).

In northern India at the time of Gotama Buddha, the dominant (though not universal) presupposition underlying the religions of the period was that all living beings were subject not only to death, but to rebirth and redeath (*saṃsāra*). In Buddhism, this is encapsulated in the teaching of the three characteristics (*ti-lakkhaṇa*) of all phenomena, not just living beings. The first characteristic is ***dukkha***, literally "insecure," often translated as "suffering." The term suffering conveys one sense of the term *dukkha*, but, even though it has become a very widespread translation of this term into English, it is misleading in this context. For the adjective *dukkha* in Buddhism applies as much to pleasant and happy experiences as to negative ones. It also applies to objects (so not only to experiences). All these things, whether pleasant, neutral, or unpleasant, are insecure, *dukkha*, in that they cannot last so cannot be relied upon. The second characteristic is that everything is ***anicca*** "impermanent." Thirdly, everything is characterized by ***anattā*** "lack of enduring self," or, put conversely, there is nothing that can be identified as an enduring self. This definition of the true character of all phenomena is an explicit rejection of other religious encapsulations of the truth that circulated in India at that time, including the notion of a pure, blissful, enduring and unchanging self. For Buddhism any aspect of humanity or human experience identified as a self can be shown on closer analysis either to be subject to change or to be a projection of an imagined entity onto what is in fact a separate function. In Buddhism, an inert "self" or "soul" is irrelevant, since there is no way of experiencing or engaging with it and it has no function.

The soteriologies – doctrines relating to the path to salvation – that developed around the time of early Buddhism struggled with the fundamental question of what binds us to *saṃsāra* (the round of rebirth) and how to escape it. One path open to those seeking the answers to these questions was to become a "renouncer," one of the wandering religious seekers who had left their home and possessions behind in the quest for spiritual truth. Gotama Buddha took this path, and so Buddhism is sometimes referred to as a "renouncer" tradition. Gotama tried out and excelled in the available teachings and practices of different renouncer traditions available in north India at the time, from **meditation** to various kinds of asceticism (the practice of austerities, such as extreme fasting – a practice reflected in skeletal depictions of the Buddha). Dissatisfied with their effect and realizing their limitations, Gotama gave up the extreme fasting he had been practicing and accepted food from the laywoman Sujātā, a favored scene in Buddhist depictions of his life (Herbert 1993: 35). Gotama then entered a state of meditation, which led to him achieving Awakening, *Bodhi/Sambodhi*, or Enlightenment, *Nibbāna*. This scene is one of the most common depictions in art and sculpture: in its simplest form the Buddha touches one hand to the ground to call the earth to witness his Enlightenment (Griswold 1957: 23, 31–41, Herbert 1993: 37). In more elaborate depictions, the earth goddess is shown ringing out her long hair beneath the Buddha, while Māra, the god who represents the temptations of *saṃsāra*, and his armies crowd the scene (Herbert 1993: 38–39). To some extent, the representation of the Buddha has become more standardized in Theravada as it has become more narrowly defined as an aspect of national identity, and we shall explore some of that process of defining the Buddha in the rest of the chapter. Yet it can be seen as an ongoing process in relation to Burmese depictions, for example. Charlotte Galloway observes that the diversity of Burmese Buddhism's past and its present has been whittled down in its art. Twelfth-century Burmese art depicting the life of the Buddha was not confined to the Theravada sources we have identified here, and the rich and ongoing presence of ***nat*** (Burmese gods) and animist beliefs of Burmese Buddhism has only been excluded from the reform categories of Buddhism in the modern period. She writes, "[Since] Burmese Buddhism has consolidated as a Theravada tradition, (and) the iconography has become standardized and far less variable. To the casual viewer, the apparent sterility of later images, primarily in the earth-touching *mudrā* [hand gesture] and devoid of any subtleties of design, is misleading in the extreme" (Galloway 2002: 52).

In the earliest corpus of Theravada sacred literature, the **Pali Canon**, there are three *sutta* (teaching) texts in the ***Sutta Piṭaka***, the second division of the canon, which give an account of Gotama's Enlightenment. These are the *Bhayabherava Sutta*, "The teaching, Fear and Terror," the *Ariyapariyesana Sutta*, "The teaching, the Noble Search," and the *Dhammacakkappavattana Sutta*, "The teaching, the Setting in Motion the Wheel of the Dhamma" (also called "The First Sermon"). There is also an account of his Enlightenment in the *Mahāvagga* of the ***Vinaya Piṭaka***, the first division of the canon which explains the rules for monks and **nuns** (Anderson 1999: 56). The accounts of the Buddha's Enlightenment in these texts vary. In the *Bhayabherava Sutta*, the Buddha describes how he entered and progressed through the different meditative states called ***jhāna*** (see Chapter 6). In the first, desire and negative states of mind disappear and the meditator experiences joy and happiness, while at the same time engaging in reasoning and deliberation. In the second, the distraction of reasoning and deliberation disappear and he achieves concentration and one-pointedness of mind. In the third, joy disappears, and in the fourth, the meditator no longer experiences happiness, but the purity of equanimity and mindfulness. These first four *jhāna* are called the *jhāna* of form and are equated with parallel cosmological realms (see Chapter 6). The next four *jhāna* are called the formless *jhāna*, again equated with parallel cosmological realms. The formless *jhāna* are the spheres of infinite space, of infinite consciousness, of nothingness, and of neither perception nor nonperception. After these, Gotama then experiences the state of the cessation of perception and sensation. Returning from these states the Buddha then progresses through the form *jhāna* again and at the fourth attains Enlightenment. In the first watch of the night, while in the fourth *jhāna*, he directs his memory to his previous births, this being the first of the three knowledges he attains through his Enlightenment. In the second watch, he understands the coming into being and passing away of all beings, the second knowledge. In the third and final watch of the night, he realizes the four noble truths (see later text) and attains the destruction of the ***kammic*** "influxes," *āsava*, that keep one in *saṃsāra* (Anderson 1999: 58). The other accounts of the Buddha's Enlightenment differ in detail. In the *Ariyapariyesana Sutta*, the Buddha relates how the Buddha left his previous teachers after achieving high levels of meditative experience, but which did not lead to an end of *saṃsāra*. He then sat down in a wood. Continuing his quest for "*nibbāna* 'where there is no birth', 'where this is no old age', 'where there is no illness', 'where there is no death', 'where there is no grief' and 'where there is no stain'. ... the Buddha attained *nibbāna* and proclaimed: 'Knowledge and vision arose in me: release is unshakable for me, this is the last birth, there is no more becoming'" (Anderson 1999: 60).

The four noble truths are taught in more detail in the *Dhammacakkappavattana Sutta*. The first truth is the "truth of suffering or pain" (or "insecurity," as I proposed earlier): "Birth is pain; old age is pain; illness is pain; death is pain; sorrow and grief; physical and mental suffering; and disturbance are pain. Association with things not liked is pain; separation from desired things is pain; not getting what one wants is pain; in short, the five aggregates of grasping are pain" (Anderson 1999: 65). The second truth, "the truth of arising," identifies craving for desire, existence, and the fading away of existing as the cause of pain and rebirth. The third truth, "the truth of cessation," identifies that by letting go of craving, pain may end. The fourth truth, "the truth of the path," names the "eightfold path" that must be followed in order to end pain. The eight components of the path are "right view, right intention, right speech, right action, right livelihood, right effort, right mindfulness and right concentration" (see Chapter 5). It has been suggested that these four truths are in the form of a medical formula that first describes the symptoms (suffering or pain, *dukkha*), then diagnoses the cause, then gives a prognosis of the possibility for recovery, and finally prescribes the treatment that will lead to that recovery (Gombrich 1988: 59). Carol Anderson points out that this analysis, which was introduced into Western scholarship in the late 1880s, became popular in spite of the lack of evidence for the Buddha drawing on a medical model (Anderson 1999: 189). The four truths have also often been treated as being the core teaching of Buddhism or as encompassing all the teachings. In her study of the variety of uses within the Theravada textual tradition, Anderson concludes that their simplification and popularity in Western writings is part of the colonial project of gaining control over Buddhism (Anderson 1999: 197). This way of reducing Buddhist teachings to a simple, single rationalized account has parallels in the ways in which the life of the Buddha was variously reinterpreted in earlier Western literature from a solar god, on the one hand, to a normal human being shorn of his supernatural or superhuman attributes, on the other hand.

In the *Dhammacakkappavattana Sutta* account, the universe is shaken by the event of the Buddha's Enlightenment and then by the Buddha teaching the four truths to his five former companions (Anderson 1999: 2). According to the *Ariyapariyesana Sutta*, on realizing what he had achieved, the Buddha initially felt disinclined to teach, lest the profundity of his realization was too difficult for others to grasp. He was persuaded to teach by three things: the god Brahmā appeared to persuade him that unless he made the effort to teach the world would be lost; the Buddha realized that the world contains people at different stages of spiritual maturation, likening this to a lotus pond in which different colored lotuses are at different stages of emerging from the mud, with some full blown above the surface; he remembered five former companions who had striven with him until they abandoned him for giving up his asceticism and who were now at a receptive stage of spiritual development (Anderson 1999: 60–62). He responded to these prompts because a Buddha is characterized by infinite wisdom *and* compassion. So Gotama returned in search of his former companions at the deer park in the town known as Sarnath in north India, where he taught the first sermon. These five men became his first disciples: while he taught two of them, the other three took turns to go and beg for alms food. The term for monk in Buddhism derives from this activity: ***bhikkhu***, "monk" (Pali; *bhikṣu* Sanskrit), literally means "a man who desires a share / begs." The female equivalent for *bhikkhu* is ***bhikkhunī***. The first monk to join the Buddha's monastic community, **Sangha**, is the first of these five companions, Aññāta Kondañña. The Sangha was later augmented by the nuns, the first of whom was Gotama's aunt and foster-mother **Mahāpajāpatī Gotamī** (see Chapter 9).

A function of the narratives about the Buddha's lifetime prior to his Enlightenment is "to establish that the *bodhisatta* chooses renunciation from a position of power more broadly. He is the best at everything to which he turns his hand. He could have [achieved] the highest goals a man in *saṃsāra* can wish for: a kingdom, wealth, wives, sons. Nothing that a man should achieve is left unachieved. He does not leave out of failure, but in order to choose a higher state of power. … [He] practiced the greatest extremes of asceticism and experienced the highest meditative states that other teachers had achieved, but he found them wanting. He had to seek his unique path, the only one that truly bestowed freedom from death" (Crosby 2012: 94).

During his journey in search of the five former companions, the Buddha had come across two merchants, Tapussa and Bhallika, to whom he gave four hair "relics" (*dhātu*) or physical reminders (***cetiya***). These, though, were not the first relics or reminders of the Buddha. Those were the topknot of hair he had cut off when he renounced to signify leaving behind the life of a householder which was taken by Sakka, king of the gods (Jayawickrama 1990: 86–97), and the golden bowl from which he had eaten the meal given by Sujātā, which found its way, through a whirlpool in the river, to the underworld of the *nāgas* (Jayawickrama 1990: 93), a class of semi-divine beings in the form of king cobras, who can take on the guise of human form and, like gods, became incorporated into Buddhist cosmology as protectors of the Buddha and his teachings. The hair relics given to Tapussa and Bhallika are particularly important for Theravada: the merchants took them to Burma and enshrined them in what was to become the Shwedagon pagoda, one of the two most important religious sites in Burma (Strong 2004: 76–80). This story is recorded in the fifteenth-century Kalyani inscriptions of King Dhammaceti now housed in a separate shrine at the Shwedagon, while the story of the two merchants is the subject of carvings on the eastern stairwell of the **pagoda** (Moore 1999: 142). The other bodily relics of the Buddha are from his funerary remains.

The narratives that the Theravada tradition has transmitted about the Buddha develop these themes: his extraordinary realization, his cognitive and physical powers; his compassion and his ability to read the needs and spiritual capacity of others; his connections with the sacred geography not just of north India but also of the regions in which Theravada flourished (Sri Lanka and mainland Southeast Asia) in part mediated through his relics; his position in relation to the rest of the universe that is still subject to *saṃsāra*, including the supporting cast of a rich pantheon of gods; his place in a lineage of those not subject to *saṃsāra*, namely, the previous Buddhas and the future Buddha Metteyya who will come when Gotama's own teaching has disappeared. Finally, Theravada accounts for its own position in relation to the Buddha, identifying itself as the tradition that has continuously preserved the teaching, Dhamma, and the monastic discipline, *vinaya*, that began in the deer park where he met with his former companions and began to teach them. It regards its male monastic (Sangha) lineage as unbroken since Aññāta Kondañña.

The Buddha's departure from this life, his *parinibbāna*, which results from him choosing to give up his lifespan, is described in a canonical text called the ***Mahāparinibbāna Sutta*** (*Dīgha Nikāya sutta* 16). In the *Mahāparinibbāna Sutta*, the Buddha names the Dhamma and *vinaya* as his successors to teach the community rather than naming any individual. He confirms the truth of impermanence – that even a Buddha's lifetime, though extendable, must end – yet in the same text also gives instruction on how to treat his physical remains, including the relics that remain from his cremation and the benefits of worshipping them. This leads to an interesting dichotomy in the tradition between his absence and ongoing presence, a subject of much debate in scholarship, which we shall explore in Chapter 2. We therefore have three kinds of legacy from the Buddha: Dhamma, the teachings; *vinaya* and the Sangha, that is, the monastic code along with those whose lives are governed by it; and physical reminders (*cetiya*) or remains of him (*dhātu*). These together form the three "refuges" of Buddhism: the Buddha (represented in living practice by his *dhātu* and other physical reminders of him), Dhamma, and Sangha. Each ritual occasion, each text in the Theravada tradition begins with a statement of homage to the Buddha, from a simple *namo buddhāya* to elaborate hymns of praise, often directed toward one of the Buddha images ubiquitous in Theravada societies, followed by the taking, three times, of the "three refuges": *buddhaṃ saraṇaṃ gacchāmi*, "I take refuge in the Buddha," *dhammaṃ saraṇaṃ gacchāmi*, "I take refuge in the Dhamma," and *Sanghaṃ saraṇaṃ gacchāmi*, "I take refuge in the Sangha."

The Changing Character of the Buddha

While in each text the Buddha comes across as an individual with a specific character, his character varies in the different genres of literature that reflect these three legacies – the Buddha *dhātu*, the Dhamma, and the Sangha.

The earliest sacred canon of literature for Theravada is the collection of works preserved in the Pali language, known as the Pali Canon or ***tipiṭaka*** (see Chapter 3). In the texts of the *Vinaya Piṭaka*, the first of the three main divisions of the Pali Canon, Gotama Buddha is the great authority to whom the mistakes of individual monks are reported, leading him to set up rules. There are no rival authorities to consider – the Buddha's word is law (Huxley 1996: 142–144). While the *Vinaya* may have developed over centuries, and there are significant variations between the different *vinayas*, each rule and variation on it is attributed to him. His word is absolute. His concern in establishing the rules relates to two main issues: whether or not the behavior in question is conducive to spiritual development and whether or not it enhances the reputation of the Sangha in relation to the broader community that supports it and from which members are recruited into it.

A body of commentaries on the *Vinaya Piṭaka* had developed by the fifth-century CE and continued to be written throughout Theravada history. The commentaries tackle what could have been meant by different, potentially conflicting statements, showing an awareness of a chronological development within the Buddha's lifetime. One well-known development is the distinction that developed between the initial ordination procedure, the Buddha's personal invitation to come and follow him, and the more formalized ordination ritual. A division into two kinds of ordination also developed during the compilation of the *Vinaya Piṭaka*. What was initially regarded as a single process of "going forth (from household life)," ***pabbajjā***, and "approaching (a teacher)," *upasaṃpadā*, became staged according to the fifth-century **commentary**, with the result that the *pabbajjā* now referred to the first "lower ordination," that could be undertaken by children as well as adults, and the *upasaṃpadā* referred to the "higher ordination" taken only by men and women over the age of 20 (Crosby 2000: 464). Only after the latter ordination are monks and nuns subject to all the rules contained in the *Vinaya Piṭaka*. All these changes are attributed to the Buddha.

When statements of the Buddha's are too concise to avoid future ambiguity, the commentaries extrapolate the meaning, but still with close reference to other statements by the Buddha in the *Vinaya*. The Buddha's position as the ultimate authority on *vinaya* matters is emphasized in the commentaries and throughout the periodic reforms seen within the Theravada tradition. For example, the *Samantapāsādikā*, the fifth-century commentary attributed to Buddhaghosa, rejected the wording for ordination rituals that had developed since the closing of the canon, insisting that only rituals performed using the words prescribed by the Buddha in the canon were valid (Crosby 2000). This then sets a precedent for later reforms, which have been an ongoing feature of Theravada history (see Chapters 3, 8, and 12). An entire monastic lineage could be destroyed if their rivals could demonstrate that they were not practicing *vinaya* according to the word of the Buddha, even though in the normal course of events *vinaya* is always adapted to the circumstances. Only the more serious rules are usually regarded as crucial, although great emphasis is also placed on rules and expectations of decorum, which might be regarded as minor and are slightly different in different cultural contexts, even in different Theravada societies.

The *Sutta Piṭaka*, the second section of the Pali Canon, records the teachings of the Buddha mainly as sermons in response to specific occasions. The sermons are set in a narrative framework noting the place where, and occasion on which, the Buddha taught them, and to whom. In these *Sutta Piṭaka* texts, unlike in the *Vinaya Piṭaka*, his authority is often not assumed but established during the course of each text. He is persuasive, winning over those not necessarily convinced, ousting in competitions of wit, wisdom, or the performing of miracles, any rival teachers or worldviews. His compassion is expressed through his anticipation of the needs and potential of those he encounters, by identifying their psychological dispositions and by establishing the values (rather than the rules) by which monks and nuns should live for the ongoing spiritual well-being and health of the Sangha.

In later parts of the *Sutta Piṭaka*, as we shall see later, the Buddha moves from being an individual and authority for the teachings conveyed in each text to being the representative of a type, one in a line of Buddhas, the extraordinary manifestation of aeons' of determined effort, full of conviction regarding his future destiny. While the existence of former and future Buddhas is mentioned elsewhere in the canon, for example, in earlier *Sutta Piṭaka* texts such as in the "lion's roar of Sāriputta" cited later, details about them are rare (Collins 2010: 109). It is the later *Sutta Piṭaka* texts, such as the *Buddhavaṃsa* and the *Cariyāpiṭaka*, that offer details of a line of specific Buddhas with specific careers, families, and followers. These later texts are confident statements about the position of Buddhism and the Buddha. They exemplify the workings of ***kamma*** over time, offer teachings about meritorious action and the rewards available in future lifetimes, including the possibility of being reborn as members of a future

Buddha's family and retinue. The narratives and life summaries contained in these later texts communicate the extraordinary nature of the historical Buddha, and set the context for the aspiration to realize one's own full potential in the presence of the future Buddha Metteyya if one fails to do so under Buddha Gotama's teaching. This aspiration would come to dominate later Theravada expressions of spirituality, when *arhatship*, personal Enlightenment, had come to be considered rare, if not impossible.

One of these later *Sutta Piṭaka* texts, the ***Jātaka*** collection (see Chapter 4), contains the stories of the lifetimes of the Buddha-to-be (*bodhisatta*), understood by later tradition in terms of him fulfilling the ten perfections of Buddhahood. In the *Jātaka*, the Buddha's character is to some extent inconsistent, perhaps indicating the strain to accommodate stories that circulated in other milieux into the monastic corpus. In some stories, the *bodhisatta* is the ideal renouncer, in some he performs great acts of generosity or forbearance, so fulfills the "perfections." In other stories, he is heroic, but he may even be identified as the villain of the story or as a completely insignificant character merely observing the events of the narrative.

Like the *Sutta Piṭaka*, the ***Abhidhamma Piṭaka***, the third collection of the canon, also contains expositions of the Dhamma, the doctrinal teaching. But, for the most part, it is not in the same narrative or poetic format. It does not employ the Buddha as the framing narrative. However, with its emphasis on the details of causality and the path to Buddhahood, unsurprisingly we find the very nature of the Buddha analyzed in the ***Abhidhamma*** (see Chapter 7). Indeed, the *Abhidhamma* culminates in its final book, the *Paṭṭhāna (Conditional Relations)*, with an attempt to encapsulate the Buddha's understanding of causality. Moreover, important defining features of the Buddha in Theravada in contrast to in other forms of Buddhism are found in the *Kathāvatthu (Points of Controversy)*, the fifth book of the *Abhidhamma Piṭaka*. The aim of the *Kathāvatthu* is to refute heretical views, including views held by other Buddhist groups, that had developed by the time it was composed, 218 years after the *parinibbāna* of the Buddha, in the middle of the third-century BCE. One of the "heresies" refuted is that there might be more than one Buddha at a time (Shwe Zan Aung and Davids 1915: 354–355). Those who composed the doctrinal treatises and commentaries within Theravada consistently rejected the presence in the world of more than one Buddha at any time. To suggest otherwise is, for them, to suggest that Gotama Buddha is somehow an inadequate Buddha. The term **Mahayana**, literally "great way / vehicle" is a term that refers to a number of branches of Buddhism that identified themselves as such in relation to their acceptance of certain doctrinal positions and new texts that began to develop around the first-century BCE to first-century CE (Skilton 1994: 93). The forms of Buddhism now found in the Himalayas, Central and East Asia, though containing many variant forms of Buddhism, all identify themselves as Mahayana. In some forms of Mahayana, we also see the idea that certain Buddha realms are better than others. The Theravada understanding that all Buddhas were equal already appears in earlier sections in the Pali Canon. In a number of texts of the *Sutta Piṭaka*, including the *Mahāparinibbāna Sutta*, we find the "Lion's roar of Sāriputta," in which the Buddha asks Sāriputta, one of the two chief disciples of the Buddha, to account for his assumption that there is no one greater than him (the Buddha):

> Sāriputta, you in fact have no direct experience in this matter regarding the enlightened fully Awakened Ones of the past, future, or present. So how can you feel such certainty that you roar the roar of a lion, saying, "Lord, I have this conviction regarding you, the Lord Buddha: that there has never been another wandering holy man or priest with greater supramundane wisdom than you, Lord, in respect of perfect Awakening; nor will there ever be, nor is another such currently found"?

> It is true, Lord, that I have no such direct experience, but I have witnessed the logical consequences of the Dhamma. Suppose, Lord, a king has a fortified city at the frontier, with solid foundations, solid walls and portal, and only a single gate. Suppose there was a clever gatekeeper, experienced and astute, stopping all strangers, and allowing those familiar to enter. On following the path all the way around that city he would not find a single break in the wall, nor a single hole, even big enough for a cat to slip through. He would be conscious of the fact that, whatever living beings that are visible to the naked eye enter or leave this city, they must all enter or leave by this very gate alone. This, Lord, is how I have witnessed the logical consequence of the Dhamma. Lord, all the Lord Buddhas in the past, have awakened to the highest full and perfect Awakening. Similarly, Lord, all the Lord Buddhas will awaken to the highest full and perfect Awakening. Similarly, Lord, the Lord Buddha who has become the enlightened fully and perfectly Awakened One now has awakened to the highest full and perfect Awakening. (*Mahāparinibbāna Sutta*, abridged, translation Crosby)

In this passage, while the sameness of the attainment of Buddhahood is confirmed, it is not clear if this is a direct response to the question of whether there can be different levels of Buddhahood. However, the *Jātakanidāna*, a commentarial text that we shall examine in more detail later, does address this issue. Based on the late *Sutta Piṭaka* text, the *Buddhavaṃsa*, it gives an account of the 28 Buddhas culminating in Gotama Buddha. Each has a specific lifespan, physical body, named parents, wife, children, disciples, and a specific number of followers. Of the Buddha Maṅgala, the *Jātakanidāna* text states,

> Whereas with other Buddhas their bodily radiance spreads to the distance of eighty cubits, it was not so with him, for the radiance of that Blessed One remained all the time suffusing the ten thousand world-systems. Trees, the earth, mountains, oceans, not excepting cooking pots and so forth, appeared as though covered with a film of gold. And his life-span was ninety thousand years. ... Beings went about their business at all times in the light of the Buddha as they do by day in the light of the sun. (Jayawickrama 1990: 39)

This passage suggests that Maṅgala Buddha is better than the other Buddhas, and the following passage of the text seeks to correct this impression:

> Do not the other Buddhas also possess this power? It is not that they do not: if they so wish they could fill with their radiance the ten thousand world-systems or more. But on the other hand, as a result of a former resolution of the Blessed One Maṅgala, his bodily radiance remained permanently filling the ten thousand world-systems even as that of other Buddhas was confined to the depth of a fathom. (Jayawickrama 1990: 39)

In fact, the discussion about whether Buddhas differ continues in Theravada from the commentarial period to the modern day. The commentary on the *Khaggavisāṇa Sutta* of the *Suttanipāta* discusses whether a future Buddha is strong in wisdom, faith, or energy. Among the many vernacular biographies of the Buddha is one in Burmese called the *Maha-bokda-win* (*The Great Chronicle of the Buddha*). It is by the first "Tipiṭaka" monk of modern Burma, Ven. Vicittasārābhivaṃsa Tipiṭaka **Sayadaw** (1911–1993) (see Chapter 3). In it, he explains that Gotama Buddha needed a relatively short timeframe overall, between the moment of his prediction as Sumedha (see later text) to his Enlightenment, to perfect his perfections compared with other Buddhas, because he began stronger in wisdom (Vicittasārābhivaṃsa, 1960–1972, "Chapter VII on Miscellany" English translation U. Ko Lay and U. Tin Lwin, Section 14.1).

There is a genre of postcanonical texts that might be said to represent most the ongoing presence of the Buddha. These are the various types of **chronicles**: the Pali chronicles (*vaṃsa*) and the vernacular chronicles. Theravada chronicle literature tends to make a connection between the Buddha, across time and space, to the place or institution and in particular to the relics (*dhātu*) that are the focus of the *vaṃsa*. The Sri Lankan *vaṃsa*, for example, describe the Buddha visiting the island on three occasions, on one of the visits leaving behind the footprint at Siripāda that remains one of the most important pilgrimage sites in Sri Lanka to this day. The *Tamnan* vernacular chronicles of the Lanna region of northern Thailand record the history of individual relics and images. Angela Chiu explains, "there is an integral relation between place and Buddha agency; it is through place that Buddha agency is activated and expressed. The location of a relic is essential to its role in expressing Buddha agency" (Chiu 2012: 121). The arrival of the Buddha, his relics, or his image in a particular place is a sign of the merit of that place (Chiu 2012: 144). We shall see that this applies both to relics and images, especially images of historical, cultural, or political significance.

In the chronicles, the Buddha foresees the future greatness of a place, its importance to the future history of his teaching, so he visits and bestows a relic or allows his likeness to be sculpted as an image. Alternatively, his relics and images themselves express agency in choosing their location. Sometimes they remain invisible until a ruler worthy to be their custodian comes to the throne. Sometimes they decline to be enshrined in places they deem inappropriate and even change location with shifts in what we might term secular power. In the Chronicle of the Great Relic of Haripuñjaya (modern Lamphun in northern Thailand), the circa twelfth-century King Āditta discovers the relic when he tries to relieve himself in the outhouse at his new palace. He is thwarted in the execution of this objective by a crow attacking him. The crow reveals the reason:

> Phraya White Crow, my grandfather, said that the Lord Buddha, when he was still alive, one day came to sit here and eat myrobalan [a kind of plum] and predicted that when the Tathāgata had gone to *nibbāna*, this place will be a great city called *mueang* Haripuñjayapuri, indeed. The place where the Tathāgata was sitting will be the dwelling place of the Suvaṇṇacetiya [golden relic chamber] of the Tathāgata's relic of the chestbone, the relic of the fingerbone and granular relics of the Tathāgata filling one bowl which will be established here through Phraya Āditta. My grandfather then had me come here to guard and not let animals and people harm this dwelling place. (translation Chiu 2012: 129)

Even after the King has the palace moved, and digs down to retrieve the relics they retreat deeper into the ground, until he performs appropriate worship and invites the relics to emerge (Chiu 2012: 128–129). When the Arakanese Mahāmuni images allowed themselves to be moved in the eighteenth century, it marked a shift of power, the rise of Burmese over Arakanese supremacy, and the stories about the fate of these images continue to be contested (see Chapter 2).

These texts associate the Buddha's visits, relics, and images with centers of power, that is, with a particular king, place, or region. Here the character of the Buddha reflects his physical and territorial authority. Three key Pali chronicles record the first of the Buddha's three visits to the island of Laṅkā (modern Sri Lanka): the fourth-century *Dīpavaṃsa*, "Chronicle of the Island," the fifth-century *Mahāvaṃsa*, "Great Chronicle," and the *Vaṃsatthapakāsinī*, "Illumination of the Meaning of the Chronicle," the commentary on the *Mahāvaṃsa* of uncertain date, judged to be either ninth- or eleventh- to thirteenth century (von Hinüber 1996: 92). It is in these texts that we see the most striking alteration in the character of the Buddha. When the Buddha arrives on the island of Laṅkā, he encounters *yakkha*, the native inhabitants of the island. *Yakkha* are a kind of nature spirit, some benign and connected with fertility and wealth, others threatening and demon-like. Mostly, in Buddhist texts, the *yakkha* are converted to support the Buddha and his teaching. In the Pali Canon, when the Buddha tames nonhuman beings such as *yakkha*, he does so through kindness, as he does humans. In striking contrast to this, in these Sri Lankan chronicles he subjects and then exiles the *yakkha* using trickery and aggression. He uses his supernatural powers to conjure up torrential rains, hurricanes, stones, weapons, embers, ashes, mud, winds, storms, and darkness. He agrees to relieve the *yakkha* from this onslaught in return for space, but continues to afflict them with cold. When they request an end to this, the rug on which he is seated emits such heat that the *yakkhas* are driven to the coast while the Buddha and his rug expand to fill the entire island. Only then, when the *yakkhas* are terrified and vanquished, does he show any compassion. He brings the neighboring island Giridīpa "Craggy Island" close to them, allowing them to settle there, then moves it away from Laṅkā again (Gunawardana 1978: 97–98).

Gunawardana suggests that the *vaṃsa* account of the Buddha in this context is a political charter authorizing the later use of violence by Sri Lankan rulers in the name of the Buddhist religion (*sāsana*). The story reconciles the teaching of nonviolence in the Canon and the distain for kingship represented in *jātakas*, because of the violence it entails, with the justification of extreme violence in the hands of the political powers that patronize Buddhism recorded in the later stages of the chronicle. Here the character and actions of the Buddha serve to teach that "violence is not invariably associated with evil, and that a distinction has to be drawn between violence committed in the interest of the *sāsana* and that motivated by greed" (Gunawardana 1978: 99–100).

The relics and images in Pali and vernacular chronicles represent the ongoing presence of the power of the Buddha, but may also have lives and adventures of their own. They extend the biography of the absent Buddha to new places and times. "They help legitimate empires here on earth and they further spread the dharma to places that the living Buddha never visited" (Strong 2004: 7). Chronicle literature tends to commence with a brief biography of the Buddha that then, through the Buddha's visits, predictions, and authorization of relics and images of the narrative's present, catapult us forward into the locality and time of the *vaṃsa's* composition.

Finally, another important genre of Theravada literature in both Pali and vernacular languages is praise and devotional literature. In these texts, the most salient aspect of the Buddha's character is his power, power derived from his status as one who has mastered *saṃsāra* (the round of rebirth). Such texts are used to harness that power, for *puñña* (literally "merit"), for protection, for personal assistance, or to install the powers of a Buddha into a Buddha image (see Chapter 2).

In their simplest form texts offering praise of the Buddha, *Buddhavandanā*, simply list the qualities of the Buddha. The most famous of these is the "Mirror of the Dharma" or "*itipiso*," which lists nine qualities of the Buddha and was taught by the Buddha to his attendant the monk Ānanda in the *Mahāparinibbāna Sutta*: "Thus indeed is that Lord Buddha, enlightened, fully and perfectly awakened, endowed with wisdom and conduct, a Sugata, knower of the world, the unsurpassed trainer of men to be tamed, the teacher of gods and men, the Awakened, the Lord Buddha" (Endo 1997/2002: 167. See also Chapter IV on the individual components of this list.) These qualities of the Buddha, followed by parallel statements on the qualities of the Dhamma and Sangha, have become a standard component of Theravada litany.

Biographies of the Buddha

While a full biography of the Buddha as such is not found in the canon, episodes from his life are described in several *suttas*, as well as the introductory section of the *Mahāvagga* of the *Vinaya Piṭaka*, the division of the Canon that deals with monastic rules. As observed earlier, certain later canonical texts such as the *Jātaka*, *Buddhavaṃsa*, and *Cariyāpiṭaka* add a cosmic, multilife framework for the events in his present life. They explain his attainment of Enlightenment, his mastery over *saṃsāra* (the round of rebirth), as the culmination of many lifetimes of conscious effort. This effort began as a vow taken many lifetimes earlier to become a Buddha to save other beings from *saṃsāra*. To do this, the Buddha-to-be declined the opportunity to gain his personal Enlightenment, *arhatship*, under a previous Buddha. These texts also authorize his achievement through predictions of this future greatness in the mouths of 24 out of 27 previous Buddhas.

The earliest single, continuous biography found in the Theravada tradition, the *Jātakanidāna*, draws on the fragmentary information found across all these canonical works. The *Jātakanidāna* is the introduction to the commentary on the *Jātaka* book of the canon. The *Jātakanidāna* is mainly a prose text with quotations of verses that recount the same narrative more succinctly with the addition of a certain amount of commentary. As a biography, the *Jātakanidāna* is incomplete in that it does not extend up to the end of the final lifetime of the Buddha. It ends with the donation of a park to the Buddha by the lay devotee Anāthapiṇḍika. The end of the Buddha's lifetime is found in the *Mahāparinibbāna Sutta* in the *Dīghanikāya*, the first section of the *Sutta Piṭaka* division of the Pali Canon (see Chapter 3). It provides a continuous account of the Buddha's final three months. However, the *Jātakanidāna* is complete at the other end of the Buddha's career, the start. It tells the story of his lifetimes from "Four *asaṅkheyyas* (periods beyond all reckoning) and a hundred and thousand aeons ago" (Jayawickrama 1990: 3) when he was born as the **brahmin** Sumedha, first took the vow to achieve Buddhahood and was predicted as destined to Buddhahood by the Buddha of the time, Buddha Dīpaṃkara.

The story of Sumedha forms the opening episode of *The Distant Epoch*, the first of the three sections of the *Jātakanidāna*. It is one of the most popular scenes depicted in Buddhist art. The *bodhisatta*, born into a wealthy brahmin family, realizes that the only way to take wealth with him to the next life is by giving it away in this. He does so, then lives as an ascetic. One day he comes across people repairing holes in a road in preparation for the Buddha Dīpaṃkara's visit. Rather than use his magical powers to join in the repairs, he fills the potholes by prostrating his body, asking the Buddha Dīpaṃkara and the 400,000 monks accompanying the Buddha to walk across him so that he may sacrifice his life to them. While lying there he makes the decision not to become a monk and gain arhatship under Dīpaṃkara's guidance, but to become a Buddha himself. The Buddha Dīpaṃkara recognizes that Sumedha is making the resolution to become a Buddha, and predicts his future success as the Buddha Gotama. Dīpaṃkara witnesses that the whole universe confirms the future success of his vow:

> The omens that were seen when Bodhisattas of yore seated themselves cross-legged, they are seen to-day.
>
> Cold is dispelled, heat is allayed. … The ten thousand world-systems are silent and motionless; High winds do not blow, streams do not flow. … Forthwith bloom flowers sprung on land and in water; today all of them have bloomed; All creepers and trees are at the same

> time laden with fruit. ... Jewels sparkle. ... Simultaneously are heard strains of earthly and heavenly music ... the mighty ocean bends low. ... Ten thousand fires in hell are extinguished instantaneously. ... The sun shines bright and all stars are visible ... you certainly will become a Buddha. (Jayawickrama 1990: 22–23)

This event then is the beginning of Gotama's path to Buddhahood. For, encouraged by this, he ponders on the factors that lead to Buddhahood and realizes that he must fulfill each of the ten perfections, beginning with *dāna*, generosity:

> Just as an overturned water-pot discharges its water holding back nothing ... so by giving everything in charity to supplicants that come to you ... without regard to wealth or fame or wife or child or one limb or the other of the body, you will become a Buddha, seated at the foot of the Bodhi tree. (Jayawickrama 1990: 25)

The examples of generosity presage future *jātaka* stories, including his final lifetime before the Enlightenment, the famous ***Vessantara Jātaka*** (see Chapter 4), in which the *bodhisatta* gives away his wife and two children as the ultimate display of generosity. Each Buddha in turn must prove his ability to make this sacrifice. A variation of this story, shocking from the perspective of the rights of wives and children, is repeated in the *Jātakanidāna*, for the Buddha Maṅgala. Buddha Maṅgala is the third of the list of 24 Buddhas, who each achieved Enlightenment in turn during the career of Buddha Gotama from the lifetime in which he vows to become a Buddha, and who each predict Gotama's future Buddhahood. There is a longer a list of 27 previous Buddhas, which includes 3 who precede Gotama's "career."

> Thereupon a yakkha by the name of Rough Fangs hearing of the Great Being's inclination towards charity went to him in the guise of a brahmin and asked him for his two children. The Great Being, who was overjoyed with the thought of giving his children to the brahmin, gave both his children away. ... The yakkha ... devoured the two children like a bundle of lotus roots while the Great Being looked on. No grief, not even to the extent of a hair's tip arose in the great Being as he looked at the yakkha and saw his mouth when he opened it disgorging a stream of blood like flame. But great joy and satisfaction rose from within his body as he reflected on the well-conferred gift. (Jayawickrama 1990: 40)

Such stories convey the Buddha-to-be's extreme capacity for generosity in comparison to the – by these standards – ordinary *dāna* of more ordinary mortals. They also convey the extent to which children and wives are seen as instruments in the religious career of their fathers or husbands, rather than as agents in their own right. This picture, however, is turned on its head at the culmination of the Buddha's career. After Buddha Gotama's own Enlightenment, he returns to his family home and, in appreciation of the crucial sacrifice his former wife had repeatedly made on his behalf, by enabling him to repeatedly abandon her, he helps her become a nun and achieve arhatship herself. He does the same for other members of his family, including his son Rāhula, who sets the model for childhood ordination (see Chapter 8). Whereas some northern Buddhist texts explain the suffering of the Buddha's wife and son as resulting from bad deeds in previous lifetimes, Theravada narrative, while still emphasizing the pathos of their plight, a pathos that sustains the popularity of these stories today, attributes their experience to lifetimes of good deeds. Just as a *bodhisatta* undergoes hundreds of lifetimes pursuing the perfections, so his wife and child/children accompany him on that journey, rehearsing time and again their role in relation to him. They make their own vows and receive their own confirmations that they will be reborn in the family of the future Buddha Gotama (Crosby 2012: 84–88).

In another story about the Buddha Maṅgala as a *bodhisatta*, he sees a Buddha shrine and decides to turn himself into a human candle and sacrifice himself as a light offering to it. This theme is more familiar from Mahayana texts, especially the story of Bhaiṣajyagururāja in the *Lotus Sūtra*. They inspired the famous self-immolations of the 1960s protesting against the treatment of Buddhists by the Catholic Diem regime in Vietnam and then against the American/Vietnamese War and those in contemporary Tibet (see Benn 2007).

The account of Sumedha's vow in the *Jātakanidāna* and the predictions of his future Buddhahood by the 24 previous Buddhas is followed by brief allusions to key *Jātakas* (stories about the Buddha's former lifetimes) in which he fulfilled each of the ten perfections, based on the reorganization of select *Jātakas* in another late canonical text, the *Cariyāpiṭaka*. The culmination of his *bodhisatta* career is marked by his birth in Tusita heaven, where he remains till reborn as the baby of Māyā. These events are all retold as the first section of the *Jātakanidāna*, the "Distant Epoch."

The "Intermediate Epoch" opens with the destruction of the world, part of the cycle of time that marks the end of the religion, Dhamma, of the previous Buddha, but presages the arrival of a new Buddha. All the powerful gods then visit the *bodhisatta* in the Tusita heaven to prompt him that the time has come for him to become a Buddha. The *bodhisatta* then selects the most appropriate time, country, family, mother, and lifespan for his final lifetime. The intermediate epoch then covers the extraordinary events associated with his conception and childhood so familiar from Buddhist art. For the conception his mother Māyā is purified by the gods and dreams of a white elephant entering her right side. Soothsayers predict that the child will become an all-powerful emperor (*cakkavattī*) or a Buddha. Māyā gives birth to him standing clasping a Sāl tree as he emerges pure and standing upright (in this version we do not yet have him emerging from her right side). Two streams of water fall from the sky to anoint him. He takes seven strides and announces "I am the chief of the world" (Jayawickrama 1990: 71). The story continues with other auspicious signs and examples of the Buddha-to-be's prowess, and then his father's attempts to keep him from seeing the four sights mentioned earlier, the sick man, old man, corpse, and renouncer, to prevent his renunciation. Then follow two famous scenes: of the birth of his son Rāhula to his wife Yasodharā, and his disgust at seeing his dancing girls fallen asleep, the veneer of beauty removed, "some of them with saliva pouring out of their mouths, … some grind their teeth, some others with their clothes in disorder revealing plainly those parts of the body which should be kept concealed for fear of shame" (Jayawickrama 1990: 82). Finally, he takes a last look at his son, resolving to return after his Enlightenment, and departs on the back of his horse Kanthaka, deities muffling the sounds of the horse, placing their hands under its hooves in order to avoid the departure being discovered. The story of his struggles with austerity, his battle with Māra, the representative of death and *saṃsāra*, who tries to both tempt and to terrify the Buddha into staying within *saṃsāra*, and finally his Enlightenment complete the "Intermediate Epoch." It concludes with the Buddha's recognition of the significance of the omniscience he has gained, two verses also found with the collection of poems of the *Dhammapada*, another book of the *Sutta Piṭaka* division of the Pali Canon:

> Seeking the builder of the house I sped along many births in Saṃsāra but with no avail, ill is birth again and again.

> O builder of the house, you are seen. Do not build the house again! All your beams are broken and the ridge pole is shattered. The mind that has gone beyond things composite has attained the destruction of the cravings. (Jayawickrama 1990: 100)

The "Recent Epoch" recounts the experience of the Buddha after his Enlightenment, including two of the scenes most frequently depicted in art: the attempts to seduce him by Māra's daughters, "Craving, Aversion and Lust," and the Nāga (King Cobra) Mucalinda wrapping himself around the Buddha and spreading his hood over him to protect him from a storm in the seventh week of his Enlightenment. Rather than emphasizing the teachings of the Buddha, as found in the first four collections (***nikāya***) of the *Sutta Piṭaka*, the account in the *Jātakanidāna* emphasizes four things: the role of the gods in affirming and serving the Buddha; his encounter with the two ascetics who would be his chief disciples, Sāriputta and Moggallāna; his reconciliation with his family; and his acceptance of the first donations of monastic land for the Sangha, culminating with the purchase by the generous layman Anāthapiṇḍika of Jeta's grove at Sāvatthi by covering it in pieces of gold. At this point the text ends by praising the benefits accrued by the donor who dedicates monasteries, and on recalling the precedent set for this by the chief sponsors of the previous Buddhas (Jayawickrama 1990: 126–127). Thus, this last section is a form of *ānisaṃsa*, a text praising the benefits of specific types of donation. This testifies to the early development of the *ānisaṃsa* genre, a genre that has remained popular to this day but is usually classified as noncanonical and tends to be preserved in a mixture of Pali and vernacular language. The popularity of *ānisaṃsa* reflects its function in celebrating and affirming the relationship between the three gems (the Buddha and Sangha, who provide the gift of salvific teaching, the Dhamma), on the one hand, and the laity who provide all the material needs for the Buddha and Sangha, on the other hand. As we shall see in Chapter 2, to some extent the Buddha image takes on the role of receiving gifts and ensuring the ongoing presence of the perfections and the Dhamma for the 5000 years that the Dhamma endures after the Buddha's *parinibbhāna*.

Later Biographies of the Buddha

The Buddha's biography continued to evolve and find new forms in Pali as well as in vernacular languages. Buddha biographies in Pali include two ornate Pali poems, the twelfth-century *Jinālaṃkāra* by Buddharakkhita (translation Gray 1894) and the thirteenth-century *Jinacarita* by Medhaṅkara (translation Duroiselle 1906), as well as the eighteenth-century *Mālāṅkāra Vatthu* (Jayawickrama 1990: xiii) and the circa fourteenth- to eighteenth-century *Jinamahānidāna*, which covers the same period as the *Jātakanidāna* but continues to include the distribution of the relics after the Buddha's *parinibbāna* (von Hinüber 1996: 180). The biography that seems to have the widest distribution in Southeast Asia is the *Paṭhamasambodhi*, which dates at least as far back as the sixteenth century and possibly several centuries earlier. There are at least ten different versions of the *Paṭhamasambodhi*. It is recorded in Pali as well as at least eight vernacular languages. Earlier versions cover the *bodhisatta's* descent from the Tusita heaven, that is, his conception to his Enlightenment, hence its title, which means "First Awakening." Later versions extended it to include Brahmā's invitation to the Buddha to teach and the first sermon. Later still the text is extended to include the death of the Buddha (Laulertvorakul 2003: 27–30). An example of an extensive, relatively recent vernacular biography is the Burmese

Maha-bokda-win, mentioned earlier, composed by Vicittasārābhivaṃsa Tipiṭaka Sayadaw at the request of U Nu, commenced the year of the Sixth Council in 1956 and published between 1960 and 1972. The narrative period covered is from the prediction of Sumedha's future Buddhahood up to the distribution of the relics found in the *Mahāparinibbāna Sutta*. Vicittasārābhivaṃsa draws material from across the canon and commentaries, and discusses highly technical aspects of the nature of the Buddha and the perfections. He also provides biographies of the previous 24 Buddhas and some of the early monks and nuns. The resulting work is immense, covering over 5500 pages and published in six volumes. It was translated into English as *The Great Chronicle of the Buddha* (Lay and Lwin 1991).

The biography of the Buddha is also included in texts that seek to harness the power of the Buddha. "The Consecration of the Buddha," a text recited to empower Buddha images in Thailand (see Chapter 2) retells the key events of the Buddha's biography to the new image while transferring the power of each great event into the image. Visual biographies are probably more familiar to most Buddhists than written ones. **Temple** wall paintings, sculptures, and temporary festival art often depict key events in the Buddha's life. Some visual images appear not to be intended for display. John Strong has reported on a find of bronze figures representing scenes in the life of the Buddha concealed in a pagoda in northern Burma. The figures were intentionally hidden from view and only revealed after its collapse in 1912:

> These included representations of the first jātaka, the story of Sumedha prostrating himself at the feet of the past Buddha Dīpaṃkara; images of all the other twenty-eight previous buddhas venerated by the Buddha in his past lives; figurines depicting the Buddha's mother, Mahāmāyā, giving birth to him, the seven steps he took immediately after he was born; the signs of the old man, sick man, dead man, and ascetic that prompted him to go forth on his "great departure"; scenes of him cutting off his hair with his sword and of Indra receiving that hair relic in heaven; statuettes showing his Enlightenment and the events of each of the seven weeks following it; the first sermon he preached to his first five disciples' and various events from his teaching career, ending with the scene of his death and parinirvāṇa. (Strong 2004: 6)

Here, then, we have the story as told in the *Jātakanidāna*, but with the biography completed by the events right up to the *parinibbāna*.

The Buddha's biography, including the extended biography, informs many other forms of artistic expression and popular performance, from dance to shadow plays and puppet shows and songs, from popular communal songs to highly sophisticated court compositions. More recently, these scenes have recurred in comics, story books, novels, and films. Some modern retellings convey a particular socialist or egalitarian perspective, such as the controversial 1973 novel *Bawa tharanaya* (Worldcat OCLC number 486931505) by the Sri Lankan writer Martin Wickramasinghe (1891–1976), or performances among the Dalit **Ambedkarite Buddhists** of India (see Chapter 12), who are strongly influenced by Theravada.

Western films, like Western biographies until recently, tended to focus on the quest in this lifetime, from the four sights to his Enlightenment under the *bodhi* tree. While this may reflect a Western trope in the biographies of "great men," namely, "the quest," Skilton's analysis of Bertolucci's 1994 film *Little Buddha* reveals that the early availability of Buddha biography in the West plays a part: It seems that the screen play is influenced by the northern Sanskrit poetic biographical poem about the Buddha, the *Buddhacarita*, even though Theravada imagery is used, for example, Theravada robe colors for the Buddha. Only the first half of the

Buddhacarita was translated relatively early on into English, and so it is this first half that informs the screen play (Skilton 2011). Despite his later associations with the Theravada revivalist Anāgarika Dharmapāla (see Chapter 12), Edwin Arnold's highly influential biography of the Buddha, *The Light of Asia*, which became a best-seller when it was published in 1879, was likewise based on a northern Buddhist Sanskrit text. Arnold had been the principal of the Government Sanskrit College in Pune, India.

Buddha Nature in the *Jātakanidāna*

Jayawickrama observes that even though the *Jātakanidāna* biography of Gotama Buddha is later than some of the Sanskrit parallels, it nevertheless "is more faithful to the original Pali tradition" (Jayawickrama 1990: xv). It includes "some of the principles of Mahāyāna seen to occur already in works like the *Buddhavaṃsa* and *Cariyāpiṭaka*. The Pāramitās are recognized, but there is no reference to the ten *bhūmis* which find mention even in a work like the *Mahāvastu*, a book that marks the transition from early Buddhism to Mahāyāna" (Jayawickrama 1990: xv). The *pāramitā* or "perfections" are the qualities – ten in the fullest list – that a *bodhisatta* must perfect to become a Buddha in the developed scheme of the Buddha path. The *bhūmi* are ten levels of increasingly elevated stages of being a *bodhisatta* culminating in Buddhahood, the higher levels being hard to distinguish from Buddhahood, and this schema reflects an even more developed understanding of the path to Buddhahood important in Mahayana treatises. Jayawickrama points to the absence in the *Jātakanidāna* of the "docetic tendency" found in Mahayana Buddhism. **Docetism** is the belief a religious figure – in our case, the historical Buddha – was not in fact a real person present in the world, but an emanation of a divine being. "This [docetic] aspect is greatly accentuated in the Lalitavistara [c. 1st C BCE text of Sarvāstivādin Buddhism] where Buddha's appearance on earth is termed an "act of sport" (lalita), and he is exalted as a divine being. ... [In the *Jātakanidāna*, by contrast] the human character of the Buddha stands out pre-eminent. ... He is superior to all devas [gods] and men but is not a divinity who resides in Sukhāvatī [Pure Land/heaven of a Buddha]. The doctrines of the Tathāgatagarbha and Trikāya are foreign to the Nidānakathā" (Jayawickrama 1990: xiv–xv]. The doctrines identified as absent in the *Jātakanidāna* are doctrines associated with different forms of Mahayana. The Tathāgatagarbha doctrine is the doctrine that we all have the potential for Buddhahood within us, which possibly developed in the third-century CE (Skilton 1994: 132). The *Trikāya* doctrine is a doctrine of *yogācāra* philosophy, which teaches that there are three (*tri*, Sanskrit) bodies (*kāya*) of a Buddha. There is the body of his perfected non-dual consciousness (*dharmakāya*, Sanskrit). There is his "enjoyment" body (*saṃbhogakāya*, Sanskrit), that is, his actual embodiment in heavens. Finally, the Buddha that people saw in the world preaching was not real. Rather it was his magical creation or emanation body (*nirmānakāya*, Sanskrit) (Skilton 1994: 127–128). This last is the most obvious example of doceticism in Buddhism, that Gotama Buddha was a magical creation, not physically present in the world. The absence of such doctrines in the *Jātakanidāna* allows us to see that Theravada's beliefs about the Buddha are distinctive from some of those which developed in Mahayana schools, and appear to be more conservative. Nonetheless, we do find that the Theravada understanding of the Buddha develops, and we shall return to those developments later.

Western Preconceptions of the Theravada Buddha

While it is true that Theravada never develops the level of docetism found in Mahayana, the Theravada understanding of the Buddha and its further development can be understood in terms, not perhaps of docetism, but **apotheosis**, the transformation into a god. For it is not only across genres that we see an alteration in the character of the Buddha, but also across time. While in the West there was a tendency to stress the humanity of the Buddha, the Theravada tradition has always grappled with his superhuman nature, the ways in which he was beyond ordinary humanity, as well as how one could gain access to him or his power after his *parinibbāna*, a topic to which we shall return in Chapter 2.

For Westerners the legacy of the Victorian and Edwardian view of the Buddha as a "rational renouncer," who taught a message of universal truth and is now absent from the world remains strong. It is a view that suits convert Buddhism in the strongly atheistic or protestant context of much Anglophone western culture. Donald Lopez writes of this view emerging at the end of the nineteenth century, when Westerners began to realize that Buddhism was not the "primitive idolatry" it had first been categorized as, but a sophisticated religion:

> What would become essential for Europe and America ... would be the Buddha's humanity; what once appeared to be the legend of another idol was in fact the portrait of an individual, an individual whose humanity would transcend the confines of ancient India, humanize the continent of Asia, and inspire the world by showing what can be done by a man who is not a god. For the Buddhist traditions of Asia, however, it was his identity with the Buddhas of the past ... that was his essence. (Lopez 2005: 31)

Certainly, as we shall in Chapter 2, Western scholars until recently combined this view of Buddhism as a rational religion with the assumption that Theravada is a representative of it in its early, uncorrupted form. This combination was then used to critique how Theravada was actually practiced in modern Asia. Embedded within this response was the colonial attitude of claiming direct access to the scriptural authorities of the religion and thus being in a position to judge "the natives." A descendant of both protestant and colonial attitudes may be seen in a tendency in scholarship to "test" current practice against the texts, an aspect of which we will examine in the next chapter when we look at Buddha worship. This "testing" against the texts, however, is a possibility of all religions "of the book." It has its precursors in the history of Theravada and also its parallels within modern Theravada. Sometimes, then, Western protestant academic responses converge with reform approaches within Theravada itself. In terms of understanding the nature of the Buddha, there is substantial support for the emphasis on impermanence and a "common-sense" religion focused on the here and now in some parts of the canon. However, the canon also attests to the belief in supernatural beings, the assumption of before- and after-lives, in the effectiveness of *kamma* across lifetimes and in the efficacious power of the Buddha and the Dhamma. Furthermore, one can trace in Theravada literature a process of refinement of what it means to be a Buddha.

In theological terms, some of the processes we see in the development of the status of the Buddha might be regarded as the natural processes of divinization applied to a human founder. As the Buddha becomes more and more exalted, his achievements are no longer seen as the outcome of an extraordinary individual's quest of a single lifetime. Rather such greatness must be the grand culmination of hundreds of lifetimes of effort marked by auspicious signs, predictions of greatness, periods in heaven, noble descent, superhuman characteristics and a supporting cast of deities and royalty. One might see this also as an outcome of religious rivalry – just as kings acquired the accolades of rivals, the conquered, and the emulated, attributes initially attributed to an important figure in one religious tradition are claimed by rivals and emulators in relation to their own saints. One group attributes to its saints qualities beyond those of its rivals' saints. We can see that the Theravada development of its expression of what it means to be a Buddha is not an unthinking accumulation of all qualities imagined possible for a super or divine being, however. For example, the definition of the meaning of omniscience, "knowledge of everything," an attribute of the Buddha, is developed in Theravada, but never to the extent that it literally means knowing everything all the time from all times. Such an understanding of omniscience was attributed to the Jina early on in Jainism. Jainism was a rival sect at the time of the Buddha – the Buddha refers to the Jina as a contemporary of his – so Buddhists were familiar with the Jain definition of omniscience, but that definition, which makes sense in terms of the Jain understanding of the soul, does not make sense in terms of the Buddhist understanding of no-self and of the processes involved in consciousness. That definition was therefore rejected (see later text) (Jaini 1974: 84–85).

The developing status of Buddha in Theravada literature

The term Buddha

We now think of the term Buddha, meaning "awakened," as specifically referring to one who has become enlightened according to all the teachings of Buddhism. In Theravada it refers to the 27 previous Buddhas, Gotama Buddha, and the future Buddha Metteyya. But the term occurs in early Jain texts to refer to sages of both Jainism and other religious traditions. In contrast, in the Buddhist poems regarded as being among the earliest material in the *Sutta Piṭaka* the term is not used, even of the Buddha. At a relatively early phase of the Pali Canon, the term *buddha* occurs alongside others such as seer (*isi*) or brahmin (*brāhmaṇa*) to refer to different, respected holy men. It seems to go through a phase of meaning a very eminent person before becoming a term for Gotama Buddha in the narrative referring to the present, and then to the lineage of 28 Buddhas and the future Buddha Metteyya, when referring to the past and future (Endo 1997/2002: 7). The Buddha then uses the term to differentiate himself from all other beings, including separating himself off from humans: "I am not a god, not a gandharva [*gandhabba* in Pali, 'heavenly musician'], not a yaksa [*yakkha* in Pali, see Chapter 2] not a human, but a Buddha." Other terms used for the Buddha include *Bhagavā* "fortunate," often translated as "The Blessed One," *Sugata*, literally "gone to/in a good state," and *Tathāgata*, "gone to/in such," both usually left untranslated.

Over the course of the development of Theravada literature, there was a tendency to emphasize the universality of Buddhahood seen in the *Buddhavaṃsa*, one of the later texts of the *Sutta Piṭaka*. The *Buddhavaṃsa* describes a parallel path to Buddhahood for all 28 past Buddhas. There was also a tendency toward the elevation of the Buddha over the *paccekabuddha* and ***arhat*** (also known as the *sāvaka* – the "listener" or "disciple").

Sometimes, in Western scholarship, the term *śrāvakayāna* (Sanskrit) is used as a nonpejorative term to refer to pre- and non-Mahayana forms of Buddhism including Theravada. However, the fifth-century author Buddhaghosa, who compiled the *Visuddhimagga*, often regarded as the epitome of Theravada orthodoxy, characterized the Buddhism he represented (that of the **Mahāvihāra** monastery of Anuradhapura in Sri Lanka, which would later come to define

Theravada) as consisting of these three soteriological paths (*yāna*): the path of the Buddhas, *buddhayāna*; the way of the individually enlightened, *paccekabuddhayāna*; and the way of the disciples or *arhats*, *sāvakayāna* (e.g., Ñyāṇamoli 1976: 43–44, citing the *Paṭisambhidāmagga*, on which see Chapter 7). Although one of the definitions of Mahayana in early Mahayana *sūtras* is that it is the great (*mahā*) way (*yāna*) because it includes all these three paths, such statements have come to be reified as historically accurate distinctions between Mahayana and non-Mahayana. The distinction appears to be pan-Buddhist and it predates the emergence of Mahayana as a separate pathway within Buddhism (Dhammajoti 2011: 155). The fact that Theravada, too, explicitly includes these three paths challenges this widely accepted dichotomy. A distinction that is valid is that Theravada regards the *bodhisatta* (*bodhisattva*, Sanskrit) on the Buddha path as rare, whereas those forms of Buddhism identified as Mahayana came to formalize the *bodhisattva* vow to achieve Buddhahood as a vow that all should undertake.

Body and mind

While there is a tendency in Western literature to treat Buddhism as a religion of the mind, particularly Theravada with its relative lack of docetism, Theravada itself consistently understands the perfection of the Buddha in psychosomatic terms. In other words, they defined the Buddha in terms of both his wisdom or spiritual attainments, literally his "knowledge-power" (*ñāṇabala*) and his physical attainments, literally "body-power" (*kāyabala*). (See Endo 1997/2002: Chapters II and III respectively.)

One of the *ñāṇabala* attributes is his omniscience, in Pali *sabbaññutā*, a compound of *sabba* "all" and *(ñ)ñutā* "knowing/science" and so a literal equivalent of the Latin-derived English term "omniscience." The main issue that arises in defining the Buddha's omniscience, however, is understanding the referent of *sabba*: "all," for example, whether it refers to all three times, that is, everything in the past, present, and future. A secondary issue is the nature of the "knowing," for example, whether it means being constantly conscious of "all."

In the canon, we find the following six "higher knowledges" (*abhiññā*) attributed to the Buddha: magical powers, divine ear (clairaudience), knowledge of the mind of others, remembrance of former existences, divine eye, and extinction of all influxes or defilements. The last three of this list are the three "knowledges" that the Buddha realized on his Awakening (see earlier text). The terms influxes and defilements translate the Pali words *āsava* (Sanskrit *āśrava*) and *kilesa* (Sanskrit *kleśa*). Both terms are evidence of the uptake in Buddhism of terms from the broader Indian religious milieu. The term *kilesa* literally means "stain," but in Buddhism means the spiritual defilement of the individual as a result of their previous bad actions, *kamma*. The term *āsava* literally means "flowing towards," so "influx." In Buddhism, it means the taints or obstruction generated by engagement with sensual pleasure, life, ignorance, and false views. They predispose one to further *kammic* engagement and so it is only when one has destroyed them that one is free from further continuation in *saṃsāra*. The literal meaning of influx comes from a more materialistic understanding of *karma*, action, in the Indian religious context of the time. Traditions such as early Jainism regarded the influxes as a kind of karmic dust that colored, and weighed down the soul, the color and weight reflecting the relatively positive or negative quality of the action that generated this dust (Norman 1997/2006: 45–46).

As the distinction between the Buddha and the *arhat/sāvaka* becomes more marked, it is expressed through two different lists of ten knowledge-powers (*ñānabala*). The Buddha's ten powers are that he knows (i) what is possible and impossible; (ii) causal connections in past, present, future; (iii) causal actions of all states of rebirth; (iv) the world and its elements;

(v) the spiritual states of human beings; (vi) the maturity of the spiritual faculties of other individuals; (vii) the higher meditative states; that he has (viii) retrocognitivity across several aeons; (ix) clairvoyance that allows him to see the death and rebirth of other beings in terms of their *kamma*; and (x) achieved the liberation of mind and of wisdom from destroying all mental defilements (Endo 1997/2002: 20–21, de Silva 1987: 39).

In contrast, the *arhat's* ten powers are (i) realization of all composite phenomena as impermanent; (ii) seeing all sense pleasures as a pit of burning embers; (iii) the inclination to renunciation; and then, listed as items 4–10, the 37 factors of awakening (*bodhipakkhiyadhamma*, see Chapter 6), which summarize different ways of formulating or aspects of following the path to *arhat*ship (Endo 1997/2002: 20–21). The powers attributed to the *arhat*, then, all relate to the individual's realization of Enlightenment, a possibility in a single lifetime, in contrast to the Buddha's understanding of the spiritual situation and needs of all other beings, developed over multiple lifetimes. In early canonical material, this distinction is not made. The Buddha's disciples achieve the same realization, the same Enlightenment as him (Anderson 1999: 63).

The Buddha's achievements in the canonical text, the *Mahāsīhanāda Sutta*, are phrased in terms of "Four Confidences" that relate entirely to the soteriological path. They are that no one can (i) accuse the Buddha of not being fully enlightened; (ii) accuse the Buddha of not being completely free of defilements; (iii) claim that what he declares are obstructions are not; and (iv) claim that the Dhamma he teaches does not lead to the cessation of *dukkha* (Endo 1997/2002: 24).

The physical powers, *kāyabala*, attributed to the Buddha in the canon include a range of statements about his great beauty and how his physical appearance reflects the occasion. In the *sutta* of the first sermon, *Dhammacakkappavattana Sutta*, the Buddha's five former companions in the deer park initially plan to spurn him for having given up his asceticism, but when they see him they realize from his physical appearance that he has achieved greatness, so they welcome him. In the *sutta* on the last three months of the Buddha's life, *Mahāparinibbāna Sutta*, the Buddha comments on how he changes his appearance to pass unnoticed in the context where he is teaching, including among the different assemblies of gods. Toward the end of the same text, he is presented with a pair of golden robes. When Ānanda, the Buddha's attendant, wraps the robes around the Buddha, he observes how the Buddha's skin appears to glow. The Buddha replies,

> There are two occasions, Ānanda, when the hue of the Buddha's skin is so very pure, so cleansed. The first is the night on which the Buddha awakens to the unsurpassed full and perfect Awakening. The second is the night on which he attains final *parinibbāna*. Today, Ananda, in the last watch of the night, between a pair of Sal trees in the Sal grove of the Mallas, the final *parinibbāna* of the Buddha will take place. (translation Crosby)

The physical attributes of the Buddha become formalized into a famous list of 32 marks of a great man. These include such attributes as wheels on his feet (mark no. 2), the whorl of hair between the eyebrows (no. 31), the distinctive bump on the Buddha's head, shaped like a royal turban (no. 32), a chest like a lion's, and long arms (no. 9). These are distinctive features on much Buddhist sculpture and in the last instances may even reflect the effects of the material sculpture on the conception of the Buddha's physical appearance. Other attributes reflect Indic ideals of beauty, such as his golden complexion (no. 11), a chest and jaws like a lion's (nos. 17 and 22), and long eyelashes shapely like those of a cow (no. 30). Still others are harder to explain, such as a long and flexible tongue (no. 27) and "privities within a sheaf" (Endo 1997/2002: 46).

Although these 32 attributes are listed in the *Lakkhaṇasutta*, a text in the *Sutta Piṭaka*, other texts in the *Sutta Piṭaka* are mostly unfamiliar with them (Endo 1997/2002: 45–47). In contrast, later texts, such as the *Buddhavaṃsa* and ***Apadāna*** (a text that provides the stories of the former lifetimes of key characters in the Buddha's life), refer to them and also extend the list of 32 major marks with an additional list of 80 minor marks (Endo 1997/2002: 46–47). Moreover, not only the Buddhas, but their sons have the marks. For example, the *Apadāna* of Gotama Buddha's son Rāhula explains that Rāhula made the vow to become the future Buddha's son in a lifetime when he was serving food to a previous Buddha, and was filled with admiration for that Buddha's young son, whom he recognizes on account of these marks (Crosby 2012: 89).

Late *sutta* texts such as the *Jātaka*, *Buddhavaṃsa*, and *Apadāna* extend the lives of the Buddha and his immediate family and followers, providing them with extraordinary preparatory careers, including him in a list of other Buddhas, each of whom has a specific Buddha field where his Dhamma takes effect (as noted earlier). Two very late *Sutta Piṭaka* texts, the *Patisambhidāmagga* and *Niddesa*, are in effect early commentaries on the canon and seem to belong to the metaphysical *Abhidhamma* in genre (Chapter 7). This means that they seek to systematize and analyze the attributes to the Buddha found in earlier works. They further define the knowledge of a Buddha as uniquely including knowledge of the maturity of spiritual faculties, knowledge of the disposition of living beings, the ability to perform the twin miracle, and the attainment of great compassion, omniscience, and unobstructed knowledge.

The twin miracle is a feat performed by the Buddha at Sāvatthi in response to a challenge by a rival wandering renouncer. When described in the canon (e.g., in the *Pāṭika Sutta* of the *Dīghanikāya*, DN III, 27), the miracle is relatively simple, in that the Buddha rises up into the air and emits fire. However, the commentary extends the description, such that the Buddha produces multiple miracles in pairs, multiplies himself, preaching different sermons directly suited to those present. At the end of performing the miracle, the Buddha then takes three enormous strides, traversing the earth, atmosphere, and heaven (similar to a feat elsewhere attributed to one of the incarnations of the Indic god Viṣṇu), to visit the deity his mother Māyā has become. It is on this occasion that he preaches to her, giving us the *Abhidhamma Piṭaka* (Chapter 7). It is called the twin miracle because "it requires the production of flames from the upper part of the Body and water from the lower part, then water from the upper part and flames from the lower part" (Anālayo 2009: 776, citing the *Paṭisambhidāmagga*). These texts and the early postcanonical text the *Milindapañha* (*The Questions of King Milinda*, translation Rhys Davids 1890–1894) state that this miracle can only be performed by a Buddha. However, a passage in the *Saṃyuktāgama* of the Sarvāstivādin canon mentions this miracle being performed by the *arhat* Dabba Mallaputta before dying, whereas the parallel passage in the Pali *Udāna* describes Dabba as rising in the air and cremating his own body, not performing the twin miracle. The Buddha's aunt, Mahājāpatī Gotamī (see Chapter 9) either alone or with 500 nuns, performs the twin miracle according the *Ekottarika Āgama*, also of the Sarvāstivādins, and the *Kṣūdrakavastu* of the *Mūlasarvāstivādin Vinaya* (Anālayo 2009: 776–777). Peter Skilling has traced narratives of the twin miracle across a large range of Buddhist literature and concludes, "The Mūlasarvāstivādins, Sarvāstivādins, Lokottaravādins, Mahīśāsakas, Aśvaghoṣa, and Asaṅga along with the *Ratnaguṇasaṃcaya*, *Eottarikāgama*, *P'u yao ching*, and *Book of Zambasta*, agree against the Theravādins that an auditor [*arhat*] as well as a Buddha could perform the *yamakaprātihārya* [twin miracle] ... The narrative literature of these schools or authors contains examples of the prodigy being performed by monks as well as nuns" (Skilling 1997: 315). The claim that the twin miracle can only be performed by the Buddha therefore appears to be a particularly Theravada attempt to carve out a unique definition for the Buddha.

Omniscience in the canon is expressed in terms of the Buddha knowing everything that is relevant to spiritual progress. In a famous passage of the *Sutta Piṭaka* (in the *Cūḷa-Māluṅkya Sutta, Majjhima Nikāya* 63), the Buddha rejects the relevance of a list of 14 metaphysical questions and replies with his famous imagery of a man shot by a poisoned arrow. The man refuses to have the arrow removed until he understands everything about who shot it, the bow that fired it, the arrow itself, how the arrow was made, and so dies. Similarly, monks should not waste their time on irrelevant metaphysical speculation since it does not lead to Enlightenment. By the time of the commentaries, however, the Buddha's omniscience includes knowledge of metaphysical matters, including all aspects of the universe, and the past *and* future as well as the present, in addition to complete knowledge about doctrinal matters.

The inclusion of the future, that is, of prescience or precognition, had a significant effect on commentarial interpretation. For example, in the opening scene of the *Mahāparinibbāna Sutta*, the Buddha is approached by an advisor to King Ajātasattu who wants advice on whether or not to make war against the Vajjī confederacy. The Buddha comments that the Vajjī are so strong because of the harmonious and consultative way they meet and make decisions, among other things. The adviser understands this to mean that the King will first need to sow dissent to weaken the Vajjī before making war. The advice "allows the king to conquer the Vajjī, a historical event attested in other accounts. Commentator Buddhaghosa is at pains to point out that the Buddha speaks as he does in order to postpone the inevitable, gaining the Vajjīs more time to make merit" (Crosby 2012: 86, note 14). As we move into early postcanonical texts such as the *Milindapañha* "Questions of King Milinda," we find that this ability to know the future begs the question of why the Buddha laid down the *vinaya* rules one at a time, when by looking ahead he could have prevented the wrongdoing that, on being reported to him, is the occasion for him establishing each rule. The answer given is that although a Buddha can know anything without obstruction, he must advert his mind to the object of his knowledge. This is in line with the analysis of the causal factors involved in the creation of the consciousness in the *Paṭṭhāna* of the *Abhidhamma Piṭaka* (see Chapter 7). A mind, including a Buddha's mind, must take something as its object to be conscious of it. Even for the Buddha, omniscience is not omnipresent.

The theme of great compassion as an attribute specifically of the Buddha develops from the story of the Buddha choosing to teach, yet is also used in the commentaries to explain why the Buddha did things and appeared to experience needs that were clearly unnecessary for a *mahāpurisa*, a "great man." He behaves as if he is subject to the usual requirements of human life in order to make monks in the future feel better about their own needs.

We noted earlier some of the aspects of Buddhahood addressed in the *Abhidhamma Piṭaka*. The *Kathāvatthu's (Points of Controversy's)* attempt to prevent some layers of docetism and apotheosis apparent in other schools is seen in the rejection of the following teachings: that the Buddha's ordinary speech is supramundane; that he never lived in the world; that he preached through a created figure; that he felt no compassion; that everything of him was fragrant; that Buddhas differ from each other; and that multiple Buddhas are present in all directions. The *Kathāvatthu* also contains refutations of attempts to downgrade the status of the *arhat* further than the Theravada differentiation between Buddha and *arhat* allowed (Endo 1997/2002: 168). *The Paṭṭhāna* (*Conditional Relations*) attempts to capture the content of the Buddha's omniscience about causality (see Chapter 7). *Abhidhamma* commentaries also develop the understanding of how the Buddha is physically transformed by his Enlightenment (his *kāyabala*), such that his body becomes entirely pure.

In the commentaries, we find further distinctions between the *arhat*, *paccekabuddha*, and *Buddha*. For the Buddha, the *vāsanā* "fragrance" or impressions of defilements (*kilesa*) no longer exert an influence, whereas on the arhat they do. The term *vāsanā* is more familiar in the *yogācāra* philosophy of Mahayana Buddhism, yet, through the commentaries, is also found in Burmese Buddhism. This needs to be distinguished from the ongoing effect of *kamma*, which does influence even the Buddha. This ongoing effect of *kamma* can be seen in *Apadāna* stories about the Buddha's former bad deeds that explain a headache or backache or other bad experience in the Buddha's current life (Walters 1990) – although this possibility is contested in a number of commentaries (Appleton 2010: 26) – as well as in chronicles that explain damage to certain images of him (see Chapter 2).

A further development is the description of the Buddha as perfect even within the womb, where he awaits birth seated upright in meditation. We also see the increased emphasis on relics and their role in mediating the ongoing presence of the Buddha (see Chapter 2).

The Three *Parinibbāna* of the Buddha

According to the fifth-century commentaries, the Buddha undergoes three different levels of *parinibbāna* "Enlightenment" or "extinction." The first *parinibbāna* is the Enlightenment under the *Bodhi* tree, when the Buddha's defilements (*kilesa*) are extinguished. The second *parinibbāna* is when the Buddha gives up the five "aggregates" *khandha*, the psychosomatic constituents that make him a physically present person interacting in the world. In human terms, this is his death. The relics (*dhātu*) left after his cremation are then his only physical remains. The third *parinibbāna*, not mentioned in the canon, is the *parinibbāna* of those relics (Strong 2004: 223). For when the new Buddha Metteyya is about to begin his teaching the relics of the previous Buddha, Gotama, gather together and deliver a final sermon at Mahābodhi, the seat of the Buddha's original *parinibbāna*. The belief in this final *parinibbāna* reflects an understanding of the Buddha's ongoing presence in his relics and other physical reminders, that is, symbols and images. The development in understanding of the Buddha's "bodies" continues in later Theravada literature. In addition to the physical body (*rūpakāya*) and the body of his teachings (*dhammakāya*) in the second layer of commentaries (such as those by Dhammapāla, circa eighth- or ninth-century CE) we find that the *dhammakāya* includes the spiritual qualities. There are three types of physical reminder of the Buddha, the physical relics, *dhātu*, that is, hair, nails, and bones, given either before or after death, the objects used by the Buddha, such as the bowl in which Sujātā offered the meal, and thirdly, indicators of the Buddha, such as footprints and even images. To this, the *Paṭhamasaṃbodhi* (see earlier text) adds a fourth type of physical reminder, that of the Dhamma, teaching. This type is more familiar from Mahayana Buddhism and noted in the packing of images with sacred texts in Tibetan Buddhism, for example. Yet the wearing of excerpts of sacred texts as protection and their insertion into ***stūpas*** and images are also found in Theravada Buddhism.

Surveying these developments in the understanding of the Buddha and the redefining of his uniqueness, we can see that Theravada, on the one hand, denies some of the docetism and apotheosis found in other Buddhist traditions. Nonetheless, it does reflect such tendencies and in some instances, for example with its emphasis on the Buddha's monopoly on the performance of the twin miracle, goes beyond other forms of Buddhism in emphasizing the Buddha's special character, and in denying such cultic status to any potential rival.

Summary

This chapter examined the core teachings, biography, and status of the Buddha. It did this in relation to the religious views that pertained in north India in sixth- to fourth-century BCE, explaining also how this date for Gotama Buddha, the Buddha of our era, is calculated. The way in which the character of the Buddha alters synchronically, adapted for the needs of different genres of literature, and diachronically, reflecting developing understandings of Buddhahood and the spread of Buddhism, allows us to see the Buddha as a figure representing different kinds of authority and expectations of what it means to have mastered *saṃsāra*, the realm of rebirth and suffering/insecurity. The notion of Buddhahood as an achievement taking multiple lifetimes is developed in later canonical literature to provide a defined career similar for all 28 past Buddhas and all future Buddhas. We also examined the evidence of the commentaries, chronicles, and later Pali and vernacular biographies. Other genres of literature related to the Buddha were noted, including their use in empowerment. The developing notions of and refinements to the definition of Buddha qualities, his wisdom, compassion, and physical attributes, were examined in some detail, allowing us to observe that aspects of apotheosis and docetism are found within Theravada since the earliest times and are the attention of exploration and expansion in the Theravada tradition, even while some such tendencies found in other forms of Buddhism are rejected. This was contrasted with Western emphases on the Buddha's humanity and a mistaken assumption that there is a Theravada "orthodoxy" that concurs with this view. Stories about the Buddha, his visits, images, and relics acted as political charters in the spread of Theravada and its patronage or "protection" by those holding worldly power – kings and, later, governments. They provide a link between the historical Buddha and Buddhists of the present. Representing the ongoing presence of the Buddha, they will come together for the Buddha's third and final *parinibbāna*, and his last sermon, in anticipation of the future Buddha Metteyya.

References

Anālayo, Bhikkhu. ( ). 'Yamakapāṭihāriya' in W.G. Weeraratne (ed.), *Encyclopaedia of Buddhism*, vol. 8, no. 3. Sri Lanka: Department of Buddhist Affairs, 776–777.

Anālayo, Bhikkhu. (2010). 'Paccekabuddhas in the *Isigili-sutta* and its *Ekottarika-āgama* Parallel', *Canadian Journal of Buddhist Studies* 6: 5–36.

Anderson, Carol S. (1999). *Pain and Its Ending: The Four Noble Truths in the Theravada Buddhist*. Canon: Curzon Press.

Appleton, Naomi. (2010). *Jātaka Stories in Theravāda Buddhism, Narrating the Bodhisattva Path*. Farnham: Ashgate Publishing.

Bechert, Heinz. (2004). 'Buddha, Life of the' in Robert E. Buswell, Jr. (ed.), *Encyclopedia of Buddhism*. New York: Macmillan Reference USA, 82–88.

Benn, James A. (2007). *Burning for the Buddha Self-Immolation in Chinese Buddhism*. Honolulu: University of Hawai'i Press.

Chiu, Angela Shih Chih. (2012). 'The Social and Religious World of Northern Thai Buddha Images: Art, Lineage, Power and Place in Lan Na Monastic Chronicles (*Tamnan*)'. PhD thesis, School of Oriental and African Studies, University of London.

Collins, Steven. (2010). *Nirvana: Concept, Imagery, Narrative*. Cambridge: Cambridge University Press.

Coningham, Robin A.E. (2013). 'Dating the Buddha: New Archaeological Evidence from Lumbini (Nepal) the Birth Place of the Buddha'. Paper Delivered in the South and Southeast Asian Art & Archaeology Research Seminar. London: SOAS, March 20, 2013.

Crosby, Kate. (November 2000). '*uddis* and *ācikh*. The Inclusion of the *sikkhāpada* in the *pabbajjā* Liturgy According to the *Samantapāsādikā*', *Journal of Indian Philosophy* 28: 461–477.

Crosby, Kate. (2012). 'The Inheritance of Rahula: Abandoned Child, Boy Monk, Ideal Son and Trainee' in Vanessa Sasson (ed.), *Little Buddhas: Children and Childhoods in Buddhist Texts and Traditions*. Oxford: Oxford University Press, 97–123.

Cunningham, A. (1877). *Corpus Inscriptionum Indicarum. Volume 1. Inscriptions of Asoka*. Calcutta: Government of India.

Dhammajoti, K.L. (2011). 'From Abhidharma to Mahāyāna: Remarks on the early Abhidharma doctrine of the three *yāna-s*', *Journal of Buddhist Studies Centre for Buddhist Studies Sri Lanka* IX: 153–169.

Duroiselle, Charles. (1906). *Jinacarita, or 'The Career of the Conqueror' A Pāli Poem*. Rangoon: British Burma Press.

Endo, Toshiichi. (1997/2002). *Buddha in Theravada Buddhism: A Study of the Concept of Buddha in the Pali Commentaries*, 2nd edn. Dehiwala: Buddhist Cultural Centre.

Galloway, Charlotte. (2002). 'Relationships Between Buddhist Texts and Images of the Enlightenment During the Early Pagan Period' in Alexandra Green and T. Richard Blurton (eds.), *Burma Art and Archaeology*. London: The British Museum Press, 45–54.

Gombrich, R.F. (1988). *Theravada Buddhism: A Social History from Ancient Benares to Modern Colombo*. London: Routledge & Kegan Paul.

Gray, James. (1894). *Jinālaṃkāra or Embellishments of Buddha by Buddharakkhita*. London: Luzac & Co.

Griswold, A.B. (1957). *Dated Buddha Images of Northern Siam*. Ascona: Artibus Asiae.

Gunawardana, R.A.L.H. (1978). 'The Kinsmen of the Buddha: Myth as Political Charter in the Ancient and Early Medieval Kingdoms of Sri Lanka' in Bardwell L. Smith (ed.), *Religion and the Legitimation of Power in Sri Lanka*. Chambersburg: Anima Books, 96–106.

Hartmann, Jens-Uwe. (1991). 'Research on the Date of the Buddha: South Asian Studies Published in Western Languages' in Heinz Bechert (ed.) *The Dating of the Historical Buddha, Die Datierung des historischen Buddha*, Part 1. Göttingen: Vandenhoeck & Ruprecht, 27–45.

Herbert, Patricia. (1993). *The Life of the Buddha*. London: British Library.

von Hinüber, Oskar. (1996). *A Handbook of Pāli Literature*. Berlin/New York: Walter de Gruyter.

Huxley, Andrew. (1996). 'The *Vinaya*: Legal System or Performance-Enhancing Drug?', in T. Skorupski (ed.), *The Buddhist Forum*, vol. IV. London: SOAS, 141–163.

Jayawickrama, N.A. (1990). *The Story of Gotama Buddha (Jātaka-nidāna)*. Oxford: The Pali Text Society.

Laulertvorakul, Anant. (2003). 'Paṭhamasambodhi in Nine Languages: Their Relation and Evolution', *Manusya: Journal of Humanities* 6.2: 11–34.

Lopez, Donald S. (2005). 'Buddha' in Donald S. Lopez (ed.), *Critical Terms for the Study of Buddhism*. Chicago: University of Chicago Press, 13–36.

Moore, Elizabeth Howard. (1999). *Shwedagon: Golden Pagoda of Myanmar*. London: Thames and Hudson.

Murti, G. Srinivasa and A.N. Krishna Aiyangar. (1951). *Edicts of Asoka*. Madras: The Adyar Library.

Norman, K.R. (1997/2006). *A Philological Approach to Buddhism*, 2nd edn. Lancaster: The Pali Text Society.

Ñyāṇamoli, Bhikkhu. (1976). *The Path of Purification*, 2 vols. Boulder/London: Shambhala.

Rhys Davids, T.W. (1890–1894). *The Questions of King Milinda*. London: Oxford University Press.

Shwe Zan Aung and Rhys Davids. (1915). *Points of Controversy or Subjects of Discourse Being a Translation of the Kathā-Vatthu from the Abhidhamma-Piṭaka*. London: The Pali Text Society.

de Silva, Lily. (1987). 'The Buddha and the Arahant Compared', in M. Hiran F. Jayasuriya (ed.), *Pratidāna Mañjarī*. Colombo: Gate Mudaliyar W.F. Gunawardhana Commemoration Committee, 37–52.

Skilling, Peter. (1997). *Mahāsūtras: Great Discourses of the Buddha*, vol. II, Parts I and II. Oxford: The Pali Text Society.

Skilton, Andrew. (1994). *A Concise History of Buddhism*. Birmingham: Windhorse Publications.

Skilton, Andrew. (2011). 'Words or Pictures? The Life of the Buddha in Gupta / Pala India and Walt Disney'. Paper delivered at Buddhismus und Film: Aspekte und Perspektiven einer medial vermittelten Religion. Freie Universität, Berlin, June 2, 2011.

Strong, John S. (2004). *Relics of the Buddha*. Princeton: Princeton University Press.

Thomas, Edward. (1858). *Essays on Indian Antiquities, Historic, Numismatic, and Palæographic, of the Late James Prinsep, F.R.S., Secretary to the Asiatic Society of Bengal; to Which are Added His Useful Tables, Illustrative of Indian History, Chronology, Modern Coinages, Weights, Measures, Etc*. London: John Murray.

Vicittasārābhivaṃsa Tipiṭaka Sayadaw. (1960–1972). *Maha-bokda-win*. English translation *The Great Chronicle of the Buddha* by U. Ko Lay and U. Tin Lwin. Yangon: Tipitaka Nikaya Sasana Organisation. 1991. Reprint Selangor Buddhist Vipassana Meditation Society of Malaysia 1997, http://www.holybooks.com/great-chronicle-buddhas/ (retrieved June 28, 2013).

Walters, Jonathan S. (1990). 'The Buddha's Bad Karma: A Problem in the History of Theravāda Buddhism', *Numen* 37.1: 70–95.

Further Reading and Watching

Endo, Toshiichi. (1997 / 2002). *Buddha in Theravada Buddhism: A Study of the Concept of Buddha in the Pali Commentaries*, 2nd edn. Dehiwala: Buddhist Cultural Centre.

Herbert, Patricia. (1993). *The Life of the Buddha*. London: British Library.

Jaini, Padmanabh S. (1974). 'On the *Sarvajnatva* (Omniscience) of Mahavira and the Buddha', in L. Cousins, Arnold Kunst, and K.R. Norman (eds.), *Buddhist Studies in Honour of I.B. Horner*. Dordrecht: D. Reidel Publishing Co., 71–90.

Jayawickrama, N.A. (1990). *The Story of Gotama Buddha (Jātaka-nidāna)*. Oxford: The Pali Text Society.

Lopez, Donald S. (2005). 'Buddha', in Donald S. Lopez (ed.), *Critical Terms for the Study of Buddhism*. Chicago: University of Chicago Press, 13–36.

Reynolds, Frank E. (1977). 'The Several Bodies of Buddha: Reflections on a Neglected Aspect of Theravada Tradition', *History of Religions* 16.4: 374–389.

Strong, John S. (2001). *The Buddha: A Short Biography*. Oxford: Oneworld.

Strong, John S. (2004). *Relics of the Buddha*. Princeton: Princeton University Press.

2

Buddha Worship

Overview

The physical reminders of the Buddha include physical remains (*dhātu*), items he used, reminders of him, that is, symbols, images, and paintings and texts containing his teachings. They represent the Buddha's ongoing influence in the world following his *parinibbāna* (death), populating the Theravada realm, as well as authorizing and providing spiritual and secular power there. In this chapter, we shall explore in some depth one of the main expressions of Buddhist faith, namely, Buddha worship. We shall examine scholarly arguments questioning the appropriateness and function of worship in Buddhism, arguments that have been regarded as pertinent to Theravada due to its relative lack of docetism in relation to the person of the Buddha (see Chapter 1). Such arguments coincide with the tendency to downplay or eschew devotion to the Buddha and to gods in **reform Buddhism** where notions of what constitutes Buddhism become **essentialized** in the context of political, ethnic, and religious rivalry. Yet such arguments oversimplify Buddhist religiosity and impose on it an essentialist notion of what it means to be Buddhist. Worship in its many forms, of many different types of Buddha image and other sources of power, such as spirits, and historic figures, constitute many aspects of religious and social expression for individuals and groups, whether constituted temporarily or over centuries. The process of empowering Buddha statues and the authorization of such empowerment in Theravada literature will be described. The importance of worship is observed in relation to merit-making, power, protection, preparation for meditation, building communities, and shaping the experience and economics of pilgrimage routes. The place of some specific images and physical relics in Theravada national identities and communities is explored. Finally, we note the way in which some Theravada images have taken up residence in new homes, including in museum collections around the world.

Theravada Buddhism: Continuity, Diversity, and Identity, First Edition. Kate Crosby.

The Ubiquity of Buddha Worship in Theravada

Before Western observation of Buddhism reached its understanding of the Buddha as an inspirational human, it initially viewed Buddhism as primitive idolatry. For early observers from Abrahamic religious backgrounds, the ubiquitous presence of images was one of the most striking aspects of Buddhism.

> In the first quarter of the sixteenth century, Portuguese proto-orientalist Duarte Barbosa (died 1521) wrote that the King of Siam, like the kings of Burma, Arakan, and Pegu, was "a Heathen ... , a worshipper of idols of whose temples he has very many." Near the end of the seventeenth century, ibn Muḥammad Ibrāhīm, secretary to the envoy sent by Shah Sulaimām the Safavid to King Narai of Ayutthaya, recorded that, "The Siamese persevere in worshipping idols. ... They are not even like the other idolators who worship one special idol which has a determined shape and form. In Siam anyone who please [*sic.*] makes an image of out plaster, wood or mud, sets it up in a particular spot and worships it. ..." (Skilling 2012: xvii–xviii)

The practices described by the foreign observers continue much the same today: simple salutations, or the offering of flowers, rice, incense, water, candles, or – in the case of important images – a full daily routine of waking, washing, dressing in monastic robes, feeding, entertaining and retiring for the night (Kyaw and Crosby 2013). Such worshipping of Buddha images confounded Western scholars in the light of their understanding of the Buddha as a mortal. It appeared to them, and to some Western convert practitioners, to be particularly contradictory in Theravada, given its relative lack of docetism (the understanding that a sacred person is solely a projection of the divine rather than a living being) in comparison with other forms of Buddhism (Chapter 1). If the formal doctrinal position in Theravada is that the Buddha was mortal and has died for the last time, then surely he is no longer accessible as an individual to his followers? (Gombrich 1988: 120) In which case, what is going on when Buddhists worship his image? In the second half of the twentieth- and the twenty-first century, there have been scholarly debates concerning Buddha worship and there are varied Theravada perspectives on the function of such worship.

The ubiquity of Buddha images over the centuries gives us some of our earliest evidence for Buddhism in Sri Lanka and Southeast Asia. Their perpetual presence means that the periodization of the art of the region's different countries is mainly defined through the proportions, physiognomy, and details of Buddha images and the buildings in which images and relics have been enshrined. An art form characteristic of a perceived golden era is then reinvoked in later centuries, for example in the fashion in nineteenth- to twentieth-century Burma when Buddhism was under threat of decline under the expansion of British imperialism, for images made in the twelfth- to thirteenth-century style of the "golden era" of the Pagan period.

Leadership After the *Parinibbāna* of the Buddha

The absence of an omnipotent, creator god, and the understanding of the Buddha as mortal have led Buddhism to be identified as a form of atheism. Authority for this is found in the Buddha's advice to his disciple Ānanda concerning who would take his place after his death. This advice is recorded in the canonical *Mahāparinibbāna Sutta (Dīgha Nikāya sutta* 16), the *sutta* describing the last three months of the Buddha's life:

> Then the Lord Buddha addressed the venerable Ānanda, saying, "It might be, Ānanda, that you might think, 'The teaching is teacherless. There is no Teacher.' But it should not be viewed like this, Ānanda. That which I have taught you, made known to you, as the Dhamma and the Vinaya, that shall be your teacher after I am gone." (translation Crosby)

According to Theravada historiography, these two teachers, the Dhamma ("truth/teaching") and *Vinaya* ("monastic discipline"), were collected together in a meeting of monks immediately after the Buddha's death. This meeting is called the "First Council." The texts preserved by the First Council form the Pali Canon. The canon is also known as the "Three Baskets," *Tipiṭaka*, because it is divided up into three sections: (i) the *Vinaya Piṭaka*, containing the rules; (ii) the *Sutta Piṭaka*, containing the teaching; and (iii) the *Abhidhamma Piṭaka*, containing the systematization of the teachings. The Buddha's advice to Ānanda means that there is no lineage of teachers inheriting the Buddha's mantle as leader of the religion: authority rests in the Canon (see Chapter 3).

The passage cited earlier is in tune with the temperament of other teachings of the Buddha recorded in the canon that have been much drawn upon by exegetes of one kind or another wishing to emphasize Buddhism as a philosophy rather than a "religion." The Buddha used the term *kamma* (Sanskrit *karma*) to refer to intentional action of the body, speech, and mind. He rejected an earlier understanding of *kamma* found in Vedic Hinduism meaning ritual action because he rejected the efficacy of such ritual. In the Pali canonical text, the *Sigālovāda Sutta* "Sutta of Advice to Sigāla," the Buddha tells the brahmin Sigāla that the effective way to perform worship of the six directions is to look after the six directions, not to make offerings to them. (This may be a reference to a Vedic ritual to worship the serpent-deities of the four cardinal points, plus above and below.) The Buddha then reinterprets each of the six directions as a different set of people with whom one is involved in the normal course of one's daily life. Rather than make offerings to the directions, one should conduct one's relations with parents (east), teachers (south), wife and children (west), friends and colleagues (north), servants (below), and renouncers and priests (above) in a skillful and appropriate fashion. In other words, one looks to one's own behavior to avoid problems arising "from the directions" rather than trying to appease unseen forces beyond one's control. The advice is practicable, like that to rely on the Dhamma and *Vinaya* after the Buddha is no longer available, given in the *Mahāparinibbāna Sutta*.

On the other hand, in this same text that identifies the Dhamma and *Vinaya* as the teacher, the *Mahāparinibbāna Sutta*, the Buddha also advocates worship of himself and his remains. At one point he asks those near him to move aside to make way for all the deities who have come to worship him but are invisible to the eyes of most mortals. At another, he gives instructions on how his mortal remains should be cremated then enshrined in funerary mounds, *stūpa*. He describes the advantages of worshipping the *stupa*. (*Stūpa* is the Sanskrit term now commonly used in English. The term in the text is Pali ***thūpa***. Other terms commonly found are Pāli *cetiya*, Sanskrit, *caitya*, Burmese *ceti*, Sinhalese *dāgaba*, and Thai *cedī*. The word used for *stūpa* in early translations into English is "cairn.") That the cult of the Buddha and things connected with him goes back to the very earliest history of Buddhism appears to be confirmed by recent finds below, that is, prior to, the Mauryan layer in archeological digs at Lumbinī, regarded as the birth place of the Buddha (Coningham 2013).

The idea that worship and the making of offerings are good actions, or meritorious activities, that have a transformative effect on one's state of mind and lead to benefits later in this life or in a subsequent life is also the basis of Buddhist "merit making."

> People build a *stūpa*, a commemorative funeral mound, for the universally powerful king at the crossroads where four great roads meet. This, Ānanda, is how people treat the physical remains of a universally powerful king. The physical remains of the Buddha should be treated in the same way as those of a universally powerful king, Ānanda. A *stūpa* should be built for the Buddha at the crossroads where four great roads meet. Any who place a garland or perfume or paint there, or pay their respects there, or experience serene faith in their minds there, it will be to their lasting benefit and happiness. (translation Crosby)

The *Mahāparinibbāna Sutta* also advocates pilgrimage. Pilgrimage should be undertaken to places associated with a list of events in the Buddha's life, a list that grew and altered but centered on eight "great moment": his birth at Lumbini, his Awakening at Bodh Gaya, the first sermon at Sarnath, the monkey offering at Vaishali, the taming of the wild elephant at Rajagriha, the performance of miracles at Shravasti, the return from preaching to his mother in heaven at Saṃkāśya, and his death at Kusinara. These formed the core itinerary for Buddhist pilgrimage in India and Nepal. The rediscovery of the sites in the modern period (although a number of the identifications are disputed) means that they are again the basis of modern Buddhist pilgrimage for Buddhists from all over the world, including from Theravada countries. There are additional, local pilgrimage sites in Theravada countries. These are authorized through stories in the noncanonical chronicle literature (see Chapter 1) relating further incidents in the life of the Buddha interposed between the canonical events. The religious practice of paying homage to the remains of the Buddha authorized in the *Mahāparinibbāna Sutta* is also extended to other types of physical reminder of the Buddha. There are then four types of physical reminder: the physical remains of the Buddha ("relic"/*dhātu*), objects used by him, reminders of him, for example, footprints and statues, and his Dhamma, that is, teachings in the form of texts. The fourth item in the list appears to be a later addition to the more common list of three (Bizot 1994: 104). While some relics are particularly famous and receive mention in chronicles (see later text), many temples also have their own relic, with or without a story of its provenance. Relics are believed to have the ability to multiply or to appear spontaneously.

Worship of *stūpa* as described in the *Mahāparinibbāna Sutta* continues to this day. It is done quite simply. People circumambulate them and perhaps place flowers and incense before them. Other representations of the Buddha, such as the carved single footprint, either plain or bearing 108 symbols of the Buddha's attributes, found at many sites throughout Southeast Asia and Sri Lanka, are also worshipped in this simple way (Cicuzza 2011). It is to a statue of the Buddha that one usually makes more elaborate offerings and addresses prayers. The ubiquitous worship of Buddha statues in Theravada has led to a considerable amount of academic discussion, and parallel criticisms within reform Buddhism, of the apparent discrepancy between the advice concerning the Buddha's lack of availability after his death/his giving up of this life in the *Mahāparinibbāna Sutta* and the practice of treating him as if he were still available. In particular, a contrast is made between this doctrinal position and that of **Hinduism**, in which a Hindu deity may be regarded as present in its *mūrti*, its "embodiment" (the Sanskrit term used for a Hindu image). Is the Buddha somehow regarded as present in the statue by those who worship the statue? Does this imply a belief the Buddha is still "out there" and able to respond with them, in the same way as a god in iconic theism? (Crosby 2005: 247)

There are, nonetheless, a number of aspects of Buddha worship that are unproblematic and authorized in the canon. Recollection of the Buddha is a key Buddhist meditation (Chapter 6). One advantage is psychological: it calms the practitioner and, in particular, allays fear.

The Buddha is worshipped for his achievements as the ultimate role model, and some Western practitioners have preferred to use verbs such as "venerate" or "revere" in this context, to avoid the connotations of obeisance to a supreme power contained within the term "worship" (e.g., King 1964/1990: 174). Perhaps the egalitarian values of the post-world war period have added to the discomfort of the translation "worship" for verbs such as *pūjeti* (*pūjayati* Sanskrit). Moreover, within Buddhism it is almost universally accepted that paying homage to the Buddha is beneficial because it is a meritorious activity, as described in the *Mahāparinibbāna Sutta* earlier. It constitutes a good action (*kamma*) that will lead to a beneficial outcome in this or a future life.

Theravada Groups That Eschew Buddha Worship

There are exceptions to the widespread acceptance of the role of Buddha worship. Some modern practitioners avoid practices that could be construed as superstitious or could make one reliant on another instead of striving for oneself. A variety of early modern to modern Buddhist groups have downplayed or even eschewed image worship altogether. Monastic-centered groups that have done so include various reform sects in Burma, such as the Zawti sect started in the sixteenth to seventeenth centuries (Khur-Yearn 2012: 60), the Santi Asoke movement founded in Thailand by Photirak in the early 1970s (Swearer 2004a: 238, 246) and, most recently, the monk Sumaṅgala Thera within the Mogok meditation system in Burma (personal communication Pyi Phyo Kyaw, see Chapter 6). Lay groups that have de-emphasized worship include practitioners of the Burmese *vipassanā* meditation method popularized by Goenka (b. 1924) and practitioners associated with the meditation center Nilambe in highland Sri Lanka. What all of these groups have in common is a dedication to in-depth meditation practice. The monastic-centered groups also share the aspiration to return to what they perceive as the early role of the Sangha, namely, a simple "forest life" dedicated to the pursuit of spiritual transformation. A general tendency emerged for modern, reform Buddhism to define Buddhism in relation to modern science and notions of rationality, particularly as Buddhism came to be associated with independence and anti-colonial movements. In defining Buddhism as a scientific religion in contrast to Christianity and other theistic religions, worship in general was downplayed.

The belief in and worship of gods was even more contentious: their importance was also downplayed in nineteenth- to twentieth-century reform Buddhism. Their prevalence in Buddhist literature, art, and practice still often comes as a surprise to Westerners. The controversy over the worship of gods was recently revived as an issue in Sri Lanka, given voice by the highly popular monk Gangodawila Soma Thera (1948–2003), again drawing on notions of Buddhism as a scientific and rational religion. While Soma Thera was critical of Christian evangelism in Sri Lanka, a controversial issue in recent years, he particularly criticized Sinhalese Buddhists for worshipping gods of "Hindu" origins, that is, who reflect the Indian background shared between the two religions (Holt 2004: 334–343). His polemics can be understood as part of the way Sinhalese Buddhists sought to distance themselves from their broader Indic heritage as part of the increasing essentializing of what it meant to be a Buddhist that took place in response and in contribution to the civil war (1983–2009) between government forces and the separatist militant group the Liberation Tigers of Tami Eelam.

The influence of Western expectations and of nineteenth- to twentieth-century reform Buddhism continues to be visible in the different approaches taken by different Theravada temples in the West. For example, in London, the London Buddhist **Vihāra** in Chiswick founded in the early twentieth century, at the height of reform Buddhism, and which caters to an international congregation mainly made up of professional, Anglophone Sinhalese and Westerners, may be contrasted with the Sri Saddhatissa Temple, an offshoot of the London Buddhist Vihāra but catering primarily to the broader Sinhalese Diaspora community. While both are served by Sri Lankan monks, only the latter has a shrine to a god (Azzopardi 2008: 174).

The Benefits of Buddha-Worship

While there have been a number of groups and individuals critical of the worship of the Buddha (and of the broader pantheon of deities associated with Buddhism), Buddhist narrative literature from the *Mahāparinibbāna* onward abounds with stories exemplifying the benefits of paying homage and making offerings to the Buddha, *paccekabuddhas* or any other sanctified beings, including members of the Sangha. Even the devotion of a dog is meritorious activity: the thirteenth-century Sinhalese text, the *Saddharmaratnāvaliya*, is a collection of stories concerning the results of good and bad deeds. It includes the story of a man called Ghoshaka, who has enjoyed not only being a god in one lifetime but, in the next, is rescued from the certain death of being abandoned as a baby on a rubbish heap: he is the male, and therefore unwanted, child of a courtesan. To what did he owe this especially fine fortune? In the previous lifetime, as a dog, he had regularly guided a *paccekabuddha* through the jungle to pick up his alms food (Obeyesekere 2001: 31).

The belief that worship earns merit is not confined to popular literature: it is also accepted in Buddhist philosophy, even if schools differ in their understanding of the nature of the Buddha's presence after *parinibbāna*. This shared belief is in evidence in the debate between opposing Buddhists in the seventh-century *Bodhicaryāvatāra*, a text belonging to the Madhyamaka school of Mahayana philosophy. In response to an objection to the proposed illusory nature of the Buddha as manifest or the phenomenal world, the protagonist retorts: "Merit comes from [worshipping] the Conqueror (Buddha) who is like an illusion in the same way as it would if he was truly existent" (Chapter 9, v. 9, Crosby and Skilton 1996: 116). His statement has to be accepted by the opponents because no Buddhists contest that worshipping a Buddha brings merit, irrespective of whether he is present, dead, or illusory (Crosby 2005: 247). Underlying the belief in this merit is the understanding that the action may transform the mental state of the individual. Since it is a universal Buddhist belief that "mind is the forerunner of all acts" (*Dhammapada* Chapter 1, v. 1–2), an improvement in the continuum of an individual's stream of consciousnesses may have a profound impact on that person's success on the spiritual path as well as on his/her future rebirths. This role of the transformative effect of the mind is seen in the explanation for *stūpa* building given in the *Mahāparinibbāna Sutta*, cited earlier:

> When people experience a mind full of serene faith on thinking, "This is the stūpa of the Buddha, the worthy one who had attained full and perfect Awakening," they then, after the breaking up of the body after death, will be reborn in a good state, in a heavenly world. (translation Crosby)

The conjunction of these benefits of Buddha worship can be understood more fully when seen in the light of Theravada philosophy of mind, that is, *Abhidhamma*. According to *Abhidhamma*, the mind can be conscious of a mental object that is past, present, or future, and the object does not necessarily have to be physically present within the reach of one's other senses (see Chapter 7). Therefore, the mind of a worshipper takes the Buddha as its object, whether the Buddha is present, dead, or illusory. The worshipper can then perform meritorious veneration through bodily action (e.g., offering flowers and food), verbal action (e.g., chanting), or mental action (e.g., thinking about the qualities of the Buddha) with good volition/intention (*cetanā*). As in the passage from the *Bodhicaryāvatāra* cited earlier, the nature of the Buddha who is the object of this worship is immaterial to the effectiveness of the meritorious action. The act of taking the Buddha as one's mental object coupled with good volition inevitably leads to merit. In addition, the good volition acts as an uplifting factor that improves one's states of consciousness. The fact that a mental object is not confined to temporal and spatial boundaries allows the believers to engage with the Buddha whether or not he is currently accessible or present in the image (Kyaw and Crosby 2013).

To sum up, the advantages of Buddha worship that are doctrinally unproblematic and widely accepted are venerating the ideal and exemplary model, allaying fear, merit making, and changing one's mental or emotional state.

Practices That Treat the Buddha as Present in His Image

Sometimes the interaction between worshipper and worshipped either falls short of or extends beyond these doctrinally unproblematic interpretations of Buddha worship. For example, some worship might be ritualized to such a degree that none of the aforementioned considerations of mental or emotional process come into play. At the other extreme, the worshipper asks the Buddha for forgiveness or assistance, as if it were still possible to interact with the Buddha as present.

The pardoning of sins and intervention by a superior power may be regarded as contrary to the doctrine of *kamma*, namely, that the good or bad consequences of one's actions are unavoidable. (On other practices that seem to circumvent this doctrine, see Chapter 5.) The requests of the worshipper also seem to indicate that the Buddha is in some way present and accessible still, particularly in images.

During fieldwork conducted in Sri Lanka in the late 1960s, Sinhalese Buddhists gave a variety of reasons as to why they worship statues of the Buddha. They confirmed the understanding that the Buddha is no longer present and the significance of the attitude of the worshipper's mind for the outcome (Gombrich 1971: 141). Richard Gombrich analyzed the contrast between such understanding and the request for the Buddha's intervention as a distinction between cognitive and affective responses, between a rational understanding that he is dead, and an emotional interaction with him as if he were divine and still accessible. "For the Sinhalese the Buddha is cognitively human but affectively divine" (Gombrich 1971: 10). For Gombrich, this "inconsistency" can be explained in terms of psychological need: "Theravādin doctrine has never wavered from the position that the Buddha is dead and no longer active in the world; in moments of great crisis some individuals do pray to him for help, but that is the spontaneous outburst of emotion and in their calmer moments they know that it can do no good except as a psychological relief to themselves" (Gombrich 1988: 120).

Some Sinhalese villagers, however, offered a different explanation. "If pressed they reveal that although the Buddha is dead there is a certain Buddha force (*Budubalaya*), which will exist until, at the end of this dispensation in another 2500 years, the Buddha's relics (including images) will collect ... and after a last sermon the Buddha will finally disappear. ..." (Gombrich 1971: 167). This answer reminds us of the postcanonical belief in the three *parinibbāna* of the Buddha mentioned in Chapter 1. For Gombrich, this answer is also problematic, "because this *Budubalaya* does not seem to operate outside the ritual context as part of the world at large, but only in the presence of images; it is virtually a force inherent in the image" (Gombrich 1971: 167).

The apparent inconsistencies in doctrine and practice are similar throughout the Theravada world, even if the details in practice vary from region to region. The views of monks on the apparent dichotomy between doctrine and emotional need were recorded by Winston L. King in Burma in the early decades after independence. He quotes the Burmese monk U Pyinnya Dipa, who explains worship in terms of reverence of the Buddha as a role model. According to King, Dipa expresses "the Buddhist apologetic for physical symbolism" as follows: "Simple or average people require simple doctrines and are able to conceive an idea only through a symbolic image or ceremony" (King 1964/1990: 154). Like Gombrich, King points out that it is the statue that is the locus of the ongoing presence of the Buddha or his power (King 1964/1990: 177–178).

We find here a view that the treatment of the Buddha as present is a development in response to the broader religious needs of those not able to confront the more austere view that the Buddha is absent. Evidence that appears at one level to support such a view can be found not only in some canonical passages, but in later Theravada literature. The following story comes from the mediaeval Pali poem, the *Sīhalavatthu-Prakaraṇa*:

> The monk Phussadeva asks Māra, the personification of death and worldly temptation, to take on the form of the Buddha. When Māra does so, Phussadeva is overcome by emotion at the sight of the Buddha and begins to worship him while recollecting the Buddha's virtues. But Māra interrupts the vision, reminding Phussadeva of the truth of impermanence, "Such is the wholly enlightened Jina, the best of all beings, but he has succumbed to impermanence, gone to destruction; one cannot see him." Phussadeva continues his description of the Buddha's physical qualities, but adds that each is "gone to destruction and not seen." This recognition of impermanence leads Phussadeva to attain enlightenment. (Strong 1993: 138)

In this story, Phussadeva experiences a powerful emotional response to the appearance of the Buddha offered by Māra, the embodiment of death and temptation. (This transformation of Māra from the tempter who tries to keep people trapped in the round of rebirth, *saṃsāra*, into an aide for Buddhists is a theme that crops up in texts of a number of different schools. See Skilton 1998.) Prompted by Māra, Phussadeva combines this recollection the Buddha's virtues, one of the standard meditations in Buddhism, with another important meditation, the meditation on the impermanence of that very thing to which he feels attachment. What is interesting here, however, is that it is Phussadeva's devotion in combination with the knowledge of impermanence that is the key to his spiritual success and he achieves the highest goal, enlightenment. A version of this story, with interesting differences that emphasize the value of seeing the Buddha's glory for spiritual development, occurs in the commentary of the division of the Pali Canon that deals with monastic rules (*Vinaya*). There Phussadeva is not so engrossed but rather uses the beauty of Māra's impersonation to reflect on how much greater the Buddha must have been. It is this inspiration that helps his development of insight and attainment of *arhatship* (Steven Collins, personal communication concerning his draft article on *rūpakāya* in preparation, April 2013). The theme of attachment to the person of the Buddha as both inspiration and as a hindrance is also found in stories of disciples of the Buddha during his lifetime. The monk Ānanda does not achieve enlightenment until the Buddha's death forces him to confront the truth of even his (the Buddha's) impermanence, yet his devotion to the Buddha was crucial to his spiritual journey. The monk Vakkali follows the Buddha everywhere, so engrossed was he in the Buddha's visible beauty (see Chapter 1). The advice the Buddha then offers him is one of the most well-known affirmations that it is in the truth of the Buddha's teachings, rather than in himself as an individual, that his significance is to be found:

> What is to you, Vakkali, this foul body that you see? He who sees the Dhamma he it is that sees me. For seeing the Dhamma he sees me, and seeing me he sees the Dhamma. (*Theragāthā* 105, adapted from C.A.F. Rhys-Davids, 1951: 197. See further King 1964/1990: 152–153)

Consecration of Buddha Images

While these stories seem to confirm the contrast between doctrine and practice, or cognitive and affective, outlined earlier, the situation is not so simple. The consecration rituals for Buddha statues in much of Southeast Asia (Bizot 1994, Swearer 1995a, 2004a: Chapters 4–6) explicitly bring the powers of the Buddha (not the Buddha himself) into the statues. A.B. Griswold observes of the making of metal images, "Important castings, which take place in monastery precincts at an auspicious moment chosen by astrologers, are accompanied by a life-giving rite. The purchasers of routine images, cast without ceremony in the craftsman's shop, arrange for them to share in such a rite in a monastery at the first opportunity" (Griswold 1957: 46). The consecration rituals in Khmer-Tai-Lao are more elaborate than those found elsewhere, but the most important moment in the empowerment of an image, found in all Theravada countries except Burma, is the "opening of the eyes," representing the Buddha's Awakening. In Sri Lanka, the eyes are painted by an artisan from a specific caste that has the entitlement to perform this ritual (Gombrich 1971: 134). In mainland Southeast Asia, the moment is enacted though the removal of wax or cloth covering the eyes.

In the rituals of Cambodia and Thailand, the image is empowered through the recitation of texts by monks holding on to a sacred thread, one end of which is tied to the Buddha image. Texts recited on such occasions include ***paritta***, the *Dhammakāya* "Body of the Dhamma" text that equates physical attributes of the Buddha with elements of Buddhist doctrine (Choompolpaisal *et al.* in preparation), and biographies of the Buddha such as the *Paṭhamasambodhi* (see Chapter 1) and the "Consecration of the Buddha" (Swearer 2004b: 122–137). The new image is thus taught the life story and achievements of the Buddha. Then the powers of the Buddha associated with these achievements are invited to enter the image:

> May all his qualities be invested in this Buddha image. May the Buddha's boundless omniscience be invested in this image until the religion ceases to exist. May all of the transcendental states of the Blessed One … be invested in this image. May the boundless concentration and the body-of-liberation of the Buddha be invested in this image for five thousand years during the lifetime of the religion. May the supermundane reality discovered by the Buddha during

> his enlightenment under the bodhi tree be invested in this image for the five thousand years of the religion. May all of the miracles performed by the Buddha after his enlightenment in order to dispel the doubts of all humans and gods be invested in this image for all time. May the powers of the reliquary mounds miraculously created by the Buddha at the places of his enlightenment in order that humans and gods might worship him be invested in this image for five thousand rains-retreats. (Swearer 1995a: 57)

The text culminates in the request, "May all the gods, together with Indra, Brahmā, Māra, and all people protect this Buddha image, as well as the relics and the religion for 5000 years for the welfare of all human beings and gods" (Swearer 1995a: 38) The consecration supports the beliefs underlying the practices and comments mentioned earlier: the association of the image with the Buddha's power, as well as with the relics and the duration of the Buddha's teaching.

The Making of the First Statue

A further level of authorization for the power of the Buddha statue is found in consecration ceremonies of Cambodia and Thailand. An older statue is invited to transmit its powers into the new statue (Griswold 1957: 47). The actions involved and terminology used parallel those used in the ordination ceremony for monks (Bizot 1994: 109). The idea that images, like monks, have a lineage similar to monks is suggested by the legend of the first image: "When the Buddha entered final *nibbāna*, he conferred his own ten perfections on a Buddha statue, so that the religion might be protected and endure for 5000 years" (Bizot 1994: 115, translation from the French, Crosby). Although the worship of his relics and *stūpas* is authorized in the *Mahāparinibbāna Sutta*, no mention of statues is made in this or other canonical texts, but by the time of the commentaries references to monks looking after the shrine room indicate that the Buddha image had, by the fifth-century CE, become an unremarkable feature of the monastery. The commentary to the *Majjhima Nikāya*, the second division within the *Sutta Piṭaka* of the Pali Canon, describes how an offering should be made to the Buddha, represented by an image: "An image (of the Buddha) containing relics should be placed on a seat facing the two Orders [monks and nuns], and a stand put there, and when the offering of water … and the rest have been made, everything is first to be offered to the Teacher" (Ps. V.73 from Swearer 2004a: 14, citing Collins 1998: 246).

Later texts provide the legend of how the first Buddha image came to be made. Here is a summary translation of one such text:

> One day King Pasenadi of Kosala arrived at the Jetavana, the grove in which the Buddha resided, bringing the usual paraphernalia for worship such as incense, candles and flowers, in order to pay homage to the Buddha. The Buddha, however, was away teaching. Finding the grove deserted, King Pasenadi felt despondent, as if the Buddha had already entered *parinibbāna* (final enlightenment/last death). In the Buddha's absence, he made his offerings to the place where the Buddha usually sat.
>
> On meeting with the Buddha at a later time, King Pasenadi explained the emotions he had experienced and gained the Buddha's permission to make a statue of him to worship during any future absence of the Buddha.
>
> Using the costliest sandalwood the King had a statue made in the Buddha's likeness and placed it on a shrine in his palace. He then invited the Buddha to see the statue.

> When the Buddha arrived at the palace, the statue noticed his arrival and thought, "I am myself a statue of the Buddha without consciousness (*viññāṇa*). Right now, the Buddha is alive and is present here. It is not right for me to be raised up on a shrine. So I shall get down and pay homage to the Buddha." As the statue descended from the shrine to worship the Buddha, however, the Buddha stopped him saying, "Younger brother, statue of the Buddha, do not get down, remain elevated on the shrine. The religion of the Buddha should endure for 5000 years. I entrust it to you. Once the Buddha has entered *parinibbāna*, you will remain in the Buddha's place to save all beings for those 5000 years." (Bizot 1994, abridged translation from the French, Crosby. See also Gombrich 1978 and Chiu 2012: 49–50, 80–81 with notes 67 and 68.)

Here, the image is assigned the task of protecting the Dhamma and making sure salvation remains a possibility. The term younger brother with which the Buddha addresses the statue is a translation of term *āvuso*, taught by the Buddha as the appropriate term of address to be used by a senior monk addressing a junior monk. The verb used for the Buddha's prediction of the future role of the statue is the same term used for the prediction by Dīpaṃkara Buddha of the future Buddhahood of the *bodhisatta* Sumedha (see Chapter 1) (Crosby 2005: 257).

From this story and the consecration rituals, it is clear that the statue is empowered not through the Buddha himself being immanent in the statue, but through a process of empowerment, in which the Buddha's powers are transmitted into the statue, that is believed to go back to the Buddha himself. This validates the treatment of Buddha statues as powerful, although it is debatable whether it satisfactorily accounts for all features of image worship, such as requests for intervention or to pardon sins/transgressions. While it is the postcanonical texts that authorize image worship, canonical texts describe the worship of the Buddha during his lifetime and authorize the worshipping of his relics after his death, as seen earlier. The later texts also identify the role of the image as safeguarding the Dhamma and *Vinaya* that the Buddha in the *Mahāparinibbāna Sutta* states that the monks are to rely on after his final *parinibbāna*.

Devotion and Meditation Contrasted

While references to images and the story of the first Buddha image first make their appearance in postcanonical literature, the authorization for worship of the Buddha and his relics is canonical, occurring in the same text that insists that monks rely on the Dhamma and *Vinaya* as their teacher. In the *Mahāparinibbāna Sutta* and the legend of the first Buddha image, it is the laity that carries out the division of relics, construction of *stūpas*, and the manufacture of the Buddha image. This has contributed to a view in scholarship and some forms of reform Buddhism that worship is an activity for laypeople rather than monks. It may be that this narrative is in fact to establish a protocol for interaction between the monastic community and the laity, especially royalty, a linking of the fortunes of the two. Nevertheless, we shall now examine the assumption that there are two different types of practitioner in Buddhism, the *nibbāna*-oriented practitioners seeking spiritual transformation (traditionally monks and nuns) and the spiritually less advanced (traditionally laypeople). In other words, we shall examine the assumption that requests for intervention and forgiveness from the image reflect a broadening out of the Buddhist teaching to supply the emotional needs of the latter group, while the former group should remain entirely self-reliant and eschew such activity (Gombrich 1988: 120, King 1964/1990).

Examining this point in terms of self-reliance, it is noteworthy that, in some representations of Theravada, meditation has been emphasized as the ultimate tool of spiritual transformation (see Chapter 6) and other aspects of religious practice, that is, devotional and ethical aspects, have been played down. In such accounts, self-transformation is set in direct contrast with devotional practices that indicate a reliance on the Buddha. From this perspective, meditation as representative of the *nibbānic* path for those seeking release from *saṃsāra* is contrasted with devotion as representative of the path for those seeking improved present and future lives within *saṃsāra* (sometimes referred to as *kammic* or *kammatic* Buddhism). This distinction is found in the scholarship cited earlier and among the groups, also mentioned earlier, which eschew Buddha-worship while emphasizing meditation. Moreover, Theravada meditation is taught around the world today without any devotional context. Its techniques have been applied beyond the Buddhist context and their effectiveness tested in cognitive science (see Chapter 6).

Since Theravada has been regarded as an essentially atheistic religion both by outside observers and by reformers within the tradition, the methodology of meditation practice can be regarded as effective in transforming the individual irrespective of that individual's beliefs. Winston King, who had taken up *vipassanā* practice in Burma in the early stages of the global and secular popularity of Theravada-derived meditation practices, opined,

> (Since) the effort and attitude of the meditator, which are absolutely essential to any salvific result, ... are not exclusively determined by creedal affirmations, formal adherence to a given statement of faith is of lesser importance than in most Christian sacramental contexts. (King 1989: 251)

King defines a sacrament as "an outward and visible sign of an inward and spiritual grace" and the "appointed means of receiving salvific grace" (King 1989: 251). He rejects the idea that there might be parallels in Buddhism on the basis that salvation in Buddhism is reached without grace from an external source. This has been one of the ongoing attractions of Buddhism for those converting or drawing on it from within a Christian culture. Seeming to confirm this view is the absence of any reference to devotional practices in two standard modern texts on the subject, King's own *Theravāda Meditation: The Buddhist Transformation of Yoga* (1980) and Vajirañāna's *Buddhist Meditation in Theory and Practice* (1962), both of which provide detailed explanations of meditation practice.

Like many academic descriptions of Theravada meditation, as well as a number of Theravada meditation revival practices, King's and Vajirañāna's books are based on the *Visuddhimagga* (*The Path of Purification*, Ñyāṇamoli 1976). The *Visuddhimagga* is a fifth-century Theravada treatise on the spiritual path compiled by Buddhaghosa, the monk-scholar often regarded as most representative of Theravada orthodoxy (see Chapter 3). The entire structure of the *Visuddhimagga* is based on the individual's development, progressing from general morality to meditation then wisdom. It analyzes the path to salvation into a series of three progressive stages, these being moral conduct (*sīla*), meditation (*samādhi*), and wisdom (*paññā*). In this progression, morality is regarded as the necessary preparation for successful meditation that leads to spiritual progress. Other more immediate preparations for meditation mentioned by modern texts on the basis of the *Visuddhimagga* include finding an appropriate place, sitting in a comfortable position, and receiving an appropriate meditation subject from an appropriate teacher. Worship of the Buddha as a preparation for meditation is ignored in these modern writings based on the *Visuddhimagga*. Yet we shall see later that this is not so in the *Visuddhimagga* itself.

Devotion and Meditation Combined

In contrast to this modern separation of meditation and devotion, a number of pre- and early modern meditation manuals provide liturgies and instructions for devotion to the Buddha: "Whoever practises meditation, whether a yogin, layperson, or a monk, who desires the fruits of meditation from both trance [samatha] and insight [vipassanā] should begin with certain dedicatory preparations" (Paññāwongsa circa 1900 in Swearer 1995b: 209). Manuscripts from across the Theravada provide evidence that related devotional materials were associated with meditation was utilized throughout the Theravada world in the pre- and early modern periods (Bizot 1992, Crosby 1999: Chapter 6).

A Litany for Devotional Practices in Preparation for Meditation

One such manual is the *Samatha-Vipassanā-Bhāvanā-Vākkapprakaraṇa*, which means "Liturgy for Tranquility and Insight Meditation." It instructs the practitioner to undertake extensive Buddha worship in the course of the meditation. A further liturgy is provided in the meditation manual that accompanies it for the devotional exchange between the student of meditation and his/her teacher (Crosby 2000: 185).

The instructions can be summarized as follows. The practitioner gathers the offerings for worship: flowers, incense, rice, water, and candles. He (or she) then worships the Buddha, Dhamma, and Sangha, makes the offerings to the Buddha and reflects on the qualities of the Buddha. He ritually undertakes pure moral conduct *sīla*, and then asks for success in meditation (*samādhi*) and attaining wisdom (*paññā*). He then transfers the merit generated through his devotion to all beings that all may escape *saṃsāra*. He invites the four guardian gods of the world to rejoice in the merit he has generated and remain attentive, so that the Buddha's teaching will last a full 5000 years. He recites some protection (*paritta*) texts (see Chapter 5). He confesses his faults, confirms his belief in the possibility of achieving *nibbāna*, and seeks the protection of the Buddha, Dhamma, Sangha, teacher, and meditation practice. He then asks the Buddha for the specific meditation exercise that he is undertaking at each stage in his practice, as well as for success in achieving the meditation experiences to which it should lead. The practitioner then vows to perform the practice successfully or die. He then repeats a sacred Pali formula relevant to the specific practice he is about to undertake hundreds or thousands of times, focuses his mind on his heart and makes a final request for success, that the meditation attainments become an inalienable part of his person and the cause of his attaining *nibbāna*. On completion of this act of worship to and request for intervention from the Buddha, the practitioner performs another ritual of devotion, this time to the meditation teacher.

The following extract from the section of litany pertaining to moral conduct gives a flavor of the technical detail and mood of the devotional preparation:

> Venerable omniscient Gotama, since these fourteen unwholesome factors, namely, delusion, unscrupulousness, shamelessness, distraction, greed, false view, pride, hate, envy, selfishness, restlessness, torpor, languor, and doubt, have flooded my mind, like a blind man

> or one deranged, I do not see the path of the four truths. Therefore, I cannot follow the Buddha's advice.
>
> Venerable, omniscient Gotama, out of compassion for me accept my material offerings.
>
> Venerable, omniscient Gotama, ascertain any defect in my three gateways. If, on investigation, there is one, then take it and place it before me. After placing it there, weaken it either by overcoming it with its opposite or by overcoming it by starving it. Destroy it. Annihilate it. Make me pure without blemish. When I have been made pure like silver or gold burnished in the mouth of a furnace, may I have a radiance like the spotless orb of the moon over Mount Yugandhara. (abridged from Crosby 1999: Chapter 6)

This extract reveals a number of aspects that are unexpected if we accept the dichotomizing arguments cited earlier. Firstly, the attainment of purity of moral conduct is ritualized: granted by the Buddha through devotion. Secondly, it is highly technical, based on the understanding of human weakness and spiritual development to be found in the *Abhidhamma*, the highly technical analysis of the Buddha's teachings of causality that constitute the third division of the Pali Canon (see Chapter 7). The list of "fourteen unwholesome factors" is an analysis of the root causes of our entrapment in *saṃsāra* (the round of rebirth) that is common in *Abhidhamma* (e.g., the second chapter of the *Abhidhammatthasaṅgaha*). The "four truths" are the truth of suffering, the arising (of suffering), the cessation (of suffering), and the path (to the cessation of suffering), which constitute an early, classical summary of the soteriological truth to be realized in Buddhism (see Chapters 1 and 5). The "three gateways" are the eye, the mind, and the body (Crosby 1999: Chapter 6 note 12): it is necessary to be rid of any faults or obstacles in these avenues of contact with the external world before beginning the meditation since, in Theravada, the mental images and experiences in meditation are initiated by external phenomena, even though they can become independent of them. The meditator will not be able to develop the higher results of meditation if he cannot see without fault the initial meditation subject. The methods of removing the obstacles are also technical processes described in *Abhidhamma* analyses of the meditation process.

From the contrast drawn in some modern contexts between devotional and meditational practices, it might have been expected that the devotion would derive from the most simple level of Theravada doctrine, but the devotion's degree of technicality indicates that it derives from what one might regard as the most advanced interpretation. The entire path toward practitioner's goal of achieving *nibbāna* is broken down into a progressive series of requests to the Buddha through the different stages of morality, meditation, and wisdom (*sīla*, *samādhi* and *paññā*) found in Buddhaghosa's *Visuddhimagga*. This culminates in the "four paths and fruits," of stream entry, once-returner, nonreturner, and arhatship (Crosby 2005: 266).

What is the purpose of the worship and requests for assistance found in this litany? The liturgy summarizes the entire spiritual path including the specific expectations of the results of each meditation exercises. As such it reminds the practitioner of the details of the practice being undertaken. It also reminds him of the overall purpose and what to expect. It is possible to understand the worship of the Buddha in terms of the "cognitive" explanation of venerating the Buddha as the ideal, and the practitioner does identify himself as a future Buddha by undertaking a vow to die, parallel to that taken by the Buddha-to-be in the *Jātakanidāna* (see Chapter 1). Furthermore, a debate embedded in the text about whether it is possible to gain *nibbāna* given that the Buddha has entered final *nibbāna* confirms an awareness that the Buddha is not directly accessible:

> Whether he is present or has entered *nibbāna*, the "fruit" in the mind is equal. People go to a good rebirth as a result of the accumulated wholesome states (*kusala*) of their mind. The teaching lasts as long as the Blessed One is present in the world. The greatly compassionate Blessed One established the teaching so that it would endure for five thousand years in order to release those beings yet unperfected. Moreover those unperfected beings who had [by the time of the Buddha's death] reached stream entry or one of the other [stages which make arhatship inevitable] were caused to attain *nibbāna* [after he had died]. (abridged from Crosby 1999: Chapter 6)

Alternatively the litany can be interpreted as the opposite, as the ritualization of the entire path including the ethical preparation, here provided by Buddha then meditation teacher, in contrast to the ethicization of ritual seen in the *Sigālovāda Sutta's* reinterpretation of the worship of the six directions seen earlier. The Buddha and meditation master remove the moral impurities of the practitioner at his request so that he can achieve the meditation results. It may be that this interpretation should be taken further, that the practitioner is performing a ritualization not only of the path to *arhatship* in one life, but the multilife path to Buddhahood. The practitioner's makes a vow parallel to that of a Buddha and elsewhere in the text repeatedly makes explicit that his aim is to gain omniscience rather than just to become an *arhat* (enlightened disciple of the Buddha). The practitioner may be ritually enacted path to Buddhahood, which is the same for all Buddhas (see Chapter 1) and includes worshipping at the feet of a previous Buddha, making the vow to achieve Buddhahood in the presence of a previous Buddha, and receiving the prediction of Buddhahood by a previous Buddha. In the ritual prescribed in this litany, the practitioner invokes aid of the Buddha as if present and treats him both as if he can intervene, and as if he is the source of the meditation instruction. Devotion to the Buddha as present is an essential preparation for the attainment of Buddhahood (Crosby 2005: 269).

The Importance of Devotion to the Buddha in the *Visuddhimagga*

Although the modern accounts of meditation based on Buddhaghosa's *Visuddhimagga* do not mention devotional practices, the *Visuddhimagga* itself does offer some guidance on devotion to the Buddha in preparation for meditation. A passage about choosing a meditation teacher gives the following hierarchy of teachers to choose from:

> It is only the Fully Enlightened One who possesses all the aspects of the Good friend. Since that is so, while he is available only a meditation subject taken in the Blessed One's presence is well taken.
>
> But after his final attainment of nibbāna, it is proper to take it from any one of the eighty great disciples still living. When they are no more available, one who wants to take a particular meditation subject should take it from someone with cankers destroyed, who has, by means of that particular meditation subject, produced the fourfold and fivefold jhāna, and has reached the destruction of cankers by augmenting insight that had that jhana as its proximate cause. .... If not, one should take it from a Non-returner, a Once-returner, a Stream-enterer, an ordinary man who has obtained jhāna, one who knows three Piṭakas [the three collections of texts that make up the Pali Canon], one who knows two Piṭakas, one who knows one Piṭaka, in descending order. If not even one who knows one Piṭaka is available,

> then it should be taken from one who is familiar with one Collection together with its commentary, and one who is himself conscientious. For a teacher such as this who knows the texts guards the heritage, and protects the tradition, will follow the teachers' opinion rather than his own. (Ñyāṇamoli 1976, vol.1: 99–100)

On the one hand, it is best to receive meditation instruction from the Buddha, as prescribed in the litany examined earlier. On the other hand, to offer alternative meditation teachers is to accept the Buddha as absent. In this advice is found one of the explanations suggested here for the details of the litany given earlier: the rehearsal ensures that the practitioner is reminded of the expected practice and outcome in accordance with authoritative texts and does not therefore follow the wrong path. This concern underlies an ongoing debate within Theravada about the relative merits of textual study (*pariyatti*) and practice (*paṭipatti*) and whether or not one can pursue the latter without the former.

The use of the Buddha image as a proxy for the Buddha is sometimes extended in contexts where a suitable person is lacking, in ways that offer insight into the use of image worship in meditation. During the 1970s in Cambodia, where monks had to disrobe for fear of being murdered by the Khmer Rouge, those who could not find a person to whom they could safely announce their disrobing (as prescribed in the *Vinaya* monastic regulations), instead announced their disrobing to the Buddha (Crosby, fieldwork 2009–2012). Although this is not an option given in the *Vinaya*, it made sense to the monks in question and did not bar them from getting reordained at a later stage.

The *Visuddhimagga* also offers a short statement on dedicating oneself to the Buddha and one's teacher before undertaking a meditation practice, again not found in modern texts based on it.

> The meditator should dedicate himself to the Blessed One, the Enlightened One (Buddha), or to a teacher, and he should ask for the meditation subject with a sincere inclination [of the heart] and sincere resolution.
>
> Herein, he should dedicate himself to the Blessed One in this way: "Blessed One, I relinquish this my person to you." For without having thus dedicated himself when living in a remote abode he might be unable to stand fast if a frightening object make its appearance, and he might return to a village above, become associated with laymen, take up improper search and come to ruin. But when he has dedicated himself in this way no fear arises in him ..., in fact only joy arises in him. (Ñyāṇamoli 1976, vol.1: 118)

Here the most important benefit of such dedication is freedom from fear, also one of the advantages identified in the *Visuddhimagga* description of the benefits of the meditation on the qualities of the Buddha, *buddhānussati*. Additional benefits are that the practitioner can endure hardships and conducts himself better through the creation of the sense of the Buddha's presence. This confirms the psychological importance of Buddha worship, but not in terms of neediness. Rather, it is all the more important for those seeking to achieve the most difficult goals of the Buddhist path:

> When a monk is devoted to this recollection of the Buddha ... he attains fullness of faith, mindfulness, understanding and merit. He has much happiness and gladness. He conquers fear and dread. He is able to endure pain. He comes to feel as if he were living in the Master's (Buddha's) presence. And his body, when the recollection of the Buddha's special qualities dwells in it, becomes as worthy of veneration as a shrine room. His mind tends towards the plane of the Buddhas. When he encounters an opportunity for transgression, he has awareness

of conscience and shame as vivid as though he were face to face with the master. And if he penetrates no higher, he is at least headed for a happy destiny.

Now when a man is truly wise,
His constant task will surely be
This recollection of the *Buddha*
Blessed with such mighty potency.
(Ñyāṇamoli 1976, vol.1: 230)

The importance of the relationship between monastics, and not only laypeople, and the Buddha as if present, that is emphasized in the stories and meditation manuals discussed here, is reflected in the final episode of the story about the first Buddha image, discussed earlier. After the Buddha explains to the image its role in protecting the Dhamma and providing access to salvation for the future 5000 years, it is the Buddha himself and the 500 monks accompanying him who lead the worship. Just as stories of the conduct of kings and gods in relation to the Sangha provides the protocol for that of laypeople, so protocol for the conduct of monastics is provided by stories about the Buddha himself:

> [The Buddha] extended his right arm, which was like [the celestial elephant] Erāvaṇa's trunk, and restrained [the image from standing up to worship him]. To do it honour he offered it handfuls of jasmine flowers, and likewise both five hundred monks? whose defilements were destroyed and the ordinary unenlightened people offered various fragrant flowers. At that moment Sakka, Suyāma, Santusita, Brahmā and the rest [of the gods] offered that image their own respective material offerings. The Four Great Kings [another class of deities] took up guard on all sides. All gods and men shouted thousands of hosannas. (Gombrich 1978: 298. Additions in square brackets. A fuller exploration of the aforementioned texts in relation to devotion is found in Crosby 2005.)

Nondoctrinal Analyses of Buddha Worship

The aforementioned discussions provide an overview of doctrine and practice in relation to Buddha worship on the part of individual practitioners. We shall turn to further aspects of worship for communities later. However, in entering this debate on Buddha worship, it is worth examining the terms of reference set by earlier scholarly attitudes to Buddha worship. Those attitudes presupposed it to be reasonable to expect consistency and a very specific type of rationality in relation to worship on the part of Theravada Buddhists. There are ways of challenging the debate simply by challenging those terms of reference. Tannenbaum, disregarding doctrinal concerns, reaches an overall assessment of a consistent worldview in terms of "power-protection" among the Shan Theravada Buddhists in whose communities she conducted her fieldwork. The Buddha is a great source of power that can be drawn on for protection irrespective of doctrinal or ethical considerations. Building up power and providing or seeking protection is a common thread connecting an entire range of practices that cross over between animate and inanimate, sacred and mundane, spirit and human worlds, as well as explaining relations within each of these realms. The Buddha has a place at one end of this spectrum, and forms a range of relationships within it (Tannenbaum 1995). Interesting from a psychological and ethical perspective is that this suggests a convergence between "good" in the sense of being based on the three "skillful" states of nongreed, nonhatred, and nondelusion and "good" as in the sense of omnipotent. While in Tannenbaum's analysis potency is the key theme irrespective of ethics, and Buddhism is harnessed within that, in Buddhist narratives and treatises dealing with themes of good and evil, the rewards of appropriate conduct are often valorized through reference to a range of outcomes, including potency. Likewise "bad" actions in the sense of those rooted in greed, hatred, and delusion result in the experience of outcomes that are "bad" in that they are experiences of vulnerability and weakness, or lack of potency. This indicates that the teachings are constructed to impact the different motivational drives and human character types on the spectrum from altruistic through masochistic to narcissistic and psychopathic. Even relatively simple canonical passages show awareness of such variations in its analysis of persons into four kinds:

> one who benefits neither himself nor another; one who benefits another but not himself; one who benefits himself but not another; and one who benefits himself and another. Of these four the Buddha praises the last, as "chief and best, foremost, highest and supreme." (Saddhatissa 1975: 1, citing *Aṅguttara Nikāya* II 94ff.).

We see elsewhere, for example in the understanding of the *Jātaka* in terms of the Buddha's progress on the path, how the understanding of altruism includes a nuanced sense of benefiting oneself: when the Buddha-to-be sacrifices himself for the benefit of another, he also gains by his progress on the path to Buddhahood.

Returning to the aspect of harnessing the power of the Buddha in terms of protection, we can see that this applies to a vast range of devotional and protective activities. Protection or beneficial proximity and interaction is sought with Buddhas, gods, *arhats* (enlightened beings) including monks, nuns, and other highly regarded individuals, whether dead or living, memorabilia associated with them, powerful texts, trees, a variety of **amulet** types, even ghosts, mummies, and corpses (see Chapter 7 and McDaniel 2011: Chapter 4). Within these various categories not all are equal nor drawn on for the same purpose. It can be what they represent, their associations, their reputations, or what they are made of that makes them attractive and potent. They may be of value for different needs, work on specific days of the week or different times of or occasions in the year and need to be treated in specific ways. A type of lightweight image of a Buddha or monk commonly found in Burma and northern Thailand is the "Holy Lord with Lotus and Needles" covered in black lacquer and either gold leaf or paint (Penth 2006: 181). They may have a little knob on their forehead and elsewhere, in which are inserted needles, and a water lily, lotus, or fish below. They bring luck and prosperity and protect from illness and wicked people. They are given vegetarian offerings and may be kept in a shallow tray of water. The power of these images does not relate so much to the Buddha but to a complex story of love, violent death, alchemy, a magic boat, mistreatment of a former image (of which they are a copy) and special ingredients that account for their power. They have to be kept in their place using the pins or they will return to the Inle Lake (Shan State) to the shrine of the original image (Penth 2006). (For more on images expressing displeasure at being moved, see later text.)

Another way of looking at such ritualistic or devotional behavior is to see it as having a cultural continuity that is more enduring than the meaning ascribed to it. In other words, even if the belief about the way in which the super being (divine or mortal) is or is not present alters, practices may be constant. Thus in this case, the worship of images continues throughout South and Southeast Asia. The similarities between the installation and treatment of Buddha images by Buddhists and Hindu images by Hindus are obvious. It is only after one assesses such practices in terms of specific doctrine or belief that one seeks to explain the similarity in light of the contrasting theologies.

We might also question the way in which worship finds little place in current models of ethics. Modern writers on Buddhist ethics have tended to expound them in terms of the precepts, especially the five precepts of the layperson, not to kill, steal, lie, commit sexual misconduct, or take intoxicants (see Chapter 5). However, Stephen Berkwitz, in his study of the chronicle literature that places worship of Buddhist relics in the present in a relationship with the compassionate prescience of the Buddha and other virtuous agents of the past, demonstrates that "such a view of Buddhist ethics is too narrow, since it presumes all moral acts are reasoned out and evaluated by a Buddhist agent for the sake of attaining *nirvāṇa*. Instead, the *Sinhala Thūpavaṃsa* [13th-century chronicle] depicts how the notion and actualisation of virtue are constructed out of an awareness of his or her place in history. … Buddhist historiography in late medieval Sri Lanka invests ritualized devotion with moral significance, expanding upon the notion of ethics to include reflecting upon one's obligations that arise out of learning what was done in the past. … Significantly, the act of *pūjā* [worship] is generally presented as a technique for remembering the Buddha and showing gratitude for what he did in the past" (Berkwitz 2004: 274. See also Kyaw 2010.) Azzopardi, in his study of religious attitudes of the Sinhalese Buddhist Diaspora in the United Kingdom, further demonstrates the multivalency of feelings and interpretations associated with devotion, undermining the assumption that one can categorize the religious behavior such as worship, on the one hand, or devotion, on the other hand, in terms of fixed goals (Azzopardi 2008: 304–306). This point is reflected in devotional verses and texts praising offerings, which, like the biographies of the Buddha, see devotional behavior and the accrual of merit as virtues that lead both to an enhanced experience of life within *saṃsāra* (the round of rebirth) as well as eventual release from it.

Similarly, just as the interpretation of Buddhist ethics as an active, conscious response to a set of precepts has been too limited, these debates on worship may be based on an over-narrow understanding of what constitutes and contributes to the active pursuit of personal transformation. Are such debates based on reductionist parameters, dismissing too quickly the complexities of religious experience? The current trend for drawing on Buddhist meditation for psychological and medical treatments reflects an appreciation that the Buddhist tradition has analyzed, developed, and practiced for centuries processes of directed transformation that have only in recent decades become the object of Western empirical research. Might we see in devotional aspects of the Buddhist tradition other ways in which it has developed understandings of how to direct personal transformation that still remain beyond the current stage of research in Buddhist studies or other fields?

The Relic and Image as Creators of Communities

The presence of relics, images, and other representations of the Buddha across the Theravada world allows the worshipper to make a connection across time with the Buddha and with the events and sacred landscape of the past (see Chapter 1 and Berkwitz 2004: 274). This brings the Buddha and the power he offers into the present creating a new landscape in which his inspiration and protection are accessible. This in turn allows the Buddha, either in general or through specific images, relics, or other reminder, to act as a frame of reference for community building, from the village level to the national or international level. At the level of local communities, the collective focus on Buddha worship then creates a safe, harmonious space in which people are well-disposed and cooperative.

The type of Buddha worship that requires more than a momentary effort is a collective affair. It is at the center of relationships of symbiosis, cooperation, and exchange. The dynamics of ritual space, level of participation, and degrees of sponsorship related to the worship at a specific site establish hierarchies across the sacred and human realms. A person's participation in the worship of the Buddha and the broader pantheon of deities with which a particular Buddhist community interacts is an expression of belonging and a shared recognition of certain values and sources of power. A village that builds a Buddha shrine makes a statement of belonging to the broader, shared civilization. Building shrines and installing Buddha images continues to be a mechanism for incorporating "tribal" groups into Burmese or Thai national identity.

The passing on and sharing in the worship of images and relics of the Buddha function to create communities at an international level. Economic, political, and military relationships may be negotiated behind the allegiances displayed in relation to images and relics. Such relationships and anxiety about them influenced decisions about the retaining and handing over of relics on the part of the British during the archaeological investigations that "rediscovered" India's Buddhist past in the early twentieth century. The restoring of relics from museums in Britain to Buddhist custodianship as Britain's colonial rule came to an end after WWII formed part of the reshaping of relationships between Britain and newly independent Asian states (Bond 1988: 76). More recently, relic tours have formed part of the relationship between China and Burma, in support of the Burmese *junta's* aspirations to be seen as righteous rulers who protect the country's Buddhist legacy (Schober 1997b: 225–226). In the modern trend of combining museum and relic shrines in Thailand, the treatment of the remains of famous **forest monks** known for their meditational attainments allows military and political rulers to accrue to themselves the power and appeal of such sacred figures through association with their remains (Gabaude 2003).

Participating in the worship of relics, images, and other symbols that are of significance beyond the local community is particularly meritorious. Sacred landscapes and pilgrimage routes are created around sites which the Buddha visited or which are the location of important images or relics of the Buddha.

Some of these sacred geographies fade from broader significance as the people from the relevant area become marginalized, but may yet be retained by the local group. In relation to the sacred landscape of the Dawei (Tavoy) ethnic group of Burma, Elizabeth Moore has recently demonstrated how the complexity of history may contribute to such developments. The landscape commemorates a visit from the Buddha recorded in the Dawei chronicle (the *Dawei Yazawin*). The writer Shwei Wei Ei published a compilation of the different versions of this chronicle in an attempt to protect Dawei culture from the upheavals of the twentieth century, such as the British and Japanese occupations and the insurgency of 1960s and 1970s (Moore 2013).

Sacred geographical networks can also grow in significance, forming part of a national identity that then becomes recognized internationally. Substantial economic advantage can be gained from supplying or controlling a pilgrimage site as pilgrims do not stint on the offerings they make and also require a number of services, from accommodation to assistance in performing their rituals. In colonial Burma in the 1930s, the Young Monks' Association (*Yahan Pyo Apwe*, Burmese) was financed in its militant anti-colonial activities by its control of the pilgrimage sites associated with the charismatic monk U Khanti (Schober 2011: 106–107).

In Sri Lanka, the sacred sites associated with the Buddha semi-crystallized in the medieval period into a set of 16 pilgrimage sites. The set includes 12 sites on the itinerary of the Buddha during the three visits he made to the island during his lifetime according to the fifth-century chronicle, the *Mahāvaṃsa*, and Buddhaghosa's fifth-century commentary on the *Vinaya Piṭaka*, the *Samantapāsādikā*; the other four sites came to be associated with him later. The sites are spread across Sri Lanka. They include Mahiyangana, where he left hairs and where a neck bone was later acquired; Siripāda, the second highest mountain in

Sri Lanka, where he left his footprint; and Nāgadīpa, an island in the north (Gombrich 1971: 128–129). The location of Nāgadīpa, where the Buddha left two "enjoyment" reminders – the preaching seat and the tree that shaded him – is in the area that the LTTE (see earlier text) had hoped to demarcate as a separate Tamil homeland. The extension of the sacred geography into this disputed territory added to the implications drawn from the *vaṃsas* ("chronicles") in the modern narrative of Sinhalese national identity. While the chronicles are of interest as historical and religious documents, their narrative of connecting the Buddha and Buddha relics with expressions of military power of past kings has inspired some scholars, journalists, and discussants to "have singled out these texts as the early sources for more recent political and ethnic conflicts ... [thereby] positing a dubious continuity between violent acts some two thousand years apart" (Berkwitz 2004: 30–31).

Devout Sri Lankan Buddhists hope to make the pilgrimage to these 16 sites at some point during their lifetime. While the pilgrimage used to be an arduous journey made on foot either on their own or in groups, the modern practice of visiting them as part of a bus party means the trip, or part of it, is also a common community, temple, school, college, or work place outing. This broadens out its appeal, extends the role of the sites in Sinhalese national identity, and enhances, while altering, the economic advantages to be gained from association with such sites. The economic activity of pilgrimage sites is further accentuated as they become part of the holiday experience for both Buddhist and non-Buddhist tourists.

A sacred site in Sri Lanka not included in the set of 16 is the Temple of the Tooth in Kandy, which houses a Buddha's tooth relic. Its association with national identity has made it the repeated object of attack by those seeking to undermine the power of those in whose custodianship it rests. Culturally protestant foreigners such as the British dismissed its power. When the American Colonel H.S. Olcott, the theosophist regarded by some as the "founding father of Protestant Buddhism" (Buddhist modernism), dismissed the relic as that of an animal, it caused an irreparable rift between him and his Sri Lankan protégé, David Hēvāvitarana (1864–1933), who later became the leader of Sri Lankan Buddhist revivalism, Anāgārika Dharmapāla (Gombrich and Obeyesekere 1988: 204–206). Others sought to destroy its power more violently. In the sixteenth century, the Portuguese invaders, as Catholics, had greater respect for the power inherent in relics. In fact our term relic for *dhātu*, which literally means "element" or "essence," is drawn from Catholic religiosity. In spite of its literal meaning, its use is sometimes extended in English to refer to all four types of reminder, not just the physical remains. The Portuguese captured what they believed to be the tooth relic in Jaffna in 1561 and took it to the Portuguese territory of Goa in Southwest India where the Archbishop publicly pulverized, cremated, and then dispersed it in the river (Strong 2004: 1 and 193, Strong 2010: 187). Fortunately the item they had captured was either a decoy or the relic of someone other than the Buddha, one story being that it was that of the monkey god Hanuman, more important to Hindus than Buddhists. According to the custodians of several historically significant relics, the practice of maintaining decoys to safeguard important relics continues to this day (personal communication) and is attested historically (Strong 2010: 189). An alternative story was that, since a relic is indestructible, it survived: "it miraculously slipped through the bottom of the vessel and, passing through the earth itself, re-emerged on a lotus blossom on its original shrine." After this event several people claimed to be in possession of the real relic including one claimant to the throne of Kandy, its home today (Strong 2010: 189–190). The British, capturing the Temple of the Tooth, also used it to claim the right to rule, initially acting as custodians of the tooth relic with the British resident in Kandy participating in its veneration until succumbing to Christian pressure to desist (Strong 2010:

197–198). More recently, the Temple of the Tooth has been a target of attacks by Tamil separatists. With a truck bomb, which killed 11 people and injured 20 others, they succeeded in seriously damaging the building, though not the relic, which is kept within gold and silver caskets at the heart of the complex. The timing of the attack may have been deliberately chosen to derail planned elections in the Jaffna peninsula and to disrupt the visit of Prince Charles to the country a fortnight later (news.bbc.co.uk, retrieved January 25, 1998; www.independent.co.uk, retrieved February 4, 1998).

Since the hosting of significant relics and images is an expression of power, a source of prestige and also a source of revenue, such relics and images have become the objects of acquisition on the part of warring parties. On the other hand, the networks they represent may also be underplayed when at odds with other power dynamics. We can see both responses exemplified in the history of the Mahāmuni image of Mandalay, the most important image in modern Burma, and the brother images associated with it.

The foundation myth of the Mahāmuni image relates how, during a visit by the Buddha to King Candrasuriya of Arakan, the image was made by the King of the Gods, Sakka, and the divine artisan Vissakamma (Indra / Śakra and Viśvakarman in Sanskrit). At a later point four younger "brothers" were cast from the remaining metal creating a family or network of images. Famously, the Buddha transferred some of his bad *kamma* into the original image. At a future date the thigh and back of the image would become damaged as a result of the Buddha's cruelty in a past life when he broke the thigh-bone of his gardener and sliced flesh from the back of a prince (Schober 1997a: 268). King Candrasuriya goes on to make a prediction that no one may move the statue except he himself. In the eighteenth century, following the defeat of Arakan by the Burmese, Sīhasūra, the son of King Bodawphaya succeeded in moving the Mahāmuni image. From a political perspective, this indicated the waning of Arakanese power. From a religious perspective, the powerful image permits itself to be moved so that it may be associated with the new center of power: Sīhasūra is in fact the incarnation of King Candrasuriya come to move the image in fulfillment of the prediction he had made in its presence during the visit of the Buddha.

The most sacred Buddha image in Bangladesh, the Chitmarong image, is located in what was formerly part of Arakan and regarded by some local Buddhists as one of the Mahāmuni brothers. However, in the current political climate, this connection with Burma is downplayed. There are repeated border clashes between Bangladesh and Burma, and the status of the Buddhism of the Chittagong Hill Tracts is marginalized within the predominantly Muslim Bangladesh (Kyaw and Crosby 2013).

The Buddha in the Museum

One of the Mahāmuni brothers, the Man Aung Myin Muni of Zalun, however, is celebrated as the image that returned to its native land. A metal statue of the Buddha, it was due to be melted down to make coins in India under the British until Queen Victoria suffered a headache. The source of the headache – the maltreatment of the image in her name – was revealed to her in a dream and the image was restored to its rightful home in modern day Burma (Kyaw and Crosby 2013). The fate of other Buddha images under colonial rule varied. The national museums of the former European colonial powers of the Theravada regions reflect their former territories. The Musée Guimet in Paris (www.guimet.fr) houses one of the largest collections of Asian art outside of Asia, including a fine collection of Buddhist sculptures from former French Indochina (areas of modern Cambodia, Laos, northern Thailand and Vietnam). The holdings of the British Museum and Victoria and Albert Museum in London reflect British colonial history in Sri Lanka, Burma, and Arakan.

The currently burgeoning interest in Asian art coupled with the desire to express power and elicit economic advantage through the ownership of Buddha images continues to drive their collection by both Buddhists and non-Buddhists, fuelling the international art trade. While there have been attempts to regulate and police this trade, the accessibility of statues and the ease of removing the heads, which can be sold in isolation, make them easy prey for thieves. Buddhist heritage is particularly vulnerable in areas affected by warfare and economic deprivation such as Bangladesh, Cambodia, and the regions of ethnic minorities such as the Shan in Burma.

Just like the relics and images of the past which decided when and where they would take up residence in their current locations, some of those now to be found in museums have also chosen to be there. The Tasmanian Mercury of March 1912 gave the following report of how an Arakanese image found its way into the collection of the Victoria and Albert Museum in the words of the curator:

> A sea captain acquired it in Lower Burma about 1833. He sailed with it for England. Near Liverpool the ship caught fire, and the superstitious sailors, believing the Buddha to be the cause, threw it overboard. The ship was brought safely into harbour, and three weeks later the Buddha was washed up on the Welsh coast. When the captain died it passed to his daughter. Everybody in her house had become frightened of the Buddha. The servants stated that at night it walked about the house; friends who stayed with her declared that its eyes haunted them, and at times appeared to move. Her children were scared out of their lives. She was therefore compelled to part with it. Its behaviour here [at the V&A], however, has so far been exemplary. (abridged from citation in Kyaw and Crosby forthcoming)

Summary

This chapter explored the ubiquitous Theravada practice of Buddha worship. We examined debates that have arisen in the modern period about the function and validity of such worship. Some scholars and some reformist groups have regarded the practice as antithetical to the Buddhist teachings of impermanence and self-reliance, particularly in the light of the Buddha's *parinibbāna*. Yet a range of meditation texts indicate that devotion was regarded as a crucial part of the process of self-transformation and was to be undertaken not just by laypeople but also monks and nuns, including by those committed to in-depth meditation practice. The Buddha as a source of power to be harnessed for a variety of ends leads to his inclusion, through the medium of his statue, in rituals aimed at protection. Potent images and relics across the lands of Theravada bring the Buddha into the present, form the bases of – and align themselves with – communities and networks, particularly through communal worship. Well-known images may also be important sources of revenue and expressions of power, and as such have been sought after through war or as spoils of war. While representative of the power of the Buddha, as indicated through their generic and specific foundation myths, images and relics may also express agency in their own right, as we see in the lifestories of images and relics who refused to be moved or destroyed or, in contrast, chose to take up new allegiances and residences.

References

Azzopardi, David. (2008) 'Religious Belief and Practice among Sri Lankan Buddhists in the U.K.' PhD thesis, School of Oriental and African Studies, University of London.

Berkwitz, Stephen C. (2004). *Buddhist History in the Vernacular. The Power of the Past in Late Medieval Sri Lanka*. Leiden/Boston: Brill.

Bizot, François. (1992). *Le chemin de Lankā*. Textes bouddhiques du Cambodge I. Paris: l'École française d'Extrême-Orient.

Bizot, François. (1994). 'La Consécration des Statues et le culte des Morts' in François Bizot (ed.), *Recherches nouvelles sur le Cambodge*. Paris: l'École française d'Extrême-Orient, 101–127.

Bond, George. (1988). *The Buddhist Revival in Sri Lanka: Religious Tradition, Reinterpretation and Response*. Columbia: University of Carolina Press.

Chiu, Angela Shih Chih. (2012). 'The Social and Religious World of Northern Thai Buddha Images: Art, Lineage, Power and Place in Lan Na Monastic Chronicles (*Tamnan*)'. PhD thesis, School of Oriental and African Studies, University of London.

Choompolpaisal, Phibul, Kate Crosby, and Andrew Skilton. (in preparation). 'The Significance of the Phitsanulok *Dhammakāya* Inscription for *borān/yogāvacara* Meditation in Theravada'.

Cicuzza, Claudio. (2011). *A Mirror Reflecting the Entire World: The Pāli Buddhapādamaṅgala or 'Auspicious Signs on the Buddha's Feet'*. Bangkok: Fragile Palm Leaves Foundation, Lumbini International Research Institute.

Collins, Steven. (1998). *Nirvana and Other Buddhist Felicities: Utopias of the Pali Imaginaire*. Cambridge: Cambridge University Press.

Coningham, Robin A.E. (2013). 'Dating the Buddha: New Archaeological Evidence from Lumbini (Nepal) the birth place of the Buddha'. Paper delivered in the South and Southeast Asian Art & Archaeology Research Seminar. London: SOAS, March 20, 2013.

Crosby, Henrietta Kate. (1999). 'Studies in the Medieval Pali Literature of Sri Lanka with Special Reference to the Esoteric Yogavacara tradition'. DPhil thesis, University of Oxford.

Crosby, Kate. (2000). 'Tantric Theravada: A Bibliographic Essay on the Writings of François Bizot and other literature on the *Yogāvacara* Tradition', *Contemporary Buddhism* 1.2: 141–198.

Crosby, Kate. (2005). 'Devotion to the Buddha in Theravāda and its Role in Meditation' in John Brockington and Anna King (eds.), *The Intimate Other: Love Divine in Indic Religions*. New Delhi: Orient Longman, 244–277.

Crosby, Kate and Andrew Skilton. (1996). *Śāntideva The Bodhicaryavatara, World's Classics Series*. Oxford: Oxford University Press.

Gabaude, Louis. (2003). 'Where Ascetics Get Comfort and Recluses Go Public: Museums for Buddhist Saints in Thailand' in Phyllis Granoff and Koichi Shinohara (eds.), *Pilgrims, Patrons, and Place: Localizing Sanctity in Asian Religions*. Vancouver-Toronto: University of British Columbia Press, 103–123.

Gombrich, R.F. (1971). *Precept and Practice: Traditional Buddhism in the Rural Highlands of Ceylon*. Oxford: Clarendon Press.

Gombrich, R.F. (1978). 'Kosalabimbavaṇṇanā' in H. Bechert (ed.), *Buddhism in Ceylon and Studies on Religious Syncretisim in Buddhist Countries*, Abhandlungen der Akademie der Wissenschaften in Göttingen, Phil.Hist. Klasse 3. Folge, Nr.108. Göttingen: Vandenhoeck & Ruprecht, 281–303.

Gombrich, R.F. (1988). *Theravada Buddhism: A Social History from Ancient Benares to Modern Colombo*. London: Routledge & Kegan Paul.

Gombrich, Richard and Gananath Obeyesekere. (1988). *Buddhism Transformed: Religious Change in Sri Lanka*. Princeton: Princeton University Press.

Griswold, A.B. (1957). *Dated Buddha Images of Northern Siam*. Ascona: Artibus Asiae.

Holt, John Clifford. (2004). *The Buddhist Visnu. Religious Transformation, Politics and Culture*. New York: Columbia University Press.

Khur-Yearn, Jotika. (2012). 'The Poetic *Dhamma* of Zao Amat Long's *Mahāsatipaṭṭhāna Sutta* and the Place of Traditional Literature in Shan Theravada Buddhism'. PhD thesis, School of Oriental and African Studies, London.

King, Winston L. (1964 [reprint 1990]). *A Thousand Lives Away: Buddhism in Contemporary Burma*. Berkeley: Asian Humanities Press.

King, Winston L. (circa 1980). *Theravāda Meditation: The Buddhist Transformation of Yoga*. University Park: State University Press. Reprint, New Delhi: Motilal Banarsidass, 1992.

King, Winston L. (1989). 'Sacramental Aspects of Theravāda Buddhist Meditation', *Numen* XXXVI. Fas. 2: 248–256.

Kyaw, Pyi Phyo. (2010). 'A Good Business Person and/or A Good Buddhist: A Study of Business Practices of the Burmese in the Context of the'Right Livelihood' *(Sammā-ājīva)* in Modern Burma.' MA dissertation, SOAS, University of London.

Kyaw, Pyi Phyo and Kate Crosby. (2013). 'The Buddha and his Brothers: Expressions of Power, Place and Community by the Network of Mahāmuni Images of Arakan, Bangladesh and Burma' in David Park and Kuenga Wangmo (eds.), *Proceedings of the Buddhist Art Forum (Courtauld Institute of Art, April 2012)*. London: Archetype Publications.

McDaniel, Justin. (2011). *The Lovelorn Ghost & The Magical Monk. Practicing Buddhism in Northern Thailand*. New York: Columbia University Press.

Moore, Elizabeth Howard. (2013). 'The Sacred Geography of Dawai: Buddhism in peninsular Myanmar (Burma)', *Contemporary Buddhism*.

Ñyāṇamoli, Bhikkhu. (1976). *The Path of Purification*, 2 vols. Boulder & London: Shambhala.

Obeyesekere, Ranjani. (2001). *Portraits of Buddhist Women: Stories from the Saddharmaratnāvaliya*. Albany: State University of New York Press.

Penth, Hans. (2006). 'Phra Bua Khem Images in Lān Nā' in Lagirarde and Koanantakul (eds.), *Buddhist Legacies in Mainland Southeast Asia: Mentalities, Interpretations and Practices*. Paris/ Bangkok: Ecole Française d' Extrême-Orient/Princess Maha Chakri Sirindhorn Anthropology Centre, 181–205.

Rhys Davids C.A.F. (1951). *Psalms of the Sisters*. London: Luzac.

Saddhatissa, H. (1975). *The Birth-Stories of the Ten Bodhisattas and the Dasabodhisattuppattikathā Being a Translation and Edition of the Dasabodhisattuppattikathā*. London: The Pali Text Society.

Schober, Juliane. (1997a). 'In the Presence of the Buddha: Ritual Veneration of the Burmese Mahamuni Image' in Juliane Schober (ed.), *Sacred Biography in the Buddhist Traditions of South and Southeast Asia*. Honolulu: University of Hawai'i Press, 259–288.

Schober, Juliane. (1997b). 'Buddhist Just Rule and Burmese National Culture: State Patronage of the Chinese Tooth Relic in Myanmar', *History of Religions* 36.3: 218–243.

Schober, Juliane. (2011). *Modern Buddhist Conjunctures in Myanmar. Cultural Narratives, Colonial Legacies, and Civil Society*. Honolulu. University of Hawai'i Press.

Skilling, Peter, Jason A. Carbine, Claudio Cicuzza, and Santi Pakdeekham. (eds.). (2012). *How Theravāda is Theravāda? Exploring Buddhist Identities*. Chiang Mai: Silkworm Books.

Skilton, Andrew. (1998). 'Māra the Malign: An Episode from the *Śūraṃgamasamādhisūtra*', *The Journal of the Buddhist Society* 73: 143–152.

Strong, John S. (1993). 'Buddha Bhakti and the Absence of the Blessed One' in J. Ryckmans (ed.), *Premièr Colloque Étienne Lamotte*. Louvain-la-Neuve: Institut Orientaliste, 131–140.

Strong, John S. (2004). *Relics of the Buddha*. Princeton: Princeton University Press.

Strong, John S. (2010). '"The Devil was in that Little Bone": The Portuguese Capture and Destruction of the Buddha's Tooth Relic' in Alexandra Walsham (ed.), *Relics and Remains*. Past and present Supplement 5. Oxford: Oxford University Press. 184–198.

Swearer, Donald K. (1995a). 'Consecrating the Buddha' in Donald S. Lopez (ed.), *Buddhism in Practice*. Princeton: Princeton University Press, 50–58.

Swearer, Donald K. (1995b). 'The Way to Meditation' in Donald S. Lopez (ed.) *Buddhism in Practice*. Princeton: Princeton University Press, 207–215.

Swearer, Donald K. (2004a). *Becoming the Buddha: The Ritual of Image Consecration in Thailand*. Princeton/Oxford: Princeton University Press.

Swearer, Donald K. (2004b). 'Signs of the Buddha in Northern Thai Chronicles' in David Germano and Kevin Trainor (eds.), *Embodying the Dharma: Buddhist Relic Veneration in Asia*. Albany: State University of New York Press, 145–162.

Tannenbaum, Nicola. (1995). *Who Can Compete Against the World? Power-Protection and Buddhism in Shan Worldview*. Ann Arbor: Association for Asian Studies Inc.

Vajiranana, Mahathera. (1962). *Buddhist Meditation in Theory and Practice: A General Exposition According to the Pali Canon of the Theravāda School*. Colombo: M.D. Guansena.

Further Reading and Watching

Films

Riley-Smith, Tristram. (circa 2004). *Birth of a Buddha: Art and Ritual in central Thailand*. Rivers Video Project. DVD. London: Meridian Trust.

Reading

Berkwitz, Stephen C. (2004). *Buddhist History in the Vernacular. The Power of the Past in Late Medieval Sri Lanka*. Leiden and Boston: Brill.

Crosby, Kate. (2005). 'Devotion to the Buddha in Theravāda and its Role in Meditation' in John Brockington and Anna King (eds.), *The Intimate Other: Love Divine in Indic Religions*. New Delhi: Orient Longman, 244–277.

Gombrich, R.F. (1971). 'The Buddha' in *Buddhist Precept and Practice: Traditional Buddhism in the rural highlands of Ceylon*. London and New York: Kegan Paul International.

Kyaw, Pyi Phyo and Kate Crosby. (2013). 'The Buddha and His Brothers: Expressions of Power, Place and Community by the Network of Mahāmuni Images of Arakan, Bangladesh and Burma' in David Park and Kuenga Wangmo (eds.), *Proceedings of the Buddhist Art Forum (Courtauld Institute of Art, April 2012)*. London: Archetype Publications.

Schober, Juliane. (1997). 'In the presence of the Buddha: Ritual Veneration of the Burmese Mahamuni Image' in Juliane Schober (ed.), *Sacred Biography in the Buddhist Traditions of South and Southeast Asia*. Honolulu: University of Hawai'i Press, 259–288.

Strong, John S. (1993). 'Buddha Bhakti and the Absence of the Blessed One' in J. Ryckmans (ed.), *Premièr Colloque Étienne Lamotte*. Louvain-la-Neuve: Institut Orientaliste, 131–140.

Strong, John S. (2004). *Relics of the Buddha*. Princeton: Princeton University Press.

Swearer, Donald K. (1995). 'Consecrating the Buddha' in Donald S. Lopez (ed.), *Buddhism in Practice*. Princeton: Princeton University Press, 50–58.

Swearer, Donald K. (2004). *Becoming the Buddha: The Ritual of Image Consecration in Thailand*. Princeton and Oxford: Princeton University Press.

Part Two
Dhamma

3

Literature, Languages, and Conveying the Dhamma

Overview

The highest textual authority in Theravada Buddhism is the Pali Canon, much of which is regarded as the word of the Buddha. While it includes some very early material, the Canon as we have it is highly organized and also includes some material accepted as centuries later than the Buddha. The Pali Canon contains a collection of works on monastic rules, the *Vinaya Piṭaka*, a collection of works containing stories and poetry conveying the Buddha's teaching, the *Sutta Piṭaka*, and a collection of works on metaphysics, psychology, and philosophy, the *Abhidhamma Piṭaka*. Theravada is the only living branch of Buddhism to accept the *Abhidhamma Piṭaka* as an expression of the ultimate truth. This is one of the reasons Theravada is regarded by many as an early form of Buddhism. The Pali Canon is extremely long and in a language that most people do not understand. A long tradition of handbooks, summaries, and commentaries has kept the material accessible to the relatively few trained in Pali. For most Theravada Buddhists, Pali texts are symbolically and ritually important. People are more likely to access Buddhist teachings through vernacular literature, oral teachings, sermons, art, and performance. Today modern media such as cartoons, films, and the Internet, including YouTube, are also important methods of promulgating Buddhist teachings. Theravada Buddhists mostly regard Pali as the language spoken by the Buddha and as sacred. As such it is used for ritual, for protective statements, and in protective symbols including tattoos.

The Pali Canon

Although most Theravada Buddhists access teachings through vernacular, local texts and discourses, their highest and shared textual authority is a collection of texts in the Pali language, which is an ancient literary language of north India related to Sanskrit but – as far as we can tell – restricted to Theravada culture. The Pali Canon is called the *Tipiṭaka*, "three baskets," in Pali. The three baskets are the *Vinaya Piṭaka*, *Sutta Piṭaka*, and *Abhidhamma Piṭaka*. The *Vinaya*

Theravada Buddhism: Continuity, Diversity, and Identity, First Edition. Kate Crosby.

Piṭaka contains monastic rules or "discipline" *(vinaya)*. The *Sutta Piṭaka* contains the Buddha's teachings, the Dhamma, mainly in the form of "teaching texts" or "discourses" (*sutta*) and poetry. The *Abhidhamma Piṭaka* is the systematization and further analyses of those teachings (*abhidhamma* "about the Dhamma" or "higher Dhamma"). The Pali Canon is believed by Theravada Buddhists to be the word of the Buddha (*buddhavacana*) and the first two *Piṭaka* were believed to have been collected rehearsed shortly after the Buddha's death (second *parinibbāna*, see Chapter 1) at a gathering called the "First Council." The council was formed of 500 *arhat* (enlightened) monks, headed by the Buddha's senior-most disciple still living at the time, the monk Mahākassapa.

The Vinaya Piṭaka

At the council, the foremost expert on monastic discipline (*vinaya*), the barber Upāli, confirmed the validity of the rules in the *Vinaya Piṭaka*, "The Basket of the Discipline." The *Vinaya Piṭaka* contains rules for individual monks and nuns to follow. The rules are provided within a narrative frame telling the story of how and why the Buddha established each rule. It also contains collective rules that apply to the running of the Sangha (the monastic community) as a whole and the liturgies to be used for the collective rituals or legal procedures (***saṅghakamma***) of the Sangha. The *Vinaya Piṭaka* additionally contains some other narratives, including the stories of the First Council, mentioned earlier, and of the Second Council. The list of rules monks and nuns must obey also exists as a separate text called the ***Pāṭimokkha Sutta***. This is the rules for individual members of the Sangha, excluding the collective rules, and is extracted from the narrative framework in which they are embedded in the *Vinaya Piṭaka*. The *Pāṭimokkha Sutta* is recited by monks at the ***uposatha*** (holy day) ceremonies, traditionally held fortnightly on the days of the new and full moons. (For more details about the Sangha and *Vinaya*, see Chapter 8.)

The Sutta Piṭaka

The Buddha's attendant Ānanda reported the teachings that he had heard the Buddha deliver. The stories of the Buddha delivering these teachings form the core of the *Sutta Piṭaka*, "The Basket of the Teaching." One meaning of the word *sutta* is "instruction," another meaning is "well-spoken." Each *sutta* text begins with the famous phrase "Thus have I heard." The "I" refers to Ānanda, who then describes the place where the Buddha was at the time when he gave the teaching that Ānanda witnessed. The *Sutta Piṭaka* also contains poems and other texts attributed to enlightened followers of the Buddha.

The *Sutta Piṭaka* is arranged into five subdivisions (*nikāya*). In modern translations, it fills about 35–40 volumes. The first four *nikāya* contain narrative *suttas* that are mainly in prose presenting teachings given by the Buddha or rarely, Sāriputta (one of the Buddha's closest disciples). The first two divisions, the *Dīgha Nikāya* (*Long Discourses*) and *Majjhima Nikāya* (*Middle Length Discourses*), are organized according to decreasing length. Well-known *suttas* from the *Dīgha Nikāya* include the *Mahāparinibbāna Sutta*, an account of the Buddha's last three months (see Chapter 1), and the *Mahāsatipaṭṭhāna Sutta* ("Great Discourse on the setting up of Mindfulness"), one of the most important texts on meditation practice (see Chapter 6).

A shorter version of it, the *Satipaṭṭhāna Sutta*, is found in the *Majjhima Nikāya*. The *Saṃyutta Nikāya* ("Connected Discourses") is organized according to form (e.g., in the first section, *suttas* containing verses are brought together) and topic (e.g., in the fourth section, all the *suttas* are about the sense organs and their objects). The fourth *nikāya* is called *Aṅguttara Nikāya*. *Aṅguttara* means "one component (*aṅga*) more (*uttara*)," referring to its arrangement according to the number of items in the topic being discussed. Thus, book one of the *Aṅguttara Nikāya* has *suttas* on topics such as *nibbāna* (of which there is only one), while book four has texts on the "four noble truths" (see Chapters 1 and 5) and even on the four types of marriage.

The fifth subdivision of the *Sutta Piṭaka* is called the *Khuddaka Nikāya*, *Minor Anthologies*. Although the term *khuddaka* means "small" (hence "minor" in the title of the English translation), this *nikāya* is in fact extremely long, containing 15 separate works, or 18 in the Burmese tradition. These works vary from some of the earliest material in the canon to some of the latest. One of them, the *Suttanipāta*, is a collection of poems containing what may well be the earliest verses in the canon, expressions of spiritual experience that predate the formulation of the schematic meditation systems and descriptions of meditative experience found elsewhere in the canon (see Chapter 6). In contrast, the *Niddesa* is really a commentary and has been dated to somewhere between the third-century BCE and second-century CE (von Hinüber 1996: 59), and the *Paṭisambhidāmagga* is an early *Abhidhamma* text (see later text). The *Apadāna*, *Cariyāpiṭaka*, and *Buddhavaṃsa* contain stories about the virtuous careers over multiple lifetimes of the Buddhas or of important people in early Buddhism. They all show a late stage in the development of the understanding of the Buddha (see Chapter 1). The stories of the Buddha's former lifetimes, the *Jātaka*, are also found here in the *Khuddaka Nikāya*. Given their ongoing popularity in art and performance, we shall look at the *Jātaka* separately (Chapter 4). Like the *Cariyāpiṭaka*, which is a rearrangement of a selection of *jātakas*, the *Khuddakapāṭha* "short readings/recitations" is a collection of material mainly found elsewhere in the canon. It appears to be a handbook providing the texts necessary for basic rituals and simple teachings: it includes a text for taking the three refuges, three texts containing basic teachings including a simple meditation text and several *paritta*, texts used for protective chanting.

As may be gathered from the description so far, the format of many of the texts in the *Khuddaka Nikāya* differs from the *suttas* of the first four *nikāya*, as well as from each other. Some works, such as the *Suttanipāta* (see earlier text) and the *Dhammapada* "Words of the Dhamma," which contains pithy summaries of doctrine and comments on the human condition, are entirely in verse.

The *Abhidhamma Piṭaka*

The third collection of texts in the Pali Canon, the *Abhidhamma Piṭaka* ("Collection of Higher Teaching"), is purported to have been realized by the Buddha in the fourth week of his Enlightenment. He then first preached to his mother Māyā, who had died seven days after his birth and been reborn as a deity in the *Tāvatiṃsa* heaven. The Buddha's disciple Sāriputta then met the Buddha on his visits back to the human realm for his daily **alms-round** and passed on the parallel section of the *Abhidhamma Piṭaka* to 500 monks who were his pupils. Although, from this story, the *Abhidhamma Piṭaka* is also the word of the Buddha, some texts within it are recognized by the Theravada tradition itself to be later. It is not mentioned in the account of the First Council in the *Vinaya Piṭaka*. The fifth book of the *Abhidhamma Piṭaka*, called the *Kathāvatthu* ("Points of Controversy"), is ascribed to Moggaliputtatissa who presided over the "Third Council" 218 years after the Buddha's *parinibbāna* during the reign of Emperor Asoka in the third-century BCE (von Hinüber 1996: 71). Current scholarship dates the gradual composition of *Abhidhamma Piṭaka* to a period between 200 BCE and 200 CE (von Hinüber 1996: 64). On the other hand, it seems to have been an approach to the Dhamma that was already emerging during the compilation of the *Sutta Piṭaka*. The *Abhidhamma Piṭaka* systematizes material contained in the *Sutta Piṭaka* and there are texts within the *Sutta Piṭaka* that are *Abhidhamma* in style. For example, the *Paṭisambhidāmagga* is an *Abhidhamma* work, but is included in the *Khuddaka Nikāya* of the *Sutta Piṭaka*. This may be because it is a relatively late text, post-dating the closing of the *Abhidhamma Piṭaka*: the *Khuddaka Nikāya*'s miscellaneous corpus continued to be open for new additions or rearrangements of existing material. Traditionally ascribed to the disciple Sāriputta, the *Paṭisambhidāmagga* may be an early handbook attempting to summarize the *Abhidhamma Piṭaka*.

Unlike the other two *Piṭaka*, the *Abhidhamma* texts are neither narrative nor poetic in style. The purpose of the style in most of the works in the *Abhidhamma Piṭaka* is to provide a systematic and mathematical arrangement of the constituents (*dhamma*) into which human experience of the universe can be analyzed and the way in which they are causally related to each other.

Theravada means the "doctrine of the elders" and it is in the *Abhidhamma Piṭaka* that the doctrine is most systematically formulated. So we can say that of the three collections of the Pali Canon, the *Abhidhamma* is the most distinctively Theravada. However, the non-narrative, rather dry format of the *Abhidhamma Piṭaka*, the technical nature of its content and the difficulty of translating or understanding many of the technical terms mean that it has in fact been drawn on least in the academic study of Theravada. (For more on *Abhidhamma*, see Chapter 7.)

Oral Performance and Transmission, and the Writing Down of the Canon

The word in Pali that we translate as "council," as in "First Council," *saṃgīti*, literally means a "singing together," yet we do not associate monks with melodic singing. Perhaps the word was already archaic in its use: listening to performances of singing is prohibited in the ten precepts for novices, monks, and nuns. When monks "perform" canonical texts throughout the Theravada world, they usually chant them. There are a few regional exceptions of monks singing in the performance of popular texts, such as those of *Jātaka* in parts of northern Thailand. Even when not sung, the quality of the chanting is important to the audience, and certain monks are sought after to perform chanting because of their reputation for having sonorous voices that carry. The phonetic accuracy, especially of *Vinaya* texts, has at times been regarded as crucial for the validity of certain rituals. This means that the sound of chanting for rituals such as ordination or consecrating sacred space may differ from chanting done for other purposes. Chanting styles and the pronunciation of Pali also vary by region and ordination lineage. On the whole monks in Burma pronounce Pali as if the consonants are Burmese, but when performing a *vinaya* ritual such as consecrating a sacred enclosure (***sīmā***) they might use the South Asian pronunciation regarded as more authentic (Nagasena 2013: §7.7). The most striking difference is the Pali "s" (IPA: s), which becomes "soft th" (IPA: θ) in Burmese pronunciation. For example, the word *saṅgho* ("Buddhist monastic community") is pronounced, according to the Burmese pronunciation, as *thaṅgho* with a "soft th" sound as in the English word "thought" while it is pronounced as *saṅgho* in the South Asian pronunciation. Consideration of this issue varies and is more likely to come to the fore at a point of crisis. In Bangladesh, *saṅgho* is pronounced with the Bengali sibilant *sh* "*shaṅgo*." In Tai-Lao, pronunciation voiced and unvoiced consonants, for example, *t* and *d*, are often pronounced with the reversed voicing. In Cambodia, the pronunciation of Pali on the whole follows Khmer style, in which the vowel pronunciation changes markedly according to whether it follows the "big" or "little" consonants into which the alphabet is divided, for example, the long *ā* in *sālā* "hall" stays the same, but becomes the dipthong "ee-a" (IPA: iɚ) in *vihāra* "monastery/temple," which becomes "*vihear*." While traditional Pali pronunciation was criticized by the reform wing of the Cambodian Sangha in the nineteenth and early twentieth centuries, that traditional pronunciation is seen as crucial to the validity of their rituals by the traditionalist (*borān*) wing (Marston 2008: 103, 106).

Highly sophisticated techniques for the memorization of extensive textual material already existed in India at the time of early Buddhism. The brahminical methods for the oral transmission of the Vedic Hindu hymns and Sanskrit literature are still used to this day. It is generally accepted that Buddhist texts were also orally transmitted, and we know that individual monks specialized in particular sections of the canon, but we do not know by what method, nor – in the early days – in what form (Allon 1997: 354–357, 398; Norman 1997/2006: 62–63; Wynne 2004). The Vedic texts, the earliest of which are verse hymns to the gods, have been accurately transmitted for over 3000 years. The format of the Pali Canon is mostly quite different: it is lengthy, often repetitive, and much of it is in prose.

Certain distinctive features of Theravada prose texts such as the use of synonyms in increasing numbers of syllables have been identified as helpful for memorization, although they also help clarify meaning. Other features, such as repeat passages, may help memorization as well as indicate the use of texts for performance (Crosby 2007: 169). Passages that move the narrative on, recited by those most familiar with the text, alternate with choruses in which all the monks can participate. The emphasis on meaning over form in early Buddhism may mean that the mode of memorization was initially quite fluid. This appears to be confirmed by differences between the extant form of texts in the Pali Canon and quotations in the third-century BCE inscriptions of the Emperor Asoka in India and the fifth- to sixth-century gold plates of Burma (Stargardt 1995). We see this also in more recent texts. For example, one Cambodian *ānisaṃsa* "benefits" text in Khmer language, which praises the benefits of the gift of toilets to the Sangha contains Pali textual passages that are recognizably from the *Majjhima Nikāya (Middle Length Discourses)* and its commentary, but it is the meaning and not the wording that is identical (Crosby and de Bernon unpublished analysis 2004). Such a fluid process of oral memorization may lie behind the *Jātaka* "Birth Stories" collection in the *Sutta Piṭaka* (see Chapter 4). The *Jātaka* contains stories of the Buddha in his former lifetimes as the *bodhisatta*. Although only the verses are considered canonical, the prose sections, which are considered "commentarial" (see later text), and so dated to a millennium after the Buddha, are crucial to convey the story and must be based on earlier narrative material.

In response to a period of ongoing famine in the first-century BCE, a crisis point was reached in Sri Lanka and, with the number of monks dwindling, a decision was made to write the Pali Canon down in order to ensure its preservation. This story relates to Sri Lanka and we do not know exactly what was written down nor whether oral or written means continued to dominate the transmission of the texts. It is quite possible that the Pali Canon continued to develop. It is only in the fifth century, with the composition of the commentaries on the Pali Canon, that we can establish the canon as a fixed collections of texts (Rahula 1956: xix).

Texts of the Pali Canon and Their Translations into English

The following is a table of texts of the Pali Canon with brief descriptions of the main sections and some of the translations available in English (adapted from Skilton, in preparation).

The Pali Canon: the tipiṭaka		
Vinaya Piṭaka *"monastic discipline"*	Sutta Piṭaka *"discourses/teaching texts"*	Abhidhamma Piṭaka *"higher doctrine"*
This section contains the rules that govern the behavior of monks and nuns and also the monastic community as a whole.	This section contains texts of various lengths representing the teachings given by the Buddha in historical settings, arranged in five major sub-subdivisions called *Nikāya*.	This section contains seven volumes of the teachings given by the Buddha arranged and abstracted according to technical principles. Texts toward the beginning analyze into constituent elements, while the final text addresses how these elements inter-relate.
Khandaka "the chapter," starting with a biography of the Buddha, it offers an account of the development of the monastic community and of the rules that cover its collective life. Part history and part legal document, this is a rich source of information about the development of the Buddhist community.	*Dīgha-nikāya* "long section," 34 long texts, including the *Mahāparinibbāna Suttanta*, the account of the final three months of the Buddha's life. *Dialogues of the Buddha* (Rhys Davids, 1899). *The Long Discourses of the Buddha* (Walshe 1987). *Majjhima-nikāya* "medium section," 152 medium length texts. *Middle Length Sayings* 3 vols (Horner 1954)	*Dhammasaṅganī* "Enumeration of Phenomena," lists all ultimate realities that can be discerned. *Buddhist Psychological Ethics* (Rhys Davids 1900). *Vibhaṅga* "The Analysis," continues the analysis of the former. *The Book of Analysis* (Thittila 1969). *Dhātukathā* "Discussion of the Elements." *Discourse on Elements* (Narada 1962).

(*Cont'd*)

The Pali Canon: the tipiṭaka		
Vinaya Piṭaka *"monastic discipline"*	Sutta Piṭaka *"discourses/teaching texts"*	Abhidhamma Piṭaka *"higher doctrine"*
Sutta-vibhaṅga "analysis of the *sutta*," that is, a commentary on the *Pāṭimokkha Sutta*, the rules governing the conduct of individual monks (227) and nuns (311). Each is set in an historical context explaining its origin and purpose. *Parivāra* "the ingredients," a thematically organized summary of the contents of the previous two sections. *Book of the Discipline, Vols I-VI* (Horner 1938–1966).	*The Middle Length Discourses of the Buddha* (Ñyāṇamoli and Bodhi 1995). *Aṅguttara-nikāya* "incremental section" several thousand short texts arranged by increasing numbers referred to in the contents of each. *The Book of the Gradual Sayings* 5 vols. (Woodward and Hare 1932). *Aṅguttara Nikāya: Numerical Discourses of the Buddha* (anthology) (Nyanaponika Thera and Bhikkhu Bodhi 1999). *Saṃyutta-nikāya* "connected section," several thousand short texts arranged thematically. *The Book of the Kindred Sayings* 5 vols. (Rhys Davids and Woodward 1917). *The Connected Discourses of the Buddha* (Bhikkhu Bodhi 2000). *Khuddaka Nikāya* "minor section," 15–18 texts, including some of the most famous, for example, *Dhammapada*: a collection of gnomic verses; *Jātaka*: a collection of 547 stories of previous lives of the Buddha; *Thera- and Therīgāthā*: poetry composed by historical disciples of the Buddha. These last, along with parts of the *Sutta Nipāta* constitute some of the very oldest Pali texts. Various translations.	*Puggalapaññatti* "Description of individual types," descriptions of personality types. *A Designation of Human Types* (Law 1922). *Kathāvatthu* "Matters of Discussion," compiled by Moggaliputtatissa (C3rd BCE) lays out 200+ doctrinal disputations from Theravāda viewpoint. *Points of Controversy* (Aung and Rhys Davids 1915). *Yamaka* "The Pairs," examines various doctrinal categories through pairs of questions. No translation. *Paṭṭhāna* "Relations," describes 24 *paccayas*, or types of conditionality through which *dhammas* interact. *Conditional Relations* 2 vols (Narada 1969/1981).

Manuscripts, Councils, Printing, and Digital Dhamma

The Buddha taught that the disappearance of the Dhamma ushers in an apocalyptic age, in which lifespans are short, warfare, disease, and natural disasters great. For this reason, and to maintain the possibility of access to the Buddha's teaching, great emphasis is placed on the importance of ensuring the Dhamma continues to be available. Therefore, copying texts into new manuscripts or, in the modern period, sponsoring the printing of books is seen as a highly meritorious activity. In some cultures, such as the Shan, sponsoring a scribe to copy a book and donating it to the monastery is a way of transferring merit (see Chapter 5) to the recent deceased, and so is done to commemorate anyone who has died in the previous year (Khur-Yearn 2012: 32). The printing and distribution of free Dhamma books is a common way to mark the anniversary of a death.

The practice of copying the Dhamma means that most Theravada temples have a small collection of manuscripts, while some temples have several thousand. Collections tend to combine works in Pali with those in vernacular languages. The selection of Pali manuscripts available in most temples reflects their ritual use, so it is common to have manuscripts of the texts for ordination, the texts for protective *paritta* rituals, whichever texts are important at funerals in the region (see Chapter 5), perhaps texts relating to the history of that temple, and texts important as the basis for sermons. This means that most temples do not keep copies of the entire Pali Canon. Temples that have been important administrative centers, or centers of learning, have hundreds and occasionally thousands of manuscripts.

In more recent times, museums and libraries have developed collections based not on local use, but on collecting. The colonial and colonizing powers of the nineteenth and early twentieth century, among which we may include Thailand, all developed their own substantial collections. Examples include the British Library in London, the Bibliothèque Nationale in Paris, and the National Library in Bangkok. The manuscript collection of each library reflects the general area of the Theravada world over which the colonial power ruled: Burma and Sri Lanka in the British Library; Cambodia, Laos, and Vietnam in the Bibliothèque Nationale; and the different regions of what came to be Thailand in the National Library in Bangkok. Many other smaller collections were built up during this period and these large institutions continue to add important material as it comes to light. Hugh Nevill, a civil servant in Sri Lanka at the end of the nineteenth century, had a love of Sri Lanka's rich botanical and cultural heritage, and an exceptional eye for rare material. While the botanical specimens he collected for London's Kew Gardens perished, the Nevill collection of over 2000 manuscripts, including many rare Pali and Sinhalese Buddhist texts, is now housed in the British Library (Somadasa 1987–1995). For a list of titles of Pali works in Sri Lankan temple collections, see Nyanatusita (2008). The collection in the National Library in Bangkok contains over 100 000 manuscripts from all over Thailand gathered in the mid-nineteenth to early twentieth centuries, which are as yet largely unexplored and difficult to access (Choompolpaisal archival work 2012). The sheer numbers and the collecting process that must have created this archive belies the stories taught in Thailand that many texts in the vernacular were destroyed and suggests an alternative approach was taken to these powerful objects.

Manuscripts are also sold into the art and tourist trade, frequently divided up or with any illuminations or illustrations extracted and sold separately. The Fragile Palm Leaves Foundation was set up in Bangkok in 1994 to try to prevent the loss of manuscripts in this manner. It focused on manuscripts from the Union of Burma that were being sold on the Burma–Thai border in the aftermath of the 1988 uprising, a market that was further driven by Burma's poor economic standing (www.palitext.com, retrieved August 30, 2012). The collection now contains over 10896 Pali/Pali-Burmese manuscripts containing 22 600 titles (http://fpl.tusita.org/manuscripts/). While a handful of catalogues of Pali and other Theravada manuscripts have been published, many remain uncatalogued. In places, work on cataloguing and digitizing continues, currently including projects by Chiang Mai University, the École française d'Extrême-Orient, the Digital Library of Laos Manuscripts in Vientiane (http://www.laomanuscripts.net), the Fragile Palm Leaves Foundation (http://fpl.tusita.org), and the Bodleian Revealing Hidden Collections project (http://www.bodleian.ox.ac.uk/sers/projects, retrieved December 9, 2012). Important conservation, microfilming, and conservation work was conducted by EFEO in Cambodia in the 1990s in response to the massive destruction of manuscripts during the Khmer Rouge period (www.khmermanuscripts.org, de Bernon *et al.* 2004). While staff at Wat Unnalom in Phnom Penh, where this project was based, maintain the expertise for this work, funding ran out and newly revealed collections that had been kept safe during the Khmer Rouge period, often at great person risk, are now at risk from the lack of conservation resources and the demise of the expertise within the ***achar*** (lay specialist) tradition to continue the maintenance of such traditions (Crosby and Long fieldwork January 2013). Manuscripts may also be neglected and temple collections are particularly at risk not just from poverty and political upheaval, but from pilfering for sale to tourists, insects, lack of use, and lack of relevant skills among monks resulting from changes in monastic education and technology. Traditional uses for worn out manuscripts were inclusion inside images or as papier mache images, and being burnt or ground up as one of the ingredients in amulets.

Theravada manuscripts are preserved on a variety of materials and in a variety of scripts. In the Shan collections of northeast Burma and northern Thailand, Pali texts tend to be in Burmese script and, as elsewhere, on prepared palm leaf, mostly from the Talipot palm, *Corypha Umbraculifera Linn*. The letters are cut with a sharp stylus into the prepared manuscript leaves, which are naturally pale cream or yellow, and these are then smeared with soot that darkens the incision making them easier to read. Palm leaves are usually only a couple of inches in height and perhaps 12–18 inches in width. (The term width is used here from the reader's perspective. One might also say "length" in that it is the longest measurement.) The writing on them is quite small, with say nine lines along the length of each side of a leaf. Even so, a standard, complete palm leaf manuscript, which may contain from one text, or a part of one, to a collection of several, can be anywhere from 20 to 200 leaves. Some are even longer. They are held together either by sticks or strings passed through two string holes toward the center of each leaf (or one string hole in the case of the smaller practice manuals carried on the person), and the whole may be clamped between two wooden boards. Illustrations on palm leaf manuscripts are not very common, although the boards offer more scope and may be highly decorated with paintings or even with semi-precious gems. In areas where Burmese script is used for Pali, a more rounded form of it (tamarind seed script) is used for ordination texts. These ordination manuscripts are far more highly decorated than is the norm. Just as Burmese script is used for Pali manuscripts by some neighboring non-Burmese ethnic groups such as the Shan, Cambodian script was used for Pali in some neighboring Tai regions until the modern period, with variations on Tham script in northern Tai and Lao regions (Iijima 2009).

A variety of scripts and manuscript form may be used. For example, while the ritual texts in Pali held in Shan temple libraries may be in Burmese script and on palm leaf, Shan vernacular texts are written in Shan script, with the occasional use of Burmese script for Pali terms, on a large format paper made from the back of the *streblus asper* form of mulberry (*sā*, Shan; *khoi* Thai). *Streblus asper* is found throughout mainland Southeast Asia, where it also has a number of medicinal uses. Consequently, large format mulberry paper manuscripts are found throughout Burma, Cambodia, Laos, and Thailand, but not in Sri Lanka. Typically, an individual page measures up to 12 in. in height and 24 in. wide. The pages are glued together to form a continuous sheet, folded into pages with a concertina-effect ("leporello"). The text reads continuously along one side of this sheet, for 100 pages for more, and the book may then be opened the other way around to continue reading, now on the other side of the sheet. The writing on this type of manuscript is much larger than on palm leaf and there is greater scope for paintings. More elaborate paintings are of popular themes, such as the *jātaka* tales of the Buddha's former lifetimes (see Chapter 4). They may be done by artists rather than by the scribes who copied the manuscript and they do not necessarily relate to the content of the manuscript. In Cambodia, which traditionally uses long and short palm-leaves as well as *streblus asper* paper-folded leporello style for manuscripts, modern school notebooks began to be used even before the Pol Pot period such that even quite rare texts such as the guides for performing traditional style (*borān*) rituals and meditation may be preserved in them.

The extent to which manuscripts continue to be copied even where printing has become common varies from region to region. In Shan Buddhism, only the most popular texts have been printed and having a new manuscript copied to commemorate someone's death is still common (Crosby and Khur-Yearn 2010). In Sri Lanka, creating manuscripts is now quite rare and is mainly done for astrologies. The format of astrologies for individuals is quite different (a single leaf curled along its length). There are some attempts to ensure that the skills required for producing and writing manuscripts are not lost, for example in Laos (http://www.laomanuscripts.net/en/about/collection). However, inevitably, given the widespread use of printing, digital scanning, and computers and the demands on monks to develop other skills, in most Theravada regions the creation and use of manuscripts are not now part of monastic training.

The royal patronage of the printing of the *Tipiṭaka* that took place in several countries in the modern period (see later text) is a continuation of a long tradition. In the past the ruling family of a region sponsored textual scholars and also sponsored councils, *saṅgīti*, to ensure the complete collection and purity of the Pali Canon. In Burmese reckoning, there have been six councils. The First Council was the one to record the Buddha's Dhamma, teachings, and *Vinaya*, monastic rules, that took place shortly after the Buddha's death. Like the First Council, the Second Council is described in the *Vinaya Piṭaka*. It took place in Vesālī in northern India about 100 years after the death of the Buddha and involved rejecting lax practices among monks. Some of the practices, such as monks handling money and monks within the same *sīmā* holding different *uposatha* ceremonies (see Chapter 8), reflect ongoing developments as Buddhism became a more settled and institutionalized religion and as societal norms changed. There have been reactions against such practices but also widespread acceptance of monks handling money over the centuries. But the significance of other of the "lax practices" is now obscure, for example, the storing of salt in a horn! Different branches of Buddhism hold different accounts of the councils, but agree that it is from this point that schisms emerge in the Sangha. The variation between accounts has been useful for the studying of the development of early Buddhism (Prebish 1974). For Theravada Buddhists, the Third Council took place under the Emperor Asoka in the mid-third-century BCE at his capital in Pāṭaliputra (modern Patna) and concerned matters of doctrine. It was headed by Mogaliputtatissa. The *Kathāvatthu*, the fifth book of the *Abhidhamma Piṭaka*, is attributed to him and was added to the canon when it was recited at this council. It is after this that, according to Theravada chronicles, Asoka sent missions to establish Buddhism in Sri Lanka and Southeast Asia. This council is extremely important for Theravada identity. It is also important in establishing a precedent for royal (and later government) intervention in Sangha affairs (see Chapter 12). The Fourth Council in Theravada is the event that took place in Sri Lanka in the first-century BCE at which the Pali Canon was committed to writing to preserve it during a time of famine and constant warfare.

Although there were other periods at which the Pali Canon was reviewed between the fourth council in the first-century BCE and the Fifth and Sixth Councils in the nineteenth and twentieth century, respectively, these are not counted as councils in the Burmese reckoning, which has now become the standard list. Tilman Frasch has suggested that such reviews took place in anticipation of important anniversaries in the lifespan of the Dhamma, that is, since the death of the Buddha, out of anxiety for the consequences should the Dhamma be allowed to decline (Frasch 2012: 579). Two other important periods of textual production stand out. The first is the writing of the commentaries under the auspices of the Mahāvihāra monastery in Anuradhapura in Sri Lanka in the fifth-century CE (see later text). The second took place in the twelfth century when King Parākkamabāhu I of Sri Lanka forcibly unified the various Sangha of Sri Lanka under the Mahāvihāra fraternity. The Mahāvihāra nikāya, in part in competition with South India rivals following the wars between Coḷa and Sri Lanka, became more cosmopolitan in outlook, modeling new Pali writings on the Sanskrit literary cultures of Indian elite culture more broadly (Gornall 2013: 236). A large number of manuals and subcommentaries were written following this event, establishing the Mahāvihāra's credentials for correct *vinaya* practice, grammar, and textual scholarship (Crosby 2003: 94–96, Gornall 2013: 11). Moreover, there was an attempt in this period to use Pali beyond the religious arena, for subjects traditionally written in Sanskrit. Sanskrit, which is closely related to Pali, had become a language of court and learning throughout South Asia since at least the Gupta period (third to sixth century). As such it was used alongside Pali, which seems to have been confined to religious literature. As a result grammatical, medical, mathematical, and other technical texts were preserved in Sanskrit even when being used by Theravada monks. In the twelfth century, an attempt was made to expand the use of Pali to these areas also, although it appears that in the long run this was successful only in a limited range of topics, such as grammar. The literature valued and produced in this period had a great impact on the Theravada of Southeast Asia. The demise of Buddhism in much of India at this time, the rise of Islam as the religion of the Asian maritime trade network (the maritime "Silk Route"), and Sri Lanka's victory against the Coḷa kingdom of Southeast Asia contributed to Sri Lanka's influence as a source of Buddhist authority from the twelfth century until the advent of European colonialism in the sixteenth century. At points of crisis, and in cases of rivalry, groups of monks from Southeast Asia would travel to Sri Lanka in search of "uncorrupted" ordination lineages and texts. This coincided with the period during which Theravada became more widespread and adopted by kings as the religion at court in mainland Southeast Asia.

Further examples of such measures taken to ward off the decline of the Dhamma took place in Southeast Asia and Sri Lanka in the fifteenth century, approaching the end of the second millennium since the death of the Buddha. Monks from Burma, Thailand, Cambodia, and possibly Bengal studied and received texts from Sri Lanka in the 1420s, receiving fresh ordination in Sri Lanka on a raft in the River Kalyāṇī. They returned, with Sri Lankan monks, to Southeast Asia, introducing Sri Lankan lineages such as that headed by Ñāṇagambhīra in Chiang Mai, where King Tilokarāja would convene a council and recitation of texts in 1455. In 1476–1479, King Dhammaceti instigated a series of reforms in the Sangha in lower Burma, explicitly citing his concern about the decline of the Dhamma in an inscription that marks the event. This event became the model for future Burmese kings (Frasch 2012: 584–586).

In spite of repeated events such as those in Sri Lanka in the fifth, twelfth , and fifteenth centuries, where various branches of the Sangha sought to reexamine the Pali Canon, commentaries and *Vinaya* practice, it is not until the modern period that the two events identified as the Fifth and Sixth Councils took place. They both took place in Burma. The Fifth Council took place in 1871 in Burma under the reign of King Mindon. The texts had been inscribed on 729 marble slabs in 1860–1868. Over a period of five months (i.e., after the inscription of the slabs), the texts were examined in detail comparing different manuscripts to produce a new edition and then recited (Braun 2008: 60).

The Sixth Council lasted from 1954 to 1956, culminating with the 2500th anniversary of the *parinibbāna* (death) of the Buddha. Like the Fifth Council, it took place in Burma, in Rangoon (now Yangon). Coinciding as it did with recent independence from European colonialism for Burma (1948), Sri Lanka (1948), and French Indochina (1954), it was a pan-Theravada celebration and collaboration, with monks and manuscripts from all Theravada countries. The resulting edition is regarded as the most authoritative of the critical editions created in the modern period. It is also the basis of the Vipassanā Research Institute's (VRI) Chaṭṭha Saṅgāyana online edition of canonical, commentarial, and other Pali literature (www.tipitaka.org).

There have been a number of printed editions of the Pali Canon. The first was the 28-volume Chulachomklao Tipiṭaka published in 1893 under the patronage of King Chulalongkorn (Rāma V, 1853–1910), who also founded the first two modern monastic universities of Thailand: Mahāchulalongkorn Royal University (associated with the **Mahānikāya** lineage of the Thai Sangha) in 1887 and Mahamakut University (associated with the Dhammayuttikanikāya lineage) in 1893. (For a history of the different editions, see Skilton in preparation: Chapter 12.) Until the availability online of the VRI edition, most Westerners accessed the Pali Canon through the editions in Roman script produced by the Pali Text Society, founded in 1881 by T.W. Rhys Davids (www.palitext.com) mainly published in first half of the twentieth century.

Since the 1990s, the quest to ensure the continued availability of the Dhamma has led to the production of CD ROMS and, now, internet sites, such as the VRI site mentioned earlier. Recently an international team based at the monastic complex of Wat Phra Dhammakaya in Pathumthani, Thailand, under the direction of Dr. Ven. Thanavuddho and Prof. G. A. Somaratne has begun working on a new edition using a sophisticated system of double-blind checking that ensures accuracy, and referring variants of any complexity to an international panel of scholars (http://www.ocbs.org, retrieved September 2011).

The Decline of the Dhamma

In spite of all these efforts to preserve it, the Dhamma will disappear. The process of gradual decline starts with the death/*parinibbāna* of the Buddha. It becomes increasingly rare for anyone to become an *arhat* and eventually no one attains any insight (*paṭivedha*) into the four noble truths (Chapter 4) taught by the Buddha. The next stage is the loss of *paṭipatti*, practice, which culminates in monks failing to keep even the four ***pārājika*** rules: not to have sexual intercourse, kill, steal, or falsely claim superhuman powers (see Chapter 8). The stage after this is the loss of study of the *Tipiṭaka* (*pariyatti*). During this stage, the texts of the Pali Canon begin to disappear in reverse order from that in which they are organized, as listed earlier. So the first work to disappear is the last book of the *Abhidhamma Piṭaka*, the *Paṭṭhāna*, followed by the other *Abhidhamma* books. The *Sutta Piṭaka*, beginning with the *Khuddaka Nikāya*, the fifth subdivision, disappears next. Finally, the *Vinaya Piṭaka* disappears. The short *Pātimokkha Sutta* that lists all the rules is the last text to disappear (Strong 2004: 222–223). After this the visual reminders of Buddhism disappear, culminating in the Buddha's relics coming together to give a final sermon (described in Chapter 1).

The Pali Canon in Relation to Other Buddhist Canons

The Pali Canon is the only canon to survive as a complete collection in an Indic language. The other early schools of Buddhism were mainly preserved in the two other Indic literary languages, Sanskrit and **Prakrit**; a large number of their texts only survive in Chinese and Tibetan translations. There are also a number of texts preserved in a variety of Central Asian languages.

All branches of Buddhism had *Vinaya* and *Sutta* (Sanskrit *sūtra*) collections. The *Vinaya* texts of different branches of Buddhism have much in common. Many of the rules are the same, particularly the more serious rules, such as those that, if broken, warrant expulsion from the Sangha. The interpretation of the rules and visual practice differs more than the rules themselves. Significant differences of practice include the prohibition on meat-eating for East Asian monastics, whereas Theravada monks and nuns eat meat, unless they are vegetarian by personal choice (see Chapter 5). Another development in *Vinaya* has been the development of married priesthoods not bound by the *Vinaya* in various forms of Himalayan and Japanese Buddhism.

Much of the *Sutta* material is common to all branches, but those schools that identify themselves as Mahayana ("great way or vehicle") include later or "rediscovered" *sūtra*, which purport to teach new material either that the Buddha realized people were not ready to hear at the time of his Enlightenment or that came from other Buddhas. Some elements that we find included as *sūtra* material in Mahayana texts are found in commentaries in the Theravada tradition.

Not all forms of Buddhism have an *Abhidhamma* (Sanskrit *Abhidharma*) collection. Indeed, some of the Mahayana philosophies that developed specifically reject *Abhidharma*, especially the *Abhidharma* of the Sarvāstivāda branch of Buddhism (see Chapter 7). While no longer extant as a philosophical school in its own right, Sarvāstivāda *Abhidharma* was extremely important for the formation of Madhyamaka and Yogācāra, two branches of Mahayana philosophy. For this reason, Sarvāstivāda *Abhidharma* continues to be studied in some forms of Mahayana Buddhism, for example as part of the curricula in Tibetan advanced monastic education. Some "Perfection of Wisdom" *sūtra* (*Prajñāpāramitāsūtra*), the highest textual authorities for Madhyamaka Buddhism, may have originally been composed as treatises rejecting Sarvāstivāda *abhidharma* analyses of reality, which were then reshaped into a *sūtra* format, most notably through Ānanda's "Thus have I heard" framing device (see earlier text).

The aspect of Sarvāstivāda most criticized by Madhyamaka is its doctrine on the enduring nature of the constituents of the universe (also termed *dhamma*), a doctrine also rejected in Theravada *Abhidhamma*. We shall return to this difference between these two types of *Abhidhamma* in Chapter 7. Nonetheless, Sāriputta (Sanskrit Sāriputra) is the disciple of the Buddha associated with all forms of *Abhidhamma*, and features in the Mahayana rejection of *Abhidhamma*. Thus in certain narratives in Mahayana *sūtras*, such as the *Lotus Sūtra*, Śāriputra appears as the fall guy, portrayed as the arrogant monk who thought he was enlightened but was in fact so misguided that he can be upstaged by laymen or seven-year-old girls (in fact, a *nāga* – serpent deity – princess) (Watson 1993: Chapter 12). He is himself transformed into a woman by a goddess in the *Vimalakīrtinirdeśa Sūtra* in order to show him up for his fixation on such characteristics as gender, one of the constituents of reality (*dhamma*, *dharma*) (Thurman 1976: 61–62). Such narratives are parables in Madhyamaka teaching for the superiority of its own doctrine of "emptiness" (Sanskrit *śūnyatā*), that is, that no entities have independent, enduring existence, over what they regarded as the reification of the fundamental constituents of the universe (*dhamma*) in Sarvāstivāda *Abhidharma* (see Chapter 7).

The Criteria for Canonical Inclusion and Apocryphal/ Noncanonical *sutta* Texts

Even at the First Council, according to the account of proceedings in the *Vinaya Piṭaka*, not all monks or texts were included. The monk Purāṇa arrived too late to participate and did not accept the First Council's selection of texts. The *Itivuttaka*, one of the works of the *Khuddaka Nikāya*, was not based on the recollections of Ānanda, but on those of a laywoman who heard the Buddha preach at Kosambi. So presumably it must have been included in the Canon after. The assumption that texts would continue to be added underlies the "four great criteria" *mahāpadesa* for knowing what to include and what not to include. According to the *Mahāpadesa Sutta* of the *Dīgha Nikāya* (DN ii.123ff.), texts should be regarded as authentic if they are (i) heard directly from mouth of Buddha; (ii) heard directly from a Sangha containing *thera* "elders," (iii) heard directly from a group of "elders" who are specialists in a *Piṭaka*; and (iv) heard directly from a single specialist in a *Piṭaka*. This means that while additions are possible, the canon is relatively closed. This contrasts with the attitude of Mahayana tradition that adopts the inclusive approach that whatever inspired speech is connected with the Teaching (*Dharma* Sanskrit), destroys defilements, and reflects the qualities of *nirvāna* not *saṃsāra* is the word of the Buddha. This allows for the inclusion of later material as the word of the Buddha in the Mahayana branches of Buddhism, although specific branches may then focus on specific *sūtra* as the most authoritative for them.

Even within Theravada, there are many Pali texts, which local Buddhists regard as *sutta* or *Jātaka* spoken by the Buddha himself, that are not included in the Canon. Such texts have been dubbed apocryphal although there is no sense that those who preserved them saw them as such. While on the whole such texts are judged to be later, it is difficult to know whether such assessments are necessarily correct, when they could be the product of branches of textual transmission separate from those that came to be represented in the Pali Canon. (On apocryphal Pali literature, see Crosby 2006a, Hallisey 1990, 1993, and Jaini 1992.)

Commentarial and Other Postcanonical Pali Literature

According to Theravada tradition, the 500 *arhats* who established the Canon at the First Council also created commentaries explaining the meaning. The son of Emperor Asoka, the monk Mahinda, who took Buddhism to Sri Lanka in the third-century BCE, is believed to have translated these commentaries into the vernacular language of the island to make them accessible to people there.

In the fifth century, the scholar-monk Buddhaghosa, whose name means "voice of the Buddha," "retranslated" the commentaries back into the "pure" Pali language that Theravada Buddhists believed was spoken by the Buddha. Buddhaghosa is attributed with the *Samantapāsādikā*, which is the most important commentary on the *Vinaya Piṭaka* and continues to be consulted in matters of monastic dispute to this day. He is also attributed with the commentaries on the first four *nikāya* of the *Sutta Piṭaka* and on the *Abhidhamma Piṭaka*. Scholars tend to agree, however, that differences in style and even point of view mean that the global attribution of all these commentaries to a single author must have come at a later date (Jayawickrama 1990: xii). Several of the commentaries on books contained in the *Khuddaka Nikāya*, the fifth division of the *Sutta Piṭaka*, are attributed to Dhammapāla, who probably lived circa ninth century, judging from his references to philosophical developments that had taken place by that time in north India (Pind 1997: 523–527).

The term for a "commentary" in Pali is *aṭṭhakathā*, which translates as "discussion or explanation (*kathā*) of the meaning (*aṭṭha*)." A commentary provides different types of explanation of meaning. Sometimes they clarify the meaning of obscure words, old-fashioned grammar, and complex sentences. In the case of *Vinaya* commentaries, great care is taken to ensure that all ambiguities about how to practice the *vinaya* are resolved. The wording of litanies used for rituals is reformed to exclude phrasing not found in the Pali Canon itself, phrasing that presumably reflects variations that had developed since the time of the Buddha. For example, Buddhaghosa rejects the inclusion of the phrase meaning "lifelong" from the liturgy for ordination on the basis that this is not the wording given by the Buddha in the canon. Presumably the option of using the term lifelong reflects alternative types of commitment to ordination, or perhaps variations within different branches of Theravada. Other types of explanations in a commentary include the provision of stories that give the reason why something happened. For example, the commentary on the rule requiring parental consent for the ordination of children relates the story of Suddhodana, the Buddha's father. Suddhodana had felt great grief when the Buddha left home in search of Enlightenment. When the Buddha's son Rāhula is ordained, Suddhodana feels his grief reawakened and requests that this rule be established: it is in response to Suddhodana's request that the Buddha establishes the rule (Crosby 2005). A commentary might also explain why the Buddha appeared to behave in ways that seem unnecessary for a Buddha. Such explanations were necessitated by developments in expectations of what it meant to be omniscient or perfect by the time the commentaries were compiled (see Chapter 1).

Attitudes to the importance of commentaries vary between different Theravada countries. In Thailand, although the study of commentaries is included in Pali examinations, the reform of the nineteenth to twentieth century focused very much on the canonical texts, to the extent that the great monk-scholar Ven. Prince Vajirañāṇavarorasa (1860–1921) felt it reasonable to dismiss the reading of the commentaries in favor of a "common sense" understanding of the canon. This is in contrast with Burma, where the canon is always read through the commentaries and apparent discrepancies between the two are resolved to accommodate both (Nagasena 2013: 58). While the monastic education of other Theravada countries now includes secular subjects, this is not the case in Burma. Burma also has a long history of the king and the state judging members and branches of the Sangha on their knowledge of Theravada literature and correct practice of *Vinaya*. To this day there are Dhamma and *Vinaya* court cases, although there is usually a broader political reason when people are brought before such courts. For example, the monk in question may have gained great popularity or the allegations of misconduct may have come from a rival monk or group. These two factors of monastic education in Burma – its nonsecular nature and the importance placed on being well-trained in the canon and commentarial texts – mean that it is Burma that has retained the most in-depth and widespread expertise in the canon and in the full range of commentarial literature from the earliest times to the present. Burma grants high status and privilege to those few monks (currently nine) who succeed in memorizing the entire *Tipiṭaka*. The first monk to hold this title in the modern period was Mingun Tipitaka Sayadaw Ven. Ashin Vicittasārābhivaṃsa (1911–1993). (For a biographical inscription of this monk, see Dhammasami and Kyaw 2012.)

Given the size of the canonical and commentarial *corpi*, it is unsurprising that another development in Pali literature was the creation of handbooks or summaries. Buddhaghosa compiled the most important Pali handbook, a summary of the Theravada spiritual path called the *Visuddhimagga, The Path of Purification* (Ñyāṇamoli 1976), which remains an important work to this day. It is structured on the basis of a set of seven types of purity gained through following the Dhamma described in the *Ratha-vinīta Sutta* of the *Majjhima Nikāya* (MN24): "purity in terms of virtue, mind, view, the overcoming of perplexity, knowledge and vision of what is and is not the path, knowledge and vision of the way, and knowledge and vision" (Thanissaro 2010: note 2). These types of purity are organized into three divisions that represent aspects of practice on the spiritual path: *sīla* (moral conduct), *samādhi* (meditation), and *paññā* (wisdom). It was regarded as such a perfect work that although the gods tested Buddhaghosa by repeatedly removing the entire text, he reproduced it word for word each time. When the gods restored all three copies, they were found to be identical. The *Visuddhimagga's* central section on meditation, which takes up half of the text, systematizes the meditations described in Pali canonical and commentarial literature into a list of 40 meditation exercises, ***kammaṭṭhāna***. The work is referred to in meditation manuals throughout Theravada and has been a source for the transmission of meditation into the West. Summaries of meditation practice in English based on it tend to omit the stories and interpretations that do not fall into a rationalist interpretation of Buddhism (see Chapter 6). The next most important manual for Theravada is the *Abhidhammaṭṭhasaṅgaha*, a concise summary of *Abhidhamma*, composed in the tenth/eleventh century by Anuruddha (see Chapter 7).

Buddhaghosa was working under the auspices of the Mahāvihāra monastery in Sri Lanka, which from the twelfth century onward came to dominate Theravada Buddhism not only in Sri Lanka but also in mainland Southeast Asia. In the twelfth century, there was a new spate of commentary writing, with a focus on subcommentaries and handbooks that further commented on and summarized the commentarial works attributed to Buddhaghosa. One of the most important writers of the time was the monk Sāriputta, named after the Buddha's famous disciple. He wrote several works based on Buddhaghosa's, including a reorganization of the legal material from Buddhaghosa's *Vinaya* commentary, the *Samantapāsādikā*. In his summary (*saṅgaha*), Sāriputta ordered the practical information according to the *vinaya* ritual being discussed and discarded all the broader explanations and stories, retaining only that which was directly relevant to correct practice. His summary goes by the catchy title *Pālimuttakavinayavinicchayasaṅgaha*,"Compendium of Pronouncements of Vinaya Independent of the Order of the Canonical Text" (Crosby 2006b: 50).

Commentaries, manuals, and literature on a broader range of subjects that refer to earlier Pali material continue to be written in Pali and in vernacular languages to this day. The most recent high point in production was in the nineteenth and early twentieth centuries, a direct response to the threat of European colonialism to the patronage and position of Buddhism. Pali has also been used as a *lingua franca* in person and in letters between Theravada Buddhists of different mother tongues, a practice that goes back at least to the time of Buddhaghosa: he contrasts the use of Pali in ritual to that of the monks' mother tongues, such as Tamil or Sinhala, used to explain the meaning of Pali texts. The practice of Pali as a shared medium continued into the modern period. The Burmese scholar monk Paññāsāmi wrote his *Sāsanavaṃsa*, which has been much used as a resource for Burmese history and Pali literature, for a delegation of monks from Sri Lanka in 1864 preliminary to the establishment of the Rāmaññanikāya (see Chapter 8) in Sri Lanka (Pranke 2004: 29–30). Nowadays, Pali is still used as a *lingua franca* among monks who have achieved a high level of traditional education, and in recent years Pali-medium scholarly conferences or conference panels have been held in Burma and Thailand. But English is now the more common shared medium in broader circles, including for university and meditation teaching among the relatively high number of visiting lecturers and student monks on exchanges between the different Theravada countries. A summary exemplifying the range of literature composed in Pali is given in the following table (adapted from Skilton in preparation). It is not an exhaustive list.

The *Tipiṭaka*: ***Vinaya-piṭaka*** ***Sutta-piṭaka*** ***Abhidhamma-piṭaka***	While all three *piṭakas* are attributed by Theravada tradition to the Buddha, these are clearly of piecemeal composition of various dates, some material possibly being contemporary with the Buddha. The collection as a whole is clearly highly edited, although when and by whom is still a matter of guesswork. Even relatively conservative estimates place the *Abhidhamma* several centuries after the time of the Buddha. Parts of both the *Sutta* and *Abhidhamma Piṭakas* remain untranslated: *Mahāniddesa*, *Cūlaniddesa*, *Apadāna*, *Yamaka*, *Paṭṭhāna*.
Commentaries ***Aṭṭha-kathā***	Based on around a dozen no longer extant precursors of unknown date, the commentaries were redacted and translated into Pali by Buddhaghosa in Sri Lanka, with further contributions by Buddhadatta, Dhammapāla, Mahānāma, Upasena *et al.* These remain largely untranslated into a European language. The translations of the *Jātaka* (Cowell 1895–1913) and *Dhammapada* commentaries (Burlingame 1921) leave out passages.
Subcommentaries ***ṭīkā***	After some time, particularly in the twelfth century, it was thought that useful information could or should be added to that offered by the commentaries and this resulted in the composition of subcommentaries. These are mostly untranslated.
Paracanonical texts	There are various texts adjunct to the canon that are necessary to the functioning of the community. These include the *Pāṭimokkha Sutta* and numerous ***kammavācā***, or ritual texts that set out, for example, the wording of the ordination procedures, etc.
Manuals	Over the centuries various manuals were compiled in an attempt both to organize canonical materials into a more accessible format and/or to update guidance in a particular practical area. These are by their nature pragmatic rather than theoretical in their approach. Three subjects well-represented in this category are *Abhidhamma*, legal/*Vinaya* issues and meditation. These texts are mostly untranslated although the *Visuddhimagga* and *Abhidhammaṭṭhasaṅgaha* have inspired multiple translations. An early exception is the mixed Pali-Sinhala *Yogāvacara's Manual*, a meditation manual belonging to the ***borān kammaṭṭhāna/ yogāvacara*** tradition that was ubiquitous throughout Southeast Asia prior to more recent reforms. From the 1970s onward related manuals were translated into French by Bizot *et al.* (Crosby 2000).

(*Continued*)

(Cont'd)

Path summaries	Encyclopedic summaries of the Buddhist Path are a feature of most Buddhist cultures and traditions. The most famous is the *Visuddhimagga*, written by Buddhaghosa. Less well known is the *Vimuttimagga*, now only known in Chinese translation and possibly composed in Pali. Both are translated into English, but other such treatises survive only in manuscript form.
Chronicles	The two national chronicles of Sri Lanka, the *Mahāvaṃsa* and *Cūlavaṃsa*, are translated as are a number of other major chronicles, for example, the *Thūpavaṃsa* "Chronicle of the Stūpa" and the nineteenth-century *Sāsanavaṃsa* "History of the Teaching." There are, however, numerous local chronicles in Pali and local languages throughout the Theravada world that remain largely unexamined, although this is a genre that has received greater attention than other material of the same period, initially for its historic interest, more recently for what it tells us about Theravada religion historically in relation to material culture.
Technical literature	Pali has been used for the composition of a wide range of technical literature: cosmology, medicine, grammar, lexicography, prosody, monastic boundary *(sīmā)*, and other kinds of legal text.
Literary texts	As we should expect, a high status-language like Pali was also used for often elaborate literary compositions known as *kāvya* ("high literature"), also anthologies, poetics, *Jātaka* collections, etc. The composition of encomia in Pali continues into the present day.
Southeast Asian literature	There is an increasingly recognized body of Pali literature composed in Southeast Asia. Previously this was on the whole ignored by Western scholars who imposed an essentially "biblical" approach that emphasized a formal idea of "the canon" at the expense of other religious literature. This category includes various kinds of so-called "apocryphal" literature including *Jātaka*s and *sutta*s. The most notable translation is Horner and Jaini's *The Paññāsa Jātaka*.
Letters	Monastics and educated people corresponded in Pali and a number of such missives are known, although the genre remains relatively unexplored. Some important examples have been translated in the Journal of the Pali Text Society.
Epigraphy	There are many inscriptions made over the centuries to mark important events, edicts, statements, etc., that employed Pali. These are translated piecemeal if at all.
Translations	Particularly from the twelfth century onward translations and adaptations into Pali of Sanskrit texts from India were made. These include grammar, poetry, technical literature, etc., and in some cases may offer us insights into Indic literature now lost in its original language. The bible was translated into Pali in the 19th century.

Pali Language and Its Use

Although the Pali Canon is the highest authority on orthodoxy ("correct belief/teachings") and orthopraxy ("correct practice") for Theravada Buddhists, it would also be a mistake to assume that Theravada Buddhists regularly use or are familiar with Pali texts (Collins 1992: 103). Even monks who use it for ritual purposes may understand relatively little of the content and it may be the correct pronunciation and its use on the correct occasion that is considered most important (de Bernon 2006: 57–8). Pali is an elite language of learning and a sacred language. Even in vernacular commentaries there may be extensive use of Pali: such texts are heteroglossic and as such, while they mediate between Pali and the use of the vernacular to create practical canons for local communities, they may still be the preserve of those with specialist training (McDaniel 2008: 119–122ff.). The practical canon of Theravada varies from region to region, even from temple to temple, as does the extent of Pali knowledge, as well as the relative emphasis on vernacular materials (McDaniel 2008: 85). Charles Keyes observes, "[T]he evidence from monastery libraries in Laos and Thailand… reveals that what constitutes the Theravādin *dhamma* for people in these areas includes only a small portion of the total Tipiṭaka, some semi-canonical commentaries such as Buddhaghosa's *Visuddhimagga*, a large number of pseudo-jātaka and other pseudo-canonical works, histories of shrines and other sacred histories, liturgical works, and popular commentaries. Moreover, for any particular temple-monastery in Thailand or Laos, the collection of texts available to the people in the associated community are [sic] not exactly the same as those found in another temple-monastery" (Keyes 1983: 272, cited Collins 1992: 103). Even when there has been a re-emphasis on Pali literature and learning, and on the authority of the Pali Canon, "there was no single text or set of texts identified as the distinctive doctrinal point of orientation" as Blackburn has observed in relation to elite monastic education in the revivalist period of eighteenth-century Sri Lanka (Blackburn 2001: 11). This makes a striking contrast with Chinese Buddhism that tended to select one particular text as having defining significance for its monastic practice and doctrine. Moreover, a re-emphasis on Pali has often been mediated through the flourishing of vernacular commentaries (Blackburn 2001: 194–195).

Although vernacular languages are more important in accessing and conveying the Dhamma for most Theravada Buddhists, and the emphasis on Pali literature has varied between locality and institution and with time, an education in Pali is highly valued. Most monks will be familiar with a number of Pali texts used ritually and aware of the contents of others, whether directly or through vernacular versions or oral teachings. Again, these vary according to region, institution and even individual monks. In Burmese and other Southeast Asian languages used for Theravada, Pali is the source of many loan words relating to matters of practice and doctrine, although the meaning of those words in the vernacular may be quite different from their meaning in early Buddhist literature and may include neologisms (Houtman 1990: 323). In most Southeast Asian languages and Sinhala, loan words and neologisms are in fact more likely to come from Sanskrit because of that language's history as a language of learning in the region, and even within Buddhist contexts the extent to which Pali terms are Sanskritized in their usage varies.

The traditional name for Pali is Māgadhī, meaning "language of Magadha," the area of north-east India including modern Uttar Pradesh and Bihar, where the Buddha lived and taught. It seems that Pali in its current form was never a lived language, used in day-to-day life, though the language of the third-century BCE inscriptions of the emperor Asoka, who ruled over much of India, is clearly closely related. Because of the evidence of those inscriptions, as well as the evidence of other languages preserved from around that time, we can identify differences between western and eastern Prakrits. Prakrit is the name given to a group of Indo-European languages closely related to Sanskrit. Pali as we have it appears to combine features of both western and eastern Prakrits. In the main it is a northwestern dialect of Prakrit but it contains older, eastern forms that are closer to the dialects of the area of India in which the Buddha lived (Norman 1997/2006: Chapter 4). Pali also shows signs of being related to the earlier Vedic form of Sanskrit, retaining forms found in Vedic that are no longer used in classical Sanskrit (Crosby 2008b: 114). On the other hand, it has many Prakrit features, marking its difference from Sanskrit – a lack of consonant clusters and final consonants and a more limited range of verb forms.

The name "Pali" that we use for the language that early Theravada texts call "language of Magadha," literally means "text." The term is found in the fifth-century commentarial literature when contrasting a canonical text, *pāḷi*, with its commentary, *aṭṭhakathā*. It is also used to mean the specific wording of the canon. When Buddhaghosa discarded later liturgies for the ordination ceremony, insisting that the word of the Buddha found in the canon be used, he used the term *pāḷi* to refer to that wording. The term *pāḷibhāsā*, "language (*bhāsā*) of the text (*pāḷi*)," originally referred specifically to the language of the canon. The term is used by Buddhaghosa in describing his task of discarding the vernacular, into which the commentaries had been translated into by Mahinda, and "re-encasing" the meaning of the commentaries in the "cover" of the language of the canon. The transition from using the term *pāḷibhāsā* to refer to the language of the canon to using it as a language name proper occurred in the specific context of commentaries being written on texts that were not canonical in the eleventh/twelfth century. *Pāḷibhāsā* then became one of several synonyms for Māgadhī, and the usage spread throughout Southeast Asia with the importation of literature and Sangha lineages from Sri Lanka (Crosby 2003). The English use "Pali language," in its short form "Pali," is taken over from the famous portrait of Siam by the seventeenth-century French ambassador to Siam, de la Loubère. It is not yet clear when the shortened form also came to be used in vernacular Asian languages.

The fact that Theravada uses a frozen, literary language may seem surprising given the Buddha's emphasis on the preservation of the meaning of language in contrast to the form. This flexible attitude of early Buddhism was a rejection of the use of Vedic Sanskrit for rituals by brahmanicial Hindus. The outcome of this attitude is that Buddhist texts have been preserved in a large number of languages over the centuries and across its broad geographic spread. However, Theravada Buddhists, at least from the time of Buddhaghosa, came to regard Pali as a sacred language and made for it some of the claims made by Hindus for Sanskrit. This process may have been part of a process of claiming authority for the Mahāvihāra monastic lineage. It was in competition against rival Buddhists, such as the Abhayagirivihāra, and rival brahmins, both groups that used Sanskrit. Theravada Buddhists believed Pali to have been the living language spoken by the Buddha, but also to have special additional qualities often attributed to a sacred language. Pali is pure; a *lingua franca* across worlds understood by gods, hell-beings and animals; an innate language, such that a child abandoned in the wilderness without parents would naturally start to speak it; and – in nonreform Theravada (*borān*, see Chapter 6) – a cosmogonic principle, underlying the creation of the universe, from which both the Dhamma of the Buddha and all aspects of creation emerge. This means that the Pali alphabet is regarded as having a role in the creation of a new universe.

These beliefs about Pali underlie its use in a number of contexts. Even though most Theravada Buddhists access their understanding of Buddhism through vernacular literature, art and other visual media, performance and the spoken word, including sermons, Pali is omnipresent in Theravada practice. It is heard regularly by most Theravada Buddhists. It is used for litanies in monastic rituals; for the recitation of *paritta*, the protective texts at the heart of the Theravada community rituals; for the phrases used in meditation to accompany visualization and inculcate the appropriate experience; to convey sanctity in vernacular texts; and to create protective symbols (*yantra*) including the protective tattoos popular among the Tai, Lao, and Khmer ethnic groups in mainland Southeast Asia (Vater and Thaewchatturat 2011). In all of these contexts, it is the sanctity and form of Pali, not the semantic meaning, that is of utmost importance. Understanding the semantic meaning may even be regarded as a hindrance, for example, in the nonreform meditation practices taught at Wat Ratchasittharam in Thonburi, Thailand (see Chapter 6). This harnessing of the power of Pali and related visual imagery, for example portraying the form of the Buddha with Pali letters, can lead to some unexpected associations. A broad range of men who are involved in dangerous activities, such as soldiers, but also including professional criminals such as drug dealers and hit men, wear protective *yantras* and sport tattoos of the Buddha (as well as of mythological figures and animals) to ensure protection from the weapons of others (Terwiel 1975: 92).

Vernacular Literature and Sermons

Local languages, vernaculars, are the most common medium for Buddhist teachings, whether through works of literature, commentaries, or through sermons delivered in the temple by monks at special events and on holy days (see McDaniel 2008: Chapter 4 on varieties of vernacular commentaries). There is a far greater volume of Theravada literature in vernacular languages than in Pali. In vernacular literature, Pali terms and phrases are often used. These give the text the right feel for a work on Dhamma, function as an emblem on the basis of which to expound a topic, and provide technical terms to do with Buddhist doctrine or meditation experience. While vernacular teachings may be very simple, ad hoc, and accessible, as in the case of most sermons, vernacular Dhamma literature may also be highly complex. For example, the Shan literary works for teaching the Dhamma are in a lengthy, ornate poetic style. They are called *lik long* "great writings." Scholars train for many years, often since childhood, to be able to copy, compose, and read out the writings. At first a new member of the audience finds the texts difficult to understand. It is only gradually, after weeks if not years of listening, that they come to understand the poetry, especially the poetry that deals with more complex topics (Crosby and Khur-Yearn 2010, Khur-Yearn 2012).

A difficulty with accessing the content of nonmodern Buddhist vernacular literature is that fewer scholars study early vernaculars than the classical languages such as Pali. Moreover, literature in a vernacular that is no longer current is less likely to be copied. Even so, in Sri Lanka we have evidence of vernacular, mixed Pali and Sanskritic-Sinhala preaching materials from the early medieval period to the modern day. This includes the Sinhalese literary works used in the twin-pulpit preaching, in which two priests alternate in reciting the text, that was still popular in the nineteenth century when it was witnessed by European observers (Deegalle 2006).

Even to this day, preaching in Sinhala can be quite formal, involving literary texts or using a form of literary Sinhala. However, for the most part sermons are accessible teachings. It is still the practice in many parts of mainland Southeast Asia to have longer or more complicated sermons mediated through a leading member of the audience. This representative of the audience asks questions of and gives answers to the monk who is giving the teaching. This person may in fact give more teaching and lead more recitation than the monks. Such a person is usually an experienced member of the congregation, usually male, often a lay manager of the temple. He will be quite knowledgeable on Buddhism and aware of the correct way to respond to the monk and acknowledge the monk's teaching. In all languages throughout the Theravada world, a hierarchical terminology has been used for addressing monks and for referring to their activities; the lay leader will be familiar with this language. The lay manager or functionary of a Cambodian temple (*achar vat*) has a number of different roles, including organizing temple festivals and rituals and as an astrologer (Harris 2005: 77). There may be several *achars*, with different areas of expertise, in any given temple.

Throughout the Theravada worlds, sermons given by monks may be based on a specific Pali or vernacular literary work. Alternatively, they draw on stories and doctrine from the canon and later literature to teach about an issue directly related to the mood of the occasion and the needs of the audience on the day (Tannenbaum 1995: Chapter 6). A sermon after the 2004 tsunami might discuss the reasons why such a dreadful event could happen relate it to past tsunamis in Sri Lanka, the coming of the future Buddha Metteyya, and how best to develop sufficient merit through helping others to be reborn in a position to take advantage of the teaching of the future Buddha Metteyya (Crosby 2008a: 65–66). A sermon on the occasion of a significant donation or after the annual ***kaṭhina*** (robe-giving) ceremony might talk about the advantages of making gifts to the Sangha, relate it to similar activity in the time of the Buddha, and emphasize the importance of the relationship between the Sangha and laypeople. A sermon addressed to soldiers about to go into battle might reinterpret killing the enemy in terms of protecting one's parents from being killed (see Chapter 12). The ability of a monk to give a sermon that speaks directly to the needs and the sentiments of the audience and the occasion not only affects his popularity and the number of attendees at the temple, it may also affect recruitment into the Sangha. In his recent study of Sri Lankan Buddhism, Samuels describes how the popular monk who is the focus of the study, whom he refers to by the pseudonym Ven. Sumedha, used a well-attended event at the temple commemorating the anniversary of a notable death to encourage monastic recruitment. Ven. Sumedha extolled the merits of a recently ordained monk; reminded the audience that being born as human is down to meritorious actions in past lives and offers a great opportunity to make further merit, congratulating them on achieving that status. He reminded them that Sri Lanka is the island of Buddhism, but that there is a shortage of monks and encouraged them to have their sons enter the Sangha.

> Sumedha's sermon – his choice of words, his tone, his use of pregnant pauses, his fluctuating voice, his calm demeanour, and his idyllic appearance – was impressive. The mass of heads continually nodding up and down as well as the frequent, approving cries of "*sādhu, sādhu, sā*" ("it is good, it is good, it is good") suggests that Sumedha more than succeeded in attracting his audience's hearts. Moreover, by colorfully depicting his students' accomplishments (especially Sumanamangala, whom Sumedha implicitly likened to the Buddha by referring to the young novice as a prince), Sumedha was able to trigger specific emotional responses: pride for Sumanamangala's family members and longing or even envy or jealousy for outsiders who do not *yet* have a buddha-like son or relative in the *sangha*. Finally, by discussing Buddhism's decline on the island in general, and the recent closing of the village's temple in particular, Sumedha was able to conjure up such affective states as dismay, sadness, and feelings of loss and, in the process, legitimate his request for new recruits. (Samuels 2010: 40)

The spontaneous or responsive nature of such sermons, in contrast to more formal preaching and reading of texts, means that successful monks, particularly the abbots of temples, may develop close relationships with their parishioners and take up leadership roles in which they may both guide and act on behalf of their congregations. This may entail guiding them in religious conduct and helping them to process certain feelings, such as grief. It may mean that the abbot is the person in the community who spearheads community activities such as cleaning up after a natural disaster or maintaining local roads. The monks may also lead responses to threats from local and even national political developments. The potential effect of this relationship was seen in Burma's Saffron revolution of 2007 when the response of monks to the suffering inflicted on their parishioners by the ruling *junta's* escalation of fuel prices turned into full-scale demonstrations that attracted international attention.

The potential power of eloquent preachers is seen in the repressive response of the *junta*. Whereas the lay scholars who read the *lik long* of Shan Buddhism are free, since their teaching is very conservative and book-based, to perform at any temple in Burma, monks, whose sermons usually reflect the *Zeitgeist*, are not. Here is a description of the hurdles faced by popular monks in Burma in the words of two monks speaking in 2010:

> To give a talk as a monk at another temple, you need permission from six levels: commander of the division, military intelligence, chief of police at division level, chief of police at township level, then the civilian council also at both district and town level. To get the permission from these people, the first thing you need is a "green light," a piece of paper/sponsor letter from the township Sanghanayaka (head monk of the Sangha of that area). To give one *dhamma* talk, the permit may cost the equivalent of £4–500 UK, because at each level a bribe is required from the devotees who want the talk to be given.... After the talk a copy has to be sent to the military intelligence. At a *dhamma* talk 2–3 military intelligence or police officers will usually be present. If the event lasts more than one day, one must get a permission for each day. (Crosby and Khur-Yearn 2010: 16)

The most popular monks draw large audiences. CDs and DVDs of the sermons of popular monks are sold at street stalls, in convenience stores, and in supermarkets in Burma and Thailand, as well as being downloadable from websites. The use of humor can be important. Part of the popularity of the British monk **Ajan** Brahm ordained within the Thai forest tradition (see Chapters 6 and 9) stems in part from the sense of humor he uses in his sermons. The head monk Venerable Dhammajayo (Phrathepyanmahamuni) of the highly influential and well-attended Wat Phra Dhammakaya in Pathumthani currently gives daily live televised sermons from 19:30 to 22:00 Thai time (www.dmc.tv), which combine cartoon stories on traditional topics, songs familiar to the Dhammakaya audience to which they clap and sing along, a back-and-forth exchange between the abbot and a member of the audience who has the honor of fulfilling the traditional role of interlocutor for a certain number of nights and a repartee that has the congregation in fits of laughter.

Summary

This chapter has surveyed the diverse ways in which Theravada literature has been transmitted, the range of genres, different approaches to canonical, commentarial, and vernacular texts, attitudes to language, and the position of Pali as a sacred language. We identified different functions and style of different sections of the canon. While we do not know the exact shape of the Pali Canon before the fifth-century commentaries written on it confirmed its wording, the belief that the canon and the commentaries go back to the first Council and the 500 enlightened disciples who held the council respectively is important to the Theravada Buddhist sense of identity as the preservers of early Buddhism. A direct connection is made in Theravada between the rehearsal of the canonical texts under the patronage and protection of the Emperor Asoka in the third-century BCE, the form of Buddhism transmitted to Sri Lanka at that time and the modern forms of Theravada. The disappearance of the Pali Canon and practice of the Dhamma is believed to usher in the next apocalypse. The anxiety to preserve the Dhamma against corruption and loss, particularly at times of political and astrological crisis, has led to repeated reviews (councils) and large-scale rehearsals of Pali literature, while the practical canon in any given place relates to ritual use, local practice, and audience expectations. Within the practical canons, local vernacular literatures, whether written or oral, dominate. Sponsoring the copying and composition of texts is an important merit-making activity at the local level, often undertaken to commemorate the recently deceased. More recently, digitization and online resources have increased access to the Dhamma globally. Sermons, while drawing on traditional literature, respond to the immediate needs and context of the congregation. This dynamic may bring popularity, but also be perceived as a political threat. While sermons are one of the more direct points of access to the Dhamma for most people, art and performance also play a significant role. In order to examine the range of ways in which literature may manifest and hold different types of meaning for different audiences and actors, the next chapter (Chapter 4) will look more closely at just one genre, the *Jātaka* stories, that recount the adventures of the Buddha-to-be in previous lifetimes.

References

Allon, Mark. (1997). *Style and Function: A Study of the Dominant Stylistic Features of the Prose Portions of Pāli Canonical Sutta Texts and Their Mnemonic Function*. Studia Philologica Buddhica Monograph Series XII. Tokyo: The International Institute for Buddhist Studies.

Aung, S.Z. and C.A.F. Rhys Davids. (1915). *Points of Controversy*. London: H. Milford.

de Bernon, Olivier. (2006). 'The Status of Pāli in Cambodia: From Canonical to Esoteric Language' in François Lagirarde and Paritta Chalermpow Koanantakool (eds.), *Buddhist Legacies in Mainland Southeast Asia: Mentalities, Interpretations, and Practices*. Paris: École française d'Extrême-Orient, 53–66.

de Bernon, Olivier, Kun Sopheap, and Leng Kok-An. (2004). *Inventaire provisoire des manuscrits du Cambodge*, vol. 1. *Materials for the Study of the Tripiṭaka*, vol. 2. Paris: l'École française d'Extrême-Orient.

Blackburn, Anne M. (2001). *Buddhist Learning and Textual Practice in Eighteenth-Century Lankan Monastic Culture*. Princeton: Princeton University Press.

Bodhi, Bhikkhu. (2000). *Connected Discourses of the Buddha: A new Translation of the Saṃyutta Nikāya*. Oxford: Pali Text Society in Association with Wisdom Publications.

Braun, Erik C. (2008). 'Ledi Sayadaw, Abhidhamma, and the Development of the Modern Insight Meditation Movement in Burma', PhD dissertation, Harvard University, Cambridge.

Burlingame, E.W. (1921). *Buddhist Legends*. Harvard Oriental Series 28–30. Cambridge: Harvard University Press. Reprint, London: Pali Text Society, 1979.

Collins, Steven. (1992). 'On the Very Idea of the Pali Canon', *Journal of the Pali Text Society* XV: 89–126.

Cowell E.B. (ed.) (1895–1913). *The Jātaka or Stories of the Buddha's Former Births*, 6 vols. Cambridge: Cambridge University Press.

Crosby, Kate. (2000). Tantric Theravada: A Bibliographic Essay on the Writings of François Bizot and Other Literature on the *Yogāvacara* Tradition', *Contemporary Buddhism* 1.2: 141–198.

Crosby, Kate. (December 2003). 'The Origin of the Language Name Pāli in Medieval Theravāda Literature', *Journal of Buddhist Studies* 2: 70–116.

Crosby, Kate. (2005). 'Only if You Let Go of that Tree: Ordination Without Parental Consent According to Theravāda Vinaya', *Buddhist Studies Review* 22: 155–173.

Crosby, Kate. (2006a). 'A Theravada Code of Conduct for Good Buddhists: The *Upāsakamanussavinaya*', *Journal of the American Oriental Society* 126.2: 177–187.

Crosby, Kate. (2006b). 'Sāriputta's Three Works on the *Samantapāsādikā*', *The Journal of the Pali Text Society* XXVIII: 49–59.

Crosby, Kate. (2007). '*Saṅkhepasārasaṅgaha*', *The Journal of the Pali Text Society* XXIX: 169–174.

Crosby, Kate. (May 2008a). 'Karma, Social Collapse or Geophysics? Interpretations of Suffering Among Sri Lankan Buddhist in the Immediate Aftermath of the 2004 Asian tsunami', *Contemporary Buddhism*, 9.1: 53–76.

Crosby, Kate. (2008b). Review of Norman (1997 [2006]), *Buddhist Studies Review* 25.1: 113–115.

Crosby, Kate and Jotika Khur-Yearn. (2010). 'Poetic *Dhamma* and the *zare*: Traditional Styles of Teaching Theravada Amongst the Shan of Northern Thailand', *Contemporary Buddhism* 11.1: 1–26.

Deegalle, Mahinda. (2006). *Popularising Buddhism. Preaching as Performance in Sri Lanka*. Albany: State University of New York Press.

Dhammasami, Khammai and Pyi Kyaw. (2012). 'The Centennial Commemorative Inscription of the Most Venerable Mingun Tipiṭakadhara Sayadaw U Vicittasārābhivaṃsa'. To be inscribed at Dhammanāda Pariyatti Sarthintike, Mingun Village.

Frasch, Tilman. (2012). 'The Theravada Buddhist Ecumene in the 15th Century: Intellectual Foundations and Material Representations' in Tansen Sen (ed.), *Buddhism Across Asia: Networks of Material, Intellectual and Cultural Exchange*, vol. 1. Singapore: ISEAS, 291–311.

Gornall, Alastair. (2013). 'Buddhism and Grammar: The Scholarly Cultivation of Pāli in Medieval Laṅkā'. PhD thesis, University of Cambridge.

Hallisey, Charles. (1990). 'Tuṇḍilovāda: An Allegedly Non-Canonical Sutta', *Journal of the Pali Text Society* XV: 170–195.

Hallisey, Charles. (1993). 'Nibbānasutta: An Allegedly Non-Canonical Sutta on Nibbāna as a Great City', *Journal of the Pali Text Society* XVIII: 117–124.

Harris, Ian. (2005). *Cambodian Buddhism. History and Practice*. Honolulu: University of Hawai'i Press. Reprint, Chiang Mai: Silkworm 2006.

von Hinüber, Oskar. (1996). *A Handbook of Pāli Literature*. Berlin/New York: Walter de Gruyter.

Horner, I.B. (1938–1966). *The Book of the Discipline*, 6 vols, vols 1–3, 1938, 1940, 1942. London: Oxford University Press; vols. 4–6, 1951, 1952, 1966. London: Luzac.

Horner, I.B. (1954, 1957, 1959). *Middle Length Sayings*, 3 vols. London: Luzac.

Houtman, Gustaaf. (1990). 'Traditions of Buddhist Practice in Burma'. PhD thesis, School of Oriental and African Studies, London.

Iijima, Akiko. (2009). 'Preliminary Notes on "the Cultural Region of *Tham* Script Manuscripts"', *Senri Ethnological Studies* 74: 15–32.

Jaini, Padmanabh S. (1992). '*Kāravattārasutta*: An "Apocryphal" *Sutta* from Thailand', *Indo-Iranian Journal* 35: 193–223.

Jayawickrama, N.A. (1990). *The Story of Gotama Buddha (Jātaka-nidāna)*. Oxford: The Pali Text Society.

Keyes, C.F. (1983). 'Merit-Transference in the Kammic Theory of Popular Theravada Buddhism' in C.F. Keyes and E.V. Daniels (eds.), *Karma: An Anthropological Inquiry*. Berkeley: University of California Press, 261–286.

Khur-Yearn, Jotika. (2012). 'The Poetic *Dhamma* of Zao Amat Long's *Mahāsatipaṭṭhāna Sutta* and the Place of Traditional Literature in Shan Theravada Buddhism'. PhD thesis, School of Oriental and African Studies, London.

Law, B.C. (1922). *A Designation of Human Types*. London: Oxford University Press.

Marston, John. (2008). 'Reconstructing 'Ancient' Cambodian Buddhism', *Contemporary Buddhism* 9.1: 99–121.

McDaniel, Justin Thomas. (2008). *Gathering Leaves and Lifting Words: Histories of Buddhist Monastic Education in Laos and Thailand*. Seattle / London: University of Washington Press.

Nagasena, Bhikkhu. (2013). 'The Monastic Boundary (*Sīmā*) in Burmese Buddhism: Authority, Purity and Validity in Historical and Modern Contexts'. PhD thesis, School of Oriental and African Studies, London.

Narada, U. (1962). *Discourse on Elements*. London: Luzac.

Narada, U. (1969 / 1981). *Conditional Relations*, vol. 1, London: Luzac; vol. 2, London: Pali Text Society.

Norman, K.R. (1997 [2006]). *A Philological Approach to Buddhism*, 2nd edn. Lancaster: The Pali Text Society.

Ñyāṇamoli, Bhikkhu. (1976). *The Path of Purification*, 2 vols. Boulder / London: Shambhala.

Ñyāṇamoli, Bhikkhu and Bhikkhu Bodhi. (1995). *The Middle Length Discourses of the Buddha: A New Translation of the Majjhima Nikāya*. Boston: Wisdom Publications in association with the Barre Center for Buddhist Studies.

Nyanaponika, Thera, and Bhikkhu Bodhi. (1999). *Numerical Discourses of the Buddha: An Anthology of Suttas from the Aṅguttara Nikāya*. Walnut Creek / London: AltaMira Press.

Nyanatusita, Bhikkhu. (2008). *Reference Table of Pali Literature*. http://resolver.sub.uni-goettingen.de/purl/?gr_elib-66 (retrieved July 31, 2011).

Pind, Ole. (1997). 'Pāli Miscellany' in *Studies in Honour of Heinz Bechert on the Occasion of his 65th Birthday*. Swisttal-Odendorf: Indica et Tibetica Verlag, 515–536.

Pranke, Patrick Arthur. (2004). 'The "Treatise on the Lineage of Elders" (*Vaṃsadīpanī*): Monastic Reform and the Writing of Buddhist History in Eighteenth-Century Burma'. PhD thesis, University of Michigan.

Prebish, Charles S. (1974). 'A Review of Scholarship on the Buddhist Councils', *Journal of Asian Studies* 33: 239–254.

Rahula, Walpola. (1956). *History of Buddhism in Ceylon: The Anurådhà Period, 3rd Century BC–10th Century AC*. Colombo: M.D. Gunasena.

Rhys Davids, T.W. (1899, 1910, 1921). *Dialogues of the Buddha*, 3 vols. London: Oxford University Press.

Rhys Davids, C.A.F. (1900). *A Buddhist Manual of Psychological Ethics: Being a Translation, Now Made for the First Time, of the First Book in the Abhidhamma piṭaka, Entitled Dhammasaṅgaṇi (Compendium of States or Phenomena)*. London: Royal Asiatic Society.

Rhys Davids, C.A.F. and F.L. Woodward. (1917, 1922, 1925, 1927, 1930). *The Book of the Kindred Sayings (Saṃyutta Nikāya) or Grouped Suttas*, 5 vols. London: Oxford University Press.

Samuels, Jeffrey. (2010). *Attracting the Heart: Social Relations and the Aesthetics of Emotion in Sri Lankan Monastic Culture*. Honolulu: University of Hawai'i Press.

Somadasa, K.D. (1987–1995). *Catalogue of the Hugh Nevill Collection of Sinhalese Manuscripts in the British Library*, 7 vols. London / Henley on Thames: British Library / Pali Text Society.

Stargardt, Janice. (1995). 'The Oldest Known Pāli Texts, 5th–6th Century: Results of the Cambridge Symposium on the Pyu Golden Pali Text from Sri Ksetra, 18–19 April 1995', *Journal of the Pali Text Society* 21: 199–213.

Tannenbaum, Nicola. (1995). *Who Can Compete Against the World? Power-Protection and Buddhism in Shan Worldview*. Ann Arbor: Association for Asian Studies Inc.

Terwiel, B.J. (1975). *Monks and Magic: An Analysis of Religious Ceremonies in Central Thailand*. Lund / London: Studentlitteratur / Curzon Press, 4th revised edn. Copenhagen: NIAS Press, 2012.

Thanissaro, Bhikkhu. (2010). 'Ratha-vinita Sutta: Relay Chariots' (MN 24), translated from the Pali by Thanissaro Bhikkhu. *Access to Insight*, http://www.accesstoinsight.org/tipitaka/mn/mn.024.than.html (retrieved December 11, 2012).

Thittila, U. (1969). *The Book of Analysis*. London: Luzac.

Thurman, Robert A.F. translator. (1976). *Vimalakirti Nirdesa Sutra*. University Park/London: The Pennsylvania State University.

Strong, John S. (2004). *Relics of the Buddha*. Princeton: Princeton University Press.

Vater, Tom and Aroon Thaewchatturat. (2011). *Sacred Skin: Thailand's Spirit Tattoos*. Hong Kong/ Enfield: Visionary World.

Walshe, M. (1987). *Thus Have I Heard: The Long Discourses of the Buddha*. London: Wisdom. Re-published (1995) as *The Long Discourses of the Buddha: A Translation of the Dīgha Nikāya*. Boston: Wisdom.

Watson, Burton. (1993). *The Lotus Sūtra*. New York: Columbia University Press.

Woodward, F.L. and E.M. Hare. (1932, 1933, 1934, 1935, 1936). *The Book of the Gradual Sayings: Or More-numbered Suttas*, 5 vols. London: Oxford University Press.

Wynne, Alexander. (2004). 'The Oral Transmission of the Early Buddhist Literature', *Journal of the International Association of Buddhist Studies* 27.1: 97–127.

Further Reading and Watching

Examples of Ajan Brahm's weekly lectures: www.youtube.com/user/BuddhistSocietyWA?-feature=g-user-u (retrieved June 25, 2013).

For Samples of Pali literature in Translation

www.accesstoinsight.org (retrieved June 25, 2013).

Gethin, Rupert. (2008). *Sayings of the Buddha: a selection of suttas from the Pali Nikāyas*. Oxford: Oxford University Press.

On Pali Literature

Collins, Steven (1990). 'On the Very Idea of the Pali Canon'. *Journal of the Pali Text Society* XV: 89–126.

von Hinüber, Oskar (1996). *A Handbook of Pali Literature*. Berlin: Walter de Gruyter.

Norman, K.R. (1983). *Pāli Literature*. Wiesbaden: Harrassowitz.

Skilton, Andrew. (in preparation). *Pālibhāsā, The Pali Language: an introduction to reading and studying Pali language and literature*.

Webb, Russell. (1975). *Analysis of the Pali Canon*. Kandy: Buddhist Publication Society.

On Vernacular Literature

Crosby, Kate and Jotika Khur-Yearn. (2010). 'Poetic *Dhamma* and the *zare*: traditional styles of teaching Theravada amongst the Shan of northern Thailand', *Contemporary Buddhism* 11.1: 1–26.

Godakumbura, C.E. (1955). *Sinhalese Literature*. Colombo: Colombo Apothecaries.

Jacob, Judith, M. (1996). *The Traditional Literature of Cambodia: a Preliminary Guide*. Oxford: Oxford University Press.

McDaniel, Justin Thomas. (2008). *Gathering Leaves and Lifting Words: Histories of Buddhist Monastic Education in Laos and Thailand*. Seattle and London: University of Washington Press.

San, Sarin. (1975). *Les Textes Liturgiques Fondamentaux du Bouddhisme Cambodgien Actuel*. Thèse E.P.H.E. Paris: La Sorbonne.

On Councils

Cousins, L.S. (1991). 'The "Five Points" and the Origin of the Buddhist Schools' in T. Skorupski (ed.), *The Buddhist Forum* II. Seminar Papers 1988–1990. London: SOAS: 27–60.

Frasch, Tilman. (2012). 'The Theravada Buddhist Ecumene in the 15th Century: Intellectual Foundations and Material Representations' in Tansen Sen *et al.* (eds.), *Buddhism across Asia: Networks of Material, Intellectual and Cultural Exchange*, vol. 1. Singapore: ISEAS: 291–311.

Lay, U. Ko. (1986). *Guide to Tipiṭaka*. Rangoon: Burma Piṭaka Association.

Prebish, Charles S. (1974). 'A Review of Scholarship on the Buddhist Councils' *Journal of Asian Studies* 33: 239–254.

Skilton, Andrew. (1994). *A Concise History of Buddhism*, Glasgow: Windhorse Publications, 45–49.

On Orality and Textual Transmission in the Early Period

Skilling, Peter. (2009). 'Redaction, Recitation, and Writing: Transmission of the Buddha's teaching in India in the early period' in Stephen C. Berkwitz, Juliane Schober, and Claudia Brown (eds.), *Buddhist Manuscript Cultures: Knowledge, Ritual and Art*. London: Routledge: 53–75.

On Preaching and Sermons

Deegalle, Mahinda. (2006). *Popularising Buddhism. Preaching as Performance in Sri Lanka*. Albany: State University of New York Press.

Tannenbaum, Nicola. (1995). *Who Can Compete Against the World? Power-Protection and Buddhism in Shan Worldview*. Ann Arbor: Association for Asian Studies Inc.

4
The *Jātaka*

Overview

In this chapter, we focus on the *Jātaka*, the stories of the Buddha's former lives. They are a form of narrative popular across Buddhist cultures. They teach the ethical values of Buddhism. They have a frame story, the "story of the present time," which relates the occasion on which the Buddha taught the story – usually a problem that arose for his monks or lay followers, or an aspect of someone's conduct worthy of comment. Then they contain the "story of the past," the main *Jātaka* story in which the Buddha relates a moral tale from his past (in a previous lifetime) in order to comment on the conduct, explain the problem, or illustrate a way forward with it. The *Jātaka* form part of the canonical corpus and the commentaries ascribed to Buddhaghosa, yet are used far more widely than this. They are found in apocryphal literature, vernacular retellings, performance, temple art, temporary street and festival art, films, comics, and cartoons. The purpose of this chapter is to see some of the many aspects of a single genre of Theravada literature and to recognize the many avenues through which Theravada Buddhists may access the stories and teachings contained within that literature.

The Buddha and His Contemporaries in the *Jātaka*

On reaching Awakening the Buddha gained three types of knowledge: remembrance of his former existences, the "divine eye," and the realization of the extinction of all his kammic defilements. The first of these knowledges, the recollection of his former lifetimes, allows for the inclusion of stories relating these previous lifetimes in Buddhist literature. They are recorded as *Jātaka* "birth-stories," a form of narrative popular across Buddhist cultures. In each story, the Buddha relates something that he did or witnessed in one of the hundreds of lifetimes through which he pursued the spiritual career that had begun when he vowed to become a Buddha. During these lifetimes, he developed the qualities that made it possible for him eventually to gain supreme Awakening or Enlightenment. At the end of the story, the Buddha identifies which character he was and which of his contemporaries the story's other

Theravada Buddhism: Continuity, Diversity, and Identity, First Edition. Kate Crosby.

characters have now become. Bad characters often turn out to be the Buddha's evil cousin Devadatta, who is representative of jealousy or rivalry. Good characters prove to be the Buddha himself or other senior monks and nuns, although there are also stories in which the Buddha-to-be did something bad in a previous life (Walters 1990). Members of the Buddha's family such as his wife Yasodharā and son Rāhula also rehearse those roles in the *Jātaka* (Crosby 2012: 87). Thus, the community of the Buddha's final lifetime spent, like him and alongside him, many lifetimes working up to its final roles, relationships, and achievements. From this perspective, *Jātaka* tales reveal that *kamma* (action) and its consequences are not merely individualistic concerns but have an impact on groups and societies (Walters 2003). Related beliefs that continue to this day are that one's current relationships and encounters may be continued from previous lifetimes, and that making merit with someone (i.e., performing good *kamma* such as making offerings together) will lead one to be reborn with that person, that is, meet up with them in another lifetime in the future.

In many of the stories, the Buddha-to-be plays a relatively minor role. This, as well as the often tenuous link made with the ten "perfections" (perfected qualities) of Buddhahood, and the fact that many of the stories have parallels in other folklore, has led to the view that the inclusion of these stories in Buddhist literature is a somewhat artificial method for incorporating popular literature into the Buddhist canon (Ohnuma 2004: 400–401). Parallels to a number of *Jātaka* can also be found in **Brahmanical**, Hindu, and to a lesser extent Jain literature (Meiland 2003: 21–22). The form the *Jātaka* stories take in the Buddhist setting tells us a great deal about Buddhist values, understandings about rebirth and kammic consequences, the concerns of the monastic community, the ways in which Buddhists dealt with the narratives of other religious groups, and even about how one form of Buddhism differs from another. Andrew Skilton has looked at the contrasting values conveyed by multiple parallel versions of the tale of the "Forebearance-espousing *bodhisattva*" Khantivādin or Supuṣpacandra (*Jātaka* no. 313 in the Pali canonical collection). The story focuses on an ascetic who teaches the king's harem when they come across him in the royal park. He thus rouses the murderous jealousy of a king but shows no anger even as the king's executioner hacks off different parts of his anatomy, because he is one who espouses forbearance. One of the conflicting values identified by Skilton is the contrast between world-renouncing, ascetic Buddhism and community (village/urban)-oriented Buddhism. The Theravada text also shows a stylistic preference for gore. A dramatic difference is that while in the Pali version the Buddha identifies himself as the hero, in a version in the Mahayana *Samādhirājasūtra* the Buddha-to-be is the bad king, whose remorse is the spur for his undertaking the spiritual path. Seeing one value represented in Theravada at one time, however, does not mean that that is universally representative of Theravada. If we look at the story of the Buddha's wife in the biographical introduction to the *Jātaka* collection, for example, we find her feelings are played down – she is on the whole supportive of the path the Buddha took, in contrast to the grief and bitterness found in other Buddhist canons (Tatelman 1999). However, a later Thai rendering (Swearer 1995b) shows that Theravada could also represent the Buddha's wife as experiencing these emotions (Crosby 2012: 85).

Because the stories retold in the *Jātaka* mostly take place in the time before Buddha Gotama made the Dhamma available, the highest spiritual practice available to characters seeking to improve themselves and society is the five precepts of the layperson (see Chapter 5). This also means that, in the absence of Buddhism and Buddhist monks, the Buddha-to-be appears as other types of religious practitioner, for example, as an ascetic or a brahmin practicing fire-worship (Meiland 2003: 7–8). He also appears in the form of a variety of humans, animals, and spirits.

The Place of *Jātaka* Narratives

The performance, retelling, and visual representation of *Jātaka* remain central Theravada practices to this day. They now also feature in books, cartoons, and films, especially for children, although – like fairytales in Europe – they were not always considered children's literature. The Pali Canon does contain other literature intended for children and young people ordained into the Sangha (Crosby 2012: 102–104).

When the stories found in the *Jātaka* are found elsewhere in world literature, they sometimes seem to come from a – perhaps shared – pre-Buddhist source, as is the case with Aesop's fables (Lüders 1897). In other instances, the stories were borrowed from Buddhist *Jātaka*, as in the case of the circa tenth-century Shi'ite Muslim theologian Ibn Bābūya's inclusion in his work of the story of the king being confronted by his first grey hair "the messenger of death" found in the *Makhadeva Jātaka*, *Nimi Jātaka*, and *Cukka-Sutasoma Jātaka*. The post-Buddhist status of these narratives is apparent because they are told alongside an adapted episode from lifestory of the Buddha, in which he experiences horror at his harem and departs from his father's palace to seek his Awakening. In Ibn Bābūya's narrative, this becomes the story *Balawhar wa-Būdāsf*. The same story had a wide circulation and became incorporated into Christian narrative with Balawhar and Būdāsf becoming the two apostles of Christianity in India, Joasaph and Barlaam (Stern and Walzer 1971).

The Buddhist *Jātakas* circulate in collections, as well as individually, in written and in oral form, in performance and in painting. The largest single Theravāda collection of *Jātaka* is found in the Pali Canon. It contains 547 *Jātaka* stories, perhaps an extension of an earlier collection of 500 (von Hinüber 1996: 57). The full number is supposed to be 550, thus 3 are lost, although at least 1 of these appears to be embedded elsewhere in the canon as the *Mahāgovindasutta* (von Hinuber 1996: 55). There are various *Jātaka* scattered throughout other parts of the canon (Meiland 2003: 3, note 3). Another *Jātaka* that may have originally been one of the canonical 550 but found nowhere in the canon is the *Vijjādhara Jātaka*. Versions of it are found in Sanskrit literature. It had been believed to be lost in its Pali version, but has been rediscovered by Jacqueline Filliozat in three Cambodian Pali manuscripts (Skilton 2009: 4 and note 6).

Only certain verses and rare sections of prose embedded in the *Jātaka* narratives are supposed to be the canonical "word of the Buddha." The main narratives are regarded as "commentarial" because their wording was fixed later (Meiland 2003: 9). Nonetheless, this collection is generally referred to as the "canonical *Jātaka*."

In non-Theravada Buddhist literature, we find *Jātaka* both of the Buddha and those associated with him embedded within other literature (Skilton 2002). The *Mūlasarvāstivāda Vinaya*, a text of monastic rules for the ordination lineages that still continue in Tibet, contains stories of former lives in the main body of the text to explain aspects of certain rules or why the rules were established (Panglung 1981). In contrast, only a few such stories are still embedded in the Pali Canon more broadly. Most of them were collected into the dedicated collections. Parallel to the Buddha's *Jātaka* is the *Apadāna* collection, one of the final books to be added to the canon (von Hinüber 1996: 61). It gives former life stories for other significant figures, including important monks and nuns in the Buddha's immediate circle and family members such as his son Rāhula (Crosby 2012: 88–89). The *Apadāna* explain how events, good conduct, vows, and predictions in previous lifetimes enabled the protagonists to achieve the extraordinary blessing of being associated with the Buddha in his final lifetime, when he attained Buddhahood.

The *Jātaka* and *Apadāna* are both found in the *Khuddaka Nikāya*, the fifth and most diverse division of the *Sutta Piṭaka*. Another collection in the *Khuddaka Nikāya* is the *Cariyāpiṭaka, The Basket of Conduct* (Horner 1975). The *Cariyāpiṭaka* contains verse forms of 35 *Jātaka*, 33 of which are versions of canonical *Jātaka*. In contrast to the main *Jātaka* collection, which is organized in incremental order of the number of verses embedded within the narrative, the *Cariyāpiṭaka* is presented as the Buddha's response to a question posed by his attendant, the monk Ānanda. Ānanda asks him about his undertaking to become a Buddha and his attainment of the *pāramī*, the "perfections," that is, the qualities that must be perfected on the path to Buddhahood. The first question, how the Buddha undertook his quest to become a Buddha, is answered in the closely related text, the *Buddhavaṃsa, Chronicle of the Buddhas* (Horner 1975). The *Buddhavaṃsa* offers a summary of the life and careers of all the 24 Buddhas who preceded Gotama Buddha in this world cycle. It was the first of these, Dīpaṃkara, who predicted that the brahmin Sumedha, who offers his body for Buddha Dīpaṃkara and his followers to walk on, would become the future Buddha Gotama. It is the second part of Ānanda's question, how the Buddha attained the *pāramī* (perfections) that is answered in the *Cariyāpiṭaka*, which organizes the stories according to six of the *pāramī*. This list is expanded to the fuller list of ten perfections in an appendix to the commentary on the text (von Hinüber 1996: 63). It is probably from this work that we understand the *Jātaka* in terms of the perfections. The diversity of the fuller collection, the marginal role sometimes played by the Buddha, and the more practical wisdom they contain makes an early association with the perfections unlikely.

There are many noncanonical, so-called "apocryphal" *Jātaka*, one collection of which is a fluid collection of "50" (*Paññāsa*) popular in Cambodia and elsewhere in Southeast Asia (one version of which is found in Horner and Jaini 1985). They copy the canonical format but are closer to *Apadāna* in style and biographical detail. There is also a collection of *Jātaka* of ten future Buddhas, beginning with *Metteyya*, which though less well-known today clearly circulated widely in the Theravada world (Saddhatissa 1975). The stories are narrated by the Buddha to his disciple Sāriputta in order to illustrate how each of these future Buddhas gained prowess in the different "perfections," particularly that of generosity. Thus while these days we tend to think of there just being one future Buddha in Theravada, namely, Metteyya, such literature allows for an indefinite number of future Buddhas, and therefore for a number of *bodhisattas* on their journey toward Buddhahood, acting concurrently.

In addition to Pali-language *Jātaka*, we find numerous vernacular versions, from simple retellings to some of the most ornate and complex poetic compositions of Sri Lanka and Southeast Asia (Godakumbura 1955: 99ff.). One such poetic rendering is the *Kavsiḷumiṇa*, a rendering of the *Kusa Jātaka* (canonical *Jātaka* No. 531) in archaic Sinhala (*eḷu*) in the thirteenth century by King Parākkamabāhu II. It is the story of the love that forms between King Kusa and his beautiful wife Pabhāvatī in spite of his extreme ugliness. Because the poem conforms to poetic conventions, the frame story is discarded. Moreover, the hero's ugliness – contrary to epic expectations of male beauty – is not mentioned until late on in the poem even though it is crucial to the plot (the heroine is not allowed to see her husband by day and then runs away when she finds out what he really looks like). Other aspects of the plot are altered to allow some of the erotic scenes and detailed exploration of female beauty expected of epic poetry to be included (McAlpine and Ariyapala 1990: xiv–xvi). The complexity of the lengthy poem, which is almost 800 verses long, in part reflects the ways in which classical Sinhalese poetry is composed with visual arrangements of syllables providing the structure, such that the syllables of each verse conform with circular, anthropomorphic, or other graphic notation (e.g., see McAlpine and Ariyapala 1990: 145–149).

While the commentary on the *Jātaka* in the canon allows us to date the "canonical" *Jātaka* to some extent, and to compare them with the noncanonical renderings of the same story, we cannot assume that other Pali and vernacular *Jātaka* are necessarily later. We do not know what criteria were used to set the parameters for inclusion in the canonical collection. The crucial issue may have been simply geography: those *Jātaka* circulating in Sri Lanka at the time, for example, were the ones included in the "canonical" collection and supplied with a full Pali narrative and commentary in the fifth century, perhaps in simple ignorance of those found elsewhere in the Theravada world.

The Audience and the Message

The *Jātaka* contain many "entertaining yarns" (Skilton 2002: 121) and are the subject of many and varied popular retellings. This aspect has led many, including scholars, to assume that *Jātakas* are predominantly lay-orientated, as if monks were not to be entertained. Justin Meiland warns that we should be skeptical of this tendency of scholarship (Meiland 2003: 14). The format of the *Jātaka* in fact suggests that their original inclusion in the canonical collection was primarily for the benefit of monks. In addition to the 227 *pātimokkha* rules monks should follow (see Chapter 8), there are many variations on those rules and hundreds of additional minor rules. There are highly specific expectations concerning decorum, ways of dealing with tricky situations, and ideals of proper conduct and self-control that pertain both to monks as individuals and to the Sangha as a collective whole. It is a lot to manage and keep in mind. Each *Jātaka is* framed by a story which explains why the Buddha was prompted to tell the *Jātaka*. Many of these framing stories relate to how monks should behave. Some are even connected to specific rules in the Vinaya. The way that in Theravada these stories are mostly gathered into a single collection is expressive of the degree of organizational editing the Pali Canon enjoyed subsequent to the creation of its contents. In this process, stories that were initially beneficial to a monastic audience were repackaged in a form that coincidentally facilitated their transmission to lay audiences as well.

To give an example of *Jātaka* as models for monastic behavior, there are two that focus on the conduct in former lifetimes of the Buddha's son, Rāhula, which teach how novices and more senior monks should relate to each other. The first is the *Tipallatthamiga Jātaka* (no. 16). *Tipallatthamiga* means "deer in three postures" and the main story relates how in a previous life Rāhula-to-be was a fawn entrusted by his mother to the head stag (the Buddha-to-be) for education. One day the fawn is caught in a hunter's trap in the woods. He adopts the three positions the head stag had taught him. Posture one: he moves the leaves around him so that he can answer the call of nature without it being spotted. Posture two: he breathes only through the nostril on the side he is lying on, keeping his visible nostril still. Posture three: he bloats out his stomach. Seeing him in this state when he comes to check his traps, the hunter believes the fawn has been dead for a few days and has begun to putrefy in the heat. He unhooks the young deer's leg to start preparing the carcass, giving the fawn the chance he needed to scamper off to freedom.

The second is the *Tittira Jātaka* (no. 319 – not to be confused with *Jātaka* 37 of the same name). *Tittira* means "partridge": Rāhula-to-be is a decoy partridge used by a hunter to help catch wild partridges. The decoy partridge's attempts to warn the wild partridges have the opposite effect, attracting the partridges to within the hunter's reach. When he tries to stay silent to avoid this, the hunter beats him and his squawks once more attract the wild partridges. The decoy manages to ask a sage – the Buddha-to-be – whether or not it is his fault that the other partridges are caught by the hunter. He is told, no, it is not his fault:

> If no sin lurks in the heart,
> Innocent the deed will be.
> He who plays a passive part
> From all guilt is counted free.
> (Cowell 1895–1913: vol 3: 44)

Even in these abbreviated forms we can see the stories' entertaining nature, the Buddha-to-be playing a relatively minor role, and the stories' layers of meaning: that mothers hand over their sons for training; the importance of studying well and being smart; the cruelty of killing; that one is innocent of a cruel act if one's involvement is inadvertent and unintentional. However, the ultimate reason for the story's inclusion in the canon is to remind monks that they must provide suitable accommodation for any novices in their charge and to remind novices that even when they are unfairly reprimanded by their seniors, they should not protest, but be modest and compliant. How can we say this when no such thing is mentioned in the story? The framing story tells us that the Buddha told these stories after finding Rāhula asleep in his toilet. When laypeople had criticized monks for having novices sleeping in the same room as them, the monks had simply kicked the novices out. Rāhula, not wanting to use his status to kick up a fuss, sleeps in the only shelter he can find with no monk in it: the toilet (though, of course, it is the Buddha's toilet). Similarly, we are told, spiteful monks deliberately throw rubbish about and blame it on Rāhula for failing to do his duty of sweeping up the temple compound, but Rāhula meekly apologizes and sets about cleaning up. In response to these events, the Buddha establishes the rule about monks providing accommodation for novices, found in the *Vinaya Piṭaka* (see Chapters 3 and 8). Here the unremarkable rule and some guidance on appropriate novice decorum are made memorable by entertaining stories, as well as a rather disgusting one: a high-status person spending the night on the floor of a toilet (Crosby 2012: 97).

Similarly unremarkable expectations of monastic conduct are made memorable by the *Guṇa* ("Qualities") *Jātaka* (no. 137). It tells the story of a jackal saving a lion that had become stuck in the mud. The lion repays the favor by inviting the jackal to hunt with him and the jackal's whole family to stay in his cave. The lion sticks to his vow to repay the favor even when his wife, the lioness, seeks to cast doubt on what to her seems like an unhealthily unequal relationship. This story is used to rehearse two aspects of receiving and giving gifts for monks. The frame story begins with King Bimbisāra becoming irate when his harem bestows 500 expensive pieces of cloth – a gift they had in turn just received from the king – on the monk Ānanda, known for his popularity with female practitioners (see Chapter 9). When the harem turns up to attend the king at breakfast wearing their old dresses, the king suspects Ānanda of using his popularity to run a fabric business. The jealous and suspicious king is a popular trope in the *Jātakas*. The king is assuaged, however, when he hears how monks recycle even the most worn out robes for other things – and here Ānanda repeats the monastic rule about recycling robes as cloaks, shirts, etc., down to mixing the shreds with clay to make daub in the construction of buildings "because it is not permitted to waste the gifts of the faithful" (Cowell 1895–1913: 18). The king is so moved by this story that he gives Ānanda a further 500 robes. Having shared the previous 500 with his 500 companions, Ānanda gives all of the second set to a novice who has fulfilled all the duties for Ānanda that one might expect an ideal novice do provide for a senior monk – here we hear listed all of the duties of a novice, including cleaning. The novice in turn shares them with his 500 fellow novices, but they in turn question whether it had been proper for Ānanda to bestow favors on a novice in this way. The *Jātaka* story teaches that it is permissible and not an impropriety for one good deed (the good service provided by the novice) to be rewarded with another (a large gift of robes from the monk). The simple story about the lion (a metaphor for a senior monk) favoring the jackal (a metaphor for a novice) who cannot easily hunt alone allows the complex nuances of gift redistribution and monk–novice relationships within the Sangha to be more straightforwardly grasped and highlights ways of dealing with the tendency to suspect impure motives in the offering and receiving of gifts.

A survey of the "stories of the present" in the canonical *Jātaka*, that is, those framing stories that introduce the reason for the telling of the *Jātaka* itself, reveals that fewer than a fifth are addressed to laypeople (Crosby and Kong, in preparation). Some make clear the *Jātaka's* connection with a specific *vinaya* rule, whereas many others convey important teachings for monks. The message imparted includes the recurrent praise for renunciation (Meiland 2003: 31–32), an ideal that pervades even community-oriented monasticism, to details of day-to-day monastic arrangements. The ongoing importance of the *Jātaka* to monks can be observed to this day in, for example, the incorporation of extensive *Vinaya* passages into the Shan version of the *Vessantara Jātaka* (Pannyawamsa 2007); the taking up of the *Temiya Jātaka* (no. 538) in which the Buddha-to-be fulfills the perfection of renunciation (by pretending to be a deaf-mute rather than inherit the throne) as an inspiration by the forest monks who dedicate themselves to a life of meditation in modern-day Sri Lanka (Carrithers 1983: 94ff. cited Meiland 2003: 15 note 63); similarly as a model for renunciation for the forest monks of Burma (Rozenberg 2010: 36) and as a basis of meditation practice for a former Khmer Rouge soldier who had taken ordination (Crosby and Long fieldwork 2012).

Nonetheless, *Jātaka* telling did not remain – and almost certainly never was – restricted to the confines of the Sangha. *Jātaka* soon became central in conveying Buddhist values to a broad audience through entertaining narrative and art. They often constitute the protective *paritta* recitation at the heart of Theravada rituals (see Chapter 5). Historically they also functioned, as chronicle literature did later (see Chapter 2), to tie Buddhism to specific places in the landscape to which it spread: a place becomes validated by having been visited by the Buddha or a previous Buddha in one of their lifetimes (Meiland 2003: 5–6). Perhaps the most famous validation of place is the telling, in the *Sutta Pitaka*, of the Buddha's former lifetime in the place of his final death, Kusinara. Ānanda tries to dissuade the Buddha from dying in such a backwater as Kusinara. In the *Mahāsudassana Sutta*, the Buddha reassures the distressed Ānanda that while Kusinara may seem like a backward, nowhere place now, in one of the Buddha's former lifetimes it was a great and glorious city, and thus is fully worthy to be the place of the Buddha's *parinibbāna*. The *Mahāsudassana Sutta* goes on to tell the story of Kusinara's glorious past, and another former lifetime of the Buddha.

Merit-Making, Depictions, and Performance

Because of the importance of *Jātaka* in popularizing Buddhism, the sponsorship of their performance, copying or depiction is seen an act of great merit and their representation is at the heart of many annual and event-specific celebrations. They are depicted in temple murals, on manuscripts, and in temporary festival art. For example, at **Wesak** in Sri Lanka, different communities, businesses, and temple groups compete to create the most interesting depictions of individual *Jātaka*. These take the form of large more or less two-dimensional story boards, often lit up with an array of lights, and add to the festivity of the occasion as people continue to enjoy the Wesak activities into the night. Sometimes the *Jātaka* depicted is well known;

other times the group challenges their audience with one that is rarely told (personal discussions with pandol-makers, Colombo, Wesak 2002).

The set of the ten *Jātaka* that tell of the final ten lifetimes of the Buddha-to-be before he became Gotama, in each of which he completes his fulfillment of one of the ten perfections, is popularly depicted as wall paintings in temples and pagodas and in illustrating manuscripts. Curiously, they do not seem to appear in manuscripts containing the texts of the *Jātaka* themselves. In Thailand, they are included on the manuscripts used by monks for reciting at funerals (Ginsburg 2000: 54ff.). Such funerary manuscripts tend to contain extracts or summaries of each of the seven books of the *Abhidhamma Piṭaka* (see Chapter 7), followed by the story of the monk Phra Māleyya who visits the different hells (Brereton 1995). *Jātaka* also influence and inform other forms of literature. As Mabel Bode comments in relation to Burmese literature, "The Jātaka has found its way everywhere, from law codes and chronicles to popular plays" (Bode 1909: 60, 82).

Women in the *Jātaka*

The most commonly performed *Jātaka* of all is the *Vessantara Jātaka*. It is the tale of the Buddha-to-be's final life before his sojourn in the Tusita heaven where he will await the life in which he will become Enlightened (Meiland 2003, Chapter 6; translation from Pali, Cone and Gombrich 1977; from Shan, Pannyawamsa 2007). As Prince Vessantara, the Buddha-to-be perfects the crucial quality of generosity by making the ultimate sacrifice of giving up all he possesses and loves. He gives away wealth and power by giving away the kingdom's magic white elephant. He gives away his nearest and dearest, giving first his children as slaves for the greedy brahmin **Jūjaka**, and then also giving away his wife. Modern readers have frequently baulked at the handing over of wife and children, concerned at what this says about attitudes to women (Tilakaratne 2008). Overall, women are indeed negatively portrayed throughout the *Jātakas*. Helga Rudolf points out, "By far the most frequent complaint against women is that they are temptresses and therefore hindrances to holiness. Many stories are responses to the complaints of women, including their former wives" (Rudolf 2001: 199). This and the pervasive "**ascetic misogyny**" (see Chapter 9) confirms the importance of *Jātakas* for monks, observed earlier. Women are also portrayed as unfaithful, deceitful and capricious, manipulative, prone to jealousy, and best ignored. Their beauty is presented as problematic and their vanity in it leads to lowly rebirths as insects (Rudolf 2001: 200–201). In the "Soft Hands" *Jātaka* (no. 262), even the Buddha-to-be, reborn as a King, is tricked by his own daughter by substituting a soft-handed page boy for herself while bathing, even though her father is so concerned to control her that he always keeps hold of at least one of her hands even while she is taking a bath. In dismay on finding the page boy in place of his daughter, he cries,

> Though soft of speech, like rivers hard to fill,
> Insatiate, nought can satisfy their will:
> Down, down they sink: a man should flee afar
> From women, when he knows what kind they are.
> Whomso they serve for gold or for desire,
> They burn him up like fuel in the fire.

To this the commentary adds a verse highlighting the danger of women having power, whether over a man or more generally:

Where women rule, the seeing lose their sight,
The strong grow weak, the mighty have no might.
Where women rule, virtue and wisdom fly:
Reckless the prisoners in durance lie.
Like highway robbers, all they steal away
From their poor victims, careless come what may –
Reflection, virtue, truth, and reasoning
Self-sacrifice, and goodness – everything.
As fire burns fuel, for each careless wight
They burn fame, glory, learning, wit, and might.
(Cowell 1895–1913, volume III: 226)

The Buddha-to-be never appears as a female character in the Theravada *Jātakas* (Jones 1979: 20). Indeed, according to some noncanonical sources from Southeast Asia, the Buddha-to-be tries to receive the prediction of future Buddhahood while a woman in a lifetime before his rebirth as Sumedha. He is told that he cannot receive this prediction as a woman and must first be reborn as a man (Derris 2008). This means that for the entirety of his career as a Buddha-to-be, he is always male, regardless of what kind of being, whether animal, human, or some kind of spirit. In a few *Jātaka*, however, although as exceptions, women are presented positively, as generous, virtuous, or wise (Rudolf 2001: 198–199). One of the more positive representations of women appears in the *Mahā-ummagga Jātaka* (no. 546), in which the Buddha-to-be and Yasodharā-to-be are husband and wife. There the wife Amarādevī is portrayed as being as wise as her husband. A genre of children's stories of the pair solving puzzles is popular in Burma to this day (Pyi Phyo Kyaw, personal communication).

The *Vessantara Jātaka*

The giving away of Yasodharā-to-be in the Vessantara in fact proves the Buddha-to-be is capable of the ultimate sacrifice, to renounce the most important thing possible (Tilakaratne 2008: 85). Prince Vessantara gives up his children and wife when living in the forest to which he had been exiled for giving away the city's white elephant that ensured the rain. That the story is intended to emphasize the perfection of his generosity and renunciation is confirmed in the biography of the Buddha provided in the introduction to the canonical *Jātaka*, the *Jātakanidāna*. There the Buddha acknowledges that without the help of his wife, Yasodharā, in previous lifetimes, he would never have been able to develop this crucial final perfection. Thus, her role in allowing herself to be abandoned and given away in several lifetimes is crucial to the Buddha's achievement of Awakening. We can see in this story the notion of the man as agent and the wife as instrument found in Vedic and other early Indian religions. The twist in this tale is that the Buddha then, in his final lifetime, enables Yasodharā's own agency, so that she can become a nun and *arhat* (see Chapter 9). Fortunately, in the *Vessantara Jātaka*, it turns out that the gods have been offering a helping hand to the Buddha to ensure that he will become enlightened and make the Dhamma available once more. The king of the gods, Sakka, who had disguised himself to take Vessantara's wife reveals his true identity and restores her to Vessantara. Two deities, disguising themselves as the children's parents, take care of them and lead them back toward the city so that their grandfather, King Sivi, recognizes them and pays a ransom for them. The evil brahmin Jūjaka, now fabulously wealthy, dies from gorging himself on an excess of food. Vessantara and his family are welcomed back to the city. In performances, Jūjaka is a source of great entertainment. In Thailand, he even takes the form of an amulet.

The *Vessantara Jātaka* has been portrayed in some of the most spectacular paintings to grace the walls of Theravada temples. The text has appeared in many vernacular renderings (on which, see Collins 2014, Introduction). The individual chapters have also become works in their own right, such as the eighteenth-century Sangharāja Suk Kai Thuen's rendering of the popular Forest chapter, which features the greedy brahmin Jūjaka, held in Wat Ratchasittharam in Bangkok (personal communication, Ven. Veera of Wat Rajasittharam, August 2011).

In Tai cultures, the sponsorship of the reading or performance of the *Vessantara Jātaka* is considered the greatest act of merit. It may be combined with the annual harvest festival (Tambiah 1970: 160–161) or sponsored in honor of deceased parents (Pannyawamsa 2009, Swearer 1995a: 35). In Laos, Burma's eastern Shan states, and north-eastern Thailand, in particular, the *Vessantara Jātaka* is performed in a series of 18 episodes over several days. The performance may be bilingual, in Pali and the local vernacular, or simply in the vernacular (Swearer 1995a: 36). It may take years for people to save enough money for all the expenses of sponsoring a performance, including the performers, the feasting, and the offerings to monks, but it earns them great merit and great praise in the community. Many Shan of the region aspire to sponsor such a performance at least once in their lifetime (Pannyawamsa 2009: 125). The performance of *Jātaka*, especially the *Vessantara Jātaka*, is also a popular way of raising funds for a temple and its community – but it is more than that, it is a way of bringing the community together. A form of temporary art is created for the *Vessantara* telling. Key episodes are also painted as temporary art on long stretches of cotton and hung either horizontally or vertically in Tai temples (Ginsburg 2000: 54). One practice is the representation of the entire narrative on lengthy scrolls, depicting the story in great color and detail with local touches. These scrolls are processed as part of the festivities (Lefferts and Cate 2012). This forms the central event of the festivities and occurs on the first afternoon. The participants carry the scroll "to an area they have designated as the 'forest'. There, as subject of the king Muang Sivi, the city in which Phra Wet (Vessantara) was born and from which they requested he be exiled they perform… a ritualised negotiation with the prince to return from exile to his kingdom. After a brief ceremony by which the people take the Five Precepts… they perform the invitation, unroll the scroll, form a procession, and return to the wat, the monastery and community centre at the heart of Theravada social life" (Lefferts and Cate 2012: 41). The jubilant emphasis on this part of the story at Vessantara's triumphant return to the city thus appears to celebrate not renunciation as such, but the return to society. It is usually performed in the middle of the dry season and anticipates the coming of the rains. The scroll procession is the highlight of the activity, not the telling of the story which follows, and "attracts the most participants: young and old, women and men, children and dogs" (Lefferts *et al.* 2012: 47).

Jātakas Today

The popularity of *Jātakas* continues to this day and attempts are being made to preserve the traditional skills required for their performance. In the past decade in Laos, for example, a school was set up outside Vientiane to save the traditional method of recitation used for *Jātakas*. This recitation method was at risk of being lost following the secularization of Sangha education in the 1970s that came after the revolution. Throughout these traditional performances, periods of recitation may be punctuated by a burst of energetic activity, such as laymen carrying the monk who has been reciting aloft on a palanquin. They process around the recitation hall three times, to the accompaniment of musicians playing loud, festive music on traditional instruments. *Jātaka* are now frequently also the basis of children's books and cartoons. (Cartoons of *Jātakas* in a wide range of languages can be found on the Internet.)

Summary

In this chapter, we saw how *Jātakas*, the stories of the Buddha's former lifetimes, initially collected in the Pali Canon to make complex teachings accessible and memorable to monks, came to inform almost every aspect of Theravada religiosity. With countless versions in Pali and vernacular languages and every possible medium of telling from high literature through temporary art festivals to cartoons, they convey the values of Buddhism and teach the workings of good and bad *kamma* at both the individual and the collective level. They also emphasize the status of the Buddha, members of his family and community, who underwent many lifetimes rehearsing and perfecting the qualities needed to fulfill their roles in the final lifetime of Gotama Buddha. *Jātaka* also exist for other Buddhas and there are *Jātaka* stories embedded in non-*Jātaka* literature.

Certain *Jātaka* have gained great popularity, being associated with particular festivals, most notably the *Vessantara Jātaka*, the story of the Buddha-to-be's final lifetime fulfilling the perfections, the last of which, generosity (*dāna*), he completes by handing over his two children and his wife as slaves, a sacrifice that has come under scrutiny – as have other *Jātaka* – for the questionable portrayal of women.

Jātakas combine many aspects of Theravada Buddhism: monastic, ascetic, and ethical values; protection and merit-making; celebrations to mark the cycles of the religious and agrarian calendars; the building of status and community in this life and across lives. They reveal the complex way in which Buddhist values and practices elevate, enrich, and intertwine with the lives of Theravada individuals and communities. The variety of ways in which the stories are conveyed informs and benefits from the variety of artistic, musical, and other creative skills preserved and developed within Theravada communities.

References

Bode, Mabel. (1909). *The Pali Literature of Burma*. London: Royal Asiatic Society.

Brereton, Bonnie Pacala. (1995). *Thai Tellings of Phra Malai: Texts and Rituals Concerning a Popular Buddhist Saint*. Tempe: Arizona State University Press.

Carrithers, M. (1983). *The Forest Monks of Sri Lanka: An Anthropological and Historical Study*. Calcutta: Oxford University Press.

Cone, Margaret and Richard Gombrich. (1977 [2011]). *The Perfect Generosity of Prince Vessantara*. Bristol: Pali Text Society.

Cowell E.B. (ed.). (1895–1913). *The Jātaka or Stories of the Buddha's Former Births*, 6 vols. Cambridge: Cambridge University Press.

Crosby, Kate. (2012). 'The Inheritance of Rahula: Abandoned Child, Boy Monk, Ideal Son and Trainee' in Vanessa Sasson (ed.), *Little Buddhas: Children and Childhoods in Buddhist Texts and Traditions*. Oxford: Oxford University Press, 97–123.

Crosby, Kate and Man Shik Kong. (in preparation). '*Jātaka* as monastic literature'.

Derris, Karen. (2008). 'When the Buddha was a Woman. Reimagining Tradition in Theravāda', *Journal of Feminist Studies in Religion* 24.2: 29–44.

Ginsburg, Henry. (2000). *Thai Art and Culture: Historic Manuscripts from Western Collections*. London: The British Library.

Godakumbura, C.E. (1955). *Sinhalese Literature*. Colombo: Colombo Apothecaries.

von Hinüber, Oskar. (1996). *A Handbook of Pāli Literature*. Berlin / New York: Walter de Gruyter.

Horner, I.B. (1975). *Chronicle of the Buddhas (Buddhavaṃsa) and The Basket of Conduct (Cariyāpiṭaka). The Minor Anthologies of the Pāli Canon III*. London: Pali Text Society.

Horner, I.B and Padmanabh S. Jaini. (1985). *Apocryphal Birth-Stories: Paññāsa Jātaka*. London: Pali Text Society.

Jones, Garrett John. (1979). *Tales and Teachings of the Buddha*. London: Allen & Unwin.

Lefferts, Leedom and Sandra Cate with Wajuppa Tossa. (2012). *Buddhist Storytelling in Thailand and Laos: The Vessantara Jataka Scroll at the Asian Civilisations Museum*. Singapore: Asian Civilisations Museum.

Lüders, H. (1897). 'Die Sage von Ṛṣyaśṛṅga' in *Nachrichten von der Königlichen Gesellschaft der Wissenschaften zu Göttingen*. 87–135.

McAlpine, W.R. and M.B. Ariyapala. (1990). *The Grest-Gem of Poetry: Kavsilumina*. Colombo: The Royal Asiatic Society of Sri Lanka.

Meiland, Justin. (2003). 'Buddhist Values in the Pāli *jātakas*, with particular reference to the theme of renunciation'. Doctoral dissertation, University of Oxford.

Ohnuma, Reiko. (2004). 'Jātaka' in Robert E. Buswell, Jr. (ed.), *Encyclopedia of Buddhism*. New York: Macmillan Reference USA, 400–401.

Panglung, Jampa Lobsang. (1981). *Die Erzählstoff des Mūlasarvāstivāda Vinaya. Analysiert auf Grund des tibetsichen Übersetzung*. Studia Philologica Buddhica Monograph Series 3. Tokyo: The Reiuukai Library.

Pannyawamsa, Sengpan. (2007). 'The Tham Vessantara-jātaka: A Critical Study of the Vessantara-jātaka and its Influence on Kengtung Buddhism, eastern Shan State, Burma'. PhD thesis, Postgraduate Institute of Pali and Buddhist Studies, University of Kelaniya, Sri Lanka.

Pannyawamsa, Sengpan. (2009). 'Recital of the Tham *Vessantara-jātaka*: A Social-cultural Phenomenon in Kengtung, Eastern Shan State, Myanmar'. *Contemporary Buddhism* 10.1: 125–139.

Rozenberg, Guillaume. (2010). *Renunciation and Power. The Quest for Sainthood in Contemporary Burma*. Translated from the French by Jessica Hackett. New Haven: Yale University Southeast Asia Studies.

Rudolf, Helga. (Spring 2001). ' "Once Upon a Time when Brahmadatta Reigned in Benares" Reflections on the Jataka Tales with Special Attention to the Portrayal of Women', *Relgiologiques* 23: 193–202.

Saddhatissa, H. (1975). *The Birth-Stories of the Ten Bodhisattas and the Dasabodhisattuppattikathā Being a Translation and Edition of the Dasabodhisattuppattikathā*. London: The Pali Text Society.

Skilton, Andrew. (2002). 'An early Mahāyāna transformation of the story of Kṣāntivādin: "The Teacher of Forbearance" ', *Buddhist Studies Review* 19: 115–136.

Skilton, Andrew. (2009). *"How the Nāgas were Pleased" by Harṣa & "The Shattered Thighs" By Bhāsa*. New York: New York University Press.

Stern, S.M., and Sofie Walzer. (1971). *Three Unknown Buddhist stories in an Arabic Version*. Columbia: University of South Carolina Press.

Swearer, Donald K. (1995a). *The Buddhist World of Southeast Asia*. Albany: State University of New York Press.

Swearer, Donald K. (1995b). 'Bimbā's Lament' in Donald S. Lopez Jr. (ed.), *Buddhism in Practice*. Princeton: Princeton University Press, 550–551.

Tambiah, S.J. (1970). *Buddhism and the Spirit Cults in North-East Thailand*. Cambridge: Cambridge University Press.

Tatelman, Joel. (1999). 'The Trials of Yaśodharā: The Legend of the Buddha's Wife in the Bhadrakalpāvadāna (from the Sanskrit)', Buddhist Literature 1: 176–126.

Tilakaratne, Asaṅga. (2008). 'Trying to Understand the Donation of Wives and Children and Related Matters in Theravāda Buddhist Ethics', *The Mahachulalongkorn Journal of Buddhist Studies* I: 71–89.

Walters, Jonathan S. (1990). 'The Buddha's Bad Karma: A Problem in the History of Theravāda Buddhism', *Numen* 37.1: 70–95.
Walters, Jonathan S. (2003). 'Communal Karma and Karmic Community in Theravada Buddhist History', in John Clifford Holt, Jacob N. Kinnard, and Jonathan S. Walters (eds.), *Constituting Communities: Theravada Buddhism and the Religious Cultures of South and Southeast Asia*. Albany: State University of New York Press, 9–39.

Further Reading

Translations

Cone, Margaret and Richard Gombrich. (1977 [2011]). *The Perfect Generosity of Prince Vessantara*. Oxford: Clarendon Press. (See also Collins, 2014, Introduction.)
Cowell E.B. (ed.) (1895–1913). *The Jātaka or Stories of the Buddha's Former Births*. Cambridge: Cambridge University Press. Available online at http://www.sacred-texts.com/bud/j1/index.htm (retrieved June 10, 2013) (Almost complete translation of entire canonical collection.)
Horner, I.B and Padmanabh S. Jaini (1985). *Apocryphal Birth-Stories: Paññāsa Jātaka*. London: Pali Text Society.
McAlpine, W.R. and M.B. Ariyapala. (1990). *The Grest-Gem of Poetry: Kavsilumina*. Colombo: The Royal Asiatic Society of Sri Lanka.
Saddhatissa, H. (1975). *The Birth-Stories of the Ten Bodhisattas and the Dasabodhisattuppattikathā Being a Translation and Edition of the Dasabodhisattuppattikathā*. London: The Pali Text Society.
Shaw, Sarah. (2006). *The Jatakas: Birth Stories of the Bodhisatta*. New Delhi/New York: Penguin. (*Abridged translation of 26 of the canonical Jātaka*)

Studies

Appleton, Naomi. (2010). *Jātaka Stories in Theravāda Buddhism, Narrating the Bodhisattva Path*. Farnham: Ashgate.
Collins, Steven (ed.). (2014). *Vessantara Jataka*, Readings in Buddhist Literatures. New York: Columbia University Press.
von Hinüber, Oskar. (1998). *Entstehung und Aufbau der Jātaka-Sammlung: Studien zur Literatur des Theravāda Buddhismus*. Mainz/Stuttgart: Akademie der Wissenschaften und der Literatur.
Kapur-Fic, Alexandra R. 2010. *The Jātakas. Times and Live of Jātakas*. New Delhi: Abhinav Publications.
Lefferts, Leedom, Sandra Cate with Wajuppa Tossa. (2012). *Buddhist Storytelling in Thailand and Laos: The Vessantara Jataka Scroll at the Asian Civilisations Museum*. Singapore: Asian Civilisations Museum.
Meiland, Justin (2003). 'Buddhist Values in the Pāli *Jātakas*, with particular reference to the theme of renunciation.' Doctoral dissertation, University of Oxford.
Rudolf, Helga. (Spring 2001). ' "Once Upon a Time when Brahmadatta Reigned in Benares" Reflections on the Jataka Tales with Special Attention to the Portrayal of Women', *Relgiologiques* 23: 193–202.
Skilling, Peter. (2006). 'Jātaka and Paññāsa-jātaka in South-East Asia', *The Journal of the Pali Text Society* xxviii: 113–173.
Skilton, Andrew. (2002). 'An early Mahāyāna transformation of the story of KΣāntivādin: "The Teacher of Forbearance" ', *Buddhist Studies Review* 19: 115–136.
Walters, Jonathan S. (2003). 'Communal Karma and Karmic Community in Theravada Buddhist History', in John Clifford Holt, Jacob N. Kinnard, and Jonathan S. Walters (eds.), *Constituting Communities: Theravada Buddhism and the Religious Cultures of South and Southeast Asia*. Albany: State University of New York Press, 9–39.

5

The Good Buddhist

Overview

This chapter explores what it means to be a good Buddhist in theory and in practice. It explores such core Buddhist activities as precept-taking, merit-making, and merit transference. It examines how the ideals of the precepts are affected by practical considerations and how Buddhists understand such practices as the transference of merit in the light of the well-known Buddhist doctrine of personal responsibility. Western expectations of how Buddhists behave are often informed by the five precepts of laypeople, but in some Theravada communities it is possible for these precepts to be undertaken temporarily or only at certain stages of life. Ways in which Theravada Buddhists accommodate keeping the precepts in the face of the practicalities of life are considered. Practices examined here include ritual practices such as *paritta* recitation, treatment of the gods and spirits, funerals and offerings to ancestors. Specifically Buddhist religious practice involving the pursuit of the "ten skilful actions," such as attendance at temples, making offerings to monks, and acts of service and reverence – including filial piety – coexists with strategies for dealing with life that are not specifically Buddhist, including the interactions with deities, ancestors, spirits, astrology, and numerology, but that pervade and are inseparable from Buddhist culture. Buddhist temples have traditionally been important in education and in social and community welfare projects. However, some of the ways in which monastics and laypeople have engaged with personal, communal, and political crises under the emblem of Buddhism in the past 50 years have collectively been termed "**(socially) engaged Buddhism**," a phrase coined by the Vietnamese (Mahayana) monk Thich Nhat Hanh in the 1960s. Engaged Buddhism focuses on addressing social and political causes of suffering in this life, rather than on multilife solutions to suffering.

Theravada Buddhism: Continuity, Diversity, and Identity, First Edition. Kate Crosby.

Correct Conduct

The truth that the Buddha realized and taught in his first sermon is often encapsulated as the "Four Truths," more fully known as the Four Noble Truths, or the "Four Truths of the Noble Ones" (see Chapter 1). The fourth of the truths is the "the truth of the path." This is the path to eliminate craving, the cause of suffering, and to put an end to the cycle of death and rebirth (*saṃsāra*). The path is summarized as the "noble eightfold path." The eight components that this refers to are (1) right view, (2) right intention, (3) right speech, (4) right action, (5) right livelihood, (6) right effort, (7) right mindfulness, and (8) right concentration. These eight are sometimes subsumed by a more succinct summary of the path having three components: moral conduct (*sīla*), meditation/concentration (*samādhi*), and wisdom or "understanding," *paññā* as given next.

Three components of the path	*Eight components of the "noble eightfold path"*
1. Wisdom *paññā*	1. Right view
	2. Right intention
2. Moral conduct *sīla*	3. Right speech
	4. Right action
	5. Right livelihood
3. Meditation/concentration *samādhi*	6. Right effort
	7. Right mindfulness
	8. Right meditation/concentration

The constituents of the path are not to be followed purely sequentially, but to some extent simultaneously, in that each supports the other. A degree of wisdom, which might be seen as the culmination of the path, is needed at the outset in order to see the value of pursuing the path. Wisdom requires both a correct view about which mental states are wholesome or skilful (***kusala***) and which unwholesome (*akusala*) (Collins 1982: 90), and also correct intention, that is, the desire to act in accordance with ethical values and to make progress on the path. These aspects can then be refined through meditation and the use of analysis to develop greater levels of experiential wisdom.

Since meditation is discussed in Chapter 6, and wisdom is discussed in the chapter on the Buddha (Chapter 1) and the chapter on *Abhidhamma* (Chapter 7), here we focus on *sīla*, moral conduct, that is, the components right speech, right action, and right livelihood, and how they are understood in Theravada.

Kamma, "action"

The teaching that underlies the Buddhist understanding of what constitutes moral conduct is the doctrine of *kamma*, "action." One's current experience is the result of previous actions. The actions one performs now will have consequences in one's future, either in this life or in a future existence.

In Vedic/brahmanical Hinduism, one of the dominant religions at the time of the Buddha, the word *kamma* (*karma*, in Sanskrit) denoted ritual action and referred to actions performed by or on behalf of the sponsor of a ritual. Such rituals, which are still performed today, involve sacrifice and oblations into one or three sacred fires. A sacred household fire, from which the other two may be drawn, is established by a high-caste male Hindu householder who follows this tradition on becoming married. These ritual actions were believed to create one's future body in the afterlife, and also feed one's departed ancestors. Buddhism rejected this understanding and the practice of sacrifice, but in the course of either rejecting or adapting these ideas some Buddhist terminology and practice echoes them. The Hinduism attested in the Upaniṣad texts from circa sixth-century BCE began to reinterpret Vedic understandings of *kamma*, moving toward a notion of *kamma* in terms of individual conduct. The sacrificial fire was symbolically internalized and interpreted in terms of the functions of the human body, particularly the breath. Buddhism arose around the same time as the early Upaniṣads and reflects this trend toward "internalization." It takes the trend a stage further: in Buddhism, *kamma* refers to any intentional action of body, speech, or mind. In its emphasis on intention, Buddhism offers an ethical reinterpretation of the pan-Indian *kamma* doctrine.

Buddhism teaches that there is no enduring, permanent soul or self (*attā, ātman* in Sanskrit). In doing so, it is rejecting the Hindu and Jain concepts of a soul. In the light of its doctrine of no-self, *anattā*, Buddhism had to explain how it was that there could be continuity of *kammic* repercussions in the absence a single entity (a soul) that continues across lifetimes. For Hinduism and Jainism, such continuity is provided in the concept of a self. Early Buddhism answered this question using imagery to give examples of causes and effects in a stream of continuity (*santāna*). Analogies offered include that of a mango seed that once planted gives rise to a mango tree and fruits; a flame that spreads from one source of fuel to another; or a boy who becomes an old man. In each case, we recognize that there is a continuity between the seed and the fruit, from the one flame to another, and from the boy to the man. But the cause or precursor is not the same as the result. That which we think of as "I" is similarly a continuum of interconnected causes. How this then relates to moral responsibility is indicated in the following images for continuity in the absence of a permanent self given by the monk Nāgasena in the early postcanonical work, the *Milindapañha*, when discussing the topic of no-self with the King Milinda:

> The monk continues by adducing a number of comparisons; a man who has stolen some mangoes claims himself to be innocent of theft, on the grounds that the mangoes he stole were different from the mangoes the owner had planted. A man lit a fire to warm himself, and left it alight when he went away; it burned a neighbour's field, but the man claims himself to be innocent on the grounds that the fire he failed to put out was different from the fire which burned the field… Finally, a man who bought some milk from a herdsman left it for a day, during which time it turned to curds; on returning the next day, he demanded the milk he had bought, claiming that he had bought milk, not curds. In all these cases, the king is made to agree that the arguments are not to be accepted, as the phenomena in sequence are connected, the latter being "produced from" the former. (Collins 1982: 185)

The nature of causality was defined more technically within *sutta* texts (see Chapter 3) as the chain of dependent origination, which expresses causality in terms of 12 causal links in a chain, a chain that is cyclical, representing *saṃsāra*. Each gives rise to the next. The 12 items are (i) ignorance, (ii) volitional mental formations (*saṅkhāra*), (iii) consciousness, (iv) name and form, (v) the six sense bases, (vi) contact, (vii) sensation, (viii) craving, (ix) clinging, (x) becoming, (xi) birth, and (xii) aging and death. Within *Abhidhamma* this was further defined:

impermanence was analyzed into a theory of relative momentariness of the mental and physical constituents that make up human experience. Causality was further analyzed into 24 types of causal relationships between conditioning and conditioned phenomena (see Chapter 7). At the more immediately practical level, however, the understanding of causality that underlies the doctrine of *kamma* emphasizes that individuals are responsible for their actions. The intentions that impel those actions shape that individual's future, and the person's current experience is a reflection of intentional actions in the past. The quality of those intentions depends on whether they are rooted in the three "fires," greed, hatred, and delusion, that keep us trapped in *saṃsāra*, or their opposites. Here we see how Buddhism first draws on the Vedic imagery of the "three (sacrificial) fires" that maintain the universe, then uses them as a metaphor and ultimately rejects them. Indeed, one of the meanings of *nibbāna*, the term we translate as Enlightenment, is "extinction," that is, the extinguishing of the three fires of greed, hatred, and delusion.

After death an individual (or the next stage in the causal continuum that makes up an individual) may be reborn in any one of the realms of Buddhist cosmology (see later text). The quality of their new life is a result of the fruition of their previous actions. Certain types of action are regarded as "weightier" and come to fruition more quickly than others. Actions and mental states close to death are particularly pertinent to the immediate rebirth state (see Chapter 7). The destiny in the next life may be one of the "fortunate realms," either in a heaven or as a human, or in one of the unfortunate realms, in a hell, or as a "hungry ghost" or as an animal.

To avoid the bad rebirths one must follow the Buddhist precepts and store up a repository of "merit" from good actions. There are also ways of assisting deceased relatives by "making merit" on their behalf. "Transferring merit" is an important part of Theravada funeral and death commemoration rituals. Most Theravada cultures also have other rituals to try to assist those of the departed who are stuck as ghosts to proceed to their next rebirth. Alternatively, since they may be causing harm to the living, they may be contained, in Cambodia, for example, by inviting them to take up residence in the base of a Buddha image (Harris 2005: 55), or dispelled to a safe distance from the community, in Shan cultures through an annual village rite (Eberhardt 2006: 69. See also later text, Chapter 7).

The reason why those writing in English tend to use the term rebirth when discussing Buddhism instead of the more familiar term reincarnation is because the latter term implies a soul taking on flesh, that is, taking up a new body. In Theravada, the five aggregates, *khandha*, that make up the individual include consciousness, mental constituents, and form, which are each forever changing. The cessation of them in one life leads to a new set of five *khandha* in the next. Thus, not only are the material aspects of the individual impermanent and replaced, but the cognitive aspects too.

Although *kamma* tends to be interpreted as an individualistic affair, Jonathan Walters has demonstrated that there are concepts of group *kamma* that explain shared fates and current formations among social groups. He has also shown that the *kamma* of leaders, in particular, affects their followers, creating a kind of "overflow *kamma*" (Walters 2003). The modern application of such notions was noticeable in the responses to the 2004 tsunami in Asia, where Buddhists regarded the corruption in government and the conduct of warfare on the part of the Sri Lankan government and/or the Tamil Tigers as contributory factors (Crosby 2008: 64).

Finally, although *kamma* is described as an automatic process in the Pali Canon, Yama, the god of death and the afterlife, who features in Pali canonical literature, is popularly regarded in Southeast Asia as the keeper of records of each person's *kammic* history (Bizot 1976, Crosby 2000: 146).

Precepts

To guide right action there are several sets of precepts. The basic set of five precepts given in the following table is undertaken by laypeople. They are usually taken in a ritual context in Pali and in front of a monk. First one pays homage to the Buddha, then one "takes the three refuges," that is, makes the Buddhist statement of faith, three times: "I go to the Buddha as my refuge, to the Dhamma as my refuge, to the Sangha as my refuge." After that the five precepts are recited.

The five precepts (*pañca sīlāni/sikkhāpadāni*) of laypeople

Pali	*English*
1. *pāṇātipātā veramaṇī sikkhāpadaṃ samādiyāmi*	1. I undertake not to cause the death of living beings.
2. *adinnādānā veramaṇī sikkhāpadaṃ samādiyāmi*	2. I undertake not to take what is not given.
3. *kāmesu micchācārā veramaṇī sikkhāpadaṃ samādiyāmi*	3. I undertake to refrain from sexual misconduct.
4. *musāvādā veramaṇī sikkhāpadaṃ samādiyāmi*	4. I undertake to refrain from lying.
5. *surāmerayamajjapamādaṭṭhānā veramaṇī sikkhāpadaṃ samādiyāmi*	5. I undertake to refrain from intoxicants.

Some people will try to follow these precepts at all times, some may take them or a few of them for a specific period; for others they may be merely formulaic, while still others avoid taking them knowing that they would break them. (This applies in Tai-Lao cultures in which vows are more likely to be taken for a specific period in order to avoid breaking them.) Some people postpone undertaking them until later in life (see later text). The term for precept in Pali is either *sīla* "moral conduct" or ***sikkhāpada*** "rule of training."

How the precepts are interpreted varies. In particular, understandings of what constitutes sexual misconduct vary between cultures and change with fashion and politics (see Chapter 10). The drinking of alcohol by laymen is usual in most Theravada communities and it may even be expected as part of a ritual that is otherwise Buddhist. For example, drinking and gambling at funerals is traditional in Tai-Lao cultures (Eberhardt 2006: 53), even though there have been attempts since the nineteenth century to reform such practice. The "bodyguards" that carry the young boys around in the elaborate ceremonies that precede novice ordination in Shan cultures also expect to be paid in alcohol by the sponsors and to drink as part of the proceedings (Eberhardt 2006: 134). At Buddhist festivals in Burma, the consumption of alcohol outside pagodas has become more pronounced since the 1990s with large beer companies such as Tiger Beer and Myanmar Beer adopting a new approach of selling large amounts wholesale at stalls set up for the occasion using young, female sales staff to attract custom. We shall return to variations in the undertaking of the first precept, not to cause the death of living beings, in later text and in Chapter 12. Variations in understandings of the third precept on sexual misconduct, particularly for women, are also considered in Chapter 10.

Laypeople may undertake an extended set of precepts, usually eight, when, for example, staying at the temple on a holy day. Holy days traditionally fall on the new moon or full moon. It varies from country to country whether this is adhered to or whether the nearest weekend day is used instead, to accommodate the modern working week. Some full-moon holy days are particularly important; one such is the ***pāvāraṇā*** that marks the end of the three-month monastic "rains" retreat. The *kaṭhina* festival, at which laypeople present monks with new robes, is then held within the following lunar month. Throughout the Theravada world it is the most important event in monastic-laity relations in the annual calendar. It falls in October or November. Another important full moon, which falls in May, is the Wesak full moon, celebrating the Buddha's birth, enlightenment, and *parinibbāna*. It has been particularly important in Sri Lanka and far less so in mainland Southeast Asia. However, it is increasingly seen as a pan-Theravada celebration.

The eight precepts are the same as the ten precepts for novice monks, with the exception of the handling of gold and silver. The number eight is arrived at by combining two of the precepts (those on spectating shows and wearing adornments). The eight-precept keeper is therefore part-way between layperson and monastic. For their third precept is a vow of chastity, not just the avoidance of sexual misconduct as found in the set of five precepts. For practical reasons, some nuns who stay permanently at the monastery (or at a nunnery if one is available) only take on the eight precepts and not the full set of ten undertaken by all male novices, monks, and some nuns. This leaves eight-precept nuns free to act as managers/housekeepers for monks and allows them to buy food, like laypeople, in situations where there is insufficient lay support for nuns (see Chapter 9). A relatively recent development is the keeping of eight precepts while otherwise outwardly following a normal lay life, as is done by many of the practitioners associated with the modern Dhammakaya Movement in Thailand. The practical advantages are that one can undertake the additional religious commitment while not changing one's outward appearance (unlike precept-keepers at temples, who change their dress, and nuns who additionally shave their heads) and while still being able to transact financial affairs. (Depending on which monastery and lineage they are ordained in, some monks may in fact handle money and transact financial affairs.)

The interpretation of the monastic precept not to listen to or watch singing, dancing, and music varies considerably. For example, some monks are involved in administering performances in honor of Buddha images (see Chapter 2), which is not normally seen as contravening this precept. In Thailand, it is common for opera and other musical entertainment to be put on in the temple grounds. In Burma, such entertainment groups are an attractive feature of pagoda festivals up and down the country. These theatrical groups occupy grounds and streets surrounding the pagodas, attracting some monks and nuns, as well as many laypeople. In all Theravada regions, certain types of music, singing, and dance are used to convey Buddhist teachings. Monks may choose to listen to music personally, also. Generally speaking, less attention is paid to the two precepts on entertainment and adornment than to the other precepts.

A comparison of eight precepts and ten precepts.

Eight precepts for laity keeping the holy day/ for some nuns/ for committed lay practitioners	*Ten precepts for novices and monks and some female novices and nuns*
1. Not to cause the death of living beings	1. Not to cause the death of living beings
2. Not to take what is not given	2. Not to take what is not given
3. To abstain from sex	3. To abstain from sex
4. To refrain from lying	4. To refrain from lying
5. To refrain from intoxicants	5. To refrain from intoxicants
6. To refrain from eating at the wrong time (after noon)	6. To refrain from eating at the wrong time (after noon)
7. To refrain from spectating singing, dancing, music, or wearing garlands, perfume, make-up, adornments	7. To refrain from spectating singing, dancing, music
8. To refrain from high and luxurious beds and seats	8. To refrain from wearing garlands, perfume, make-up, adornments
	9. To refrain from high beds and seats
	10. To refrain from handling gold and silver

Meritorious Action

The precepts discussed earlier provide a list actions from which one should refrain. The list of ten wholesome actions (*dasa kusala kamma*) provided in the following table is less well known because it is not part of the most common litanies, yet it better reflects the range of activities in which people try to engage in order to "make merit," that is, build up a history of good *kamma*. The table lists the action alongside a summary of how this action is realized in Theravada practice.

Ten wholesome actions	*Practice*
1. Generosity (*dāna*) (a) Motivated by respect (b) Motivated by pity	(a) *dāna* is mostly performed through giving "the four requisites" to monks; food, clothing, shelter, and medicine. The focus is on giving alms food to monks, and increasingly nuns, which may happen on a daily basis, and other offerings, such as robes on specific occasions. The Pali term *dāna* is familiar throughout the Theravada world. (b) Giving to the needy, although an important part of Theravada ethics, is less emphasized than giving to monks. It is sometimes mediated by monks to enhance the merit of the gift. Monks are thus are able to motivate community action to relieve distress. The Sri Lanka Engaged Buddhist organization Sarvodaya encourages social action as "*śramadāna*," the gift of effort, a Gandhian phrase applied within Buddhism to draw on the understanding of *dāna* as highly meritorious.

(*Cont'd*)

Ten wholesome actions	*Practice*
2. Moral conduct (*sīla*)	Keeping the precepts (discussed earlier) to avoid harm. The precepts are regarded as a "universal" ethics, that is, ethical principles that apply to all, in contrast to tribal codes of conducts, or that of brahminical Hinduism, which ascribes appropriate behavior according to gender, age, and status. Scholars regard this common code as a contributory factor in the uptake of Buddhism as a religion of trade, and hence its spread throughout Asia. While this is true to some extent, the different lists of precepts, the extent to which in practice expectations of behavior vary according to sex, age, and station in life, must modify this theory about Buddhism.
3. Meditation (*bhāvanā*)	Meditation is seen as a meritorious activity as well as transformative in its own right. Most Buddhists do not practice meditation to any great extent, although this varies (see Chapter 6). A small amount is often embedded into other rituals.
4. Transferring merit	Performing meritorious activities such as feeding monks or sponsoring the recitation or copying of religious texts in the name of someone who has died, or in the name of all living beings.
5. Rejoicing in merit	When people engage in communal activities, even if they are not the main sponsor, their rejoicing in the merit of others is an important act in itself. The phrase *sādhu sādhu sā[dhu]* 'It is good. It is good. It is good." is heard throughout the Theravada world as people touch offerings about to be made or rejoice at the good deeds performed before them.
6. Rendering service to others	An important part of most laypeople's involvement in Buddhist practice, also embedded in monastic duties, is looking after others.
7. Honoring others	Showing appropriate deference, particularly to the Buddha, Dhamma, and Sangha and to seniors, including parents. Outwardly this is often done by placing the palms of the hands together as in prayer, perhaps bowing the head or by kneeling down and touching the head and/or palms of hands to the ground, usually three times. On Buddha worship, see Chapter 2.
8. Preaching	The gift of the *dhamma* is regarded as the highest gift (see Chapter 3 on preaching and sermons).
9. Listening to Dhamma	Attending the temple to hear the recitation or reading of texts and listen to sermons is one of the main merit-making activities for Theravada laypeople.
10. Having correct views	Correct views includes understanding the three marks of existence: impermanence, suffering and no-self; the four noble truths (see Chapter 1) and skilful from unskillful conduct/mental states.

This table explains the main activities included under the ten skilful actions. Rather than repeat that information here, what follows will explore particular emphasis and variations. Accommodations with other aspects of religious culture in Theravada communities and with the practicalities of daily life will also be considered.

Of the ten skilful merit-making actions, in practice the most emphasis is placed on worship and offerings to the Buddha, particularly by attending the temple on the annual holy days (see later text), on *dāna*, on listening to the *dhamma* and on filial piety. Buddha worship can include pilgrimage to worship at important sites (though pilgrimage is not emphasized in the same way that it is in, say, Islam) and participation in the annual processions or relics (*perahera*, Sinhala) held throughout Sri Lanka. The most well known of these is that of the Tooth relic in Kandy. The building of temples and pagodas (*stūpas*) is an important larger-scale merit-making activity: the *dāna* of providing the requisite of accommodation. Much collective, community wealth is invested in the building of temples, which then become a form of common property, giving individuals of modest means the opportunity to share in grander projects and space than would otherwise be possible. In Burma, the festive culmination of the building process is the popular and highly festive "hoisting of the finial," the umbrella that crowns the tip of the pagoda (Moore 2000, filmed in the opening of Kawanami 1996). In Cambodia, an important public moment in the founding of a new temple is the *sīmā* ceremony, to which local politicians must be invited (Kent 2008: 82). One way of making the merit of building pagodas for those unable to afford to sponsor a real pagoda is through the building of sand pagodas (Gabaude 1979).

Filial piety includes showing respect and doing service to one's parents and transferring merit to them after their death. One expression of filial piety for boys and men is to become ordained. In Tai, Lao, and Cambodian communities, being ordained as a novice is regarded as the way for the son to pay back "the mother's milk," for the mother is the main beneficiary of the merit generated by the son's ordination (Eberhardt 2006: 95, 136). People without children may form a quasi-parental relationship with a boy or man by sponsoring his ordination; thus, all members of the community can participate in this very important merit-making activity.

The emphasis on generosity to the Sangha over other recipients reflects the view that the benefits of *dāna* are affected by the experience of giving. A person's joy at offering *dāna* is affected by the worthiness of the recipient, the pleasing atmosphere, the ability of the monk/s in question to receive gracefully, the extent to which these aspects combine to allow the donor to rejoice in their own merit and for those also participating in the merit-making activity to rejoice (Samuels 2008: 128–132). A text taught in the Pali Canon referred to as the "Mirror of the Dhamma" or the *itipisogāthā* describes the qualities of each of the three refuges, the Buddha, Dhamma, and Sangha, and forms a common part of ritual litanies throughout the Theravada world. In it the Sangha is described as being the "highest field of merit," that is, the most beneficial objects of meritorious giving. In Sri Lanka, where going on an alms-round is no longer the usual way for monks to receive food, formalized alms-rounds are organized so that laypeople can enjoy the romance and aesthetics of the traditional alms-round. The stricter teaching monasteries and nunneries in Burma, renowned for their adherence to *vinaya* and the visible appearance of this through a uniform dress code, are often fully booked by laypeople seeking to give alms because of the pleasing aesthetics and atmosphere created during mealtimes. This has now become one of the most popular and photographed tourist attractions in modern Burma, as has the breakfast alms-round in Luang Prabang in Laos.

In all Theravada communities, the merit generated through *dāna* is formally marked and transferred to the intended recipients – participants themselves, or their deceased relatives, or all the beings in the universe – by the ritual pouring of water at the end of the ceremony. This may be done by pouring the water slowly from one vessel into another, or onto the ground, while making a statement dedicating the merit. In Sri Lankan funerals, the following verses from the *Petavatthu*, the primary canonical authority for the transference of merit, are spoken while transferring the merit:

> As water rained on the uplands flows down to the low land, even so does what is given here benefit the petas (departed spirits / hungry ghosts)...
>
> Just as swollen streams swell the ocean, even so does what is given here benefit the petas. (translation Masefield 1980, 26, cited Langer 2012: 29)

In mainland Southeast Asia, the pouring of this water onto the ground is an offering to the earth goddess *Thorānī* (Thai, Lao, Khmer; Pali *Dhāranī*; also known as *Vasuṃdharā*), who is witness to one's merit. This is the same goddess who in some depictions of the scene is shown witnessing the Buddha's Enlightenment (Guthrie 2004: 22). In Southeast Asian iconography, she is depicted as a beautiful young woman wringing water from her long hair (Guthrie 2004: 19). Sometimes the armies of Māra are depicted drowning in the resulting flood of water.

The important merit-making activities of preaching and listening to the Dhamma encompass the preservation of the Dhamma through the sponsorship of textual performances and of the copying of texts (see Chapter 3). It is most often done as part of death rituals. Sponsoring the performance or ritual reading of the *Vessantara Jātaka* is one of the most important merit-making activities in Tai-Lao Buddhism; it may be done as part of the annual festival calendar or to transfer merit to a deceased parent (see Chapter 4). A standard component of Theravada ritual is the recitation of *paritta* "protection" texts, described in greater detail next.

Within Theravada Buddhism, which is often portrayed in Western literature as being solely focused on personal development, there is in fact considerable emphasis on the giving of service to others, which is widespread and takes a number of forms. Service may be Dhamma-oriented, in that monks may see their primary duty as making sure the Buddha's teaching is available to local people. Nancy Eberhardt records how Shan children see a way of making merit in helping older people to practice temple-sleeping, for example, by carrying what they need to the temple for them (Eberhardt 2006: 162). Monks may persevere with their ordained life specifically because of the position it gives them in leading the community, and assisting it in secular matters also (see Chapter 8). Before they were taken over by government agencies, communal activities such as road-mending were traditionally organized by the monastery, which acted as a central repository for the community as a whole, lending out equipment and substitute work animals for agriculture when the need arose. This continues in some areas to this day. For example, in 2002, three of the "Tipiṭaka" monks (who have won the prestigious title after being tested on their ability to recite the entire Pali Canon, see Chapter 3) led the collective construction of a tarmac road between Sagaing Town and Migun village in upper Burma (Dhammasami and Kyaw 2012). These days monasteries may be at the heart of protests to protect the local community, as in the case of the tree ordinations to protect the local forests in Thailand (Darlington 1998, Tannenbaum 2000), the organization of relief work after natural disasters such as the 2004 Asian tsunami (Crosby 2008) and Cyclone Nargis in 2008.

In the modern period, Theravada Buddhism has received criticism from both within and without that the amount of "social work" done by monks was insufficient. The development of "socially engaged Buddhism," which places greater emphasis on tackling contemporary concerns such as human rights, social justice, and the environment, is a global development in Buddhism that took place from the second half of the twentieth century onward. It tends to focus on this-life solutions, rather than future life solutions (also regarded as a trend more broadly within modern Buddhism), and advocates monks becoming involved in social, welfare, environmental, and, where relevant, political issues. As such it can be seen, in Western terms, as a shift from virtue and duty ethics toward a more utilitarian approach that assesses the outcome of action in practical terms. An example of more active engagement on the part of monks is the late Mahāghosānanda from Cambodia. In 1993, he led the peace march termed *dhamma-yātra* ("dharma journeys," a traditional term for pilgrimage) that ended the stand-off between the Khmer Rouge and the Cambodian and Thai governments, which had trapped thousands of Cambodians in refugee camps on the Thai borders for years after the Khmer Rouge's period of rule (Harvey 2000: 282). In subsequent years, he led further *dhamma-yātra* highlighting other social problems in the country such as the rise in prostitution and the HIV epidemic. Other developments in more active engagement include such organizations as the NGO Sarvodaya Śramadāna movement ("Gift of effort for the uplift for all") founded by A.T. Ariyaratne in Sri Lanka in 1958 and now active in villages throughout Sri Lanka (Bond 1988: Chapter 7, Gombrich and Obeyesekere 1988: 243–248), and attempts by monks such as Payutto and Buddhadāsa, and the outspoken critic and human rights activist Sulak Sivaraksa to develop liberal reform in Thailand (Harvey 2000: 218). Among monks at the forefront in ensuring the provision of welfare services in Burma, Sītagu Sayadaw Ven. Dr. Nyanissara has been able to use his international reputation to establish the Sītagu Āyudāna Hospital. Begun in the 1980s, this hospital now has one of the best facilities for eye operations. International doctors from the United States and United Kingdom work alongside Burmese doctors in its health care programs.

Whether it is correct to see "Engaged Buddhism" as a radical departure from traditional Buddhism is open to debate. Thus, Ariyaratne regarded his activities as reinvoking a Sri Lankan village tradition of collective social work that had fallen out of practice by the 1950s (Gombrich and Obeyesekere 1988: 244). It may be that the essentializing notions of the roles of Buddhist monks that developed in the reform movements of the modern period first confine the scope of monastic activity and then subsequently critique that confinement. Because of the rhetoric of colonial and Christian superiority that often informs them, there are difficulties in interpreting early modern external observations of monastic conduct. Nevertheless, the assumed division between the role of the monk and welfare work means that those monks who do engage in such activities may then be criticized for not keeping to their traditional roles. In Sri Lanka, after the 2004 tsunami, monks who helped in immediate relief work by collecting bodies for safe disposal were criticized by some for breaking with traditional expectations, such as those that monks should not drive (Crosby 2008: 56). In Cambodia, monks such as Mahāghosānanda were initially mistrusted as representative of foreign influence: a divide was perceived between traditional Buddhism and the type of modernist Buddhism involved in work funded by foreign NGOs, even though monks in traditional monasteries were often also involved in servicing the welfare needs of their congregations. This assumed polarization appears to have reduced in recent years. Perhaps it is more useful to observe that Buddhism, like other religions, is a form of social capital that can be harnessed in the service of emerging needs. The Theravada world's social needs were radically altered over the last century by modern warfare, new diseases, evolving drug and alcohol markets and the advent of modernization, industrialization, and globalization. As such the Sangha and the emerging lay Buddhist movements became instruments of response for the promotion of social and public politics, education, community development, and environmental protection (Litalien 2010: 109ff.). So far there has been only limited research into the extent to which the aspirations of the Sangha and other Buddhist organizations to assist communities, individuals, and the environment are effective, but much grass-roots activity is conducted at the local community level by such groups, running environmental projects and youth groups, providing shelter and education, supporting the disadvantaged and offering treatment for addiction.

Right Livelihood, Vegetarianism, and the First Precept

"Right Livelihood" means making a living in an honest way without harming others. Specifically there are five occupations that Buddhists must avoid. These are "Business in weapons, business in human beings, business in meat, business in intoxicants, and business in poison" (*Vanijja Sutta*, Thanissaro 2010). All of these activities, weapons trading, human trafficking including slavery and prostitution, the meat industry, making and selling alcohol and drugs, and the provision of poisons are found within Theravada cultures.

The most widespread of these wrong livelihoods is clearly "business in meat" and Buddhists who have such occupations do regard the killing involved in being a fisherman, butcher, or even farmer as bad *kamma* leading one to experience of suffering. In Sri Lanka, early attempts to interpret the 2004 tsunami considered such issues. One response reported from inland farmers at the time was, "Any livelihood that kills is bad. Ours is bad enough, but fishing, that is beyond the pale." Others saw the violence of the civil war and the increase in prostitution, that is, other types of wrong livelihood, as causal factors (Crosby 2008). It sometimes comes as a surprise to those outsiders who are aware of the Buddhist emphasis on compassion and avoiding harm to others that vegetarianism is rare among Theravada Buddhists, including monks and nuns. It is traditionally only found as part of specific rituals, such as the first-menstruation ceremony for girls in Sri Lanka (Wickremeratne 2006: 79) and in ancestral rites among ethnically Chinese Buddhists in Southeast Asia. Some modern Theravada practitioners, such as Buddhadāsa and members of Santi Asoke (see later text), have also chosen to be vegetarian as a logical interpretation of the emphasis on avoiding harm. Monks who have chosen the forest life in Burma may take it on as an additional ascetic practice, "eating only that which is free from any killing" (*thet-that-lut sa-*), beyond the set of thirteen ascetic practices, which include other food restrictions, found in the *Visuddhimagga*, which they may also follow (Rozenberg 2010: 28).

Vegetarianism is one of the major differences between East Asian and Theravada monastic practice (Kieschnick 2005). Whereas Theravada monastic practice strictly observes the precept of not eating after noon such that those who break this precept take care to keep it a secret, East Asian monks and nuns are strictly vegetarian and likewise seek to conceal any breaking of this monastic regulation, but do not keep the precept of eating only in the morning. (Tibetan and other Himalayan monks and nuns, like their Theravada counterparts, eat meat.) According to East Asian Buddhism, the Buddha was vegetarian and the food from which he became ill, as described in the *Mahāparinirvāna Sūtra* (Sanskrit; *Mahāparinibbāna Sutta*, Pali), may have been some kind of fungus (Strong 2012). For Theravada Buddhists, the Buddha died from eating rancid pork and the term means "tender pork." An "apocryphal" *Jātaka* that circulates in Cambodia relates how the Buddha was destined to die as a result of eating this specific pig because in a previous lifetime the Buddha had, at his mother's behest, killed a fearsome *yakkha* (demon-like creature) that was terrorizing the kingdom. Even though the Buddha-to-be had acted out of filial piety and compassion for many people, his act of killing was still a bad deed. The fearsome *yakkha* was later reborn as the pig whose flesh poisoned the Buddha (Martini 1972).

In Theravada, although monks and nuns may eat meat, they are not supposed to eat it if they know it has been slaughtered specifically for them, but other than that they should eat what is offered. There have been prohibitions on certain types of meat at different times and in different places, such that in Sri Lanka monks often do not eat beef. The various lists of meats to avoid, perhaps including the meat of animals regarded as belonging to the king, appear in texts from the fifth century onward, but there has been no prohibition on meat-eating as a whole (Kong in preparation). Theoretically monks should express no preference in what food is offered, but in practice a simple hand gesture covering the alms bowl is the way to decline too much food or an unwanted dish. Consumable offerings to the Buddha tend to be water and rice, and many deities receive offerings of fruit, but some of the deities that receive offerings from Theravada Buddhists are believed to have an active preference for flesh offerings, requiring meat, or even animal sacrifice, and some have a preference for alcohol. Human sacrifice in Cambodia was recorded as late as 1877, but has become replaced with the sacrifice of bulls (Harris 2005: 54–55). Reform movements have repeatedly focused on ending Buddhist participation in blood sacrifice to the gods, aware of the contradictions with Buddhist doctrine and the criticism of sacrifice found in the Pali Canon. In healing/rebalancing treatments in Tai and Lao culture (see later text), the spirits, both the bad type that sometimes possess the body and cause illness, and the positive spirits necessary to maintain health, may also be partial to similar foods that humans like, so meat- and fish-based foods may be used to entice them to enter or leave the body of the person being treated, as appropriate (Eberhardt 2006: 35).

With meat-eating forming such a part of the human, divine, and spirit diets, how do Theravada Buddhists in general deal with the fact that not to kill is the first of the five precepts and dealing in meat is one of the five wrong livelihoods? Different communities deal with it in different ways. In Tai-Lao communities, great emphasis is placed on the dangers of breaking a vow. Therefore, rather than take all five precepts all the time, individuals might only take a few of them, or only take them for a limited time (Terwiel 1975/2012: 196). For example, a farmer who knows he is to plough a field later in the day and will inevitably kill at least insects might not take that precept when attending the temple earlier in the day or might take it for a limited time. In Shan Buddhism, people only give up hunting, rearing animals for slaughter, and killing animals once they have taken on the role of being a "temple-sleeper" (Eberhardt 2006: 156), a senior member of the community usually aged over 45 who undertakes periods of staying at the monastery whilst observing the eight precepts. When they decide to do this, younger members of the family have agreed to take over those aspects of the farming that involve killing (Eberhardt 2006: 158). In Cambodia, Buddhists commonly recite a prayer over the animal as they kill it, wishing for its better rebirth, for example a wish that the duck should be reborn as a heavenly *haṃsa* (a divine goose or swan). Smaller animals are sometimes given to younger children to kill, since they are regarded as being less responsible for their actions (Harris 2005: 179).

In some communities, butchery, especially of large animals, is left to non-Buddhists, such as Muslims, whose religion does not include such prohibitions. In Thailand, this has been formalized in that all slaughterhouses must by law use Muslim halal slaughter methods. Thus, the avoidance of the act of killing by Buddhists in fact leads to greater suffering for animals since halal slaughter does not use the stunning method generally regarded as more humane in international discussion on enhancing slaughterhouse practice.

The avoidance of large-animal killing is not the only "good" Buddhist behavior in relation to animals that may contribute to animal harm. A traditional merit-making activity practiced throughout Buddhism, including Theravada, is the ritualized buying of birds, fish, or animals to release them, rather than kill them (Shiu and Stokes 2008). This may relate also to a long-standing practice of giving people freedom as a meritorious act – from the Emperor Asoka giving the condemned enough time to make merit, to the releasing of slaves so that they might be ordained. It is now generally undertaken as a longevity practice. Ironically the practice of releasing animals has created a market in livestock being trapped or bred for this purpose: stalls selling appropriate caged livestock for release used to be found outside important temples, such as in the stalls that appear in the afternoons outside the Silver Pagoda next to the royal palace in Phnom Penh, or the royal temple Wat Phra Kaew ("the Emerald Buddha" temple) in Bangkok. It can also adversely affect biodiversity and so has been banned in Singapore (Shiu and Stokes 2008). Singaporeans are now among those who visit the royal cattle release project in Pathumthani, an hour's drive from Bangkok in Thailand, a highly organized redistribution of healthy cattle to poor farmers run by one of Thailand's meat-producing companies (Crosby and Choompolpaisal fieldwork 2013). George Orwell, who spent five years in the British colonial police in Burma, refers to this practice cynically in his novel critical of British rule in Burma, *Burmese Days*, in which the wife of the corrupt Burmese official Ko Po Kyin pleads with him to refrain from so much evil. Ko Po Pyin has already consoled himself with a plan to build pagodas later in life to make up for his bad deeds (in fact he dies before managing to do this) and then tells his wife to mind her own business. At that she requests that, if he will not desist from evil, then he should at least make more merit:

> Well, I do not know. I am your wife and have always obeyed you. But at least it is never too soon to acquire merit. Strive to acquire more merit, Ko Po Kyin! Will you not, for instance, buy some live fish and set them free in the river? One can acquire much merit in that way. Also, this morning when the priests came for their rice they told me that there are two new priests at the monastery, and they are hungry. Will you not give them something, Ko Po Kyin? I did not give them anything myself, so that you might acquire the merit of doing it. (Orwell 1935: Chapter 1)

An interesting aspect of the Buddhist teaching on merit, perhaps inadvertently adverted to by Orwell in this dialogue between corrupt husband and devout wife, is that it indicates the ways in which Buddhist understandings of meritorious activity can motivate not just the selfless but also the selfish person to do good deeds.

Killing fellow humans is a far more serious sin than killing an animal. (Nonetheless, see Harvey (2000: 329–332) on the relatively high number of abortions in some Theravada countries even though authoritative Theravada literature, unlike that of some other forms of Buddhism, places feticide and homicide in the same category (Agostini 2004: 64).) Sometimes, having committed murder or having killed fellow humans during active service as a soldier or policeman is a motivating factor in ordination: although a monk or nun who commits murder is defrocked and disqualified from ordination for life, someone who killed while still a layperson may still become a monk or nun. Khmer Rouge soldiers who later became monks have spoken of doing so as expiation for their roles in the killing during the Democratic Kampuchea period. They cite the story of the serial killer Aṅgulimāla who, according to the Pali Canon, was converted by the Buddha and achieved arhatship in spite of murdering 999 people (Crosby and Long, fieldwork 2012). The issue of how to evaluate killing in the name of protecting others, particularly in Buddhist justification of war, is explored in Chapter 12.

Paritta

At the heart of many Theravada rituals is the chanting of *paritta*. *Paritta* is a Pali word meaning "protection" that refers to a type of text that is recited to protect against misfortune and ensure prosperity. *Paritta* recitation and ceremonies are at the heart of many Theravada Buddhist festivals and rituals. The use of protective texts in this way is authorized in the Pali

Canon. For example, the Peacock *Jātaka* (*Mora Jātaka*) protects against seduction because the peacock in the *Jātaka* was caught on being enticed by the song of the peahen – but only when he forgot to recite the *paritta*. The *Khandha Paritta* teaches the recitation of verses to counter snake bite. The *Aṅgulimāla Sutta*, in which the Buddha advises a former murderer on how to use a truth-statement to save a woman and child from a dangerous delivery during childbirth (see later text), is recited to help ensure safe pregnancy and childbirth.

Paritta texts are mainly extracted from the Pali Canon and are therefore regarded as the word of the Buddha (*buddhavacana*). Important canonical *paritta* texts include the *Peacock Jātaka*, the *Aṅgulimāla sutta*, the ***Mettā sutta***, and the *Maṅgala sutta*. The *Khuddakapāṭha* "minor recitations," one of the later books within the fifth division of the *Sutta Piṭaka*, includes a number of *paritta* texts, which confirms that whether or not *paritta* was in fact taught by the Buddha, it had become a standard part of Theravada practice relatively early, during the centuries in which the Pali Canon was formed. Each country or region has a standard *paritta* collection. For example, in Sri Lanka, the most popular book of *paritta* texts is the *Catubhāṇavāra*, "4 recitations," which contains 29 *suttas* for *paritta* chanting. A *bhāṇavāra* is a "recitation" of a specific length, equivalent to 250 verses. We know that this particular collection goes back at least as far as the early tenth century, as it is mentioned in an inscription in the ancient capital Anuradhapura dated to the reign of King Kassapa IV. The inscription indicates the importance of *paritta*, for it states that only men who know the text may be ordained as monks (Perera 2000: v). Although most *paritta* texts are canonical, there are some composed relatively recently: Saraṇaṃkara, the great reformist monk of eighteenth-century Sri Lanka, composed *paritta* that were included in the litanies used for devotion to the Buddha in preparation for meditation practice (personal communication Amal Gunasena. See Chapter 2).

One of the most important noncanonical *paritta* is a short text of around 14 verses called the *Jinapañjara gāthā* "Verses on the Victor's Amour," which names different Buddhas, enlightened disciples of the Buddha (*arhats*), and canonical *paritta* texts as located on different parts of the body. Found throughout the Theravada world, it is the most well-known and used protective text in Thailand, and possibly of northern Thai origin. It is advocated by the present Supreme Patriarch, learnt by people from all strata of society and backgrounds, ubiquitous as both an aural and visual text, including in the form of protective diagrams (*yantras*) (McDaniel 2011: 77–85).

In Burma, there is a set of 11 *paritta* recited by individuals in the context of Buddha worship or as part of a vow to recite the *paritta* a certain number of times. To keep count when chanting people use a "rosary," a string of beads of a significant number, such as 108. *Paritta* are not the only texts chanted for protection. The qualities of the Buddha, Dhamma, and Sangha in the form of the *itipisogāthā* (see earlier text) is a common recitation throughout the Theravada world. In Burma, the 24 conditions explained in the seventh book of the *Abhidhamma Piṭaka* are also recited in this way (see Chapter 7).

Paritta chanting can vary from a brief statement to a recitation lasting seven days and nights. The following *paritta* verse taken from the noncanonical *Mahājayamaṅgalagāthā* (Langer 2012: 35), found in standard Sri Lankan *paritta* books, is commonly used by either monks or laypeople, for example when they are tying *paritta* string (string empowered in a *paritta* ceremony) around the wrist of another:

> *sabb'itiyo vivajjantu, sabbarogo vinassatu,*
> *mā te bhavat'antarāyo, sukhī dīghāyuko bhava.*
> May all calamities be averted, all disease perish.
> May no obstacle confront you. Be happy and long-lived.

Seven-day *paritta* chanting is usually undertaken by monks (and increasingly nuns). The performance can be continuous or broken up into 12-hour blocks. Loudspeaker systems are sometimes set up so even those unable to attend the temple may benefit from the sound broadcast around the neighborhood throughout the night. To sustain the chanting for this length of time, the monks join in the chanting on rotation. They are kept refreshed with drinks and whatever other nourishment is counted as "medicine." (Certain types of sweets or drinks, depending on the region, are regarded as "medicine" and can be consumed without breaking the rule not to eat after noon.)

The chanting of *paritta* on more formal occasions is performed in a temporary enclosure, typically made from long banana leaves with other greenery, either square, rectangular, or octagonal. In Sri Lanka, a white canopy covers the top of the enclosure. Inside this there may be an "*indrakīla*," a sacrificial post tied between the two chairs placed at the center of the enclosure (de Silva 1991: 143), reflecting the incorporation of features from the broader religious milieu in which Buddhism developed. Other items inside the enclosure include offerings, a palm leaf manuscript of the *paritta* (even if the monks use printed copies), and a Buddha relic. More chairs are packed tightly inside the enclosure for the monks joining in the chanting. Before the *paritta* ceremony starts, the gods are invited to attend. Sometimes this is done by delivering to the nearby shrines letters addressed to the various deities important in that community.

In addition to the items and people necessary for the performance of the ceremony, items to be empowered through the sound of the *paritta* are also placed inside the enclosure or close to it. The main items blessed are water, string, and, in some regions, sand. People may also place their personal items that they want empowered, such as household Buddha images and amulets. The string is tied from the center of the enclosure to touch the various sacred objects and the objects for blessing and then continues out into the temple compound to the people listening to the *paritta*. They may hold on to the string while listening. Those attending the ceremony find the overall effect of the canopy of greenery, the string, the lights strung up in the night around the canopy, and the sight and sound of the monks chanting aesthetically highly pleasing. Older people who do not have to go to work the next morning are more likely to be able to attend the full ceremony than workers who usually just drop in for a short time. Grandchildren attending with their grandparents, falling asleep in their laps while the adults do their best to stay awake is a familiar scene. Childhood memories of this calm environment and the happy atmosphere at the temple sometimes draw people back to attending the temple later in life.

Most *paritta* ceremonies culminate with *dāna*, the formal feeding of the monks who performed the chanting. At the end of the ceremony, the merit accrued is formally dedicated. Then the string is cut up and distributed. It can be tied onto objects to bless them (e.g., around the steering wheel of a new car), or around people's wrists either to be left on until it breaks or to be cut off after a period of seven days. String around wrists can be a sign of having attended a *paritta* ceremony or having visited a monk and received it as a blessing. However, it is also used in "calling the spirits" ceremonies in Tai-Lao religious culture (see later text) and so is a practice that extends beyond Buddhism in some regions. The water blessed during the *paritta* ceremony can be drunk or used to bless other items. The sand is scattered on the rooftops or around the grounds of the homes of those who attended.

There are many occasions on which a *paritta* ceremony may be conducted or a recitation of *paritta* incorporated into another type of ceremony: it forms part of the main events in the annual festival calendar; it is a component of Buddha consecration ceremonies, funerals, death anniversaries; it may be used at the opening of a new business to inaugurate any new secular or religious building, or a new item, particularly an expensive one such as a car or motorbike; it is also used to varying degrees in exorcism and healing. *Paritta* harnesses the power of the sacred texts and monks and may be performed before other rituals at which monks do not officiate or even attend. For example, Theravada monks are not usually involved in weddings (although exceptions are found, particularly in adapting to expectations of converts in the West). Traditionally it is inauspicious for monks to attend weddings because they are associated with the renunciation of lay life and with death and funerals. Nonetheless, monks may be invited to chant *paritta* in advance of the wedding to ensure that all proceeds well.

Some social anthropological studies of Theravada have identified *paritta* as an apotropaic ("magically protective") ritual that goes against the doctrine of *kamma*, that is, the teaching that each individual's experience is based on their earlier actions in this or former lifetimes. This interpretation sees it as an accommodation of Buddhism to the needs of dealing with everyday life, a need supplied by most religions regardless of their core teachings. The practice of *paritta* therefore continues the use of the types of ritual, which is seemingly rejected in such texts as the *Sigālovāda Sutta* (see Chapter 1). In other words, early Buddhism appears from the perspective of some texts to eschew ritual and focus on personal conduct. On the other hand, most Theravada Buddhists use ritual, and this use sometimes also finds authority in Pali canonical texts as in the case of *paritta* rituals.

Nicola Tannenbaum has suggested that trying to interpret the ritual practices of Buddhists in terms of Buddhist doctrine is an inappropriate approach and proposes that one could rather see the entire range of practices found among Theravada Buddhists in terms of power and protection. Her study is of the Shan of northern Thailand, but it applies well to other Theravada groups. Power may be built up through various means including in the practice of restraint (in the Buddhist aspect through monastic vows, following the eight precepts or keeping other vows) and this offers a potential source of protection which people bestow or seek out.

From the Buddhist perspective, however, *paritta* is efficacious as a speech act, the use of which is authorized by the Buddha in the Pali Canon. This understanding of "right speech" goes beyond the fourth precept, not to lie, and other teachings on the importance of harmonious speech and avoiding harsh and idle speech. The efficacy of *paritta* draws on various concepts. Firstly, the content of the texts recited are comprehensible to gods and spirits (Pali being the universal *lingua franca*, see Chapter 3) and so converts potentially malevolent forces who might have otherwise disrupted the lives of those attending the ceremony, but who now adopt the Buddhist, compassionate attitude. Secondly, the power of the Buddha, Dhamma and Sangha are efficacious in dealing with aspects of *saṃsāra* and may be harnessed for specific purposes and also transferred into material objects. Thirdly, there is a belief that truth statements are efficacious in their own right (Kong 2012).

This belief in the efficacy and protective power of truth is an ancient belief, one that underlies the legal process of "trial by ordeal" found in many cultures around the world. In trial by ordeal, if someone truthfully declares they are innocent of a crime the truth of their statement will protect them from the punishment for that crime, such that fire, for example, will not burn them. The theme recurs in the different forms of Hinduism that form the background to the development of Buddhism, attested to in the **Vedas**, Upaniṣads, Purāṇas, and other important Hindu religious literature, as well as in narrative texts of the Pali Canon such as the *Vimāna Vatthu*, "*Vimāna Stories*" (Masefield 1989). In Buddhism, the importance of truth statements thus reflects the emphasis on acts of body, *speech*, and mind in the interpretation of the doctrine of *kamma* and the inclusion of right speech in the eightfold path. The power of such truth statements may be harnessed to benefit others. For example, the verses of the *Aṅgulimāla Sutta* are regarded as particularly beneficial *paritta* for women in childbirth. In this *sutta*, the serial killer Aṅgulimāla "Finger-Necklace," who has murdered 999 people, is converted by the Buddha and, ordained as a monk, gains enlightenment. He helps a pregnant woman who is having a difficult delivery by using the following truth statement, "Sister, since I was born with the noble birth, I do not recall that I have ever intentionally deprived a living being of life. By this truth, may you be well and may your infant be well" (Ñyāṇamoli and Bodhi 1995/2001: 714). Even though Aṅgulimāla was a murderer, his statement is true because he has harmed no one since his "new birth" as a monk in the Sangha. The truth statement allows the women a safe delivery and, as a result of this story, the verses of this *paritta* continue to be recited throughout the Theravada world to ward off harm in a number of contexts, including childbirth. Although the content of truth statements is usually significant, the idea that truth, regardless of the nature of the truth, is efficacious, is seen in a spoof on truth-statements in *Jātaka* 354. A boy had died and when other efforts to revive him fail, the three main characters of the story make three rather unexpected truth statements: the sage admits that he has long since regretted becoming a monk; the boy's father admits that he resents feeding monks and does it is only because it is family tradition; the boy's mother admits that she has no feelings for her husband and has remained faithful only because women in her family are not in the habit of taking on lovers. Yet these statements, being true, work and the boy is restored to life (Crosby 2012: 87, note 19). A story of *paritta* saving a child from death is also found in the commentary to the *Dhammapada*. *(Dhammapada Verse* 109 *āyuvaḍḍhanakumara Vatthu*. http://www.tipitaka.net/tipitaka/dhp/verseload.php?verse=109*)*.

In contrast to such stories of truth statements restoring life found in the commentarial literature is the more well-known story of the distraught mother Kisā Gotamī who brings her dead child to the Buddha asking him to bring the child back to life. The Buddha agrees to do so if the woman can bring him a cup full of mustard seed, one taken from each household where there has been no experience of death. Of course, the woman is unable to find any household unaffected by death, which brings her to a realization of impermanence and the inevitability of death. She then becomes a nun and achieves arhatship, and her story is recorded in the *Therīgāthā* (see Chapter 9).

Merit transference and commemorating the dead

Another practice critiqued by observers as going against the doctrine of *kamma* is the practice of transferring merit, such that living beings, especially the recently deceased, may benefit from the meritorious actions performed by others. In giving to monks in the name of the intended beneficiary, there is a continuity in the ritual process of sponsoring sacrifice found in Vedic Hinduism and local religious practice. Just as the brahmin priest performs rituals on behalf of the sponsor, who either reaps the benefits in this or the next life or whose ancestors benefit, so monks, in receiving gifts, act as the priest through whom the sacrifice is made, to the benefit of the donor or their deceased relatives. In practice, often after someone's death, relatives provide food through both means: leaving it out for the deceased, and by making offerings to monks. Similarly, in the annual fête of the ancestors (*pchum ben*, Khmer) in Cambodia, people feed monks and make offerings of rice balls directly to the ancestors in fields by throwing the rice balls into the air. The practice of making offerings to the ancestors is not found among Buddhists in Sri Lanka, but is pervasive in Southeast Asian religion, in common with Chinese religion, and not specific to Buddhists. Yet among Buddhists, the close association between feeding deceased relatives and donating to monks, and the way in which the Buddhist Sangha has negotiated its position as intermediary, is seen in the following story in praise of alms-giving recounted in a sermon by a Shan monk in northern Thailand as part of a death-commemoration:

> Once there was a very wealthy man who had a son ... When the child died unexpectedly the father was heartbroken. He asked his servant to take a bowl of rice for his son's spirit to eat on the other side of a stream that ran next to their house. ... One day the stream flooded and [the servant] was unable to cross... While he was wondering what to do, he saw a line of monks with alms bowls approaching along the road. [So the servant, rather than waste the food, offered it to the monks.]...That night the father had a dream. His dead son appeared to him and said, "Father! Don't you love me? I haven't received any rice from you for a long time and have been very hungry. Today is the first day you gave me anything to eat!" (Eberhardt 2006: 51–52)

In fact, the transference of merit, like *paritta*, is authorized in the Pali Canon. The *Petavatthu*, "Stories of the Departed," is dedicated to stories of departed spirits who, on account of previous bad deeds, are trapped as ghosts that haunt the living and who can only be released by a living person making offerings to the Sangha in their name. The *Petavatthu* is a book of the *Khuddaka Nikāya*, the fifth subdivision of the *Sutta Piṭaka* of the Pali Canon (see Chapter 3). From a doctrinal perspective, the transference of merit draws on similar ideas found in explanations of *paritta*. It is also explained by the fifth of the ten meritorious actions, "rejoicing in merit." When the departed spirit witnesses the good action being done in his/her name, he/she rejoices in the merit. The mental action is then transformative – a good action in itself, but also setting off a chain of changes in mental state that then affect the state of rebirth. The departed spirit as a result may move on from its unfortunate rebirth to a more fortunate one. Monks in Burma, often questioned about the benefits from merit-transference, explain that it works only for those in the *peta* realm, because those in hells, animal realm, human realm, and *deva* planes cannot reap the benefits as they will be unaware that such an act is being done for them. The canonical authority the monks refer to for this practice is the *Jāṇussoṇī Sutta* in the *Aṅguttara Nikāya*.

The main occasions for transferring merit to the deceased are in the days immediately after their death, including the funeral, the first anniversary of their death and, in many Theravada cultures, in the annual festival of commemoration of ancestors. In Cambodia, this annual festival, called Pchum Ben, mentioned earlier, is the biggest festival in the annual cycle, lasting 15 days and taking place in October or November, depending on the lunar calendar. During this period, *peta*, departed spirits, are thought to be particularly receptive to offerings as at this time each year the gates to hell are opened by Yama, the god of the afterlife.

Funerals usually take place within a few days of death, although in the case of high-status monks and member of the royal family, for example, funeral may take place even months later. Funerals are preceded by various merit-making activities. Whereas other rituals in the lifecycle of a Theravada Buddhist are usually performed by other types of priest or just by senior members of the community, monks are the main officiants at funerals and still take center stage when the labor is shared with other types of priest.

While theoretically rebirth is instantaneous, there are a variety of beliefs about this. In Sri Lanka, it is thought that rebirth usually takes place after seven days, making the initial week after death the most important merit-making period. Among the Shan and some Burmese there is a belief in the 49-day intermediate period, like that found in Tibetan Buddhism: this suggests that historically Shan and Burmese Buddhism may also have been influenced by the Sarvāstivāda Buddhism of north India (Jotika Khur-Yearn, personal communication). This possibility is also suggested by a number of other interesting variations in the Buddhism of northern Burma and northern Thailand, such as the pervasive cults of the monk Gavāṃpati and the monk/novice Upagupta (Strong 1992: 175–182). Gavāṃpati is regarded as having been a contemporary of the Buddha who brought Buddhism to Southeast Asia in a story that acts as an alternative to the story linking the arrival of Buddhism with Soṇa and Uttara in the time of Asoka. Upagupta is regarded as a contemporary of Asoka's missionaries, in Southeast Asia regarded as either the offspring of an ascetic and a fish or of the Buddha and a *nāgī*, a mythical serpent, which swallowed the semen the Buddha ejaculated into a stream (Strong 1992: 16, 175–182). He is widely associated with magical powers as indicated in the popular depiction of him eating from his alms bowl while looking up the sky – he is ensuring that the sun stays below the zenith so that he can continue eating without breaking the rule about not eating after afternoon.

This association of monks with funerals reflects the fundamental Buddhist teachings on impermanence (Williams and Ladwig 2012: 2–3), teachings drawn on in the texts recited on these occasions. Canonical texts recalling the three characteristics of all phenomena – impermanence, suffering, and no-self (*anicca*, *dukkha*, *anattā*) – and the fact that all beings will die from the litany of all Theravada funerals. *Paritta* may also be recited. In Tai-Lao funerals, *Abhidhamma* texts that deal with impermanence and causality are chanted. Usually the texts selected are excerpts from the first and last or from all seven of the books of the *Abhidhamma Piṭaka*, or from *Abhidhamma* summaries. In addition to the usual offerings of food to monks, it is common for monks to receive a robe from the deceased, called a "rag robe" *paṃsukūla*. Although these days new robes are used, placed on the coffin and then removed by monks, the term refers to an ascetic practice described in the Pali Canon in which monks wear rag robes taken from corpses (Langer 2012).

Gati: Places of rebirth in Buddhist cosmology

Death rituals and merit-transference focus on fears that the recently deceased may be suffering either because of bad deeds they may have committed or because they experienced a sudden, violent, or premature death. In the latter case, the departed spirit may haunt the living, causing them harm, and so additional ritual precautions are taken to deal with such deaths. People worry that their relative may be a *peta* or wandering spirit (a ***phī*** in Tai-Lao cultures), or an animal, or may have entered one of the eight major hells of Buddhist cosmology. When people are regarded as having died a good death or as being spiritually advanced, they are believed to have been reborn in one of the good rebirths, either in one of the Buddhist heavens, or as a human being. Because they made merit with other family members and are likely to have retained an interest in them after death, deceased members of a community are likely to be reborn within that same community. It is common to interpret current relationships and the characters of young children in terms of past lifetimes, and to identify children as specific deceased members of the community reborn. In Cambodia, this understanding of children as having previously belonged to other mothers, and therefore taking a while to attach to their mothers in this life, lies behind the traditional practice of mothers interpreting any signs of discomfort in their newborn as possible interference from the mother in its previous lifetime. They rush outside to yell curses at the previous lifetime mother, thereby scaring her away and keeping the new baby safely with them.

An individual's stay in any of these potential realms of existence may last a short time or an incalculably long time but will eventually come to an end as the *kamma* that put them there is exhausted. Scenes of hell are popularly depicted in temple murals, and to some extent reflect the known torture methods of the period in which they were painted, including the present day: some recent Cambodian wall paintings of hells are immediately recognizable as scenes from the "killing fields" of the Khmer Rouge.

In total there are four different planes of existence in Buddhist cosmology. The lowest is the woeful plane, which includes the hells, *peta*-realm and animal realm and also the realm of the antigods, the *asura*, which is mentioned in canonical texts but features less in popular belief. Above this is the fortunate plane, which includes the human realm and lowest three heavens. These first two planes of the fortunate realms of rebirth are both within the "sphere of sensual form." Above this are a series of further heavens that make up the third sphere of "non-sensual form" and finally the sphere of no-form (Na Rangsi 1976: 32ff.). It is generally believed that it is possible to visit hells and other planes of existence through meditation.

Depictions of heavens, the human realm centered around Mount Meru and hells are omnipresent in the art and architecture of the Theravada world. Depictions of Mount Meru range from the enduring 10 meter high representation carved into the rock face at the remote Po-win-daung cave complex in the Lower Chindwin District of Burma to the temporary art of Burmese funerals for important monks, at which the catafalque bearing the coffin is topped by a giant paper or bamboo model of the mountain (Herbert 2002: 77) and the sand models and temporary mazes with Meru at the center in Cambodia. Hell scenes adorn manuscripts and temple walls and are depicted in films. The eight principal hells include the "screaming hell," *roruva*, where culprits are immersed in fire for having spoken ill of the Dhamma, been miserly or committed adultery; the "scalding hell," *tapana*, where beings are transfixed by heated stakes, and the "unremitting hell," *avīci*, the lowest and most commonly depicted hell, in which beings are boiled in a flaming cauldron of oil (Herbert 2002: 90–91). A common depiction of the punishment for adulterers is being impaled on trees of thorns. Such hell scenes also adorn the manuscripts and comics of the story of Phra Malai, the monk who visits the different realms of heaven and hell to explain the workings of *kama*, traditionally retold at Thai funerals (Brereton 1995: 16). (For details of correlations between specific bad actions and rebirth in specific hells, see Na Rangsi 1976: 32ff.) A recent extension of the enthusiasm for hells scenes is the building of hell theme parks depicting all the tortures and denizens of the different layers of hell in several places in Thailand (McDaniel 2011: 122).

"Non-Buddhist" religious and ritual practice

Within all Theravada communities, religious practices and festivals can be found that are not specific to Buddhism, with priests and other kinds of ritual specialists who are not Buddhist monks performing rituals and healing or acting as mediums. Community-wide festivals, such as harvest festivals and New Year celebrations, may or may not involve Buddhist monks, temples, or themes. Of the lifecycle rituals, birth rituals, naming ceremonies, first-feeding rituals,

rituals for the commencement of education or training, girls' coming of age ceremonies and marriage are usually conducted without Buddhist monks, though monks might be asked to perform *paritta* or be consulted about possible auspicious names for new-born babies. Some protective rituals such as lower-body tattooing are also usually done by lay tattooists, even though some tattooists are monks, who will tattoo the upper body (Terwiel 1975 / 2012: 84, 92).

There are usually different regional, national, and local deities and spirits, as well as planetary and tutelary deities in the Theravada pantheon in any given community. Some are recent additions to the pantheon, some attended Buddhism's arrival, and others predated it. The Indic gods spread with Buddhism and so are found across the Theravada world. Deities and spirits receive offerings and present threat or protection depending on how they are treated. Mediums may become possessed by them and allow messages to pass between the spirit realms and human realm. Traditional medicine often combines a range of herbal medicine with exorcism or the restoration of the body's various spirits. Buddhist practices may or may not feature in such medicine. A common practice in Tai-Lao communities is the dispelling of dangerous spirits (*phī* in several Tai-Lao languages) through exorcism from the body or "beating the boundaries" of a community; and the calling of "spirits" (*khwan* in several Tai-Lao languages) to return to the body. When someone undergoes a difficult experience or is ill, it is believed that one or more of the 32 spirits associated with the body has quit the body and needs to be coaxed into returning (Eberhardt 2006: 32–43). In Cambodia, there are 19 such spirits (***praling*** in Khmer) connected with the body and an individual's well-being (Harris 2005: 59). Non-Buddhist communities also use these practices, which tells us that they preceded the spread of Buddhism to the region.

Though dismissed by some modernists, and unfamiliar to most Western converts, astrology is also very important in traditional Theravada communities. It may affect decisions about when to conduct a ceremony, when to begin an undertaking, or who suitable marriage partners might be. Ordination into the Sangha is a traditional a way of having a new "birth" to overcome an inauspicious birth chart. Various forms of numerology are also found: in Burma, decisions may be made on the basis of auspicious and inauspicious numbers; in mainland Southeast Asia, the day of one's birth may influence life-decisions and the selection of a child's name or the preceptor's selection of a new monk or nun's ordination name. Such skills as spirit-calling, astrology, healing, numerology, and even martial arts were among the subjects traditionally taught in Buddhist temples before a combination of nonmonastic state education, the secularization of monastic education, and the reform of Buddhist education to a more essentialized core radically altered the syllabus taught within the monastic system (Dhammasami 2004: 270).

Some of the practices described earlier are commented on as un-Buddhist, either by reformers who develop an essentialized view of Buddhism or by scholars mindful of such Buddhist doctrines as self-reliance and no-self. Nonetheless, Buddhism seems to have been intermingled in this way from its earliest origins. Part of its success in being adopted so widely seems to be down to its capacity for accommodating those local religious expressions that allow it to dominate the soteriological realm (i.e., teachings connected with the ultimate goal of escaping *nibbāna*) and hold a high, if not the highest, position in the overall hierarchy. This hierarchy is reflected in temple layout, with shrines to the broader spiritual pantheon usually subordinated visually, placed in peripheral and / or lower locations than the shrine to the Buddha and the other core Buddhist figures. Some of these spirits, such as *phī* (Tai languages) and some *nat* (Burmese), may have little iconic representation, being relatively uninstitutionalized (Holt 2009: 17–19). The popularity of Buddhist teachers including monks and nuns may reflect their reputation for these aspects of religion (McDaniel 2011: 65). The process of adapting to new religious space, events, and ideas constantly continues. Wei-yi Cheng reports on a recent development in

Taiwan, where in the past two decades Theravada has gained some popularity: Theravada Buddhist monks from Sri Lanka, which does not have an annual fête of the ancestors (unlike most Southeast Asian communities), perform the traditional Taiwanese ghost festival to accommodate the religious needs of their local congregation (Cheng 2012). The notion of the body containing different spirits, or of there being an entity that continues on death, does not contradict Buddhist doctrine of no-self, since the no-self doctrine is specifically rejecting the notion of a permanent, unchanging self, rather than the possibility of continuity from one existing state to another. However, the cult of ancestors is a more ambiguous case if one pursues the path of seeking absolute consistency across religious practice. Throughout much of mainland Southeast Asia, alongside the understanding that one's deceased relatives will have been reborn (and even identified among the new arrivals in a community) either immediately or within 7 or 49 days, and in contrast to the Burmese teaching about hungry ghosts mentioned earlier, offerings are given on the family shrine or at the annual festival to ancestors who are treated as in some way accessible within the ancestral lineage and needful of offerings.

Summary

This chapter explored what it means to be a good Buddhist, focusing on lay practice that comes under the "good conduct" (*sīla*) aspect of the eightfold path, that is, right speech, right action, and right livelihood. The precepts and ten wholesome actions (*kusala*) and how these are understood in practice were summarized, then specific aspects examined in more detail. We looked at how Buddhists in Theravada countries accommodate the practicalities of daily life with such religious goals. We noted how in the twentieth century there was a shift in emphasis from personal virtuous conduct toward a more utilitarian approach on the part of both laypeople and monks, a development collectively termed "Engaged Buddhism." To some extent, the understanding of Buddhist monks and practice as removed from issues of social welfare and the environment may be the result of an over-essentializing of what it means to be Buddhist in the modern period. On the other hand, some popular practices, such as animal release, may be considered harmful to the animals they are meant to benefit, if one considers the practice from a this-life perspective.

The ritual practices at the heart of Theravada religiosity include merit-making, merit-transference, protective rituals, and the feeding of ancestors. Buddhist practices vary regionally, in part in line with other religious aspects within the host culture. In examining ritual, we see how some practices that have been regarded as antithetical to Buddhism may be understood in relation to specific Buddhist understandings of the nature of intention, consciousness, speech, truth, and the power of Buddha, Dhamma, and Sangha.

References

Agostini, Guilio. (2004). 'Buddhist Sources on Feticide as Distinct from Homicide', *Journal of the International Association of Buddhist Studies* 27.1: 63–95.

Bizot, François. (1976). *Le figuier à cinq branches*. Recherches sur le bouddhisme khmer I, PEFEO CVII. Paris: l'École Française d'Extrême-Orient.

Bond, George. (1988). *The Buddhist Revival in Sri Lanka: Religious Tradition, Reinterpretation and Response*. Columbia: University of Carolina Press.
Brereton, Bonnie Pacala. (1995). *Thai Tellings of Phra Malai: Texts and Rituals Concerning a Popular Buddhist Saint*. Tempe: Arizona State University Press.
Cheng, Wei Yi. (2012). 'Theravadizing Ghost Festival in Taiwan', *Contemporary Buddhism* 13.2: 281–299.
Collins, Steven. (1982). *Selfless Persons. Imagery and Thought in Theravāda Buddhism*. Cambridge: Cambridge University Press.
Crosby, Kate. (2000). Tantric Theravada: A Bibliographic Essay on the Writings of François Bizot and Other Literature on the *Yogāvacara* Tradition', *Contemporary Buddhism* 1.2: 141–198.
Crosby, Kate. (May 2008). 'Karma, Social Collapse or Geophysics? Interpretations of Suffering Among Sri Lankan Buddhist in the Immediate Aftermath of the 2004 Asian Tsunami', *Contemporary Buddhism*, 9.1: 53–76.
Crosby, Kate. (2012). 'The Inheritance of Rahula: Abandoned Child, Boy Monk, Ideal Son and Trainee' in Vanessa Sasson (ed.), *Little Buddhas: Children and Childhoods in Buddhist Texts and Traditions*. Oxford: Oxford University Press, 97–123.
Darlington, Susan M. (1998). 'The ordination of a tree: The Buddhist ecology movement in Thailand', *Ethnology* 37, 1: 1–15.
Dhammasami, Khammai. (2004). 'Between Idealism and Pragmatism – A Study of Monastic Education in Burma and Thailand from the Seventeenth Century to the Present'. DPhil thesis, University of Oxford.
Dhammasami, Khammai and Pyi Kyaw. (2012). 'The Centennial Commemorative Inscription of the Most Venerable Mingun Tipiṭakadhara Sayadaw U Vicittasārābhivaṃsa'. To be inscribed at Dhammanāda Pariyatti Sarthintike, Mingun Village.
Eberhardt, Nancy. (2006). *Imagining the Course of Life. Self-Transformation in a Shan Buddhist Community*. Honolulu: University of Hawai'i Press.
Gabaude, Louis. (1979). *Les Cetiya de sable au Laos et au Thaïlande*. Paris: l'École française d'Extrême-Orient.
Gombrich, Richard and Gananath Obeyesekere. (1988). *Buddhism Transformed: Religious Change in Sri Lanka*. Princeton: Princeton University Press.
Guthrie, Elizabeth. (2004). 'A Study of the History and Cult of the Buddhist Earth Deity in Mainland Southeast Asia'. PhD thesis, University of Canterbury, Christchurch.
Harris, Ian. (2005). *Cambodian Buddhism. History and Practice*. Honolulu: University of Hawai'i Press. Reprint, Chiang Mai: Silkworm 2006.
Harvey, Peter. (2000). *An Introduction to Buddhist Ethics*. Cambridge: Cambridge University Press.
Herbert, Patricia. (2002). 'Burmese Cosmological Manuscripts', in Alexandra Green and T. Richard Blurton (eds.), *Burma Art and Archaeology*. London: The British Museum Press, 77–97.
Holt, John Clifford. (2009). *Spirits of the Place. Buddhism and Lao Religious Culture*. Honolulu: University of Hawai'i Press.
Kawanami, Hiroko. (1996). *Keepers of the Faith: Nuns of the Sagaing Hills*. London: Royal Anthropological Institute. Order No. RAI-200.341.
Kent, Alexandra. (2008). 'Peace, Power and Pagodas in Present-Day Cambodia', *Contemporary Buddhism* 9.1: 77–97
Kieschnick, John. (2005). 'Buddhist Vegetarianism in China' in Roel Sterckx (ed.), *Of Tripod and Palate. Food, Politics, and Religion in Traditional China*. New York: Palgrave Macmillan.
Kong, Choy Fah. (2012). *Saccakiriyā. The Belief in the Power of True Speech in Theravāda Buddhist Tradition*. Singapore: Choy Fah Kong.
Langer, Rita. (2012). 'Chanting as '*bricolage* technique': A Comparison of South and Southeast Asian Funeral Recitation', in P. Williams and P. Ladwig (eds.), *Buddhist Funeral Cultures of Southeast Asia and China*. Cambridge: Cambridge University Press, 21–58.

Litalien, Manuel. (2010). 'Développement social et Régime providentiel en Thaïlande: La Philanthropie religieuse en tant que nouveau Capital démocratique'. PhD thesis, Université du Québec à Montréal (UQAM), Quebec.

Martini, G. 1972. 'Un Jātaka Concernant Le Dernier Repas De Buddha', *Bulletin de l'Ecole Française d'Extrême-Orient* 59: 251–256.

Masefield, Peter. (1980). *Elucidation of the Intrinsic Meaning: So Named the Commentary on the Peta-Stories*. London: The Pali Text Society.

Masefield, Peter. (1989). *Vimana Stories, Translation of the Commentary, with the Verses Embedded*. Oxford: Pali Text Society.

McDaniel, Justin. (2011). *The Lovelorn Ghost & The Magical Monk. Practicing Buddhism in Northern Thailand*. New York: Columbia University Press.

Moore, Elizabeth Howard. (2000). 'Myanmar Religious Practice and Cultural Heritage', *The Journal of South East Asian Studies* 18: 285–300.

Na Rangsi, Sunthorn. (1976). *The Four Planes of Existence in Theravada Buddhism*. Reprinted as The Wheel Publication No. 462. 2006. Kandy: Buddhist Publication Society.

Ñyāṇamoli, Bhikkhu and Bhikkhu Bodhi. (1995/2001). *The Middle Length Discourses of the Buddha: A New Translation of the Majjhima Nikāya*. Boston: Wisdom Publications in association with the Barre Center for Buddhist Studies.

Orwell, George. (1935). *Burmese Days*, 1st edn. London: Victor Gollancz Ltd. Available at www.george-orwell.org (retrieved November 3, 2012).

Perera, G. Ariyapala. (2000). *Buddhist Paritta Chanting Ritual: A Comparative Study of the Buddhist Benedictory Ritual*. Dehiwala: Buddhist Cultural Centre.

Rozenberg, Guillaume. (2010). *Renunciation and Power. The Quest for Sainthood in Contemporary Burma*. Translated from the French by Jessica Hackett. New Haven: Yale University Southeast Asia Studies.

Samuels, Jeffrey. (May 2008). 'Is Merit in the Milk Powder? Pursuing of Puñña in Contemporary Sri Lanka', *Contemporary Buddhism* 9.1: 123–147.

Shiu, Henry, and Leah Stokes. (2008). 'Buddhist Animal Release Practices: Historic, Environmental, Public Health And Economic Concerns', *Contemporary Buddhism: An Interdisciplinary Journal* 9.2: 181–196.

de Silva, Lily. (1991). 'The Paritta Ceremony of Sri Lanka: Its Antiquity and Symbolism' in David Kalupahana (ed.), *Buddhist Thought and Ritual*. New York: Paragon House, 139–150.

Strong, John S. (1992). *The Legend and Cult of Upagupta. Sanskrit Buddhism in North India and Southeast Asia*. Princeton: Princeton University Press.

Strong, John S. (2012). 'Explicating the Buddha's Final Illness in the Context of his Other Ailments: The Making and Unmaking of Some Jātaka Tales', *Buddhist Studies Review* 29: 17–33.

Tannenbaum, Nicola. (2000). 'Protest, Tree Ordination, and the Changing Context of Political Ritual', *Ethnology* 39.2:109–127.

Terwiel, B.J. (1975 [2012]). *Monks and Magic: An Analysis of Religious Ceremonies in Central Thailand*. Lund/London: Studentlitteratur/Curzon Press, 4th revised edn. Copenhagen: NIAS Press.

Thanissaro, Bhikkhu. (2010). 'Vanijja Sutta: Business (Wrong Livelihood)' (AN 5.177), translated from the Pali. *Access to Insight*, http://www.accesstoinsight.org/tipitaka/an/an05/an05.177.than.html (retrieved November 1, 2012).

Walters, Jonathan S. (2003). 'Communal Karma and Karmic Community in Theravada Buddhist History', in John Clifford Holt, Jacob N. Kinnard, and Jonathan S. Walters. (eds.), *Constituting Communities: Theravada Buddhism and the Religious Cultures of South and Southeast Asia*. Albany: State University of New York Press, 9–39.

Wickremeratne, Swarna. (2006). *Buddha in Sri Lanka. Remembered Yesterdays*. Albany: State University of New York Press.

Williams, Paul and Patrice Ladwig. (eds.). (2012). *Buddhist Funeral Cultures of Southeast Asia and China*. Cambridge: Cambridge University Press.

Further Reading and Watching

Films

Ladwig, Patrice. (2010). *Caring for the Beyond. Two Lao Buddhist Festivals for the Deceased.* http://www.bristol.ac.uk/religion/buddhist-centre/projects/bdr/films/laofilm.html (retrieved June 25, 2013).

Obeyesekere, Gananath (1973). *Kataragama, A god for all seasons.* Order No RAI-200.22

Reading

Crosby, Kate. (May 2008). 'Karma, Social Collapse or Geophysics? Interpretations of suffering among Sri Lankan Buddhist in the immediate aftermath of the 2004 Asian tsunami', *Contemporary Buddhism*, 9.1: 53–76.

Eberhardt, Nancy. (2006). *Imagining the Course of Life. Self-Transformation in a Shan Buddhist Community.* Honolulu: University of Hawai'i Press.

Endo, Toshiichi. (1987). *Dana. The Development of its Concept and Practice.* Colombo: Gunasena.

Harvey, Peter. (2000). *An Introduction to Buddhist Ethics.* Cambridge: Cambridge University Press.

Hayashi, Yukio. (2003). *Practical Buddhism Among the Thai-Lao. Religion in the Making of a Region.* Kyoto Area Studies on Asia. Kyoto: Kyoto University Press.

Kalupahana, David (ed.). (1991). *Buddhist Thought and Ritual.* New York: Paragon House.

McDaniel, Justin. (2011). *The Lovelorn Ghost & The Magical Monk. Practicing Buddhism in Northern Thailand.* New York: Columbia University Press.

Saddhatissa, H. (1970). *Buddhist Ethics: Essence of Buddhism.* New York: George Braziller.

Samuels, Jeffrey. (May 2008). 'Is Merit in the Milk Powder? Pursuing of Puñña in Contemporary Sri Lanka', *Contemporary Buddhism* 9.1: 123–147.

Spiro, Melford. (1971). *Buddhism and Society: A Great Tradition and its Burmese Vicissitudes.* London: George Allen & Unwin.

Sizemore, R.F. and D.K. Swearer (eds.). (1990). *Ethics, Wealth and Salvation: A Study in Buddhist Social Ethics.* Columbia: University of South Carolina.

Terwiel, B.J. (1975 [2012]). *Monks and Magic: An Analysis of Religious Ceremonies in Central Thailand.* Lund/London: Studentlitteratur/Curzon Press. 4th revised edition, Copenhagen: NIAS Press.

Walters, Jonathan S. (2003). 'Communal Karma and Karmic Community in Theravada Buddhist History', in John Clifford Holt, Jacob N. Kinnard, and Jonathan S. Walters. (eds.), *Constituting Communities: Theravada Buddhism and the Religious Cultures of South and Southeast Asia.* Albany: State University of New York Press, 9–39.

6

Meditation

Overview

Buddhist meditation is a technology of transformation. It encompasses a range of guided techniques toward self-mastery and understanding that build on the centrality of our mental states in conditioning all aspects of our experience. In other words, each of the many forms of meditation available applies a specific technique to a specific end, whether that is a simple calming practice to relax the body and mind, or a practice designed to inculcate the realization of one of the key Buddhist truths, such as the truth of impermanence. So while in some forms of Chan/Zen-derived and *dzog chen* meditation there may be such a practice as "just sitting," this is most unlikely in a Theravada context. Theravada has inherited and developed a complex range of techniques, which, while they may or may not attempt to prejudge the experience of the goal to be attained, certainly give detailed direction on how to practice toward that goal. Most Theravada meditation practices are aimed at a range of effects, while other "side effects," such as health benefits, supernatural powers, or disarming of potentially malevolent beings, are also widely ascribed to them. From the earliest period of Buddhism, there was understood to be a correlation between the states attained and different cosmological realms, even to the extent of enabling the practitioner to visit such realms.

Theravada meditation practice varies considerably both in terms of the subject of meditation and in terms of the ways of approaching the technique for meditating on those different subjects. For the former, there is a standard list of forty meditation subjects though more can be found both historically and in the present. In the case of the latter, there is an unknown number, for variety of that kind is harder to detect and quantify. We shall summarize the different subjects and look at some of the main traditions of technique visible in the modern world in this chapter.

In the modern period, meditation has become intrinsically associated with Buddhism, particularly Theravada, such that it is often mistakenly assumed that most Theravada Buddhists meditate. At the same time, meditation has been extracted from the Buddhist framework in order to harness its established benefits for a wide range of applications. It has found its way into the laboratory and into therapy as cognitive scientists and psychologists attempt to apply it to range of mental and psychosomatic health issues. It has also

Theravada Buddhism: Continuity, Diversity, and Identity, First Edition. Kate Crosby.

had applications as the basis of discourse between and across communities, and across other barriers, for example, within prisons as a basis of personal freedom and for generating a sense of shared trust. While we might regard meditation as a world-renouncing activity, at least at the moment of its practice, it has been used as a political tool and suppressed as a political threat.

Pali Terms Used for "Meditation"

A number of Pali terms are translated as "meditation." The word *samādhi* literally means "bringing together," "focus," or "concentration." The word *bhāvanā* is from the verb *bhū* to become, and literally means "causing to become" or "cultivation." The word *jhāna* is well known also in its forms in other languages: Sanskrit *dhyāna*, Chinese "Chan" and Japanese "Zen." While it came to refer to specific Buddhist traditions with a focus on meditation in East Asia, its use in Pali texts may be translated as "meditative state," "meditative absorption," or "altered state of consciousness." It refers to the more refined levels of consciousness achieved through meditation (see later text). The term *kammaṭṭhāna* literally means "place/object of work," referring to the individual meditation practices or subjects. Many postcanonical Pali and vernacular treatises on meditation have the name *kammaṭṭhāna* in the title. Three other Pali terms often associated with meditation are *sati*, *samatha*, and *vipassanā*. The word *sati*, cognate with the verb "to remember," means "mindfulness" or "awareness," referring to the heightened state of nonjudgmental awareness or seeing things from a detached perspective "as they really are." This heightened awareness is a quality generally aimed at, not just in meditation, but because it is the opposite of being heedless or careless. It is just one aspect of some forms of meditation and also a meditation goal in its own right. This term is familiar in Pali from the title of the *locus classicus* for Theravada meditation practice, the *(Mahā)Sati-paṭṭhāna Sutta* (see later text), and is now also familiar through the English term "mindfulness," applied to a range of approaches beyond Buddhism, applying the basic concept of heightened awareness. The term *samatha* means "calming," that is, the calming of physical and mental agitation and activity and the discarding of unwholesome states of mind. The term *vipassanā*, often translated as "insight meditation," means "seeing through," "investigating," or "analysis," referring to the investigation into the true nature of phenomena. Its adaptation in modern therapeutic contexts is usually termed "mindfulness." Originally the two terms *samatha* and *vipassanā* referred to two different effects of meditation in tandem and *samatha* was regarded as a prerequisite for the full development of *vipassanā*. This can be seen from the following categorization of individuals fulfilling the path to liberation from the *Puggalapaññatti*, the fourth book of the *Abhidhamma Piṭaka*, in which someone can succeed in morality and *samatha* without succeeding in insight, but there is no such thing as a person succeeding in insight without also succeeding in morality and *samatha*:

> A man who fulfils the moral laws [*sīla*], but incompletely practises meditation [*samatha*] and the way of insight [*vipassanā*]. A man who fulfils the moral laws, completes the practice of meditation, but incompletely practises the way of insight. A man who fulfils the moral laws, completes the practice of meditation, but completely practises the way of insight. (Law 1922: 10, cited Orsborn 2007: 10)

However, the terms *samatha* and *vipassanā* came to be applied to a classic division of meditation types, at least from Buddhaghosa onward (see later text). They are also now commonly applied to different meditation traditions, especially in relation to systems in or derived from Burma. In Burma, the term *samatha* has also become associated with practices at the more "magical," power-enhancing end of the spectrum of Buddhist meditation practices, such as Burmese ***weikza***. Although not stated so explicitly, the same association of more traditional practices with power, including worldly power, has been one of the motivations behind the suppression of traditional practices in Thailand, Cambodia, and possibly Laos. Modern Burmese *vipassanā* is now more widespread than other techniques within Southeast Asia and globally.

The Place of Meditation in Theravada Buddhism

The image of Gotama Buddha in meditation is fundamental to the visual imagery of Buddhism including Theravada. The developed Theravada biography of the Buddha has the fetal Buddha-to-be seated in meditation even while in the womb during his mother Māyā's pregnancy. His enlightenment is said to have followed on from his entering meditative states, and the account of his final relinquishing of life, his *parinibbāna*, also relates him entering the different stages of *jhāna* (discussed later) before breathing his last.

For those following the model and teaching of the Buddha, meditation is a fundamental technique for self-transformation, central to an important threefold schema describing the path as consisting of moral conduct, meditation, and wisdom, *sīla, samādhi, paññā* (see Chapter 5). The centrality of mind in guiding our behavior (and so in shaping *kammic* consequences) and our experience is recognized from the earliest Pali texts, such as the poems of the *Dhammapada* and *Suttanipāta* contained within the *Khuddaka Nikāya* of the *Sutta Piṭaka*. Chapter III of the *Dhammapada* is a collection of verses on the nature of the mind or consciousness (*citta*):

35. Wonderful, indeed, it is to subdue the mind, so difficult to subdue, ever swift, and seizing whatever it desires. A tamed mind brings happiness.

37. Dwelling in the cave (of the heart), the mind, without form, wanders far and alone. Those who subdue this mind are liberated from the bonds of Mara [the deity representing *saṃsāra* and our weaknesses].

40. Realizing that this body is as fragile as a clay pot, and fortifying this mind like a well-fortified city, fight out Mara with the sword of wisdom. Then, guarding the conquest, remain unattached.

42. Whatever harm an enemy may do to an enemy, or a hater to a hater, an ill-directed mind inflicts on oneself a greater harm. (Buddharakkhita 2012a)

Meditation involves working on one's mental states typically either by calming the mind, or by developing new capacities, or by creating a certain degree of objectivity or estrangement from the individual self and thus a heightened awareness of one's own habitual identifications and responses. This last aspect leads to the ability not to respond automatically in habituated ways, and thereby to master one's responses to impulses. It is this with the calming aspects of meditation that makes it a useful tool for treating a range of mental, psychosomatic, and behavioral problems, including addiction. In a sense, many of our behavioral "problems" can be seen as lower level but strongly compulsive addictions.

Meditation tends to be discussed in terms of mental states and mental culture; the modern independence and nationalist movements emphasized the superiority of Asian *mind* culture. However, neither the process nor the effects are confined to the mental realm. Meditation practices presume a psychosomatic, even cosmic whole, although the degree to which the practices are seen in somatic terms or involve physical movements varies from tradition to tradition.

It is recognized that many of the techniques of meditation developed in Buddhism came from the broader religious milieu of north India at the time of the Buddha. The Buddha is described as rejecting the meditation practices of his former teachers, Aḷāra Kālāma and Uddaka Rāmaputta, as not leading to the goal of liberation from *saṃsāra*, yet the states they achieved are part of the range of meditation experiences recognized in Buddhism. Meditation experiences can be pleasant and desirable pursuits in their own right, as we shall see in the story of the monk Nanda later, and they are also traditionally regarded as bestowing the ability to exert power over the world. However, if part of the Buddhist path, meditation practices must contribute to the uprooting of the three root causes of our entrapment in *saṃsāra*, namely, greed (or "inclination toward"), hatred ("repugnance/aversion away from"), and delusion about the true nature of the world. Delusion is the failure to understand that the world, and the components that make us up as individuals are unsatisfactory and impermanent and that what we experience cannot be identified as an enduring self.

To address these three root causes of our entrapment, early Buddhist meditation practices brought together trends within the renouncer traditions of ancient India. One trend saw the mechanism that traps people in *saṃsāra* in terms of our passions. The appropriate response to this is to engage in practices that lead to calm (*samatha*) and to withdrawal from our engagement with our responses to the world. The other trend identifies delusion as the mechanism entrapping us. This is to be addressed through practices aiming at insight, *vipassanā*. These two different approaches are still visible in the Pali Canon, with both types of practice being seen as leading to liberation from *saṃsāra*, but they were systematized into a single system in the fifth-century *Visuddhimagga* (see later text), which came to dominate later lists of meditation subjects. The division between the two types has been reified much more strongly in the modern period (see later text).

There is great variety not just of different meditation subjects, that is, the topics on which one may meditate, but also of different meditation techniques, that is, ways of practicing those meditation subjects. The variety between topics is relatively easy to differentiate, because they are recorded in the Pali Canon and some of them were systematized by the fifth century into a well-known set of 40 different named practices. This common enumeration of 40 topics in the *Visuddhimagga* refers only to the practices described in the *samādhi* section of the text (see later text). Sometimes the enumeration is longer because it includes the practices contained within the *paññā* section, for example, in the *borān yogāvacara kammaṭṭhāna* in Cambodia. For although identified as a *samatha* practice system in contrast to Burmese *vipassanā*, *borān kammaṭṭhāna* includes both *samatha* and *vipassanā* (Crosby and Long interviews, Cambodia, December 2012).

The variety between techniques, that is, the details of the technique applied to the meditation subject, is more difficult to identify and very difficult to trace through history: techniques were refined within different teaching lineages and may not have been committed to writing or named. For example, many practice traditions advocate mindfulness of breathing (*ānāpānassati*) but how each teacher teaches is specific to their lineage, and – except in famous cases – the specifics are not differentiated by a different name. Famous cases that are named include the Burmese *vipassanā* system of the teacher Mahāsī Sayadaw (1904–1982), whose method of mindfulness of breathing is sometimes referred to as "rising and falling," referring to the way breathing in and out is watched in the abdomen, as it causes the abdomen to inflate and deflate. Even such labeling tells us little about the details of how each practice understands transformation to take place, how it deals with the obstacles of meditation (such as distraction and anxiety), or how it interprets the experiences within meditation. There are cases where a meditation tradition that appears entirely orthodox in terms of the Pali terminology and the *kammaṭṭhāna* practices came to be identified as heretical because of the method applied or the emphasis on supernatural powers (see discussions of *borān kammaṭṭhāna* and *weikza* given later). Meanwhile, many different forms of meditation in Burma (and more recently elsewhere) have received the name *vipassanā*, which may mask substantial variation in practice. In part this is to benefit from the popularity of *vipassanā*, in part an attempt to safeguard against the very real threat of prosecution by the State Sangha Council.

Usually assessments of orthodoxy and heterodoxy by the Sangha or state hierarchy (see Chapter 12) are made within a specific political context. Meditation has become, certainly in the modern period, an aspect of Theravada identity, with adherence to specific methods defining a broader loyalty or belonging. The uptake of a particular method or switching between methods by high-ranking or ambitious monks and political figures has played its role in indicating a shift of allegiance. It has been used as a method of setting up a new power base with meditation as an element through which followers will express allegiance. In the colonial period, meditation was advocated as an aspect of national identity and a way of working to maintain the religion against colonial suppression. While harnessed politically, meditation movements were in fact often less politicized that other reform trends, reflecting a search for meaningful explorations of the Dhamma, or seeking an internal space safe from external politics. The extent to which individual followers have understood the political context of their choices varies greatly. The focus on meditation during the colonial period was also in part a reactionary statement about the superiority of Asian, specifically Buddhist, mind-culture (meditation technology) in contrast to the recognition of the prevailing superiority of Western somatic culture (medical and military technology). This dynamic may have favored those types of meditation practice that focused more on the mental and psychological aspects of meditation rather than those that were more holistic or geared more toward somatic aspects. It also altered the perceived relationship between meditation, healing and – to a lesser extent – cosmology.

The rise in the fashion for rhetoric about "rationality" and empirical knowledge over "superstition" in the competition between local and colonial religion and cultural values also had an impact on meditation. In the dialogue with modernity and in defense against colonialism, Buddhism was defined as a scientific, rational religion or philosophy, with an emphasis on empirically verifiable effects, and a de-emphasis of supernatural outcomes. The rhetoric of empiricism contributed to the acceptance of meditation as a technique that may be applied beyond the Buddhist context with verifiable results, and as a topic of public discourse. The public down-playing of elements that cannot be reproduced in a manner that easily conforms to empiricism means that, while practitioners continue to believe in and speak of supernatural outcomes, that discourse is at a more private level and often an expression of adherence to a particular practice, teacher or lineage. Thus, we have, on the one hand, publicly accessible meditation and meditation discourse on the former model, a kind of neutral space in which any may engage, and, on the other hand, a hierarchy above the publicly taught techniques through levels requiring greater commitment, expressions of belonging, and testing of meditative attainments and psychological aptitude in both individual teacher–pupil relationships and in mass meditation movements. For example, in two widely employed methods, the Goenka *vipassanā* from

Burma and the Dhammakāya *vijjā dhammakāya* from Thailand, the lower levels are well known and public, even – especially in the Dhammakāya case – available through online teachings, including through cartoons for children, and other media. In both systems, the higher levels are restricted and not the subject of public discourse. Since it is at the higher levels that we find the greatest variety and fine-tuning of techniques, this adds to the difficulty of conducting research on the richness and variety of Theravada meditation practices. The result is that much academic writing on the subject is naturally confined to the either textual, loosely descriptive or peripheral matters. In other words, studies almost inevitably veer away from dealing with actual experience. Even where the focus of research is the process and effectiveness of transformation, that is, in cognitive science and therapeutic applications, the scope may be quite narrowly circumscribed or, in the latter case, restricted by the difficulty of such issues as the setting up of control groups, negotiating the medical ethics of conducting experiments on "live subjects," and the reproduction of experiments in high-enough numbers to produce statistically significant results.

There have then been a number of developments in the past two centuries that have led to changes in the popularity of the different types and lineages of practice, particularly in the twentieth to twenty-first centuries. These developments, outlined earlier, include the use of meditation in politics and identity formation, the shift away from somatic to mind-culture, "rationalized" forms of meditation, the emphasis on meditation as an empirically verifiable technique, and its function in negotiating private and public space. A further reason for the rise in popularity of *vipassanā* and *dhammakāya* methods is that they offer, at the more introductory levels, a simplified form of meditation that requires little of the ritual or teacher–disciple commitment of more traditional forms.

A further difficulty in conducting research is that the inevitable gap between what is expressed or written and what is experienced in practice is especially wide with meditation. The gap between the experience of practice and the written word is reflected in the traditional distinction between *paṭipatti*, practice, and *pariyatti*, study or knowledge of textual authorities. Not unexpectedly, Sangha and state hierarchies have generally favored *pariyatti*. This preference has a long history in Theravada, going back to a famine in the first-century BCE in Sri Lanka. A decision was made to prioritize the preservation of texts, the role of *gantha-dhura* ("book-duty") monks, over the meditation practice of *vipassanā-dhura* ("insight-duty") monks. This moment in history is famous as the occasion for the writing down of the Pali Canon (see Chapter 3). The rationale for prioritizing the preservation of the text is that the Dhamma thereby remains accessible to all and for longer, with the further benefit that a teaching's reliability may be assessed against those textual authorities, to check that it is in accord with the teaching of the Buddha. A corollary is that textual knowledge is easier to control and impose on a greater scale, and thus the logical preference of large centralized institutions. These may have motivations that are mixed and include the preservation of order, the maintenance of control and a distrust of others. As a consequence practitioners have been judged against textual sources that were possibly never intended to cover the level of content of practice being scrutinized. This has resulted in practitioners being forced to adopt the terminology of the texts considered authoritative by the centralized Sangha hierarchies. While the rhetoric of purity at points of dispute has been consistently compelling throughout Theravada history, it can be seen as an attempt to arrest the influence of popular religious leaders. It is no coincidence that it is currently seen most in Thailand and Burma, where the centralization of Buddhist education, authority, and hierarchy was such a key element of the state centralization and nation-building of the nineteenth and twentieth centuries (see later text and Chapter 12).

Authoritative Meditation Texts: Canonical

There is a wide range of texts explaining meditation in the Pali Canon and a great diversity of meditation practices advocated in different manners. Some texts give extensive instruction. The most famous and most drawn-upon canonical text is the lengthy *Mahāsatipaṭṭhāna Sutta* ("Great (*Mahā*) Discourse (*sutta*) on Establishing (*paṭṭhāna*) Mindfulness (*sati*)") in the *Dīghanikāya* of the *Sutta Piṭaka*. It provides details of how to practice mindfulness on the four objects of mindfulness, namely, "body" (*kāya*), "sensations" (*vedanā*), "states of consciousness" (*citta*), and "objects of consciousness" or "constituents of reality" (*dhamma*). This last category allows for the inclusion of many other meditation practices taught independently elsewhere in the Canon, allowing the *sutta* to be used as a complete guide to meditation. The *Mahāsatipaṭṭhāna Sutta*, along with the commentary on it attributed to the fifth-century scholar monk Buddhaghosa, therefore became the basis for later, often vernacular meditation manuals. In contrast, the *Karaṇīyametta Sutta* ("Discourse (*sutta*) on how loving kindness (*mettā*) should be practised (*karaṇīya*)"), from the *Sutta Nipāta* (I.8) within the fifth division of the *Sutta Piṭaka* (see Chapter 3), provides a brief poem of ten stanzas extolling the benefits of the practice of loving kindness, *mettā*, as a kind of narrative, with a relatively brief though effective description of how to extend the feelings of love a mother has for her only son to the entire universe.

> Who seeks to promote his welfare,
> Having glimpsed the state of perfect peace,
> Should be able, honest and upright,
> Gentle in speech, meek and not proud.
> Contented, he ought to be easy to support,
> Not over-busy, and simple in living.
> Tranquil his senses, let him be prudent,
> ...
> (Then let him cultivate the thought:)
> May all be well and secure,
> May all beings be happy!
> Whatever living creatures there be,
> Without exception, weak or strong,
> Long, huge or middle-sized,
> Or short, minute or bulky,
> Whether visible or invisible,
> And those living far or near,
> The born and those seeking birth,
> May all beings be happy!
> Let none deceive or decry
> His fellow anywhere;
> Let none wish others harm
> In resentment or in hate.
> Just as with her own life
> A mother shields from hurt
> Her own son, her only child,
> Let all-embracing thoughts
> For all beings be yours.
> Cultivate an all-embracing mind of love

For all throughout the universe,
In all its height, depth and breadth—
Love that is untroubled
And beyond hatred or enmity.
...
It is deemed the Divine State here.
Holding no more to wrong beliefs,
With virtue and vision of the ultimate,
And having overcome all sensual desire,
Never in a womb is one born again.
(abridged extract from
Buddharakkhita 2012b)

The *Karaṇīyametta Sutta* advocates the practice as a way of ending the cycle of rebirth, that is, attaining Enlightenment, but in developed Theravada it came to be subordinated as preparatory to other practices (see Chapter 11). It continues to be used in its canonical form, particularly as a protection text (*paritta*), even in political contexts: during the 2007 Saffron Revolution it was chanted by the protesting monks (see Chapter 12). It has multiple functions, being particularly poignant in the context of a protest in defense of the oppressed, in that it seeks to convert those with malevolent minds to a love for all beings.

The practice "recollection of the [qualities of the] Buddha," *buddhānussati*, is also said, in the prose narrative of the *Apallaka Jātaka*, to lead to *Nibbāna*, but in the *Visuddhimagga*, it is attributed with only a limited benefit, namely, leading to the first *jhāna* (Meiland 2003: 9, also Orsborn 2007: 18). This makes dubious the ascription of the prose narratives of the *Jātaka* to Buddhaghosa, to whom the *Visuddhimagga* is also ascribed (Meiland 2003: 9). Man Shik Kong has recently identified a similar discrepancy between the canonical and the *Visuddhimagga* assessment of various of the *saññā* ("perception" or "contemplation") practices, such as the *āhāre paṭikūlasaññā*, "perception of repulsiveness in relation to food." In various canonical passages, they are said to lead to elevated states of spiritual attainment, including *Nibbāna*, but Buddhaghosa again relegates them to a subordinate position on the spiritual path in his *Visuddhimagga* (Kong in preparation).

Authoritative Meditation Texts: Postcanonical

The most famous and influential postcanonical compendium of meditation practices is the *Visuddhimagga*, "The Path of Purification," by the fifth-century Indian commentator Buddhaghosa working under the auspices of the Mahāvihāra, "Great Monastery," of Sri Lanka (see Chapter 3). While containing a substantial amount of material on meditation that has been used as the basis of practice at least in the modern period, the *Visuddhimagga* does not see itself as supplanting the need for a practice tradition, that is, meditation based on a teacher–disciple relationship. It explicitly refers to the contemporaneous existence of secret meditation manuals but not to their content (Cousins 1997: 193). The commentary on the *Mahāsatipaṭṭhāna Sutta*, also attributed to Buddhaghosa, though less well known in the West, has similarly had a very far-reaching impact on practice, especially in Burmese and Shan meditation traditions, including the modern *vipassanā* traditions.

The *Visuddhimagga* is organized around the threefold schema mentioned earlier: *sīla*, *samādhi*, and *paññā*. A range of meditation practices, *kammaṭṭhāna*, described in the canon is systematized by Buddhaghosa and reduced to a list of 40 *kammaṭṭhāna* (see later text), presented in the central *samādhi* section of the text. It is here that Buddhaghosa subordinates most of the meditation practices, terming them *samatha*, to wisdom (*paññā*) in the sense of insight or understanding, the focus of the final third of the *Visuddhimagga*. That final third draws heavily on *Abhidhamma* (see Chapter 7). This distinction was later taken a step further in the *vipassanā* insight traditions of Burma that developed in the nineteenth and twentieth centuries. A key advocate was Ledi Sayadaw (see Chapter 7), who taught that the development of insight was sufficient and did not need to be supported by the practices labeled as *samatha* (Braun 2008: 5–6)

There is sometimes an apparent disjunction between the actual function of the *kammaṭṭhāna* and their categorization into *samatha* and *vipassanā*. Thus, methods for understanding the impermanence of the body or the ultimate unsatisfactory nature of food are labeled as *samatha*, when they are clearly about inculcating insights into the Buddhist understanding of reality. The *Visuddhimagga* interpretation of which category a method falls into is based on the quality of the meditative state to which each can lead. In fact, analyses related to the practices found in the *samādhi* section are provided in the *paññā* section but taken further through the application of *Abhidhamma* analysis (see Chapter 7).

In the period between the *Visuddhimagga* and the present, there have been numerous meditation texts, both manuals and descriptive treatises. Many of the texts found in manuscript collections relate to meditation, some on a single, simple subject such as the recollection of the qualities of the Buddha, others more complex. Little research has been done to assess their variety. One difficulty is that meditation manuals as such are often in a mixture of a classical language, that is, Pali, and a vernacular that may or may not be a currently used language. Also, actual manuals often contain prompts or reminders rather than an in-depth explanation. In recent years it has emerged that there is still extant a relatively high number of manuals and related texts pertaining to a system of meditation called – among other things – *borān kammaṭṭhāna* or *yogāvacara* (see later text). Its core text, the *Mūla-kammaṭṭhāna* "original, fundamental or basic meditation practice," circulated under a number of different titles, or without a title, throughout the Tai–Lao–Khmer and Sri Lankan Buddhist worlds. Some versions of this text are simple lists of *kammaṭṭhāna* and from that perspective look entirely in accord with the *Visuddhimagga* or Theravada *Abhidhamma* texts. Other versions contain extensive narratives, explanations of symbolism, and of the somatic locations involved in the practice that make it clear that we are dealing with techniques of practice not described in the Canon or *Visuddhimagga* (Crosby 1999: Chapters 3 and 6; Crosby *et al.* 2012).

The crisis created by the European colonial expansion into South and Southeast Asia, especially in the nineteenth and early twentieth centuries, saw a spate of meditation texts being produced within the reformist wings of Theravada, seeking to strengthen Buddhism and often looking back to such texts as the *Mahāsatipaṭṭhāna Sutta*, its fifth-century commentary and the *Visuddhimagga*. We also see attempts in Thailand in the early twentieth century and in Cambodia in the mid-twentieth century to preserve and investigate the "ancient" *borān* system that was threatened by both colonialism and reformism. With the increasing availability of the printing press, the attempt at preservation led to the production of books as well as manuscripts reflecting that tradition (e.g., Yasotharat 1935/1936; see also Bizot 1976). New works on meditation also proliferated in Burma during this period. In addition to works about meditation and guides to meditation, two genres of histories also emerged in Burma – histories of meditation practices of a particular region and hagiographies of individual teachers (Houtman 1990: 79).

The international interest in Eastern meditation, to become more widespread later, also began to inspire works in English from the very end of the nineteenth century, such as Rhys Davids' *Manual of a Mystic* (1896) translated by Woodward in 1916. The *Manual of a Mystic* was based on a copy of a manuscript that the Sri Lankan leader of the Buddhist revival, Anāgārika Dharmapāla, who was at that time experimenting with various forms of meditation, had handed over to Rhys Davids during a visit to England. The earliest publications show an uncertainty about the subject and an assumption, influenced by theosophy, that there was a shared mysticism between different religious traditions (Lounsbery 1935, Rhys Davids 1896, Woodward 1916). They also indicate the early interest in the possible overlap between Buddhist meditation and psychology (Tillyard 1927). During the 1950s and 1960s, more definitive understandings of Theravada meditation based on the *Mahāsatipaṭṭhāna Sutta* (Nyanaponika 1953), the Pali Canon, and the *Visuddhimagga* (Conze 1956 and Vajirañāṇa 1962) began to appear. A boom in production in the 1960s was inspired by the recent wave of independence, the establishment of the World Fellowship of Buddhists in 1950 in Colombo, the Buddha Jayanti celebrations including the Sixth Council in the mid-1950s (see Chapter 3), international interest in Burmese *vipassanā* movements, and experimentations with altered states of consciousness as an aspect of the counter cultural revolution. Gustaaf Houtman observes that the first anthropological study to consider Theravada meditation in any detail also dates from this period: the unpublished Cornell Ph.D. by John F. Brohm, *Burmese Religion and the Burmese Religious Revival*, 1957 (Houtman 1990: 48).

Given the accessibility of well-known authoritative textual sources such as the *Mahāsatipaṭṭhāna Sutta* and *Visuddhimagga*, it can sometimes be difficult to assess whether a text or practice of the past or even present is based on a long living tradition or is a relatively recent revival based on texts. In-depth familiarity with the texts is obvious in both the northern Thai forest tradition and the Burmese *vipassanā* traditions. In contrast, the *borān kammaṭṭhāna* (also referred to as *yogāvacara*) mentioned earlier, though widespread throughout Southeast Asia and Sri Lanka during the Ayutthaya and Kandyan periods (eighteenth century), has since – in ignorance of this history – been accused of being a corrupt tradition or one invented on the basis of a misunderstanding of the texts.

Who Meditates?

While central to the gradual, progressive soteriological path advocated in Theravada (although cases of instantaneous enlightenment are also described in the Pali Canon), most Theravada Buddhists do not really practice meditation. While it is often central in reform movements and convert Theravada, within Theravada communities it is more often a specialist vocation or undertaken for a special period. For monastics, the extent to which they practice meditation very much depends on their motive for ordination, the tradition into which they are ordained or even the attitudes of the abbot and lay managers of the individual temple in which they reside. Western converts to Theravada, especially those who become ordained, are very likely to undertake meditation practice, the personal transformation it appears to offer being one of the main reasons for their attraction to Buddhism.

Within most Theravada cultures there are monastic traditions and specific monasteries, monks, and other individuals that focus more on meditation than others: some cater for meditation as a dedicated vocation. These include the wandering forest monks of northern Thailand (Tiyavanich 1997), the *weikza* monks and lay ascetics in Burma (Rozenberg 2010) and the northern Thai forest tradition, a modern form of which has spread around the world through the lineage of Ajan Chah. The label "forest monk" does not always refer to practitioners of a meditation lifestyle, but to a specific lineage. A forest monastery has a technical definition in the *Visuddhimagga*, which defines it as being established at least 50 bow lengths from the nearest village. At times monks belonging to the forest lineage have been at the heart of political affairs and at court. However, there are still monks who attempt to renounce society and dedicate themselves to their spiritual transformation, especially through meditation. The decision to focus on meditation/*nibbāna* entails a decision not to fulfill the central social roles played by monks. This can create tensions either through accusations of selfishness or through heightened popularity, as the act of taking on greater levels of *vinaya* and meditation discipline makes monks more attractive for laypeople seeking to make merit through donations to more worthy monks, as described by Carrithers in relation to forest monks in Sri Lanka (Carrithers 1983). On the other hand, some monks who dedicate themselves to the forest life / meditation, such as the *weikza* in Burma, while not providing the education and religious services of the village monk, continue to provide others services. They are particularly known for rebuilding derelict shrine and temples, and for offering services, such as blessing, healing, longevity practices, predictions, and astrology.

The annual three months rains retreat has traditionally been a period for training in a variety of subjects including meditation and, reflecting the early tradition, this is the most likely time for most monks to meditate. It seems that in nonreform Buddhism, such as that among the Shan and in pre-Khmer Rouge Cambodia, spending more time engaged in such activities as meditation comes with age as people are freed up from more manual work and child-raising. Thus in Shan Buddhism, the women from their mid-40s and above and men upward of 50 who spend more time as "temple sleepers" may also practice meditation at the local monastery (see Chapter 5). The French scholar François Bizot, who did more than any other outsider to document the detail of the traditional *borān kammaṭṭhāna* meditation practices immediately prior to the Khmer Rouge period, first became aware of it because his Cambodian mother-in-law would regularly go to a hut in her garden to practice (Bizot 1976). In the surviving traces of this tradition, teaching to laypeople is mainly offered for periods lasting between nine days and three months during or toward the end of the rains retreat, or in January after the rice harvest, when there is less farm work to be done (Crosby and Long, fieldwork December 2012).

Since the 1950s, meditation centers separate from monasteries have been built throughout the Theravada world and further afield. These were typically in urban centers, allowing laypeople access while also following a modern working life, but some have been built in rural settings to offer laypeople, as well as monastics, the opportunity for intensive practice. Such centers began in Burma and inspired similar centers in other Theravada countries. They facilitated the exportation of Buddhist influence outside of the usual monastic lineages and networks, as centers were set up, firstly in India and other Asian countries and then globally, for example through the Goenka network. Taking advantage of the perception of Theravada's authority as an authentic, early form of Buddhism, and as more strict in terms of practice, Theravada meditation centers have also been established in East Asia.

From the end of the nineteenth century in Burma, and, under the influence of Burmese traditions elsewhere from the 1950s, there was an increasing participation of laity, including young laypeople, in meditation, a trend that has continued. Because of this and the association of the setting up of meditation centers with reform and revival movements, it has sometimes been stated that the practice of meditation by laypeople is a modern phenomenon, and not in conformity with traditional Theravada. However, the example of the Shan and Cambodian lay practice of meditation, especially by women, as well as the biographies of some of the early modern *vipassanā* teachers, suggests that this is not true. Wat Preah Meas in Kompong Cham traces its teaching of meditation to both monks and laypeople back to the establishment of the monastery by a wandering ***thudong*** monk in 1412, although this date is yet to be verified

(Crosby and Long fieldwork December 2012). The main issue for laypeople is finding time free from other duties – hence the tendency to commence such practice in late middle age and the popularity of simplified methods in recent decades. Centralization of Buddhism by the Thai government in the nineteenth and early twentieth centuries obscured prior practice and practice relationships. The focus on centralized exams and study emphasized that a monk's esteem lay with the passing of exams, including Pali exams, while the laity's role should be expressed through supporting the temple. This, and the suppression of wandering forest monk practice (see later text), undermined both lay meditation practice and monastic practice that had not been approved by the centralized monastic hierarchy. While Bizot and others documented prerevolution practice in Cambodia, little has been documented for the same period in Laos.

While the sharpening of the lay-monastic divide seems to be an aspect of some neotraditionalist forms of reform Buddhism, others advocate lay engagement. In Sri Lanka, the early modern revival of the preindependence period emphasized lay involvement in high-level practice, as in Cambodia, but under G.P. Malalasekera's leadership in the 1950s, the All Ceylon Buddhist Congress took a neotraditionalist stance (Bond 1988: 84). Nonetheless, looking into the canonical and commentarial texts from which neotraditionalism takes its authority, we find no discouragement for laypeople. Even in the fifth-century commentary on the *Mahāsatipaṭṭhāna Sutta*, the ideal country is one where laypeople also meditate. The region where the Buddha teaches the *sutta* resembles the mythical country of Uttarakuru because

> When people are at the weavers or ford, they don't stand about gossiping, they ask one another about their meditation practice. If a woman answers that she doesn't practise they criticise her for the lost opportunity of being born as a human in the time of the Buddha's teaching. (abridged translation Crosby).

Buddhaghosa even includes a story to exemplify animals practicing meditation:

> A young parrot gets left behind by a wandering circus and is taken in by some nuns. The abbess tells the parrot, "Nobody is idle in my convent,' and so gives him the meditation on 'bones," one of the stages of decomposition of the body in the *asubha* meditation practices (see below). The parrot meditates repeating the phrase "bones, bones." [Repeating a phrase as an aid to meditation is a standard practice.] One day the parrot is sunning himself on the top of the high gateway of the convent when he is snatched by an eagle. The nuns set off in pursuit. As the parrot is carried along in the talons of his captor he has the detached realisation, as a result of his meditation, "A cage of bones is carrying a cage of bones," and as a result feels no panic at his predicament. The eagle drops him and he is able to relay his experience to the nuns. (Adapted, abridged translation Crosby)

Basic Overview of Practices

The two most commonly taught meditation practices are mindfulness of breathing and the "divine abidings," *brahmavihāras*, in which one develops different types of (nonsexual) love toward oneself and others. Both are regarded as appropriate for beginners. In mindfulness of breathing one observes one's breathing in and out, by paying attention to where it enters and exits the body or to the rise and fall of the chest/abdomen or by counting the breaths to ten. There are four kinds of *brahmavihāra*: loving-kindness (*mettā*), pity (*karuṇā*), sympathetic joy (*muditā*), and equanimity (*upekkhā*) (see Chapter 11). In these practices, one develops each of the attitudes in turn to oneself, to someone of whom one is fond, to someone to whom one has neutral feelings, then to someone one dislikes. One then generates the attitude equally to all four, after which one may extend it to the entire universe.

A meditation well known because of its shocking nature and its representation in art is the set of ten meditations on *asubha* "impurity." By meditating on the stages of decomposition of the body one compares a corpse with one's own body and therefore recognizes one's own impermanence. In the Pali Canon and the *Visuddhimagga*, the meditation on the corpse/impurity is described in the context of charnel grounds where bodies are left exposed. The practice is still found today using artistic representations and "skeleton walks." A skeleton walk is a short walkway, smoothed for walking back and forth along it barefoot, with a skeleton on display at one end. Until quite recently in Cambodia a man might donate his body to the Sangha (monastic community) on death. It would be placed in a bamboo cage to protect it from scavenging animals, then left to rot so that monks could meditate on it. In Burma, King Mindon kept items made from human bones near him as well as models of skeletons made of wood with functioning joints in order to sustain his awareness of the *asubha* practice on bones (Houtman 1990: 39 with note 48). It is still common to see a model of a corpse with its eyes and tongue being pecked out by crows, a scene described in the commentary to the meditation on the corpse practice in Buddhaghosa's commentary on the *Mahāsatipaṭṭhāna Sutta*. It is sometimes used to represent the corpse that is the third of the "four sights" that inspired the Buddha to undertake his quest for Enlightenment (Chapter 1). Martin Seeger points out that while men meditate on the bodies of others for *asubha* practice, women may meditate on their own body. He cites the examples of Ambapālī, the canon's famous prostitute-turned-nun (see Chapter 10), and Mae Chi Kaew, a famous **precept nun** in modern Thailand (2010: 591, see Chapter 9).

The forty meditation practices given in the *Samādhi* section of the *Visuddhimagga* are outlined in the following table:

Meditation Type	*Practice*
10 *kasiṇa* "visual objects": Earth Water Fire Air, wind Blue Yellow Red White Space Light	The practitioner constructs a round, flat meditation object out of sticks and matting or leather, making it the appropriate color for the specific *kasiṇa*. He then places it on the ground (some meditation centers fix them onto the wall) to gaze upon. He removes analytical thought about the nature of the object, but uses the repetition of a phrase that aids total focus on the object, for example, "fire, fire" or "bright, bright" in the case of the fire *kasiṇa*. In the case of water, one uses a pot of water, in the case of fire, a small fire; wind becomes the *kasiṇa* by noticing its effect, for example where it touches the body or a plant; light where moonlight falls on the floor or by projecting lamplight onto a wall; space by a hole in a wall, a piece of leather or a mat.

(cont'd)

Meditation Type	Practice
10 *asubha* "impure aspects" of the body decomposing The bloated The livid The festering The cut up The gnawed The scattered The hacked and scattered The bleeding The worm infested A skeleton (Ñyāṇamoli 1976: 169 ff.)	The practitioner, once mentally prepared, goes to a graveyard or wherever else she/he has heard a corpse is lying, making sure someone responsible knows what she/he is doing so that s/he can be looked after if adversely affected. She/he observes a corpse in different stages of decomposition, dismemberment and scattering, and each time compares that corpse with his/her own body. Care is taken in the selection of the corpse, so as to avoid problems such as a beautiful body of the opposite sex that might arouse inappropriate attraction.
10 *anussati* "recollections": (1) The Buddha (2) The Dhamma (3) The Sangha (4) Moral conduct (5) Generosity (6) Gods (7) The body (8) Death (9) Breathing (10) Peace	This is the most varied set of practices. The practitioner reflects in detail on the characteristics of each of the ten objects. The Buddha *anussati* involves recollection of all the good aspects and achievements of the Buddha. The recollection of the body is the analysis of it into 32 constituents. The recollection of death is on its inevitability.
4 *Brahmavihāra* "divine abidings": (1) *mettā*, loving kindness (2) *karuṇā*, pity (3) *muditā*, sympathetic joy (4) *upekkhā*, equanimous appreciation	The practitioner develops the attitude or disposition in question to his/her self, a loved one, a neutral person, an enemy, then all four together equally, and expands this disposition to the entire universe (see earlier text and Chapter 11).
4 formless *jhāna*: (1) Infinite space (2) Infinite consciousness (3) Infinite nothingness (4) Neither perception nor nonperception	The practitioner may use the *kasiṇa* as the starting point for this practice but develops a dispassion for materiality and discards its limitations to achieve the experience of unbounded space; then discarding that, focuses on attaining infinite consciousness, pursuing this and the other two in turn as more peaceful than the previous.
1 *āhāre paṭikūlasaññā* the perception of repulsiveness in relation to food	In the Theravada tradition, this is subdivided into the unpleasant actions and effort involved in seeking alms. This is different from other traditions, which may regard food itself as repulsive, that is, perform a kind of *asubha* meditation in relation to food (Kong in preparation). Mindfulness not to over-eat because of the adverse psychological and physical effects is mentioned in the *sīla* "good conduct" section of the *Visuddhimagga*.

(Continued)

(cont'd)

Meditation Type	*Practice*
1 *mahābhūta*, meditation of the four elements: earth, water, fire, air	The practitioner regards the different aspects of his body in terms of the elements. She/he sees hard aspects being the element earth, fluid and moist aspects as the element water; whatever creates heat, is consumed or burnt up as the fire element; whatever winds and breath are in the body as the air element.

Jhāna and *Nimitta*

In the altered mental states, *jhāna*, the practitioner becomes further and further removed from the sensual, external realm around us. In the *Visuddhimagga*, the first four *jhāna*, called the form *jhāna*, result from various of the *kammaṭṭhāna*, whereas the higher *jhāna*, the formless *jhāna* are listed as *kammaṭṭhāna* in their own right. These increasingly elevated experiences are regarded as being parallel to cosmic planes of existence, as indicated in the next section. The *jhāna*, while not regarded as salvific in their own right in the *Visuddhimagga* presentation of the path, are incorporated from the practice traditions that did regard them as such. They have a prominent place in the descriptions of the Buddha's own Enlightenment, where, however, they precede the gnostic liberating insight into the fundamental reality encapsulated as, for example, the four truths (see Chapters 1 and 5). Here is one such account, from the *Majjhima Nikāya*, in which the Buddha describes his experience of the *jhāna* in the lead up to his Enlightenment.

> Aloof from the pleasures of the senses, aloof from unskilled states of mind, I entered into the first meditation which is accompanied by initial thought and discursive thought, is born of aloofness and is rapturous and joyful. By allaying initial and discursive thought, with the mind subjectively tranquillised and fixed on one point, I entered into and abided in the second meditation which is devoid of initial and discursive thought, is born of concentration and is rapturous and joyful. By the fading out of rapture, I dwelt with equanimity, attentive and clearly conscious and I experienced in my person that joy of which the ariyans say: "Joyful lives he who has equanimity and is mindful," and I entered into and abided in the third meditation. By getting rid of joy, by getting rid of anguish, by the going down of my former pleasures and sorrows, I entered into the fourth meditation which has neither anguish nor joy and is entirely purified by equanimity and mindfulness. (Horner 1954 I: 27–28)

Both the four *jhāna* of the form realms and the four "formless" *jhāna* are included in the description of the Buddha's death in the *Mahāparinibbāna Sutta*. However, before discarding life, the Buddha returns to the form *jhāna*. This is parallel to descriptions of his initial Enlightenment in which it is understood that insight *vipassanā*, or liberating knowledge, arises when one has attained the calm focus of the fourth *jhāna*.

The *Visuddhimagga* classifies 22 of the 40 *kammaṭṭhāna* as leading to the experience of *jhāna*, based on what kind of "sign" or "mental image" (***nimitta***) result from the meditation (Orsborn 2007: 18). The *nimitta*, a postcanonical systematization, analyses the stages of progress in using an external object as a basis for meditation, into the preliminary sign, learning sign, and counterpart sign. The first is when the meditator is reliant on the external object, the second when she/he is able to see the object with his/her eyes shut as clearly as with them open. The third is when the meditator generates a mental image of the meditation object which she/he can manipulate independently of the initial object.

In the third division of the *Visuddhimagga*, dedicated to wisdom, *paññā*, the different levels of insight and purification are acquired by utilizing *Abhidhamma* analyses of the psychophysical experience (see Chapter 7) on the basis of the mindfulness of breathing and the four *satipaṭṭhāna* described in the *Mahāsatipaṭṭhāna Sutta*. Liberation is defined in terms of the thirty-seven "factors of liberation," also given in the *Mahāsatipaṭṭhāna Sutta*, which constitute different lists of aspects of enlightenment found elsewhere in the canon. The thirty-seven factors of liberation are the four foundations of mindfulness, the four right endeavors (for the non-arising of unskillful states, for their abandonment, for the arising of skilful states, for their maintenance), the four roads to power (will, energy, consciousness, discrimination), the five faculties and five powers of faith, energy, mindfulness, concentration, wisdom; the seven enlightenment factors (mindfulness, investigation, energy, joy, tranquility, concentration, equanimity), and the Noble Eightfold Path (see Chapter 5) (Ñyāṇamoli 1976: 707).

Correlation Between Mental States and Cosmological Realms

The understanding that some of the meditation practices give the successful practitioners access to corresponding realms of the cosmos is found in canonical narratives about meditation, such as the *Kevaddha Sutta* (*Dīgha Nikāya* 11), the *Mahāgovinda Sutta* (*Dīgha Nikāya* 11), and the *Nanda Sutta* (*Udāna* 3.2) (Andrew Skilton, current research). Such access can be through temporary visits or, in the case of death in the corresponding state, rebirth. In the *Kevaddha Sutta*, a monk visits the god Mahābrahmā in his heaven, accessible through the first *jhāna*, to ask the him cosmological questions, only for the god to take him aside, admit that he does not know the answers, and send him back to the Buddha. In the *Nanda Sutta*, the Buddha lures his cousin Nanda away from his beautiful bride with promises of more alluring nymphs in heaven, to be accessed through meditation practice. Once ordained, Nanda becomes very adept at meditation, solely with this purpose in mind, but is then shamed by other monks into pursuing meditation for more spiritual purposes. Correspondences between specific realms of the cosmos and meditation states had been fully worked out by the fifth-century CE (King 1980: 86) as had durations of rebirth and effects of subtle differences in *jhānic* experience (Bodhi 1993: Chapter V). Thus the four highest levels of the cosmos, the "formless realms" (*arūpaloka*) are accessed through the parallel "formless *jhāna*." The names of these formless realms are the same as the realms of the equivalent *jhāna*. In descending order from highest or most elevated to lowest they are: realm of Neither Perception nor Non-Perception, realm of Nothingness, realm of Infinity of Consciousness, realm of Infinity of Space. The realms of form (*rūpaloka*) are then paired with the four (sometimes five) *jhāna*. The fifth *jhāna* comes from subdividing the fourth *jhāna* into two levels. Thus, the highest six heavens in this realm, all identified by the type of deity residing in them, are paired with the fourth (or fourth and fifth) *jhāna*. The third heaven from the bottom of these six heavens is the heaven of the "Effortless Gods." It is here that nonreturners, at the third spiritual level en route to arhatship, are reborn and stay until achieving *nibbāna*. The next three heavens below these six heavens, inhabited by different levels of "lustrous" gods, are paired with the third *jhāna*. Below them, the three classes of "radiant" gods are paired with the second *jhāna*. Finally, the lowest of the form realms is made up of three classes of *brahma* gods, the Mahābrahma deities, below which are the "Ministers to Brahma" and then the "members of Brahma's retinue." These three are paired with the first *jhāna*.

Extensive tabulations of the aforementioned parallels, including the lower *kāmaloka* "sensuous world," can be found in King 1980: 85, Bodhi 1993: 212–213 and Na Rangsi 1976: 32ff. Na Rangsi provides duration of rebirths and additional causes for rebirth in the different realms.

The realms of the sensuous world, the *kāmaloka*, which includes further heavens, as well as the human realm, animal realms, and hells, are also accessible to meditators, as is seen in stories about the Buddha and monks such as Phra Māleyya, whose exploits visiting different realms is the subject of popular narratives at traditional Tai funerals. It is also a belief found in the present day, as Martin Seeger describes in relation to Mae Chi Kaew. Mae Chi Kaew achieved *arhatship* after following the advice of the famous northern Thai meditation monk Ajan Mahabua, who told her to turn the focus of her meditation from the outside to the inside. He had received similar advice himself from his teach Ajan Man. This meant that Mae Chi Kaew should meditate on her own body and mental states (i.e., follow the practice described in the *Mahāsatipaṭṭhāna Sutta*), rather than interact with ghosts, spirits, mythical snakes (*nāgas*), and the cosmological realms to which her seven years of meditation had given her access (Seeger 2010: 571):

> The hagiographies also mention cosmological tours that Mae Chi Kaew undertook in her meditation. These took her to various levels of heavens and the lower realms of the rebirth cycle in Theravāda Buddhist cosmology. Such superhuman experiences allowed her to study and understand the working of the kammic law. (Seeger 2010: 589)

A Burmese meditation tradition called "Maung-taung Myae Zin" (also known as "Kani") also teaches practitioners how to access and observe different realms of the cosmos. Some meditation teachers comment on the ease with which children, who they say are less prone to impose meaning or construct experience, access these realms when taught meditation (personal communication). This point ties in well with a proposition by Johannes Bronkhorst that meditative experiences such as *jhāna* reflect the accessing of reality without the intermediary of the constructions of language (Bronkhorst 2012), even if the resulting assessment of the significance of such experience is radically different from a practitioner perspective.

Prerequisites and Preparations for Meditation

Canonical and commentarial texts present a traditional formulaic list of secluded places suitable for undertaking meditation that includes the foot of a tree and an empty shrine. The upright, cross-legged (half-lotus) posture appropriate to most meditations is also described.

Adaptations to these have probably been made from the earliest times: monasteries developed as complex sites with individual cells or huts for monks as well as shrine rooms in which one can meditate facing the Buddha image. The adaptation has continued in the modern period with the teaching and practice of meditation in a broader range of contexts. While the traditional cross-legged seated posture on the ground might be adapted for those uncomfortable on the floor by providing chairs, for example, some practitioners regard posture as more important than comfort, relating it to awareness of suffering and to energy flows.

The importance of these rudimentary physical preparations for meditation is acknowledged even in the most reformed and applied types of practice. However, in reform Buddhism and where meditation has been extracted as a technique to be applied outside of Buddhism, a range of prerequisites and preparations traditionally regarded as necessary for meditation are often ignored. These include the practice of moral conduct (*sīla*) as a prerequisite, and the assessment of the moral or mental state of an individual by the meditation master in order to decide the type and level of meditation practice. Both of these aspects of preparation are hard to ensure in the teaching of meditation to large groups. One of the texts of the *Abhidhamma Piṭaka*, the *Puggalapaññatti* (*"Designation of Human Types*)," provides guidance on how to determine an individual's disposition from their behavior, proclivities, and mannerisms; which of the root problems (greed, hatred, or delusion) this disposition most relates to; and what to select as an appropriate meditation subject for that type. There are manuals within traditional meditation (*borān kammaṭṭhāna*) that hint at the interpretation of *nimitta* (see earlier text) in relation to the student's readiness for different levels of practice.

In his *Visuddhimagga*, Buddhaghosa points out the necessity of a teacher, ranking them in a hierarchy of spiritual attainments, from the best, the Buddha himself, down to someone who at least is familiar with one of the three *Piṭaka* of the Pali Canon, so that the teaching will, at least, not be in conflict with the Dhamma. Here we see perhaps see a merging of the hierarchies of learning and experiential wisdom, a merging that is not unproblematic. Today there are still contrasting emphases. The *borān kammaṭṭhāna* lineage of the former Thai supreme patriarch Suk Kaithuean (1733–1822), now continued at Wat Ratchasittharam in Thonburi, Bangkok, emphasizes the importance of studying meditation experience not in book form but through the discussion of one's experiences within a teacher–pupil relationship (Ong 2011: 161). The Dhammakāya Movement's meditation system is based on that established by Luang Pho Sot (1896–1956), an erstwhile student at Wat Ratchasittharam, and is clearly closely related to it (Newell 2011: 104). One of the key differences is that it teaches a simplified form of the earliest stages of meditation to mass audiences, rather than in a close pupil–teacher relationship. Nonetheless, they emphasize the importance of experience over study: the main temple of the movement, Wat Phra Dhammakāya, is set up in ways that accommodate the thousands of literate and illiterate followers equally and the movement flaunts the nonliterate status of the precept nuns whose meditation instruction lies at the heart of the temple's practice lineage (see Chapter 9). Meanwhile, the movement's arch-critic, the celebrated scholar monk Phra Prayudh Payutto (b.1938), emphasizes the importance of study (*pariyatti*) as a basis for practice (*paṭipatti*), dismissing the movement's practices and teachings as lacking canonical authority (Seeger 2009).

Another preparation Buddhaghosa mentions is the importance of dedicating oneself to the Buddha before commencing practice (see Chapter 2). Worship of the Buddha traditionally takes place before undertaking meditation and it is interesting to see that, in the more extensive litanies for Buddha worship extant from meditation traditions, the moral status of the practitioner is one area in which the practitioner, through the worship, asks for intervention of the Buddha and the meditation teacher. The importance of devotional practice and the ritual chanting of Pali texts at the soteriological, meditational end of the religious spectrum contradicts Western preconceived notions of early Buddhist teachings on worship and ritual (see Chapters 2 and 5); these misconceptions appear to be associated with the rationalization of Buddhism in the modern period on the part of both orientalist scholars and Theravada apologists. The importance of the devotional activities and chanting does not appear to have been questioned before the modern reform period. They necessitate the procuring and making of the offerings. In the *borān kammaṭṭhāna* tradition, in which engagement in the different levels of meditation is marked by fresh rituals and chanting, these offerings are extensive and can be costly, one of the reasons identified by practitioners in twenty-first-century Cambodia for its failure to compete with the increasingly popular *vipassanā* system (Crosby and Long, fieldwork 2012).

Central to the practice of meditation is the achievement of an appropriate mental state and a major aspect of the development of the capacity to meditate is dealing with the "hindrances" to such a state, traditionally a set of five:

1. Covetousness/craving for sensual pleasure
2. Ill-will
3. Sloth and torpor
4. Restlessness and anxiety
5. Doubt

One can see how the ritual, precept-taking and moral and merit-making practices can help prepare mental states that avoid these hindrances. Different traditions have different ways for dealing with the hindrances when they occur. Some just observe them and let them pass; others actively focus on them, labeling them, as in the naming of distractions three times in the Mahāsī Sayadaw tradition.

Benefits

In addition to the self-transformation for which it is advocated, meditation has a number of other benefits widely accepted within Buddhism. Meditation is regarded as a meritorious activity in its own right. Some practices combat fear and prevent danger; some assist the dead. Examples of the latter include the cemetery practices of wandering northern Thai forest monks in the early twentieth century (Tiyavanich 1997), the pride of place at the head of the funerary procession given to a *borān kammaṭṭhāna* monk in Cambodia in the pre-Khmer Rouge period (personal communication, Samdech Preah Krou Om Bunheng, December 14, 2012) and the mass gatherings of about 3000 monks performing chanting and practicing meditation outside the Royal Palace in Phnom Penh organized by the Cambodia Ministry of Cults and Religions for the benefit of the late King Sihanouk in the period between the return of his body from China and its cremation on February 4, 2013 (personal communication, Phra Sok Buntheoun, December 11, 2012). The benefits to health and stress management were emphasized in the promotion of *vipassanā* in newly independent Burma, for example by U. Nu (1907–1995), several time prime minister before the military coup of 1962. More direct applications in terms of health are its use in the treatment of addiction in Thailand and elsewhere, and in the healing applications of the *borān kammaṭṭhāna* (see later text). A widespread understanding that meditation attainments bestow the kind of power that can be used for withstanding attack from enemies is found in the legends associated with the practices (probably *borān kammaṭṭhāna*) of King Taksin (1734–1782), the sole ruler of Thailand in the Thonburi period, known for his successful campaigns against the Burmese who had sacked the previous capital of Siam, Ayutthaya, in 1767. Advanced meditation practitioners are regarded as having gained powers (*iddhi* in Pali), sometimes translated as "miraculous power." While they are regarded as natural side effects of meditation, in Thailand and Burma, *samatha* meditation and practices such as *weikza* (see later text) are sometimes regarded with suspicion, as being practised primarily with *iddhi* in mind.

This range of benefits attributed to meditation blurs the distinctions made in Western scholarship and some reform Theravada between the *nibbāna* aspect of religion, entailing meditation, the *kammic*, entailing meritorious activity, and the apotropaic aspect, entailing protective practices such as *paritta*. The transformative impact of the broader devotional, chanting and ritual activities in which Theravada Buddhists engage including as a component of meditation has received little attention in contrast to the empirical research on meditation. The traditional cognitive–somatic divide in Western medicine and the variable validation of the different aspects of Theravada practice by both reformers and outside observers have contributed to this imbalance in research.

Variety of Methods

A number of meditation traditions have become well known or widely popular in the modern period. At the same time, the tradition that appears to have been most widespread and dominant in court-sponsored Buddhism in the eighteenth century, *borān kammaṭṭhāna* "traditional meditation," has virtually disappeared. Some of the most important and well known traditions of the early modern and modern period are identified next:

(a) *Borān yogāvacara kammaṭṭhāna*, shortened to *borān kammaṭṭhāna* here, was the dominant form of meditation at court and in court-sponsored Buddhism in the eighteenth century in Cambodia, Laos, Sri Lanka, and Thailand, as attested by the evidence of manuscripts and manuals belonging to the supreme patriarchs and members of the royal families (Yasoatharat 1935/1936, Crosby *et al.* 2012). Written evidence for it dates back to the sixteenth-century Dhammakaya inscription in Phitsanulok. This is earlier than evidence for any of the other meditation systems currently widespread in Theravada (Choompolpaisal *et al.* in preparation). Although the tradition was transmitted from the court of Ayutthaya to Sri Lanka in the 1750s (Crosby *et al.* 2012), after the sack of Ayutthaya by the Burmese and the end of the Thonburi rule of King Taksin, the new Chakri dynasty of Bangkok began to promote the new Thammayutika Nikāya founded by Prince Mongkut in 1833. This Nikāya, which was given institutional priority throughout Thailand and was also established in Laos (1850) and Cambodia (1864), represented Thai royal and national interest. As part of this transition, the traditional meditation associated with the more established "Mahānikāya" was discouraged. This process of undermining the tradition in Cambodia continued under French colonial rule. The French promoted a reform faction within the Mahānikāya there. The combination of the spread of Burmese *vipassanā* and the Marxist revolutions in Laos and Cambodia led to the virtual elimination of this tradition. It now continues among only a few temples in Cambodia (de Bernon 2000, Crosby and Long fieldwork December 2012, Marston 2008) and Thailand (Ong 2011).

The simplest *borān kammaṭṭhāna* practices are akin to the *kasiṇa* practices described earlier. The more complex *borān kammaṭṭhāna* methods are interesting in that they apply to the components that make up the spiritual and meditative path, as found in the *Visuddhimagga*, the methods of directed transformation that also developed in other sciences such as medicine, mathematics, alchemy, and linguistics. The method for physically internalizing the components of the meditative qualities sought on the path to Buddhahood (through visualizing them as spheres of light/syllables entering the "womb" via energy centers from the nostril down to the navel) is recognizably akin to the obstetrical treatment of babies in the womb practised in traditional ayurveda. The use of group theory mathematics to combine these elements is familiar from the *Paṭṭhāna*, the seventh book of the *Abhidhamma Piṭaka*, but also from ayurvedic pharmaceuticals. In the former case, the mathematics is used to explore the causal combinations understood by the Buddha through his omniscience. In the latter case, the mathematics is used to calculate the exact balance of medicine required to treat medical conditions caused by an imbalance in the three "humours" (*dosa*) in relation to the four material elements that make up the body. The parallel between this and treating the spiritual imbalance caused by the three fires of greed, hatred, and delusion in combination with the four material elements suggests a shared view of the process of bringing about change (Crosby, ongoing research). The overlap extends to the use of *borān kammaṭṭhāna* to healing of both oneself and others. It appears in some accounts to work on the basis of clarifying disturbances in the "humours" (*dosa*) and movement in the energy channels (Mettanando 1998).

Other features of *borān kammaṭṭhāna* include the use of *Abhidhamma;* a rich symbolism; rituals including "rebirthing" rites; its esoteric nature, in that it relies on initiation and teacher–pupil teaching and harnesses the power and hidden meaning of symbolic language and concepts familiar in their exoteric interpretations in Theravada more broadly; and language as a cosmogonic power. The tradition also uses a rich mythology and narrative representations of the path and of meditation practice. These include the mind personified as a young princess (sometimes a prince and princess) the body as a five-branched fig tree (Bizot 1976, Crosby *et al.* 2012) and the spiritual quest in the form of an esoteric retelling of the Indic epic popular in Southeast Asia, the *Rāmāyana* (Bizot 1989).

There are some interesting reports of differences between the experience of *Visuddhimagga* and *borān kammaṭṭhāna* practices even when the instructions appear quite similar. Practitioners described their experience of the *asubha* meditation in which rotting corpses are visualized in different stages of decomposition, as also found in the *Visuddhimagga* (see earlier text) and akin to the northern Thai practice as taught by Mahabua (Kornfield 1977/2007: 175), as so realistic that they included even the smell of the corpse and the physical symptom such as sweating and horripilation (Crosby and Long, interviews with former practitioners and grandchildren of now deceased practitioners, December 2012). Although the periods before the Khmer Rouge were not without warfare, violence, and death, one might speculate that the horrors of the Khmer Rouge period were so overwhelming as to have contributed to an unwillingness to re-engage with this practice. The perception of the "new" *vipassanā* system as a fresh beginning more generally is confirmed by the testimony of those who switched to *vipassanā*.

The practices are not confined to soteriological applications. The levels of initiation, the importance of teacher–student interaction, the physical incorporation of qualities, the creation of Buddha within, the use of symbolic language, and the fetal imagery all add up to remind the outside observer of tantric Buddhism as found in the Buddhism of the Himalayas. With the diverse history of Buddhism in the region, there has been plenty of opportunity for influence from Śaiva and Vajrayāna traditions, yet so far in the meditation manuals of *borān kammaṭṭhāna* no non-Theravada nomenclature has been uncovered, no rich pantheon of gods, *bodhisattvas* or other beings that we might expect from a direct borrowing (Crosby 2000). An interesting exception to this within Cambodian Pali *paritta* (rather than in *borān kammaṭṭhāna* meditation) is the *Mahādibbamanta Sutta*, where we find reference to the non-Theravada pantheon (Jaini 1965/2001: 505). Rather, Theravada *Abhidhamma* and traditional medicine form the framework within which this practice is constructed, suggesting the possibility that Theravada *Abhidhamma* developed within it types of practice reminiscent of those that developed elsewhere because of a pan-Asian scientific worldview that applied as much to meditation as to medicine.

(b) The *weikza* tradition of Burma includes practices aimed at spiritual transformation, the prolongation of life and this-world advantages. Details of *weikza* are hard to trace before the nineteenth century even though their presence in narrative goes back at least two centuries further (Pranke forthcoming). The term *weikza* derives from the Pali term *vijjā* "knowledge," and, like the term in Pali has the connotations both of liberating knowledge and magical knowledge. The longevity practice are based on the stories of immediate enlightenment, or at least entrance on to one of the four stages of the path (stream-entrant, one-returner, nonreturner, or arhatship/enlightenment), on hearing the Buddha preach in person. Practitioners therefore seek to avoid missing out on the next opportunities to hear a Buddha preach in person by prolonging their life as a human, thus avoiding being in a bad rebirth as a hellbeing or animal on those occasions. The first such opportunity is the occasion when, at the end of his teaching in about 2500 years time, Gotama Buddha's relics gather together for him to give a final sermon (see Chapter 1). The subsequent occasion is the arrival of Metteyya Buddha. Like *borān kammaṭṭhāna*, the manipulation of significant numbers and letters, and the chanting of powerful phrases is an important aspect of *weikza* (Rozenberg 2010: 48–50). Because of the reliance on the future preaching of a Buddha for enlightenment and the use of his/her (almost always his) supernatural power to intervene in mundane matters, they are described in Burmese Buddhism as referring to the mundane (*lawki*, Burmese, *lokiya/lokika* Pali) realm as opposed to the supramundane (*lawkoktara* Burmese, *lokuttara* Pali). Such magical powers as telepathy and flying or being able to travel to remote places, both in this realm and in the universe, are attributed to them. Because of this association with the acquiring and use of magical powers, *weikza* may be spoken of disparagingly by opponents, including those who advocate *vipassanā* (see later text), the more well-known practice within Burmese Buddhism, which does not aim at such powers. However, a distinction is also made within *weikza* between an emphasis on the mundane and the supramundane goals (Rozenberg 2010: 53). Ascetic practices, including extreme fasting and meditation in the remote forest, are important aspects of the supramundane *weikza* path, and there are *weikza* today who are regarded as being *arhats* (*yahanda* Burmese).

Like *borān kammaṭṭhāna*, the *weikza* path is esoteric, requiring initiation under a master (Pranke forthcoming). The meditation practices followed by *weikza* are routinely described as *samatha* "tranquility" practices, in contrast to *vipassanā* "insight" practices. That means that in the current characterizing of the distinction between *samatha* and *vipassanā* in Burma, which draws on the distinction made in the *Visuddhimagga* (see earlier text), *weikza* draws on the forty *kammaṭṭhāna* described by Buddhaghosa in the *samādhi* ("meditation/concentration") section of the *Visuddhimagga*. While I have been told of the use of breathing techniques and repetition of the phrase *araham̩*, these are presumably initial techniques. Current publications on *weikza* available to me do not clarify the nature of the *samatha* practice nor how *weikza* engage with it. In other words, we are unusually confronted with problems in both ways of describing meditation practice, not only the distinctive method applied (as is the case with most traditions), but also the specific subjects, which usually we can identify. While this reflects the general tendency for writings on meditation to focus on what, from a practitioners perspective, are the peripheral matters, with *weikza* this has greater justification in that the importance and attractiveness of *weikza* in Burmese mythology and present narrative is very much the non-soteriological, "mundane" (*lowki* Burmese) practices and the benefits of these both for ordinary people and in maintaining Buddhism.

As with *borān kammaṭṭhāna* (see earlier text) there have been accusations of heterodoxy and of Mahayana and Tantric influence on *weikza*, and some practitioners accept that as the case. There has been plenty of opportunity for the forms of Buddhism we now label as Theravada, Mahayana and **Vajrayana** to influence one another, having existing side by side including in the territories we now designate at Theravada. However, Guillaume Rozenberg has pointed out that one of the aspects seen as most heterodox, the extension of the lifespan, finds authority in the Pali Canon. He observes, "there is doctrinal foundation in Theravāda Buddhism itself for the idea of being able to prolong one's life due to one's spiritual accomplishment ... found not in an obscure and incomprehensible passage of the canon but in the *Mahāparinibbāna Sutta* and the *Cakkvatti–Sīhanāda Sutta*, among the most well-known and studied canonical texts. In the *Cakkvatti-Sīhanāda Sutta*, the Buddha tells his monk disciples that one who practices the roads to supernatural powers (*iddhis*) "may, if he so desires, live for an aeon, or the remainder of an aeon" and that it constitutes a true way to live according to his doctrine" (Rozenberg 2010: 66). In spite of such accusations of heterodoxy and non-Theravada influence, and without recourse to such authorizing statements, "most Burmese people, whatever the social milieu, simply grant – without question – Buddhist legitimacy to *weikza*. The common presence of famous *weikza* portraits on domestic Buddhism shrines attests to this fact. Rather than belonging to an indefinable "normative Burmese Buddhism," the *weikza* represent a cultural phenomenon; within Burmese society they constitute a central focus of practice, discourse, and controversy" (Rozenberg 2010: 67).

(c) The Northern Thai forest monks, called *thudong* monks, meaning followers of one or more of the 13 permitted "ascetic practices" (such as never lying down, or eating only one meal day) kept to practices such as living in the forests and pursuing an itinerant lifestyle dedicated to meditation. They were often attributed with great magical and spiritual powers (Jackson 1988/2003: 157). Some of the details of their meditation practice, such as recitation of certain phrases (*buddho* and *sammā araham̩*) and the images that may appear to practitioners, suggest a possible relationship with the *borān kammaṭṭhāna* methods. The devotional litanies transmitted for use in preparation for meditation are akin to those that have circulated with *borān kammaṭṭhāna* methods in Cambodia and Sri Lanka (Crosby 1999: Chapter 6, Swearer 1995). Until further research on this is undertaken, the extent of the relationship remains a matter for speculation.

It is unclear to what extent the practice of *thudong* monks throughout Southeast Asia was interconnected. An important *thudong* monk of Bangladesh was Sādhanānanda Mahāthera. His ordained name means "joy in meditating." Born in 1920 he spent at least 12 years meditating in the forest having been disappointed with the level of spiritual learning available at the local monasteries. On the basis of his period in the forest, he is popularly known as Bana Bhante (*bana* is the Bengali/Chakma pronunciation of Pali/Sanskrit *vana* "forest" and *bhante* is a Pali word for addressing a senior monk) meaning "Spiritual Teacher from the Forest." From 1977 to his death he lived at Vana Vihāra in Rangamati, where a large and well supported complex of monastic and meditation buildings grew up around him offering training to monks, precept nuns, and laypeople. The monks are renowned for their strict observance of monastic discipline, including not handling money. His meditation in the forest may have been forms of mindfulness of breathing and recollection of the gods, though he also became familiar later with the *satipaṭṭhāna* methods that are the basis of *vipassanā*. His teaching focuses on the nature of suffering (*dukkha*) (fieldwork Crosby and Nagasena Bhikkhu, February 2009; personal communication of Nagasena Bhikkhu with Bangladeshi monks December 2012).

The stories and practices of the lives of earlier monks from the northern Thai tradition live on mainly in comic books and hagiographical stories, since the tradition for the most part died out in the early to mid twentieth century, excepting the lineage connected to Thammayutikanikāya that included the famous monks Ajan Sao and Ajan Man, and the latter's Ajan Mahabua. However, while, Ajan Sao and Ajan Man are credited with the foundation of the forest tradition within the Thammayutikanikāya, and Ajan Sao studied with the earlier forest monks (Tiyavanich 1997: 263–264), the narratives of their activity include the conversion of forest monks adhering to earlier meditation practices associated with supernatural powers to the practice of Ajan Sao's and Ajan Man's methods (Taylor 1993: 111–112). Once again, then, the hagiographies are more informative about the great powers to the forest monks than their actual meditation practices. We know that they used recitation of verses and rosaries to count the repetitions (Tiyavanich 1997: 325, note 66), but this is a widespread practice for meditation methods involving repetitions of phrases such as "*Buddho*" or "*arahaṃ*" and it appears to have continued among some Thammayutika forest monks also. The Thammayutika forest monks seem to have accepted living in the forest but to have taken on the *samatha* practices as described in the Pali Canon and the *samādhi* section of *Visuddhimagga*.

Mahabua taught that the *samatha*, calming or concentration practices, were a necessary precursor to the insight practices:

> In a place where there are few trees and each one is standing on its own, if a man wanted to cut one down he could do so and make it fall where he wanted. He could then take it and use it as he wished with no difficulty.
>
> But if he wanted to cut a tree down in a forest where its branches were entangled with other trees and creepers, he would find it difficult to fell the tree and to make it fall just where he wished. (Kornfield 1977/2007: 177)

However, those people who found it hard to achieve calm might first use insight about the reasons for their agitation as a precursor to calm. The insight practice he taught involves observing the body and how one acts based on attachment to it (including one's interactions with others). This causes one to lose attachment to the body and thus also lose one's attachment to and hatred toward others. At the more advanced level, the insight meditation includes the meditation on the aggregates as given in the wisdom (*paññā*) section of the *Visuddhimagga*.

The threats to the older tradition of northern Thai/Lao forest monks came from a number of developments – not just the Thammayutika-oriented reforms, but also the political developments in Thailand and Laos and the economic use made of the forest. The centralization of Sangha education and hierarchy and attempts to impose Bangkok Thai as the medium for teaching the Dhamma undermined the status of practice-oriented monks and the monk–lay relationship that supported them. The forests ceased to be free for people to roam in. This loss of habitat began as a result of the anticommunist policies under General Sarit after the military coups of 1957–1958, targeting the northeast as the poorest region and as that closest to Laos and China, and thus more susceptible to Communism. From the 1960s, money from the United States for rural development in the region further undermined the habitat. After the loss of half of the forest area by the 1980s, the Thai government closed the forest in 1989, controlling felling. The deforestation had led to floods in the south, but later replanting in the deforested areas was often with eucalyptus, reflecting Japanese commercial interests. A ban on people living within the conservation areas led to the forced relocation of an estimated three to five million forest dwellers, mainly from the around the Chiang Mai and Maehongson areas. (http://www.ldinet.org/2008/index.php?option=com_content&task=view&id=217&Itemid=32, retrieved December 10, 2012).

The great human cost this entailed included the loss of the habitat and communities that had supported traditional forest monks. Only the livelihood of a relatively small number of *thudong* was protected.

One monk who studied with both Ajan Man and Ajan Mahabua was Ajahn Chah (1918–1992). He was instrumental in popularizing the tradition not only in Thailand but internationally. Through him, the northern Thai forest tradition adapted to modern developments and attracted a significant number of Western converts. The first monastery in this lineage in the West was Cittaviveka, opened in Chithurst, England, in 1979, with Ajahn Chah's American disciple Ajahn Sumedho as its first abbot. Further centers have followed in the United Kingdom, including Amaravatī near Hemel Hempstead, opened in 1984, and further afield, including centers in the United States and Australia.

(d) Burmese *Vipassanā*. The Burmese *Vipassanā* movement that has spread worldwide dates back, in its current form, to the developments in Buddhism that took place in Burma from the end of the nineteenth century to the middle of the twentieth century as the last kings of Burma strove to stave off the British (see also Chapter 7). It continued to flourish as Burma strove for independence and then in the creation of the newly independent Burma after 1947. The two teachers who appear to have done most to popularize the lay engagement characteristic of modern *vipassanā* are Ledi Sayadaw in Upper Burma (1840–1923, see Chapter 7) and Mingun Sayadaw in Lower Burma (1868–1955).

There had been attempts in Burma to popularize meditation at least from the eighteenth century but with no long-term effect (Braun 2008: 65). In the second half of the nineteenth century, the number of monks meditating in the monasteries in the Sagaing Hills southwest of Mandalay increased in response to King Mindon's effort to impose the ethos of forest-dwelling monks on the Burmese Sangha as a whole. Mindon's chief queen sponsored one of the most effective meditation monks there, Htut-kaung Sayadaw (1798–1890) (Braun 2008: 66). At this stage, meditation began to be promoted more widely among monks. The reformist monk Hngettwin Sayadaw (1831–1910), who moved to the Sagaing Hills in the late 1860s, not only advocated meditation as a daily practice for monks, but also for laypeople on the fortnightly holy days (Braun 2008: 66).

At the same time, meditation texts had become a topic for new scholarly works, such as the commentary *Mahāsatipaṭṭhāna Sutta Nissaya* written by the Burmese monk Cakkinda in 1873 (Khur-Yearn 2012: 209ff.). It drew heavily on Buddhaghosa's fifth-century commentary on the *Mahāsatipaṭṭhāna Sutta*, rather than being a commentary directly on the canonical text. Cakkinda's work in turn influenced other authors including his pupil the Shan scholar Zao Sra Naminda and Naminda's student Zao Amat Long (1854–1905). In 1875, Zao Amat Long (a name acquired later in life when appointed as a minister of one of the Shan states) composed a Shan version of Cakkinda's *Mahāsatipaṭṭhāna* commentary in Shan *lik long* style. At that time the 21-year-old Amat Long had disrobed and was working as a travelling *zare*, a composer-scribe, under the sponsorship of the rulers of various Shan States. The meditation text he composed was written for public reading as part of the temple-sleeping tradition in which laypeople join monks on holy days to stay overnight at the temple and undertake intensive religious practice (see Chapter 5). This means that at the time *vipassanā* was on the brink of becoming popularized among both monks and lay members of the different ethnic groups of Burma, including Shan laypeople, it was already part of Shan lay practice (Khur-Yearn 2012: 91–96). It seems to be based on a longer tradition of *Abhidhamma* study and meditation practice by Shan laity (that may also have been found among other groups in Burma), although centers derived from the Burmese popularization of *vipassanā* would also spread to the Shan states with the spread of the Mingun tradition to all parts of Burma in the 1930s (Khur-Yearn 2012: 74). The practice of establishing meditation centers independent of monasteries seems to have started with the followers of Mingun Sayadaw, who set up a center in Myohla in 1911 or 1913 (Houtman 1990: 43).

The two most internationally well-known *vipassanā* teachers to emerge in the early independence period were U Ba Khin (1899–1971) and Mahāsī Sayadaw (1904–1982). U Ba Khin was the first Accountant-General of Burma. He traced his teaching lineage to Ledi Sayadaw via Saya Thetgyi (1873–1945). Mahāsī Sayadaw was a pupil of Mingun Sayadaw. The modern style of teaching meditation in designated meditation centers began to be popularized more widely after independence under the initial patronage of U Nu. Mahāsī Sayadaw opened a center in Rangoon in 1949, shortly followed by U Ba Khin whose center opened in 1952. In 1955, *vipassanā* was included in the syllabus of the Sangha University and from 1957 it was introduced into prisons (Houtman 1990: 47). This was long before the uptake of *vipassanā* by political prisoners from the 1980s onwards (Houtman 1999).

U Ba Khin's most famous disciple is the layman S.N. Goenka, born in Mandalay in 1924 to a family of Indian ethnicity. Goenka, advocating it as a scientific system that is not restricted to Buddhists, has been responsible for its spread worldwide. Hundreds of thousands of people train in the method annually through the courses he designed. While closely based on the *Mahasatipaṭṭhāna Sutta*, the *vipassanā* methods all incorporate *Abhidhamma* analyses into the four *satipaṭṭhāna*, as also found in the third division *Visuddhimagga* even though not all traditions accept the *Visuddhimaga* as a correct authority. There are variations in the way mindfulness, and any preparatory *samatha*, are to be developed. One of the characteristic methods of the Goenka tradition is the scanning of the body used in the initial stages of practicing mindfulness of the body.

Most modern traditions trace back to either Ledi or Mahāsī Sayadaw. In part, this is because of the way approval for running meditation centers was granted with reference to the centers established in Rangoon. The Mogok Tradition is independent of the Ledi and Mahāsī lineages, going back to the Mogok Sayadaw Ven. U Vimala (1900–1962) who had studied *Abhidhamma* under Sayagyi U Ohn (see Chapter 7). His meditation focuses on dependent origination and *cittānupassanā* "observation or identification of the moments of consciousness." Since the Mogok Sayadaw did not receive state support, his following grew less quickly. A dedicated center was opened by some of his followers only following his death, but there are now over 300 branches in Burma.

Another important tradition is the Pa-Auk lineage, headed by Pa-Auk Sayadaw Āciṇṇa (b. 1934). His teaching currently attracts many foreigners to his forest center near Mawlamyine (Moulmein). His teaching follows the *Visuddhimagga* strictly and therefore requires students to stay for three to six months. He also teaches long courses internationally.

The Burmese *vipassanā* traditions began to gain popularity throughout the Theravada world before its broader global spread. It spread among monks and laypeople through teaching lineages to Thailand and Sri Lanka in the nineteenth and early twentieth centuries. In Thailand, the female lay meditation master Ajan Naeb (1897–1983) began learning from Pathunta U Vilāsa in 1932, a Burmese monk resident in Bangkok. She founded several centers in Thailand, where she continued to teach a straightforward form of *vipassanā* that focused on observing the cause and effect of suffering in our daily lives. Jack Kornfield reports, "She may first instruct the visitors to sit comfortably and then ask them not to move. Shortly, of course, one automatically begins to change position. 'Wait, hold it. Why are you moving? Don't move yet.'" She then points to how moving away from and finding distraction from pain guides all our daily actions (Kornfield 1977/2007: 137–138). Most of the modern style *vipassanā* meditation centers in Thailand were influenced directly by the centers of U Ba Khin and Mahasī Sayadaw in the early 1950s, with a *Vipassanā* Meditation Centre opening in Bangkok as early as 1951.

The Sri Lankan forest monks of the end of the nineteenth and twentieth centuries were part of the reform movement in Sri Lanka, which was closely aligned to the independence movement, as in Burma. The forest monks were in the newly introduced Amarapura and Rāmañña Nikāya ordination lineages from Burma, which unlike the powerful Siyam-nikāya were not restricted by caste (see Chapter 8). Their meditation practices were eclectic, based on *Suttas*, the *Visuddhimagga*, and other manuals. This meant that the *borān kammaṭṭhāna* meditation introduced with the Siyam Nikāya from Ayutthaya in the 1750s (Crosby *et al.* 2012) was not transmitted in these new meditation lineages. Although *borān kammaṭṭhāna* continued to be practised during the nineteenth century, it seems to have died out at the very end of the nineteenth century (Crosby 1999, Woodward 1916).

The *vipassanā* tradition in Sri Lanka was introduced by laypeople who had visited Burma and supported a group of Burmese monks of the Mahasī Sayadaw lineage who initially taught from a private house in Colombo. The rural center established at Kanduboda with facilities designed to maximize time spent in meditation was opened to both monastics and laypeople in 1956 (Gombrich and Obeyesekere 1988: 238). Its first head was the Sri Lankan monk Kahatapitiya Sumathipāla Thera, a member of Amarapura Nikāya (Bond 1988: 133). Initially there was some vociferous opposition to *vipassanā*, partly in resentment of it as a foreign intrusion. The most vociferous adversary was the monk Kheminda Thera, who criticized it for a number of reasons including the absence of *samatha*, that it does not require Dhamma study as a preparation, that it is not in accordance with the *Visuddhimagga* vision of progression or practice, and that the breathing exercises focusing on the rising and falling of the breath in the abdomen were unorthodox. Counter-arguments pointed to the diversity of meditation teaching to be found in the canon and commentaries, and thus to the possibility of textual authorities other than the *Visuddhimagga* for *vipassanā* practices. In spite of this initial response, the

Kanduboda center has gone on to be highly influential among monks and laity alike, every year hosting hundreds of practitioners on intensive meditation training, usually of a fortnight's duration. (For examples of other types of meditation practised in Sri Lanka in the postindependence period, see Bond 1988: Chapter 5.)

In Cambodia, Burmese *vipassanā* had been introduced in the early twentieth century by U Pandidama, a pupil of Mingun Sayadaw (Houtman 1990: 44), and possibly even early by Preah Thamma Vipassana Kong, a senior monk who lived on Phnom Santuk in the late eighteenth/early nineteenth century (Ian Harris, personal communication March 27, 2012). This transmission was disrupted by the events of the 1960s culminating in the devastation of the Khmer Rouge period. Some people within this early transmission revived *vipassanā* after the Khmer Rouge period, in part as a way of coping with the stress of so much killing. However, the current popularity of *vipassanā* in Cambodia mainly stems from the lineage of the monk Sam Buntheon. In spite of his still unsolved murder in 2003, his impact has been so widespread that, by 2012, the Udong *vipassanā* tradition had almost completely eclipsed the traditional *borān kammaṭṭhāna*, which initially looked set to make a comeback after the freeing up of religious practice in the 1990s (Crosby and Long fieldwork 2012). The success is in part due to the organization of training at the large and specialist facilities at Udong. More recently, Goenka centers have also been established in Cambodia.

(e) The influential Thai social activist and religious reformer, Buddhadasa (1906–1993), holding an attitude much in common with the early *vipassanā* movement, rejected the monastic-lay divide of "traditional" Thai Buddhism. While he advocated *vipassanā* over *samatha* methods because of the association of the latter with *jhāna* and magical powers (a view found in both Thailand and Burma), he did not advocate intensive, formal meditation for laypeople. He was highly critical of *Abhidhamma* and the *Visuddhimagga* as overly complex and regarded the *vipassanā* systems from Burma as also too complex. He advocated a more rational and engaged form of Buddhism that emphasized not identifying any aspect of our bodies or our experiences as "self," with a simplified mindfulness of breathing meditation that should be applied in daily life (Jackson 1988/2003: 110ff.). Jackson writes,

Buddhadāsa emphasized the general accessibility of the practice of *chit wang* or non-self-centred mindfulness, and thus the accessibility of salvation, by maintaining that if it is practised correctly the mindfulness of *chit wang* can itself lead to *nibbāna*. Buddhist doctrine details a series of stages on the path to ending suffering and Buddhadāsa claims that each of these stages follows on from one another in a natural succession, starting from the fundamental mindful practice of *chit wang* or non-self-centredness. He claims that it is "just by making our own daily living so pure and honest that there develop in succession spiritual joy, calm, insight into the true nature of things, disenchantment, withdrawal, escape, purification from defilements, and then peace of *nibbāna*." (Jackson 1988/2003: 163, abridged.)

Buddhadāsa's emphasis on awareness in daily life and on sitting still bear similarities to the teachings of Vietnamese Mahayana monk Thich Nhat Hanh and was criticized in Thailand for being influenced by Zen (Gabaude 1988: 92 note 101). However, although the term emptiness (*suññatā*, Pali; *śūnyatā* Sanskrit) is more familiar from the Mahayana context, Pyi Phyo Kyaw has pointed out that Buddhadāsa's teaching of *suññatā*, "emptiness" (of notions of selfhood) through the advocation of *chit-wang*, literally "void-mind" is closer to the teachings of *suññatā* found in the Pali Canon (Kyaw 2011).

(f) The *borān kammaṭṭhāna* method outlined first earlier, as the oldest method for which we have evidence for an ongoing tradition, has been popularized in a simplified form in the modern period as the Dhammakāya method (*vijjā dhammakāya*). The monk who developed this branch of the practice was Candassāro Bhikkhu, referred to by followers of the practice as Luang Pho Sot, who became abbot of Wat Paknam in Bangkok. Although there were attempts to spread the *vijjā dhammakāya* method internationally by Wat Paknam in the 1950s (Skilton 2013), its current popularity worldwide is down to the activities of the Dhammakaya Foundation based at Wat Phra Dhammakāya in Pathumthani, near Bangkok (Newell 2011).

It is not yet clear to what extent the intensive meditations of *vijjā dhammakāya* undertaken by their most advanced practitioners differ from those of the *borān kammaṭṭhāna* tradition more broadly since it is only the simplified methods, on the theme of visualizing a sphere of light within the center of the body, that are made public. One of the adaptations is a very simplified form for children. It explains the meditation object as a sun-like globe of light through the medium of cartoons, as a way of giving children a sense of inner peace and security in the context of their troubles. Adult followers enjoy the cartoons too. A very similar simplified meditation practice is found in northern Thai traditions, seen in the practice briefly taught at the initiation of novices filmed by Verkerk (2006). An interesting possible scientific investigation would be to assess the potential of this kind of meditation, akin to installation techniques in the treatment of psychological trauma, for creating inner security for troubled children with unstable home lives. To date it is mainly mindfulness practices that have been studied for their usefulness beyond the Buddhist context (see later text).

In spite of the widespread teaching of Luang Pho Sot's method internationally (see, e.g., Cadge 2004), the meditation practices themselves have been little studied by outsiders who have favored examining the institution of the Dhammakaya as a new religious movement. The high degree of attention the Dhammakaya Foundation has received as an organization in modern studies of Thai Buddhism is a response to a number of factors (McDaniel 2010): its phenomenal financial success, taking traditional generosity to the Sangha to unprecedented levels (Scott 2009); its staggering organizational capacity, demonstrated by such large-scale events as the hosting of one million school children from across Thailand on a single day at its Pathumthani headquarters on December 8, 2012 (http://ireport.cnn.com/docs/DOC-892624) and its alignment with high-profile public figures.

Modern Applications: Meditation Beyond Tradition

The heightened awareness and interruption to habitual patterns of thinking that define the mindfulness generated through Buddhist meditation practice have been investigated in a number of fields beyond Buddhism to assess the applicability of mindfulness to health, business, education, social problems, and communication. While Theravada forms of meditation, including *vipassanā*, have been important in this research, it is eclectic, drawing on other forms, including Zen (Kristeller 2007: 394).

The extent to which researchers seek to distance themselves from the Buddhist origins of mindfulness varies. Two reasons for doing so are firstly the desire to emphasize the evidence-based (rather than faith-based) nature of findings and applications; and secondly, the resistance or active hostility to the use of mindfulness by those who perceive it as a threat to Christianity, as seen, for example, in protests against the use of meditation to reduce stress and behavioral problems in prisons in the United States.

Scientific and social-scientific research in this area began in the 1970s. The resulting applications have been many and varied, and continue to expand exponentially. (For a chart of this growth in terms of scientific publications, see Williams and Kabat-Zinn 2011: 3.) One aspect of such research has been in the area of cognitive science using brain-imaging and other methods to confirm the effects of meditation practice in both experienced and novice practitioners. These have also been used to further map and theorize about cognitive and emotional processing. In broader application, the methods used to induce mindfulness, although originally drawn from meditation practice, are now designed in many ways that do not require meditation practice.

When meditation is used, it tends to advocate paying attention to internal experiences, that is, the bodily sensations, thoughts, and emotions arising in each moment, akin to the *satipaṭṭhāna* practice described in the *Mahāsatipaṭṭhāna Sutta*, or to external stimuli, such as sights and sounds. In either case, these stimuli should be observed with nonjudgmental acceptance (Baer 2003: 125). Ruth Baer describes the "mindfulness-based stress reduction programme" (MBSR) as follows:

> The program is conducted as an 8- to 10-week course for groups of up to 30 participants who meet weekly for 2–2.5 hr for instruction and practice in mindfulness meditation skills together with discussion of stress, coping and homework assignments... Several mindfulness meditation skills are taught. For example, the body scan is a 45-min exercise in which attention is directed sequentially to numerous areas of the body while the participant is lying down with eyes closed. Sensations in each area are carefully observed. ... Participants in MBSR are instructed to practice these skills outside the group meetings for at least 45 min per day, six days per week. ... For all mindfulness exercises, participants are instructed to focus attention on the target of observation (e.g. breathing or walking) and to be aware of it in each moment. When emotions, sensations, or cognitions arise, they are observed non-judgmentally. When the participant notices that the mind has wandered into thoughts, memories, or fantasies, the nature or content of them is briefly noted, if possible, and then attention is returned to the present moment... An important consequence of mindfulness practice is the realization that most sensations, thoughts, and emotions fluctuate, or are transient, passing by "like waves in the sea." (Baer 2003: 126–127)

Mindfulness-based cognitive therapy (MBCT) builds on this type of training with the additional intervention of cognitive therapy, to instill the understanding "thoughts are not facts" and "I am not my thoughts" in order to reduce relapse into the habitual, negative thought patterns that cause or exacerbate depressive conditions (Baer 2003: 126). Important differences between mindfulness training and cognitive behavioral therapy include the absence in mindfulness of the assessment in CBT of particular ways of thinking as distorted and the striving for specific behavioral outcomes (Baer 2003: 130). The effectiveness of such interventions has been confirmed in a number of studies, although it is hard to draw statistical data from the small number and variable methods used for testing. (See Baer 2003: 131–132 for a chart of studies to test effectiveness for a range of conditions, and her summary of findings on the following pages. See Bogart 1991 for an overview of debates about the use of meditation within a psychotherapeutic context. See Williams and

Kabat-Zinn 2011 for a range of articles from different types of practitioner and academic on recent developments in and responses to mindfulness.)

There is another field of mindfulness training that is not based on meditation, but shares some features in that it may also deroutinize habitual thought patterns. Altering language use, the design of a task or work routine and using particular forms of questioning may be used enhance nonjudgmental mindfulness. Ellen Langer and Mihnea Moldoveanu define mindfulness as the "drawing of novel distinctions" that sets up the opposite of mindless behavior routinized on the basis of established categories that may be outdated. They identify the advantages of this drawing of novel distinctions as "(1) a greater sensitivity to one's environment, (2) more openness to new information, (3) the creation of new categories for structuring perception, and (4) enhanced awareness of multiple perspectives in problem solving. The subjective 'feel' of mindfulness is that of a heightened state of involvement and wakefulness or being in the present" (Langer and Moldoveanu 2000: 2). Other generalized advantages include an enhanced perceived sense of control in one's life and day-to-day activities, reduced boredom and anxiety and the switching between those states, and greater ability to focus by viewing the object of focus from altering perspectives rather than in fixed way (Langer and Moldoveanu 2000: 3).

Both forms of mindfulness training have been applied in psychotherapy for a range of purposes, including pain management, addiction treatment, dialectical therapy for the treatment of borderline personality disorders (Lineham 1993a, 1993b), and the treatment of depressive, anxiety-related conditions and eating disorders.

Developments in Theravada Meditation Among Western Converts

There has been a dramatic increase in the number of Westerners who come into contact with Theravada meditation now that many teachers within the various Thai and Burmese traditions have attracted an international following and now that meditation is extensively used in therapeutic contexts. There have also been developments within the lineage of those initial converts who adopted Theravada meditation in the United States in the 1970s, in part reflecting these broader developments. The Insight Meditation Society founded by Joseph Goldstein, Jack Kornfield, Sharon Salzburg, and Jacqueline Schwartz, who had all studied in the Burmese *vipassanā* or Thai forest traditions, has bifurcated into those who retain the early emphasis on intensive retreat advocated by the Burmese teacher Mahāsī Sayadaw and those who advocate a more eclectic approach (Gleig forthcoming). This latter approach incorporates insights from modern psychology in areas such as interpersonal relationships and self-esteem issues that are not addressed and might even be bypassed by meditation, according to such advocates as Jack Kornfield (Gleig forthcoming). Adaptations to meditation to address such issues can also be found, for example, in Ajahn Brahm's teaching people to develop *mettā* first to a neutral or lovable person, and later to oneself in order to develop self-acceptance. Other mindfulness-related developments have taken place within a new generation of Buddhist converts and second-generation converts. Richard Seager notes four examples of such developments: the online project Buddhist Geeks cofounded by Vince Horn in 2007, Ethan Nichtern's online Interdependence Project (IDP), Noah Levine's Dharma Punk Nation, and David Ingram's Dharma Overground (DhO), which, in Ingram's words, focuses on "mastery of the traditional hardcore stages of the path rather than some sort of vapid New Age fluff" (Seager 2012: 66–71).

Summary

There is an extensive range of meditation practices within Theravada. While they often draw on early canonical and commentarial sources, the most widespread of the current practices are of relatively recent origin. Practitioners adapted existing methods, drawing on newly available sciences and technology in order to encourage meditation in the face of the threats to Buddhism posed by colonialism, other forms of oppression and modernity. The great variety in practice traditions is hard to document because of the natural discrepancy between discourse and practice, the closed teacher–pupil relationship at higher levels of teaching and the imposition of centralized norms by the powerful Sangha hierarchies in the past and the present. Scientific studies have verified some of the effects of meditation in altering brain patterns, while an increasing number of social scientific studies have positively evaluated the usefulness of both mindfulness meditation and mindfulness-based applications in areas such as business, communication, education, and health. Traditionally meditation was the pursuit of the relative few who could afford the time to undertake it and was practised within certain periods of life or at a specific time of year. The modernized practices that have gained popularity in recent years, including Burmese *vipassanā* and Thailand's *vijjā dhammakāya*, offer simplified methods, stripped of the extensive traditional ritual and initiatory stages that accompanied some older forms. This has enabled the uptake of meditation by large numbers of people, which in turn has created a sufficient demand for the running of intensive programs for a relatively high number of practitioners. The application of meditation in therapeutic contexts has both drawn from and encouraged this increasing popularity. While to some extent meditation practice represents a search for the highest values that Buddhism has to offer, an arena that transcends physical, ethnic, national, and personal boundaries, its transmission has often been circumscribed by politics and been highly politicized.

References

Baer, Ruth A. (2003). 'Mindfulness Training as a Clinical Intervention: A Conceptual and Empirical Review', *Clinical Psychology: Science and Practice* 10: 125–143.

de Bernon, Olivier. (2000). 'Le Manuel des Maîtres de *kammaṭṭhān*, Études et présentation de rituels de méditation dans la tradition du bouddhisme khmer'. PhD thesis, Institut National des Langes et Civilisations Orientales, Paris.

Bizot, François. (1976). *Le figuier à cinq branches*. Recherches sur le bouddhisme khmer I, PEFEO CVII. Paris: l'École Française d'Extrême-Orient.

Bizot, François. (1989). *Reamaker ou L'Amour Symbolique de Rām et Setā*. Recherches sur le Bouddhisme Khmer V. Paris: l'École Française d'Extrême-Orient.

Bodhi, Bhikkhu. (1993). *A Comprehensive Manual of Abidhamma: The Abhidhammattha Sangaha of Ācariya Anuruddha*. Kandy: Buddhist Publication Society.

Bond, George. (1988). *The Buddhist Revival in Sri Lanka: Religious Tradition, Reinterpretation and Response*. Columbia: University of Carolina Press.

Braun, Erik C. (2008). 'Ledi Sayadaw, Abhidhamma, and the Development of the Modern Insight Meditation Movement in Burma'. PhD dissertation, Harvard University, Cambridge.

Bronkhorst, Johannes. (2012). *Absorption. Human Nature and Buddhist Liberation*. Wil/Paris: University Media.

Buddharakkhita, Acharya. (2012a). 'Cittavagga: The Mind (Dhp III)'. Translation *Access to Insight*. http://www.accesstoinsight.org/tipitaka/kn/dhp/dhp.03.budd.html (retrieved December 9, 2012).

Buddharakkhita, Acharya. (2012b). 'Karaniya Metta Sutta: The Hymn of Universal Love (Sn 1.8)'. Translation from the Pali by Buddharakkhita. *Access to Insight*. http://www.accesstoinsight.org/tipitaka/kn/snp/snp.1.08.budd.html (retrieved December 9, 2012).

Cadge, Wendy. (2004). *Heartwood: The First Generation of Theravada Buddhism* in *America*. Chicago: Chicago University Press.

Carrithers, M. (1983). *The Forest Monks of Sri Lanka: An Anthropological and Historical Study*. Calcutta: Oxford University Press.

Choompolpaisal, Phibul, Kate Crosby, and Andrew Skilton. (in preparation). 'The Significance of the Phitsanulok *Dhammakāya* Inscription for *borān/yogāvacara* Meditation in Theravada'.

Conze, Edward. (1956). *Buddhist Meditation*. London: Allen and Unwin.

Cousins, L.S. (1997). 'Aspects of Southern Esoteric Buddhism', in Peter Connolly and Sue Hamilton (eds.), *Indian Insights: Buddhism, Brahmanism and Bhakti. Papers from the Annual Spalding Symposium on Indian Religions*. London: Luzac Oriental, 185–207.

Crosby, Henrietta Kate. (1999). 'Studies in the Medieval Pali Literature of Sri Lanka with Special Reference to the Esoteric Yogavacara Tradition'. DPhil thesis, University of Oxford.

Crosby, Kate. (2000). 'Tantric Theravada: A Bibliographic Essay on the Writings of François Bizot and Other Literature on the *Yogāvacara* Tradition', *Contemporary Buddhism* 1.2: 141–198.

Crosby, Kate, Andrew Skilton, and Amal Gunasena. (2012). 'The Sutta on Understanding Death in the Transmission of *borān* Meditation from Siam to the Kandyan Court', *Journal of Indian Philosophy*, 40.2: 177–198.

Gabaude, Louis. (1988). *Une herméneutique bouddhique contemporaine de Thaïlande: Buddhadasa Bhikkhu*. Paris: l'École française d'Extrême-Orient.

Gleigr, Anna. (forthcoming). 'From Theravada to Tantra: The Making of an American Buddhist Tantra?' *Contemporary Buddhism*.

Gombrich, Richard and Gananath Obeyesekere. (1988). *Buddhism Transformed: Religious Change in Sri Lanka*. Princeton: Princeton University Press.

Horner, I.B. (1954, 1957, 1959). *Middle Length Sayings*, 3 vols. London: Luzac.

Houtman, Gustaaf. (1990). 'Traditions of Buddhist Practice in Burma'. PhD thesis, School of Oriental and African Studies, London.

Houtman, Gustaaf. (1999). *Mental Culture in Burmese Crisis Politics. Aung San Suu Kyi and the National League for Democracy*. Tokyo: Institute for the Study of Languages and Cultures of Asia and Africa.

Jackson, Peter A. (1988 [2003]). *Buddhadasa: Theravada Buddhism and Modernist Reform in Thailand*. Chiang Mai: Silkworm Books.

Jaini, Padmanabh S. (1965 [2001]). '*Mahādibbamanta*: A *Paritta* Manuscript from Cambodia', *BSOAS* XXVIII.1: 61–80.

Khur-Yearn, Jotika. (2012). 'The Poetic *Dhamma* of Zao Amat Long's *Mahāsatipaṭṭhāna Sutta* and the Place of Traditional Literature in Shan Theravada Buddhism'. PhD thesis, School of Oriental and African Studies, London.

King, Winston L. (circa 1980). *Theravāda Meditation: The Buddhist Transformation of Yoga*. University Park: State University Press. Reprint, New Delhi: Motilal Banarsidass, 1992.

Kornfield, Jack. (1977 [revised reprint 2007]). *Living Buddhist Masters*. Kandy: Buddhist Publications Society.

Kristeller, Jean L. (2007). 'Mindfulness Meditation' in P. Lehrer, R.L. Woodward, and W.E. Sime (eds.), *Principles and Practice of Stress Management*, 3rd edn. New York: Guildford Press, 393–427.

Kyaw, Pyi Phyo. (2011). 'Emptiness Through *dhammas* or Emptiness of *dhammas*: Understanding of Emptiness in *Theravāda* Meditation Traditions', *Journal of International Buddhist Studies* 3: 115–130.

Langer, Ellen J. and Mihnea Moldoveanu. (2000). 'The Construct of Mindfulness', *Journal of Social Issues* 56.1: 1–9.

Law, B.C. (1922). *A Designation of Human Types*. London: Oxford University Press.

Lineham, M.M. (1993a). *Cognitive-behavioral Treatment of Borderline Personality Disorder*. New York: Guildford Press.

Lineham, M.M. (1993b). *Skills Training Manual for the Treatment of Borderline Personality Disorder*. New York: Guildford Press.

Lounsbery, Grace Constant. (1935). *Buddhist Meditation in the Southern School*. Reprint with a foreword by W.Y. Evans-Wentz. London: Luzac 1950.

Marston, John. (2008). 'Reconstructing 'Ancient' Cambodian Buddhism', *Contemporary Buddhism* 9.1: 99–121.

McDaniel, Justin. (August 2010). Review of Scott 2009, *H-Buddhism*. http://www.h-net.org/reviews/showrev.php?id=29580 (retrieved June 20, 2012).

Meiland, Justin. 2003. 'Buddhist Values in the Pāli *jātakas*, with particular reference to the theme of renunciation'. Doctoral dissertation, University of Oxford.

Mettanando, Bhiikkhu. (1998). *Meditation and Healing in the Theravada Buddhist Order of Thailand and Laos*. PhD thesis, University of Hamburg.

Na Rangsi, Sunthorn. (1976). *The Four Planes of Existence in Theravada Buddhism*. Reprinted as The Wheel Publication No.462. 2006. Kandy: Buddhist Publication Society.

Newell, Catherine. (2011). 'Two Meditation Traditions from Contemporary Thailand. A Summary Overview', *Rian Thai. International Journal of Thai Studies* 4: 81–110.

Ñyāṇamoli, Bhikkhu. (1976). *The Path of Purification*, 2 vols. Boulder/London: Shambhala.

Nyanaponika, Thera. (1953). *Satipaṭṭhāna. The Heart of Buddhist Meditation. A Handbook of Mental Training Based on the Buddha's 'Way of Mindfulness', Etc*. Colombo: "Word of the Buddha" Publishing Committee.

Ong, Pei Wen Patrick. (2011). 'Examining and Analysing the Meditation System Passed Down by the Supreme Patriarch Suk Kaithuean, Now Taught at Wat Ratchasittharam', *Rian Thai. International Journal of Thai Studies* 4: 115–189.

Orsborn, M. (Shi Huifeng) (2007). *Samatha and Vipassanā as Presented in the Theravāda Abhidhamma*. Published online. www.stefan.gr/.../samatha-vipassana-in-the-theravada-abhidhamma.pdf (retrieved June 20, 2012).

Pranke, Patrick Arthur. (forthcoming). 'On Saints and Wizards: Ideals of Human Perfection and Power in Contemporary Burmese Buddhism' in Rozenberg et al.

Rhys Davids, T.W. (1896 [reprint 1981]). *The Yogāvacara's Manual*. London: Pali Text Society.

Rozenberg, Guillaume. (2010). *Renunciation and Power. The Quest for Sainthood in Contemporary Burma*. Translated from the French by Jessica Hackett. New Haven: Yale University Southeast Asia Studies.

Scott, Rachelle M. (2009). *Nirvana for Sale? Buddhism, Wealth, and the Dhammakāya Temple in Contemporary Thailand*. Albany: State University of New York Press.

Seeger, Martin. (2009). 'Phra Payutto and Debates "On the Very Idea of the Pali Canon" in Thai Buddhism', *Buddhist Studies Review* 26.1: 1–31.

Seeger, Martin. (2010). '"Against the Stream": The Thai Female Buddhist Saint Mae Chi Kaew Sianglam (1901–1991)', *South East Asia Research* 18.3: 555–595.

Seager, Richard Hughes. (2012). *Buddhism in America*, revised and expanded edition, The Columbia Contemporary American Religion Series. New York: Columbia University Press.

Skilton, Andrew. (2013). 'Elective Affinities: The Reconstruction of a Forgotten Episode in the Shared History of Thai and British Buddhism – Kapilavaḍḍho and Wat Paknam' in Brian Bocking, Phibul Choompolpaisal, Laurence Cox, and Alicia Turner (eds.), *Pioneer Western Buddhists and Asian Networks 1860–1960*. Contemporary Buddhism Special Issue.

Swearer, Donald K. (1995). 'The Way to Meditation' in Donald S. Lopez (ed.), *Buddhism in Practice*. Princeton: Princeton University Press, 207–215.

Taylor, James L. (1993). *Forest Monks and the Nation-State: An Anthropological and Historical Study in Northeastern Thailand*. Singapore: Institute of Southeast Asian Studies.

Tillyard, Aelfrida Catharine Wetenhall. (1927). *Spiritual Exercises and their Results: An Essay in Psychology and Comparative Religion*. Society for Promoting Christian Knowledge. London/New York/Toronto: Macmillan.

Tiyavanich, Kamala. (1997). *Forest Recollections: Wandering Monks in Twentieth-Century Thailand*. Honolulu: University of Hawaiʻi Press.

Vajirañāṇa, Mahathera. (1962). *Buddhist Meditation in Theory and Practice: A General Exposition According to the Pali Canon of the Theravāda School*. Colombo: M.D. Guansena.

Verkerk, Mark (2006). *Buddha's Lost Children*. EMS Films.

Williams, J. Mark G. and Jon Kabat-Zinn (eds.). (2011). Mindfulness: Diverse Perspectives on Its Meaning, Origins, and Multiple Applications at the Intersection of Science and Dharma. *Contemporary Buddhism* 12.1. Special Issue.

Woodward, F.L. (1916). *Manual of a Mystic Being a Translation from the Pali and Sinhalese Work Entitled The Yogāvachara's Manual*. London: Pali Text Society.

Yasotharat, Phramaha Chai (= "Jai"). (1935/1936). *Nangsue phuttha-rangsi-thrisadi-yan wa duai samatha lae vipassana-kammathan si yuk* (Thai), Bangkok B.E. 2478.

Further Reading and Watching

Films

Ariel, Eilona and Ayelet Menahemi. (1997). *Doing Time. Doing Vipassanā*. On the use of *vipassanā* meditation in prisons in India.

Phillips, Jenny, Andrew Kukura, and Anne Marie Stein. (2007). *The Dhamma Brothers*. On the use of *vipassanā* meditation in one prison in the USA.

Primary Sources

Bronkhorst (2012, see below) includes translations of 'The Main Texts with a Psychological Commentary' Appendix I: 176–201.

Shaw, Sarah. (2006). *Buddhist Meditation: An Anthology of Texts*. London: Routledge.

The *Visuddhimagga* by Buddhaghosa. Translation: Ñyāṇamoli, Bhikkhu (1976). *The Path of Purification*, 2 vols. Boulder/London: Shambhala. (Multiple reprints including and free distributions. Available as free pdf from www.accesstoinsight.org) (retrieved June 25, 2013).

Secondary Sources

Baer, Ruth A. (2003). 'Mindfulness Training as a Clinical Intervention: A Conceptual and Empirical Review', *Clinical Psychology: Science and Practice* 10: 125–143.

Bogart, Greg. (1991). 'Meditation and Psychotherapy: A Review of the Literature.' *The American Journal of Psychotherapy* XLV: 383–412.

Bond, George D. (1988). *The Buddhist Revival in Sri Lanka: Religious Tradition, Reinterpretation and Response*.

Braun, Erik. (forthcoming). *The Birth of Insight: Meditation, Modern Buddhism, and the Burmese Monk Ledi Sayadaw*. Chicago: University of Chicago Press.

Bronkhorst, Johannes. (2012). *Absorption. Human Nature and Buddhist Liberation*. Wil/Paris: University Media.

Conze, Edward (1956). *Buddhist Meditation*. London: Allen and Unwin.
Cook, Joanna. (2010). *Meditation in Modern Buddhism: Renunciation and Change in Thai Monastic Life*. Cambridge: Cambridge University Press.
Crosby, Kate. (November 2000). 'Tantric Theravada: A bibliographic essay on the writings of François Bizot and other literature on the *Yogāvacara* Tradition', *Contemporary Buddhism* 2: 141–198.
Crosby, Kate, Andrew Skilton, and Amal Gunasena (2012). 'The Sutta on Understanding Death in the Transmission of *borān* Meditation from Siam to the Kandyan Court', *Journal of Indian Philosophy*, 40.2: 177–198.
Houtman, Gustaaf. (1990). 'Traditions of Buddhist Practice in Burma'. PhD thesis, School of Oriental and African Studies, London.
Houtman, Gustaaf. (1999). *Mental Culture in Burmese Crisis Politics. Aung San Suu Kyi and the National League for Democracy*. Tokyo: Institute for the Study of Languages and Cultures of Asia and Africa.
Jordt, Ingrid. (2007). *Burma's Lay Meditation Movement: Buddhism and the Cultural Construction of Power*. Athens: Ohio University Press.
King, Winston L. (1980). *Theravada Meditation: The Buddhist Transformation of Yoga*. University Park, Pennsylvania: State University Press.
Kornfield, Jack. (1977 [reprint 2007]). *Modern Buddhist Masters*. Kandy: Buddhist Publications Society.
Kristeller, Jean L. (2007). 'Mindfulness Meditation' in P. Lehrer, R. L. Woodward, and W.E. Sime (eds.) *Principles and Practice of Stress Management*, 3rd edn. New York: Guildford Press, 393–427.
Langer, Ellen J. and Mihnea Moldoveanu (2000). 'The Contruct of Mindfulness', *Journal of Social Issues*. 56.1: 1–9.
Ong, Patrick Pei Wen. (2011). 'Examining and Analysing the Meditation System Passed Down by the Supreme Patriarch Suk Kaithuean, Now Taught at Wat Ratchasittharam', *Rian Thai. International Journal of Thai Studies*. 4: 115–189.
Rozenberg, Guillaume. (2010). *Renunciation and Power. The Quest for Sainthood in Contemporary Burma*. Translated from the French by Jessica Hackett. New Haven: Yale University Southeast Asia Studies.
Taylor, James L. (1993). *Forest Monks and the Nation-State: An Anthropological and Historical Study in Northeastern Thailand*. Singapore: Institute of Southeast Asian Studies.
Tiyanavich, Kamala (1997) *Forest Recollections*. Honolulu: Hawai'i University Press.
Williams, J. Mark G. and Jon Kabat-Zinn (eds.). (2011). 'Mindfulness: Diverse Perspectives on its meaning, origins, and multiple applications at the intersection of science and dharma', *Contemporary Buddhism*. Special Issue. 12.1.

7

Abhidhamma

Overview

Abhidhamma (*Abhidharma*, Sanskrit) is the systematization of Buddhist doctrine through analysis of the components (*dhamma*, *dharma* in Sanskrit) that make up reality and the way they interrelate. It explains the world as experienced by living beings, including its ethical manifestations (good and evil), *saṃsāra* (the round of rebirth) and the path to *nibbāna*. In Theravada Buddhism, the term *Abhidhamma* is interpreted to mean "higher Dhamma," that is, the higher teaching. The third division of the Pali Canon contains seven books dedicated to *Abhidhamma* and is called the *Abhidhamma Piṭaka*. *Abhidhamma* literature continues to be systematized and developed. In Burma in the nineteenth and early twentieth centuries, new writings also accessible to Westerners flourished. Drawing parallels between *Abhidhamma* analyses and Western science, they helped take methods of personal transformation in Buddhist meditation beyond the borders of Buddhism. New *Abhidhamma* texts, the study of *Abhidhamma*, and its application in meditation continue to thrive in Burma, even in popular Buddhism. *Abhidhamma* also forms the basis of nonreformed meditation systems and continues as a more specialist interest elsewhere in the Theravada world. It also underlies some popular Buddhist practices. It was in *Abhidhamma* that a distinctive Theravada doctrine emerged, yet most general studies of Theravada Buddhism pay it scant attention.

Theravada is an *Abhidhamma* school, in that it takes *Abhidhamma* to be the most direct expression of ultimate reality, *paramattha*, but it is to be distinguished from the ultra-realist *Abhidharma* (Sanskrit) of the now extinct but historically important Sarvāstivāda branch of Buddhism. When the literature of the self-styled "great way" (*mahāyāna*) emerged in the first centuries of the first millennium CE, it was Sarvāstivāda understandings of reality that were criticized as an inferior way (*hīnayāna*). The Pali spelling *Abhidhamma* will be used below when speaking of *Abhidhamma* generically and in the Theravada context. The Sanskrit spelling *Abhidharma* is used when discussing the Sarvāstivāda tradition and its relationship to Mahayana schools of philosophy.

Theravada Buddhism: Continuity, Diversity, and Identity, First Edition. Kate Crosby.

Schools of *Abhidhamma*

When people describe Theravada Buddhism as the earliest surviving school of Buddhism, they might put it better by saying that Theravada is the only surviving *Abhidhamma* school. For while many traditions of *Abhidhamma* developed in the early centuries, only three "schools" of *Abhidhamma* have left behind a substantial body of literature: the Dharmaguptaka, the Sarvāstivāda, and the Theravada (Bodhi in Karunadasa 2010: xii). Living traditions of *vinaya*, monastic practice, containing these names do survive forming the main two *vinaya* traditions other than the Theravada: the *Mūlasarvāstivāda vinaya* lineage of Tibetan Buddhism and the Dharmaguptaka *vinaya* lineage of East Asian Buddhism. But Theravada is now the only school that takes *Abhidhamma* as the best representation of the highest truth or ultimate reality (*paramattha*). For the Theravada tradition, the estimation of *Abhidhamma* as the representation of the highest truth is also seen in the belief that, when the Dhamma begins to disappear (see Chapter 3), it is the *Abhidhamma Piṭaka*, beginning with the final book, that disappears first (Braun 2008: 32).

Although Theravada is the only "living" tradition of *Abhidhamma*, *Abhidhamma* remains important in other traditions. It continues to be a crucial aspect of the training in the Mahayana philosophies of Madhyamaka and Yogācāra in Tibetan Buddhist education. In that context, *Abhidharma* is studied not because it is regarded as the ultimate truth but because it is rejected or qualified by Mahayana philosophies. The way it was rejected indicates its importance: the statements concerning ultimate reality in Madhyamaka and Yogācāra accept *Abhidharma* terms of reference. They reject *Abhidharma* in different ways. Although both reject its realism, Yogācāra can be seen a resurgent form of *Abhidharma* with the physical components of *Abhidharma* analysis of reality reinterpreted as also being an aspect of consciousness, that is, it advocates a form of *Abhidharma*-derived idealism. *Abhidharma* is so crucial to the development and formulation of Madhyamaka and Yogācāra forms of philosophy that they cannot be understood without reference to it. So while no independent Sarvāstivāda philosophical school survives, its *Abhidharma* had a great impact on the forms of Buddhism that developed and continue to thrive in Central and East Asia (Bhikkhu Bodhi in Karunadasa 2010: xii–xiii). Only in Theravada is *Abhidhamma* a living tradition, taken to be expressive of ultimate reality and the Buddha's omniscience, and a basis for religious practice, ritual, and philosophical engagement.

The Inaccessibility of *Abhidhamma*

Since much *Sutta* material overlaps with that found in the *Sūtra* collections of other Buddhist traditions, it is the *Vinaya* (monastic discipline) and *Abhidhamma* that are the most distinctive formal aspects of Theravada Buddhism, unique to Theravada. In the case of the *Vinaya*, the actual list of regulations is very close to that of other Buddhist traditions: it is the minor rules (*sekhiya*) and the interpretation and physical manifestation of the rules that are distinctive. In the case of the *Abhidhamma*, both the content and practice are distinctive.

Despite its being a distinguishing feature of Theravada, relatively little has been published on *Abhidhamma* in English writings about Theravada in general (Braun 2008: 82, Crosby 2005: 47). There are a number of reasons for this. For example, Theravada is often equated with early Buddhism and, as a later development, *Abhidhamma* is then ignored. However, *Abhidhamma* emerged as a distinctive tradition as early as the time in which the major branches of the Sangha (monastic community) began to divide, and so the history of Theravada and the history of *Abhidhamma* as distinctive, traceable entities coincide. However, the foremost reason for the poor representation of *Abhidhamma* in English writings on Theravada is the difficulty of engaging in a topic that requires not just linguistic expertise but specialist training achieved through years of consistent dedication. The terminology of *Abhidhamma* is also difficult to translate. If terms that have no equivalent in English are not to be left untranslated, they have to be represented by neologisms, and so new vocabularies are created by each scholar who tries to bridge the language divide. *Abhidhamma* has sometimes been dismissed as dry or even irrelevant scholasticism, an assessment that ignores the way in which *Abhidhamma* evolved to solve such core problems as continuity in the absence of perpetuity, its history of responding to changes in scientific understanding and the way that it underlies most advanced Theravada meditation systems – both the pre-reform methods and those born of Burma's engagement with colonialism and modernity that have gone on to inform practice globally.

The difficulty of understanding *Abhidhamma* is acknowledged in early Theravada narratives. In current Burmese practice, much time is given to learning it verbatim, as a basis for more analytical study or practical use (Kyaw 2012b). The following story is found in the commentary to the *Dhammapada*, the book of short verses encapsulating core Buddhist teachings and values found in the *Khuddaka Nikāya* of the *Sutta Piṭaka*: the first 500 monks to learn the *Abhidhamma Piṭaka* taught by Gotama had unwittingly prepared for this honor and difficult task by listening to it, although without any comprehension, in a previous lifetime:

> [In] the dispensation of the Buddha Kassapa they [the 500 monks] were little bats. On a certain occasion, as they hung over a mountain-cave, they overheard two monks reciting the Abhidhamma as they walked up and own their walk and straightway fell in love with their voices. As for the expressions "These aggregates of being, these elements of being," they did not know what they meant; but solely because they had fallen in love with their voices, when they passed from that state of existence they were reborn in the World of the Gods. … afterwards they were reborn in Sāvatthi in the households of families of distinction. Receiving faith in the Twin Miracle (see chapter 1), they became monks under the Elder and were the first to obtain mastery over the Seven Books. (Burlingame 1921, III: 52)

The Significance of *Abhidhamma*

Theravada Buddhists would accept *Abhidhamma's* depiction as demanding in nature but would be surprised at the view that it is irrelevant to practice, for it is at the heart of Theravada and has been so from a very early period. While the *Abhidhamma Piṭaka* is later than the majority of the texts included in the *Vinaya Piṭaka* and *Sutta Piṭaka*, *Abhidhamma* as a system for organizing, systematizing, and remembering the Buddha's teaching is undoubtedly early, appearing in a number of *suttas*.

Abhidhamma developed in response to a number of factors, not just the attempt to systematize and work out how the existing analyses of early Buddhism could be taken further. It also incorporates developments in the understanding of the world, the human mind and body.

Alongside analyses of momentariness and how different mental states relate to each other are analyses of the development of the embryo in the womb that parallel understandings within medical science (Kim 1999). While the development of the fetus in early *Abhidhamma* reflects understandings in *Ayurvedic* medicine of the time, modern *Abhidhamma* incorporates developments in obstetrics in Western "allopathic" medicine (McDaniel 2009). This process of aligning Western scientific knowledge with existing Burmese knowledge systems (Charney 2006: 233) has incorporated new data into works on *Abhidhamma* and, in turn, meditation. This process can be seen in the writings that mark the transformation of *Abhidhamma* learning and meditation practice in Burma in the nineteenth century. This same transformation foreshadowed the subsequent uptake of Burmese meditation technologies within Western cognitive science (see Chapter 6). An example is the work of the Burmese minister Hpo Hlaing, a mentor of and significant influence on Ledi Sayadaw (1846–1923, see later text) and author of three meditation books. In his *Meditation on the Body* (*Kāyānupassanā*, written in 1875), Hpo Hlaing attempted to reconcile the anatomical information provided in an Italian anatomy textbook that he had had translated into Burmese with the anatomical descriptions that he found in *Abhidhamma* commentaries; the results in turn formed the focus of the meditation practice (Braun 2008: 64–68).

The reason for *Abhidhamma's* responsiveness to scientific developments is that it is the Theravada attempt to plumb the depths of human experience: it represents the profundity of the Buddha's omniscience concerning the processes of transformation, making them available to those seeking to make progress through the latter toward the former. As new sciences enhance humanity's self-understanding, they should then be harnessed in the service of this transformation. The final book of the *Abhidhamma Piṭaka*, the *Paṭṭhāna*, attests to new developments in group theory mathematics that took place in South Asia in the first millennium CE (Crosby, current research). In other strands of Asian society, these mathematical innovations were harnessed to enhance medical and commercial applications. In the *Paṭṭhāna*, the new mathematics is applied to the quest to capture every possible causal combination that must have been recognizable to the Buddha. For an aspect of the Buddha's omniscience is his understanding of all the causal connections that either lead people to be trapped in *saṃsāra* or allow them to emerge from it. The number of combinations and permutations made possible by the new mathematics are calculated to be in their millions, which means that this text is never written in full. Rather, examples of the calculations and their results are given.

At a general level, the Theravada understanding of causality in the absence of an enduring self is expressed through analogies: an action (*kamma*, *karma* in Sanskrit) produces a specific result (*vipāka*) like a mango seed produces a mango tree, and a person continues in a continuum of cause and effect like a flame moving from one fuel to another (see Chapter 5). The causality is not random, but the later entity is not the same as the earlier. Another analogy is like that of a boy compared with the man the boy becomes. They are not the same, but they are part of a linked process. There is a stream of connected causes and results. *Abhidhamma* seeks to take these analogies further, to investigate the more technical descriptions of causality provided by the Buddha in the *suttas* and scrutinize how they function in fine detail. In order to grasp Theravada causality in any depth, then, it is to *Abhidhamma* one must turn. Therefore, while it can be treated as a form of philosophy or scholasticism, it – like other forms of Buddhist philosophy – develops and is used within the context of trying to enhance soteriological (salvific) practice (Nyanaponika 1949: Chapter 1).

Burma's long history of engagement with *Abhidhamma*, commentarial literature, meditation, and scholarship responded to the distinctive conditions of the rise of European scientific learning and the British colonial period in ways that led to the popularization of *Abhidhamma* in Burma. In modern-day Burma, large numbers of both monastics and laypeople study *Abhidhamma*, including on intensive residential courses. Its popular appeal is related to the popularity of lay meditation practice: an understanding of *Abhidhamma* is regarded as a necessary prerequisite for some, but not all meditation practices (Kyaw 2012a).

Abhidhamma as a basis for ritual and protective practices

The importance ascribed to *Abhidhamma* has other implications for Buddhist practice: especially in Burma its sponsorship is highly meritorious, and its protective powers are important. The set of seven sacred syllables drawn from the *Abhidhamma*, each representing one book of the *Abhidhamma*, are used as protective formulae in chants and yantras (Bizot and Lagirarde 1996: 191, Swearer 1995a). The syllables are *saṅ* (for *Dhammasaṅgaṇi*), *vi* (for *Vibhaṅga*), *dhā* (for *Dhātukathā*), *pu* (for *Puggalapaññatti*), *ka* (for *Kathāvatthu*), *ya* (for *Yamaka*), and *pa* (for *Paṭṭhāna*). These syllables are also used as tools in the nonreform meditation (*borān kammaṭṭhāna*) still practiced in Cambodia and at some temples in Thailand (see Chapter 6). The *Saddavimala*, a text of the *borān kammaṭṭhāna* tradition, teaches the set of seven syllables, then explains how each particular book of the *Abhidhamma Piṭaka* bestows specific benefits. For example, the *Dhammasaṅgaṇi* allows one to discern good and evil, the *Dhātukathā* bestows the benefit of smelling pleasant scents, and the *Puggalapaññatti* inspires one to preach the teaching fluently (Bizot and Lagirarde 1996: 218–219).

The *Abhidhamma* is drawn on in funerals, for even an unanalytical appreciation of the words of the *Abhidhamma* can lead – as in the case of the 500 bats – to heavenly rebirth (Langer 2007: 46). In Thailand, summaries of the seven books of the *Abhidhamma* are recited at funerals (Swearer 1995b) in texts that culminate in the story of Phra Māleyya (Brereton 1995).

The Special Place of *Abhidhamma* in Burmese History

In spite of the importance of *Abhidhamma* in Theravada's history, identity, and religious application, the only part of the Theravada world in which the popular study and the composition of *abhidhamma* texts is still significant to this day is Burma. Several factors have led to the ongoing commitment in Burma to the training required to master the complexity of *Abhidhamma*. Whereas in Sri Lanka, Laos, Thailand, and Cambodia, the twentieth century saw the secularization of monastic education to varying degrees, the education system for monks in Burma has never been secularized. Moreover, throughout Burma's long history of reform and royal or state scrutiny, the Sangha has consistently defended its authority and sanctity with reference to its conservative practice of *Vinaya* and its in-depth familiarity with Buddhist doctrine. Under the final kings of Burma during the Konbaung dynasty (1752–1885) and particularly under Bodawpaya (r. 1782–1819) and Mindon (r. 1853–1878), royal/state scrutiny of monastic practice and knowledge intensified in response to the various threats posed by the Anglo-Burmese wars and British colonialism. To this day, accusations of shortcomings in *Vinaya* or suspicions that teachings or meditation do not accord with orthodoxy can result in court cases in these two areas, called *Vinaya-vinicchaya* and *Dhamma-vinicchaya*, respectively.

Most Theravada countries that, in response to European colonialism, underwent text-based reforms judge familiarity and compliance with Buddhist doctrine and practice with reference to the Canon, especially the *Vinaya* and *Sutta Piṭakas*, even where the study of the commentaries was advocated. In Burma, while the *Sutta* and *Vinaya Piṭakas* are important, their interpretation is based on detailed, comprehensive study not just of the Pali Canon, including the *Abhidhamma Piṭaka*, but the commentaries and handbooks as well. Thus, both the canonical and postcanonical *Abhidhamma* literatures have retained their importance. Starkly put, we can see a contrast between a simplification of Buddhist doctrine in most reform Buddhism and the retention of more complex systems in Burma and in nonreform Buddhism elsewhere.

In Burma, correct practice based on a thorough understanding of the Dhamma is not only a defense against accusations and state intervention but also a medium for rivalry between different monastic groups and an instrument for personal advancement. A complex system of examinations has evolved in Burma. In addition to the government-sponsored exam systems that have a long history, there are nongovernment exam systems organized by monasteries and the many lay organizations that have developed since the late nineteenth century (Kyaw 2012b), when the laity were encouraged to take over roles previously ascribed to the court. Intensive study programs are organized to help monks, nuns, and laypeople prepare for these examinations.

The understanding that the *Abhidhamma Piṭaka* will be the first part of the Buddha's Dhamma to disappear also contributes to an anxiety to preserve *Abhidhamma*. This anxiety intensified when Burmese Buddhists faced the insecurities of the British colonial period. In the late nineteenth century and the first half of the twentieth century, pioneers such as Ledi Sayadaw (1846–1923), whose monastery had been responsible for the rehearsal of the *Abhidhamma Piṭaka* at the Fifth Council in 1871 (Braun 2008: 57), made connections between Western science and *Abhidhamma*, took advantage of the newly available printing technology, and encouraged *Abhidhamma* learning on a massive scale, not just among monks but also among laypeople. Ledi made a direct link between the conduct of laypeople and the sufferings of the nation (Braun 2008: 32), concluding that individual laypeople should commit to personal spiritual transformation to a degree more commonly envisaged traditionally for meditating forest monks.

In encouraging this degree of involvement of laypeople through the newly established lay associations, Ledi was arguing for laypeople to take up the gap created in 1885 when the British banished the king, the traditional sponsor of Buddhism (Braun 2008: 33). This development went on to have a considerable impact on the popularization of insight meditation practice (*vipassanā*), which was closely based on *Abhidhamma* in its earlier formulations. This in turn gave rise to the conditions that enabled the spread of Burmese insight meditation throughout the world. The laity's filling of the vacuum in patronage of the Sangha helped create the triangular relationship that characterizes Burmese Buddhism today between state (including the military government), the Sangha, and the populace, and is a factor in the role taken up by monks in representing lay concerns through political protest.

The emphasis in Burma on preserving the *Abhidhamma*, on learning as a means of defense, competition, and rivalry, on the individual's responsibility to make spiritual progress for the sake of the nation, has meant that expertise in *Abhidhamma* can flourish on the basis of a broad educational support in Burma and a willing audience. Expertise in both Pali and *Abhidhamma* are still rewarded through position and prestige.

Another reason for Burma's *Abhidhamma* expertise may be the attendant expectation on the part of audiences that listening to the Dhamma can and *should* be demanding, an expectation that in turn may relate to economic conditions. Differences in receptiveness to *Abhidhamma* between audiences in Burma and those in neighboring countries were identified in a recent study of current practices of listening to Buddhist poetry among the Shan ethnic groups (see Chapter 3). While Shan audiences across the borders in northern Thailand and southern China prefer to listen to narrative stories and easier materials, audiences within the Shan State in the Union of Burma continue to request *Abhidhamma* topics. As a result, Shan poetic texts (*lik long* in Shan) continue to be commissioned and composed on *Abhidhamma* subjects (Crosby and Khur-Yearn in preparation). Thailand's greater variety of entertainment and the alternatives for career development available to young men in Thailand were cited by Shan poet-performers familiar with the requirements of these different audiences as possible reasons for this contrast. Another possible explanation is that the different audience cultures may reflect the varied approaches taken to the reform of Buddhism in Theravada countries since the nineteenth century.

Abhidhamma texts

According to Theravada commentaries, the Buddha realized the *Abhidhamma* during the fourth week after his enlightenment (e.g., *Atthasālinī* p.13, *Majjhima Nikāya Aṭṭhakathā* II, p. 184). This is depicted in Buddhist art as the fourth in a series of seven postures of the Buddha, each one representing one of the 7 weeks after the Buddha's Enlightenment. In the Abhidhamma week, his hands are sometimes crossed facing him at chest level (Griswold 1957: 42, Stratton 2004: 68). This set of seven differs from the increasingly popular set of nine or seven Buddha postures found in many Thai temple compounds, associated with the nine planets or the different days of the week and used for astrological predictions and merit making on the basis of the day of the week on which one was born (Stratton 2004: 69).

Although the Buddha had realized the Abhidhamma in the fourth week of his Enlightenment, he did not teach it at the first sermon. His first audience was his mother, who had been reborn as a deity in the Tāvatiṃsa heaven. After performing the twin miracle at Sāvatthi in north India (see Chapter 1), the Buddha went to visit her. His visit lasted the three months of the annual rains retreat. During this period, he taught the *Abhidhamma Piṭaka* to her, each day leaving a double of himself in his place to continue the teaching while he would go on the alms round for food in the Himalayas. On his return, his disciple Sāriputta would visit him. He would inform Sāriputta of how far in the *Abhidhamma Piṭaka* he had reached and tell him to teach the same section to a group of 500 disciples who had recently taken ordination under Sāriputta. These disciples – the ones who had already overheard the *Abhidhamma* in a previous lifetime when they were bats – were the first monks to become versed in the seven books of the *Abhidhamma Piṭaka* (Burlingame 1921, III: 47–52).

Although this story of the origin of the *Abhidhamma Piṭaka* authorizes it by placing it in the mouth of the Buddha, both scholars and the *Abhidhamma* tradition itself in fact recognize that the *Abhidhamma Piṭaka* took its current shape at a far later date, perhaps between 200 BCE and 200 CE (von Hinüber 1996: 64). The fifth book of the *Abhidhamma Piṭaka*, the *Kathāvatthu*, is explicitly attributed to Mogaliputtatissa at the time of the Emperor Asoka in the mid-third-century BCE. *Abhidhamma* as a process, as a way of representing doctrine in an impersonal way on the basis of summary lists (*mātikā*, *mātṛkā* in Sanskrit) without the narrative of much *Sutta Piṭaka* representation of doctrine, is attested in the *Sutta Piṭaka*. For example, in the *Saṅgīti Sutta* (*Dīgha Nikāya sutta* 33), when Sāriputta teaches he organizes lists of concepts according to number. Passages that use such doctrinal lists are found in many places in the *Sutta Piṭaka* (Skilton 1994: 85). The *Paṭisambhidāmagga* in the *Khuddaka Nikāya* of the *Sutta Piṭaka* is a book that is *Abhidhamma* in both the content and in the way it is presented (Karunadasa 2010: 2; Mizuno 1997).

The titles of the seven books of the *Abhidhamma Piṭaka* are *Dhammasaṅgaṇi*, *Vibhaṅga*, *Dhātukathā*, *Puggalapaññatti*, *Kathāvatthu*, *Yamaka*, and *Paṭṭhāna*. (See the table of canonical works in Chapter 3 for the titles of translations into English of each text.) These seven works are organized by process or type of analysis (see later text). The *Dhammasaṅgaṇi* opens with the *mātikā*, the list of categories that provide the framework for the *Abhidhamma* as a whole. It then enumerates all the *dhamma* into which reality and experience can be analyzed, beginning with types of consciousness and their concomitant mental factors (*citta* and *cetasika dhamma*), and finishing with material *dhamma* (*rūpa*). The final section of the text offers explanations of all the terms in the *mātikā*. The second book, the *Vibhaṅga*, is made up of 18 chapters, each of which addresses an important Buddhist category, such as the aggregates (*khandha*), the foundations of mindfulness (*satipaṭṭhāna*), aspects of meditative experience, different types of knowledge, and expounds them first from the perspective of *Sutta* text and then from an *Abhidhamma* approach. Book three, the *Dhātukathā*, analyses *dhamma* with reference to the aggregates (*khandha*), sense bases (*āyatana*), and elements of consciousness (*dhātu*) (see later text). The *Puggalapaññatti*, the fourth book, is a more discursive work analyzing different types of personality in relation to *Abhidhamma* categories, particularly different assessments of ethical state, explaining how these are manifest and identifying appropriate practice for them. Book five, the *Kathāvatthu*, defends Theravada doctrine against developments in other Buddhist schools that had arisen by the third-century BCE. An overview of the doctrinal positions defended is provided by Bareau in his seminal analysis of the differences between early schools of Buddhism (Bareau 1955/2013: 275–326). The penultimate book of the *Abhidhamma Piṭaka*, the *Yamaka*, uses a form of interrogation of the technical terms of *Abhidhamma* to resolve ambiguities and define the terms very precisely. The final book, the *Paṭṭhāna*, explores the permutations generated by the 24 types of causal relationship between the *dhamma* (constituents of reality, see later text). Although never written out in full, its Sixth Council edition takes up 2500 pages (Bodhi *et al.* 1993: 11–13).

The fifth-century commentaries on the *Abhidhamma Piṭaka* are the *Atthasālinī*, translated into English by Pe Maung Tin (1976) and into German as *Die Darlegung der Bedeutung* by Nyanaponika (2005), which comments on the *Dhammasaṅgani;* the *Sammohavinodanī*, which comments on the *Vibhaṅga* (translated into English by Nyāṇamoli as *The Dispeller of Delusion* 1987, 1991); and the *Pañcappakaraṇaṭṭhakathā*, which comments on the remaining five books. The commentaries integrate information from the different parts of the *Abhidhamma Piṭaka* when commenting on an individual text, so that the analysis into *dhammas* is combined with the synthesis through *paccayas* (see later text) in order to explain how *Abhidhamma* works. There are also "handbooks," which summarize the *Abhidhamma* either as a whole or in relation to specific subjects. Of all the "handbooks," the most significant has been Anuruddha's terse summary, the *Abhidhammatthasaṅgaha*, composed in Sri Lanka in perhaps the eleventh- to twelfth-century (Bodhi *et al.* 1993). It has been the key text for studying *Abhidhamma* ever since, continuing to influence the structure also of modern books on the subject. The fifth-century *Visuddhimagga*, which is often paired with the *Abhidhammatthasaṅgaha* to form a comprehensive overview of Theravada doctrine and spiritual practice, is also to some extent an *Abhidhamma* manual. Its final section (Chapters XIV–XVII), which is dedicated to *paññā* (wisdom), offers an explanation of the categories of analysis, beginning with the five aggregates (*khandha*) that make up the psychosomatic individual, drawing on *Abhidhamma* (Karunadasa 2010: 2). The *Abhidhammatthasaṅgaha* is counted as one of the nine so-called "little-finger manuals" (*let-than* in Burmese). The others are the *Abhidhammāvatāra*, *Nāmarūpapariccheda*, *Paramatthavinicchaya*, *Rūpārūpavibhāga*, *Saccasaṃkhepa*, *Mohavicchedanī*, *Khemappakaraṇa*, and *Nāmacāradīpaka* (Karunadasa 2010: 3).

Manuals have continued to be produced into the modern period. One of the most prolific *Abhidhamma* authors of the early modern period was Ledi Sayadaw (see earlier text). Seeking to relate *Abhidhamma* to the newly emerging worldviews of modern science and world religions, he both defended Burmese Buddhism from the effects of Western encroachment and also made *Abhidhamma* accessible and exciting to westerners. Another well-known nineteenth- to twentieth-century author on *Abhidhamma* was the Shan poet Naṅ Khaṃ Ku, daughter of Zao Kang Suea, who also composed Shan poetic texts on the subject (see Chapter 10).

Analysis (*bheda*) and Synthesis (*saṅgaha*)

Abhidhamma concerns itself with ultimate truth (*paramattha-sacca*), rather than conventional truth (*saṃvuti-sacca*). In other words, there are two ways of speaking about the world. In day to day life one can speak in terms of "I" and of relationships such as "mine." This is conventional truth. *Sutta* texts analyze the individual thus referred to into a set of five aggregates. This analysis expresses the ultimate truth that there is no real entity of "I" or "mine." *Abhidhamma* breaks such concepts and analyzes down further into constituents or factors of reality called *dhamma*. Such *dhamma* are categorized into unconditioned reality and conditioned reality, the former being *Nibbāna*, the state of enlightenment. As unconditioned, *Nibbāna* is not subject to causality, impermanence, or the other laws of *saṃsāra*. It is beyond time and beyond *saṃsāra*. The other *dhamma*, while conditioned, are nonetheless considered to really exist in Theravada. In Indian philosophical terms, they have *svabhāva* – "own being," yet are empty (*suñña*) of self (*attā*) in that they are conditioned. The self, *attā*, being dismissed in this context is the concept of an enduring, independently existent entity. Dhamma, by contrast, are mutually dependent on each other, cannot exist "in a vacuum," and are temporary, swiftly coming to an end to be replaced by newly arisen *dhamma*; nonetheless, they are the ultimate constituents into which all phenomena can be analyzed. Other than these *dhamma*, all that is perceived is a conceptual construct or abstraction (Karunadasa 2010: 13).

From the perspective of both Theravada and the Madhyamika school of Mahayana Buddhist philosophy, the Sarvāstivāda school of *Abhidharma* went too far in reifying these *dhamma*. The Sarvāstivādins ("those with the theory that everything exists") developed the theory that the "substance of the *dharmas* persists in the three divisions of time, future, present, and past" (Karunadasa 2010: 8). The theory arose in part to address the problem of such matters as memory: if one remembers something in the past, then in some sense the thing remembered still exists in the present. The Sarvāstivādins considered the manifestations of *dharma* in past, present, or future as temporal aspects of an underlying nature that continued across these three times (Karunadasa 2010: 28). They were therefore criticized as teaching a form of eternalism, in contradiction of the fundamental Buddhist teaching of impermanence. In response, the *Perfection of Wisdom Sūtras* of early Mahayana Buddhism, and the Madhyamaka philosophy for which those *sūtras* are the core texts, emphasized the doctrine of no-self to mean not just "no-self of individuals" (*pudgala-nairātmya*, Sanskrit) but also no-self of *dharmas* (*dharma-nairātmya*, Sanskrit). Theravada *Abhidhamma* was similarly careful to emphasize the temporal and dependent nature of *dhamma*. Chapter 6 of the *Kathāvatthu*, compiled at the Third Council, criticized the *Sarvāstivāda* theory of tri-temporality. For the Theravada, all conditioned reality is the result of and subject to causality. All *dhamma* are momentary and no *dhamma* can exist independently of others. Rather they are the limit of the analytical process to divide up experience into its constituent factors. One must then also analyze the way in which they interconnect to constitute causality.

The term Dhamma has been used in other chapters of this book to mean the "truth" realized by the Buddha or the "teaching" expounded by the Buddha. The term *dhamma*, used in the plural, in the *Sutta Piṭaka* can just mean "things" and it is also the term given to the objects of the conscious mind, so "thoughts." In *Abhidhamma*, it is used in the technical tense to mean "the basic factors into which all things can be resolved" (Karunadasa 2010: 15).

There are a number of ways of analyzing human experience and causality that were developed in early Buddhism and that continued to be used alongside the *dhamma* theory. A basic analysis was into "name and form" (*nāma-rūpa*), a very early Indian analysis of the mental and physical aspects of human experience. In Buddhism, *nāma-rūpa* is one of the 12 links in the ***paṭiccasamuppāda*** ("chain of dependent origination") that explains the causal continuity of the individual across lifetimes, and *viññāna* "consciousness" is another link in this chain. Thus in Buddhism, the pair *nāma-rūpa* is not seen as covering the entire psychosomatic experience. Rather, the "naming" cognitive aspect (*nāma*) is understood as the five mental factors feeling, apperception, volition, contact, and attention (*vedanā, saññā, cetanā, phassa*, and *manasikāra*) that arise with consciousness; the physical aspect (*rūpa*) encompasses the four material elements, earth, wind, fire or heat, and water, and the more complex physical forms that develop out of them (Karunadasa 2010: 16–17).

The most well-known and widely found analysis of the individual in early Buddhist texts is into five psychosomatic aspects, the *khandha* ("aggregates"), which identify the different aspects of experience moving from what we might term the external level (the physical world and physical sense organs), through the various levels of the more cognitive aspects of human experience and response. The five *khandha* are form (*rūpa*); feeling (*vedanā*); perception or apperception, that is, the labeling of incoming sense data (*saññā*); mental formations (*saṅkhāra*), that is, the volitional responses to the incoming data; and consciousness (*viññāna*). This analysis of the individual is used to counter the notion of the self as a single entity with an enduring essence.

Another analysis of empirical reality is into six elements (*dhātu*): the four fundamental elements of physical existence, earth, wind, heat and water, plus space and consciousness. Two analyses that focus on the relationship between the external world and consciousness are the analysis into the twelve "bases" (*āyatana*) on which experience relies, and an extension of this analysis, the 18 elements (*dhātu*). The twelve *āyatana* are the six sense organs, that is, eye, ear, nose, tongue, body, and mind, and the objects of each of these: the visible, sound, smell, taste, touch, and thoughts or mental objects. The list of 18 *dhātu* adds to this set of 12 the 6 corresponding types of consciousness that arise from the contact between each organ and its object, that is, visual, auditory, olfactory, gustatory, tactile, and mental consciousness (Karunadasa 2010: 17). Note that the term *dhātu* ("element") is, like the term *dhamma*, used in a variety of ways. It can mean material "element," as in the four or six elements, or "essence," as a term for the relic of a Buddha, or a constituent, as in the set of 18 constituents that make up human experience. In all of these analyses, consciousness is identified not as a "self" at the heart of and separate from all experience but simply as "consciousness of" interactions, and thus part of a mutually dependent system of components rather than a static independent essence that could be misconstrued as an enduring entity.

Abhidhamma takes these various ways of analyzing our psychophysical experience further scrutinizing the connections between them and how they relate to the concept of cause and effect, including the doctrine of *kamma*. The analysis of psychophysical experience into *dhamma*, constituents of reality, resulted from the attempt to further reduce even these various analyses to the ultimate breakdown of their components, beyond which no further analysis was possible. The result in Theravada *Abhidhamma* was a list of 169 conditioned *dhamma*. (Sometimes the list is enumerated in a way that makes this list longer – see later text.) The conditioned *dhamma* are of three kinds: form/physical (*rūpa*), mental factors/aspects of consciousness (*cetasika*), and types of consciousness (*citta*). *Rūpa* is analyzed into 28 material *dhamma*. There are 52 *cetasika*. Finally, there are 89 varieties of consciousness (*citta*). If this *dhamma* analysis is compared with the *khandha* analysis, the first *khandha* is *rūpa*, also the first of our groups of *dhamma*. The next three *khandha* are aspects of consciousness (*cetasika*). Then the fifth *khandha*, consciousness, is the equivalent of the 89 varieties of consciousness (*citta*) in the *dhamma* analysis of *Abhidhamma*.

This parallel between the *dhamma* analysis and *khandha* analysis is as shown in the following table:

Khandha *analysis*	*Form*	*Feeling*	*Perception*	*Mental formation*	*Consciousness*
Dhamma analysis	28 *rūpa dhamma*		52 cetasika *dhamma*		89 citta *dhamma*

The 28 *rūpa dhamma*, material constituents of reality, are as shown in the following table:

Rūpa *group*		*Name of* rūpa dhamma	*Numbers of* rūpa
Real dependent matter	The great elements	Earth, water, heat, air	4
	The sense organs	Eye, ear, nose, tongue, body	5
	The sense objects	Visible form, sound, smell, taste, {tangibility is analyzed further into earth, heat, air, and thus is not enumerated here separately}	4
	The gender distinctions	Femininity, masculinity	2
	The physical base of the mind	Heart-base	1
	The physical aspect of ensuring the continuity of life	Life faculty	1
	Sustenance	Nutriment	1
Nominal dependent matter	The matter of limitation	Space	1
	The aspects of communication	Bodily intimation, vocal intimation	2
	The mutable phenomena	Lightness, malleability, wieldiness	3
	The characteristics of materiality	Production, continuity, decay, impermanence	4
	Total number of *rūpa*		28

Of these, the first four are the basic elements and the others are all derived from those four.

Another way of classifying these 28 *rūpa* is according to how they are produced. The first 18 *rūpa dhamma* are material products of one or a combination of the four causes (*rūpa-samuṭṭhāna*), namely, *kamma*, mind (*citta*), season (*utu*), and nutriment (*āhāra*) (*Abhidhammaṭṭhasaṅgaha* 6.9). They are therefore called "real dependent matter." The second ten *rūpa dhamma* are not produced from those four causes and exist merely as qualities or modes of the real dependent matter, and thus these are classified as "nominal dependent matter."

Cetasika, mental factors, arise together with consciousness and have intrinsic characteristics that determine the ethical quality of consciousness. The 52 *cetasika dhamma* are subdivided into 13 ethically variable *cetasika*, 14 unwholesome *cetasika*, and 25 "beautiful" (*sobhanasa*) *cetasika*. The 13 ethically variable *cetasika* can arise together with both beautiful (or wholesome) *citta* and unwholesome *citta*. They are further divided into two groups: seven universal *cetasika*, that is, they arise with every consciousness, and six particular *cetasika*, which are present only in some consciousnesses. The 14 unwholesome *cetasika* arise only with unwholesome consciousness, and the 20 beautiful *cetasika* arise with wholesome *citta*, resultant *citta*, and functional *citta* (see later text for different types of *citta*). The details of 52 *cetasika dhamma* are as shown next.

14 unwholesome cetasika:	*13 ethically variable* cetasika:		*25 beautiful* cetasika:
Delusion	7 universal *cetasika*	Contact	Faith
Shamelessness		Feeling	Mindfulness
Fearlessness of doing wrong		Perception	Shame
		Volition	Fear of doing wrong
Restlessness		One-pointedness	Nongreed
Greed		Life faculty	Nonhatred
Wrong view		Attention	Neutrality of mind
Conceit			Tranquility of mental body
			Tranquility of consciousness
Hatred			Lightness of mental body
			Lightness of consciousness
			Malleability of mental body
Envy			Malleability of consciousness
			Wieldiness of mental body
Avarice			Wieldiness of consciousness
			Proficiency of mental body
Worry			Proficiency of consciousness

(*Continued*)

(Cont'd)

Sloth	6 particular *cetasika*	Initial application	Rectitude of mental body
Torpor			Rectitude of consciousness
Doubt		Sustained application	Right speech
			Right action
		Decision	Right livelihood
		Energy	Compassion
		Zest/delight	Appreciative joy
		Desire	Wisdom faculty

Citta is the process of being conscious of something. An overview of the 89 *citta dhamma* is given in the following table. The list is subdivided into the four levels of planes of existence, seen in both cosmological and – here – psychological terms. The four are the mundane levels, which include the realm of sense pleasure; the realm of nonsense pleasure, which includes the material realm (realm of form) and immaterial realm (realm of no-form); and the supramundane level. There are further subdivisions according to unwholesome, wholesome, resultant, and functional (see following).

89 *citta*	81 mundane *citta*	54 sense-realm *citta*	12 unwholesome	8 rooted in greed
				2 rooted in hatred
				2 rooted in delusion
			18 rootless (see following)	7 unwholesome resultant
				8 wholesome resultant
				3 rootless functional
			24 wholesome sense-sphere	8 wholesome
				8 resultant
				8 functional
		27 nonsense realm *citta*	15 material realm	5 wholesome
				5 resultant
				5 functional
			12 immaterial realm	4 wholesome
				4 resultant
				4 functional
	8 supramundane *citta*	4 path *citta*	The path of stream entry	
			The path of one-returning	
			The path of non-returning	
			The path of arhatship	
		4 "fruit" (= culmination) *citta*	The fruit of stream entry	
			The fruit of one-returning	
			The fruit of nonreturning	
			The fruit of arhatship	

The 89 *citta* are analyzed into 81 mundane *citta* and 8 supramundane *citta*. Of the 81 mundane *citta*, 54 are sense-realm *citta* and 27 pertain to the nonsense realm. The 54 sense-realm *citta* are further refined into 12 unwholesome (8 rooted in greed, 2 rooted in hatred, 2 rooted in delusion); 18 rootless (i.e., *citta* that do not have greed, hatred and delusion or their opposites as roots/primary conditions); and 24 wholesome sense-sphere *citta*. The 27 nonsense realm *citta* are further analyzed according to planes within the realm of nonsense pleasure, namely, 15 material-realm *citta;* and 12 immaterial-realm *citta*. The 8 supramundane *citta* represent the four stages of liberation up to arhatship, beginning with stream-enterer, through once-returner and nonreturner to the *arhat*. Of these 8, 4 are the path *citta* corresponding to the path of stream-entry, the path of one-returning, the path of nonreturning, and the path of arhatship. The latter 4 are the "fruit" or "culmination" *citta* corresponding to the fruits of each stage of liberation. These 8 supermundane *citta* can be further refined into a list of 40 *citta*, giving a longer list of 121 rather than 89 *citta dhamma*. (See Bodhi *et al.* 1993: 28–29.)

In these categorizations, wholesome mental states are rooted in nongreed, nonhatred, and nondelusion, while unwholesome mental states are rooted in the three "fires" of greed, hatred, and delusion. Both constitute *kamma*, intentional action, with *kammic* results. Resultant states are states that result from previous wholesome and unwholesome action. Functional states are processes of consciousness that have no *kammic* effect and are also not the result of previous *kamma*. Resultant and functional *citta* are classed as "indeterminate," because of their lack of *kammic* effect. In this categorization of *dhamma*, we see the understanding of *kamma* as volitional action taken to its logical conclusions with *kamma* understood in terms of moments of wholesome and unwholesome consciousness (Bodhi *et al.* 1993: 31–32).

Conditions and Conditioned

None of these *dhamma* exists independently of others. Even a single *citta* coexists with a minimum of seven *cetasika*. A simile for the multiplicity of factors and their interconnectedness in even a single moment of consciousness is given in the *Atthasālinī* as follows:

> But consciousness does not arise singly. Just as in saying, "the king has arrived," it is clear that he does not come alone without his attendants, but comes attended by his retinue, so this consciousness should be understood to have arisen with more than fifty moral (mental) phenomena. (Pe Maung Tin 1976: 90. See also Nyānaponika 2005: 145)

The way that *dhamma* are interconnected, the way they both condition and are conditioned by each other, is the other focus of *Abhidhamma* philosophy. This is the *saṅgaha* "synthesis" aspect. Whereas causality is expressed simply in the *suttas*, in terms of single cause and effect by the formula: "when A exists, B arises; when A does not exist, B does not arise" (Pali: *imasmiṃ sati, idaṃ hoti, imasmiṃ asati, idaṃ na hoti*). *Abhidhamma* looks at causality in terms of multiple causes and clusters of effects. It identifies 24 types of conditions (*paccaya*), which form the basis of the complex causal relationships between *dhamma*.

The 24 *paccaya*, a number of which are further subdivided, are (1) root or primary *kammic* condition, (2) object condition, (3) predominance condition, (4) proximity condition, (5) contiguity condition, (6) conascence condition, (7) mutuality condition, (8) support condition, (9) decisive support condition, (10) prenascence condition, (11) postnascence condition,

(12) repetition condition, (13) *kamma* condition, (14) result condition, (15) nutriment condition, (16) faculty condition, (17) *jhāna* (higher meditative state) condition, (18) path condition, (19) association condition, (20) dissociation condition, (21) presence condition, (22) absence condition, (23) disappearance condition, and (24) nondisappearance condition (Bodhi *et al.* 1993: 304). The names of these conditions identify the ways in which each *dhamma* interrelates with other *dhamma*, both conditioning and being conditioned by them. (For a summary of the nature of the conditional relationships for each of these, see Kyaw 2012a: 8–9.)

The root or primary condition refers to the wholesome or unwholesome mental states based on the absence of the three fires (greed, hatred, and delusion) or their presence, which then condition further mental states or even physical and verbal actions. An object condition is the condition of a corresponding cognition. For the main senses, the material objects need to exist in the present, so be contemporary to the cognition of them, but mind-consciousness can be conscious of objects of the past, present, future, as well as real or conceptual (Karunadasa 2010: 266). A conascent condition comes into being at the same times as the conditioned *dhamma* that it causes, such as a flame instantly on arising causing light and heat. The same relationship exists between *citta* and the attendant *cetasika* (Karunadasa 2010: 268). The repetition condition, which causes successive mental states to gain power, refers to the relationship between successive mental *dhammas* in the *javana* (active momentary mental states) sequence that forms a cognition (Karunadasa 2010: 272). We can see from this that the nature of the contribution of the different conditions to the conditioned state vary, and that multiple conditions are involved in creating the resulting *dhamma*.

Commentarial Developments Including Momentariness

In the commentaries on the *Abhidhamma*, there are developments that in part result from the commentarial quest to coordinate the different sections of the *Abhidhamma Piṭaka*. Some of these developments are implicitly presumed in the canonical texts but are made explicit by the commentaries. The commentaries also prevent an infinite development, limiting the number of *dhamma* even though the *Dhammasaṅgaṇi* indicates further additions are possible. Included in these developments is a detailed analysis of the specifics of the way and order in which consciousness continues. This distinguishes between a "process-consciousness" (*vīthicitta*), that is, a consciousness that is active in a cognitive process, and a process-free consciousness (*vīthimutta*), that is, a consciousness that is free from cognitive process and thus in a passive condition (Karunadasa 2010: 139). In order to ensure the continuous flow of consciousness, whenever an active process consciousness is interrupted, it is immediately followed by a passive process-free consciousness. There are three different functions performed by the process-free consciousness, namely, life-continuum (*bhavaṅga*), death (*cuti-citta*), and rebirth-linking (*paṭisandhi*), in other words a type of consciousness that explains continuity within life, a type of consciousness at death, and a type of consciousness that makes the connection between one life and the next (at which point a *bhavaṅga*-type consciousness occurs). The *bhavaṅga* is a resultant consciousness that preserves the continuity of the individual existence whenever a cognitive process subsides. "In other words, it [*bhavaṅga*] intervenes between every two cognitive processes and thus separates them as two different cognitive units" (Karunadasa 2010: 139). The *bhavaṅga* arises and falls every moment during life whenever there is no active process-consciousness. Therefore, there are two alternating streams of consciousness moments, namely, a stream of process consciousness moments and a stream of process-free consciousness moments. The commentaries here refine the notion of momentariness, with the term *khaṇa* "moment," "instant" replacing the term *samaya* "occasion," for referring to the duration of a *dhamma*, that is, the duration of both consciousness *dhamma* with their concomitant mental factors, and the duration of matter (*rūpa-dhamma*) (Bodhi 1993: 14.). A full cognitive process will consist of 17 mind-moments, beginning with the past *bhavaṅga*, moving through passive to active and determining states. Each mind-moment is then divided into arising, duration, and dissolution (Karunadasa 2010: 239, 249).

Abhidhamma has a relative understanding of momentariness, such that matter (*rūpa*) lasts longer than consciousness with its concomitants (*citta* and *cetasika*). There are 17 *citta* moments from the passive states through the active states in relation to any single *rūpa* moment. This allows for the perception of the external world and creates a type of continuity not of any individual constituent but of the flowing network of ever-replaced constituents. The understanding of momentariness as relative develops from the *paccaya* theory found in the *Paṭṭhāna*, book seven of the *Abhidhamma Piṭaka*. Two of the 24 conditions include *purejāta-paccaya*, the condition of having arisen before, or prenascence, and *pacchājāta-paccaya*, the condition of arising after, or postnascence. The former is when a *dhamma* acts as a condition to something that arises later, the latter to when a *dhamma* acts as a condition to something that has already arisen. This requires overlapping and so relative durations of the condition and the conditioned. In the case of a prenascent condition, the condition is material and the conditioned *dhamma* is mental, such that with the material *dhamma* lasting longer, both then coexist. In the case of the postnascent condition, the condition is mental and the conditioned is a material *dhamma*, that in fact arose before the condition (Karunadasa 2010: 258–259).

The Theravada theory of momentariness is the result of the analysis of the Buddhist doctrine of impermanence, found in the *Sutta* texts, in the light of the *dhamma* theory and the need to establish the detailed process of continuity in the absence of an enduring self, or, indeed, of enduring *dhamma*. It is specific to the *Abhidhamma* tradition (Karunadasa 2010: 234).

The commentaries also introduce an explicit connection between consciousness and the heart-base (*hadayavatthu*) by suggesting that it is implied in the canonical texts. The *hadayavatthu* is understood to be the physical basis of consciousness. It is possible that it developed in parallel with medical understanding (Karunadasa 2010: 48). Another development in the Pāli exegesis is the importance of the consciousness and its object at the moment of death (see later text).

Abhidhamma and popular practice

Abhidhamma offers an analysis of reality that identifies the components that make it up and the ways in which these components relate. It does so to answer core questions at the heart of the Buddhist worldview, especially the problem of continuity in the absence of permanence. This issue of continuity in the absence of permanence is of fundamental importance to the Buddhist ethical worldview because of the continuity of *kammic* consequences in the absence of a self. The aforementioned discussion focused on some of the details of such analysis, utilizing lists of the entities and causal relationships that make up human psychosomatic experience across lives. The combination of its system of discourse, the technical language used, and its attention to detail can give *Abhidhamma* the reputation of residing within the domain of scholasticism on the part of some scholars (e.g., Kalupahana 1961, cited Kyaw 2012a). However, *Abhidhamma* scholars point out that this system of analysis arose on the basis of very practical considerations and that it continues to have practical implications to this day, beyond the ritual and protective uses based on the invocation of its power: it forms the basis for the understanding of the transformative process in meditation. For some Burmese meditation masters, a rigorous understanding of

Abhidhamma is a prerequisite for successful meditation practice. Kyaw identifies three well-known teachers who currently teach *Abhidhamma* as a preliminary to insight meditation: Mohnyin Sayadaw, the Saddhammaransī Sayadaw, and the Bamaw Sayadaw (Kyaw 2012a: 9 ff.). Each explains how an understanding of *Abhidhamma's* detailed theory of causality allows the meditation practitioner to understand and improve their meditation experiences.

While the relationship between *Abhidhamma* and *vipassanā* (insight) meditation may seem natural since both are at the dedicated, *nibbāna*-oriented end of the religious spectrum, an awareness of the *Abhidhamma* can also help us understand popular Buddhist practice. An understanding of the consciousness process, continuity over lifetimes, and momentariness helps illuminate death practices that might otherwise be understood as contrary to the Buddhist teaching of *kamma*, as will now be explained.

Although there is no escaping one's *kamma*, it may be observed that Buddhists believe that two things are particularly influential on one's immediate rebirth status: one's mental state at the time of death and which *kamma* is more "weighty" at the time of death. The object of consciousness at death has an impact on the immediate consciousness of the next life. This belief can be understood in relation to the *Abhidhamma* understanding of consciousness and continuity from the moment of death to the moment of rebirth. Langer points out that the passive consciousness or mental state (*bhavaṅga* "life faculty") differs from the active one in that, while both have an object, only the active mental state is aware of that object (Langer 2007: 45–46). The *bhavaṅga* is unaware of its object and the nature of its object remains the same throughout an individual being's lifetime (Gethin 1994: 19, cited Langer 2007: 45–46). As such, "*bhavaṅga* represents what and who we are, our nature and character, it also defines our potential and limits or shortcomings, which means that however hard some beings may try, they may never achieve certain attainments in their given existence" (Langer 2007: 46). It is only at the moment of new life that the *bhavaṅga* changes significantly, and as an immediate result of the final *citta* of one's previous life. This means that the object of consciousness at the time of death has a direct impact on one's character, rebirth, and experience in the subsequent life (Langer 2007: 47). At the time of death, if one may recollect good actions one has performed, such as making offerings or building a shrine (Langer 2007: 48), this can then have a positive effect on one's immediate rebirth. Conversely having one's bad deeds as the object of one's consciousness at the moment of dying will lead to a hellish rebirth. This understanding that the dying *citta* may have the same object as the rebirth *citta* led later *Abhidhamma* commentators to discuss whether intimations of one's next-life destiny could be experienced at the end of this life (Bodhi *et al.* 1993: 224).

The *Abhidhamma* explanation of the elements of the final death moment and their relationship to the first moment of consciousness in the next life of an individual informs a number of beliefs concerning the effect of the manner of dying on the next rebirth and a number of near-death practices. Older people traditionally spend more time at the temple listening to Dhamma and undertaking meditation or devotional practices. There are special meditations to be done close to death, including the ten *anussati* "recollections," which include recollections of the qualities of the Buddha (see Chapter 2), and of the gods, and also of one's own meritorious actions in the past. A monk may visit someone who is dying in order to chant Dhamma to them. The prognostication of future destiny on the basis of experiences toward the end of life found in some traditional Theravada meditation (*borān kammaṭṭhāna*) manuals bears a resemblance to prognostications found in Tibetan postdeath guidance manuals, such as that represented by the *Tibetan Book of the Dead* (Lopez 2011). Such similarity does not confirm the conjecture made by some of a tantric influence on *borān kammaṭṭhāna*, but rather the influence of *Abhidhamma* concepts, which are found throughout the genre (Crosby *et al.* 2012: 179, 189).

A sudden or violent death or death in childbirth is seen as particularly inauspicious and extra precautions need to be taken in relation to such deaths to ensure that those who die in this way do not get trapped as ghosts (*peta/petī*) and haunt the living. In fact, in mainland Southeast Asia the idea that those who die in this way haunt the living has been drawn on in rather macabre ways. As late as the nineteenth century in places (with rumors of more recent occurrences) people, sometimes prisoners or prisoners of war, sometimes pregnant women, were sacrificed in the foundations of palaces in the belief that those murdered in this way would become protective spirits of the building built over them. The offering of drops of blood into the post holes of *sīmā* markers in Cambodia to this day may also reflect an earlier practice of human sacrifice: the hundred spirits (*bray* in Khmer) that protect the monastery Wat Vihear Thom in Kratie Province, and its head monk, are believed to be the 100 virgin maids sacrificed when the princess they served died (Harris 2005: 58). A particularly shocking practice known from Cambodia is rumored still to be used today by the political elite as well as gangsters: the use of embryo amulets (*goan krak* Khmer), made of desiccated human fetuses (Harris 2005: 61). Similarly empowered amulets are found in Thailand using oil in which the corpses of still-born children and fetuses have been mummified (McDaniel 2012: 51). One type of protective figure empowered through treatment with such oil is the figure of a woman thought not only to protect the person who possesses it but to attract women to him (McDaniel 2011: 160).

The idea that end of life experience could have such an influence on the next life in this way has been seen by scholars as a belief somewhat at odds with the Theravada doctrine of *kamma*. However, the aforementioned exploration indicates how a closer familiarity with *Abhidhamma* can lead to a reassessment of even popular beliefs.

Summary

In this chapter, we examined the importance of *Abhidhamma* in defining Theravada as the last surviving *Abhidhamma* school of Buddhism. The Theravada estimation of Abhidhamma as the highest expression of ultimate truth has contributed to its identification as early Buddhism. However, *Abhidhamma/Abhidharma* is important in the development of all Buddhist philosophy. Moreover, Theravada Abhidhamma shares with Madhyamaka (one of the philosophies within Mahayana) a critique of the over-reification on the part of *Sarvāstivāda Abhidharma* of the constituents of reality (*dhamma/dharma*) into which both *Sarvāstivāda* and Theravada sought to analyze reality.

Abhidhamma developed its *dhamma* theory in response to the various systems of analyzing the human psychosomatic experience found in *sutta* texts. The analysis into four different types of *dhamma* (*rupa*, *cetasika*, *citta*, and *nibbāna*) takes up the first books of the *Abhidhamma Piṭaka*, while the seventh and final book deals with how the *dhamma* interrelate by conditioning and being conditioned by each other. This in turn led the commentaries to develop further the understanding of *dhamma*, including by developing a theory of relative momentariness.

Burma is the country that has retained the greatest in-depth knowledge and application of *Abhidhamma*. This is due to a number of specific historical developments, including the way the different Sangha groups defended their position in the face of scrutiny from the royal court/government and rivals. *Abhidhamma* was also important in the Burmese Buddhist response to the challenges of colonialism and modernity among both the Sangha and the laity. The fact that Burmese Sangha education has not been secularized has also contributed to the maintenance of a strong educational base for expertise in *Abhidhamma*. The study of *Abhidhamma* and its application in meditation remain popular among monks, nuns, and laypeople. It was important in the development of modern *vipassanā* and its uptake beyond Burma.

Abhidhamma has practical implications beyond its use in meditation. The detailed theories of *Abhidhamma*, particularly of the death-consciousness and the factors affecting our subsequent rebirth, underlie a number of death-related practices, including prognostication of future rebirths, preparations for a good death, and the creation of protective ghosts and amulets out of those who have suffered violent or untimely death.

References

Bareau, André. (1955 [2013]). *The Buddhist Schools of the Small Vehicle*. Translated from the French by Sara Boin-Webb, edited by Andrew Skilton. Honolulu: University of Hawai'i Press.

Bizot, François and François Lagirarde. (1996). *Saddavimala. La pureté par les mots*. Paris/Chiang Mai: l'École française d'Extrême-Orient.

Bodhi, Bhikkhu. (1993). *A Comprehensive Manual of Abidhamma: The Abhidhammattha Sangaha of Ācariya Anuruddha*. Kandy: Buddhist Publication Society.

Braun, Erik C. (2008). 'Ledi Sayadaw, Abhidhamma, and the Development of the Modern Insight Meditation Movement in Burma', PhD dissertation, Harvard University, Cambridge.

Brereton, Bonnie Pacala. (1995). *Thai Tellings of Phra Malai: Texts and Rituals Concerning a Popular Buddhist Saint*. Tempe: Arizona State University Press.

Burlingame, E.W. (1921). *Buddhist Legends*. Harvard Oriental Series 28–30. Cambridge: Harvard University Press. Reprint, London: Pali Text Society, 1979.

Charney, Michael W. (2006). *Powerful Learning. Buddhist Literati and the Throne in Burma's Last Dynasty, 1752–1885*. Ann Arbor: Centers for South and Southeast Asian Studies, The University of Michigan.

Crosby, Kate, Andrew Skilton, and Amal Gunasena. (2012). 'The Sutta on Understanding Death in the Transmission of *borān* Meditation from Siam to the Kandyan Court', *Journal of Indian Philosophy*, 40.2: 177–198.

Crosby, Kate. (2005). 'What Does Not Get Translated in Buddhism and the Impact on Teaching', in Lynne Long (ed.), *Translation and Religion: Holy Untranslatable?* Clevedon: Multilingual Matters, Ltd., 41–53.

Gethin, Rupert. (1994). 'Bhavaṅga and Rebirth According to the Abhidhamma' in Tadeusz Skorupski (ed.), *Buddhist Forum III*. London: School of Oriental and African Studies, 11–35.

Griswold, A.B. (1957). *Dated Buddha Images of Northern Siam*. Ascona: Artibus Asiae

Harris, Ian. (2005). *Cambodian Buddhism. History and Practice. Honolulu:* University of Hawai'i Press. Reprint, Chiang Mai: Silkworm, 2006.

von Hinüber, Oskar. (1996). *A Handbook of Pāli Literature*. Berlin/New York: Walter de Gruyter.

Kalupahana, David. (1961). 'Prolegomena to the Philosophy of Relations in Buddhism', *University of Ceylon Review* 19.2: 169–194.

Karunadasa, Y. (2010). *The Theravāda Abhidhamma. Its Inquiry into the Nature of Conditioned Reality*. Hong Kong: Centre of Buddhist Studies, The University of Hong Kong.

Kim, Wan Doo. (1999). 'The Theravadin Doctrine of Momentariness: A Survey of its Origins and Development'. DPhil thesis, University of Oxford.

Kyaw, Pyi Phyo. (2012a). 'The *Paṭṭhāna* (Conditional Relations) and Buddhist Meditation: Application of the Teachings in the *Paṭṭhāna* in some Burmese Meditation Traditions'. Paper presented at the 2nd IABU Academic Conference, MCU, Thailand, June 2012.

Kyaw, Pyi Phyo. (2012b). 'Burmese Monastic Education in Contemporary Sociopolitical Contexts of Burma: Curricula, Motivations and Roles of Monastic Examinations'. Presented at the 10th International Burma Studies Conference, Northern Illinois University, DeKalb.

Langer, Rita. (2007). *Buddhist Rituals of Death and Rebirth: Contemporary Sri Lankan Practice and its Origins*. London: Routledge.
Lopez, Donald. S. (2011). *The Tibetan Book of the Dead: A Biography*. Princeton: Princeton University Press.
McDaniel, Justin. (2009). 'Philosophical Embryology: Buddhist texts and the Ritual Construction of a Fetus' in Vanessa Sasson and Jane Marie Law (eds.), *Imagining the Fetus*. Oxford: Oxford University Press, 91–106.
McDaniel, Justin. (2011). *The Lovelorn Ghost & The Magical Monk. Practicing Buddhism in Northern Thailand*. New York: Columbia University Press.
McDaniel, Justin. (2012). 'A Buddha in the Palm of your Hand. Amulets in Thai Buddhism' in Heidi Tan and Alan Chong (eds.), *Enlightened Ways: The Many Streams of Buddhist Art in Thailand*. Singapore: Asian Civilisations Museum, 48–55.
Mizuno, Kōgen. (水野弘元) (1997). パーリ論書研究 (in Japanese) (Pāli Ronshyo Kenkyu), 春秋社.
Nyanaponika, Thera. (1949). *Abhidhamma Studies, Researches in Buddhist Psychology*. Kandy: Buddhist Publication Society.
Nyanaponika, Bhikkhu. (2005). *Die Darlegung der Bedeutung*. Oxford: The Pali Text Society.
Pe Maung Tin. (1976). *The Expositor (Aṭṭhasālinī): Buddhaghosa's commentary on the Dhammasaṅgani, the first book of the Abhidhammapiṭaka*. Edited and revised by Rhys Davids. London: Pali Text Society.
Skilton, Andrew. (1994). *A Concise History of Buddhism*. Birmingham: Windhorse Publications.
Stratton, Carol. (2004). *Buddhist Sculpture of Northern Thailand*. Chicago/Chiang Mai: Buppha Press/Silkworm Books.
Swearer, Donald K. (1995a). 'Consecrating the Buddha' in Donald S. Lopez (ed.), *Buddhism in Practice*. Princeton: Princeton University Press, 50–58.
Swearer, Donald K. (1995b). 'A Summary of the Seven Books of the Abhidhamma' in Donald S. Lopez (ed.), *Buddhism in Practice*. Princeton: Princeton University Press, 336–342.

Further Reading

Aung, Shwe Zan. (1910). 'Abhidhamma Literature in Burma', *Journal of the Pali Text Society* 6: 106–123.
Bodhi, Bhikkhu *et al.* (1993). *A Comprehensive Manual of Abhidhamma: the Abhidhammattha Sangaha of Ācariya Anuruddha*. Kandy: Buddhist Publication Society.
Boriharnwanaket, Sujin. (2005). *A Survey of Paramattha Dhammas*. Translated by Nina van Gorkom. Bangkok: Dhamma Study and Support Foundation.
Gethin, Rupert. (1994). 'Bhavaṅga and Rebirth According to the Abhidhamma' in Tadeusz Skorupski (ed.), *Buddhist Forum* 3, 11–35.
Gethin, Rupert. (1998). *The Foundations of Buddhism*. Oxford: Oxford University Press, 202–223.
Karunadasa, Y. (2009). 'Consciousness in the Abhidhamma Psychology' in K.L. Dhammajoti and Y. Karunadasa (ed.), *Buddhist and Pali Studies in Honour of The Venerable Professor Kakkapalliye Anuruddha*. Hong Kong: Centre of Buddhist Studies, The University of Hong Kong, 43–52.
Karunadasa, Y. (2010). *The Theravāda Abhidhamma. Its Inquiry into the Nature of Conditioned Reality*. Hong Kong: Centre of Buddhist Studies, The University of Hong Kong.
Nyanaponika Thera. (1977). *Abhidhamma Studies*. Boston: Wisdom Publications.
Skilton, Andrew. (2013). 'Theravada'. *A Companion to Buddhist Philosophy*, 1st edn. Edited by Steven M. Emmanuel. Chichester: Wiley-Blackwell, 71–85.
Varma, Chandra B. (2002). *Dictionary of Abhidhammic Terms*. Ranchi: Sineru International Publications.

Part Three

Sangha and Society

8

Monks, Monasteries, and Their Position in Society

Overview

The Buddha's teachings have mainly been preserved and represented by the community of monks and nuns who are bound by the rules of the *Vinaya Piṭaka*, the first of the three "baskets" that make up the Pali Canon (see Chapter 3). The monks' Sangha sees itself as deriving from the first five monks ordained by the Buddha shortly after his Enlightenment. There are two levels of ordination: the *pabbajjā*, then the *upasampadā*. After *pabbajjā* one is a ***sāmaṇera***, a novice, committed to keeping the "ten precepts" (see Chapter 5). After *upasampadā* one is now a *bhikkhu*, a monk, bound by the 227 *pāṭimokkha* rules, plus a number of additional regulations. Ancillary literature has been written since at least the fifth-century CE to help access the vast body of *vinaya* literature. Correct *vinaya* practice has been particularly emphasized at times of reform. The number of novices and monks varies greatly between different Theravada countries. Motivations for ordination vary, with education and merit-making high on the list of priorities. In mainland Southeast Asia, temporary ordination is normal, while in Sri Lanka ordination is supposed to be for life, even though most monks are first ordained as children. In addition to providing for the ritual needs of the community and of the Buddha (in the form of images), monks often have roles as educators and community leaders. For longer-term monks, the decision to disrobe can be a difficult one since they often have important roles in their communities, yet leaving the decision to return to lay life too late can have a serious impact on the possibility of developing a career as a layman. There are many different branches of the Theravada Sangha, called *nikāya*. On the whole they cannot conduct monastic legal procedures, *saṅghakamma*, together. This chapter focuses on the place of male ordination in Theravada Buddhism. Because of specific factors and recent developments affecting nuns, female ordination is discussed separately in Chapter 9.

Theravada Buddhism: Continuity, Diversity, and Identity, First Edition. Kate Crosby.

The Establishment of the Sangha

An identifying feature of Theravada Buddhism is the monks dressed in "saffron robes," who constitute the Sangha, or monastic community. The Buddha established the community of monks by recruiting the five fellow seekers who had been his companions when he was engaged in asceticism but who had abandoned him when he gave up austere practices. He returned to them at the Deer Park in Sarnath and gave there the "first sermon" that "set in motion the wheel of the law," the *Dhamma-cakka-ppavattana Sutta* in the *Saṃyutta Nikāya* section of the *Sutta Piṭaka*. The Theravada monks regard themselves as being in a lineage that goes back to these first five monastic followers, naming one of them, Aññāta Koṇḍañña, as the first. The nuns order was initiated later at the request of the Buddha's aunt Mahāpajāpatī Gotamī (see Chapter 9). Other monks who mark important turning points in Theravada and who are also important members of that lineage for current Theravada monastic identity include Mahinda, son of the Emperor Asoka, who is believed to have taken Theravada Buddhism to Sri Lanka; Soṇa and Uttara, who took Theravada to Southeast Asia at the same time; and Shin Arahan, the eleventh-century monk credited with converting King Anawratha of Burma to Buddhism. The nun Saṅghamittā, sister of Mahinda, is revered for bringing the nuns' ordination lineage to Sri Lanka: her memory has been invoked in the various attempts to revive the nuns' lineage.

Initially, ordination was through the personal invitation of the Buddha and there was only a single ordination. Then separate rituals arose for a lower ordination and a higher ordination. The former only requires one monk. The latter historically requires ten monks. In "outlying" regions, into which category all Theravada countries fall, this requirement is lowered to five monks. Ordination also became possible for children, modeled on that of the Buddha's son Rāhula, and in fact childhood ordination became the norm throughout Theravada, with the exception of some reform movements (Crosby 2012: 84).

The number of monks within each country fluctuates according to political events, the role of Buddhism in the nation's identity, and the availability of alternative options for young men. Current estimates for each country where Theravada is the majority religion are around 320 000 monks and males novices in Thailand serving 62 million Buddhists in a total population of 67 million (Seeger 2010: 556); 500 000 in the Union of Burma serving 50 million Buddhists, in a total population of 55 million (Schober 2011: 6–8); 50 000 in Cambodia serving 14 million Buddhists in a total population of 15 million (*Pacific Daily News* May 20, 2009); 22 000 in Laos serving a Buddhist population of 3.5 million out of a total of 6.5 million; 30 000 monks in Sri Lanka serving 13 million Buddhists out of a total population of 20 million (Samuels 2010: 138). In Bangladesh, there are fewer than 1000 monks serving a Buddhist population of about three million, which is mainly located in the Chittagong Hill Tracts (personal communication, Nagasena Bhikkhu). These figures show large differences in the ratios of laypeople per monk: 100 to 1 in Burma, 160 to 1 in Laos, 200 to 1 in Thailand, 280 to 1 in Cambodia, 400 to 1 in Sri Lanka, and 3000 to 1 in Bangladesh. The relatively high proportion of monks in Burma may reflect stronger Dhamma education and a lack of education in secular subjects for novices and monks, as well as the greater difficulty in saving up money for disrobing. The low number in Bangladesh may reflect the pressures faced by monks and the Buddhist community as a whole (see later text) coupled with the lack of the state support for Buddhism that is found in all the other Theravada countries. An interesting finding is that while the temporary ordination seen throughout mainland Southeast Asia seems to increase the number of monks available at any given time, the percentage of fully ordained monks who disrobe appears to be as high in Sri Lanka as in mainland Southeast Asia. Jeffrey Samuels reports that while there are no government statistics in Sri Lanka, monastic and lay informants estimate the number who disrobe at 85–95% (Samuels 2010: 131, note 7). This correlates closely with my own findings while researching the subject in Southeast Asia. The pressure on monks in Sri Lanka to stay in the monastery for life does not ensure and may even be counterproductive in terms of actually maintaining the numbers in the Sangha. There is anxiety in most countries about the number of long-term monks. The numbers are affected by dwindling birth rates and increasing alternative opportunities for education and social mobility. The ratios of monks to laypeople do not represent a true picture of the number of monks available per capita in any given village or town because the majority of monks live in the urban centers where they are receiving their education, and rural areas are often desperately short of monks for their ritual and other religious needs.

The Place of Ordination in Society

Ordination, the Sangha and the monastery, contrary to a commonly held Western notion that Buddhist monks are "other-worldly," play an important part at the heart of Theravada communities. The rhetoric that monks should have renounced society is not confined to Westerners, but drawn on by local Buddhists also when they seek to restrict the power of popular monks in political debate. In reality, while Buddhism began as a "renouncer" tradition, Buddhist monks fulfill roles across a broad spectrum. At one end of that spectrum is the "world-renouncer" ideology, a life of meditation sought out by a small minority of monks, with relatively little ritual and social service for laypeople. Across the rest of the spectrum are ritual, preaching, educational, and social roles that we might more comfortably ascribe to "priests." Yet in all Theravada communities, there are laypeople who support the monks in their work providing an additional range of services, and others who provide alternative services, to whom we might also apply the term priest. This lack of terminological precision is also seen in the interchangeability in English of the terms monastery and temple for the place where monks live (*vihāra* in Pali). There are some temples, places of worship, and communal gathering, such as the Temple of the Tooth in Sri Lanka, and the pagodas of Burma, which are not home to monks. There are also to be found monasteries, for example residences for monks trying to follow a renouncer life, which have no Buddha shrine for laypeople to worship. For the most part, however, a complex of buildings that serves as a residence for monks will have within it a building that acts as a shrine room for both laypeople and monks: the roles of monastery and temple are fulfilled by the same set of buildings. Throughout the Theravada world the layout of each monastery is similar enough that Buddhists from one region will be able to find their way about in a monastery of another tradition or region and recognize the function of each part. There is some slight variation. For example, in Shan temples, the abbot's residence is often within the same building as the shrine room to one side behind the shrine. In some temples, the *sīmā* or *uposatha* hall, where ordinations take place, may be open to laypeople, except when a *saṅghakamma* is taking place. In others, either laypeople or female laypeople are not allowed to enter. These halls tend to be roofed and more elaborate in mainland Southeast Asia. In Sri Lanka and Bangladesh, they tend to be more simple, even open to the elements.

Scholars have often struggled to comprehend the actual life of monks and the role many monks play in their community. There is still a tendency to treat them as something "other."

The understanding of Buddhism as a world-renouncing tradition is so strong in the history of Buddhist studies that there is a blind spot when it comes to recognizing monks as full members of their society with the usual range of human aspirations and emotions and often a long list of duties and obligations that keep them closely involved with the local community. The idea of Buddhism as world-renouncing is based on the Pali Canon, but is also influenced by the nineteenth- to twentieth-century attitudes (see Chapter 12), including those of the sociologist of religion, Max Weber. His view of Buddhism as other-worldly has had a long-term impact on the sociology/social anthropology of Theravada Buddhism (e.g., Spiro 1971, see Choompolpaisal 2008). The demarcation between monk and priest in Christianity, which does not apply in Buddhism, has also influenced Western expectations.

The contrast between Western expectations of the lifestyle and aspiration of Theravada monks and reality has prompted scholars to examine the place of ordination in the lives of Buddhist men. It is now recognized that ordination fulfills a number of functions and might be inspired by a range of motivations, of which the aspiration to reach Enlightenment, *Nibbāna*, is only one. The search for *Nibbāna* is a pervasive value in a society's support of the Sangha, regardless of whether it is the immediate, primary consideration in the decision of any individual to support or undergo an ordination. The Sangha is very much a community within a community, with its own internal dynamics and its own responses to the broader issues affecting the society which hosts it.

Ordination into the Sangha can be a stepping stone to education, adulthood, and a career. This motivation can be explicit in those Theravada societies where ordination is intended to be temporary, that is, in most of Southeast Asia. Even though ordination is generally supposed to be lifelong in Sri Lanka, this same motivation is to be found there, but is not explicitly acknowledged in a neutral manner. There is a stark contrast in attitudes to ordination and ex-monks between the Theravada of Southeast Asia and that of Sri Lanka. In modern Sri Lanka, in spite of a number of attempts to reintroduce temporary ordination, leaving the Sangha is regarded as a bad thing and ex-monks may find themselves viewed with distrust. It is not clear when lifelong commitment became the expectation in Sri Lanka. It may have been during the eighteenth-century reform under the monk Saraṇaṃkara. Buddhaghosa, the fifth-century author of the commentary on the *Vinaya Piṭaka*, rejected a formula for ordination that included the phrase "lifelong" (Crosby 2000) and referred to monks ordaining and disrobing as many as 100 times without it being regarded as a problem. In Southeast Asia, the commitment in most Theravada traditions of Southeast Asia is temporary, and to have undertaken life as a monk even for a few days is regarded as highly meritorious and the merit from it is not lost on disrobing. Nonetheless, some monks do stay lifelong.

The wide range of motivations behind an individual's decision to undergo ordination includes external factors. The motivation may not be a personal one of the ordinand, but that of his family, community, parole officer, employer, etc. Contrary to the understanding in much Western literature of Theravada spirituality as essentially self-interested, relating to personal arhatship, even the personal spiritual motivations of the man who remains as a monk longer term are not limited to personal attainment of higher spiritual states or the goals of *Nibbāna*, but more often include compassionate considerations, such as ensuring the aspiration for good is there for the community, guiding and protecting. Other ways of serving society, through the provision of ritual and teaching, or ensuring the availability of the Dhamma, are also important. Such motivations often emerge *after* ordination, as one might expect given the prevalence of childhood ordination. One reason monks cite for staying in the Sangha after they had expected to return to lay life is the value of the Dhamma and Sangha for the community and society as a whole, a value they had only come to realize during their exposure to Buddhist teachings while a novice.

There is a large degree of tradition involved in the decision to become a monk: that it is traditional for all men, or for a man in each generation of the family to do so (Crosby in preparation); that it is the traditional way for a son to repay his mother for her suffering in childbirth, or both parents for the hardships they endured in raising him (Eberhardt 2006: 96); and that one has a duty to have a son ordained in order to maintain the Sangha (Samuels 2010: 45). It might be the standard coming of age ceremony for boys in that society and an important factor in improving their marriage prospects. For the most part, female coming of age ceremonies in Theravada cultures do not involve the Sangha, although there are exceptions to this. In Lamphun in northern Thailand, the tall offering "trees," distinctive, elaborately decorated poles or structures up to ten meters high bearing gifts and money for monks donated at the end of the rainy season in the Salak Yom festival, were traditionally made by unmarried women around the age of 20. Alexandra Denes reports, "According to local informants, the Salak Yom offering was a demonstration of a young woman's diligence, handicraft skills, and ability to manage the household economy – all evidence that she was ready for marriage" (Denes 2012: 59).

The Sangha traditionally played a role in providing education in a range of skills including numeracy and literacy for boys. Even with the introduction of state-run education and in places where education is free or cheap, joining the Sangha continues to ensure housing and at least subsistence throughout the period of education. Although families have to go without the labor and money a male child would bring in were they not being educated, and they may have to pay contributions to costs or for permission to ordain, this is mitigated by the monastery covering some or all of his living costs. Even children who are not ordained can benefit from the shelter and support provided by monasteries (see Chapter 10).

Monasteries also offer mobility. Novices and monks may, for example, move from rural areas to urban centers with access to secondary and higher education. This can be quite a simple process: securing the permission of the head monk or the head of that section of the monastery, perhaps through the mediation of a friend. In Burma, the process may be complicated by the need to secure the commitment of one or more families willing to provide food and other support for the new monk. Securing a place at a teaching monastery may also require having the right connections in terms of teacher lineage and lay sponsors, particularly as one rises in status and it becomes harder to break into existing chains of command in the monastery one wishes to join. In Vientiane, the capital of Laos, and Phnom Penh, the capital of Cambodia, most of the monks are from rural backgrounds and will stay in the monasteries until they have finished their education. Similarly in Burma, some monasteries in Yangon, for example, provide shelter and support including secular or monastic education to children from ethnic minority groups, such as Pa'O people from the Shan State in the north. Some of these children then go on to complete university education while staying in the monasteries as temple boys.

The mobility that the Sangha affords young men means some may undertake ordination in order to migrate to a neighboring region or country. They can then acquire language skills in that new region or country that prepare them for work when they return to their lay lives. In Thailand, many of the monasteries are dependent on illegal immigrant monks from neighboring countries, not all of whom intend to disrobe. Young men of Thailand often have a wider range of opportunities open to them; those from poor, rural backgrounds in Burma, Cambodia, and Thailand itself may be more committed to staying in the Sangha longer, in addition to wanting to take advantage of the entry into the new language, community, and culture that ordination has offered them. The use of Pali language in rituals throughout

Theravada means that migrant monks can play roles in serving the community before they have had time to learn to communicate with parishioners. Some Shan temples in northern Thailand are popular for providing blessings and *yantras* to speakers of Bangkok Thai and Tai Yuan, and the skills required of the officiating monks do not include much knowledge of the language of communication. Thai people will travel long distances to receive these services from monks who have gained a reputation for expertise in them.

The pan- and trans-national fluidity of monasticism allows monks to move from place to place for a number of reasons. Novices may seek out a head monk who acts as a good parental figure, or flee from one who has a short temper. A monastery that is popular enough with donors to provide good food, or one that provides the best training or access to schooling is also attractive. Monks of all ages will move to find teachers in their area of interest, whether that is meditation or a more "secular" interest such as carpentry, literature, or kick-boxing. They may also stay for long periods in other areas simply to take advantage of the opportunity to travel or broaden their experience. Some temples are particularly auspicious for ordination. For example, many novices become ordained at Chitmarong temple in Bangladesh, which houses a Mahāmuni image, the most sacred image in Bangladesh (see Chapter 2). The novices may then move on to stay at a temple nearer home if they remain in robes for more than a few weeks.

The floating nature of the monastic communities that results from this fluidity allows governments to send spies as monks, in the expectation that their status gives them a vantage point at the heart of a community. One monk escaping from Cambodia during the Khmer Rouge period explained how he was able to cross the border smoothly (i.e., not end up in a refugee camp) because he was in the company of Thai monks. On reaching Thailand they immediately disrobed, having only been ordained for the purposes of espionage (Crosby in preparation). The mobility can also cause problems: In areas where there is a shortage of monks, those imported from outside the community may have little knowledge of the local people, the issues they face, and how the local power structures are to be navigated. This may make them less effective in their role as community leaders and guides.

Another practical motivation for ordination is the avoidance of draft either into the national army, for example, in Thailand, or one of the rebel armies, for example, the Shan State Army in the Union of Burma. Becoming a monk to avoid "service to the king" has a long history in Theravada and has also been one of the motivations for rulers and governments to restrict and control ordination to varying degrees. In seventeenth-century Burma, King Thalun (1629–1648) not only banned ordinations from 1638 until the end of his reign but also purged a large number of monks from the Sangha in order to have more young men for military service, expeditions, and construction (Dhammasami 2004: 23 and 63). In the modern period, all Theravada countries except Sri Lanka have kept a relatively tight control on people receiving higher ordination. In Cambodia in 1981 after the Khmer Rouge period came to an end, the Vietnamese-backed government restricted ordination to those over the age of 55 for a number of years to ensure the army was sufficiently well-manned, a restriction that was lifted in 1988. Restrictions also continued in those areas that remained under the Khmer Rouge until 1997 (Crosby and Long, fieldwork 2012).

The temple is a place for "taming" wayward young men. In addition to any transformation wrought by the ritual of ordination itself, the Sangha's emphasis on decorum and proper deportment inculcates civil behavior in young men, an aspect valued in making men marriageable. Additionally, meditation encourages the ability to restrain impulsive behavior. There are exceptions to this pattern. There have been cases of violence and even violent crime on the part of monks, particularly in Cambodia, where the relative shortage of middle-ranking monks able to mediate between elderly and young monks and to guide the latter has caused problems with discipline. This problem is particularly severe in rural temples where the shortage of middle-ranking monks is at its worst.

The calming effects of monastic life on the temperament have been harnessed to treat drug and alcohol abuse and to help post-prison rehabilitation. Ordination offers a new start to men wanting to put a troubled period behind them. For young boys, widowers, and the retired, the monastery provides not only shelter but also a substitute family. In Cambodia and Laos, many elderly women live as nuns in temple compounds, although the monastery is less likely to offer shelter in this way to girls and younger women (see Chapter 10).

The process of ordination generates great merit for all involved: for the ordinand, for those who provide the items he will need as a monk and for those who sponsor the festivities. It is particularly important as a rite of passage for mothers (Eberhardt 2006: 135ff.) In Tai, Lao, and Khmer ethnic groups, lower ordination is particularly associated with repaying the mother, and higher ordination the father. Sponsoring a novice's ordination and perhaps their subsequent education can be a way for childless people to acquire quasi-children, or at least become intimately involved in the younger generations. Similarly, popular monks in Burma may undertake a kind of "strengthening" ritual for their ordination, which allows the laypeople sponsoring it to form a closer relationship with him and gain the high degree of merit this provides (see later text).

Temporary ordination is regularly undertaken as part of a funerary rite, even if just for a few days: the merit generated is then dedicated to the deceased. It is also undertaken in completion of a vow in thanksgiving for recovering successfully from an illness, averting a calamity or obtaining an award or promotion. Some monks disrobe for health reasons, if, for example, they cannot follow the regulation against eating after noon (diabetes is a common problem among longer term monks) or need nursing care; conversely it is also common to ordain for health reasons, to take advantage of the merit gained through ordination. A common motivation for having a child ordained used to be if he had an inauspicious astrological chart: joining the Sangha would give him a fresh "birthday."

The status of the monk, with their privileged position in society and access to a better lifestyle and education, is an allure that motivates boy and parents alike. A child's interest may be stimulated by playing with other novices at the local temple or developing emotional bonds with monks at the temple where they play. A temple's popularity as a meeting place and playground for children, and the regard in which the abbot is held by local people, has a strong impact on recruitment into the Sangha from the local community. Recruitment, particularly of monks intending to stay long term, is an issue for all Buddhist communities, especially those in rural regions. It has been observed by senior monks in Cambodia that former Khmer Rouge soldiers, who ordain to make a new start and to try to make recompense for their former violent pasts, often have more dedication and commitment than other monks, who typically disrobe after completing their education: the ex-soldiers had stronger religious motivations for being ordained (Crosby in preparation).

The Ordination Process

Ordination for monks is in two stages. The first is the lower ordination, the *pabbajjā*, which can be undertaken once "old enough to scare crows away," that is, from the age of seven to eight upward, although actual age varies greatly. In Thailand, boys traditionally undertook ordination as young teenager, but increasingly do so after university or during the university vacation period. Far younger boys may live at the temple as temple boys for training or to access schooling or because their parents are unable to take care of them.

All monks, whatever age, whether temporary or longer term, go through the *pabbajjā* ritual. To do so they must fulfill a number of criteria: be free from certain diseases, free men (not in debt or in service to the king, etc.), and have their parents' permission if their parents are still living. The ritual itself, especially in its more elaborate forms, is preceded by a re-enactment of Buddha's leaving society and, in Southeast Asia, incorporates brahmanical and other life-cycle rituals. There has been an emphasis – since at least the time of the fifth-century commentator Buddhaghosa – on the exactitude of the specifics of the ordination ritual, particularly the wording and pronunciation of the obligatory Pali language components (Crosby 2000). The *pabbajjā* bestows purity and status. The novice's change of status is most clearly indicated at the end of the ceremony in the reversal of parent–child hierarchy. The parents and relatives worship at the feet of their newly ordained son. This can be a very moving experience both for the relatives and for the newly ordained monks. It is rare for the same reverse in status to be granted to nuns or precept-nuns, although this is beginning to change (see Chapter 9).

An ordination can take place for one individual, or it can be a community affair, with dozens, even hundreds of novices taking ordination at the same time. In Southeast Asia, the boys who are about to be ordained are dressed up in finery and made up as princes in re-enactment of Gotama before he renounced. They are processed around the streets, perhaps on a horse or cart, or on the shoulders of older male relatives. A band plays music and as they process the novices-to-be throw coins and sweets symbolizing giving up wealth. It is a very festive occasion and the sponsors may have saved up for several years to be able to afford the musicians, the offerings for the gods, Buddha, preceptor, and other monks, the food for the monks and for the community, the outfit and gifts for the "prince," and the items such as a robe and a bowl that he will need as a monk. The boys then make their request to the preceptor that he ordain them, are taken away to have their heads shaved, and return dressed as monks. Sometimes the initial shaving of the hair is done by the preceptor monk himself and is a form of meditation, as the novice repeats after the preceptor the Pali words for the first five of the constituents of the body in the meditation on the 32 parts of the body: *kesa* (head hair), *loma* (body hair), *nakha* (nails), *danta* (teeth), and *taco* (skin) (see Chapter 6). During the ordination process, the novice must take the three refuges in Pali ("I go to the Buddha for refuge", etc.) and the ten precepts of a novice (see later text).

Not all monks remain long enough or bother to receive the higher ordination, *upasaṃpadā*. There is no difference in appearance or in rituals that a monk can perform for laypeople, but a reason for undertaking the *upasaṃpadā* is the status it bestows, both for the monk himself and for the people for whom he performs rituals. In the past, because only fully ordained monks can ordain others, the *upasaṃpadā* has been at risk and even died out in a country. This happened in Sri Lanka in the eighteenth century, even though there were mature "novices" on the island, and attempts were made to reintroduce the lineage from Arakan, Burma, and Thailand. The Siyam Nikāya ("lineage from Thailand"), which is the oldest, most powerful' and most prestigious lineage in modern Sri Lanka, results from the successful reintroduction of the *upasaṃpadā* from Ayutthaya, then the capital of Thailand (Siam) in 1753.

It is usual for longer-term monks to take the higher ordination within a few years of turning 20, and men who first become novices at this age can take the *pabbajjā* and *upasaṃpadā* in quick succession. After this ordination, the monk is committed to keeping all the rules contained in the *Vinaya Piṭaka* (see later text). During the ordination ceremony, the first four rules, the *pārājika*, breaking which entails lifelong expulsion from the order, are emphasized. (For a summary structure of the higher ordination, see Carbine 2011: 204.) Like the *pabbajjā*, the *upasampadā* ritual bestows purity and status. It is also the point at which seniority commences. Seniority for monks is calculated in terms of the number of rainy seasons, ***vassa***, that have passed since taking the *upasampadā*. In gatherings of monks unknown to each other, it is not uncommon for them to ask each other their "*vassa* age" so that they might know who is to worship whom in greeting. Many things beyond this daily display of status, including what posts one holds and whether one inherits a particular temple, depend on *vassa* age and it is this that a monk is in danger of losing if he disrobes.

Upon ordination monks are given a new Pali name by their preceptor, the person who conducts the ordination. How a monk is then referred to varies a little. Monks in Sri Lanka are known by the village in which they were ordained followed by the Pali ordination name. For example, in the name Hikkaḍuvē Sumaṅgala (an important nineteenth-century monk studied in Blackburn 2010), the first word refers to a town in southwest Sri Lanka and the second word means "Very Auspicious" in Pali and was given him on ordination. In Tai ethnic groups, a monk may have an ordained name but be referred to by a nickname or the first item of this pairing. When a monk has become well known in Burma, he may simply be referred to by the place he resides, his lineage, or by his qualification with the word "Sayadaw." For example, the case of the famous scholar-monk the Ledi Sayadaw U. Ñāṇadhaja, the word "Ledi" refers to the Ledi Forest Monastery (*Ledi-twaya* in Burmese), "Sayadaw" means "royal teacher, that is, a highly regarded monk-teacher," "U" is the Burmese male honorific, and Ñāṇadhaja is the Pali name he was given on ordination. He is most commonly referred to as simply "Ledi Sayadaw."

Rules for Novices and Monks

In the *pabbajjā* ceremony, the novice (like many precept nuns) undertakes the ten precepts:

1. Not to kill/cause killing
2. Not to take what is not given
3. Celibacy
4. Not to lie
5. Not to take intoxicants
6. Not to eat at the wrong time
7. Not to spectate dancing, singing, or music
8. Not to ornament oneself with garlands, scent, ointments
9. Not to sleep on large or high beds
10. Not to handle gold or silver

After the *upasampadā*, monks are bound to keep the 227 *pāṭimokkha* rules. For fully ordained nuns, the number of such rules is 331. *Pāṭimokkha* is the name of the fortnightly ceremony at which monks should meet and recite these rules in the form of the *Pāṭimokkha Sutta*. This is a noncanonical text but contains all the 227 *pāṭimokkha* rules, extracted from the *Vinaya Piṭaka*. The extent to which monks still conduct the *pāṭimokkha* ceremony with such regularity varies considerably.

The *Vinaya Piṭaka* contains the stories that explain why the Buddha established each rule. It also provides variations on each offence, checking whether or not it would still count as the offence in question. For example, in the case of the second rule, not to commit murder, the *Vinaya Piṭaka* describes a monk going to a house and sitting on what he thought was a pile of cloth. In fact, it was a baby and he thereby kills the baby. Because there was no intention to kill, he is not guilty of murder, but of inattentiveness.

The 227 *pāṭimokkha* rules are classified into eight different types of offense, in decreasing order of seriousness:

1. 4 *Pārājika* "defeats" ("to be driven out") – entailing lifelong expulsion from the Sangha: sexual intercourse, murder, serious theft, false claims of magical powers. There are an additional 4 *pārājika* on top of this list for nuns, as well as additional rules in the other categories.
2. 13 *Saṅghādisesa* – entailing an initial and subsequent meeting of the Sangha to determine whether a period of suspended status *mānatta* is deserved.
3. 2 *Aniyata* – "undetermined."
4. 30 *Nissaggiya-pācittiya* – requiring confession and relinquishing of a wrongly acquired item.
5. 92 *Suddhika-pācittiya* – requiring confession of a transgression for purification.
6. 4 *Pāṭidesanīya* – requiring acknowledgement of a transgression.
7. 75 *Sekhiya* – "requiring training," that is, forms of undesirable behavior, such as improper wearing of robe, but not an offence as such.
8. 7 *Adhikaraṇasamatha* – processes for dealing with disagreements, etc.

The *Vinaya* also includes other offences, beyond the *pāṭimokkha* list, conduct that is wrong but not a formal *pāṭimokkha* offence. These can be lesser versions of *pāṭimokkha* offences or different types of wrongdoing entirely. There are three kinds of non-*pāṭimokkha vinaya* offence: *thullaccaya* "a grave lapse," quite a serious offence such as an unsuccessful attempt to commit a *pārājika* or *saṅghādisesa* offence but it can be expiated through confession to another monk; *dukkaṭa* "something badly done," that is, "wrongdoing" or "improper conduct"; and *dubbhāsita* "ill spoken," improper speech.

We quite often find misconduct labeled as a *dukkaṭa* offence in the context of regulations about monastic processes, for the *vinaya* also describes how monks (and, separately, nuns) should conduct themselves as a community. For example, all the legal acts of the Sangha, the *saṅghakamma*, such as ordination, should be carried out within a ritual enclosure, called a *sīmā* (Kieffer-Pülz 1992, Nagasena 2013). The *sīmā* can be a secular village boundary, and the rituals are conducted by monks who have to be seated closely within a certain distance of each other. More often, such rituals are conducted within a formally marked or bound *sīmā* (*baddhasīmā*). Establishing a *sīmā* is often a priority for a newly formed monastery and is mentioned as one of the first matters of business conducted by Mahinda and his companions in establishing Buddhism in Sri Lanka in the third-century BCE. Even where there are *sīmā* available in the other monasteries, the abbot of a new monastery will be keen to establish a *sīmā* in his own because it gives the group of monks resident there the ability to conduct their *saṅghakamma* independently of other monasteries in the same village, town, or city. The correct consecration of a *sīmā* is extremely important. An invalid *sīmā* invalidates the lineage of the monks whose ordinations were conducted in it. In consecrating a *sīmā*, great care is taken to ensure that the demarcation markers (*nimitta*) are correct in number, material, and layout; that there is a quorum of monks (in this case a minimum of four, a *gaṇa*) who are "pure," that is, have not broken a *pārājika* rule;

that all monks in the relevant area are present or have sent their consent to ensure that the Sangha is unified; and that the litanies (*kammavācā*) are recited with the correct wording and pronunciation (Nagasena 2013: Chapter 7). The *Vinaya Piṭaka* was regarded as providing insufficient detail of how to consecrate a *sīmā* correctly, so this is one of the sets of rules where we rely on the *Samantapāsādikā*, the fifth-century commentary to the *Vinaya Piṭaka*, to know the rules clearly. Breaking these rules is a *dukkaṭa* offense. Similarly such actions as ordaining a monk without parental consent is a *dukkaṭa* offense. So although *dukkaṭa* would seem to be a minor category, the practical consequences of committing some *dukkaṭa* offences are very serious.

With all the *pāṭimokkha* and the many other rules, the *Vinaya Piṭaka* is extremely long. To help monastic communities keep on top of the rules, summary manuals that discard the narratives that explain why the Buddha established each rule have been compiled since at least the fifth-century BCE, when Buddhadatta (probably South Indian) composed the *Vinaya Vinicchaya*. During periods of crisis and reform, there is often a spate of writing new *vinaya* commentaries and manuals. For example, the twelfth-century scholar Sāriputta and his pupils composed many *vinaya* works following the unification of the Sangha of Sri Lanka under Parākamabāhu I (Crosby 2006). In their differing responses to the threat of European colonialism in the nineteenth century, Burma and Thailand were both highly productive of *vinaya* literature. The former emphasized reading the *Vinaya Piṭaka* through the commentaries, especially the *Samantapāsādikā*, whereas one of the most productive authors on *vinaya* in Thailand was Prince Ven. Vajirañāṇavarorasa (1860–1921). He had headed the editing of the *vinaya* (1969) volumes for the printed edition of the Pali Canon produced under royal patronage at that time (see Chapter 3). In part reflecting this, and also reflecting the **Thammayutika Nikāya's** emphasis on going back to the Canon, his numerous works on *vinaya* practice derive directly from the Pali Canon. Some of his works, including the *Vinayamukha*, *Entrance into the Vinaya* have been translated into English by Ven. Thanissaro (b. 1949), an American monk in the Forest tradition of the Thammayutika Nikāya and now abbot of a Thai forest monastery in California. Ven. Thanissaro has also written *The Buddhist Monastic Code: The Pāṭimokkha Training Rules Translated and Explained* (1994), allowing the growing international Sangha access to detailed information on correct *vinaya* practice. In most cases, even with all this literature, monks learn about correct conduct from other, more senior monks, through emulation and oral instruction.

The extent to which rules are adapted in the West varies considerably. Thai forest monks recreate as traditional a setting as possible, allowing them to maintain quite strict *vinaya* discipline, although even they must adapt the rules on dress. The three robes permitted in the *vinaya* are insufficient in cold climates. Adaptation of the rules has taken place for centuries. Thus with the universal use of money in modern societies it is only a few *nikāya* that keep the precept (and parallel *pāṭimokkha* rule) not to handle money (on which, see Wijayaratna 1990: Chapter 5). Some *nikāya* take a literal interpretation of the precept "not to handle gold and silver," and will use a cloth to hold the gold key to the shrine room, for example. Because of this natural process of adaptation, there are easy targets at times of reform. For example, the Thammayutika Nikāya criticized the traditional adapted robes worn in Southeast Asia, which include such items as a belt. These changes had been present for so long that a rich symbolism had developed in relation to them, but the Thammayutika Nikāya monks began wearing robes in the manner described in the canon, disregarding local heritage (Bizot 1993: 75–82).

Leaving the Sangha

In those cultures where ordination is mainly a merit-producing act or a coming of age ceremony, most novices disrobe after a short period. Some people become novices and disrobe many times. Most longer-term novices and those who have taken the higher ordination to become monks disrobe after they have completed their education found a job or are needed by their family to work in the family business or care for other family members.

The process of leaving the Sangha is relatively simple. One informs another person, ideally but not necessarily one's preceptor, that one is disrobing. One then changes into lay clothes and returns to receive the five precepts from the preceptor or from other monks, worshipping them to show one's new relative status. If one is leaving the Sangha of one's own accord, that is, not because one has broken a *pārājika* (expulsion) rule, then one must want to leave. Enforced disrobing does not count. In Burma in recent years, as part of the junta's crackdown on dissent, monks have been defrocked by the military, as a step in the process of incarceration. The validity of the defrocking is then in dispute and we hear stories of monks going to great lengths to retain their monastic vows and deportment even under such circumstances, even when unable to wear robes. It is clear that unproven accusations of violating *pārājika*, particularly the one prohibiting sexual relations, have also been acted on without due process. Guillaume Rozenberg reports, "In 1980 and 1981, with the help of the police, the government officials of the Department of Religious Affairs conducted an extensive investigation that led to the exclusion of more than three hundred monks judged guilty of grave disciplinary violgations, generally for having engaged in sexual relations. The entire procedure was led by government representatives, and a simple approval of the concerned township monastic committee was required for the execution of the decision. Monks of national renown were unfrocked. Like the famous monk of Popa, U Parama, an eminent representative of the *weikza* path [see chapter 6], certain monks left the monastery of their own volition to avoid official sanctions" (Rozenberg 2010: 128).

In Cambodia during the Khmer Rouge period, monks who feared being killed or pushed into forced marriages or made to kill others took care to undertake the disrobing ritual for themselves if they could find an opportunity. One man who did this told me that because he could not find a person, he informed the Buddha image. He wanted to be able to return to the monkhood later if possible. Had he not disrobed properly before being forced into sex or violence, as he anticipated he might be, he would never have been able to become a monk again. It is only breaking the *pārājika* (expulsion) rules (see earlier text) while one is a monk that bars one from becoming a monk again.

The story of each longer-term monk who disrobes is unique to him and is rarely of one single cause though some generalizations can be made. In some instances, one can see context-specific issues that tell us much about the actual role of monks in their communities (Crosby in preparation). Among longer-term monks, especially younger ones, it is no surprise that a key reason for disrobing is going to be love-interest – either an actual or budding relationship, or the desire to form one. Several former monks I interviewed told me this reason honestly, reminiscing with joy about how they first came to know their wife-to-be. Others glossed over such motivation with the rather general phrase "to enjoy lay life." This gloss reflects the more common situation: the monk has the desire to be open to the possibility of a relationship rather than a specific relationship already formed. Other monks emphasize aspects of the freedom of lay life other than romance or marriage, or just saw them as part a range of different experiences they were keen to explore.

The two most honorable and most cited reasons for leaving long-term monkhood are to support one's family and to serve one's community. With diminishing birth rates and, in some communities, high emigration by young men, monks can find themselves in the position of being the only able-bodied man in their family. They leave the Sangha in order to take on the financial and domestic responsibilities that that entails, including caring for young and elderly dependents.

Service to one's community may take many forms: for example, Shan monks have travelled to an army base on the Thai–Burma border to disrobe and then enlist, having witnessed atrocities at the hands of the Burmese army that, as monks, they were helpless to prevent. Several former monks in Laos could still recall their sense of urgency to join the revolution in the service of their society nearly five decades ago.

Another reason monks disrobe can be the failure to have served the community. In Bangladesh, where Buddhist communities and especially temples have suffered from the encroachment of resettled, usually Muslim, Bengali lowlanders, monks may disrobe after failing in their attempts to protect sacred sites from resettlement or simply under the pressures of being a monk in such conditions. A range of difficulties confront a diminished Sangha in a temple in any environment where the proportion of monks in the population is too low. Monks may struggle to retain charge over the infighting of lay supporters, to find sufficient support among a dwindling and impoverished population, to recruit and retain other monks. These leave some monks isolated and under impossible pressure.

In Sri Lanka, some monks leave after failing to become the abbot of a temple, realizing they would never be in charge, although the opposite may also be the case: some monks may not want the responsibility of a difficult temple.

Some monks experience a sense of disillusionment. For those who ordained as adults for spiritual reasons, this disillusionment came when, even after years of intensive meditation, they did not experience the expected enlightenment that had drawn them to the Sangha as idealistic young men. Some had experienced a sense of "spiritual failure" when they could not inspire their lay supporters to take an interest in the Dhamma, others when they learnt of flaws in the character or conduct of the monk who ordained them.

As in any type of apprenticeship, the quality of the relationship between the more junior monk and his abbot and other senior monks is obviously important in sustaining a monk's commitment or ensuring his ongoing support after disrobing (Samuels 2010: 17–18). Political allegiances may also impinge on group dynamics or exacerbate feelings of exclusion. National political party allegiances have been a factor in disrobing in a number of cases in Sri Lanka and Cambodia, shading over into coerced disrobing. In Burma, in its efforts to retain control over the Sangha, which it regards as politically threatening, the military government recruits high-ranking *Vinaya* experts from the Sangha into government positions as laymen.

Among monks of all ages in Cambodia, a common reason for disrobing is the need to access medical provision or round the clock care. Thailand has addressed this problem to some extent by establishing a hospital dedicated to the treatment of monks, but the parallel hospital in Cambodia closed down. There the elderly move in both directions: While some monks disrobe in order to be looked after by the women of their family who cannot give them the hands-on care they need while they remain monks, other elderly men become ordained to be in the supportive context of the Sangha. It is recognized in many places that monastic life can be detrimental to health, especially where nutrition is poor. The prohibition on eating after noon is seen by many as detrimental to boys in the Sangha, especially while they are still growing, yet head monks who have tried to protect their novices by adapting the *vinaya* rules have sometimes faced severe criticism from laypeople.

Another reason we see longer-term monks disrobe is personal conscience, perhaps prompted by their head monk. This may be on account of alcohol problems or because of their own misgivings for an undetected indiscretion even many years past. If an actual *pārājika* offence has gone undetected, a monk may disrobe and re-ordain as a novice if he regrets his conduct and wishes to remain in the monastery.

The challenges faced by former monks who have spent a long time in the Sangha are not to be underestimated. Some are better prepared than others. They may have money saved in preparation, or a job to go to or may be able to move into a career that relates to their role as a monk. In Amarapura in Burma in 1886, one year after the fall of all Burma to the British – a period of instability that saw many monks leave the Sangha – U Ohn (1846–1925) disrobed and went on to become famous as a teacher of *Abhidhamma* (Theravada philosophy) attracting many students – monks, nuns, and laypeople – from different parts of the country (Ghosita 1995/1999: 59). These days, among educated ex-monks who have had a choice, the caring professions – teaching, psychiatric care, NGO, or other relief work – predominate. Others have learnt the skills traditionally taught in monasteries such as high-level literacy in the literature of the local ethnic group, healing, astrology, "calling the spirits" (an important ritual in Tai-Lao and Khmer Buddhism, see Chapter 5), or carpentry, that could also serve as professions for laymen. Such training is only continued in those regions less affected by the centralization and reform of monastic education. After reaching the mid-30s, finding a job or commencing a career can be especially difficult and is a reason for many monks re-examining their life plans at around this age. This age is also a turning point in terms of finding a marriage partner. Beyond finding a partner and the issue of finances, all the activities laypeople take for granted can offer challenges. Ex-monks and monks contemplating disrobing in Sri Lanka tell of their anxiety about how to shop, or catch a bus, or sit by a woman on the bus. Some ex-monks, including some who had returned to monkhood after a period of lay life, recalled their dismay at experiencing how harshly people in normal society behave toward each other. They witnessed behavior not seen in the temple, where laypeople are always on their best, most respectful behavior. This last point gives us an insight into how the monastery is a model of civilized society not only in how monks behave but in how laypeople behave within its walls: it offers a taste of peace, order, hierarchical, and cultured conduct that is a respite from and model for daily life outside.

Hierarchy, Rivalry, and Independent Authority

No matter what positions monks may hold in the Sangha or even the government, their hierarchy within the Sangha is based solely on their monastic age. For monks who have taken the higher ordination, *upasaṃpadā*, the years spent as a novice make no difference to their monastic age, which is counted by the number of years since their *upasaṃpadā*. The *vassa*-age-based hierarchy can also have significant status consequences: one method of passing on a temple from abbot to abbot is the "teacher–pupil" succession (*paraṃparā*). It is the first surviving, still-ordained monk that the outgoing/deceased abbot ordained (perhaps decades earlier) who inherits the headship of the temple even if he was ordained long before the abbot became abbot and may now reside elsewhere (Woodhouse 1916, Crosby, fieldwork Sri Lanka 2005, Southeast Asia 2009–2011). There are alternative methods of inheritance, which seek to avoid the randomness of this selection – after all, the first ordained may have no facility for leadership or be unpopular. One such is election between qualified candidates, another is for the temple to pass to a relative, from uncle to nephew, since, if the abbot was ordained as a boy, he has no recognized children of his own (Woodhouse 1916, Crosby, fieldwork Sri Lanka 2005, Southeast Asia 2009–2011). More recently, new models of secular organization may also play a role in new management structures and temple constitutions, as the importance of leadership skills for a temple's success is increasingly recognized.

This *vassa*-age-based hierarchy is a neutral way of minimizing the effect of vested familial interests and partisan factions, one that avoids complex evaluations of different people's worth. This system of seniority is supported by a canonical *jātaka* (Chapter 4): the Buddha's senior most disciple, Sāriputta, despite being recognized as the monk most skilled at *Abhidhamma* (see Chapter 7), is excluded from overnight accommodation. A group of monks called "the Six" – a notorious group of self-serving monks who represent all the behavior monks should avoid – "hurried on ahead [of the Buddha and his entourage including Sāriputta], and, before quarters could be taken for the Elders, monopolised the whole of the available lodgings, which they distributed among their superiors, their teachers and themselves. When the Elders came up later ... even Sāriputta's disciples could not find lodgings for the Elder [Sāriputta]" (Cowell 1895: 92). As a result, Sāriputta ends up sleeping out under a tree near the Buddha's lodgings. In the morning, the Buddha hears Sāriputta coughing and is startled at him having had to spend the night outside. He calls the monks together and asks, " 'Tell me, who deserves the best lodging, the best water, and the best rice, Brethren?' Some answered, 'he who was a nobleman before he became a brother.' Others said, 'He who was originally a brahmin, or a man of means.' Others severally said, 'The man versed in the Rules of the Order; the man who can expound the Law [Dhamma]; the men who have won the first, second, third, or fourth stage of mystic ecstasy [*jhāna* –see Chapter 6].' Whilst others again said, 'The man in the First, Second, or Third Path of Salvation [stream-entrant, once-returner or non-returner, the three levels of spiritual attainment before enlightenment, arhatship], or an Arhat; one who knows the Three Great Truths; one who has the Six Higher Knowledges." Here then the monks are identifying a range of possible criteria that might be used when evaluating the relative status of monks: preordination status in terms of position in society, caste, wealth; attainments specific to ability in terms of "book learning" or achievements in meditation, spiritual progress, or spiritual insight. The Buddha dismisses all these, "Brethren, in my religion, it is seniority which claims respect of word and deed, salutation, and all due service; it is seniors who enjoy the best lodging, the best water, and the best rice" (Cowell 1895: 93). He then recalls a story from the past (the main *jātaka* story) in which "Even animals worked out that it was not proper for them to live without respect and subordination to one another." The animals in the story work out who is oldest in relation to a banyan tree. The elephant can remember the tree being a mere bush when he was young, just touching his belly as he walked over. The monkey remembers being able to stretch up and reach the topmost shoots while sitting on the ground, so is older than the elephant. But the partridge remembers an earlier banyan tree close by, on whose branches he used to sit, consuming and then excreting the banyan tree seeds. It is from one of those seeds that had passed through the partridge that their banyan tree grew and he is therefore the oldest. So the partridge is given respect and worshipped by the other two; in return he gives them advice, including teaching them the five precepts, which he himself keeps (Cowell 1895: 93–94).

As we can see from the story about Sāriputta, this hierarchy crosses student lineages – the group of six was still obliged to respect the seniority of Sāriputta even though they were not in his lineage. The same remains true today across all the Theravada ordination lineages, *nikāya*. Thus when King Parākramabāhu "unified" the Sangha of Sri Lanka in the twelfth century by making every monk from other ordination lineages (*nikāya*) reordain in the Mahāvihāra Nikāya, he was effectively demoting the non-Mahāvihāra monks, resetting their status within the monastic community at zero.

Despite the seemingly unarguable simplicity of this hierarchy, there have been plenty of attempts to circumvent or interrupt it. This happens from the local and personal level to the national level, which may affect the fortunes of an entire monastic lineage. The favoring by a new king of one branch of the Sangha over another to the extent of stopping the rival lineages, as in the case of Parākkamabāhu I (given earlier) is a clear example of this. Individual monks and groups of monks may try to set up an alternative hierarchy to circumvent the existing order and gain greater power than their status automatically confers. Thus in the nineteenth century, Ven. Vajirañāṇa, the future King Mongkut, Rāma IV of Thailand, established the new Thammayutika Nikāya so that he was at the head of a *nikāya* without having to consider too closely the hierarchy within the existing *nikāyas*. Mongkut used the rhetoric of reform and orthopraxy, but the move also allowed him to build up a power base in the run up to his taking the throne. This allowed him to remain apparently aloof from politics, as a member of the Sangha, and safer than he would have been in the palace during the period of conspiracy in the run up to the royal succession. Once Mongkut had disrobed and become king, his loyal Thammayutika Nikāya was given authority over other *nikāya* (now collectively called the *Mahānikāya* "majority ordination lineage") in the extensive centralization of the Sangha of Thailand from the mid-nineteenth to early twentieth centuries (Choompolpaisal 2011: 154–286). New criteria for remaining in the Sangha, including hierarchy based on an education system prescribed by the Thammayutika elite in Bangkok, the use of Bangkok Thai, etc., further undermined established monastic hierarchies.

During the British annexation of lower Burma, monks used the existence of two separate governments to jockey for power. Another way to circumvent existing hierarchical structures or to try to establish a new institutional ethos is to introduce a new ordination lineage from elsewhere. This happened in Sri Lanka in the eighteenth century – the Amarapura and Rāmañña Nikāya were introduced from Burma, placed greater emphasis on meditation, and were free from caste restrictions of the established Siyam Nikāya. Another way to disrupt existing hierarchies is to align oneself with a new meditation tradition, which may have been a factor in the importation of Burmese *vipassanā* to Sri Lanka and Thailand in the 1950s.

Individual monks may seek to gain power over a rival, including a senior, by garnering the support of the *dāyaka* committee, the lay supporters and managers of a temple. This is a relatively common problem and sometimes leads to splits within a monastic community, and even court cases over temple ownership or the division of a single monastic complex into several communities, as in the case of the historic monastery at Cox's Bazaar in Bangladesh.

It is possible for monks to move from one *nikāya* to another without reordaining and losing their hierarchy. This practice is used by the Burmese Shwegyin lineage when monks from lineages regarded as less prestigious or pure stay within a Shwegyin temple or join the lineage in order to hold a particular office in relation to one of the sacred sites of Burma managed by the Shwegyin. The necessary ritual is called a strengthening ritual *daḷhī-kamma*. It has been suggested that such a ritual should therefore be accepted by the Burmese Sangha (which is reactionary on the subject of female ordination) as sufficient to adapt the East Asian nuns' lineage for Theravada purposes in restarting the interrupted

Theravada nuns' lineage: that is, the nuns should be able move from an ordination lineage (*nikāya*) within the Dharmaguptaka tradition into a *nikāya* within the Theravada tradition (see Chapter 9).

The ultimate loss of status for a monk is to be defrocked for one of the *pārājika* offenses (see earlier text) because one cannot be reordained as a monk afterwards, whereas one can if one disrobes of one's own volition. Because of the severity of the sanction, one sees monks falsely accused, victims of personal vendettas (Pannapadipo 2001: 50–51). There have also been attempts to have monks who are regarded as too powerful by the state or monastic rivals convicted of a *pārājika* offense to ensure that they cannot build up a powerful support base as a monk again (see Chapter 12).

When a monk has committed a *pārājika* offence but is determined not to disrobe, it can prove difficult to enforce his defrocking, and the state may be called on to intervene. The Vinayas of other branches of Buddhism have a special category called *śikśādattaka* ("to whom the training has been given," Sanskrit), but the Pali Vinaya does not (Clarke 2009). Those in the Theravada Sangha who commit a *pārājika* can be reordained as novices only. Passages in the *vinaya* describe how even in the early days of the formation of the canon settling this and other *vinaya* disputes could prove difficult and ultimately come down to force – the need to have a larger group that can outnumber the supporters of the offending monk in question and forcibly evict him (Huxley 1996: 146–147). The tendency to deal quietly with potentially scandalous problems does not help this issue be addressed. In 2012, the head monk of the Buddhist temple near London, UK, was convicted of four counts of indecent assault on a 9-year-old girl 34 years earlier (www.thisiscroydontoday.co.uk, May 7, 2012). According to long-standing members of the Sinhala community, the monk had been told to leave the Sangha and return to Sri Lanka by the late abbot of another temple in London 35 years earlier, but had used the silence over his behavior and his popularity with some members of the congregation to remain a monk by setting up his own monastery in a town just south of London. This tactic put him, under *vinaya* rules, in a different jurisdiction. While he should have disrobed regardless, he was no longer the responsibility of the original abbot. Attitudes to sexual abuse within the Sangha range from the salacious, a theme in Thai newspaper coverage (Kapur-Fic 1998: 207), to an unwillingness to address the problem (Seneviratne 1999: 238, note 83; 297, note 21). However, the reporting of the UK case in Sri Lanka has brought some cases to court there also.

Subdivisions of the Theravada Sangha: *Nikāya* and Sub-*nikāya*

For a number of reasons, there are different divisions or "ordination lineages" within the Theravada Sangha. The word for these different branches is *nikāya*, the same word as that used for the five divisions of texts in the *Sutta Piṭaka* in the Pali Canon. These *nikāya* are then subdivided further into sub-nikāyas. For the most part, members of different *nikāya* cannot conduct monastic rituals (*saṅghakamma*) together although they can perform together rituals for laypeople. There have been many *nikāya* historically, not all of which have survived into the modern period. The names and identity of the current *nikāya* are all relatively recent, dating from the eighteenth century onwards, as branches or breakaways of earlier local lineages or as importations of lineages from other Theravada countries.

In Sri Lanka, there are three main *nikāya*. The Siyam Nikāya derives from the reintroduction of the Mahāvihāra lineage from Thailand (Siam/Siyam) in 1753. It is restricted to the highest caste in Sinhalese society, the *goyigama*. The important rituals of state including the custodianship of the Temple of the Tooth in Kandy is in the hands of the Siyam Nikāya. The other two Nikāya are also named after the place from which they were imported. The Amarapura Nikāya was also introduced from Burma circa 1803. Amarapura, now part of Mandalay, was then the capital of Burma. The Amarapura Nikāya was formed in reaction to the caste exclusivity of the Siyam Nikāya, but has itself subdivided more than either of the other Sri Lankan Nikāya and often along caste lines. The Rāmañña Nikāya was introduced from Burma in 1864, Rāmañña being a Pali word for Burma. The monks of this Nikāya have a reputation for more strict interpretations of the *vinaya* rules and can be immediately recognized by their umbrellas made of large dried palm leaf in contrast to the usual black or saffron umbrellas typically carried by other monks. The robes worn by monks of these different *nikāya* tend to reflect their national origins. Siyam Nikāya monks tend to wear orange to yellow robes like monks in Thailand, while monks of the other two nikāya tend to wear the maroon or darker orange worn by monks in Burma.

In Thailand and Cambodia, the vast majority of sub-*nikāya* are collectively termed the Mahā-nikāya, "majority lineage," in contrast to the Thammayutika Nikāya "reform" lineage founded by Prince Mongkut of Thailand in 1833. There are many different sub-*nikāya* within the Mahānikāya. In Cambodia, we can also see a division in terms of practice between the traditionalist (*borān*) and modernist camps in the Mahānikāya, a division that goes back to the French period and refers to approaches to practices, ritual, Pali, and meditation rather than to conservatism versus modernity (Marston 2008).

In Burma, nine *nikāya* were officially recognized during the reforms under Ne Win in 1980 (Carbine 2011: 75). The largest two, accounting for the majority of Burmese monks, are the Thudhamma Nikāya and the Shwegyin Nikāya. The term Thudhamma, *Sudhamma* in Pāli, derives from an ecclesiastical council, the Thudhamma Council, founded by King Bodawpaya (r. 1782–1819). Under King Mindon's reign between 1853 and 1878, the Shwegyin Sayadaw Ven. Ashin Jāgara and his disciples were freed by King Mindon from the control of the Thudhamma Council and its leader. The smaller ones are the Mahā Dwāra, the Mūla Dwāra and Anauk Chaung Dwāra, the Veluwun, the Hngettwin, the Ganawimok Gado, and the Mahāyin. The Mahā Dwāra, also known as the Dwāra, is also found in the Chittagong Hill Tracks of Bangladesh. It was established by Ok-hpo Sayadaw Ven. Ashin Ukkaṃsamālā in 1855. Two others, namely, the Mūla Dwāra and the Anauk Chaung Dwāra, splintered from it in 1900 and 1918, respectively. The Mahāyin was established in 1875 by a Mon monk, Ven. Buddhavaṃsa, who was ordained in the Thammayutika Nikāya of Thailand, and thus it is also known as Dhammayutti Mahāyin Nikāya (http://www.dhammyutmon.com/2010/03/founder-of-mahain.html). The other *nikāya* initially developed between 1875 and 1900. (See Carbine 2011: 75–77 and 199 for a brief description of divisions of the Sangha in Burma.)

Conclusion

In this chapter, we have looked at both institutional and practical aspects of monkhood and at the many roles the Sangha plays within Theravada communities. The Sangha both retains the authority of the *Vinaya* codified in the canonical texts established over 2000 years ago and displays a great deal of variety and dynamism. Boys and men enter and leave the Sangha as part of their own life structure and as expressions of familial and societal will. While the spiritual ideal is familiar as an aspiration maintained by the monkhood, the roles and outlooks of monks are many and varied. The fate of even local monks and monasteries has often been deeply affected by the broader political context at the local, national, and global level. At the same time, the Sangha is a pan-societal organization that allows for social mobility both within a country and across borders. The appearance and conduct of monks is recognizable throughout Theravada countries even if there are local, lineage and regional differences of dress, conduct, and expectations of behavior. Some developments within the Sangha have been criticized as uncanonical by reformers, usually with some level of political agenda. Yet, interestingly the main Sangha lineages that we recognize today all developed within the modern period, belying the sense of an ongoing historical continuity with the first monks ordained by the Buddha at his "first sermon" at Sarnath shortly after his Enlightenment.

References

Bizot, François. (1993). *Le Bouddhisme des Thaïs*. Bangkok: Éditions des Cahiers de France.

Blackburn, Anne M. (2010). *Locations of Buddhism: Colonialism and Modernity in Sri Lanka*. Chicago: Chicago University Press.

Carbine, Jason A. (2011). *Sons of the Buddha: Continuities and Ruptures in a Burmese Monastic Tradition*. New York: Walter de Gruyter.

Choompolpaisal, Phibul. (2008). 'Constrictive Constructs: Unravelling the Influence of Weber's Sociology on Theravada Buddhist Studies Since the 1960s', *Contemporary Buddhism* 9.1: 31–76.

Choompolpaisal, Phibul. (2011). 'Reassessing Modern Thai Political Buddhism: A Critical Study of Sociological Literature from Weber to Keyes'. PhD thesis, School of Oriental and African Studies, University of London.

Clarke, Shayne. (2009). 'Monks Who Have Sex: Pārājika Penance in Indian Buddhist Monasticisms', *Journal of Indian Philosophy* 37: 1–43.

Cowell E.B. (1895–1913). *The Jātaka or Stories of the Buddha's Former Births*, 6 vols. Cambridge: Cambridge University Press.

Crosby, Kate. (November 2000). '*uddis* and *ācikh*. The Inclusion of the *sikkhāpada* in the *pabbajjā* Liturgy According to the *Samantapāsādikā*', *Journal of Indian Philosophy* 20: 461–477.

Crosby, Kate. (2006). 'Sāriputta's Three Works on the *Samantapāsādikā*', *The Journal of the Pali Text Society* XXVIII: 49–59.

Crosby, Kate. (2012). 'The Inheritance of Rahula: Abandoned Child, Boy Monk, Ideal Son and Trainee' in Vanessa Sasson (ed.), *Little Buddhas: Children and Childhoods in Buddhist Texts and Traditions*. Oxford: Oxford University Press, 97–123.

Crosby, Kate. (in preparation). *Re-entering the World? Life-Decisions of Monks in Theravada Communities*.

Denes, Alexandra. (2012). 'Trees of Offering. The Salak Yom Festival in Lamphun Province' in Heidi Tan and Alan Chong (eds.), *Enlightened Ways. The Many Streams of Buddhist Art in Thailand*. Singapore: Asian Civilisations Museum, 56–66.

Dhammasami, Khammai. (2004). 'Between Idealism and Pragmatism – A Study of Monastic Education in Burma and Thailand from the Seventeenth Century to the Present'. D.Phil. thesis, Oxford.

Eberhardt, Nancy. (2006). *Imagining the Course of Life. Self-Transformation in a Shan Buddhist Community*. Honolulu: University of Hawai'i Press.

Ghosita, Ashin. (1995 [reprint 1999]). *Mogok Sayadaw Hpayakyi ei Ta-bha-va Tha-tha-na* (in Burmese. '*Biography of Mogok Sayadaw: One life in a Sāsana*'). Yangon: Association of Mogok Vipassana.

Huxley, Andrew. (1996). 'The *Vinaya*: Legal System or Performance-Enhancing Drug?', in T. Skorupski (ed.), *The Buddhist Forum*, vol. IV. London: SOAS, 141–163.

Kapur-Fic, Alexandra. (1998). *Thailand: Buddhism Society and Women*. New Delhi: Abhinav Publications.

Kieffer-Pülz, Petra. (1992). *Die Sīmā. Vorschriften zur Regelung der Buddhistischen Gemeindegrenze in älteren Buddhistischen Texten*. Berlin: Dietrich Reimer.

Marston, John. (2008). 'Reconstructing 'Ancient' Cambodian Buddhism', *Contemporary Buddhism* 9.1: 99–121.

Nagasena, Bhikkhu. (2013). 'The Monastic Boundary (*Sīmā*) in Burmese Buddhism: Authority, Purity and Validity in Historical and Modern Contexts'. PhD thesis, School of Oriental and African Studies, London.

Pannapadipo, Phra Peter. (2001). *Little Angels. The Real-Life Stories of Twelve Thai Novice Monks*. Bangkok: Post Books.

Rozenberg, Guillaume. (2010). *Renunciation and Power. The Quest for Sainthood in Contemporary Burma*. Translated from the French by Jessica Hackett. New Haven: Yale University Southeast Asia Studies.

Samuels, Jeffrey. (2010). *Attracting the Heart: Social Relations and the Aesthetics of Emotion in Sri Lankan Monastic Culture*. Honolulu: University of Hawai'i Press.

Schober, Juliane. (2011). *Modern Buddhist Conjunctures in Myanmar. Cultural Narratives, Colonial Legacies, and Civil Society*. Honolulu: University of Hawai'i Press.

Seeger, Martin. (2010). '"Against the Stream": The Thai Female Buddhist Saint Mae Chi Kaew Sianglam (1901–1991)', *South East Asia Research* 18.3: 555–595.

Seneviratne, H.L. (1999). *The Work of Kings: The New Buddhism in Sri Lanka*. Chicago: University of Chicago Press.

Spiro, Melford. (1971). *Buddhism and Society: A Great Tradition and its Burmese Vicissitudes*. London: George Allen & Unwin. 2nd edn, 1981, Berkeley: University of California Press.

Vajirañānavarorasa, Somdech Phra Mahā Samaṇa Chao Krom Phrayā. (1969). *Vinayamuka: The Entrance to the Vinaya*, vol. 1. Bangkok: Mahāmakutarājavidyālaya.

Wijayaratna, Mohan. (1990). *Buddhist Monastic Life According to the Texts of the Theravāda Tradition*. Translated by Claude Grangier and Steven Collins with an Introduction by Steven Collins. Cambridge: Cambridge University Press.

Woodhouse, George William. (1916). *Sissiyanu Sissia Paramparawa and Other Laws Relating to Buddhist Priests in Ceylon*. Tellipallai: American Ceylon Mission Press.

Further Reading and Watching

Films

Verkerk, Mark (2006). *Buddha's Lost Children*. EMS Films. The information afterwards refers to another film, but one that does not have a name. http://vimeo.com/50534646# (retrieved February 06, 2013). Film of the early members of the English Sangha Trust and the first black monk being ordained in Thailand.

Secondary Sources

Bunnag, J. (1973). *Buddhist Monk, Buddhist Layman: A Study of Urban Monastic Organization in Central Thailand*. Cambridge: Cambridge University Press.

Carbine, Jason A. (2011). *Sons of the Buddha: Continuities and Ruptures in a Burmese Monastic Tradition*. New York: Walter de Gruyter.

Huxley, Andrew (1996). 'The *Vinaya*: Legal System or Performance-Enhancing Drug?', in T. Skorupski (ed.), *The Buddhist Forum*, vol. IV. London: SOAS, 141–163.

McDaniel, Justin Thomas. (2008). *Gathering Leaves and Lifting Words: Histories of Buddhist Monastic Education in Laos and Thailand*. Seattle / London: University of Washington Press.

Pannapadipo, Phra Peter. (2001). *Little Angels. The Real-Life Stories of Twelve Thai Novice Monks*. Bangkok: Post Books.

Rozenberg, Guillaume. (2010). *Renunciation and Power. The Quest for Sainthood in Contemporary Burma*. Translated from the French by Jessica Hackett. New Haven: Yale University Southeast Asia Studies.

Samuels, Jeffrey. (2010). *Attracting the Heart. Social Relations and the Aesthetics of Emotion in Sri Lankan Monastic Cultures*. Topics in Contemporary Buddhism. Honolulu: University of Hawai'i Press.

Seneviratne, H. L. (1999). *The Work of Kings: The New Buddhism in Sri Lanka*. Chicago: University of Chicago Press.

Silber, I. F. (1995). *Virtuosity, Charisma, and Social Order: A Comparative Sociological Study of Monasticism in Theravada Buddhism and Medieval Catholicism*. Cambridge: Cambridge University Press.

Thanissaro Bhikkhu. (1994). *The Buddhist Monastic Code. The Pāṭimokkha Explained*. Valley Centre: Metta Forest Monastery.

Wijayaratna, Mohan. (1990). *Buddhist Monastic Life According to the Tets of the Theravāda Tradition*. Translated by Claude Grangier and Steven Collins with an Introduction by Steven Collins. Cambridge: Cambridge University Press.

9

Women in Monasticism

Overview

The movement to reinstate the lineage of Theravada nuns (*bhikkhunī*), which appears to have died out by the twelfth to thirteenth centuries, has been a major development in modern Theravada and an important motivating force in the production of Buddhist feminist and academic gynocentric writings. The issue of the *bhikkhunī* lineage has led to a re-evaluation of other forms of female "renunciation" in Theravada, especially the monastic lifestyle without full ordination that can be undertaken by girls and women in all Theravada countries. These women usually undertake the eight precepts of an *upāsikā* (female lay devotee attending the temple) or the ten precepts of a novice. The focus on "precept nuns" within Theravada communities and in scholarship reasserts female empowerment and creates a valid place for women within the religion while complying with the anti-*bhikkhunī* sentiments – and even legislation – of Sangha and state hierarchies (Seeger 2010: 558). It is thus a way of rejecting those forms of feminism some regard as Western impositions that, since they advocate personal power, may be labeled as anti-spiritual in their aspirations.

There is a danger in focusing on the *bhikkhunī* ordination and non-*bhikkhunī* parallels in Theravada Buddhism, in that it further increases the monastic bias of academic studies. Since it is only a tiny minority of women who take some form of ordination (especially relative to the number of men), we in doing so perhaps further marginalize the representation of women in Theravada society as a whole. Thus, Chapter 10 looks at the known contribution of women to Theravada literature and explores possible reasons for their apparent invisibility. It also touches on other roles for and attitudes to women in Theravada, including the role of the monastery in providing for vulnerable girls in contrast to vulnerable boys. It reviews the debate on whether Buddhism at essence offers a liberal or a patriarchal framework for women in Theravada societies.

The third chapter dedicated to women (Chapter 11) approaches the subject of the feminine in Theravada from a completely different angle. Rather than looking at what may or may not have happened historically and current developments, it redresses an imbalance in the contrasting uses made by Buddhist feminists in **existentialist** scholarly interpretations of Theravada and Mahayana sources.

Theravada Buddhism: Continuity, Diversity, and Identity, First Edition. Kate Crosby.

Spiritual Capacity of Women and the Establishment of the *Bhikkhunī* Lineage

From the time of the Buddha there have been nuns, *bhikkhunī*, as well as monks, *bhikkhu*, in Buddhist monasticism. However, within Theravada, the *bhikkhunī* orders died out during the eleventh, twelfth, and thirteenth centuries CE. Attempts to revive it in the twentieth and twenty-first centuries have met with both significant success and substantial resistance and condemnation.

In most forms of Buddhism, a woman is regarded as able to reach even the highest stage of the religious path, that is, arhatship, enlightenment or *nibbāna*. This belief was crucial to the Buddha's establishment of the *bhikkhunī* order and remains crucial to the attempts to revive the *bhikkhunī* lineage today. Underlying this belief is the fundamental theological presupposition of female agency rather than mere instrumentality in the religious and, especially, soteriological sphere. This underlies not only canonical narratives about the enlightenment and other spiritual achievements of the Buddha's female followers (see later text) but also Theravada Buddhists' belief that some women have become enlightened in recent decades in spite of the fact that Enlightenment is considered to be rare in the modern period, even for men (Seeger 2010: 571, 574–577). Neither does a woman need to be reborn as a man to achieve enlightenment, nor is her highest role to act as instrument in the spiritual progress of a man. We see both approaches to women in the religions of India, including the religions that were developing at the same time as Buddhism in the first millennium BCE. Some forms of Hinduism, including those that advocate Vedic rituals, centered around the establishment of a sacred, household fire into which offerings are made, advocate the role of the woman as instrumental in the religious success of men, especially that of her husband. Jainism, which like Buddhism is a renouncer tradition advocating the importance of leaving the household life for religious success, also instituted a nuns' order early on. A major division developed between two main branches of Jainism. The more extremely ascetic Digambara sect produced complex theological arguments in support of their belief that it is essential for women to be reborn as men to gain spiritual liberation (Horner 1930: 101, Jaini 1991). Within Theravada, Buddhism life as a woman is thought to have additional difficulties in the form of menstruation and childbirth. These two items are also found in a list of "the five hardships of women," alongside three relating to marriage: sexual submission, leaving one's home to join that of one's husband, and having to serve one's husband (interviewee precept nun, Kawanami 1996). In modern Burma, monks are familiar with this list and give women guidance to pray to be reborn as men (Bonnet 2008: 205), even though this contradicts the assumption in Theravada literature that gender tends to continue across lifetimes (Chapter 11), possibly into the lifetime in which liberation is achieved.

The belief in Buddhism that men and women both have the capacity for spiritual realization or perfection – a position Sponberg (1992) has termed "soteriological inclusivity" (the view that salvation is open to both men and women) – is pivotal to the story of the establishment of the nuns' order. The Buddha's acknowledgment of this soteriological inclusivity marked the turning point in the fortunes of the early women, whose aspiration to become renouncers in the Buddha's Sangha (monastic community) had initially floundered. In the famous foundation story for the *bhikkhunī* order recorded in the *Vinaya Piṭaka*, the Buddha three times rejects the request for ordination made by his aunt and foster mother Mahāpajāpatī Gotamī. Anālayo Bhikkhu has suggested that the Buddha's response to her request was not a rejection of her following a celibate, spiritual life, but of her becoming a homeless wanderer (Anālayo 2011: 289). The monk Ānanda, a cousin of the Buddha and his attendant, then makes the request on behalf of Mahāpajāpatī and her companions. At the Buddha's again repeated refusal, Ānanda takes a different tack and asks,

> Are women competent, Reverend Sir, if they retire from household life to the houseless one, under the Doctrine and Discipline announced by the Tathāgata [Buddha], to attain to the fruit of conversion, to attain to the fruit of once returning, to attain to the fruit of never returning, to attain to saintship? (*Cullavagga* X.1, translation Rhys Davids and Oldenberg 1885: 444, Horner 1930: 103–104)

To this the Buddha replies that women are indeed capable of attaining these, the four stages on the soteriological path culminating in "saintship," that is, arhatship or enlightenment. In response Ānanda recalls the crucial role Mahāpajāpatī has had in the Buddha's own life by nurturing him as his foster mother after his own mother died shortly after his birth, and then repeats his request for permission for her to renounce (Heirman 2001: 279, Ohnuma 2006: 867). In contrast to Buddhism being ahead of its time in relation to women, the Buddha's foster mother is in fact pursuing two forms of conduct traditional for widowed women: to move from dependency on her husband to dependency on her son, or to see out one's days in renunciation (whether at home or wandering). "Mahāpajāpatī's attempt to become a nun could be interpreted not as the act of a feminist trailblazer but instead in terms of the traditional patriarchal Indian notion that a woman should always be dependent upon her male kin" (Ohuma 2006: 887).

The passage in which Ānanda persuades the Buddha to permit Mahāpajāpatī and her followers to join the Sangha authorizes and combines two religious views of women, both as agents in their own spiritual destiny and as instruments in that of men. Confirmation of the third view of women haunting this passage, the dependency of widows on their surviving male relatives, seems to be confirmed both by the permanent subordination of nuns to monks instituted on this occasion (see later text) and by another aspect of Mahāpajāpatī's story observed by Reiko Ohnuma, namely, her conscious decision "to pass out of existence ... *before* various close male relatives have done so, such as Rāhula [her grandson], Ānanda, Nanda [her nephews], and the Buddha himself [her son]" (Ohnuma 2006: 887). In relation to the second point, women as instrumental, the Buddha's aunt played a crucial role in his own life, making his path to enlightenment possible, an instrumentality that contributed to making the Dhamma available for all. As we saw when looking at the stories of previous lifetimes of the Buddha, it is in recognition of his former wife Yasodharā's instrumentality in his own religious path, by being given up so that he can fulfill the perfection of generosity, that the Buddha assists Yasodharā on her own spiritual path on his return to his home town (Chapter 4).

In the canon, there are other statements by the Buddha indicating that gender is irrelevant to *nibbāna*. A famous example is found in the final lines of the following verse from the *Saṃyutta Nikāya* of the *Sutta Piṭaka*, in which the Buddha describes the path to *Nibbāna* using the simile of a chariot:

> "Straight" is the name that Road is called, and "Free
> From Fear" the Quarter whither thou art bound.
> Thy Chariot is the "Silent Runner" named,
> With Wheels of Righteous Effort fitted well.
> Conscience is the Leaning-board; the Drapery

Is Heedfulness; the Driver is the Norm [Dharma],
I say, and Right Views, they that run before.
And be it woman, be it man for whom
Such chariot doth wait, by that same car
Into Nibbāna's presence shall they come.
(S.N. I.5§6, translation Rhys Davids and
Woodward 1917: 45, my emphasis)

Recognizing women as having the same potential as men for spiritual liberation is not the same as advocating equality between the sexes. We see much in Pali literature that assumes an unchallenged inequality or (if we look it at from a different angle) assumes different domains of power. Such assumptions and the practical dimensions of those assumptions are encompassed by Sponberg's phrase "institutional androcentrism," the placing of men at the center of society's structures (Sponberg 1992). In the poems of early nuns recorded in the canonical text, the *Therīgāthā*, we find striking expression given to woman's spiritual capacity in the face of societal expectations of woman's inferiority and how those might affect a woman's estimation of her own ability (Rajapakshe 2000: 16, note 14). In the following poem, the nun Somā is approached by Māra, the deity that embodies death. Māra's role in this story, as in that of the Buddha's own Enlightenment, is to frighten or tempt people into staying within his grasp, that is, within the realm of repeated death, *saṃsāra*, by personifying their fears and weaknesses. Here Māra tries to discourage Somā on the basis that women are not clever enough to achieve arhatship:

That vantage-ground the sage may attain
Is hard to win. With her two-finger wit
That may no woman ever hope to achieve.

Recognizing Māra, Somā replies,

What should the woman's nature signify
When consciousness is tense and firmly set,
When knowledge rolleth ever on, when she
By insight rightly comprehends the Norm [Dharma]?
To one for whom the question doth arise:
Am I a woman [in these matters], or
Am I a man, or what not am I then?
To such an one is Māra fit to talk.
(S.N. I, V§2, translation Rhys Davids
and Woodward 1917: 161–162)

The philosophical presupposition of women's capacity for enlightenment is the basis for the Buddha changing his answer to Ānanda, in response to Mahāpajāpatī's request for ordination, an alteration of resolve unparalleled elsewhere in the canonical narratives about the Buddha. The Buddha then allows his aunt to receive ordination if all the women take upon themselves the "eight strict rules," eight rules that accept and mirror women's subordinate role in society. Mahāpajāpatī then accepts this condition and becomes not only the first nun but a female parallel to the Buddha (see Chapter 11).

Subordination of Nuns to Monks: Implications for the *Bhikkhunī* Lineage

The eight strict rules, *garudhammā*, that Mahāpajāpatī was obliged to accept subordinate nuns to monks and make the nuns' order dependent on the monks' order. They are as follows:

> I. An almswoman [*bhikkhunī*], even if of a hundred years standing, shall make Salutation to, shall rise up in the presence of, shall bow down before, and shall perform all proper duties towards an almsman [*bhikkhu*], if only just initiated. This is a rule to be revered and reverenced, honoured and observed, and her life long never to be transgressed.
>
> II. An almswoman is not to spend the rainy season (of Vassa [the three months of the year when travel for monks and nuns is restricted]) in a district in which there is no almsman. This is a rule ... never to be transgressed.
>
> III. Every half-month an almswoman is to await from the Chapter of Almsmen two things, the asking as to (the date of) the Uposatha ceremony, and the (time when the almsman) will come to give the exhortation. This is a rule ... never to be transgressed.
>
> IV. After keeping the rainy season (of Vassa), the almswoman is to hold Pavāraṇā (to enquire whether any fault can be laid to her charge) before both Sanghas – as well that of the Almsmen as that of the Almswomen – with respect to three matters, namely what has been seen, and what has been heard, and what has been suspected. This is a rule ... never to be transgressed.
>
> V. An almswoman who has been guilty of a serious offence is to undergo the Manatta [penance] discipline towards both the Sanghas (Almsmen and Almswomen). This is a rule ... never to be transgressed.
>
> VI. When an almswoman, as novice, has been trained for two years in the Six Rules, she is to ask leave for the **Upasampadā** initiation from both Sanghas (as well that of the Almsmen as that of the Almswomen). This is a rule ... never to be transgressed.
>
> VII. An almswoman is on no pretext to revile or abuse an almsman. This is a rule ... never to be transgressed.
>
> VIII. From henceforth official admonition by almswomen of almsmen is forbidden, whereas the official admonition of almswomen by almsmen is not forbidden. This is a rule ... never to be transgressed. (translation Horner 1930: 119–120)

This set of extra rules stands parallel to, rather than as part of, the *pāṭimokkha* rules that apply to monks and nuns (see Chapter 8). Those *pāṭimokkha* rules also show disparity between monks and nuns, in that there are 311 such rules for nuns, in comparison with the 227 for monks. The extra *pāṭimokkha* rules that only apply to nuns include the extra four *pārājika*, rules for which the punishment is expulsion. The nuns' *pārājika* additionally allow the expulsion of a woman for more general erotic conduct than actual sexual intercourse and for taking the side of a monk to cause a division in the Sangha. Among the additional *pāṭimokkha* rules for nuns there are also some that do in fact apply to monks as well, but are rated as less serious when broken by men, counting only as minor infractions (*dukkaṭa*) rather than the breaking of the *pāṭimokkha* rules proper. This is an example of how the assessment of Buddhist ethics/behavioral rules as universal (e.g., in contrast to the age, status, caste, and gender specific ethics of brahmanical Hinduism) breaks down when examined closely. However, it is the eight *garudhammā*, rather than the bias of the *pāṭimokkha* rules, that have the greater significance for the history of the nuns' order. In particular, the dependency of the nuns' monastic legal acts, *saṅghakamma*, such as ordination, on the monks' Sangha, as stipulated in rules II–VI, has had and continues to have implications for the restarting of the *bhikkhunī* lineage, since ordaining nuns and maintaining the *bhikkhunī* Sangha require the participation of monks. That dependency and the subordination of even the most senior nun to the most junior monk, as stipulated in *garudhamma* rules I, II, and VIII, also inform a counter argument for nuns to remain non-*bhikkhunī* precept nuns, since precept nuns are theoretically independent of monks and so may be more powerful (Seeger 2010: 558).

The *garudhammā* passage presents a challenge to feminist Buddhists who, regarding as true both the Buddha's status as an enlightened being and the inherent equality of men and women, expect the word of the Buddha to conform with an egalitarian approach to women. Consequently, the passage, which is similar across different Buddhist traditions (Heirman 2001: 279), has been examined intensively in recent years and has been both explained as a response to the institutional androcentrism of Indian society at the time and questioned as to its authenticity. In another canonical passage, for example, Mahāpajāpatī makes an offering to the Sangha of monks and nuns, but is referred to as taking the five precepts we now associate with a layperson. This may mean that there were other nuns before her and undermines the authenticity of the nuns' origination story describing her as the first nun (Williams 2000: 168–170), confirmation of which appears to be found in other textual passages (Anālayo 2011: 302), although it has also been suggested that the reference to the five precepts may be retrospective, that is, referring to Mahāpajāpatī's past as a lay devotee (Anālayo 2008: 108–109). Another inconsistency that has been pointed out is that a number of the *garudhamma* rules are also included in the *pācittiya* section of *vinaya* rules, where they have different narratives of origination (Horner 1930:158). The institutional androcentrism was already identified as a factor in the editing and selective preservation of texts by I.B. Horner in 1930. Horner pointed out the problems of examining texts preserved primarily by men for evidence of attitudes toward women. This "monk-factor," she writes, " ... partially explains the views, more favourable to monkdom than to lay-life, more favourable to men than to women, which are usually ascribed to Gotama" (Horner 1930: xx–xxi).

After Mahāpajāpatī has received her ordination, the Buddha then makes a prediction that the ordination of women will halve the lifespan of the Buddhist religion (*sāsana*). While there are other passages that predict the decline of Buddhism in relation to immoral behavior and lapse practice among monks (Nattier 1991), this passage is the most famous. Furthermore, it is a key canonical authority drawn on by Sangha hierarchies today to justify their opposition to the reinstitution of the *bhikkhunī* lineage (see later text). After making this prediction, the Buddha compares the situation of having women in the Sangha both to a house with a disproportionately high number of women that is therefore more susceptible to robbers and to a crop infected by a disease. This reflects the easy transition from institutional androcentrism, with its assumption that power and the duty to protect the "weaker sex" lies with men, to misogyny in the analogy to disease. Sponberg (1992) has questioned whether this misogynistic voice in Pali literature should in fact be seen as a specific type, namely, ascetic misogyny (a fear of women that protects self-denial). Here, then, a perceived threat, in this case the threat of women to ascetic celibacy and the independence of the monks, is reified (i.e., understood in more concrete terms) as an active threat even when in other passages the responsibility is recognized as lying with the individual who is tempted from their celibacy rather than with the object of their desire. Thus, the extreme fear of women represented in the following verses from the Pali Canon, in which even a dying woman's main objective is to ensnare men, could be seen as rhetoric specifically aimed at warning celibate monks rather than as representing a broader estimation of the character of women:

> Monks, I know no other single form ... sound ... perfume ... taste ... or touch, so enticing, so desirable, so intoxicating, so binding, so distracting, such a hindrance to winning the unsurpassed peace from effort – that is to say, monks, as the form, sound, perfume, taste and touch of a woman. Monks, whosoever clings to [them] ... for many a long day shall grieve, snared by a woman's charms.
>
> Monks, a woman, even when going along, will stop to ensnare the heart of a man; whether standing, sitting or lying down, laughing, talking or singing, weeping, stricken or dying, a woman will stop to ensnare the heart of a man. Monks, if ever one would rightly say: "It is wholly a snare of Māra", verily, speaking rightly, one may say of womanhood: It is wholly a snare of Māra.
>
> Go parley with a man with sword in hand;
> Use question with a goblin; sit ye close
> Beside th'envenomed snake whose bite is death;
> But never alone with a lone female talk!
> (AN III, 67 abridged from translation by Hare 1934, 1995: 56)

Similar verses are found in the **Upanishads**, texts that represent the renouncer tradition emerging within brahmanical Hinduism around the same time that early Buddhist texts were being formed. This confirms the identity of such verses as ascetic rhetoric, specifically ascetic misogyny. Such statements acknowledge, whether consciously or unconsciously, the difficulty of recognizing that – in Buddhism certainly – the source of temptation is ultimately internal, that is, in one's own response. While Buddhism has practices that address one's response as well as advocating that one sequesters oneself physically and thus avoids projecting one's fundamental obstacles onto women, such realization requires an elevated degree of self-scrutiny and training. Such training is found in meditations on the body such as that given in the *Bhāradvāja Sutta* (*Saṃyutta Nikāya* 35.127), which provides guidance on keeping celibacy by contemplating the 32 parts of the body and seeing form as it is, without clinging to details. Whether or not the more sophisticated reading of ascetic rhetoric was in the mind of the composers and early promulgators of such texts, an unsophisticated reading of women as deserving objects of misogyny is inevitably more obvious. Such texts therefore authorize the damaging institutionalized misogyny that pervades most societies, including Theravada ones, and continues to inform decisions made by privileged male Sangha hierarchies that affect the lives of women – especially unprivileged women – directly and through internalized compliance.

Meanwhile, in spite of the Buddha's prediction of the shortened lifespan of the *sāsana*, epigraphic evidence indicates that the nuns' order was allowed to continue and flourished for several centuries (Barnes 2000). Donative statements record nuns, as well as laywomen, contributing almost as much as men to the sponsorship of the building of *stūpa* (memorial structures for Buddhism's saintly dead) in ancient India. By the commentarial period, having either one's son or daughter ordained came to be identified as one of the most meritorious acts a parent can undertake (Crosby 2006: 185).

The origination story for Theravada in Sri Lanka directly relates to the belief in the merit to be gained from having one's son *or* daughter ordained. When the great emperor Asoka is told that his intervention to protect the purity of the Sangha by instigating the Third Council (see Chapter 3) is not as meritorious as having one's son or daughter enter the Sangha, he has both his son Mahinda and daughter Saṅghamittā ordained (Crosby 1999: Chapter 5, note 88). After Mahinda converts King Tissa of Sri Lanka to Buddhism, King Tissa's consort Anulā and

500 of her companions attain "stream-entrance," the first of the four stages of spiritual perfection that culminate in arhatship. As a result, Anulā requests ordination. To help fulfill the requirement of the ordination of women that a quorum of five *bhikkhunī* should be present as well as a quorum of monks, Mahinda sends for his sister. Meanwhile, Anulā and her 500 companions live as lay nuns in special quarters built for them by the king. When Saṅghamittā arrives with her companions to perform the ordinations, she also brings with her a sapling from the ***bo* tree** under which the Buddha was enlightened (Bartholomeusz 1994: 18–19). Even as late as the tenth century the association of nuns with the *bo* tree continued: The chief scribe Sena, during the reign of King Kassapa IV, established a convent whose resident nuns had the duty of looking after the *bo* tree at the Mahāvihāra, one of the most prestigious monastic institutions of Sri Lanka (Gunawardana 1979: 38). Descendants of the *bo* tree continue to be one of the defining features of sacred space in Sri Lankan Theravada to this day.

Incidental references in the chronicles indicate that convents within the various Sri Lankan monastic orders could be extremely wealthy and continued to attract royal patronage. As well as the estate attached to the convent charged with maintaining the *bo* tree, there are references to substantial work forces, such as the hundred staff attached to a convent established by the queen of King Aggabodhi IV in the seventh century, and to royal interventions, for example, one to restore impoverished nunneries in the tenth century (Gunawardana 1979: 39). Nevertheless, when Sri Lankan Buddhism, probably as a result of the Coḷa invasion, underwent a crisis in the eleventh century, only the monks' lineage was sustained, and reinvigorated from Burma. The nuns' order died out and was not restored, even though we know that Burma's order of nuns survived at least until the thirteenth century. Chinese sources may refer to female novices and *bhikkhunī* in Burma in the Pyu period (Luce 1937: 251), but it is in inscriptions from Burma itself that we have later evidence: references to nuns of slave parentage, and to nuns attending ceremonies such as a *paritta* recital (see Chapter 5), and, as late as 1261 CE, to the chief incumbent of a nunnery (Gunawardana 1979: 39, Than Tun 1955: 285–286). Although this information has been familiar to scholars, including scholars in Burma, for some time (Lottermoser 1991, Pyi Phyo Kyaw personal communication July 2012), it does not seem to have entered the recent discourse of the hierarchy of the male Burmese Sangha. The nuns' order may have died out in Burma in the thirteenth century, when Pagan was sacked by the Mongols (Gombrich 1988: 168).

It is generally believed that within Thai Buddhism the *bhikkhunī* lineage was never instituted (Kabilsingh 1991: 36). However, Skilling, in his survey of the datable evidence for the nuns' lineages in South and Southeast Asia, notes that it may have existed in Cambodia. A twelfth-century Cambodian inscription of memorial verses dedicated by Queen Indradevī to her late sister Jayarājadevī seems to mention that Jayarājadevī had sponsored the lower ordination of a large number of girls (Skilling 1994: 37). This means that some fully ordained *bhikkhunī* were available at the time to conduct the novice ordinations.

Reinstituting the *bhikkhunī* Sangha

Ordinations of full *bhikkhunī* require five fully ordained monks (*bhikkhu*) and five fully ordained nuns (*bhikkhunī*). The interruption in transmission of the last nuns' ordination lineage in Theravada in the thirteenth century thus seems to prevent the possibility of restoring the Theravada *bhikkhunī* lineage. Particularly in mainland Southeast Asia, the position that the interruption in the transmission of the lineage prevents its reinstitution is hotly defended.

However, the case is far from simple. A monastic lineage for nuns, using the Dharmaguptaka *vinaya*, which has minor differences from the Theravada *vinaya*, was transmitted from Sri Lanka to Nanking in China in the early fifth century CE in response to similar concerns concerning the validity of the nuns' lineage in China at the time (Gunawardana 1979: 37, Heirman 2001: 276, 295, de Silva 2004: 121). One scholar in favor of the reinstitution of the *bhikkhunī* Sangha therefore refers to the Dharmaguptaka lineage as a "sub-sect of Theravada" (Kabilsingh 1991: 52). We have extant texts of at least eight *Vinaya Piṭaka*, eight of what were presumably once many (Prebish 1994: 46). While variations emerged during the transmission and geographical spread of the *vinaya* codes, none of them envisage a divided Sangha; all are composed as if the Buddha is alive and the rules are all made in his lifetime. This means that there is no canonical prohibition preventing nuns from this East Asian lineage forming the quorum to restart the Theravada *bhikkhunī* lineage.

The argument at this point turns on the self-identity of Theravada, particularly the claim that Theravada is "early Buddhism." In the hands of Theravada apologists, this claim informs a rhetoric of purity, a claim that even modern Theravada is true to Buddhism's origins, a more pure form of Buddhism than those regarded as later developments, that is, the various forms of Mahayana. We know from the accounts of Chinese pilgrims in the first millennium CE that in ancient India differences in doctrine did not prevent monks from living in the same monastery or conducting *saṅghakamma* (monastic legal rites) together. In the mindset of some, especially in the centralized Sangha hierarchies that are most closely identified with the workings of the state, the quest for overall control has led to a conflation between matters of doctrine and *vinaya*. With its additional 37 rules for nuns, the Dharmaguptaka *vinaya* appears to be more strict than the current Theravada *vinaya* (de Silva 2004: 121). Despite this the established Theravadin hierarchies have disputed the viability of the introduction of this nuns' order, claiming that the lineage is corrupted by the Mahayana doctrines of those who have preserved it. Five Sri Lankan nuns who received a dual ordination (from East Asian nuns followed by Theravada monks) in California in 1988 were not recognized as *bhikkhunī* on their return to Sri Lanka and continued to live as precept nuns (de Silva 2004: 126).

Nonetheless, less than a decade later the East Asian Dharmaguptaka lineage in collaboration with Theravada monks ordained ten Sri Lankan women, headed by Kusuma Devendra, as *bhikkhunī*. The ceremony took place in 1996 at Sarnath in north India, the site of the Buddha's first sermon and the ordination of the first five monks. The ordination was arranged by the artist and sculptor Ven. Mapalagama Vipulasāra Mahāthera. Ven. Vipulasāra was then head of the Mahabodhi Society, which had been founded by Anāgārika Dharmapāla. Dharmapāla himself had also advocated the restoration of the *bhikkhunī* order. Ven. Vipulasāra's position, in addition to his fame as designer of Sri Lanka's national emblem, gave this event greater prestige than previous attempts. While there were adverse reactions in Sri Lanka, there were also those who spoke out in support of them (de Silva 2004: 126). Significant in making such ordinations possible was Sakyadhita, the International Association of Buddhist Women ("Daughters of the Buddha" http://www.sakyadhita.org), which has developed an international network of nuns and other Buddhist women since its foundation in 1987.

Since then well over a thousand nuns have received ordination in this reinstated Theravada lineage, including many from other Theravada countries (personal communication Wei-Yi Cheng August 2012). Among the Thais to receive ordination was the academic and activist Chatsumarn Kabilsingh. Receiving the ordination name Dhammānandā, she became a novice in 2001 and, in 2003, a *bhikkhunī*. Chatsumarn's own mother, Voramai Kabilsingh, had herself taken ordination nearly half a century earlier. Voramai first took the eight precepts in Thailand in 1959 while wearing white, after which she dressed in yellow robes. In 1971, she received full ordination in Taiwan in the Dharmaguptaka lineage (Kabilsingh 1991: 48–51). Although Voramai's ordination was not recognized in Thailand, the opposition that she experienced was at least less extreme than the treatment meted out to two nuns ordained in 1932. Sara and Chongdi Bhasit received ordination from a senior monk, and, while they have kept his identity secret, the monk suspected of performing their ordination was forced to disrobe. The most senior monk in Thailand, the Saṅgharāja, literally "king of the monastic community," intervened to try to force the nuns to disrobe. They received negative responses in the press and from monks. The monks used the "ascetic misogyny" argument discussed earlier, saying that "women were the enemy of monks' purity" (Kabilsingh 1991: 47). The two nuns were arrested and jailed for eight and four days, respectively. They eventually disrobed under the pressure (Kabilsingh 1991: 47). A law was passed on June 18, 1928 outlawing the ordination of women in Thailand. It remains a monastic offence for a monk to participate in the ordination of a woman (Department of Religious Affairs [Thailand] 1928: 157). As recently as 2003 a monk was sentenced to 76 days in prison for "causing schism" as a result of ordaining women (Thai weekly Newspaper *Matichon Sud Sapda* November 25–December 1, 2005. See http://www.asoke.info/09Communication/DharmaPublicize/Kid/k186/052.html). Although Thai women such as Chatsumarn Kabilsingh have received ordination in the Sri Lankan lineage and began to conduct *bhikkhunī* ordinations in Thailand (Lindberg-Falk 2008: 114), no Thai Sangha has as yet commenced a Thai *bhikkhunī* lineage.

A more recent development is the ordination in October 2009 of four *bhikkhunī* in Australia into the Thai Forest Tradition by the British monk Ajahn Brahm (Brahmavaṃso). Ajahn Brahm is one of the most popular international Theravada monks among both Western and Asian Buddhists; such was his standing King Bhumipol of Thailand had awarded him in June 2006 the rank of "Phra Raja Khana Fay Vipassana Thura," a title recognizing his senior position as a meditation monk. This honor was then reflected by the monastic title "Phrasuddhi Sangvorn Thera" (*Ratchakitchanubeksa* (*Royal Thai Government Gazette*) Vol. 123, Part 15kho, July 6, 2006: 12). In response to his performance of the *bhikkhunī* ordination, however, Ajahn Brahm was removed from the Thai Sangha lineage and stripped of these titles (*Matichon* newspaper December 21, 2009).

The response of the Thai Sangha has had ramifications in the broader network of Thai forest tradition temples: it brings the assumed liberalism (and with it feminism) within Western Buddhism into direct conflict with the obedience to the conservative Thai Sangha hierarchy (personal communication with lay and monastic participants at relevant meetings in the United Kingdom, 2011–2012). This highlights how Western monks gain their authority from the Thai lineage and ongoing loyalty to Thailand, and that Diaspora temples, even those served by Western monks, represent the influence of the home country of the monastic lineage, in this case Thailand, internationally. There is also an effect on the more internationalized monks within Thailand, who consider the appearance of Thai monastic conduct in the global context. This is apparent in the interview of the highly influential Thai scholar monk Phra Payutto by Sanitsuda Ekachai in the Bangkok Post in 2001 (www.budsas.org/ebud/ebdha203.htm, retrieved December 7, 2012). The highly articulate interview is also interesting in that it manages to come across as supportive and progressive while at the same time confirming a reactionary stance.

The Buddhist Society of Western Australia, an organization supportive of Ajahn Brahm, reported that during a visit to Thailand in late 2011 he was presented with a Buddha image by King Bhumibhol (media.bswa.org/documents/Thai2012.pdf. retrieved August 2, 2012). We can see this as a diplomatic move, a gesture that, on the one hand, betokens Thailand's continued inclusion, recognition, and even we might say "ownership" of Ajahn Brahm, yet, on the other hand, circumvents and has no bearing on his official standing in the Sangha. Nonetheless, the ongoing public opposition in Thailand to his actions can be seen from web discussions since 2010 that have continued to be reposted following his February and June 2012 public talks in Thailand (e.g. http://topicstock.pantip.com/religious/topicstock/2009/11/Y8530275/Y8530275.html, retrieved August 2, 2012). The main reasons given in such postings for objecting to his actions are that his view is against the mainstream, that he is disrespecting hierarchy by not obeying senior monks, and that he creates disunity.

The religious authorities in Burma, like those in Thailand, remain opposed to full female ordination. Similarly, expectations of obedience to the centralized Sangha hierarchy have a force not fully appreciated outside the country. A dramatic example of this opposition was played out in relation to the erstwhile Burmese nun Saccavādī (by 2012 voluntarily disrobed, married, and in the United States), who had received ordination in the Sri Lankan lineage alongside Chatsumarn Kabilsingh in 2003 in Sri Lanka. She had previously been ordained as a *thilashin* in Burma in 1986. Cristina Bonnet, who interviewed Ven. Saccavādī in 2006, reported that Saccavādī's attempt to have the ordination in Burma recognized was refused by the State Sangha Mahā Nāyaka Council (i.e., the State Supreme Sangha Council). A letter from the Mahanayaka Monastery in Yangon, where the monks on the Council live during their terms of office, was worded as follows:

> We, who know the right view from the wrong view as taught by the blessed one [Buddha], submit herewith: That, Ma Saccavadi, who had received Bhikkhuni ordination in Sri Lanka, has now brought forth a wrong view with the sole malicious intent to destroy the Buddha dispensation that now flourishes in Myanmar. (Bonnet 2008: 215)

That the letter goes beyond disapproval of an action to an insistence on knowing the internal workings of Ven. Saccavādī's mind is interesting from the point of view of legal discourse. As an aid to understanding such rhetoric, it is perhaps helpful to remember how important hierarchy and obedience are in Theravada Buddhism, and how even a perceived slight to the Sangha hierarchy may have Kafkaesque implications in modern Burma (Gravers 2012: 26). Moreover, the letter to Saccavādī, like other responses to the issue of female ordination, attests to an interesting continuity with the ascetic misogyny identified earlier and, in particular, the discourse concerning Māra. Here, in the absence of the *bhikkhunī* lineage of the Buddha's time that allowed an outlet for women to express the aspiration to renounce, those women most serious about the Buddhist path are tarred with the same brush as the seductress out to corrupt it. It sometimes seems as if the opposition to such an outlet for women is most strongly expressed by those holding positions in centralized institutions and those obedient to them. Not infrequently, those who seek promotion through institutional ranks are those least likely to have experience of the renouncer/spiritual aspiration; the blocking of such an outlet in women may be from a lack of empathy not only for women but for the renouncer aspiration per se. This combines with a projection of their own will for personal power onto the woman in question.

Bonnet reports that the letter to Ven. Saccavādī was followed up by punitive action against her: "When in 2005 she went to visit her ill father in Burma, she was arrested for 76 days, charged under the section 295 of the Burmese Criminal code which relates to 'abusing religion' and to the 'desecration of religious buildings and properties'. She was allowed to leave the jail after having to ask for forgiveness for her actions and after having been made to change her robes to the *thilashin's* normal robes. After this, she was taken immediately to the airport to return to Sri Lanka, where she again wore her *bhikkhunī* robes ... " (Bonnet 2008: 214).

The State Supreme Sangha Council in Burma uses canonical and commentarial texts to justify its decisions. Its response to Saccavādī is an example:

> The validity of her ordination was rejected by ... the State Supreme Saṅgha Council, on the basis of the fact that the continuity of the Order of *Bhikkhunī* ended during the reign of King Vaṭṭagāminī (103–77 BCE). ... Using a number of commentaries, ... the State Sangha Council cited ... the demise of the *Bhikkhunī Sangha* during a war that took place between the King and invaders from South India ... The last recorded mention in the commentaries is of the existence of thirteen members of the *Bhikkhunī Sangha* surviving in a village called Bhatara. ... The State Supreme Sangha Council thus believes this war led to the extinction of the *Bhikkhunī Sangha*. Leading from this, and cited as a second reason for this refusal, is that the ordination of a *bhikkhunī* may only take place when she has been approved by both *Bhikkhunī* and *Bhikkhu* Sangha. The Burmese State Supreme Sangha Council argues that since no *Bhikkhunī Sangha* has existed since that time there is no *Bhikkhunī* Sangha in existence authorised to give this approval. They ignore the East Asian *bhikkhunī* lineage, only taking into consideration the existence of Theravada. (Nagasena 2013: Chapter 1)

Their reliance on commentarial evidence leads the Council members to ignore the other inscriptional and later textual evidence cited earlier for the continuation of the nuns' lineage. Moreover, since the chronicle literature that started relatively early in Sri Lanka only developed as a genre much later in Burma, its evidence, so important for our knowledge of the *bhikkhunī* lineage, lies beyond the scope of the commentarial material deemed most authoritative in Burma. Using only commentaries and bringing forward the date of the demise of the *bhikkhunī* lineage in this way allows the Council implicitly to ignore the Dharmaguptaka lineage from Sri Lanka since it post-dates this event. This marks an interesting divergence between Burmese and broader scholarship on the commentaries. The latter uses the chronicle and inscriptional evidence for the continuation of the nuns' order to date texts on the basis that they give considerable attention to nuns to before the disappearance of the order in the eleventh to thirteenth centuries. Examples are the dating of the *Upāsakamanussavinayavaṇṇanā* (Crosby 2006) and of the Vinaya commentary, the *Vajirabuddhiṭīkā* (Kieffer-Pülz 2009: 165).

According to *vinaya* rules, a person cannot be defrocked for non-*pārājika* offenses without their willing consent. When the Burmese state has attempted to defrock monks suspected of being involved in human rights marches, this has been contested. Thus, when the Burmese Sangha attempted to defrock Saccavādī, it did so in full knowledge that this was impossible according to the *Vinaya*. The decisions of the Sangha authorities in one state may be sufficient to control monastic activity in that state, but are mostly not recognized by the Sangha in other states.

As suggested earlier, it appears to be the centralized reform traditions of Burma and Thailand that are most afraid of allowing the nuns' lineage to develop. In other words, opposition comes mainly from those whose ethos relies on control, obedience, hierarchy, and conservatism. Such groups often have great textual expertise that in part developed as they established the validity of their own lineage in relatively recent history. An interesting question not yet addressed in the extensive literature on the subject is what it is that enables certain monks to defy this fear to support *bhikkhunī* ordination. Typically they have established secure prestige or are already outside the central hierarchy. Despite "precept nuns" (see next section) being seen to be less threatening to authority, such nuns also meet with resistance. In their case too, it has often taken the voice of senior monks whose authority is established beyond question to confirm their spiritual achievements.

Precept Nuns

Theravada women have continued to undertake various forms of renunciation over the centuries without the support of the full ordination lineage. Such nuns are found in every Theravada country to this day as well as in many of the places to which Theravada Buddhism has spread in the modern period.

For these nuns, there is no single Pali word equivalent to *bhikkhunī*. Since all these women undertake a set of precepts, usually either eight or ten, I shall use the umbrella phrase "precept nuns." When the royal women of Sri Lanka retired to a convent and undertook the precepts awaiting the arrival of Saṅghamittā, they were referred to as *upāsikā* "female lay devotees," but this term is also used for women attending the temple even for a few hours, so does not suffice for precept nuns in the modern period. Rather the title given to them differs according to the local language. In Sri Lanka, such a nun is called a *dasa sīl mātāva* a "ten precept mother." Dressed in saffron robes that look like those of monks, they take on the same ten precepts undertaken by the male novice monk. In Burma, which has the highest number of such nuns, they are called *thīlashin* "precept-keeper." They dress in pink, brown, or yellow, and keep either the ten novice precepts or, more usually, the eight precepts, which allows them to handle money (see Chapter 5). In Thailand, they are called *mae chi*, "honored mother" (Collins and McDaniel 2010: 1384). Like their parallels in Laos and Cambodia, they wear white and keep either the five or eight precepts of lay practitioners. In Cambodia, they are called *don chi*. While some live in monasteries or nunneries full time, other *don chi* may spend only some of the time, for example, the three-month "rains-retreat" period at the monastery, and the rest of the time at home. Like novices and *bhikkhunī*, precept nuns shave their heads (an exception to this are the precept nuns at Bana Bhante's monastery in Bangladesh, see Chapter 6).

The history of female renunciation in the absence of a *bhikkhunī* lineage is hard to trace. This may in part be a reflection of the relative lack of study of medieval (including vernacular) Theravada records. The ambiguity of terminology, particularly of the term *upāsikā*, also obscures the history of precept nuns.

Currently, since our knowledge still relies on the observations recorded by early European visitors, we can only take the history of precept nuns back just over three centuries. In 1691, the French diplomat de la Loubère, who had headed the 1687–1688 embassy to Siam, published a book about what he learnt, *Du Royaume de Siam*. The book was so well received that it contributed to his election to the Académie Française. In it, de la Loubère describes elderly precept nuns living in temples much as we still find in mainland Southeast Asia today. The German naval physician Engelbrecht Kämpfer working for the Dutch East India Company around the same time observed that, unlike the monks, these women wore white (Kabilsingh 1991: 36). The nineteenth-century Christian minister W. Osborn Allen observed nuns with shaven heads clad in either yellow or white at the Shwedagon Pagoda in Rangoon (Bartholomeusz 1994: 28) and in the same period Bishop Coplestone observed the presence of women, wearing white, in Sri Lanka in the ancient capital at Kandy where the Buddha's tooth relic is enshrined and on pilgrimage to the holy site of the Buddha's footprint, Siripāda or Adam's Peak, although it is possible that these women were *upāsikā*, only temporarily dressed in white (LeVine and Gellner 2005: 12).

In Sri Lanka and Burma, the history of the current precept nuns can be traced to the nineteenth century. In the mid-nineteenth century, a nun founded Gutalon Gyaung nunnery, the remains of which are still visible in Sagaing, an important pilgrimage site about 12 miles southwest of

Mandalay on the Irrawaddy River (Kawanami 1996). It is from there that the current 145 nunneries and over 2000 precept nuns in the Sagaing area trace their lineage (Kabilsingh 1991: 89, Kawanami 1996). In 2012, the official figure for precept nuns during the rains-retreat was 45 353.

Like precept nuns elsewhere, *thilashin* often have an ambiguous status both socially and legally. Unrecognized as monastics by the Burmese state, they are referred to as "associates of Buddhism" (*tha-tha-na-hnwe-win* in Burmese), rather than as "insiders of Buddhism" (*tha-tha-na-win* in Burmese), the phrase used for monks on their religious identification/ID card. (See Houtman 1990: 70–71 for discussion of ambiguous terms used for different groups in Burma.) Precept nuns have a continued role as givers, like laypeople, rather than as receivers, like monks, who are seen as the most worthy recipients of laypeople's offerings. Nuns often act as servants or administrators for monks, especially when nuns's living-quarters are located within monasteries. On the whole they lack the level of donations received by monks, and their handling of money adds to their ambiguous monastic-lay status. However, this situation has changed in recent years. Firstly, some individual nuns have gained recognition for their learning and practice; secondly, the general recognition of the contribution of nuns to Buddhism has steadily increased. There are strong, increasingly respected traditions of meditation and scholarship among *thilashin*. Well-known *thilashin* meditation teachers include Sayalay Dipankara, who actively rejected the traditional role of serving monks (Bonnet 2008: 217–218) and established a meditation center called "Brahma Vihari Meditation Centre" in Maymyo, upper Burma. She is a disciple of the famous meditation teacher Pa-Auk Sayadaw Āciṇṇa (see Chapter 6). Individual nuns well known for their academic achievement include Sayagyi Daw Indavatībhivaṃsī, who completed all seven levels of one of the most demanding monastic examinations in Burma, namely, the Pariyattisaddhammapāla Examinations of Mawlamyine, and thus received the "Bhāsantara Kovida" degree in 1981 (Kyaw 2012). People do visit precept nuns as spiritual teachers. Moreover, in Burma, unlike in other Theravada countries, some parents believe that merit is gained from having their daughters become precept nuns. Similarly, many of the same broader range of motivations for ordination found among monks across the Theravada world are found for ordaining precept nuns in Burma: In addition to spiritual reasons, such as to deepen one's knowledge of the Dhamma, learn meditation, or explore dissatisfaction with some aspect of lay life or lay life in general, nuns also receive ordination to serve the Dhamma, to earn merit, to sort out health problems, and to allow relatives to generate merit.

As in the case of *bhikkhunī*, the global network of women and scholars in Theravada Buddhism has made a contribution to the development of *thilashin* too. Hiroko Kawanami, who conducted research on *thilashin* in Sagaing for her PhD (Kawanami 1991), bought the land for the Sakyadhītā Thilashin Sathintike nunnery founded in 1998, which is already well known for its scholarship (www.nri.org/projects/makingendsmeet/burma.htm, retrieved August 17, 2012). The head nuns of this nunnery, particularly Daw Pavanatherī and Daw Kusalavatī, focus on teaching Buddhist texts prescribed in the state and national monastic examinations, thus empowering future generations of *thilashin* through education.

The communities of *dasa sīl mātā*, "ten precept mothers," of Sri Lanka today derive from the *thilashin* tradition of Burma. The precept mother tradition was initiated in Sri Lanka in the context of the nineteenth-century Buddhist revivalist movement, when efforts were made to protect and revive Buddhism in response to the threat of European colonialism. In that time of crisis, a number of men and women took on an intermediary position between monastic and lay status, taking on monastic names, that is, Pali names, usually changing their dress to wear white or yellow robes, and traveling around Sri Lanka to give religious teachings. Such figures included the leading revivalists of the day, Anāgārika Dharmapāla, his American acolyte Countess Miranda de Souza Canavarro, an ex-monk called Subodhānanda, and a woman called Sīlavatī. The appropriateness of such steps was debated at the time, including in letters to newspapers (Bartholomeusz 1994: 34–37, 44–47, 59).

The first *dasa sīla mātāvo* was Catherine de Alwis (circa 1849–1939) (Cheng 2007: 14). Inspired by Burmese nuns she met in Sri Lanka, she went to Burma to receive ordination under *thilashin* there. Known as Sister Sudharmācārī she set up a center for nuns in Kandy (Bartholemeusz 1994: 92ff.). She was from a well-to-do family, and her undertaking was supported by the urban elite as a contribution toward the Buddhist revival (Bond 1988: 68). However, as elsewhere in the Theravada world, the nuns' vocation to meditate and study Dhamma came into conflict with pressure to run orphanages and hospitals. This pressure stemmed from practical needs and from societal expectations of women as carers. However, it also reflects how the independence movement reconstructed Buddhism in response to the perceived strengths of Christianity and so believed that Buddhist nuns should outdo Christian nuns in charitable and caring work. The institution of precept nuns was also transmitted from Sri Lanka to Nepal in the early twentieth century with the return of Nepalese monks who had trained in Sri Lanka and held similar views on the roles of nuns. Becoming a nun there offered an alternative to the demeaning position of being a widowed or a divorced woman in Nepalese society, although by the 1950s, at a time when meditation from Burma was also becoming popular among precept nuns, young women were also being attracted to the role (LeVine and Gellner 2005: 72).

This conflict between serious Buddhist practice and societal expectations of women to be carers remains an issue for nuns today (see Chapter 10). In other cases, precept nuns' concession to this expectation has backfired. Having conceded in the spiritual sphere they were then outcompeted in the realm of social service. In Laos, where precept nuns used to run hospitals, the professionalization of medical care has left them without jobs or income. One response has been to set up herbal, steam baths and to make these available to the growing tourism industry (Crosby interviews Laos 2009). In the case of the nunnery founded by Sister Sudharmācārī in nineteenth-century Ceylon, there was an emphasis on education for girls from the outset. After Sri Lanka's independence, the appreciation of the contribution of nuns to the maintenance of Buddhism waned, and both status and levels of education of nuns around the island were on the whole low. It was not until 1981 that a school for monastic education (*pirivena*, Sinhala) was established for nuns on a par with the many *pirivena* for monks. The general expectation was again that they should undertake domestic duties. In the late 1980s, Bartholomeusz observed, "In the majority of lay nunneries I visited, the renunciants spent hours baby sitting for those who support them … much of their religious service is confined to maintenance and support roles" (Bartholomeusz 1994: 131). Even before the recent flourishing of the *bhikkhunī* lineage matters had improved for female monastics, including precept nuns in the 15 years following Bartholomeusz study. Wei-Yi Cheng found considerable variation in the status and support accorded precept nuns, with some highly educated and well supported and others living in impoverished conditions (Cheng 2007: 17).

When asked about their decision to become lifelong (as opposed to temporary) nuns, precept nuns, like their *bhikkhunī* counterparts, often cite disillusionment with the world. Typical reasons for renunciation include bereavement, the desire to avoid what they regard as an unfulfilling life of marriage and raising children, and the experience or risk of domestic abuse (e.g., Bartholomeusz 1994: 133ff.). It is a sign of the desire throughout these patriarchal societies – a desire that reverberates throughout the world of Buddhist Studies – to undermine the status of nuns that when women give motives such as these they are often dismissed as running away from life, even though such crises can be the impetus for both men and women to reassess their lives. In the canonical *Poems of the Elders (Thera- and Therīgāthā)*, it is such experiences that are cited as the cause of the spiritual shock, *saṃvega*, that motivated the earliest monks and nuns.

In Thailand, there are around 20 000 *mae chi* in contrast to around 250 000 monks and 70 000 male novices (Seeger 2010: 556). The education of precept nuns has been designed and monitored centrally since the establishment under the Queen's patronage of the Shee Thai Foundation in 1969 by the Supreme Patriarch (Sangharāja) of Thailand. The first president of the Foundation was Mae Chi Yani Siriwoharn (1916–1976) of the temple Wat Paknam, who also went on to become the head meditation teacher there after the passing of the former abbot Luong Phor Sot (topicstock.pantip.com/religious/topicstock/2006/06/Y4449070/Y4449070.html, http://www.thainun.org/index.php?option=com_content&view=article&id=50:2010-02-03-08-17-12&catid=41:2010-02-03-08-15-55&Itemid=65, retrieved August 18, 2012).

At that time Wat Paknam was also one of the most high-profile temples internationally. The first monks of the English Sangha Trust were ordained there by Luong Phor Sot in the 1950s (Shine 2002: 33, Skilton 2013). The success of *mae chi* achievement in education in the highly regarded subjects of Pali and Abhidhamma can be seen in the number who graduate with the highest (nineth) level of government Pali exams, even though the stipendary rewards for doing so are lower for *mae chi* than for monks. *Mae chi* also make up a high proportion of professors at Abhidhamma Jotika College, the premier school of Abhidhamma studies in Thailand (Collins and McDaniel 2010: 1389).

In spite of this relatively early attempt to provide education for *mae chi* in Thailand, their royal patronage and the respect for them as meditation teachers, *mae chi*, like precept nuns in other Theravada countries, have a lower religious and social status than monks. Seeger observes, "As a consequence of the charisma they obtain through their ordination, monks may quite easily gain free shelter, food and financial support in most places in Thailand, even if they are 'strangers'. In contrast, for *mae chis*, it can be relatively difficult to find places to stay or to receive support from lay people in places other than those where they are already known" (Seeger 2010: 30, note 107).

A side effect of the broad support for the Thai Saṅgha Supreme Council's opposition to the introduction of the *bhikkhunī* lineage to Thailand is that *mae chi* are receiving greater recognition as the Thai alternative (Seeger 2010: 556–558). A recent development is the enshrinement of the relics of *mae chi* recognized for their accomplishment in meditation (Seeger 2010: 562–564). Their relics then form part of the national repertoire of Thai Buddhist worship culture in a similar way to those of important monks. For example, Mae Chi Kaew Sianglam (1901–1991) was renowned as a meditation practitioner and believed to have become an *arhat*. Since Mae Chi Kaew's death, her crystallized relics have been housed in several *stūpas*. An image of her has also been included in a building for images of enlightened figures of twentieth-century Thailand, alongside that of one other woman, Upāsikā Ki Nanayon (1901–1978), at the monastery of the Supreme Patriarch in Chonburi province (Seeger 2010). Another important meditation *mae chi* to receive such attention is Khun Yay Jan Khon Nokyung (1909–2000) (Seeger 2010: 579). At the temple Wat Phra Dhammakaya in Pathumthani outside of Bangkok, there is a pyramidal memorial containing a statue of her in meditation and a museum commemorating her life. During the lifetime of Luang Phor Sot, the founder of the Dhammakaya meditation system practiced at the temple, Mae Chi Khun Yay Jan Khon Nokyung and Mae Chi Yani Siriwoharn, the head of the national Mae Chi organization mentioned earlier, were two of the five leaders of Luang Phor Sot's meditation groups. Khun Yan Jan Khon Nokyong went on to become the teacher of the current abbot of Wat Phra Dhammakaya, the central temple of the now international Dhammakaya Foundation (see Chapter 6). *Mae chi* have been recognized through the inclusion in what is normally male-dominated material or visual culture of Thai Buddhism before this period, however.

While the protective amulets that are particularly popular in Thai Buddhism are mainly made by monks, they were also made by Mae Bunruean Tongbuntoem (1894–1964) (McDaniel 2012: 51). Mae Bunnuean is widely believed to have been an *arhat* on the bases of her achievements in meditation, her altruism, teaching, and magical abilities (Seeger 2013: 4, 10).

Although precept nuns are theoretically more independent of monks, rather than subordinated to them as *bhikkhunī* are through the eight *garudhamma*, in practice this is rarely the case in institutional settings. For example, while the ordination of *thilashin* in Burma is conducted by other *thilashin*, it is then usually blessed by a monk, who may also give the new nun her name (Kawanami 1996). Mae Chi Kaew's status and abilities have gained greater recognition because they were confirmed by two of the most highly influential forest monks in Thailand, Ajan Mahabua and Ajan Man (Seeger 2010: 565). Moreover, Mae Chi Kaew was also careful to maintain her position of subordination, placing herself lower than monks, even though she was regarded by herself and others as enlightened. The gender hierarchy instituted by the eight *garudhamma* for *bhikkhunī* influenced the placing of Mae Chi Kaew's relics, in spite of her widely recognized spiritual attainment: they were placed lower than those of monks, rather than at the pinnacle of the memorial (Seeger 2010: 581). Similarly, while recognized as an important meditation teacher at Wat Phra Dhammakāya, Mae Chi Jan Khon Nokyung also performed the traditional services conducted by precept nuns for monks, such as the provision of alms food at the temple. On the other hand, some *mae chi* such as Mae Chi Dr Thossaporn Thevaphithaktham (1958–present, www.thossaporn.com) of Wat Phitchaya Yatikaram, Bangkok, known for her meditation practice and ability to cure, manage to sustain their popularity in spite of criticism from well-known senior monks. The scholar Supaphan Na Bangchang, also known as Ajan Mae Chi Vimuttiyā, is director of the important library of Pali texts, the International Tripitaka Hall, at Chulalongkorn University in Bangkok and responsible for the development of advanced Pali programs there. She is an example of a *mae chi* who declines ordination as a *bhikkhunī* for the purpose of such independence, while having received international status and having been honored by the Thai Royal Family (Collins and McDaniel 2010: 1388). While the effects of differential status are practical, it is also worth bearing in mind that they can be seen by both male and female practitioners themselves as irrelevant in terms of the soteriological path, as found by Wei-Yi Cheng in Sri Lanka (2007) and Joanna Cook while studying the shared meditation practices of monks and *mae chi* in Thailand (Cook 2010: 170).

Summary

In this chapter, we have examined the history and current status of both fully ordained *bhikkhunī* (nuns) and precept nuns. We looked at attitudes to women in early Pali literature, including the accounts of the ordination of the Buddha's aunt Mahāpajāpatī. Various voices and attitudes are present in such texts and we noted three identified by Sponberg as soteriological inclusivity, institutional androcentrism, and ascetic misogyny. We also noted some traditional views emerging on the role of women as instruments in the lives of men rather than agents in their own right and on the status of widows. These attitudes have had a significant impact on the establishment, continuity, and attempts to revive the *bhikkhunī* order, which seems to have died out within Theravada region in the thirteenth century. The reinstated *bhikkhunī* lineage in Sri Lanka is flourishing, but the centralized Sangha (monastic) hierarchies of Burma and Thailand remain vehemently opposed to the restoration of the *bhikkhunī* order.

This latter position needs to be viewed in the light of the importance placed on obedience to the central hierarchy and the sanctions, backed up by those countries' legal systems, against those who do not comply. In response, there has been a wider acceptance and support of "precept nuns," that is, female renouncers who do not have the full *bhikkhunī* ordination, whose history is difficult to trace further than the nineteenth century. As a result, there has been an increase in the way they are viewed and represented publicly in both countries, and their standard of education and facilities have in many cases improved significantly in recent decades.

References

Anālayo, Bhikkhu. (2008). '"Theories on the Foundation of the Nuns" Order – A Critical Evaluation', *Journal of the Centre for Buddhist Studies, Sri Lanka* VI: 105–142.

Anālayo, Bhikkhu. (2011). 'Mahāpajāpatī's Going Forth in the *Madhyama-āgama*', *Journal of Buddhist Ethics* 18: 267–317.

Barnes, Nancy J. (2000). 'The Nuns at the Stūpa: Inscriptional Evidence for the Lives and Activities of Early Buddhist Nuns in India' in Ellison Banks Findly (ed.), *Women's Buddhism, Buddhism's Women: Tradition, Revision, Renewal.* Boston: Wisdom Publications, 17–36.

Bartholomeusz, Tessa J. (1994). *Women Under the Bō Tree: Buddhist Nuns in Sri Lanka.* Cambridge: Cambridge University Press.

Bond, George. (1988). *The Buddhist Revival in Sri Lanka: Religious Tradition, Reinterpretation and Response.* Columbia: University of Carolina Press.

Bonnet, Cristina. (2008). 'Brave Daughters of the Buddha: The Feminisms of the Burmese Buddhist Nuns', *Orientalia Parthenopea* VIII: 201–222.

Cheng, Wei Yi. (2007). *Buddhist Nuns in Taiwan and Sri Lanka. A Critique of the Feminist Perspective.* Abingdon: Routledge.

Collins, Steven and Justin McDaniel. (2010). 'Buddhist 'nuns' (mae chi) and the Teaching of Pali in Contemporary Thailand'. *Modern Asian Studies* 6: 1373–1408.

Cook, Joanna. (2010). *Meditation in Modern Buddhism: Renunciation and Change in Thai Monastic Life.* Cambridge: Cambridge University Press.

Crosby, Henrietta Kate. (1999). 'Studies in the Medieval Pali Literature of Sri Lanka with Special Reference to the Esoteric Yogavacara Tradition'. DPhil thesis, University of Oxford.

Crosby, Kate. (2006). 'A Theravada Code of Conduct for Good Buddhists: The *Upāsakamanussavinaya*', *Journal of the American Oriental Society* 126.2: 177–187.

Department of Religious Affairs, Thailand. (1928). *Thalang Karn Khana Song [Monastic Community Declaration]*, vol. 16. Bangkok: Department of Religious Affairs.

Gombrich, R.F. (1988). *Theravada Buddhism: A Social History from Ancient Benares to Modern Colombo.* London: Routledge & Kegan Paul.

Gravers, Mikael. (2012). 'Monks, Morality and Military. The Struggle for Moral Power in Burma– and Buddhism's Uneasy Relation with Lay Power', *Contemporary Buddhism* 13.1: 1–33.

Gunawardana, R.A.L.H. (1979). *Robe and Plough. Monasticism and Economic Interest in Early Medieval Sri Lanka.* Tuscon: The University of Arizona Press, The Association for Asian Studies.

Hare, E.M. (1934 [1995]). *The Book of Gradual Sayings (Anguttara-Nikāya) or More-Numbered Suttas* [vol. III, reprint]. Oxford: The Pali Text Society.

Heirman, Ann. (2001). 'Chinese Nuns and Their Ordination in Fifth Century China', *Journal of the International Association of Buddhist Studies*, 24.2: 275–304.

Horner, I.B. (1930). *Women Under Primitive Buddhism: Laywomen and Almswomen.* London: George Routledge & Sons, Ltd.

Houtman, Gustaaf. (1990). 'Traditions of Buddhist Practice in Burma'. PhD thesis, School of Oriental and African Studies, London.

Jaini, Padmanabh S. (1991). *Gender and Salvation: Jaina Debates on the Spiritual Liberation of Women*. Berkeley: University of California Press.

Kabilsingh, Chatsumarn. (1991). *Thai Women in Buddhism*. Parallax Press: Berkeley, California.

Kawanami, Hiroko. (1991). 'The Position and Role of Women in Burmese Buddhism: A Case Study of Buddhist Nuns in Burma'. PhD thesis, School of Oriental and African Studies, London.

Kawanami, Hiroko. (1996). *Keepers of the Faith: Nuns of the Sagaing Hills*. Order No. RAI-200.341.

Kieffer-Pülz, Petra. (2009). 'The *Ganthārambhakathās* of Upasena's *Saddhammapajjotikā* and Vajirabuddhi's *Vajirabuddiṭīkā*', *Indo-Iranian Journal* 52: 143–177

Kyaw, Pyi Phyo. (2012). 'Burmese Monastic Education in Contemporary Sociopolitical Contexts of Burma: Curricula, Motivations and Roles of Monastic Examinations'. Presented at the 10th International Burma Studies Conference, Northern Illinois University, DeKalb.

LeVine, Sarah and David N. Gellner. (2005). *Rebuilding Buddhism. The Buddhist Movement in Twentieth-Century Nepal*. Cambridge / London: Harvard University Press.

Lindberg-Falk, Monica. (2008). 'Gender and Religious Legitimacy in Thailand' in Wil Lundstöm-Burghoorn (ed.), *Gender Politics in Asia: Women Maneouvring Within Dominant Gender Orders*. Copenhagen: NIAS, 95–120.

Lottermoser, Friedgard. (Summer 1991). "Buddhist Nuns in Burma", *Sakyadhita Newsletter* 2.2. http://www.enabling.org/ia/vipassana/Archive/L/Lottermoser/burmeseNunsLottermoser.html (retrieved July 23, 2012).

Luce, Gordon H. (1937). "The Ancient Pyu", *Journal of the Burma Research Society* 27.3: 239–253.

Mae Chi Kaew Sianglam (1901–1991)', *South East Asia Research* 18.3: 555–595.

McDaniel, Justin. (2012). 'A Buddha in the Palm of your Hand. Amulets in Thai Buddhism' in Heidi Tan and Alan Chong (eds.), *Enlightened Ways. The Many Streams of Buddhist Art in Thailand*. Singapore: Asian Civilisations Museum, 48–55.

Nagasena, Bhikkhu. (2013). 'The Monastic Boundary (*Sīmā*) in Burmese Buddhism: Authority, Purity and Validity in Historical and Modern Contexts'. PhD thesis, School of Oriental and African Studies, London.

Nattier, Jan. (1991). *Once Upon a Future Time: Studies in a Buddhist Prophecy of Decline*. Berkeley: Asian Humanities Press.

Ohnuma, Reiko. (2006). 'Debt to the Mother: A Neglected Aspect of the Founding of the Buddhist Nuns' Order', *Journal of the American Academy of Religion* 74: 861–901.

Prebish, Charles S. (1994). *A Survey of Vinaya Literature*. Taipei: Jin Luen Publishing House.

Rajapakshe, Vijitha. (2000). *The Therīgāthā: A Reevaluation*. The Wheel Publication no. 436. Kandy: Buddhist Publication Society. http://www.bps.lk/olib/wh/wh436.pdf (retrieved June 8, 2013).

Rhys Davids, T.W. and Hermann Oldenberg. (1885). *Vinaya Texts*, Part III. The Kullavagga 4–12. Oxford: Clarendon Press. http://www.sacred-texts.com/bud/bits/bits099.htm (retrieved June 9, 2012).

Rhys Davids, C.A.F. and F.L. Woodward. (1917, 1922, 1925, 1927, 1930). *The Book of the Kindred Sayings (Saṃyutta Nikāya) or Grouped Suttas*, 5 vols. London: Oxford University Press.

Seeger, Martin. (2010). '"Against the Stream": The Thai Female Buddhist Saint Mae Chi Kaew Sianglam (1901–1991)', *South East Asia Research* 18.3: 555–595.

Seeger, Martin. (2013). 'Reversal of Female Power, Transcendentality, and Gender in Thai Buddhism: The Thai Buddhist Female Saint Khun Mae Bunruen Tongbuntoem (1895–1964)', *Modern Asian Studies* 47.2: 1–32.

Shine, Terry. (2002). *Honour Thy Fathers. A Tribute to the Venerable Kapilavaḍḍho and Brief History of the Development of Theravāda Buddhism in the U.K.* Buddha Dharma Education Association, Inc. www.buddhanet.net (retrieved June 8, 2013).

de Silva, Ranjani. (2004). 'Reclaiming the Robe: Reviving the Bhikkhunī Order in Sri Lanka' in Karma Lekshe Tsomo (ed.), *Buddhist Women and Social Justice: Ideals, Challenges, and Achievements*. Albany: State University of New York Press.

Skilling, Peter. (1994). 'A Note on the History of the Bhikkhunī-saṅgha (ii). The Order of Nuns After the Parinirvāṇa', *World Fellowship of Buddhism Review* XXXI.1 January–March 2537: 29–49.
Skilton, Andrew. (2013). 'Elective Affinities: The Reconstruction of a Forgotten Episode in the Shared History of Thai and British Buddhism – Kapilavaḍḍho and Wat Paknam' in Brian Bocking, Phibul Choompolpaisal, Laurence Cox, and Alicia Turner (eds.), *Pioneer Western Buddhists and Asian Networks 1860–1960*. Contemporary Buddhism Special Issue 14.1.
Sponberg, Alan. (1992). 'Attitudes Toward Women and the Feminine in Early Buddhism' in J.K. Cabezon (ed.), *Buddhism, Sexuality and Gender*. Albany: State University of New York Press, 3–36.
Than Tun. (1955). 'The Buddhist Church in Burma during the Pagan Period, 1044–1287'. PhD thesis, School of Oriental and African Studies, London.
Williams, Liz. (2000). 'A Whisper in the Silence: Nuns Before Mahāpajāpati', *Buddhist Studies Review* 17.2: 167–173.

Further Reading and Watching

Film

Kawanami, Hiroko. (director). (1996). *Keepers of the Faith: Nuns of the Sagaing Hills*. London: Royal Anthropological Institute. Order No. RAI-200.341.

Reading

Bartholomeusz, Tessa J. (1994). *Women under the Bō Tree: Buddhist Nuns in Sri Lanka*. Cambridge: Cambridge University Press.
Bonnet, Cristina. (2008). 'Bravel Daughters of the Buddha: The Feminisms of the Burmese Buddhist Nuns', *Orientalia Parthenopea* VIII: 201–222.
Chatsumarn, Kabilsingh. (1991). *Thai Women in Buddhism*. Berkeley: Parallax Press.
Cheng, Wei Yi (2007). *Buddhist Nuns in Taiwan and Sri Lanka. A Critique of the Feminist Perspective*. Abingdon: Routledge.
Collins, Steven. (2011). *Civilisation et femmes célibataires dans le bouddhisme en Asie du Sud et du Sud-Est: une 'Étude de genre'*. Paris: Éditions de Cerf.
Collins, Steven and Justin McDaniel. (2010). 'Buddhist 'nuns' (mae chi) and the teaching of Pali in contemporary Thailand', *Modern Asian Studies* 6: 1373–1408.
Horner, I.B. (1930). *Women Under Primitive Buddhism: Laywomen and Almswomen*. London: George Routledge & Sons, Ltd.
Seeger, Martin. (2010). 'Against the Stream': The Thai Female Buddhist Saint Mae Chi Kaew Sianglam (1901–1991)', *South East Asia Research* 18.3: 555–595.
Seeger, Martin. (2013). 'Reversal of Female Power, Transcendentality, and Gender in Thai Buddhism: The Thai Buddhist female saint Khun Mae Bunruen Tongbuntoem (1895–1964)', *Modern Asian Studies* 47.2: 1–32.
Skilling, Peter. (1994). "A note on the History of the Bhikkhunī-saſgha (ii). The Order of Nuns after the Parinirvāṇa", *World Fellowship of Buddhism Review* XXXI.1, January–March 2537/1994: 29–49.
Sponberg, Alan. (1992). 'Attitudes toward Women and the Feminine in Early Buddhism' in J.K. Cabezon (ed.), *Buddhism, Sexuality and Gender*. New York: SUNY Press, 3–36.
Walters, Jonathan S. (1995). 'Gotami's Story' in Donald S. Lopez (ed.), *Buddhism in Practice*. Princeton: Princeton University Press, 113–138.

10

Women in Theravada Literature and Society

Overview

This chapter explores whether the Buddhist bias in favor of monks over laypeople and in favor of men over women has an impact on evaluations of women and support provided for them in Theravada societies as a whole. It addresses some of the following questions: Is the role of women as agents in the transmission of the Dhamma less likely to be visible than that of men? How does Theravada inform attitudes to women? What characteristics are ascribed to women and how are they valued? Are Buddhist feminists right to see Buddhism as offering a template for greater egalitarianism, or does the evidence favor those who claim it supports patriarchal systems that are detrimental to women's welfare? Given the traditional role of monasteries in redistributing wealth and supporting the vulnerable, what are the practical implications of the exclusion of girls and women from monastic life?

Female Invisibility in the Production of Texts

Writing in 1930 on the position of women in the Buddhism of the Pali Canon, I.B. Horner commented on the bias the "monk-factor" creates in favor of monastics over laity and of men over women (see Chapter 9). Since the Pali Canon and commentaries were recorded and preserved mainly by monks, this bias makes it difficult to find evidence about women from a female perspective in historic sources for Theravada. While it is hard to argue from silence, a confirmation of this effect on the availability of texts can be detected in the preservation of the nuns' rules. In the *Vinaya Piṭaka*, the division of the Pali Canon that explains the monastic rules, the section explaining the rules for nuns is called the *Bhikkhunī-vibhaṅga*. It is much shorter than the text for monks even though there are more rules for nuns. This is because it only talks about the additional rules for nuns. If a rule also applies to monks, it is assumed one will look at the monks' sections. The text as we have it is written for monks who have authority over nuns as well as monks as we saw when discussing the eight

Theravada Buddhism: Continuity, Diversity, and Identity, First Edition. Kate Crosby.

garudhamma rules for nuns. We do not have a text of the rules for nuns that does not require reference to the male counterpart. It is possible, given the demise of the nuns' order, that the *Bhikkhunī-vibhaṅga* has only been preserved because of its inclusion in the text for monks – its dependency has preserved it. This begs the question of whether there was an independent transmission of literature among nuns that was lost with the loss of the lineage. The extant commentary on the rules that apply to nuns is extremely brief in contrast to the extensive commentary on the rules that apply to monks (von Hinüber 1996: 15 and 107).

A notable exception to male authorship in the Canon is the *Therīgāthā*, verses attributed to early nuns. This unique quality of the *Therīgāthā* has in recent times inspired a number of translations, paraphrases, and analyses in response to interest from new generations of women from around the world who have converted to Buddhism and are hungry for texts that speak to them. (For a reevaluation of the use made of the Therīgāthā, see Rajapakse 2000.) There is a parallel text to the *Therīgāthā*, the *Theragāthā*, which contains poems by early monks. In fact, wherever there are female-specific texts in the Pali Canon, they are gender-paired in this way, with a parallel version for men. Texts that apply to laywomen are clearly not affected in the same way as *Vinaya* literature by the demise of the nuns' order – the presence of laywomen as audiences for monastic literature continues to this day. (See Chapter 11.)

An exception to the male monopoly on the preservation of texts in the canon is the early textual history of the *Itivuttaka*. The *Itivuttaka* is a collection of short *sutta* teachings that, according to its commentary, found their way into the Pali Canon because they had been remembered by the laywoman Khujjuttarā, who had heard the Buddha preaching them in the city of Kosambi (von Hinüber 1996: 47).

It has been suggested that the circa fourth- to fifth-century CE *Dīpavaṃsa*, the earlier of the two most famous Sri Lankan Pali chronicles, was written by nuns (Bartholomeusz 1994: 18, Gunawardana 1988: 15). There is no direct evidence for this. Rather it is inferred from the striking prevalence of information about nuns in it, in contrast to their relative invisibility in the fifth-century Sri Lankan chronicle, the *Mahāvaṃsa*, in spite of the otherwise similar coverage in the two texts. The *Mahāvaṃsa* chronicle continued to be updated and maintained within the Mahāvihāra, the monastic institution that would come to dominate Sri Lankan Buddhism. The relative visibility of women in the two chronicles may therefore not reflect authorship, but the gradual demise of the nuns' order or the absence of nuns in the central Sangha hierarchy of the Mahāvihāra.

A study conducted in 2009 among the Shan ethnic group of northern Thailand offers an insight into the invisibility of women in the authorship and preservation of texts, indicating the extent to which it may arise when the perspective is that of the androcentric institutional center. Many Shan thought that only men were *zare*, the scholars who recite, copy, and, in many cases, compose Theravada literature in Shan. This belief was held by the majority of male *zare* themselves: the received wisdom is that there has only ever been one female *zare* in history, Naṅ Khaṃ Ku (1853–1918). Her virtuosity was able to flourish in a male-dominated sphere because of the influence, under very specific circumstances, of a male relative in the same field.

Similarly, while Theravada countries have produced some of the most exceptional female political figures in the world, they have all stood out as exceptions also within their own cultural milieu. Even though her education before marriage in some ways qualified her for the role, the first female prime minister in the world, Sri Lanka's Sirima Bandaranaike

(1916–2000), stepped into the role only as a response to the assassination of her husband, Prime Minister Solomon Bandaranaike, in 1959. Without this tragedy she would almost certainly have remained in the background as a politician's wife, especially given the reputed chauvinism of her circle, including that of her late husband. The chauvinism was not negligible: pandering to the religious, ethnic, and conservative biases of the Sinhalese majority was a key factor in Solomon's success (and his assassination) and ultimately contributed to bringing about the civil war that dominated the history of post-independence Sri Lanka (Rettie 2000). Quite different was the political career of their daughter Chandrika Kumaratunga (president 1994–2005). Similarly, Khin Kyi, the mother of Nobel Peace Prize winner, Burma's pro-democracy leader Aung San Suu Kyi (b. 1945), became a member of parliament after the assassination in 1947 of her husband, founder of the modern nation of Burma. Aung San Suu Kyi's own political career, despite relevant education and work experience before marriage, flourished unexpectedly, interrupting doctoral studies in Burmese literature at the University of London (Finch 2011: 12). She had returned to Burma to look after her dying mother, when a combination of the 1988 student uprisings and her position as daughter of Aung San catapulted her into the political spotlight (Michael Aris 1988, personal communication). Historically, women undertaking exceptional roles also follow similar patterns: queens such as Cāmadevī (seventh century CE) and Suriyothai (sixteenth century) both took the place of their husbands in the traditional domains of men, including battle.

To return to the case of Nang Khaṃ Ku, the nineteenth- to twentieth-century female Shan *zare*, her father was the *zare* Zao Kang Suea, regarded by many as the most gifted composer of Shan poetic literature of all time (Crosby and Khur-Yearn 2010: 6–7). Zao Kang Suea had disrobed from the Sangha at the age of 65. He then married and had his daughter when already established as one of the leading scholars and composers of his time. His daughter learnt the skills of the *zare* alongside the many pupils who came to visit their home to study with him. By the age of 22 she had become a recognized author in her own right, composing works on the demanding subject of *abhidhamma* (Buddhist metaphysics, see Chapter 7), as well as writing the famous novel *Khun Samlaw Nang Upem*. Her father's profession gave her access to training normally only available to men. Although men who are identified as having talent can continue their pursuit and practice of this expertise as laymen, most male *zare* begin their training as novice monks at the temple. As we can see in other arenas, the absence of a *bhikkhunī* lineage and the prohibition on girls, especially post-pubescent girls, spending time in the vicinity of monks (in the absence of learned nuns), restrict opportunities for women to develop skills in literacy and to benefit from other aspects of education traditionally provided by monks. (In relation to *mae chi*, see Seeger 2010: 568.) This lack of novice education for girls that has kept the number of female *zare* low historically is still relevant (even where there is state education) for two reasons: monasteries continue to provide literacy in ethnic languages not taught in schools, and they provide food and shelter to allow boys to study rather than to work to support the family. The lack of training available to women has created a vicious cycle among precept nuns. In recent decades, precept nuns in Burma and Thailand have, with considerable success, worked hard to break this cycle but we still see its impact on the status and effectiveness on nuns in Cambodia and Laos.

In spite of these restrictions on female access to literacy, however, Nang Khaṃ Ku is not – contrary to both scholarly and indigenous opinion – the only female *zare* in history. The 2009 study of about 80 *zare* in the Maehongson region identified 7 women *zare* active in that region alone (Crosby and Khur-Yearn 2010). The reason for the widespread ignorance of the existence of these female *zare* seems to lie in the listening practices that are specific to women. Most extensive performance of Shan Buddhist poetry takes place during "temple-sleeping." Temple-sleeping is when senior men and women from the community stay overnight at the local temple, dressed in white and undertaking precepts. A *zare* reads a poetic work to the temple sleepers in sessions throughout the course of their stay. During the day the men and women listen together in the main shrine room, which is also where the men set up their mats and mosquito nets to spend the night. At night the women go off to a separate residence. Unbeknownst to most of the men – and thus the male *zare* – the women would sometimes continue listening to poetry, but now read by one of their number. The female *zare* mostly performed only in front of women, either at home or in the women's temple sleeping quarters. Only one of them also performed in front of men and was asked to undertake similar roles to the male *zare*. Unusually, she had been ordained as a temporary nun as a teenager and had began her initial, intensive training under the abbot until her mother asked her to disrobe (Crosby and Khur-Yearn 2010: 8).

These Shan poetic texts contain evidence for another way in which women have contributed to the generation and preservation of texts. Unlike most manuscripts of Theravada texts, Shan poems tend to be preceded by lengthy introductions about the occasion for the copying of the text. A high number of female sponsors is mentioned, making these introductions unusual for the visibility of female history that they offer (Crosby and Khur-Yearn 2010: 3). A similar picture of women's relative importance in sponsoring religious activities is presented by inscriptions and accounts of the spread of Buddhism. Female members of the royal court played a leading role in the transmission of Buddhism to Sri Lanka, and we find similar accounts of women mediating the transmission of the Dhamma or of relics in the chronicles of Southeast Asia. The role of women as supporters of Buddhism (and as mothers, see later text) is highly visible in Theravada art and architecture, from Sujāta, who gives the Buddha his first meal after he gives up asceticism, to the earth goddess, who bears witness to his enlightenment and appears throughout Southeast Asia, incorporated constantly into the ritual pouring of water to mark the making of merit (Guthrie 2004). An early female patron of the Buddha appears in the Pali Canon. She is the courtesan Ambapālī, whose moving verses on impermanence, contrasting the beauty of her youth with the same features now that she is aged, is one of the most famous of the *Therīgāthā* poems:

> Glossy and black as the down of the bee my curls once clustered.
> They with the waste of the years are liker to hempen or bark cloth.
> Such and not otherwise runneth the rune, the word of the Soothsayer. (252)
> ...
> Gleamed as I smiled my teeth like the opening buds of the plantain.
> They with the wast of the years are broken and yellow as barley.
> Such and not otherwise runneth the rune, the word of the Soothsayer. (260)
> ...
> Full and lovely in contour rose of yore the small breasts of me.
> They with the waste of years droop shrunken as skins without water.
> Such and not otherwise runneth the rune, the word of the Soothsayer. (265)
> Shone of yore this body as shield of gold well-polished.
> Now with the waste of the years all covered with network of wrinkles.
> Such and not otherwise runneth the rune, the word of the Soothsayer. (266)

> ...
> Soft and lovely of yore as though filled out with down were the feet of me.
> They with the waste of the years are cracked open and wizened with wrinkles.
> Such and not otherwise runneth the rune, the word of the Soothsayer. (269)
>
> (Rhys Davids and Norman 1980: 100–104)

The story of Ambapālī, whose invitation the Buddha honors in spite of subsequent, more prestigious invitations, offers a template for monks on how to accept alms by invitation: one honors the first invitation accepted. Parallels have been drawn between the figure of Ambapālī and Christ's most prominent female disciple, Mary Magdalene, as an example of the inclusive tolerance of both the Buddha and Christ. This is largely because of the later (sixth century) identification of Mary Magdalene as a "fallen woman" or prostitute that became so popular in European art rather than on account of their spiritual achievements, which offer a better parallel (de Boer 2004, 2007). But Ambapālī's identification as a prostitute is within the canon itself and comes with no judgment about the profession. Rather, Ambapālī's profession explains her ability to afford to sponsor the Sangha independently in her own right.

Mothers

Other important lay figures in stories of the Buddha's life and Sangha are, of course, the Buddha's mothers, his birth mother Māyā and his foster mother Mahāpajāpatī Gotamī. His foster mother is significant as the first nun (see Chapter 9) and as a quasi-Buddha (see Chapter 11). In the developed biography of the Buddha, Māyā dies seven days after his birth. Nevertheless, this is not the end of their relationship. One of the key pilgrimage sites associated with the Buddha's life in India is Saṃkāśya. The religious imagery associated with the event of the Buddha's life at this site is of the Buddha descending a ladder, flanked by deities. He is returning from heaven where he had been teaching *Abhidhamma*, the most sophisticated representation of the Buddha's teachings (see Chapter 7), to the deity his birth mother had become. There are other ways in which the *Abhidhamma* is associated with motherhood (see Chapter 11).

In emulation of the Buddha teaching his mother, it remains a tradition in Thailand for boys undergoing temporary ordination to give their first sermon to their mother. This ties in with a commonly held belief that by receiving lower ordination a boy is – through the merit the mother gains – paying back his mother for the pain she went through in childbirth and the sacrifices she made in nurturing and caring for her son. The higher proportion of women among lay attendees at temples on holy days is in part because mothers attend to visit their sons. To be the mother of an abbot can bestow particularly high status and give the mother a place alongside other local dignitaries in ritual contexts. It may have also formed another type of network that, like the female copying and sponsoring of texts, is barely visible historically: a gift of a cushion seat from a Cambodian queen to the mother of the nineteenth-century Sri Lankan monk Subhūti, who played an important role in the development of Pali studies in the West, is still housed in the Waskaḍuwē temple of which he was abbot, testimony to a relationship and network otherwise unrecorded.

The importance and status of motherhood and a child's relationship with its mother is emphasized in all Theravada societies, and in many of them a woman's status increases on the birth of her first child. The role of mothers in providing their sons as monks to join the

Sangha is highly valued. The nurturing aspects of motherhood also function in Buddhism as positive models or analogies for qualities to be emulated by men as well: the self-sacrifice and compassion of the Buddha, and also of senior monks, are explicitly seen as maternal qualities. The metaphor of motherhood is drawn on in some of the rituals performed to consecrate important Buddha images in Thailand. The way the mould in which the image is formed is treated mirrors the traditional confinement of women during labor and after giving birth. (For further Theravada symbolism based on motherhood, see Chapter 11.) Procreation, nurturance. and compassion, then, are not only accepted but theologically and socially validated domains of female power and potency.

Protecting Men from Female Power

Attitudes to the female domain of fertility that comes with procreation are more ambivalent. In Southeast Asia, women are regarded as having special powers that can be dangerous for – although in the case of mother and son, also protective of – men. While amulets are mostly empowered by men, one made from the skirt his mother wore in childbirth is regarded as particularly powerful protection for a man. One could see the belief that women's power is dangerous for men as an extension of the "ascetic misogyny" (a fear of women that protects self-denial/celibacy) already seen in Theravada monastic literature from the earliest times (Chapter 9). Women are banned from *stūpa* (religious memorials) in which powerful Buddha relics are enshrined such as the Shwedagon Pagoda in Burma, and from some *sīmā* (the sacred enclosure for Sangha rituals) including the historic *sīmā* at Cox's Bazaar in Bangladesh (Nagasena 2013, Seeger 2010: 560, Spiro 1997: 11). Monks avoid physical contact with women, and in Thailand even when women give gifts to monks they use a special cloth to avoid direct contact (Seeger 2010: 568, note 45). However, anxiety about female power is on the whole more prevalent in Southeast Asian than South Asian cultures. In Sri Lanka, there is little concern about the effect of women's power on men, and while monks avoid contact with women, there are exceptions in the ritual context, such as when monks tie protective ritual string around the wrists of women. Moreover, such attitudes go beyond the assumptions of Theravada literature, and the fact that they affect laymen as well as monks suggests that other cultural factors contribute to these beliefs. Laymen and women avoid situations in which men will have contact or even walk below female lower body clothing, for example, in the way laundry is laid out to dry, because women's personal garments will disempower men. This belief informs famous stories about women's menstrual cloths being wrapped around weapons by female combatants or rulers to disarm male enemies (Collins 2011: 79).

A Framework for Patriarchy or Egalitarianism in Theravada Societies?

The pervasive androcentrism of most societies is also manifest in various ways in Theravada communities. Yet some writers have been pleased to point that there is little of the extreme systemic devaluation or pervasive control of women's lives found in some other societies with a conservative take on their religion, even in the most orthopractic and conservative of

Theravada contexts. Some feminist Buddhists take this further by claiming that Buddhism offers a template for greater liberty for women. Those who wish to see Theravada as contributing to a more egalitarian attitude to women point out attitudes to the birth of daughters: female children are usually as welcome as male children. It is true that in Theravada cultures there are areas in which women traditionally enjoy more equality with men than in the West. In early twentieth-century Britain, the rights of Burmese women were seen as something British women could aspire to. Given the rhetoric of equality in the West, we still see some unexpected remnants of this imbalance. For example, women's leadership in and ownership of business is prevalent in Southeast Asia. This is an area in which Buddhist monks in the West sometimes mediate between Thai wives and their Western husbands, who do not anticipate this (personal communication, two Western temples 2008).

In some parts of the Theravada world, the introduction of Western legal systems during the European colonial period, for example, under the Dutch and British in Sri Lanka, brought with it the disempowerment of women as their traditional property and custodial rights were eroded (Seneviratne 1999: 19, note 45). Here colonial influence intruded into and disrupted the very arena, namely, familial relations, which is the traditional domain of female power. While in the more modern law codes of the Western countries that imposed their patriarchal legal systems on Sri Lanka the balance has shifted toward recognizing that power domain, Sri Lanka has yet to regain the balance it enjoyed before the colonial period. Similarly, we can see the ongoing influence of Victorian values on Sri Lankan attitudes to sexuality and in the importance placed on the virginity of women on marriage, which contrasts with the values of the pre-colonial period (Gombrich and Obeyesekere 1988: 255–256). Changes in attitudes to female sexuality and to extramarital sexual relations are not only the result of colonial influence. They have varied considerably across time and between communities, with no single uniform view across Theravada cultures and history. In the earliest layers of the Pali commentaries (see Chapter 3), the interpretation of the third precept, to refrain from sexual misconduct, was not based on ideals of virginity but on notions of theft, which were differently interpreted for men and women. Women who are married break the third precept by "stealing the contact which belongs to their husbands" (Collins 2007: 263), whereas men break the third precept if they have sex with women who belong to others, which can be reversed if permission is then given to the man by the person to whom the woman belongs. "Thus, as is often the case worldwide, sexual transgressions are committed by men not directly against a woman but against those who either 'own' her or are in some other way legally responsible for her. … In the specifically Buddhist jurisprudential-ritual sense, therefore, lay single women, of any kind (the unmarried [whether young or old], divorcées, widows, and prostitutes, … do not break the Third Precept by having sex with a man" (Collins 2007: 264). Variation between the sexual mores of Theravada cultures within a single country can be seen today in contrast between the more liberal values of the Shan and the more reactionary Burman values with regard to extra and premarital sexual intercourse. Whether the Burman or Shan attitudes are the more traditional is arguable (Tannenbaum 1995, 1999, personal communication with Burmese and Shan in the United Kingdom 2007–2008). Such differences are accommodated in the very general wording of the third precept for Buddhist laypeople, which prohibits "sexual misconduct" and is construed variously in different Buddhist cultures.

Others have disagreed with the idea that Theravada promotes equality for women, pointing to the effect on women of human slavery, trafficking, restriction on movement, and prostitution in the Theravada region of Southeast Asia. It is difficult to untangle the different causal factors. All these abuses of human liberty and dignity do have a history in the region and in Buddhism's early cultural context. One text of the Pali Canon, the *Vimāna-Vatthu*, praises wives and their fathers as virtuous for employing prostitutes as substitutes to keep their husbands satisfied so that they can get on with meritorious Buddhist activity; Thailand has its own domestic sex industry servicing Thai men; and the traditional and ongoing practice of polygamy in the region could be said to inform the acceptability of prostitution (Thitsa 1980: 23). On the other hand, the notoriety of Thailand for prostitution and sex tourism, which is supplied with poor girls/women (and boys/men) from rural regions and neighboring countries, is a direct consequence of its use by American military personnel in the 1950s to 1970s. We should be wary of blaming the recently increased commodification of women in Southeast Asia on traditional Theravada culture alone: rather it reflects the internationalized sex industry in that region, and also the global shaping and sexualizing of girls' bodies in relation to the mediation of modernity through consumerism (Orbach 2011) and the broader cultural influences of the advertising and pornographic industries.

Nonetheless, one could argue that even if Buddhist doctrine does not provide a framework for patriarchy, the practice of preserving and supporting only the male Sangha exacerbates the effects of prostitution and the commodification of the female body. These issues may affect more women than men not just because of the demands of the prostitution market but also because monasteries offer a refuge from poverty and abuse for boys in Southeast Asia (see Chapter 8), which they cannot, on the whole, offer girls. Some writers, looking at the sex industry in relation to the availability of ordination for boys, have even suggested that a poor girl entering prostitution in order to supply her family with money functions as a parallel to the contribution made by boys in terms of merit by entering the Sangha (van Esterick 1982, cited in Tannenbaum 1999: 245). In Burma, the widespread availability of ordination, including temporary ordination, as a precept nun appears to provide an avenue for girls and women escaping domestic abuse. In contrast, in Cambodia and Laos, it is older women who usually become precept nuns. They do so for life and tend to be illiterate. These factors, in addition to their poverty (unlike monks they rarely receive offerings), their focus on their own Dhamma practice and on serving the needs of monks, make it difficult for them to care for girls made vulnerable by poverty or being orphaned. A combination of their age, illiteracy, and usual background in farm labor limits their value as mentors for girls in an age where the challenge is to keep girls in education. A study conducted in Cambodia in 2005 highlights how girls from vulnerable backgrounds take on the responsibility of caring for their families and start work to provide money for the family at a younger age than boys. This reduces the opportunities that education would provide to break the cycle of poverty and to lower the risk of trafficking and prostitution. Monks, who are themselves usually young and literate, can provide mentoring for boys, and boys can stay in monasteries. Monks cannot perform this service for girls, especially those who have reached puberty, even though – probably due to their relative youth and continued engagement in society – monks are often more aware of the problems facing girls than the nuns are (Ramage *et al.* 2005). We should bear in mind, however, that the availability of monasteries as a refuge does not solve the difficulties facing vulnerable boys. There is also significant use of men and boys in Southeast Asia's sex industry. Moreover, in several recent cases, monks have used the trust and access to boys granted to them to traffick children in the pedophile sex industry (e.g., http://www.pattayadailynews.com, April 3, 2010, retrieved August 2012).

The extent and direction of the influence of Buddhist theology and ideology on attitudes to women remains, then, a moot point. Women's primary association with households and nurture, mentioned earlier, in contrast to men's primary associations beyond the household (Bartholomeusz 1994: 22, Tannenbaum 1999: 244), means that the power domains as a whole tend to be different between men and women in ways not dissimilar from other cultures. These differences are often maintained, as elsewhere, even when women are equally or more active economically beyond the household. While in some Theravada cultures women have equal or shared access to money through their traditional farming or manual labor, in more recent times they may have greater access to employment, such as office and factory work in addition to prostitution. This is not as a result of a positive evaluation of women's worth. The pattern of women being regarded as harder working and accepting lower pay is widespread. Women were preferred in the newly burgeoning garment trade in Sri Lanka in the early 1990s, for example, as easier to control and cheaper. The pervasive domestic division of power domains regardless of changes in economic activity has been understood as "a dualism linking women with fertility, nurturance and attachment and men with supra-mundane power and detachment" (van Esterick 1982: 5, cited in Tannenbaum 1999: 244–245). In other words, this division of roles maps on to the Buddhist teaching that attachment keeps one in *saṃsāra* and that men have less attachment and a correspondingly greater capacity for ordination and higher spiritual states. As Tannenbaum points out, the "issue of attachment and detachment is construed as a Buddhist one" (Tannenbaum 1999: 245).

Perhaps influenced by ethnic tensions conceived in Hindu–Buddhist terms, scholars in Sri Lanka have contrasted the relatively egalitarian attitude in Sri Lanka with the less egalitarian attitude in India, attributing the former to Buddhism and the latter to Hinduism (while ignoring north–south and other Indian regional variations in this regard). Chatsumarn Kabilsingh, writing from the Thai perspective, blames Hinduism for non-egalitarian attitudes within Buddhism that are assumed to post-date the Buddha (Kabilsingh 1991: 24–26). That the two neighboring dominant cultures of India and China have been influential on the cultures that host Theravada is indisputable, but the extent to which this influences attitudes to women varies and is open to debate. Moreover, the notion found in Burmese and Tai cultures of men as spiritually powerful and women as power-draining is not, at least not consistently, in evidence in Buddhist or other classical religious sources. Attributing attitudes to a Theravada framework cannot explain the striking regional differences between, for example, Sri Lanka and mainland Southeast Asia. It would seem that there are more complex cultural issues behind the varying expressions of egalitarianism between the sexes and the relative subordination of women in different Theravada regions.

Tannenbaum has suggested that the literature on the subject of differential power between men and women, as well as on the subject of the position of women in the sex industry, is hard to assess given that authors, especially Thai authors, are projecting their own middle-class assumptions onto the subject. She suggests that the widespread popular view in Thailand that men, while being more detached, have natural sexual needs requiring an outlet, in contrast to women having no need of sexual outlet, "is a modern view: in premodern Southeast Asia both men and women were seen as sexually active and needing and deserving sexual satisfaction" (Tannenbaum 1999: 248). Given that the premodern view continues to be reflected in Southeast Asian cultures less influenced by centralized reform, even in Diaspora, we again have to consider whether the essentializing of male versus female identity (i.e., the process of attributing contrasting characteristics to men and women) has been ongoing, in part driven by the processes of nation-building, colonialism, and modernity. Tannenbaum points out that problems are created by trying to see "all aspects of Thai [more broadly 'Theravada'] culture … in Buddhist terms" (Tannenbaum 1999: 251). Nevertheless, it is clear that the male-dominated monastery benefits disadvantaged boys more than equally vulnerable girls. An unexplored possibility is that it also means that adult women are disadvantaged once problems have arisen, given the role of monks in mediating and providing guidance for those who turn to them for advice on all aspects of life, including in cases of domestic difficulties and abuse.

The essentializing of both male–female difference and the Asian "other" certainly seems to have contributed to the cognitive dissonance experienced by Western observers since the earliest times to the present when observing the high evaluation of women's economic status in Southeast Asia in contrast to her lower spiritual status, as well as the ambivalence of Buddhist texts toward women. It is worth bearing in mind that relations between men and women and differentials of power are not set in stone, nor is gender always a primary factor in establishing status. Tannenbaum points out in relation to Tai cultures, "Difference in status or rank, based on merit, are more important than gender and consequently many women rank higher than many men" (Tannenbaum 1999: 244) It may also be that for scholars assessing the "differentially privileged access to spiritual power and prestige" (Tannenbaum 1999: 254) apparent in Buddhist cultures, the areas in which men are more likely to be privileged have more in common in terms of criteria for success with the criteria for success that pertain in academic careers. In other words, in both these arenas success is measured more in terms of external and financial validation rather than internal or domestic validation and biological continuity. This applies not only to the assessment of social and sexual status but also to the spiritual realm and appears to be confirmed in the rejection by nuns, especially precept nuns (see Chapter 9) of the signifiers of power aspired to by Western and academic feminist observers on their behalf (Cheng 2007).

Summary

This chapter explored a number of issues concerning aspects of female power in Theravada. It examined questions of invisibility, drawing on counter-examples, which suggest that the nature of female expressions of learning and power and the way in which textual history has been recorded may significantly hamper our examination of such matters. This raised the question of whether prominent women in what are traditionally considered male roles are exceptions benefitting from family advantage rather than reflecting Theravada as a catalyst in gender egalitarianism. The importance placed on the role of women as mothers and nurturers was explored in relation to the Buddha's own mothers, the status of women on becoming mothers and the relationship between mothers and their sons, particularly those who have entered the Sangha. The virtues of mothers are seen as qualities emulated by the Buddha and by ideal monks. It was noted that women have traditional domains of power that vary between societies and over time, and that in Southeast Asia their power is seen as dangerous for men other than their sons. The impact was observed of colonialism, the presence of Western military, and aspects of modernity on attitudes to women, their legal status and sexual mores. While the assessment of whether Theravada offers a framework for egalitarianism or patriarchy remains a moot point, and there are difficulties in isolating judgments on this from scholars' own value systems, it is clear that the absence of a strong tradition of nuns (whether fully ordained *bhikkhunī* or precept nuns) disadvantages vulnerable girls in contrast to vulnerable boys for whom provision is often made in monasteries.

References

Bartholomeusz, Tessa J. (1994). *Women Under the Bō Tree: Buddhist Nuns in Sri Lanka*. Cambridge: Cambridge University Press.

de Boer, Esther A. (2004). 'The Gospel of Mary: Beyond a Gnostic and a Biblical Mary Magdalene', *Journal of the Study of the New Testament. 260. Supplement Series*. London: T & T Clark International.

de Boer, Esther A. (2007). *The Mary Magdalene Cover-up: The Sources Behind the Myth*. London/New York: T & T Clark.

Cheng, Wei Yi. (2007). *Buddhist Nuns in Taiwan and Sri Lanka. A Critique of the Feminist Perspective*. Abingdon: Routledge.

Collins, Steven. (2007). 'On the Third Precept: Adultery and Prostitution in Pali Texts', *Journal of the Pali Text Society* XXVIII (Festschrift for K.R. Norman): 259–280.

Collins, Steven. (2011). *Civilisation et femmes célibataires dans le bouddhisme en Asie du Sud et du Sud-Est: une 'Étude de genre'*. Paris: Éditions de Cerf.

Crosby, Kate and Jotika Khur-Yearn. (2010). 'Poetic *Dhamma* and the *zare*: Traditional Styles of Teaching Theravada Amongst the Shan of Northern Thailand', *Contemporary Buddhism* 11.1: 1–26.

Finch, Steve. (2011). 'Free', *SOAS World* 37: 10–12.

Gombrich, Richard and Gananath Obeyesekere. (1988). *Buddhism Transformed: Religious Change in Sri Lanka*. Princeton: Princeton University Press.

Gunawardana, R.A.L.H. (1988). 'Subtile Silks of Ferreous Firmness: Buddhist Nuns in Ancient and Early Medieval Sri Lanka and Their Role in the Propagation of Buddhism', *The Sri Lankan Journal of the Humanities* 14.1 and 2: 1–59.

Guthrie, Elizabeth. (2004). 'A Study of the History and Cult of the Buddhist Earth Deity in Mainland Southeast Asia'. PhD thesis, University of Canterbury, Christchurch.

von Hinüber, Oskar. (1996). *A Handbook of Pāli Literature*. Berlin/New York: Walter de Gruyter.

Kabilsingh, Chatsumarn. (1991). *Thai Women in Buddhism*. Berkeley: Parallax Press.

Nagasena, Bhikkhu. (2013). 'The Monastic Boundary (*Sīmā*) in Burmese Buddhism: Authority, Purity and Validity in Historical and Modern Contexts'. PhD thesis, School of Oriental and African Studies, London.

Orbach, Susie. (2011). 'The Body and the State: How the State Controls and Protects the Body', *Social Research: An International Quarterly* 78.2: 387–394.

Rajapakse, Vijitha. (2000). *The Therīgāthā: A Reevaluation*. The Wheel Publication no. 436. Kandy: Buddhist Publication Society. http://www.bps.lk/olib/wh/wh436.pdf (retrieved June 8, 2013).

Ramage, Ian, Gabriel Picket, and Kheang Lyhun. (2005). *Girls and Buddhist Nuns. Research Report Cambodia, 2005*. Phnom Penh: Domrei Research and Consulting.

Rettie, John. (2000). Obituary Sirimavo Bandaranaike, *The Guardian*, October 11, 2000.

Rhys Davids, C.A.F. and K.R. Norman. (1980). *Poems of Early Buddhist Nuns*, new edn (revision of Rhys-Davids C.A.F. 1951). Oxford: The Pali Text Society.

Seeger, Martin. (2010). '"Against the Stream": The Thai Female Buddhist Saint Mae Chi Kaew Sianglam (1901–1991)', *South East Asia Research* 18.3: 555–595.

Seneviratne, H.L. (1999). *The Work of Kings: The New Buddhism in Sri Lanka*. Chicago: University of Chicago Press.

Spiro, Melford. (1997). *Gender, Ideology and Psychological Reality*. New Haven: Yale University Press.

Tannenbaum, Nicola. (1995). *Who Can Compete Against the World? Power-Protection and Buddhism in Shan Worldview*. Ann Arbor: Association for Asian Studies Inc.

Tannenbaum, Nicola. (1999). 'Buddhism, Prostitution, and Sex: Limits on the Academic Discourse on Gender in Thailand?' in Peter A. Jackson and Nerida M. Cook (eds.), *Genders and Sexualities in Modern Thailand*. Chiangmai: Silkworm Books, 243–260.

Thitsa, Khin. (1980). *Providence and Prostitution: Image and Reality for Women in Buddhist Thailand*. London: Change.

Further Reading

Collins, Steven. (2007). 'On the Third Precept: Adultery and Prostitution in Pali Texts,' *Journal of the Pali Text Society* XXVIII (Festschrift for K. R. Norman): 259–280.

Gombrich, R. F. (1972). 'Feminine Elements in Sinhalese Buddhism', *Wiener Zeitschrift für die Kunde Südasiens* 16: 67–93.

Gunawardana, R.A.L.H. (1988). 'Subtile Silks of Ferreous Firmness: Buddhist Nuns in Ancient and Early Medieval Sri Lanka and Their Role in the Propagation of Buddhism', *The Sri Lankan Journal of the Humanities* 14.1 and 2: 1–59.

Guthrie, Elizabeth. (2004). 'A Study of the History and Cult of the Buddhist Earth Deity in Mainland Southeast Asia'. Ph.D. thesis, University of Canterbury, Christchurch.

Kabilsingh, Chatsumarn. (1991). *Thai Women in Buddhism*. Berkeley: Parallax Press.

Obeyesekere, Ranjani. (2001). *Portraits of Buddhist Women: Stories from the Saddharmaratnāvaliya*. Albany: State University of New York Press.

Ohnuma, Reiko. (2012). *Ties that Bind: Maternal Imagery and Discourse in Indian Buddhism*. Oxford: Oxford University Press.

Ramage, Ian, Gabriel Picket, and Kheang Lyhun. (2005). *Girls and Buddhist Nuns. Research Report Cambodia*. Phnom Penh: Domrei Research and Consulting.

Sasson, Vanessa R. (2012). *Little Buddhas: Children and Childhoods in Buddhist Texts and Traditions*. Oxford: Oxford University Press.

Tannenbaum, Nicola. (1999). 'Buddhism, Prostitution, and Sex: Limits on the Academic Discourse on Gender in Thailand?', in Peter A. Jackson and Nerida M. Cook (eds.), *Genders and Sexualities in Modern Thailand*. Chiangmai: Silkworm Books, 243–260.

Thitsa, Khin. (1980). *Providence and Prostitution: Image and Reality for Women in Buddhist Thailand*. London: Change.

Van Esterik, Penny (ed.). (1982). *Women in Southeast Asia*. DeKalb: Center for Southeast Asian Studies, Northern Illinois University Press.

11

Feminist Readings of Gender-Related Symbols

Overview

In this chapter, we explore the kinds of female-gendered and gender-inclusive symbols to be found in Theravada. This chapter responds to widespread assumptions about differences between Theravada and Mahayana and so follows the agenda set by those assumptions. Sometimes feminist writers have looked for positive feminine-gendered or gender-inclusive symbols within Buddhism; these have been assumed to be discoverable mainly within Mahayana. One feminist writer on Buddhism has taken this a step further to propose that it was attitudes to women that generated *the* historical bifurcation between Theravada and Mahayana, a proposal reconsidered and rejected here. This chapter explores a broad range of Theravada literature, adding to the evidence indicating that the mistaken equation of Theravada with early Buddhism has confined assumptions about Theravada to an over-narrow purview.

Search for Role Models and Exemplary Symbols

In Theravada countries, mythologizing and memorializing exemplary female role models has formed part of the process of nation-building and continues to this day. In Thailand, recent statues and pictures of the eighth-century Queen Cāmadevī, the sixteenth-century Queen Suriyothai, the sixteenth- to seventeenth-century Princess Suphankanlaya, and the nineteenth-century noblewoman Tha Suranari are worshipped as heroic models (Collins 2011: 79ff., Seeger 2010: 562–563). Those important female religious practitioners who do not flout the anti-*bhikkhunī* agenda of the Thai Sangha hierarchy have been similarly memorialized in recent decades (see Chapter 10). This search for evidence of strong women, renouncer or lay, in Theravada history, has also been a marked feature of feminist writings. These writings attempt both to correct the under-representation of women and to provide inspiration for the present. Some of the evidence in Theravada literature for the intended

Theravada Buddhism: Continuity, Diversity, and Identity, First Edition. Kate Crosby.

inclusion of women on the soteriological path that has informed such writings was examined in Chapter 9. However, it is the literatures of Mahayana and Vajrayana Buddhism, the forms of Buddhism that spread north of India and continue to be represented in Central and East Asia, that have so far been the more productive sources for the eliciting of feminine or gender-inclusive/neutral symbols in the creation of modern feminist readings. This is in part due to the anachronistic equation of Theravada with early Buddhism. This equation has led to an imbalance in the chronological spectrum of sources used: While the examination of Mahayana and Vajrayana literature has ranged across the centuries, the examination of Theravada sources has mostly been confined to canonical texts. Examining a broader range of Theravada literature, including a broader range of canonical texts than those usually used, alters the current categorizations of the ways in which the feminine is represented in Buddhist literature.

This chapter is mainly an exercise in existentialist interpretation, looking at the texts to see if feminist exercises carried out on other Buddhist literature can also be applied to Theravada texts. As we saw with Thailand, each Theravada country or region has its own female role models. On the whole these are role models for women as instrumental in the well-being of others or of a nation, rather than as agents in their own destiny. Where they are agents in their own destiny, they are nevertheless compliant in some way with the status quo. While the distinction between the two aspirations – instrumental or agentive – is arguable, it is symbols that unambiguously affirm the latter that are sought in feminist interpretation.

Female quasi-Buddhahood and gender pairing in Theravada

In response to the presupposition that a Buddha is a perfected male, feminist-Buddhists have observed that in Mahayana certain high-level female bodhisattvas function as quasi-Buddhas. This is important for feminist Buddhists because of statements of a pervasive theme in Buddhist literature to the effect that women are incapable of full Buddhahood. Particular attention has been paid in this regard to the Buddha-similarity of Vajrayoginī, Śrīmālādevī and the *bodhisattvas* of compassion, Tārā and the female form of Kuan-Yin (Avalokiteśvara). Vajrayoginī can function as the central figure, with whom the practitioner ritually identifies in Vajrayana practices (English 2002). Śrīmālādevī, who with her lion's roar is representative of the highest wisdom, embodies the perfect understanding of Tathāgatagarbha philosophy in the eponymous *sūtra*. In the case of Śrīmālādevī, Rita Gross – author of the seminal feminist book *Buddhism after Patriarchy* (1993) – has pointed out that scholarly debate within the Tibetan tradition, which excluded the possibility of a female Buddha, struggled to assess the relative standing of Śrīmālādevī in the ten *bhūmi* or stages of bodhisattvahood. Some allocated her to the lowest *bhūmi* and others to the eighth, a level indistinguishable from Buddhahood without extremely subtle analysis (Gross 1993: 74–75). In contrast to the discussion in Mahayana studies of the high status and Buddha-like roles of these female bodhisattvas, studies of Theravada have concluded that the Buddha or a future Buddha is never represented as female at any point in his many rebirths since the lifetime in which, as the brahmin Sumedha, he receives the prediction to future Buddhahood (for the exception before this point, see Chapter 4), noting the tendency in Theravada for individuals to retain their gender-identity across lives.

In the light of the parallel male and female trajectories in Theravada literature, it has been pointed out that Mahāpajāpatī Gotamī functions as a female Buddha or "quasi-Buddha" in the *Apadāna* of the Pali Canon. The *Apadāna* is one of the latest canonical texts. It contains the life stories of significant figures in early Buddhism. Mahāpajāpatī is the Buddha's aunt and foster mother and the first nun (see Chapter 9). Her life, enlightenment, teaching and *parinibbāna* present her not as a second class follower reluctantly acknowledged as capable of arhatship and so grudgingly admitted to the Saṅgha, but as being on a par with Gotama Buddha and in some ways preceding him. Her final demise, her *parinibbāna*, is heralded by earthquakes in just the same way as the Buddha's (Walters 1995: 116–117).

This phenomenon of gender-parallel paths or gender-pairing is reminiscent of another feature of Mahayana *sūtras*, the explicit inclusion of both female and male potential bodhisattvas as the target audience of *sūtras*, addressed as "sons and daughters of good family" (Gross 1993: 66). This form of gender-paired address is important because it indicates that the *dharma* is intended for both. In Theravada, extensive gender-pairing affects the format of entire genres of texts that exist in pairs, one for males and another for females. In addition to the separate rules for monks and nuns, the *bhikkhu/bhikkhunī-pāṭimokkha*, and their respective *vibhaṅga*, there are the "Verses of the Elders," *Thera/Therī-gāthā*, poems attributed to early monks and nuns expressing their motivation for joining the Sangha and their enlightenment experiences; and the *Peta/Petī-vatthu* (Skilling 2001: 242–250), as well as the corresponding text about rebirths in heaven, the *Vimānavatthu*. The title of the *Petavatthu* means "stories of ghosts/departed spirits." Divided according to whether the protagonist is male, *peta*, or female, *petī*, it contains the narratives of ghouls who explain how they suffer now because of their bad deeds in former lifetimes. They implore the people they haunt to perform good deeds, such as making offerings to monks, on their behalf and transferring the merit to them so that they can move on from their terrible suffering (Masefield 1980).

We also find paired forms of address within postcanonical Theravada texts. Probably – since it mentions the ordination of girls – composed before the thirteenth century (see Chapter 9), the *Upāsakamanussavinaya* explains the bad conduct that traps people in *saṃsāra* and in repeated hellish rebirths. It states that its teaching is relevant to all the beings trapped in *saṃsāra*: "be they a man of the warrior caste, a woman of the warrior caste, a male renouncer or female renouncer, a brahmin man or brahmin woman, an ordinary woman or man, a minister or the commander of an army, whether a viceroy or a town-watchman, or a merchant, a poor man or poor woman or someone with great wealth, whether of the husbandry caste, the servant caste or a beggar." Here, with the exception of the high status or military positions occupied only by men – the minister, general, viceroy, or watchman – women are explicitly included, as the text pairs male and female types (Crosby 2006: 178). This parallels the "sons and daughters of good family" observed in Mahayana literature and suggests we might rather see this as a development in the style of Buddhist literature in general that postdates the early canonical phase rather than as specific to a particular tradition.

While gender-pairing may be taken as a form of inclusivity, it is also possible to see it as a move toward greater essentializing, especially in the light of the understanding that gender usually transfers to the next rebirth. It is possible that both developments reflect the emergence of *Abhidhamma* analysis of the differences between the sexes, seen in the *Dhammasaṅgani*, the first text of *Abhidhamma* (see Chapter 7). According to the *Dhammasaṅgani*, there are two faculties of sex, the faculty of femininity (*itthindriya*) and the faculty of masculinity (*purisaindriya*). These faculties define physical appearance, marks, traits, and deportment peculiar to the state of femininity (*itthibhāva*) and the state of masculinity (*purisabhāva*), respectively. While the *Dhammasaṅgani* defines the two faculties in terms of physical appearance, etc., that are peculiar to woman and man, the commentary (the *Atthasālinī*) takes a view that these two faculties are the *causes* of female and male physical appearances, etc. Thus the fifth-century commentary reflects the essentializing of gender distinctions. Such essentializing of femininity and masculinity becomes more explicit in later commentarial literature on Theravada Abhidhamma, for example, in the eleventh- to twelfth-century handbook, the *Abhidhammatthasaṅgaha*. There the systematization of the ultimate constituents of reality (*dhamma*) (see Chapter 7) includes the faculty of femininity (*itthibhāva*) and the faculty of masculinity (*purisabhāva*) as two of the eighteen ultimate components of material experience (*rūpa-dhamma*). From the perspective of the *Abhidhammatthasaṅgaha*, the faculties of femininity and masculinity are indeed real existents and thus inherent parts of woman and man. The mere presence of faculties of femininity and masculinity in the canonical and postcanonical literature of Theravada Abhidhamma attests to gender pairing symbols in Theravada, yet the essentializing poses a challenge for those feminists who interpret all gender differentiation as social/environmental constructs (Kyaw, in preparation).

Feminine and Androgynous Symbols

Another important feature of feminist writings on Buddhism has been the search for inspirational models that offer female-gendered, **androgynous**, or gender-inclusive symbols of salvific qualities, that is, of aspects of Buddhahood or Awakening that one seeks to nurture within oneself.

By gendered symbols I mean female embodiments of salvific qualities, found in Mahayana and Vajrayana sources. Compassion is embodied as the *bodhisattvas* Tārā or Kuan-yin. Wisdom (Prajñā) is represented by the *bodhisattva*, Prajñāpāramitā, who is also an embodiment of the literature of the same name. Another embodiment of salvific qualities is Vajrayoginī, the female figure who represents empowered enlightenment and can be the central figure in tantric meditation. Even the "womb" imagery of developing Buddhahood in Tathāgatagarbha (the Mahayana and Vajrayana doctrine that everyone has the potential for Buddhahood within) has been taken as a feminine symbol.

By androgynous symbols I mean symbols of enlightenment that either explicitly discount the inherent nature of characteristics such as masculine and feminine or explicitly extol male and female characteristics as inherent and complementary. The most frequently adduced gender-excluding concept in feminist writings is *śūnyatā*: "emptiness" as the ultimate truth (see later text). The most frequently adduced androgynous symbol is the union of male and female in tantric enlightenment, which draws on the complementarity of male and female attributes. The union of male and female attributes symbolizes the realization of nondual transcendence. Writers seeking for symbols such as these, which can be productive for a feminist reconstruction of Buddhism, have tended to find them only in Mahayana and Vajrayāna sources. Yet by taking into our purview a broader spectrum of Theravada sources, we are able to find similar symbols within Theravada.

Feminine embodiments of nonego-derived responses to others

The *Visuddhimagga*, a fifth-century summary of the Theravada path, classifies some meditations as preparatory practices not salvific in their own right (see Chapter 6). Included are those practices most explicitly designed to generate positive responses to others and to eliminate the discrimination between self and other, that is, those practices aimed at developing compassion, one of the pair of perfected qualities of a Buddha, the other being wisdom. These practices are the four *brahmavihāra* or "divine abidings," loving kindness (*mettā*), pity (*karuṇā*), appreciative joy (*anumodanā*), and equanimity/impartiality (*upekkhā*). Each of these four attitudes is developed according to the appropriate form of compassion for the status of the living being toward whom they are directed. Loving kindness is the more general wish for the well-being of self and others, pity appropriate toward someone who is suffering, appreciative joy for one who is doing well, and equanimity is for one who is succeeding and not in need of one's intervention or support. Another term for these attitudes is the "unlimiteds" (*appamāṇa*, *apramāṇa* in Sanskrit) because in their perfected form they are experienced without limitation for all beings throughout the cosmos; they do not prioritize between oneself and others, nor between those one favors and those one does not.

From the earliest references to these practices in the Pali Canon and even in the *Visuddhimagga*, these unlimited states are epitomized by the attitude of mothers to their children. The ***Karaṇīyamettasutta*** (*Suttanipāta* I.8), the earliest instruction on this practice in the canon, advocates a mother's love for her only son as the model for the immeasurable love that one should aspire to feel for all beings. In the *Visuddhimagga*, a mother's love for her children is the model for all four *brahmavihāra*. A mother's awareness of her grown up son who is doing well and is no longer needy of her is the model for *upekkhā* (equanimity).

It has long been noted that the *Karaṇīyamettasutta* states that one who successfully develops the practice reaches the "peaceful state" (a synonym for enlightenment) and does not "come to lie again in a womb," that is, is not reborn. *Mettā* (loving kindness), according to this text, is salvific. (For translations, see Chapter 6 and www.accesstoinsight.org/tipitaka/kn/snp/snp.1.08, retrieved November 28, 2012.) While commentarial literature, including the *Visuddhimagga*, sought to reinterpret these statements and relegate the *brahmavihāras* to a subsidiary role, a number of scholars have recognized other passages in the canon, which confirm that the *brahmavihāra* were taught as salvific in their own right. This contradicts the *Visuddhimagga* (Conze 1956, Gombrich 1998, Maithrimurthi 1999, Skilton 1988). In earlier layers of the canon, the compassion aspect of Buddhahood is an equally viable path toward enlightenment, unlike the systematized forms of Theravada that treat it as preliminary to the insight aspect. We therefore have salvific compassion represented in Theravada by the ideal mother. This could be taken as a Theravada symbol of altruism on a par with Mahayana's Tārā or, more closely, Kuan-yin. (Although Kuan-yin is also an important object of devotion in Theravada in modern mainland Southeast Asia, in part through the influence of Burmese and Thais of Chinese descent, her cult is mostly outside of the soteriological framework.) An obvious difference is that Tārā and Kuan-yin are personified as archetypes with specific characters and attributes, but this is not possible in Theravada at the soteriological level because a core Theravada doctrine, in contrast to Mahayana that allows many or even unlimited Buddhas, is that there can be only one Buddha at a time (see Chapter 1). It is thought that some of the most popular archetypal *bodhisattvas* in Mahayana originated with the adoption of regional deities into the pantheon as beings on the path to Buddhahood (*bodhisattvas*), an option precluded in Theravada because of its one-Buddha doctrine, leaving deities, be they male or female, in supportive roles outside of **soteriology**.

Feminine embodiments of wisdom

Prajñā, "wisdom," is the other half of the pair of salvific qualities that constitute the Buddha. In Mahayana, wisdom or "the perfection of wisdom" is personified as *Prajñāpāramitā*, the "mother of all Buddhas." She embodies emptiness, the understanding of reality that transforms the unenlightened into enlightened beings, and thus creates all Buddhas and all teachings/*dharmas*.

Emptiness, *śūnyatā*, is the key doctrinal innovation – or restatement of the fundamental Buddhist truth of impermanence – in Madhyamaka Buddhism, the earliest distinctive school of Mahayana philosophy. While the origins of Mahayana may be debated, it is clear that Madhyamaka developed in reaction to *Abhidharma* (Sanskrit, Pali Abhidhamma) philosophy, which in Theravada became the third of the three Piṭakas. Abhidharma – including Theravada *Abhidhamma* (see Chapter 7) – categorized existence into entities, *dharmas*, that it considered real, to have inherent existence. Madhyamaka seeks to demonstrate that these *dharmas* do not in fact have ultimate reality. They are empty. (The type of inherent existence being disputed in Madhyamaka is in fact that found in Sarvāstivāda *Abhidharma*, not in Theravada *Abhidhamma*, as was discussed in Chapter 7). Because of its roots in a reaction to *Abhidharma*, Madhyamaka philosophy takes much of the terminology directly from *Abhidharma*. In Madhyamaka *prajñā*, salvific wisdom results from analyzing the *dharmas* of Abhidharma to reveal their inherent lack of substance or "emptiness." This *prajñā* is called "the mother of all truth/teaching" (Dharma "teaching").

Now *Abhidhamma* (Pali)/*Abhidharma* (Sanskrit) also has a "mother" of all Dharma(s), the *mātikā* (Pali, *mātṛkā* Sanskrit), which literally means both "mother" and "creator/constructor" (Gethin 1992). The *mātikā* in *Abhidharma* are the lists of *dharmas* found at the start of Abhidharma texts and that form the basis for all analyses of reality in Abhidharma. Thus *Abhidharma*, including the Pali *Abhidhamma* tradition, has an antecedent of the feminine *Prajñāpāramitā* of Mahayana. This notion of *mātikā* as mother, creating all *dharmas*, in the sense of the analytical components of reality, the truth taught by Buddhas, and the true qualities of Buddhahood was not the preserve of scholastic or philosophical texts. It was drawn on in myths and meditation practices directed at enlightenment in nonreform Theravada (Chapter 6). We noted the association of the *Abhidhamma* with the mother, in this case the Buddha's mother, in the story of its origins (Chapters 7 and 10).

A more visibly parallel embodiment of wisdom is Suntari Vāni (Sanskritic Vāṇī Sundarī transcription), who represents the *tipiṭaka* (the Pali Canon). She is worshipped in Thailand, though textual references go back to twelfth-century Sri Lanka (Collins 2011: 73–74). Practitioners say she appears in meditation in the tradition found at Wat Ratchasittharam, Thonburi. There she is depicted as a mature woman, white in color and dressed in royal garb (jewels, silks, crown, etc.), seated cross-legged on a white lotus, her right hand in the teaching gesture and her left in the meditation gesture holding a crystal sphere in front of her navel (Andrew Skilton fieldwork 2011).

Soteriological androgyny: Gender-exclusive and gender-inclusive symbols of Enlightenment

Parables from narrative sections of Mahayana literature sometimes use the motif of girls or women to illustrate the doctrines of emptiness. Such passages use the belief in women as impure and inferior to mock the fixation of male characters on phenomena (*dharma*) that do not really exist, such as masculinity and femininity. The person mocked is usually Śāriputra (Pali Sāriputta), who stands representative of Abhidharma (see Chapter 3). These parables are important to feminists because they authorize the possibilities of women being more spiritually advanced than men and of women becoming enlightened, and point out the irrelevance of gender to enlightenment. In discarding the relevance of female–male distinctions emptiness becomes a gender-excluding symbol. Such stories are reminiscent of the nun Somā's oft-quoted rebuttal of Māra, examined in Chapter 9, which also, though in a Theravada source, explicitly dismisses the relevance of the categories of female and male for Enlightenment.

While most material of this type is drawn from Mahayana literature, Sponberg refers to a Theravada canonical text, the *Aggañña Sutta*, in his analysis of male attitudes to the feminine in early Buddhist literature. He terms this category "**soteriological androgyny**" (Sponberg 1992: 24). The *Aggañña Sutta* describes the origin of human society as a gradual process of degeneration through different rebirths from pure ethereal beings to gross corporeal beings as a result of various acts of greed and selfish stupidity (see also Collins 2011: 32). Initially the beings are sexless, but at a certain point in the degeneration sexual differentiation becomes apparent. Sponberg uses this to argue that even early Buddhism recognized gender distinctions as constructed and not inherent. Thus Theravada also has a textual authority for the type of soteriological androgyny that excludes gender distinctions.

The *Aggañña Sutta* is not the only creation myth in Theravada literature, however. A completely different model is found in the *Paṭhamamūlamūlī*, "First Origins," a noncanonical Theravada text of particular importance in Southeast Asia (Peltier 1991). In this creation myth, the formation of the world is not attributed to a decline in the consciousness of beings, which arises after the creation of the earth with its elements and plant life (Peltier 1991: 198–199). Creatures are created by the first woman, who in turn arises from the earth element. She mixes her sweat (or in another version the sweat of the creator god Brahmā) with clay to create pairs of animals. Woman is primary in this creation myth, in that her existence is treated first and she has the desire to create, in part to contain the excess growth of plants. Man comes along second, spontaneously born of the fire element, sees the fun that animals have through sex and decides he would like to try it (Peltier 1991: 200–203). After this, while the woman is primary in creation, both parties consult and cooperate in the creation of subsequent generations of humans, making the three genders, male, female, and hermaphrodite (Peltier 1991: 204). They go on to create other aspects of the universe. This myth of gender-inclusive creation moves away from the earlier Iedic? understanding of progenation, which saw male semen or "seed," already containing all attributes, being planted in the woman's womb, the "field" that merely provided nourishment (Olivelle 1997: 432). This development in the understanding of procreation postdates the canonical layers of Theravada literature that, preceding this development in understanding, do not contain more inclusive myths. The understanding of male and female complementarity pervades much of Southeast Asian Theravada mythology, symbolism, and practice, such that different components of the human body are said to come from the mother or father respectively, with 12 female and 20 male components. The two levels of ordination into the Buddhist Sangha are said to represent first the mother's qualities (lower ordination), usually taken at the age of 12, and the father's qualities (higher ordination), should be taken at the age of 20. This symbolism is associated with the belief that the mother is the main recipient of merit when a boy receives the lower ordination in Tai, Lao, and Khmer forms of Theravada, and the father is the main recipient of the merit from his son receiving ordination as a *bhikkhu*. Understanding these equations – the female and male attributes that make up creation, the human body including one's own, and aspects of reality from an *Abhidhamma* perspective – are core aspects of the traditional, *borān kammaṭṭhāna* meditation practices (see Chapter 6), practices aimed at Enlightenment.

Postcanonical Theravada also offers models for gender-inclusive soteriological androgyny, which may provide parallels to those found in Vajrayana, the form of **tantra** that developed within Mahayana, which have been so important for feminist Buddhists. However, Vajrayana uses sexual union to symbolize the realization of soteriological androgyny through the spiritual union of complementary male and female aspects. Theravada does not. In the nonreform Theravada meditation tradition that has been likened to tantra, sex is still seen very much as belonging to the realm of Māra, the god of death and the realm of rebirth (Crosby *et al.* 2012: 196). Nevertheless, this same type of nonreform Theravada practice is also important in our next model drawn on in feminist Buddhist writings.

Embryonic Buddhas

Tathāgatagarbha, the Mahayana teaching that an embryonic Buddha lies within each of us, has been seen as productive for a feminist Buddhism in two ways. Firstly, the model of embryonic development is so clearly based on pregnancy, the preserve of women. From a text-historical perspective (an approach that treats texts as sources for uncovering history), the model is problematic: In Buddhist literature, the mother, particularly those parts of her that come into contact with the child during birth, is seen as impure and she is of essentially instrumental value, even once the mother's contribution to the make-up of the progeny has been recognized. The important person is the new baby.

The second and more important reason for the importance of Tathāgatagarbha for feminist Buddhism is because an embryonic Buddha lying within all means that Buddhahood is accessible to all, whether male or female. Particularly in the context of Vajrayana, which presents a method of ritual enactment of enlightenment enabling Buddhahood in a single lifetime, this confirms the possibility of Buddhahood from a female embodiment without the necessity of first going through male embodiment.

There is a type of nonreform meditation (*borān kammaṭṭhāna*, see Chapter 6) within Theravada that has practices reminiscent of Tathāgatagarbha and Vajrayana in that it employs ritual enactments to create a Buddha within and draws on the imagery of pregnancy (Crosby 2000: *passim*). The main practice is to internalize qualities and attributes of the path to Buddhahood "into the embryo" located below the naval by treating them as quasi-physical substances visualized as entering the nostril and being passed down inside the body. Practitioners thus create a Buddha inside their own body whom they may visualize / see seated there on the diamond throne of enlightenment. The process of internalization is based on traditional medical techniques for medicating the embryo while still in the womb. Thus Theravada has a parallel to the Tathāgatagarbha of Mahayana. Both men and women have practiced this system.

Implications for the representation of Theravada in broader Buddhist studies

The examples discussed here reveal that positive female and female-inclusive symbols are available in Theravada literature as well as in Mahayana and Vajrayana. They also indicate some of the rich diversity to be found in Theravada. This survey undermines the representation of Theravada as inherently more suppressive of women than Mahayana, a notion that starts and ends with the failure to maintain the full *bhikkhunī* lineage in Theravada. The findings here overturn Rita Gross' provocative suggestion that the attitude to women was *the* factor that led to a historic division into Theravada and Mahayana (Gross 1993: 57), a division questioned elsewhere in this book and on other grounds. Yet Gross' suggestion has been constructive in inspiring this hunt in Theravada literature for the kind of imagery and teachings that Buddhist feminists have drawn on from Mahayana and Vajrayana literature as symbols of empowerment. While the hunt is for symbols to apply prospectively, in the process it unveils some dimensions of Theravada that are missed when examining the material solely from a monastic or androcentric perspective.

Limitations and Revelations of Female and Female-Inclusive Symbols

While it is reassuring to find that Theravada can provide positive female and gender-inclusive or -excluding imagery, it is important to remember the limitations of a gynocentric study that seeks to extract empowering symbols for women from literature that, however diverse and however appreciative of women, remains essentially androcentric. This is an extension of the problem of using androcentric sources already noted in previous chapters (e.g., Chapter 10). The recognition of the female focuses on qualities visible where women's lives intersect with men's, where women are of crucial importance and relevance to men. The two virtues associated with woman that are emphasized in models of salvation are the concern for the well-being of others, in particular compassion, and the ability to procreate, to generate something new beyond (and potentially greater) than herself. These themes in the representation of women were already noted in the previous chapter and are used by some opposed to female renunciation to justify restricting women to such roles. The positive symbols noted here, be they feminine or gender-inclusive, are still based on these two aspects of motherhood: procreation and protective nurturing.

An appreciation of the androcentric concerns naturally reflected in the literature transmitted by monks enables us to re-evaluate the texts. For example, we can see the notorious textual passages that initially seem misogynistic as, to build on Sponberg (1992), the warnings of women's hypersexuality and cunning that form an ascetic rhetoric to affirm celibacy. Similarly, recognizing the androcentric concerns behind the development of more appreciative literature about women alerts our attention to the limitations of the spectrum and nature of female qualities represented. Thus this concentration on the compassionate qualities of the mother and the creative potential of reproduction is essentially an appreciation of what women do for society, particularly from the male perspective. Some aspects of this problem have been noted by Gross (1993) in relation to Indian and Tibetan Buddhism. She points out the limited value of such symbols for women who explicitly eschew such female roles or who fall short of these ideals. For the purposes of an existentialist interpretation of Buddhist texts, this begs the question of the validity of these religious symbols for guiding spiritual development and aspiration. Does seeing the virtues of motherhood and reproduction as absolutes require a certain alienation from women? It is generally recognized that childbirth and motherhood can be spiritual experiences and require a massive re-thinking of notions of self and other. This re-thinking informs the use of motherhood as a model for the *brahmavihāra* meditations discussed earlier. Yet even there the feelings of a mother are simplified, in that they are those "for her only son," and it is only once such sentiments can be extended equally to all beings that they become spiritual attributes (Ohnuma 2012: 16). Moreover, women may be more conscious of the limitations of the development they gain through these processes, a limitation that in some ways brings us back to the distinction between agent and instrument noted earlier (Chapter 9). Thus paradoxically these symbols may in practice be more useful for male aspiration than for a feminist reading of Theravada. Furthermore, by incorporating such symbolism as metaphors for soteriological ideals in a celibate, renouncer-oriented tradition, that tradition is appropriating motherhood and procreation from the realm of women, who represent *saṃsāra* and society in our androcentric literature. One might therefore argue that they thereby wrest power from the traditional domain of women and seek to contain it within the male realm.

Finally, a recurrent criticism of feminist readings of Vajrayana literature is that an appreciation of the feminine should not be taken as an historical valorization of women as human beings. Thus such appreciation should not be used to read a society liberated in feminist terms retrospectively back into the source society of the literary sources used. In fact, feminist writers tend to be conscious of the distinction between text-historical and existentialist exegesis. Those opposing such work might be accused of being too closed to any possibility of the historical valorization of women to see what such analyses can offer. One striking product of the search for positive female imagery in Theravada is that it actually reflects the valorization of women – although from androcentric perspectives – found in lived Theravada monasticism. While the appreciation of mothers and the esteem achieved through motherhood is a strong feature of all Theravada societies outside of the monastic context, women also have a strong presence at temples (Chapter 10). The temple is a permitted place for young women to socialize, even in Sri Lanka where ordination is lifelong and, unlike in Thailand, monks cannot be viewed as prospective marriage partners. Mothers of monks keep contact with their sons and make up a significant component of holy day temple attendance. Women often run elements of temple life, including monastic kitchens. These activities take place alongside an awareness of female businesswomen and professionals as important donors. Thus the literature drawn on in this study, particularly the literature that predates editorial systematization or has escaped the process of monastic-led reform, seems to reflect a truer picture of Theravada on the ground. This reveals that the characterization of Theravada has suffered by being based on too narrow a band of the textual tradition.

Summary

There are ways in which Theravada differs from Mahayana and Vajrayana in its representation of the feminine. Theravada came to regard femininity and masculinity as constituents of reality, *dhamma*, and saw men and women as tending to maintain the same gender over lifetimes. In Theravada, the pantheon did not extend to include female archetypal *bodhisattas*, whereas such *bodhisattvas* in Mahayana and Vajrayana are numerous, as seen in the examples of Tārā, Prajñāpāramitā, Vajrayoginī, etc. However, we can find models of gender-pairing, gender-inclusiveness, and complementarity in the Theravada discourse on Enlightenment. We also find feminine models for aspects of Enlightenment based on the imagery of motherhood and the symbolism of pregnancy. It had been assumed that such symbols had been largely lacking in Theravada because only a limited range of texts had been drawn on due to its equation with early Buddhism. By examining a wider range of Theravada literature, as well as looking at some familiar literature more closely, we can find female and gender-related imagery parallel to much of that drawn on in feminist writings based on other Buddhist traditions.

How valuable such models are for women is questionable since they draw on the essentialized positive qualities of women identified from an androcentric perspective. Moreover, the harnessing of the female power of progenation within the male monastic context can be seen as a wresting of power from women.

An unexpected outcome of pursuing an existentialist interpretation of the Theravada texts, however, is that the findings proximate better to the actual position of women on the ground in most monasteries, as mothers and caretakers of monks.

References

Collins, Steven. (2011). *Civilisation et femmes célibataires dans le bouddhisme en Asie du Sud et du Sud-Est: une 'Étude de genre'*. Paris: Éditions de Cerf.

Conze, Edward. (1956). *Buddhist Meditation*. London: Allen and Unwin.

Crosby, Kate. (2000). 'Tantric Theravada: A Bibliographic Essay on the Writings of François Bizot and Other Literature on the *Yogāvacara* Tradition', *Contemporary Buddhism* 1.2: 141–198.

Crosby, Kate. (2006). 'A Theravada Code of Conduct for Good Buddhists: The *Upāsakamanussavinaya*', *Journal of the American Oriental Society* 126.2: 177–187.

Crosby, Kate, Andrew, and Amal Gunasena. (2012). 'The Sutta on Understanding Death in the Transmission of *borān* Meditation from Siam to the Kandyan Court', *Journal of Indian Philosophy*, 40.2: 177–198.

English, Elizabeth. (2002). *Vajrayoginī. Her Visualizations, Rituals, and Forms*. Boston: Wisdom Publications.

Gethin, Rupert. (1992). 'The Mātikās: Memorization, Mindfulness and the List' in Janet Gyatso (ed.), *In the Mirror of Memory: Reflections on Mindfulness and Remembrance in Indian and Tibetan Buddhism*. Albany: State University of New York Press, 149–172.

Gombrich, R.F. (1998). *Kindness and Compassion as Means to Nirvana*. Amsterdam: Royal Netherlands Academy of Arts and Sciences.

Gross, Rita M. (1993). *Buddhism After Patriarchy: A Feminist History, Analysis, and Reconstruction of Buddhism*. Albany: State University of New York Press.

Maithrimurthi, Mudagamuwe. (1999). *Wohlwollen, Mitleid, Freude und Gleichmut: Eine ideengeschichtliche Untersuchung der vier apramaṇas in der buddhistischen Ethik und Spiritualität von den Anfängen bis hin zum frühen Yogācāra*. Stuttgart: Franz Steiner Verlag.

Masefield, Peter. (1980). *Elucidation of the Intrinsic Meaning: So Named the Commentary on the Peta-Stories*. London: The Pali Text Society.

Ohnuma, Reiko. (2012). *Ties that Bind: Maternal Imagery and Discourse in Indian Buddhism*. Oxford: Oxford University Press.

Olivelle, Patrick. (1997). 'Amṛtā: Women and Indian Technologies of Immortality', *Journal of Indian Philosophy* 25.5: 427–449.

Peltier, Anatole-Roger. (1991). *Paṭhamamūlamūlī: l'origine du monde selon les taditions du Lan Na*. Chiang Mai: Chanchirayuwat Ratchani.

Seeger, Martin. (2010). '"Against the Stream": The Thai Female Buddhist Saint Mae Chi Kaew Sianglam (1901–1991)', *South East Asia Research* 18.3: 555–595.

Skilling, Peter. (2001). 'Nuns, Laywomen, Donors, Goddesses: Female Roles in Early Indian Buddhism'. *Journal of the International Association of Buddhist Studies* 24.2: 241–274.

Skilton, Andrew. (1988). 'A Study of the Brahmavihara in early Buddhism'. BA dissertation, Bristol University.

Sponberg, Alan. (1992). 'Attitudes Toward Women and the Feminine in Early Buddhism' in J.K. Cabezon (ed.), *Buddhism, Sexuality and Gender*. Albany: State University of New York Press, 3–36.

Walters, Jonathan S. (1995). 'Gotami's Story' in Donald S. Lopez (ed.), *Buddhism in Practice*. Princeton: Princeton University Press, 113–138.

Further Reading

Readings Relevant to Theravada

Collins, Steven. (2011). *Civilisation et femme célibataires dans le bouddhisme en Asie du Sud et du Sud-Est: une 'Étude de genre.'* Paris: Éditions de Cerf.

Gethin, Rupert. (1992). 'The Mātikās: Memorization, Mindfulness and the List' in Janet Gyatso (ed.), *In the Mirror of Memory: Reflections on Mindfulness and Remembrance in Indian and Tibetan Buddhism*. Albany: State University of New York Press, 149–172.

McDaniel, Justin Thomas. (2008). *Gathering Leaves and Lifting Words: Histories of Buddhist Monastic Education in Laos and Thailand*. Seattle / London: University of Washington Press.

Ohnuma, Reiko. (2012). *Ties that Bind: Maternal Imagery and Discourse in Indian Buddhism*. Oxford: Oxford University Press.

Sponberg, Alan. (1992). 'Attitudes toward Women and the Feminine in Early Buddhism', in J.K. Cabezon (ed.), *Buddhism, Sexuality and Gender*. Albany: State University of New York Press, 3–36.

See also the various edited volumes that have been produced by Sakyadhita (see Chapter 9).

Texthistorical and Feminist Studies of Women and the Feminine in Mahayana and Vajrayana

English, Elizabeth. (2002). *Vajrayoginī. Her Visualizations, Rituals, and Forms*. Boston: Wisdom Publications.

Gross, Rita M. (1993). *Buddhism after Patriarchy: A Feminist History, Analysis, and Reconstruction of Buddhism*. Albany: State University of New York Press.

Klein, Anne C. (1995). 'The Great Bliss Queen' in Donald S. Lopez (ed.), *Buddhism in Practice*. Princeton: Princeton University Press, 139–150.

Paul, Diana Y. (1979). *Women in Buddhism: Images of the Feminine in Mahayana Tradition*, 1985 edition. Berkeley: University of California Press.

Shaw, Miranda. (1994). *Passionate Enlightenment. Women in Tantric Buddhism*. Princeton: Princeton University Press.

12

Nonharming, Politics, and Violence

Overview

Throughout Sri Lanka and Southeast Asia, Theravada Buddhism has become closely intertwined with independence, ethnic, state, and insurgency politics. This has led to the use of violence by states, majorities, and the marginalized. While this is in breach of the Pali Canon's teachings of nonviolence, texts from the fifth century onward have been drawn on in justifying violence "in defense of the Dhamma." Interpretations of what this means in terms of the doctrine of *kamma* vary because of the significance of the role of intentionality in forming *kammic* consequences. Monks find themselves in the position of needing to provide support and reassurance to soldiers. Buddhists, including monks, may see Buddhism as a tool of liberation and oppression or find themselves in entrenched positions in which their conception of Buddhism forms a crucial construct.

The use of Buddhism by the ruling elite appears to date from the earliest presence of Theravada in the region and draws authority from the narratives of the third-century BCE Emperor Asoka of northern India. Later, Buddhism was used as a tool by both colonial powers and independence movements. Dalits in India and Roma in Europe saw/see "re"-conversion to Buddhism as a way of improving group status and drew/draw on an emerging, newly self-aware global network of Buddhists. Buddhism functioned as a diplomatic tool in Asia and has been used to legitimize all the different forms of politics and economics that dominated the various Theravada countries since the end of World War II. The Sangha's attractiveness as a political tool has been enhanced by its position as an institution represented at all levels of society. The use of Buddhist missionizing in nation-building drew in part on its reputation as a rational, scientific religion, a rhetoric that was used as a weapon against dissent and also at times against established Sangha hierarchies. The specific manifestations of Theravada and the patterns of suppression have, since the 1960s, depended on the official and unofficial alignments of each country along the Cold War divide and their response to it ending. The use of Buddhism in forming state identity has contributed to tension between governments that reflect a majority franchise and both Buddhist and non-Buddhist ethnic minorities. The increase in the popular conception of Islam in terms of jihadism has led to the misconstrual

Theravada Buddhism: Continuity, Diversity, and Identity, First Edition. Kate Crosby.

of violence among southern Thailand's local Muslim majority in religious terms, in ways that prove to be self-fulfilling. The close association between government and Buddhism can stifle spiritual expression, and attempts at providing alternatives within the Buddhist fold can attract hostile responses from the establishment.

Buddhist Teachings on Nonviolence

Since the 1970s, the relationship between Buddhism and politics has been a major focus of the study of Theravada Buddhism, particularly by sociologists. The theme of violence in Buddhism then came to the fore after the widespread anti-Tamil violence by Sinhalese Buddhists in "Black July" in 1983. The violence shocked those who had regarded Sri Lanka as the exemplar among newly independent Asian nations and regarded Buddhism as a source of moderation in the region. Reflections on such violence at the hands of Buddhists were led by Buddhist studies scholars from Sri Lanka itself, including Gananath Obeyesekere, Stanley Tambiah, and Ananda Wikremeratne (Kent 2010: 160).

Outsiders, too, are surprised when they first come across violence, state violence, and wars conducted in Theravada countries by Buddhists and using Buddhism as a justification. There is a widespread understanding of Buddhism as a religion of peace. The very first precept for all Buddhists, monks, nuns, and lay people, is not to kill, "I undertake not to cause the death of living beings" (see Chapter 5). Mahinda Deegalle confirms that this expectation has ample justification in the Pali Canon, the most authoritative scriptures for Theravada Buddhism. In it the Buddha is presented teaching against violence and how to overcome violence at the level of the individual and that of society.

> On the whole, the Pāli Canon gives clear indications that physical violence cannot be accepted even as a means of solving human and social problems. … The *Dhammapada* verses 129–30 draws our attention to a common human situation and reaction in the face of all forms of violence:
>
> All tremble at violence
> All fear death…
> Life is dear to all
> Comparing oneself with others
> One should neither kill nor cause to kill.
> (Deegalle 2006: 4–5)

According to the commentary, this teaching is a response to a violent altercation between two groups of monks when one group tries to take over the monastery built by the other. Other causes of violence identified are that some people inflict violence out of pleasure (illustrated with reference to children torturing a snake); that people fight even with those to whom they are close when seeking to fulfill their own desires; and that when people's basic needs are not met and resources are unevenly distributed some people will be driven to crime (Deegalle 2006: 6–8). The immediate consequence of violence is that it escalates and everyone suffers. The *kammic* effect of violence is that those who commit it experience it themselves sooner or later as the *kammic* repercussions of their actions come to fruition. While Hindu military epic literature, such as the *Mahābhārata* (main compilation dates circa second-century BCE – second-century CE), extolled the death of warriors on the battlefield as a sure way to heaven, the Pali Canon could not. In accordance with Buddhist views on the effects of a violent death on the immediate afterlife (see Chapter 7), the Buddha in the *Yodhājīva Sutta* ("Teaching on the Livelihood of a Soldier"), initially remaining silent when questioned by a soldier on the topic, states, "those who die on the battlefield are inevitably overcome with hatred and pain and are born, according to those feelings, in a hell realm (*Saṃyutta Nikāya* XLII.3)" (Kent 2010: 157–158).

The *Mahāparinibbāna Sutta*, which describes the last three months of the Buddha's life, opens with a visit to the Buddha from Vassakāra ("Rain-Maker"), the minister of King Ajātasattu ("No-Born-Rival"). The King is in the process of building a new capital Pāṭaliputra, modern-day Patna, at a location close to the confluence of a number of rivers on the bank of the River Ganges and thus a highly strategic position for controlling trade. He is determined to annihilate the powerful confederacy of the Vajjī in the region, so jealous is he of their success. Vassakāra has come to consult the Buddha, as a wandering holy man, for a prediction on whether such a venture might prove a success or a disaster.

The Buddha does not reply directly but turns to his attendant, the monk Ānanda, and reflects with him on the qualities that give the Vajjī their strength: they regularly meet together as one, performing their duties collectively, they maintain ancient customs and laws and do not introduce new ones, they respect and listen to the elders of the community, they do not abduct or force women to live with them, they maintain their shrines, and they provide support and protection for holy men. He identifies these as the qualities that give them their strength. The commentator Buddhaghosa, writing in the fifth-century CE, points out how these qualities are beneficial. For example, the Vajjī can focus their energies on any trouble that arises by avoiding disputes among themselves; people who might otherwise cause trouble are content because they are given the opportunity to establish their innocence in the system of law and because new taxes are not imposed. The Buddha uses these qualities as a model and goes on to suggest parallel sets of seven factors that will be conducive to the future and ongoing prosperity of the Sangha, the community of monks and nuns. In other words, he takes the conduct of the Vajjī as a positive example. However, the Minister Vassakāra, on hearing about these qualities, forms a different construction. He realizes, "While the Vajjīs possess even one of these factors, the King cannot overpower them, not in battle. He must first use diplomatic overtures and undermine their alliance" (abridged translation Crosby). Pleased with the tip, he departs and we know from history that eventually the King does succeed in destroying the Vajjī. Buddhaghosa, writing centuries later and knowing the eventual outcome of the Buddha's advice to Vassakāra, reacts as we might in the light of the Buddha's teachings on nonviolence: How could the Buddha reveal the information that would cause the Vajjī's downfall? Buddhaghosa justifies it by saying that the Buddha, realizing their downfall was inevitable, was buying them time to make merit (see Chapter 5). Yet the story highlights a problem: the same analysis may be used to different ends, to emulate or destroy. In the hearts of the two interlocutors, bringing them to the same analysis, lie radically opposing motivations, to empower, on the one hand, and to overpower, on the other hand. At their extreme they are the empathetic and the psychopathic. The Buddha is endowed with the highest compassion. The King is already a patricide, having brutally murdered the father who had saved his life.

The history of Theravada Buddhist association with violence often reveals different underlying motivations that come together to form an alliance. Even in the turn to violence – of rhetoric or deed – the motivation to defend and preserve the peace, to maintain the presence of the Dhamma, forms an alliance with motivations of self-interest and control of others. The rhetoric that has encouraged much violence, in calling people to defend the Dhamma or bring justice to the disadvantaged, has therefore often proven irresistible to a broad spectrum of people, regardless of whether it is in the mouth of one experiencing genuine concern or one seeking a means to enhance their own power, a distinction not necessarily recognizable even to the speaker. This affects not only Buddhist laypeople but members of the Sangha as well. We find that the same young men motivated to join the Sangha are those motivated to valiant (which may become violent) action and vice versa. Some of those who joined the Khmer Rouge voluntarily out of idealism and ended up killing, even committing murder, have since become exemplary Buddhist monks. Is this to make up for their sins or because the same idealistic empathy led them to both courses of action? In the 1980s in Sri Lanka, it was rural younger men, sometimes monks and former monks, frustrated with poverty and what they felt to be the government's capitulation to India and the non-Buddhist Tamils, who participated in the violent Marxist uprising and murders of the 1980s, leading in turn to high numbers of extrajudicial killings by the government with an overall death toll of about 50 000–60 000 (www.unhcr.org LKA99001.ZAR, retrieved April 14, 2013), mainly young men, including monks (personal conversations with witnesses 1989, 1992–1993). In 2004, nine monks representing the J.H.U. (National Sinhalese Heritage) Party, motivated to protect Buddhism in the country, won seats in Sri Lankan elections, standing in the face of widespread criticism that they, as monks who had renounced household life, should stay out of politics (Deegalle 2004). In 2007 in Burma, it was young monks who began the nonviolent protests, called the Saffron Revolution, on behalf of a populace in desperation at hiked fuel prices. At the end of 2012, monks came to the defense of local concerns about the environmental impact of Chinese copper mining, the Burmese government apologizing for their heavy-handed treatment but at the same time arresting leading monks (www.bbc.co.uk/news/world-asia-20650576, December 8, 2012, retrieved December 11, 2012). It is unclear to what extent the rhetoric that monks should stay out of politics is in fact a modern one, promulgated by the French and British colonial powers. A British attempt to disenfranchise monks (a topic still of debate in the main Theravada countries) was defeated in the House of Commons in the 1940s due to strong opposition from Labour backbenchers (Ian Harris, personal communication, April 13, 2013).

Conflicting motivations can be detected in the evidence behind the "Buddhism" of the first "Buddhist" emperor, Asoka. The edicts he had inscribed on rocks and stone pillars around his territory give an extraordinary contemporary testimony to how he wished to be seen. Most famously he describes his remorse at the killing of 100 000 people and displacement of 150 000 others occasioned by his invasion of the region of India that is now called Orissa; his desire now to win a victory through the Dhamma rather than victory through violence; and his decision to become a Buddhist lay devotee. He describes making a pilgrimage to the site of the Buddha's Enlightenment (Norman 1997/2006: 149–150). Theravada sources give a different account, attributing his conversion to the extraordinary resilience under torture and the teaching of a novice monk. It is only on the subject of his attempts to resolve a schism in the Sangha that the evidence of the inscriptions tallies closely with the Theravada account of his involvement with Buddhism (Norman 1997/2006: 160). K.R. Norman points out that his use of the term *dhamma* appears to refer to rather general religious duties rather than specifically Buddhist doctrine (Norman 1997/2006: 151–152). A.L. Basham has compared some of the inscriptions of Asoka with passages in the *Arthasāstra*, a treatise on the exercise of political power attributed to the chief minister of Asoka's grandfather Candragupta, and likened to Machiavelli's *The Prince* in its psychology of power games. A.L. Basham suggests, for example, that Asoka's claims in "Rock Edict I" that the gods now attend him because of his religious works is a direct enactment of the *Arthasāstra* advice to pay actors to dress up as deities and accompany one in procession (Basham 1982: 133–134). Basham's point is that the religious claims made in Asoka's edicts must be read primarily with politics rather than spirituality in mind.

While there is no explicit statement in his inscriptions of the extravagant religious acts ascribed to Asoka in Theravada texts, such as his dividing up the Buddha's relics and redistributing them under 84 000 newly constructed *stūpa*, or having his son and daughter ordained, recent archaeological discoveries confirm early ritual sites in line with Buddhist religiosity beneath, that is, predating, the Asokan period remains (see Chapter 1). This appears to confirm that Asoka renovated earlier Buddhist sites. Moreover, regardless of whether or not his son and daughter were indeed the first monk and nun to visit Sri Lanka, it is from the period of Asoka that we first have historical evidence of Buddhism in India and during which Buddhism began to spread under the hegemony of Asoka's empire centered in Magadha. This was the region of India where Buddhism began and was now at the heart of the land and maritime trade routes collectively known as "The Silk Route." While Buddhism is likely to have spread piecemeal and at the level of ordinary people, perhaps migrant traders and settlers, Buddhist texts routinely describe its spread as a matter of dramatic royal conversion. Moreover, it is when rulers formed a relationship with Theravada Buddhism that historical and epigraphic sources begin to refer to it in ways that allow us to document its development clearly. In spite of Pali inscriptions dating back to the fifth-century CE in Burma, it is the use of Buddhism by kings in legitimizing their authority, expanding their territories, and, later, nation-building that structures our current histories of Theravada in the region. For Burma, this begins in the eleventh- or twelfth-century Pagan period, in Thailand with King Ramkhamhaeng in the newly independent Sukhotai Kingdom in the thirteenth century and the kingdom of Ayutthaya in the fourteenth century, and in Cambodia under King Jayavarman Parameśvara, also in the fourteenth century. A history based on inscriptions and archaeological evidence presents a much more complex picture, which is often difficult to assess, but looks set to overturn the current broad-brush stroke, court-centered historiography. Theravada / Pali Buddhism was clearly established locally in all these areas before its high-profile promotion by the courts in question. Meanwhile, inscriptions in the Pyu and Mon kingdoms from the fifth century onward, territories that were later to be absorbed into Pagan, indicate a strong presence of Pali Buddhism in the west of what is now Burma from this earlier date, although not as far back as the third-century missions described in chronicles (see later text) (Assavavirulhakarn 2010, Aung-Thwin 2005, Brown 1996, Kyaw in preparation). Inscriptions and monastic structures in the Dvāravatī Kingdom that was at its height in the seventh- to ninth-century CE in central Thailand indicate that Pali Buddhism was also one of several forms of religion present there (Skilling 2003). At present the extent of the influence of Mon, Pyu, and Dvāravatī Buddhism on the later Theravada in the region remains a matter of conjecture, however, absent as they are in the chronicle writing that emerged within monastic traditions that derived from Sri Lanka and dominate current historiography. Even in Sri Lanka, where donative inscriptions in cave dwellings for monks confirm the third-century BCE date provided by the Pali chronicles, they indicate that patronage was from different levels of society, including but not primarily from kings (Coningham 1995). It may be that some of the complexity of the archaeological evidence will be mirrored also in chronicle literature as a broader range of such material comes under scholarly scrutiny. A rather narrow repertoire of such literature has been extensively relied on since the colonial period, effectively silencing the diverse voices of the past in favor of specific monastic traditions and court dynasties. As Michael Charney has written of Burma, "This select sampling of chronicles that made the transition to print thus granted undue authority to particular chronicles, which in turn helped make the focus of historiography extremely circumspect" (Charney 2006: 7).

Territorial Authority

The Buddhist chronicle literature on which the modern historiography of Theravada has been based mainly comes from the Mahāvihāra monastic lineage in Sri Lanka from the early period and then, for the medieval period, from Sri Lankan–derived monastic lineages in mainland Southeast Asia. Such writing sought to make connections between local landscapes and the Indian mainland, particularly to centers and sources of power that would legitimize those in whose service it was composed, be that particular dynasties or monastic lineages, or the relationship between them. It did so through reference to visits of the Buddha, the presence of his relics and connections with the Emperor Asoka. Sri Lanka claims a connection through Asoka's children, the monk Mahinda and the nun Saṅghamittā. Various territories of Southeast Asia claim the visits of the missionaries Soṇa and Uttara under Asoka's auspices. Theravada's claim to orthodoxy and continuity with early Buddhism rests in large part on its account of the Third Council, at which false monks were defrocked and false views refuted with the assistance of Asoka's personal intervention. At this point the *Kathāvatthu*, the text that encapsulated Theravada orthodoxy in explicit opposition to the "heresies" of other Buddhist groups, was added to the Pali Canon. It was after this, according to Theravada chronicles, that Theravada was taken to Sri Lanka and mainland Southeast Asia, fulfilling predictions attributed to the Buddha during visits the chronicles describe him making to those regions during his lifetime.

In the literature that relates these connections between India and the future regions of Theravada, the nature of the Buddha and of the Sangha's relationship with royalty differs significantly from those described in canonical literature. In the *Māhāparinibbāna Sutta*, cited earlier, the visit of the minister to the Buddha is in keeping with a longstanding, and ongoing, tradition of people seeking blessings and insightful truths from renouncers who have left society. The minister has to walk the last stretch of the journey, leaving behind the carriages of his entourage, because of the remoteness of the Buddha's residence. The Buddha's reflections pertain to the running of his Sangha. In stark contrast, in the chronicles, particularly the *Mahāvaṃsa* and works derived from it, the Buddha has become an aggressive source of territorial power: he rousts the native *yakkha* from the island of Sri Lanka, terrorizing them into submission and evicting them so that the island can become the preserve of the Dhamma (see Chapter 1). At the Third Council, the Emperor Asoka is personally involved in the minutiae of doctrinal disputes. The commentary on the *Vinaya Piṭaka* reports on the decision to defrock half the monks in the Sangha:

> It was not difficult for the King who had already learnt the Dhamma to realise that they were not monks but heretics who belonged to other persuasions. The King gave them white garments [the garments of lay devotees in contrast to the saffron robes of monks] and expelled all of them, numbering 60 000 in all, from the community of monks. … Thereupon King Asoka told Venerable Moggaliputta Tissa Thera, "Venerable Sir, the Dispensation is now pure, let the fraternity of monks perform the *Uposatha*." (Karunadasa 2010: 283)

The *uposatha*, the fortnightly holy day on which the ceremony of reciting the *vinaya* rules and confession of faults should take place, had been postponed for six years because of the problem of "heretics" in the Sangha, and it was this which had necessitated the emperor's involvement. When Asoka's son Mahinda arrives in Sri Lanka, his first and enduring contact is the King, his entourage and then harem, a closeness of interaction that commentaries composed at the same time as the *Mahāvaṃsa* also retrospectively attributed to the Buddha and the kings of his day.

These claims to royal connections may have been in part to set protocol for Sangha-lay interactions by telling stories in which the highest authority for lay behavior, the king, plays a leading role. The texts claim authority for the Mahāvihāra monastery at Anuradhapura in Sri Lanka at which they were composed. The Mahāvihāra came to dominate Theravada monastic lineages from the twelfth century onward and thus its history became to some extent the history of much of Theravada. Regardless of the myth-building nature of such texts, the relationship they claim between Sangha and King / State went on to have far-reaching consequences in authorizing the intervention of the king or state in Sangha affairs and military and state violence in the name of protecting the Dhamma.

Perhaps the most cited textual authority for state violence is the account in the *Mahāvaṃsa* and texts based on it of the war led by King Duṭṭhagāminī of Sri Lanka, who, bearing a Buddha relic on his spear, defeated King Eḷāra from South India. The texts couched this engagement in terms of a religious war to protect Sri Lanka as the island of the Buddha's teaching. At the end of the war, when Duṭṭhagāminī expresses remorse for the massive loss of life, eight enlightened monks come to reassure him:

> From this deed arises no hindrance in thy way to heaven. Only one and a half human beings have been slain here by thee, O lord of men. The one had come unto the (three) refuges, the other had taken on himself the five precepts. Unbelievers and men of evil life were the rest, not more to be esteemed than beasts. But as for thee, thou will bring glory to the doctrine of the Buddha in manifold ways; therefore cast away care from thy heart, O ruler of men! (*Mahāvaṃsa* XXV, 109–111. Geiger 1912: 178)

While many doubts have been cast on the modern, nationalistic interpretation of Duṭṭhagāminī's war with the South Indian king Eḷāra as having been fought along ethnic lines, the *Mahāvaṃsa* came to be taken as a key source for Sri Lankan history. Despite the different ethnic and religious groups of Sri Lanka having cooperated in the independence movement to remove the British, following independence in 1948 rifts emerged as, in search of mandate, successive democratic governments increasingly pandered to the Sinhala majority's perceptions of longstanding economic disadvantage under the British. Two key stages in this process were the disenfranchising in 1949 of Tamil plantation workers brought in by the British from the nineteenth century onward to work the tea crops and the introduction in 1956 of the Official Language Act, which imposed Sinhala as the national language in place of the colonially inherited but ethnically more neutral English. As tensions and violence escalated into civil war (1983–2009), with the call for a separatist Tamil state in the north, the story of the Buddha's conquest of the island, that of Duṭṭhagāminī's war, and the passage absolving him from guilt for killing non-Buddhists were repeatedly used to authorize state violence. Among those who most vehemently opposed peace negotiations were senior Buddhist monks who held rituals for the success of the army and protection of soldiers. At the outset, senior monks, including the scholar **Walpola Rahula**, were often at the forefront of those advocating violent military intervention to a reluctant government (Abeyesekara 2002: 210–215). The importance of defending the country as the island of the Dhamma continued to be used to justify mass killings and human rights abuses even up to the point when the Sri Lankan army was essentially victorious (http://srilanka.channel4.com/).

The apotropaic practices found in Buddhism from *paritta* to amulets, yantra, and tattoos (see Chapter 5) are commonly drawn on in warfare. Thai soldiers fighting for the United States in the war in Vietnam wore Buddhist amulets. Cambodian soldiers would insert small pieces of lead that had been inscribed with potent yantras under their skin to deflect bullets. Monks ministering to the Shan State Army provide yantra cloths for the soldiers to wear under their headgear (Crosby and Khur-Yearn interviews 2009). In Sri Lanka, two important annual Buddhist ceremonies for the Sri Lankan army are held on 11 October, the anniversary of the army's founding, and on the first Sunday of October, when the flags of all the regiments in the army are blessed at the Bodhi tree in Anurādhapura, the descendant of the tree brought by Asoka's daughter, the nun Saṅghamittā, to the island in the mid-third-century BCE (Kent 2010: 158–159).

One interpretation of the reassurance given by the eight enlightened monks to Duṭṭhagāminī in the *Mahāvaṃsa* has been that, in the circumstances, what else does/can one say? The reality is that wars take place in Buddhist countries and are fought by Buddhists. Soldiers have little choice but to participate, which leaves them and the monks ministering to them with practical issues to consider: how to reduce the psychological damage to the soldiers, how to ensure that soldiers maintain a balanced mind and therefore are less at risk of killing innocent bystanders or making other costly mistakes. One monk explained to Daniel Kent, who has conducted research on this question in Sri Lanka, "When we preach to soldiers, we have to decide whether we should preach in a way that would decrease their belief, self-confidence, and pride in themselves or in a way that would increase their self-confidence" (Kent 2010: 167). In fact, some monks who minister to Buddhist soldiers in Sri Lanka confirm that killing is a negative, unwholesome act (*akusala kamma*), but others emphasize the importance of the intention. "*Cetanā* [intention] is the thing at the root. Soldiers don't take guns with the intention of killing. More than killing, they take them with the principal intention of saving the country, the race, the religion. ... Our goal is just to face the enemy with the goal of protecting our own lives and the lives of others. Our soldiers don't kill with anger" (Kent 2010: 164–165). Kent reports, "Of fifty-eight soldiers interviewed at the Sixth Sri Lankan Light Infantry camp in Mihintale, thirty-three believed that negative karma did not occur when they fired their weapons at the enemy, while twenty-five believed that it did occur. While each of these soldiers agreed that intention determines the karmic effects of particular actions, they disagreed on whether it was possible to fire weapons with a positive intention" (Kent 2010: 165).

The idea that a good intention behind killing and violence removes the presence of the unwholesome mental states (which are bad *kamma*, see Chapter 7) from the act of violence is far from universally accepted in Theravada even amidst those who deem violence necessary. This can be seen in the traditional Theravada understanding that righteous kings, who undertake violence in order to preserve law and order, are *bodhisatta* (*bodhisattva*, Sanskrit), because they take on the bad *kamma* of their role for the benefit of the many. Theravada regards the *bodhisatta* vow as a rare undertaking, whereas in Mahayana traditions it is emphasized as the ultimate goal for all Buddhists. Nevertheless, we find the concept of the *bodhisatta* in Theravada in specific contexts beyond accounts of the 28 Buddhas and the future Buddha (see Chapter 1). It occurs in discussions of kingship and particularly compassionate monks. It is also a relatively common wish in the colophons of manuscripts, where scribes dedicate the merit of copying the text to their aim of saving all beings in *saṃsāra* and reaching full

Buddhahood (rather than the goal of an *arhat*) (Crosby 2004: 841). The idea that kingship inevitably entails bad *kamma* goes back as far as the *Jātaka* narratives (Zimmermann 2002, on *Jātaka* see Chapter 4). In the *Temiya Jātaka*, the Buddha-to-be (*bodhisatta*), born as the sole heir to throne, pretends to be a deaf-mute in order to avoid being crowned king and taking on the resulting bad *kamma*.

Nineteenth to Early Twentieth Century

The Western study of Buddhism began to form as an academic subject within the context of European colonialism and the beginnings of American engagement in international affairs. The desire to understand Buddhist texts, and especially the Pali Canon, stemmed not only from interest and admiration but also from a will to claim authority over what Buddhism is. Part of the rhetoric of early Western scholarship is that the Buddhism of "the natives" is a corruption of the rational religion to be found in the texts. It was not only scholars from protestant countries that prioritized the classical texts over the vernacular and local (Hallisey 1995). In Indochina, the French promotion of Pali studies was part of a policy to form an alliance with a new, young group of monks, a reform wing within the Mahānikāya monastic lineage. They shared an interest in wresting power from the monastic establishment whose traditional meditation, and related healing and apotropaic practices, passed on through esoteric teacher–pupil lineages, was a feared source of power. These practices could be undermined by pointing out that they had no authority in the Pali Canon. This also allowed the French and Khmer scholars in this alliance to steal ground from the reformist Thammayutika Nikāya. This lineage had been transplanted to Cambodia from Thailand when the former became a protectorate of the latter, shortly before falling into French control. The Thammayutika Nikāya had been established in 1833 by the then monk Prince Mongkut, future King Rāma IV of Thailand. Similarly seeking to set up his own power base for political reasons, while circumventing the existing Sangha hierarchy, Mongkut used the rhetoric of reform through correct practice of *vinaya* (monastic discipline) and reference to the Pali Canon to justify his new monastic lineage. The extent to which this reform had an impact on the way in which Buddhism was taught at local monasteries in regional Thailand varied. In some it seems to have been minimal (McDaniel 2008: 113), while in others it created crises affecting even whether non-Thai-speaking monks received alms and that required negotiated resolutions (Crosby and Khur-Yearn fieldwork Maehongson District 2009, briefly noted 2010: 15).

Reform of Buddhism in relation to the *vinaya* and the Pali Canon was nothing new: such reforms were a part of the history of Theravada and lay behind the repeated councils (see Chapter 4). Ensuring the correct maintenance of the Dhamma has been an iterative concern at crucial junctures since the demise of the Buddha in order to prevent the Dhamma's decline and the apocalypse it would usher in. Long before the impact of Protestant Christianity it had been a standard element of regime change to switch allegiance from one monastic network to another, even persecuting or dismantling the monastic group associated with the predecessor, while justifying the switch with reference to purity of practice and textual authority (Crosby 2004: 64). The incursions of European powers from the sixteenth century onward brought fresh anxiety along these lines, while suiting the political ambitions of interested "reformers." The eighteenth-century attempts by the King of Kandy and the Sinhalese aristocracy to secure a new ordination lineage from Arakan (in modern Burma) and Siam (in modern Thailand), culminating in the establishment of the Siyam Nikāya in 1753, served multiple political purposes aside of religious revival and reform. They reflected inter-monastic rivalry, particularly between the Asgiri and Malvatu temples in Kandy (Blackburn 2001: 44). They allowed the kings of Kandy to disrupt the hold of the Dutch and British on the coastal areas by calling on native workers, including the all-important cinnamon-peelers, to attend to Buddhist practice. The importation of Siamese monks concealed an attempt to assassinate King Kīrti Śrī and replace him with a Thai prince smuggled in as a monk, a plot which once uncovered saw the monk Saraṇaṃkara, the leading light of the reform, placed in jail (Suraweera 1968). When the sack of Ayutthaya, the capital of Siam, disrupted the ongoing liaisons between the two Buddhist regions, Sri Lankan monks renewed their search for links with countries that retained a Buddhist king. This search intensified after the British took control of the entire island in 1815, after their failure to continue traditional royal sponsorship of Buddhism and their brutal suppression of the 1817 uprising. Enterprising scholar monks such as Waskaḍuwē Subhūti Thera acted as sources for the newly emerging Western scholars of Pali such as Childers, author of the first substantial Pali-English dictionary, and Fausbøll, editor of the multivolume edition of the *Jātakas*, for which project Subhūti provided manuscripts. At the same time, Subhūti was forging connections with the royal houses of Cambodia and Thailand (Burma having already fallen to the British) (Guruge 1984; personal communication Waskaḍuwē Mahindavaṃsa Thera 2005).

The convergence of religious and political motivation and the use of the rhetoric of reform as a strategy in claims of authority were centuries-old practices in the history of Theravada: a new aspect that shaped modern Theravada, particularly at the political center, was the encounter with Western technology and post-European Enlightenment notions of rational thought. Since the Sangha, which provided education and literacy, had always included members of the intelligentsia and technological innovators, leading Buddhist reformers of the day looked to the new technologies of the West and actively took on board Western ideas of early Buddhism as a rational philosophy. This entailed also adopting an understanding of religion and science as essentially separate, a relatively new development even in the West. They searched for a convergence between the new sciences and Buddhist teachings and used logical argument to convince outsiders and the local people of the superiority of Buddhist thought. Mongkut engaged in debates with American missionaries, using the rhetoric of "superstitious practices" despite continuing away from the Western gaze traditional practices such as animal sacrifice and worshipping local gods for protection (Choompolpaisal 2011: 154–203). Ledi Sayadaw eloquently attacked as irrational the beliefs in God held by Christians, Hindus, and Muslims, the main religious rivals under the British annexation of Burma (Ledi Sayadaw 1919/1954: 118–188, discussed in Pranke 2010). Perhaps the single most important victory of Buddhist reformers in this period was the Buddhist defeat of the Christians in the Pānadura debate in Southwest Sri Lanka in 1862. Reported widely in Western media its inspiration was felt internationally. In response the theosophist Colonel Olcott visited Sri Lanka and formed an alliance with the future Anāgārika Dharmapāla (1864–1933), the most influential reform Buddhist at the height of the colonial period there. In collaboration with Sir Edwin Arnold, author of the world-famous poem based on the life of the Buddha, *The Light of Asia* (1879), Anāgārika Dharmapāla led the establishment of the Mahabodhi Society that undertook to reclaim for Buddhism the site and temple at Bodh Gaya, the place of the Buddha's enlightenment in northern India, and thus organized cooperation between leading Buddhists of several countries.

Buddhism became a source of pride and a rallying point for independence movements and emerging nation-states. The reforms commenced by Mongkut in Thailand continued and, particularly under Chulalongkorn (1868–1910), became the rhetoric under which the court at Bangkok constructed a nation-state in the face of the encroaching French and British colonial powers. Promoting over the Mahānikāya the Thammayutika Nikāya, with its allegiance to the crown, and centralizing monastic education and advancement, Chulalongkorn used the Sangha's institutional presence at every level of society as a means of forging a hierarchical network that looked to Bangkok for its authority (Tiyavanich 1997: 8–9). So while, on the one hand, there was greater high-level interaction between countries in the name of Buddhism, on the other hand, there was a move toward the hardening of the borders between nations through which much Buddhist education and cross-fertilization traditionally took place.

Politics Following the Second World War

The ways in which the relationship between Buddhism and politics unfolded in the second half of the twentieth century, while influenced by various reform movements and the association of Buddhism with independence movements in the nineteenth and early twentieth centuries, also followed the contours along which Asia was shaped during the aftermath of the Second World War and the emergence of the Cold War.

In the run-up to the Second World War and in the period immediately after independence, Buddhism, as a shared source of pride among Asian nations, was a diplomatic tool in the region. Theravada monks established working relations with their counterparts in China, Japan, and Sikkim (Bocking *et al.* 2013), where interest in Theravada was in part fuelled by the understanding of "Theravada as early Buddhism": this was a view on which Western scholarship at the time and the burgeoning, often nationalistic, Theravada reform consciousness converged, and which would re-emerge as a basis of contact between East Asian and Theravada nations from the 1990s onward. With the archaeological "rediscovery" of Buddhism in India in the early nineteenth century, the establishment of Pali and Buddhist studies at prestigious universities such as those in Calcutta and Pune, and the success of the Mahābodhi Society, India, highly productive networks flourished with a new geographical awareness. One outcome of these developments was the founding in 1950 in Sri Lanka of the World Fellowship of Buddhists, which continues to this day. The Sixth Council held in Burma 1954–1956 formed a focal point for cooperation between the newly defined Theravada nations.

Following visits to Sri Lanka and then Burma, in 1956 the Indian lawyer and political leader Bimal Rao Ambedkar, inspired by previous converts in south India (Ober 2013), led 500 000 fellow "untouchables," now referred to as ***daḷits***, "the oppressed," to convert to Buddhism, which he represented as being the religion of their ancestors. He chose Buddhism as a native religion in line with his nationalism, but also as an egalitarian religion that, in his view, validated his rejection of Hindu caste divisions. This event would go on to influence other convert groups, such as the Roma of Hungary following the end of the Cold War, who have explicitly described themselves as the "*daḷits*" of Europe who are rediscovering their lost Buddhist heritage (CERF-Institute.org, August 20, 2012, retrieved March 20, 2013).

International missionizing increased, whether through the spread of meditation traditions or the sending of missionaries (***dhammadhūta***), with monasteries around the world sponsored by Burma, Sri Lanka, and Thai governments. One country to which Theravada spread was Nepal, initially among the **Newars** of the Kathmandu Valley, a process that began in the first half of the twentieth century. To some extent it has displaced their unique, ritual-focused form of Vajrayana Buddhism, already threatened by the new aspirations of a secular society (LeVine and Gellner 2005: 35). Burma and Thailand in the 1960s both developed internal missionizing programs seeking to bring non-Buddhists into the national Buddhist fold (Swearer 1999: 214). While it is still an ongoing process in both countries, in Thailand internal missionary activity in the northeastern region was in part promoted and financed as part of an anti-communist agenda as the Thai royal family and military government aligned the country with the West, and the nation emerged as the region's most important ally of the United States during the Vietnamese war.

In the newly formed Indonesian nation in 1945, following the end of the Japanese occupation, citizenship was defined in the constitution in terms of ***pañcasīla*** "five principles," of which the first was the belief in one god. (The term *pañcasīla* is the same as the term for the five precepts of a lay Buddhist, but the phrase in fact came through old Javanese, a language highly influenced by Sanskrit terminology.) While this was originally envisaged as a way of bringing together the vast and diverse nation, under Suharto it became mandatory, part of a defense against Communism that followed the brutal suppression of the Indonesian Communist party in the 1960s. This placed Indonesia to the West of the deepening Cold War fault line. While Buddhism has sometimes been defined as an atheism, because of its lack of creator god, in response to this move it was redefined as a monotheism by segments of the population newly defining themselves as Buddhists. Some converts to Buddhism were building on interests in theosophy and Japanese philosophy that had developed under the Dutch and Japanese. The vast majority of converts were among the ethnic Chinese who traditionally followed a mixture of Buddhism, Confucianism, and Taoism. Theravada monastic lineages have been established from Thailand and Sri Lanka in response to this development as part of the missionizing agenda of both countries.

The Cold War fault line has highlighted the extent to which Buddhist textual authorities can be used to legitimize a variety of types of governance and political philosophy: from socialism (Burma, Sri Lanka, and more recently, nominally, Cambodia) to monarchy (Thailand and the reestablishment of the monarchy in Cambodia); capitalism (Thailand), Marxism (especially Laos and Cambodia), and military rule (most of mainland Southeast Asia at different points). Mikael Gravers (2012) has demonstrated how Buddhism is used to authorize radically different positions in modern Burma, with very different interpretations of what it means to defend Buddhism coexisting among the three factions of generals, opposition, and young monks.

The Marxist revolution in Laos in the mid-1970s saw the recruitment of the Sangha as an instrument of the state and the sending of monks to re-education camps, and even reports of the execution of monks suspected of being anti-communist (Stuart-Fox 1999: 164–165). High-ranking monks are still party officials. In Cambodia, the dismantling of Buddhism was even more severe during the Khmer Rouge period and is now more fully documented. A majority of monks were executed or died of starvation and all were forced to disrobe (Harris 1999: 66). The re-establishment of the Sangha under the Vietnamese in 1989 was tightly controlled in the early years. Although officially there is freedom of religion in Cambodia and ordination is open to all men, membership of the Sangha is largely assumed to mean support of the ruling Cambodian People's Party, an association institutionalized through the party membership of high-ranking monks and the participation of politicians in the establishment of new temples.

Prior to the suppression or installation of Marxism on the part of governments falling to the West or East of the Cold War fault line, respectively, significant numbers of the educated elite and the rural poor throughout the region, including in India, had been attracted to Marxism as a political counterpart in accord with Buddhism or as an alternative to it. The most recent Marxist uprising was the violently suppressed JVP uprising at the end of the 1980s in Sri Lanka. It had been initially inspired by the USSR sponsorship of Sri Lankans to study at its universities, regarded as one of a number of responses to the rumored use by the US navy of Sri Lanka's deep harbor at Trincomalee for shipping and submarines (personal conversations with Sri Lankan villagers/former students in USSR late 1980s, early 1990s. On Trincomalee, see Anderson and Wijeyesekere 2011).

While the United States' political involvement in the region continues, along with US and Russian oil, commodities and other commercial interests, competition between the emerging superpowers of India and China, especially over the Indian Ocean and the Bay of Bengal, may set the scene for the coming decades (Anderson and Wjeyesekere 2011). Major human rights violations, such as the displacement of both Burmans and ethnic minorities from their villages, have been perpetrated in the course of laying pipelines between the Bay of Bengal and China (personal communication Arakanese journalists). There have been repeated reports of Burmese army activity in Shan State including the burning Shan villages and Shan Buddhist monasteries, including their libraries (personal communication Shan villagers and journalists). The dispossession and relocation of people within cities such as Mandalay for political and commercial reasons within the context of the economic role of China has been documented for over two decades now. "In Mandalay, wealthy Chinese investors, ethnic Chinese Kokang and Was drug warlords and military officials have made wholesale acquisition of real estate and homes, forcing residents to relocate" (Philp and Mercer 2002: 1597, citing Mya Maung 1994). An aspect of the relationship between Buddhism and politics in this region that has yet to be documented or explored (as far as I am aware) is the role of Khun Sa (1934–2007), leader of the Shan United Army that dominated the Shan State from the 1970s to the mid-1990s. He funded his activities through the production in the "Golden Triangle" of the high-quality opium that came to dominate the US East Coast illegal drugs market during this period, placing him high on the Drug Enforcement Administration's most wanted "warlords" list. The Burmese government's recent relaxation (2011–2012), coming so soon after the brutal suppression of the 2007 Saffron Revolution, signaled by talks with Aung San Suu Kyi, prisoner releases, parliamentary elections, and high-level diplomatic visits from the West, has been interpreted as a bid to break China's monopoly over the Burmese economy. Previously, sanctions imposed on Burma and the junta by the European Union and the United States, relaxed in July 2012 (http://www.bbc.co.uk/news/world-asia, July 12, 2012), had severely hindered economic growth and channeled the West's unofficial access to Burma's rich resources of commodities such as hardwood through neighboring Thailand.

Muslim Majorities and Minorities

Among the minorities that have suffered from the association of Buddhism with national identity in the lands where Theravada is the majority religion are a number of Muslim ethnic groups. Examining these cases can give an indication of how cultural and economic tensions can be constructed primarily in religious terms with the global essentializing of such categories as Buddhist and Islam. The border provinces in the south of Thailand are 80% Muslim, with a distinctive culture and a claim to have been a historically separate sultanate: it was annexed by Thailand in 1909 during Bangkok's creation of a nation-state to compete with British and French colonial expansion. Resistance to the Thai state's assimilation policy has led to violence by both local militants and the state itself since the 1940s. Between the 1960s and 1980s, this escalated into guerrilla warfare against the Thai state that was then reigned in by the Thai government of the 1980s putting in place special administrative and security arrangements, granting amnesty to former militants, and coopting the elite of the Muslim community. The situation deteriorated again in the 1990s, and violence escalated radically from 2001 when the prime minister, Thaksin Shinawatra (prime minister 2001–2006), did away with the arrangements that had been set up in the 1980s. Thousands have died, and the Thai state's authority was irrevocably undermined by two atrocities in 2004, when more than 100 men were killed during the siege of the historic Kru-Ze mosque and 75 unarmed protestors died in police custody. Thanks to the current global context, and with a vacuum in leadership resulting from Thaksin's attempts to blame the violence on the previously coopted Muslim elite from the region, the militancy increased, now with jihadist rhetoric, despite the conflict essentially being based, as Duncan McCargo describes, in issues of cultural not religious identity. Extrajudicial killings on both "sides" of the local population, including of Muslim religious leaders and Buddhist monks, continue and the escalation is such that attempts to reinvoke former policies that had to some extent worked are now insufficient; attempts at the assimilation of young men of the region through military indoctrination have backfired (McCargo 2008: 2–7). Meanwhile, the use of ***wats*** (monasteries) as military training grounds makes blatantly visible the identification of the national government with Buddhism. Michael Jerryson observes, "The stationing of soldiers and police ... transforms the *wat* into a military space. In doing so, it exacerbates the relations between Buddhists and Muslims in the southernmost provinces. One acute example of militant activities at *wat* [monasteries] is the armed forces' use of torture in places such as at Wat Suan Tham in Narathiwat, or Wat Lak Muang and Wat Chang Hai in Pattani. Wat Chang Hai's Batallion 24 Army has received the most complains for detaining and torturing suspected militants" (Jerryson 2011: 139–140). McCargo sums up the bleak outlook for peace in the area given the association of Buddhism with national identity and a majority mandate as follows: "Because Malay Muslims constituted only around a fortieth of Thailand's population, they were structurally doomed to impotence within the country's Buddhist-dominated political order. Bangkok sought to use representative politics to relegate Malay Muslims to permanent marginality within the Thai state, while lionizing the virtuous tokenism of individual leaders ... Yet these strategies of co-optation were fraught with danger, since the coopted elites gradually become alienated from the ordinary people of the region" (McCargo 2008: 183). Violence in the region continues despite the Thai government's declaration in August 2012 of its willingness to engage in peace talks (www.reuters.com, August 16, 2012; www.bangkokpost.com/multimedia/interactive/324868/violence-in-the-south, retrieved December 8, 2012).

Also in the summer of 2012, it was reported by the Aljazeera news channel that 80 000 people had been displaced in further human rights abuses against Burma's Arakanese Rohingya Muslim minority. The complicity of the Burmese military in ethnic violence is documented as far back as the 1940s (stream.aljazeera.com, August 1, 2012). Between 2008 and 2011, there were reports of deaths through dehydration of Rohingyas who had tried to flee to Thailand by boat but were forced back out to sea by the Thai military (www.bbc.co.uk Asia news, February 14, 2011). Their only viable refuge has been the Chittagong region of Bangladesh. While Rohingya have fled there since the 1940s and about 200 000 are currently in refugee camps on the border, Bangladesh declined to allow Rohingyas fleeing the fighting to cross the border during the most recent violence. The tensions behind this go back to the large movements of people under British colonial rule in the nineteenth and early twentieth-centuries, including a million Muslims, Hindus, and Sikhs from India, including Bengal, particularly in Rangoon (previously and now Yangon). Some arrived to work in the Indian Civil Service; larger numbers worked in banking, or as traders and as laborers more widely in Burma (Schober 2011: 43). The resentment was in part fuelled by demographic changes and economic competition, in part by seeing Muslims as instruments of British colonial power, as in the anticolonial riots of 1932 and 1938 in which Buddhists, reportedly including monks, committed assault, arson, and murder (Schober 2011: 106). A major contributory factor to the resentment was the Depression of the 1930s, resulting in the coolie riots and the creation of a newly landless peasantry. As the price of rice had fallen, many Burmese peasants lost their land that had been mortgaged to the Indian *chettyar* (Houtman 1990: 44). These tensions were revived after the suspension of the political guarantees of the modern state by the military *junta* following its brutal suppression of the popular uprising of 1988 (Schober 2011: 78). The ruling elite's rhetoric of authority deriving from reference to the founding father of the nation, Aung San, was disrupted by the arrival of Aung San Suu Kyi (see Chapter 10) after which they increasingly moved toward instituting Buddhism as a state religion and banner for national identity, turning to the large-scale sponsorship of Buddhist ritual and restoration, while at the same time implementing extensive control of and espionage on Buddhist monks (Houtman 1999; Schober 2011: 78; personal communication). The use of Buddhism as an emblem of national identity has included internal missionizing (see earlier text) and reports of forced conversion among tribal minorities, including of Muslims in Arakan (Schober 2011: 91). Anti-Muslim riots took place in 1997 in response to rumors about damage to the Mahamuni image (see Chapter 2) and violence has flared intermittently since even extending to homicide (e.g., March–April 2013). Meanwhile, in Bangladesh, human rights abuses against the Buddhist minorities in the Chittagong Hill Tracts (CHT), which have included the burning of villages by the army, have registered on human rights reports on Bangladesh since the country's formation. Already in the 1960s 100 000 Chakma Buddhists were forced to relocate without any resettlement assistance on account of the creation of the Kaptai Dam. Then, after the 1971 civil war in which CHT Buddhists had, in a bid to preserve their traditional land rights, sided with West Pakistan, the government deprived them of those rights. The resettlement, because of Bangladesh's overpopulation, of lowlander Muslims in the formerly protected highland Buddhist areas is an aggravating factor (Crosby and Nagasena fieldwork CHT 2009). More recently such violence against Buddhists has been justified as "reprisal attacks" for the violence in Burma.

Whither Spirituality?

Once the Sangha becomes an instrument of state, through what avenues can those who are spiritually motivated find expression? While there have always been multiple reasons for ordination, and support during schooling and higher education remain the key reason for staying a monk longer term, it is nevertheless out of such recruits that experienced, compassionately motivated monks with leadership skills develop. Interviews with monks in Laos revealed that the secularization of Sangha education – which initially took place in order to reverse the privilege accorded those studying in the French system – and the lack of meditation lineages, has left a dearth of motivated monks (Crosby interviews 2009). Only a tiny minority of young adult monks interviewed were considering staying in the monkhood longer term. They had by chance been exposed to spiritual experiences, through the Dhamma teaching of a senior monk or from learning meditation, experiences that would traditionally have been more common. In Burma and Thailand, charismatic monks who draw a following, perhaps because they present a more dynamic religious alternative than the mainstream court/state-sponsored Sangha, risk being perceived as a threat and may be persecuted. They may then become further politicized by this process.

Personal rivalry between monks and monasteries feeds into the ways in which monks and monasteries may become politically aligned. Monastic rivalry also provides potent political fuel that can have significant impact on the unfolding of historical events, but is often missed in Western studies because of a confusion between the ideals of enlightenment and the realities of human institutions when it comes to Buddhism. The assumption that most monks are unworldly is a problematic premise for research. Phibul Choompolpaisal has demonstrated this issue in exploring the case of the high-ranking Thai monk Phimonlatham, defrocked and imprisoned on the accusation of being a Communist in 1962. The accusation resulted from the jealousy and intrigue of other high-ranking monks who perceived him as a rival, yet this more human aspect of the case is eclipsed in narratives of the event compiled in terms of Cold War politics (Choompolpaisal 2011: Chapter 8, 287–336). In Burma, court cases against monks for "teaching against the canon" or for the use of "magical displays" (i.e., breaking the fourth *pārājika* rule (see Chapter 8)) increased from the 1980s (Houtman 1990: 52).

The close relationship between the monarchy and the Sangha in Thailand continues to this day. Donald Swearer observes, "Since the 1970s in Thailand many Buddhist groups have emerged on the periphery of the mainstream to challenge the development policies of the central government and the increasingly secular, materialist ethos of Thai society" (Swearer 1999: 218.) Among these is the Buddhist layman Sulak Sivaraksa (b. 1933), who is well known in the West. He has founded a number of NGOs addressing poverty, human rights, social justice, and ecology. In response to his outspoken criticisms, he was arrested on the charge of *lèse-majesté* in 1984 and imprisoned for four months. The use of the stringent *lèse-majesté* law to arrest perceived political opponents in Thailand increased significantly after the 2006 coup. Sulak Sivaraksa is representative of "Engaged Buddhism," a term coined by the Vietnamese monk Thich Nhat Hanh in a letter to Martin Luther King in 1963 to explain the self-immolation of Thich Quang Duc. "Engaged/Socially Engaged Buddhism" advocates intervention in, rather than withdrawal from, the world in order to address the social and political causes of suffering within the present lifetime. As such it is contrasted with both the other-worldliness and the ritualism of what is seen as "traditional Buddhism," although the extent to which it is entirely a new phenomenon is debated, and in spite of the fact that Engaged Buddhists also tend to emphasize personal transformation.

Two of the movements that emerged in the 1970s likewise seeking to circumvent the centralized control of Buddhism but with two different forms of traditionalism were Santi Asoke and the Dhammakaya Movement. Both have been much studied by Western scholars. Both movements offer a form of religion that takes spiritual development seriously and offers a controlled structure for its adherents that eschews the loose astrological and apotropaic religion of many Thai temples. They also both advocate strict *vinaya* adherence on the part of their monks and clean-living among lay followers – in a region where drugs, including permitted stimulants among the economically active, are a major problem. They are also both headed by charismatic leaders. In economic approach they are diametrically opposed. Santi Asoke is anti-consumerist. In contrast, the Dhammakāya Movement, with as its headquarters the extensive Wat Phra Dhammakāya complex in Pathumthani one hour's drive from Bangkok, has developed a global network based on large donations from followers, its expansion in part attributed to the marketing skills of its founders (Swearer 1999: 215). Both movements have been seen as a threat by the establishment, and the heads of both have been arrested and taken to court on a number of charges. One of the interesting aspects of such cases is the attempt to prove that the head of the movement in each case has broken one of the *pārājika* rules (see Chapter 8), which would allow the authorities to defrock them on a permanent basis. In the 1980s, the monk Photirak (Bodhiraksa), head of Santi Asoke, was successfully accused of breaking the fourth *pārājikā* by making false claims to spiritual attainments. He has since created his own order of monastics, unrecognized as monks by the state. The abbot of Wat Phra Dhammakāya was arrested on multiple charges, including unorthodox teachings and embezzlement. The latter would place the abbot in breach of the second *pārājika*. The extent to which the financial crisis of the late 1990s and other more personal or political factors played a role in this development remains unclear. The movement was in a stronger position than Santi Asoke because of its economic strength and political connections, and the charges were dropped in 2006. Duncan McCargo reports on the subsequent developments for both groups:

> Despite earlier attempts to close them down, both Santi Asoke and Wat Dhammakāya are now thriving – albeit in very different ways. Santi Asoke has remained more on the margins, and has recently aligned itself with mass protest movements against controversial former prime minister Thaksin Shinawatra, a billionaire telecommunications magnate, under the auspices of the self-proclaimed People's Alliance for Democracy (PAD). ... By contrast, Thaksin developed close links with Dhammakāya during the later years of his premiership (2001–2006), even holding a major party rally there in 2006. ... Dhammakāya has adopted a strategy of mainstreaming itself, in order to secure a safe and privileged space in the Thai Buddhist hierarchy. (McCargo 2008: 256)

It has been suggested that the rise of interest in *weikza* practices in Burma from the nineteenth century onward is another type of response to the over-centralizing control of the center, and the focus on the authorized Buddhism of the court/state as a rational science (Pranke 2012, Schober forthcoming). The constantly contested tension that arises between the control manifesting as authorizing discourse at the center and alternative expressions of freedom from the central control at the peripheries leads to a complex dance in which the center detects and seeks to harness the perceived power of such peripheral activities/actors and those at the periphery repeatedly seek the safety of central approval.

Summary

Our earliest evidence indicates that Buddhism, while advocating renunciation from society, maintained involvement with and in it. The tradition formalizes the relationship through narratives of interactions of the Buddha and other significant monastic figures with kings, authorizing also the king's intervention in the Sangha. Indeed, it is in part because of its ability to adapt around and be useful to the powerful that we have evidence for Buddhism and its history at dating back over two millennia. The history of Theravada currently available to us from before the modern period is in the main the history of the politically powerful, as Theravada came to be adopted and advocated as the religion at court. The conception of Theravada as a single unit across time and geography, as an identity marker of communities and nations as a whole, is a relatively recent construction that developed in the nineteenth century. Nonetheless, it takes the seminal moment of this relationship between "Theravada" and power to the intervention by Emperor Asoka in the Sangha in the third century BCE, the subsequent third council that ensured the purity of doctrine from the Theravada perspective and the arrival of "Theravada" in Southeast Asia and Sri Lanka of Asoka's missionaries, including his son and daughter, the founding monk and nun of the Sri Lankan Sangha. The extent to which monks and nuns were expected to stay out of politics historically is unclear. Statements of this kind are most often voiced by those who do not wish to see a particular expression of politics on the part of monks, that is, such rhetoric is itself an attempt at political control.

Rivalry and politics at the local level is also an important feature of Buddhism that has been overlooked in scholarship, which has tended to collude with the rhetoric of Buddhism as "other-worldly," or regarded it as politicized only at the national level. In the modern adoption of Buddhism as a signifier of national and/or ethnic identity, past legends have been reinterpreted in support of vested political interests. The variety of teachings and topics contained within Theravada canonical and commentarial literature allows the justification of a range of contrasting political and economic positions, policies, and actions. Theravada was drawn on by independence movements, and the builders of the identities of the modern nation states of mainland Southeast Asia and Sri Lanka. It has been a feature of the rhetoric within civil wars and internal political oppression, as well as the avenue through which people have sought personal and communal freedom. As Theravada has become a religion of communities, it has developed various interpretations of ethical action, including how to understand and deal with violent action, including the killing of fellow humans.

References

Abeyesekara, Ananda. (2001). 'The Saffron Army, Violence, Terror(ism): Buddhism, Identity and Difference in Sri Lanka', *Numen* 48.1: 1–46.

Anderson, David A. and Aton Wijeyesekera. (2011). 'U.S. Naval Basing in Sri Lanka?', *Small Wars Journal*. October 15, 2011. smallwarsjournal.com/jrnl/art/us-naval-basing-in-sri-lanka (retrieved June 20, 2013).

Assavavirulhakarn, Prapod. (2010). *The Ascendancy of Theravada Buddhism in Southeast Asia*. Chiang Mai: Silkworm Books.

Aung-Thwin, Michael. (2005). *The Mists of Rāmañña: The Legend that was Lower Burma*. Honolulu: University of Hawai'i Press.

Basham, A. (1982). 'Asoka and Buddhism: A reexamination', *Journal of the International Association for Buddhist Studies* 5.1: 131–143.

Blackburn, Anne M. (2001). *Buddhist Learning and Textual Practice in Eighteenth-Century Lankan Monastic Culture*. Princeton: Princeton University Press.

Bocking, Brian, Phibul Choompolpaisal, Laurence Cox, and Alicia Turner (eds.). (2013). Pioneer Western Buddhists and Asian Networks 1860–1960. *Contemporary Buddhism*. 14.1. Special Issue.

Brown, Robert. (1996). *The Dvāravatī Wheels of the Law and the Indianization of South East Asia*. Leiden: Brill.

Charney, Michael W. (2006). *Powerful Learning. Buddhist Literati and the Throne in Burma's Last Dynasty, 1752–1885*. Ann Arbor: Centers for South and Southeast Asian Studies, The University of Michigan.

Choompolpaisal, Phibul. (2011). 'Reassessing Modern Thai Political Buddhism: A Critical Study of Sociological Literature from Weber to Keyes'. PhD thesis, School of Oriental and African Studies, University of London.

Coningham, Robin A.E. (1995). 'Monks, Caves and Kings: A Reassessment of the Nature of Early Buddhism in Sri Lanka', *World Archaeology* 27.2: 222–242.

Crosby, Kate. (2004). 'Persecutions', in Robert E. Buswell, Jr. (ed.), *Encyclopedia of Buddhism*. New York: Macmillan Reference USA, 640–647.

Crosby, Kate and Jotika Khur-Yearn. (2010). 'Poetic *Dhamma* and the *zare*: Traditional Styles of Teaching Theravada Amongst the Shan of Northern Thailand', *Contemporary Buddhism* 11.1: 1–26.

Deegalle, Mahinda. (2004). 'Politics of the Jathika Hela Urumaya Monks: Buddhism and Ethnicity in Contemporary Sri Lanka', *Contemporary Buddhism* 5.2: 83–103.

Deegalle, Mahinda (ed.). (2006). *Buddhism, Conflict and Violence in Modern Sri Lanka*. London/ New York: Routledge.

Geiger, Wilhelm. (1912). *The Mahāvaṃsa or the Great Chronicle of Ceylon*. Colombo: The Ceylon Government Information Department.

Gravers, Mikael. (2012). 'Monks, Morality and Military. The Struggle for Moral Power in Burma–and Buddhism's Uneasy Relation with Lay Power', *Contemporary Buddhism* 13.1: 1–33.

Guruge, W. Ananda. (1984). *From the Living Fountains of Buddhism*. Colombo: The Ministry of Cultural Affairs.

Hallisey, Charles. (1995). 'Roads Taken and Not Taken in the Study of Theravāda Buddhism' in, D.S. Lopez (ed.), *Curators of the Buddha: The Study of Buddhism Under Colonialism*. Chicago: University of Chicago Press, 31–62.

Harris, Ian. (1999). 'Buddhism in Extremis. The Case of Cambodia' in Ian Harris (ed.), *Buddhism and Politics in 20th century Asia*. London: Cassell, 54–78.

Houtman, Gustaaf. (1990). 'Traditions of Buddhist Practice in Burma'. PhD thesis, School of Oriental and African Studies, London.

Houtman, Gustaaf. (1999). *Mental Culture in Burmese Crisis Politics. Aung San Suu Kyi and the National League for Democracy*. Tokyo: Institute for the Study of Languages and Cultures of Asia and Africa.

Jerryson, Michael. (2011). *Buddhist Fury: Religion and Violence in Southern Thailand*. New York: Oxford University Press.

Karunadasa, Y. (2010). *The Theravāda Abhidhamma. Its Inquiry into the Nature of Conditioned Reality*. Hong Kong: Centre of Buddhist Studies, The University of Hong Kong.

Kent, Daniel W. (2010). 'Onward Buddhist Soldiers: Preaching to the Sri Lankan Army' in Michael K. Jerryson and Mark Juergensmeyer (eds.), *Buddhist Warfare*. Oxford: Oxford University Press, 157–177.

Ledi Sayadaw, Mahathera. (1919 [reprint 1954]). *Sāsanavisodhanī*, vol. 1. Yangon: Hanthawadi-pitakat Pon-hniek Taik.

LeVine, Sarah and David N. Gellner. (2005). *Rebuilding Buddhism. The Buddhist Movement in Twentieth-Century Nepal*. Cambridge/London: Harvard University Press.

McCargo, Duncan. (2008). 'Review of Rory Mackenzie, New Buddhist Movements in Thailand: Towards an Understanding of Wat Phra Dhammakāya and Santi Asoke', *Buddhist Studies Review* 25.1: 254–256.

McDaniel, Justin Thomas. (2008). *Gathering Leaves and Lifting Words: Histories of Buddhist Monastic Education in Laos and Thailand.* Seattle / London: University of Washington Press.

Mya Maung. (1994). 'On the Road to Mandalay: A Case Study of the Sinonization of Upper Burma', *Asian Survey* 39: 265–286.

Norman, K.R. (1997 [2006]). *A Philological Approach to Buddhism*, 2nd edn. Lancaster: The Pali Text Society.

Ober, Douglas. (2013). '"Like embers hidden in ashes, or jewels encrusted in stone": Rāhul Sāṅkṛtyāyan, Dharmānand Kosambī and Buddhist activity in colonial India' in Brian Bocking, Phibul Choompolpaisal, Laurence Cox, and Alicia Turner. (eds.), *Pioneer Western Buddhists and Asian Networks 1860–1960*. Contemporary Buddhism Special Issue.

Pranke, Patrick Arthur. (2010). 'Against God: Ledi Sayadaw's Critique of Monotheism'. Paper delivered in Civilization and the rhetoric of 'the field' Panel II: Theravada and other religions in SE Asia at the Theravada Civilisations Meeting, Chicago.

Pranke, Patrick Arthur. (forthcoming). 'On Saints and Wizards: Ideals of Human Perfection and Power in Contemporary Burmese Buddhism' in Guillaume Rozenberg, Bénédicte Brac de la Perrière, and Alicia Turner, (eds.). *Champions of Buddhism. Weikza Cults in Contemporary Burma.*

Philp, Janette and David Mercer. (2002). 'Politicalised Pagodas and Veiled Resistance: Contested Urban Space in Burma', *Urban Studies* 39.9: 1587–1610.

Schober, Juliane. (2011). *Modern Buddhist Conjunctures in Myanmar. Cultural Narratives, Colonial Legacies, and Civil Society.* Honolulu. University of Hawai'i Press.

Schober, Juliane. (forthcoming). 'The Longevity of *Weikza* and Their Practices' in Rozenberg et al.

Skilling, Peter. (2003). 'Dvāravatī: Recent Revelations and Research' in *Dedications to Her Royal Highness Princess Galyani Vadhana Krom Luang Naradhiwas Rajanagarindra on her 80th birthday.* Bangkok: The Siam Society, 87–112.

Stuart-Fox, Martin. (1999). 'Laos: From Buddhist Kingdom to Marxist State' in Ian Harris (ed.), *Buddhism and Politics in 20th century Asia*, London: Cassell, 153–172.

Suraweera, A.V. (1968). 'The Imprisonment of Sangharāja Saranaṃkara', *Vidyodaya Journal of Arts, Sciences and Letters* I: 53–57.

Swearer, Donald K. (1999). 'Center and Periphery: Buddhism and Politics in Modern Thailand' in Ian Harris (ed.), *Buddhism and Politics in 20th century Asia*. London: Cassell, 194–228.

Tiyavanich, Kamala. (1997). *Forest Recollections: Wandering Monks in Twentieth-Century Thailand.* Honolulu: University of Hawai'i Press.

Zimmermann, Michael. (2002). 'Only a Fool Becomes a King: Buddhist Stances on Punishment' in Michael Zimmermann (ed.), *Buddhism and Violence*. Lumbini: Lumbini International Research Centre, 213–242.

Further Reading and Watching

Films

Contextual

Lemkin, Rob and Teth Sambath. (2009). *Enemies of the People*. ReesHarper. www.enemiesofthepeople.com (retrieved June 25, 2013).

Sri Lanka's Killing Fields First broadcast June 14, 2011. http://srilanka.channel4.com/ (retrieved June 25, 2013).

Sri Lanka's Killing Fields. War Crimes Unpunished. First broadcast March 14, 2012. http://srilanka.channel4.com/ (retrieved June 25, 2013).

More Specifically About Sangha Involvement in Protest
Østergaard, Anders. (2008). *Burma VJ*. Magic Hour Films.

Reading

Abeyesekere, Ananda. (2004). *Colors of the Robe. Religion, Identity and Difference*. Columbia: University of South Carolina Press.

Deegalle, Mahinda. (ed.) (2006). *Buddhism, Conflict and Violence in Modern Sri Lanka*. London/New York: Routledge.

Harris, Ian. (ed.) (1999). *Buddhism and Politics in 20th century Asia*. London: Cassell.

Harris, Ian. (ed.) (2007). *Buddhism, Power and Political Order*. London/New York: Routledge.

Jerryson, Michael. (2011). *Buddhist Fury: Religion and Violence in Southern Thailand*. New York: Oxford University Press.

Jerryson, Michael K. and Mark Juergensmeyer. (eds.) (2010). *Buddhist Warfare*. Oxford: Oxford University Press.

Philp, Janette and David Mercer. (2002). 'Politicalised Pagodas and Veiled Resistance: Contested Urban Space in Burma', *Urban Studies* 39.9: 1587–1610.

Schober, Juliane. (2011). *Modern Buddhist Conjunctures in Myanmar. Cultural Narratives, Colonial Legacies, and Civil Society*. Honolulu. University of Hawai'i Press.

Stuart-Fox, Martin. (1996). *Buddhist Kingdom, Marxist State: The Making of Modern Laos*. Bangkok: White Lotus.

Wyatt, David K. (1969). *The Politics of Reform in Thailand: Education in the Reign of King Chulalongkorn*. New Haven/London: Yale University Press.

Glossary

Abhidhamma The analysis of metaphysics and causality that characterizes Theravada philosophy and informs meditation practice. See *Abhidhamma Piṭaka*.

Abhidhamma Piṭaka The third section of the Pali Canon, which details the wisdom realized by the Buddha with analysis of reality into constituents called *dhamma*, and their synthesis through causal connections.

ācariya "Teacher."

achar The lay functionaries of temples in Cambodia, who perform some religious services.

ajan "Teacher" from Pali *ācariya*. Frequently occurs in Thai and Lao titles for monks.

akusala "Unwholesome/unskillful." An attribute of mental positive mental states that are based in greed, hatred, and/or delusion.

alms-round The traditional means by which monks and nuns receive food by laypeople offering food into the alms bowl, one of the "requisites" a monk receives at his ordination.

amulet An object that bestows some form of protection of power when worn about the person. The power comes from the substances from which it is made and the empowerments it has received, including Buddhist chanting.

Ambedkarite Buddhism The Buddhism of the "*dalits*" (q.v.) who converted to Buddhism in the 1950s following the Indian lawyer B.R. Ambedkar.

anattā "Absence of self." The doctrine that the individual has no enduring soul or self.

androgynous (a) Having neither male nor female attributes; (b) having both male and female attributes.

anicca "Impermanent." The doctrine that all phenomena are impermanent.

animism The belief that animate and inanimate objects may be inhabited by some kind of living spirit.

apadāna A story about an important character in early Buddhism explaining the events in previous lifetimes that enabled them to perform the important role or reach the achievement of the "current" or final lifetime.

apotheosis The transformation of a religious figure into a god.

arhat variant spellings *arhant, arahant*. An enlightened being who has gained enlightenment in response to the Buddha's teaching. Such a person (male or female) is no longer subject to rebirth.

Theravada Buddhism: Continuity, Diversity, and Identity, First Edition. Kate Crosby.

asceticism The practice of austerities for religious purposes. Examples of ascetic practices include denying oneself normal amounts of food or certain types of food, denying oneself shelter, clothing and other comforts, not lying down to sleep, etc.

ascetic misogyny A hatred or fear of women generated on the part of those seeking to abstain from sexual and other intimate relations either by way projecting their own responses to women onto them to blame them or in order to protect themselves from their own weaknesses by emphasizing their need to avoid women in this way. It can extend beyond the sexual aspects of women to other areas that threaten male independence.

Asoka Mid-third-century BCE emperor of north India associated with the patronage of Buddhism.

Asokan inscription A text engraved on pillars or in caves in the mid-third-century BCE conveying messages from the Emperor Asoka to his subjects.

bhikkhu (monk) Usually applied to those who have received the higher ordination, *upasampadā*.

bhikkhunī Nun who has received the higher ordination.

Bodhi "Awakening." The state of liberation or enlightenment achieved by a Buddha.

bo tree The sacred fig under which the Buddha gained enlightenment, or one of its descendants, particularly associated with the sacred landscape of Sri Lankan Buddhism and branches of Buddhism elsewhere influenced by Sri Lanka.

bodhisatta Buddha-to-be, a future Buddha; the Buddha-to-be as described in the *jātaka* stories of his previous lives.

borān kammaṭṭhāna "Traditional meditation." One of the traditions of meditation practiced in Theravada, also referred to as *yogāvacara*. One modern form of this is called *vijjā dhammakāya*.

brahmin A member of the highest, priestly class in Hinduism, although early Buddhist texts such as the *Dhammapada* also use it to refer to a holy person generally.

brahmanical An adjective for the type of Hinduism dominated by Vedic rituals and the ritual expertise and textual knowledge of brahmin priests.

canon A body of authoritative texts: (1) The Pali Canon *q.v.* (2) The practical canon, those texts treated as authoritative and used for teaching and/or ritual in a given community or monastery (following Blackburn 1999).

cedi/ceti/cetiya A sacred monument that is an object of worship, usually a *stūpa, q.v.*

chronicle A text providing the history of a particular relic, image, place, monastic lineage, etc., in Pali or a vernacular language, usually making a connection between the topic in question and the Buddha and the visits to the local region ascribed to him.

commentary A text written to provide "explanation of the meaning" (*aṭṭhakathā*) and expand on a canonical text. The "commentarial period" refers to the phase beginning in the fifth-century CE with the commentaries compiled by Buddhaghosa and other written under the auspices of the Mahāvihāra. Commentary writing has continued into the modern era.

daḷits The "oppressed." A term used by ex-untouchable communities in India, many of which embraced Ambedkarite Buddhism.

dhamma (a) The truth or teaching that the Buddha realized and taught. (b) An analyzable constituent of reality according to *Abhidhamma*.

dhammadhūta "Messengers of the Teaching": missionaries; the term occurs in Asokan inscriptions. In the modern period, it usually refers to those monks sponsored by the governments of Burma, Sri Lanka, and Thailand to missionize internally or abroad.

Thammayutika Nikāya. A division of the Thai Sangha created by Prince Mongkut in nineteenth-century Thailand.

dhātu "Element" or "essence." (a) The four material elements, earth, wind, fire, water. (b) Bases of consciousness. (c) The "relics" of the Buddha in the form of (i) the physical remains from his cremation or hairs that he gave away when alive; (ii) things he used; or (iii) symbols that represent him.

dhūtaṅga The permitted ascetic practices within Buddhism, 13 of which are listed in the *Visuddhimagga*. See *thudong*.

docetism The belief that a religious figure is/was not in fact a real person present in the world, but an emanation of a divine being

dukkha "Suffering/insecurity." The doctrine that all phenomena are insecure so a cause of suffering, whether because they are unpleasant in themselves or because, though pleasant, they will cease. It is one of the three characteristics of existence and existents according to Buddhism. The other two are *anattā* and *anicca, q.v.*

engaged Buddhism A phrase coined by the monk Thich Nhat Hanh to describe the kind of Buddhism that developed in the second half of the twentieth century in which Buddhists, including monks, prioritize current issues affecting this life, including poverty, human rights, social issues, and the environment.

essentialism/essentialize The reduction of a category to attributes that are seen as essential and necessary, to the exclusion of other attributes. In relation to Buddhism, this overlaps with reform Buddhism. The essentials identified as crucial tend to be knowledge of canonical texts, text-based meditation, and a strong division between monastic and lay roles, to the exclusion of varieties in meditation practice, a broader pantheon, ancestral rites, worship, supernatural powers, etc. In relation to women, the focus tends to be on their function as sexual objects, nurturers, and carers.

existentialist interpretation An analysis or interpretation of sources with a view as to what they say about how we should and could live now.

forest monk (a) A monk who is in an ordination lineage that has the label of "forest tradition"; (b) a monk who has left behind the normal duties of the majority of monks ("village" monks) in order to pursue spiritual practices in the seclusion of the forest, or one who has spent a considerable number of years doing this.

gati "Destiny/place to which one goes." Place of rebirth, categories into five types: human, animal, hungry ghost, hell-being, and god.

Gotama The family name of the historical Buddha and so used to distinguish between him and other Buddhas or as his name before his enlightenment.

hell One of the many hells into which one may be reborn as a result of bad *kamma*. There are eight major hells in Theravada cosmology.

Hinduism a Term used since the end of the eighteenth century to refer to the religions of India collectively; it became more narrowly defined to refer to those who took as their ultimate textual authority the Vedas or practiced their religion primarily in relation to the pantheon of the Vedas, epics, and/or Puranas as their dominant gods.

Jātaka A story about an episode in one of the Buddha's former lifetimes.

jhāna Altered state of consciousness achieved through meditation.

Jūjaka The brahmin character in the *Vessantara Jātaka* who takes Vessantara's children from him and is a comic character in modern performances.

kamm An "action," especially intentional action that then has an effect on subsequent experience. Also, a ritual as in *saṅghakamma, q.v.*

kammaṭṭhāna Meditation exercise/meditation topic.

kammavācā The litany used for a *saṅghakamma, q.v.*

kammic A neologism meaning "relating to *kamma*," *q.v.*

Karaṇīyamettasutta A text that describes how one should develop *mettā*, "loving kindness" to all beings. It is used as a protective (*paritta*) text.

kaṭhina Festival, at which laypeople present monks with new robes, held within the lunar month following the end of the "rains" retreat, *vassa, q.v.*

kusala "Wholesome/skilful.' An attribute of positive mental states that are based in nongreed, nonhatred, and nondelusion.

Mahānikāya The branches of the Theravada Sangha in Thailand, Laos, and Cambodia that are not the Thammayutika Nikāya, *q.v.*

Mahāparinibbāna Sutta The canonical text recounting the last three months of the Buddha.

Mahāvihāra A branch of the Sri Lankan Sangha that came to dominate Sri Lankan and to some extent Southeast Asia Theravada from the twelfth century afterward; named after its monastic base in Anuradhapura in the Sri Lankan dry zone.

Mahayana In the modern period, this term is used to refer to the Buddhism of East and Central Asia, including the Himalayas. Within Mahayana, Vajrayana refers to some of its tantric (q.v.) developments. There are different views on the origins of Mahayana and how these origins relate to the current varieties of Buddhism.

Mahāpajāpatī Gotamī The name of the Buddha's aunt and foster mother, who became the first *bhikkhunī, q.v.*

Māyā The name of the Buddha's birth mother.

meditation The practice of calming and/or self-transformation by altering attitudes and psychosomatic patterns through one of the many types of meditation exercise (*kammaṭṭhāna*) taught in Buddhism.

mettā "Loving kindness." The attitude of being well-disposed to oneself and all beings that is generated through the first of the *brahmavihāra* meditations and described in the *Karaṇīyamettasutta, q.v.*

monastery A place where monks live. Nuns may also live there, that is, in a separate compound within the same complex as monks. A monastery usually also has places to receive laypeople, where laypeople conduct their religious activities, including a shrine room, Buddha images, a *bo* tree.

nat The Burmese term for a god or spirit.

Newar An ethnic group in the Kathmandu valley of Nepal. Traditionally Vajrayana Buddhist, many have converted to Theravada Buddhism in the modern period.

Nibbāna A term for the Buddha's "Enlightenment." The literal connotations of the term are both "bliss" and "extinction." Other terms for the Buddha's liberation include parinibbāna, bodhi/sambodhi "Awakening," amata, the deathless state – immortality in the sense of freedom from death, but not necessarily the retention of life – and sabbaññutā "Omniscience."

nikāya "Division." This refers either to a division with the *Sutta Piṭaka (q.v.)* of the Pali Canon *(q.v.)* or an ordination lineage within the Saṅgha (*q.v.*). The Burmese term is *gaing*.

nimitta Visual experience of a meditation object.

nun See *bhikkhunī* and precept nun.

pabbajjā The lower ordination to become a novice, taken from the age of 7 upward.

paccekabuddha A "solitary Buddha" who attains *Nibbāna* but, unlike the Buddha, does not make the Dhamma available for others.

pagoda A shrine containing images and/or relics, sometimes large enough to enter and so a kind of temple.

Pali The classical Indic language in which the sacred texts of Theravada Buddhism are preserved, used as a sacred language. From *pāḷibhāsā* "language of the main text" (on which a commentary is written). Alternative name: *māgadhī* "language of Magadha," one of the areas of the north India where the Buddha lived and taught.

Pali Canon The canonical textual authority for Theravada Buddhists, preserved in the Indic language Pali. Alternative term: *tipiṭaka*.

Pañcasīla 1. "Five precepts" undertaken by lay Buddhists. 2. "Five principles" that define citizenship in the modern nation state of Indonesia.

pārājika "Expulsion." One of the four rules breaking of which requires that a monk is permanently excluded from the monastic community.

parinibbāna See *nibbāna*. In English language sources, this is sometimes taken to refer specifically to the death of the Buddha, but in Buddhist sources it is used for his enlightenment, his giving up of life, and for the coming together of his relics to give a final sermon/recitation of texts.

paritta "Protection." Protective texts, many of which are extracted from the Pali Canon, that are chanted or used in visual form to bestow protection from malevolent spirits/forces. *Paritta* chanting is a core practice in many Buddhist rituals.

paṭiccasamuppāda "Dependent origination." The principle of conditionality, expressed in brief as "This being, that becomes" and more fully in the 12 links *nidāna* that detail the conditioning process between and within lifetimes.

pāṭimokkha (1) The name of the Sutta that lists the rules that govern the behavior of individual monks and nuns. (2) The name of the fortnightly ceremony at which these rules are recited to declare the branch of the Sangha connected within the jurisdiction of a particular *sīmā* pure.

pāvāraṇā A monastic ritual that marks the end of the three-month monastic "rains" retreat, *vassa*.

phī A Tai-Lao word for a spirit.

Prakrit A range of north Indian languages or dialects related to Sanskrit, of which Pali is one.

praling A Khmer term for a spirit.

precept *sīla* or *sikkhāpada* One of the set of five, eight, or ten precepts taken by laypeople, nuns/lay people staying at the monastery, and novices and some nuns, respectively.

Precept nun A woman who undertakes the lifestyle and appearance of a nun, but usually undertaking the 8 or 10 precepts rather than receiving the *upasampadā, q.v.*

Rahula Name of the Buddha-to-be's son in his final lifetime. Also the name of the twentieth-century political scholar monk from Sri Lanka, Walpola Rahula.

relic The English word used for *dhātu*, q.v. on the basis of the closest parallel in Catholicism.

reform Buddhism The Buddhism of the modern period that seeks to essentialize what it means to be Buddhist usually by drawing on a selective reading of canonical and commentarial sources.

robes The set of garments worn by a monk, minimally including a lower robe, upper robe, and outer robe.

Sakka (Indra) King of the Gods in Buddhist narratives.

sāmaṇera a Novice monk who has received the *pabbajjā* ordination.

saṃsāra The round of rebirth/cyclic existence.

Sangha (*saṅgha*) The community of Buddhist monks and nuns.

saṅghakamma A monastic ritual or monastic legal procedure.

Sanskrit The classical language of ancient India used as a sacred language in Hinduism and some forms of Buddhism. It was also periodically used as a language of learning throughout much of the history of India and neighboring Asian countries.

sayadaw Anglicized spelling of Burmese *hsayadaw* "royal teacher" that appears in the names of some monks.

sikkhāpada "Training principle" or "precept," *q.v.*
sīla "Good conduct" or "precept" *q.v.*
sīmā "Boundary." A sacred enclosure within which *saṅghakamma* may take place. See *uposatha.*
socially engaged Buddhism See "engaged Buddhism."
soteriology Doctrine or theory about how one escapes from *saṃsāra.*
soteriological androgyny Theories or symbols of enlightenment or salvific knowledge as including male and female attributes or excluding both male and female attributes.
stūpa A funerary monument containing relics of the Buddha or another holy person.
Sutta Piṭaka The second section of the Pali Canon that contains the Buddha's teachings embedded in narratives about his life or former lives or in the form of poetry.
tantra Ritualized Buddhist practices aimed at enlightenment in this life, also used for worldly ends.
temple The place where people go to perform Buddhist rituals, acts of merit, and listen to sermons. It is often the same as the monastery, but seen from the perspective of communal and lay practice, although there are some temples that are not monasteries.
thudong The Tai-Lao word for a monk who follows one or more of the *dhūtaṅga q.v.* ascetic practices and who usually lives in the forest.
thūpa See *stūpa.*
tipiṭaka "Three baskets." The Pali term for the Pali Canon. The three "baskets" are the *Vinaya Piṭaka*, the *Sutta Piṭaka*, and the *Abhidhamma Piṭaka.*
upajjha/upajjhāya "Preceptor." The monk who ordains other monks.
Upanishad A genre of Hindu texts that bridge the ritual religion of the brahmanical religion with more speculative, contemplative, and renouncer traditions.
upasampadā The higher ordination to become a *bhikkhu* or *bhikkhunī*, taken from the age of 20 upward, calculated either from conception or birth.
uposatha The fortnightly holy days falling on the full and new moon days in the lunar calendar on which the *pātimokkha* ceremony is held and laypeople may attend the monastery for religious practice. The term is also sometimes used for the hall in which the *sīmā* is located.
Vajrayana The tantric tradition that developed within Mahayana, now predominantly associated with Himalayan and Central Asian Buddhism.
vassa "Rainy season." The monastic rains retreat lasting three months ending in October–November.
Veda A genre of hymns to gods and ritual instructions used for the practice of religion in brahmanical Hinduism. The texts predate the first millennium BCE.
Vedic Connected with the Vedas.
Vessantara The Prince Vessantara is the character of the Buddha-to-be in the last of the *Jātakas, q.v.* This is the most popular *jātaka* in art and performances to this day.
vihāra "Monastery." A place where monks and/or nuns live.
Vinaya Piṭaka The section of the Pali Canon dealing with the rules that govern the Sangha.
Wat (vat) Alternative spelling for *vat, q.v.* Tai–Lao–Khmer term for a monastery.
weikza Burmese for Pali *vijjā* "knowledge," this refers to a range of practices connected with the prolongation of life for spiritual purposes and the use of powers to help people with worldly concerns. The practitioners are also called *weikza*, short for *weikzado* (Burmese, *vjjādhara* Pali).
Wesak The full moon festival, celebrating the Buddha's birth, enlightenment, and *parinibbāna.* The most important annual festival in Sri Lanka, it is increasingly emphasized as a pan-Theravāda festival. It usually falls in May.
Yasodharā Name of the Buddha-to-be's wife in his final lifetime.

An extensive bibliography for this book is available at
www.wiley.com/go/theravadabuddhism

Index

This index is inclusive but not exhaustive in its coverage. Proper nouns – names, places and texts – are fully indexed. Themes are indexed in inverse intensity to their frequency – the more elusive, fully; the more frequent, less so. On this principle, various ethnic/cultural/state units are indexed, e.g. Arakan, and Taiwan, but not the main Theravada countries – Burma, Thailand, Cambodia, Laos and Sri Lanka, plus India – reference to each of which is so frequent as to make indexing pointless. There are no sections with a national or geographical focus as such, but each country is integrated into thematic discussions alongside others. For the same reason, 'Buddha', 'Dharma', 'Sangha' and 'monks', are not indexed. 'Nuns', being somewhat less ubiquitous, are, but not exhaustively. The index covers the main text of chapters, but not overviews, summaries, the text of quotations, or bibliographies

Theravada Buddhism: Continuity, Diversity, and Identity, First Edition. Kate Crosby.

Printed and bound by CPI Group (UK) Ltd, Croydon, CR0 4YY
16/06/2021
03073910-0001